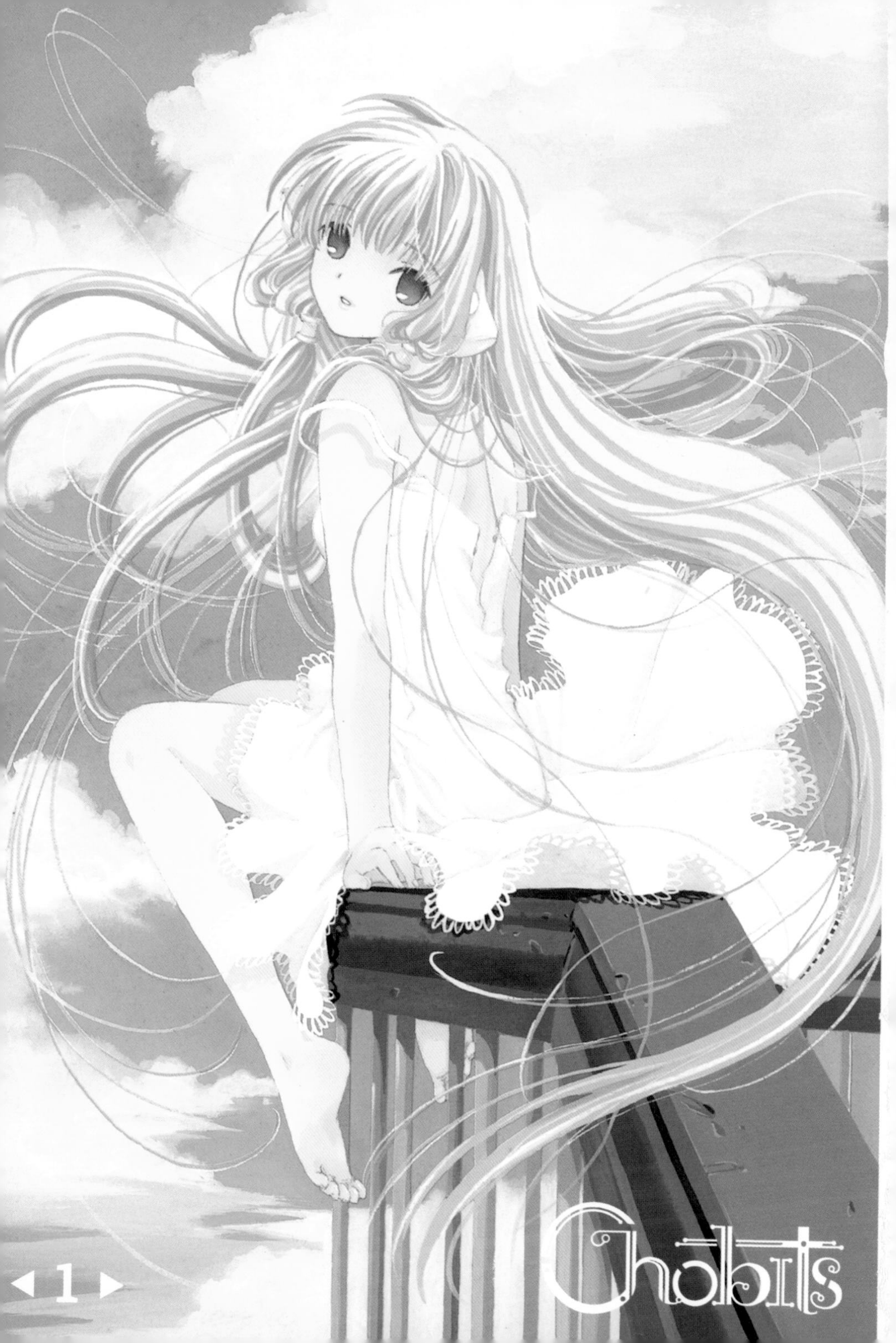

Chobits
1

CONTENTS

◄ CLAMP ►

SATSUKI IGARASHI
NANASE OHKAWA
TSUBAKI NEKOI
MOKONA

◄ Book design ►
CLAMP

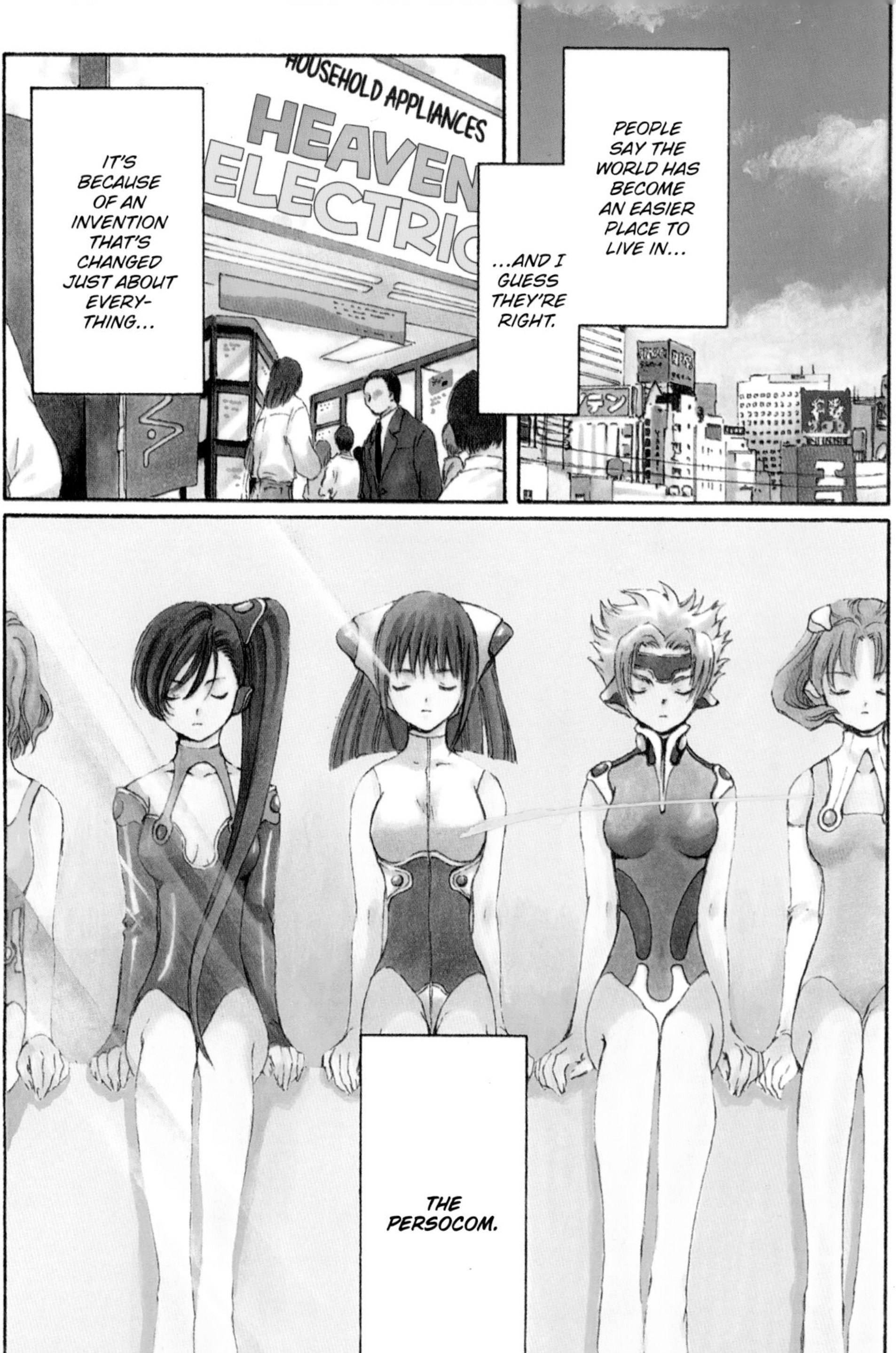
PEOPLE SAY THE WORLD HAS BECOME AN EASIER PLACE TO LIVE IN...
...AND I GUESS THEY'RE RIGHT.
IT'S BECAUSE OF AN INVENTION THAT'S CHANGED JUST ABOUT EVERY-THING...
HOUSEHOLD APPLIANCES
HEAVEN
ELECTRIC
THE PERSOCOM.

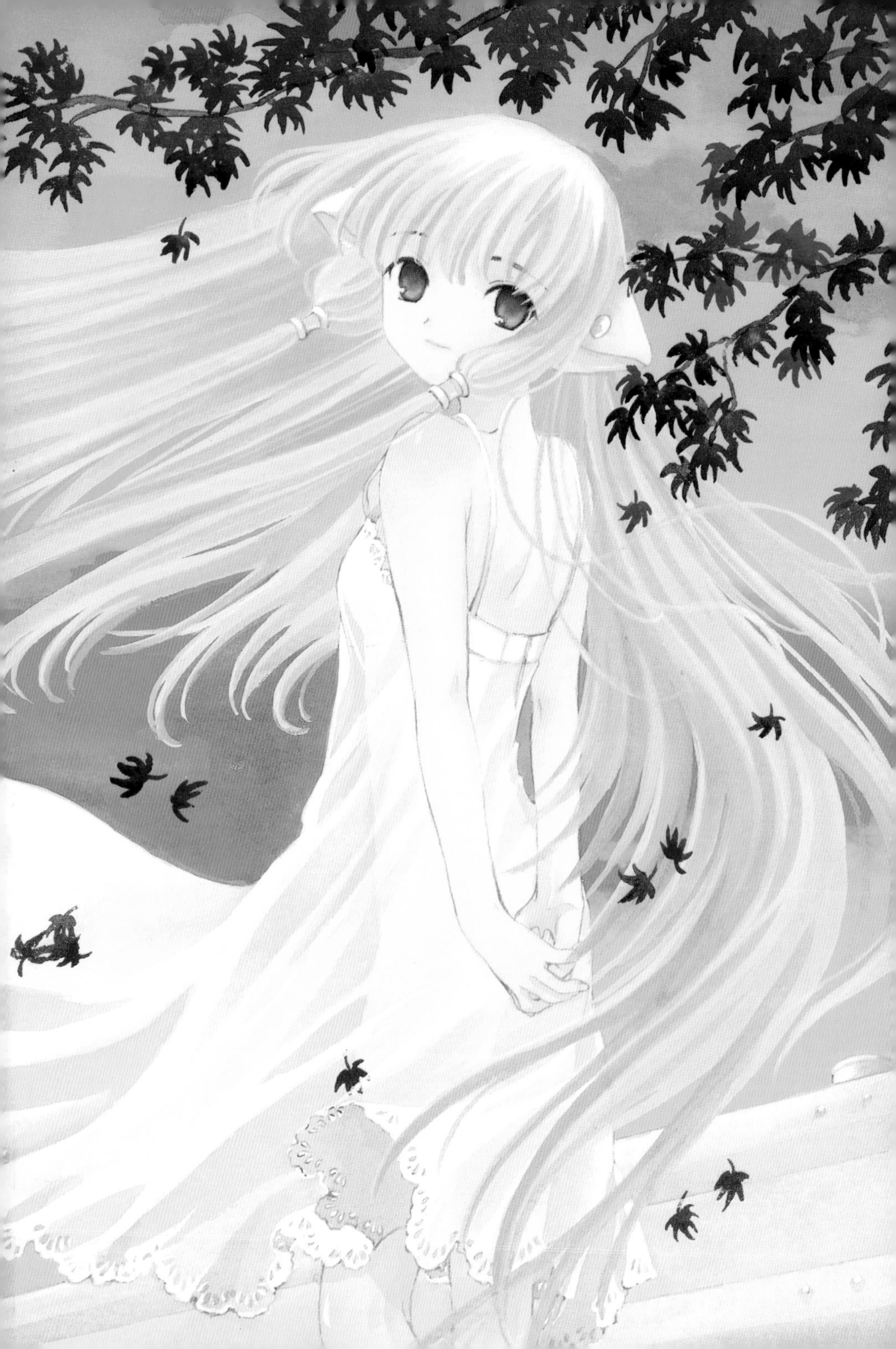

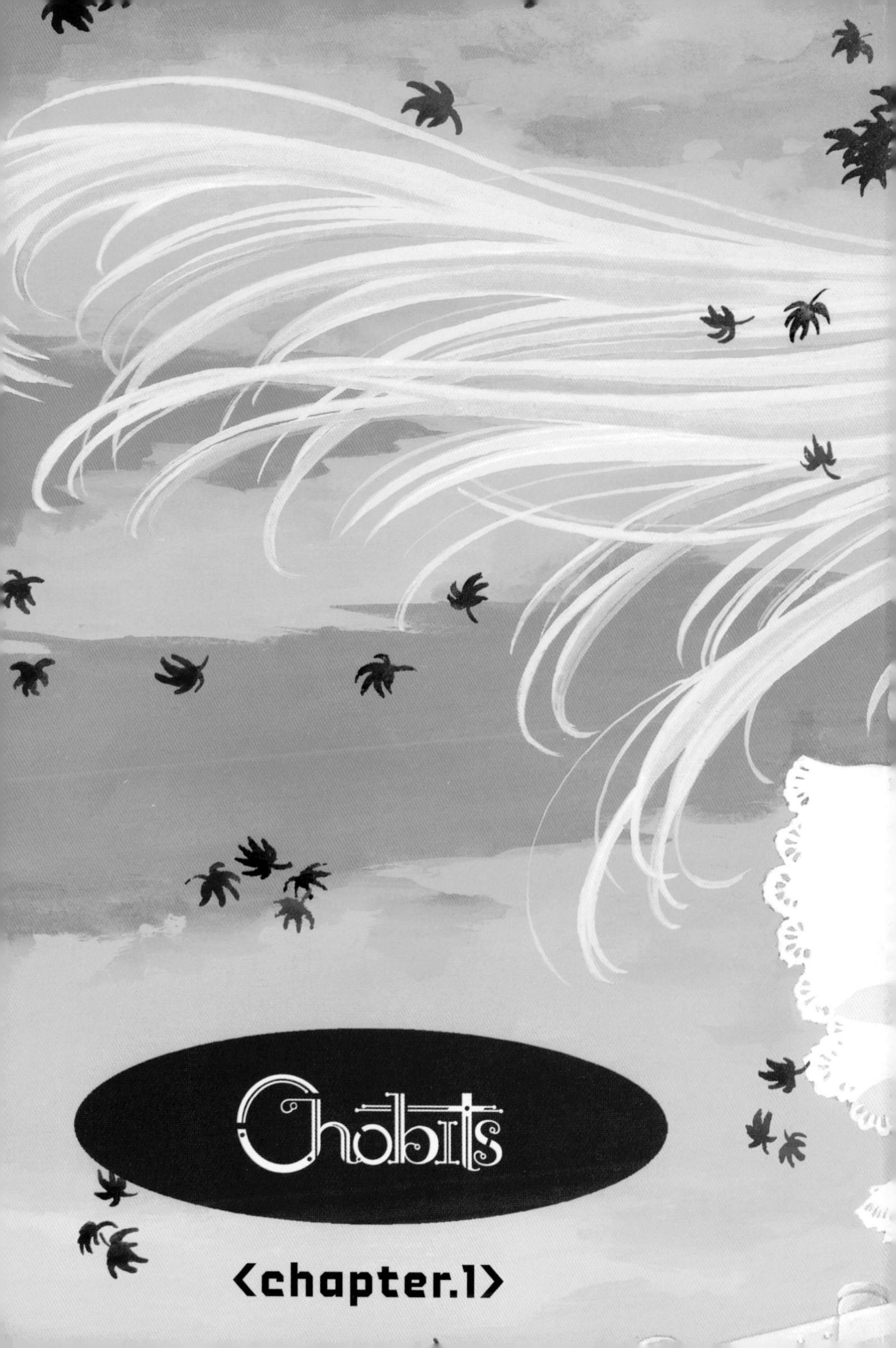

Chobits

<chapter.1>

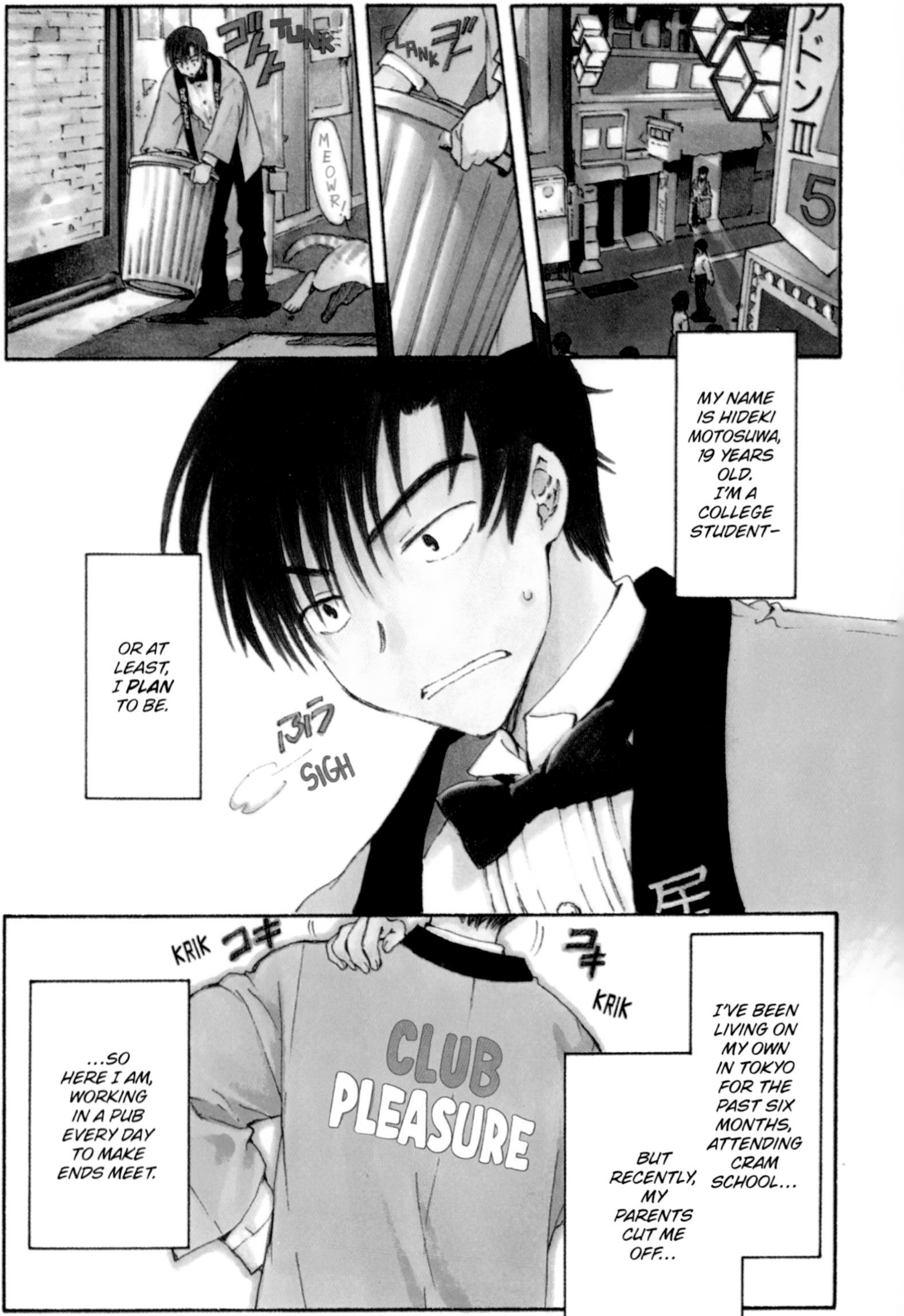
CLANK
TUNK
MEOWR!
MY NAME IS HIDEKI MOTOSUWA, 19 YEARS OLD. I'M A COLLEGE STUDENT–
OR AT LEAST, I **PLAN** TO BE.
SIGH
I'VE BEEN LIVING ON MY OWN IN TOKYO FOR THE PAST SIX MONTHS, ATTENDING CRAM SCHOOL...
BUT RECENTLY, MY PARENTS CUT ME OFF...
...SO HERE I AM, WORKING IN A PUB EVERY DAY TO MAKE ENDS MEET.
KRIK
KRIK
CLUB PLEASURE

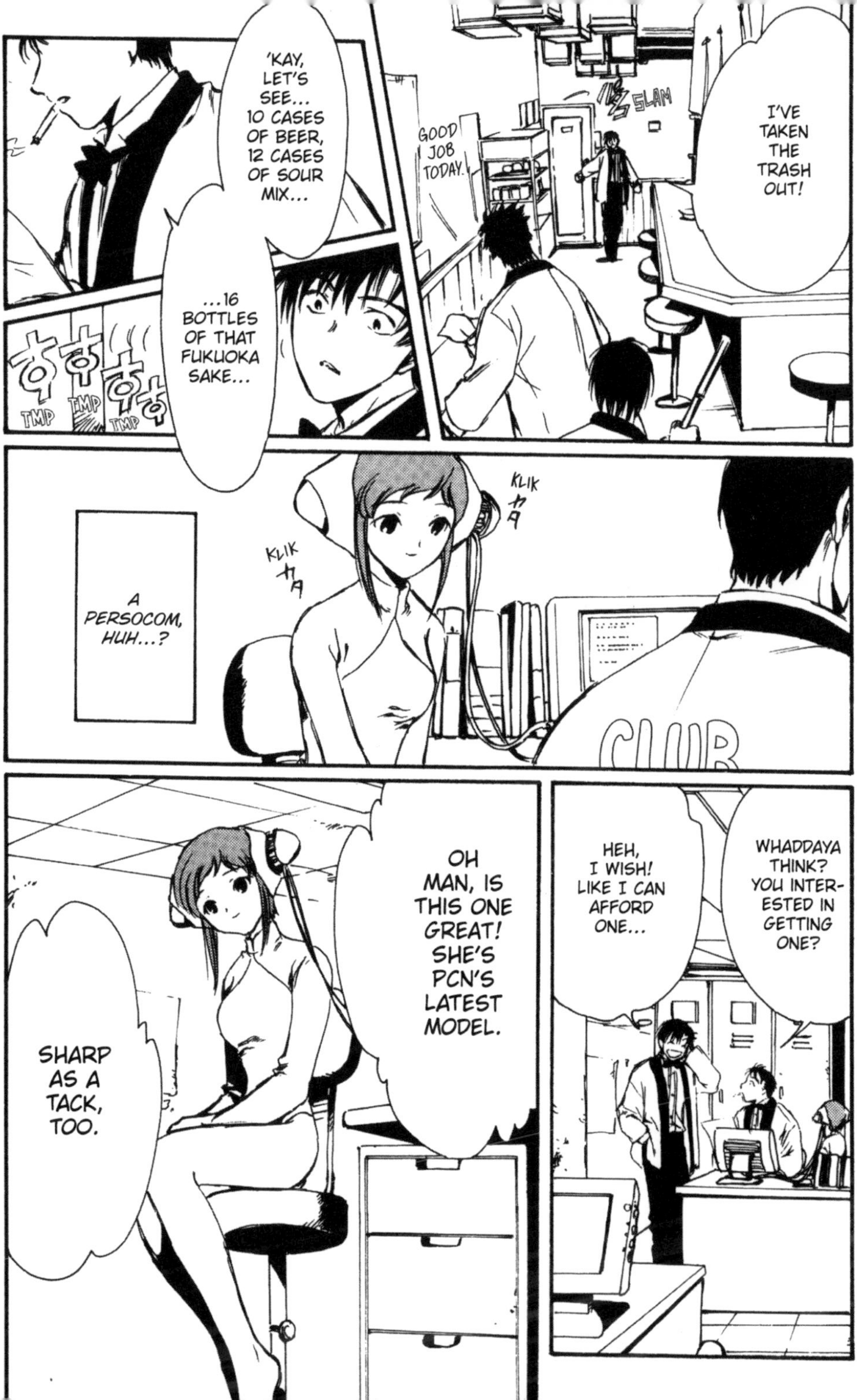
I'VE TAKEN THE TRASH OUT!
SLAM
GOOD JOB TODAY.
'KAY, LET'S SEE... 10 CASES OF BEER, 12 CASES OF SOUR MIX...
...16 BOTTLES OF THAT FUKUOKA SAKE...
TMP TMP TMP
KLIK KLIK
A PERSOCOM, HUH...?
CLUB
WHADDAYA THINK? YOU INTER-ESTED IN GETTING ONE?
HEH, I WISH! LIKE I CAN AFFORD ONE...
OH MAN, IS THIS ONE GREAT! SHE'S PCN'S LATEST MODEL.
SHARP AS A TACK, TOO.

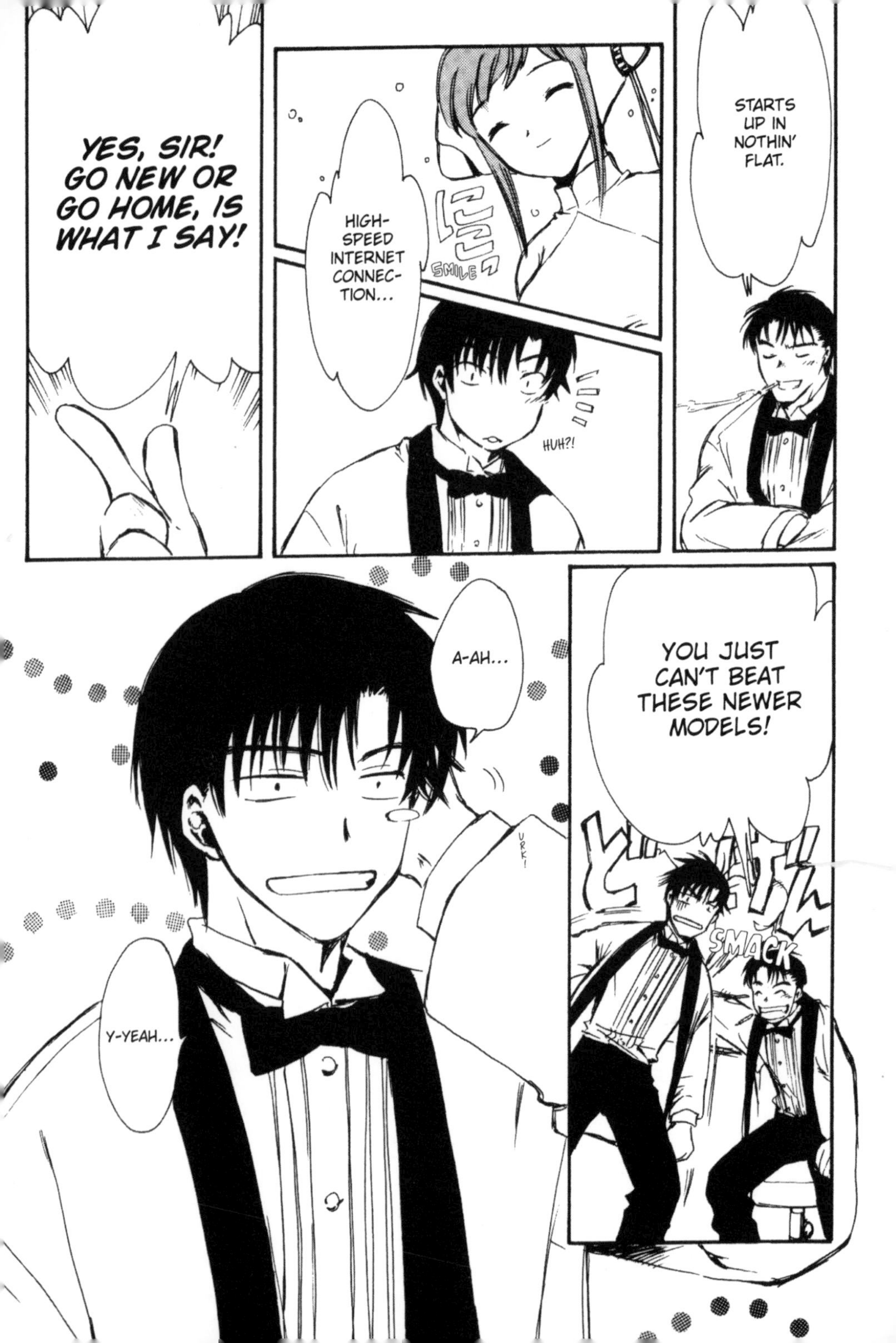
STARTS UP IN NOTHIN' FLAT.
HIGH-SPEED INTERNET CONNECTION...
SMILE
HUH?!
YES, SIR! GO NEW OR GO HOME, IS WHAT I SAY!
YOU JUST CAN'T BEAT THESE NEWER MODELS!
SMACK
A-AH...
URK!
Y-YEAH...

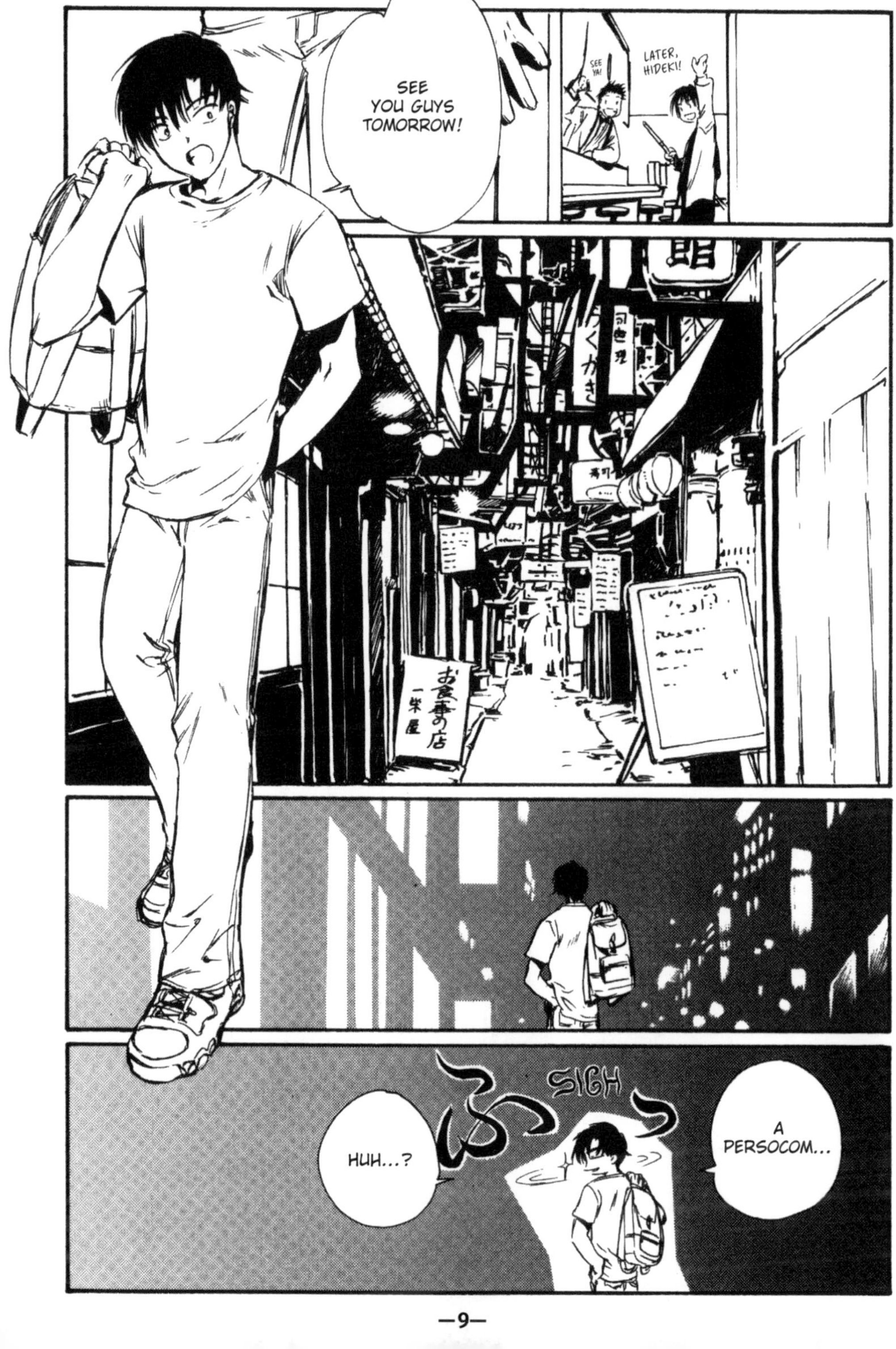
LATER, HIDEKI!
SEE YA!
SEE YOU GUYS TOMORROW!
お食事の店 一栄屋
A PERSOCOM...
ふっ
SIGH
HUH...?

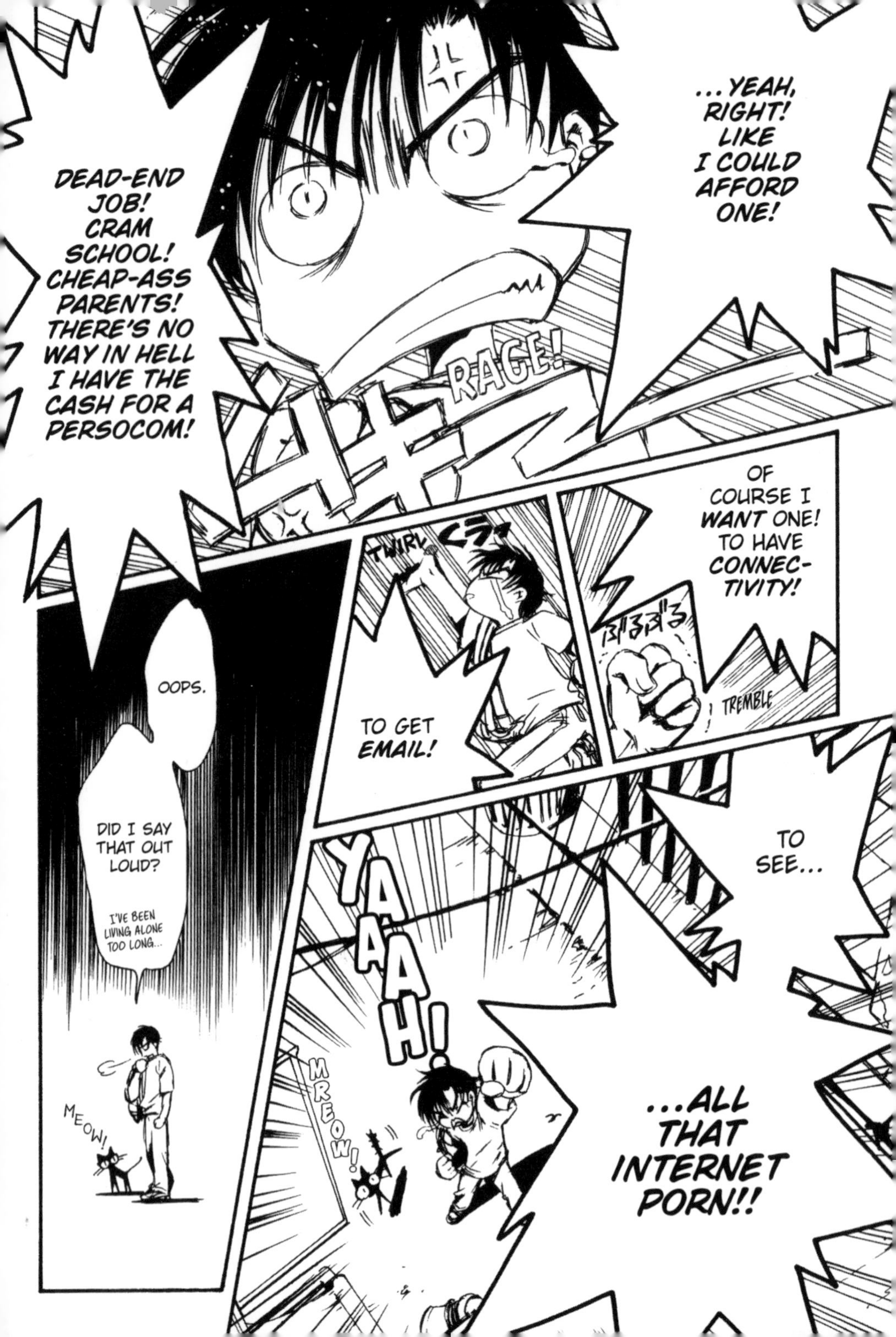

...YEAH, RIGHT! LIKE I COULD AFFORD ONE!
DEAD-END JOB! CRAM SCHOOL! CHEAP-ASS PARENTS! THERE'S NO WAY IN HELL I HAVE THE CASH FOR A PERSOCOM!
RAGE!
OF COURSE I *WANT* ONE! TO HAVE **CONNECTIVITY!**
ぶるぶる
TREMBLE
TWIRL
くらっ
TO GET **EMAIL!**
TO SEE...
YAAAAH!
MREOW!
...ALL THAT INTERNET PORN!!
OOPS.
DID I SAY THAT OUT LOUD?
I'VE BEEN LIVING ALONE TOO LONG...
MEOW!

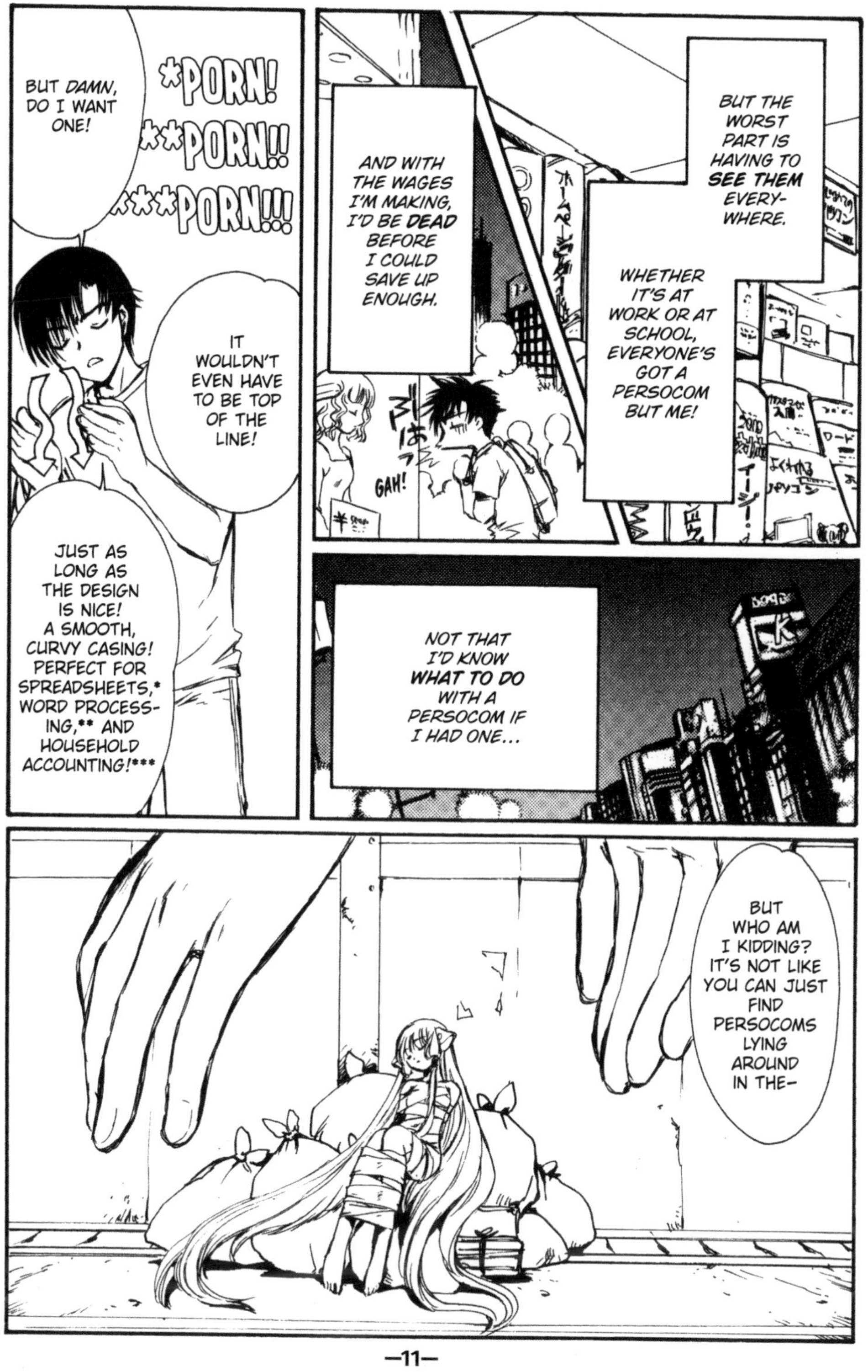
BUT THE WORST PART IS HAVING TO *SEE THEM* EVERY-WHERE.
WHETHER IT'S AT WORK OR AT SCHOOL, EVERYONE'S GOT A PERSOCOM BUT ME!
AND WITH THE WAGES I'M MAKING, I'D BE *DEAD* BEFORE I COULD SAVE UP ENOUGH.
GAH!
NOT THAT I'D KNOW *WHAT TO DO* WITH A PERSOCOM IF I HAD ONE...
*PORN!
**PORN!!
***PORN!!!
BUT *DAMN*, DO I WANT ONE!
IT WOULDN'T EVEN HAVE TO BE TOP OF THE LINE!
JUST AS LONG AS THE DESIGN IS NICE! A SMOOTH, CURVY CASING! PERFECT FOR SPREADSHEETS,* WORD PROCESS-ING,** AND HOUSEHOLD ACCOUNTING!***
BUT WHO AM I KIDDING? IT'S NOT LIKE YOU CAN JUST FIND PERSOCOMS LYING AROUND IN THE–

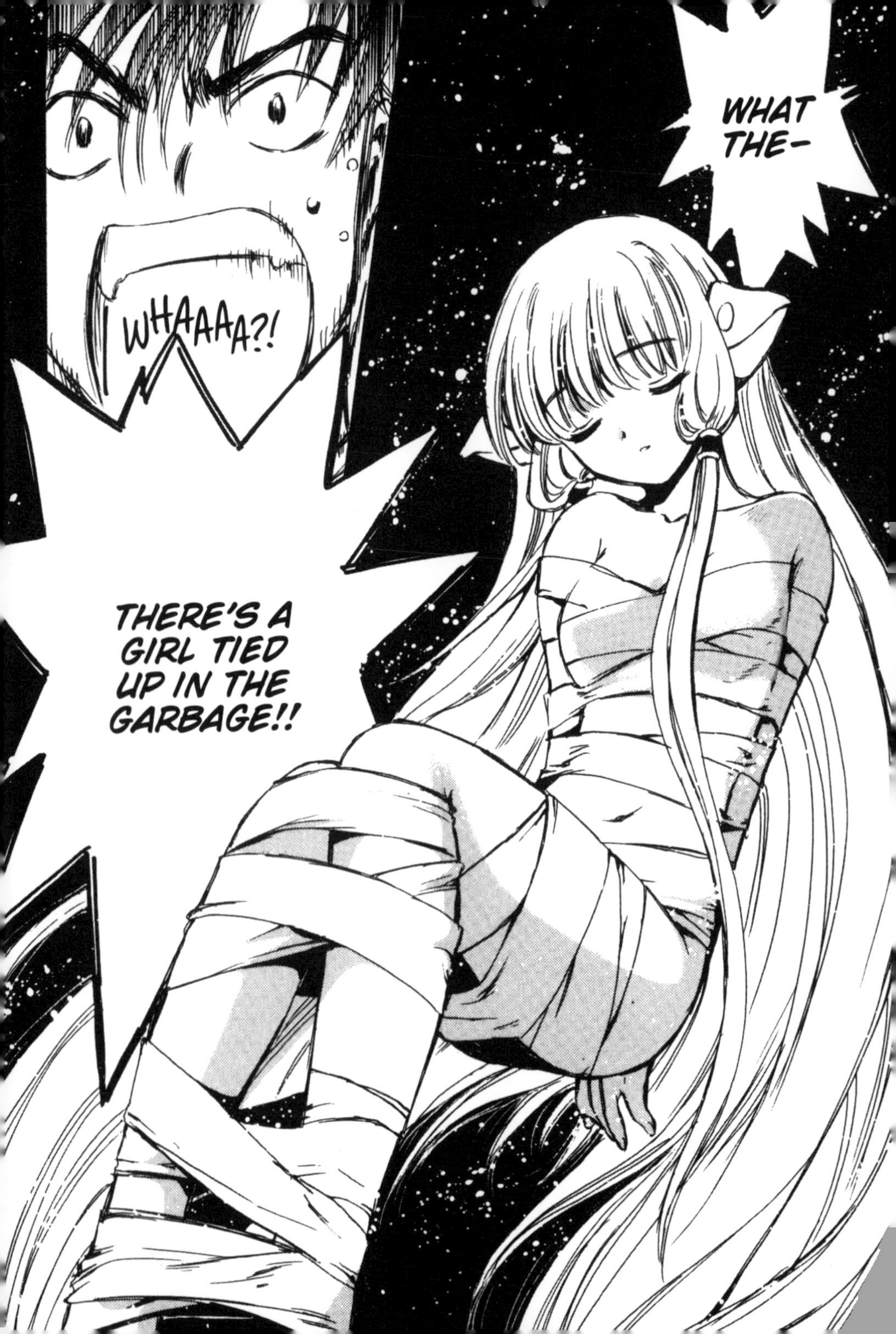
WHAT THE-
WHAAAA?!
THERE'S A GIRL TIED UP IN THE GARBAGE!!

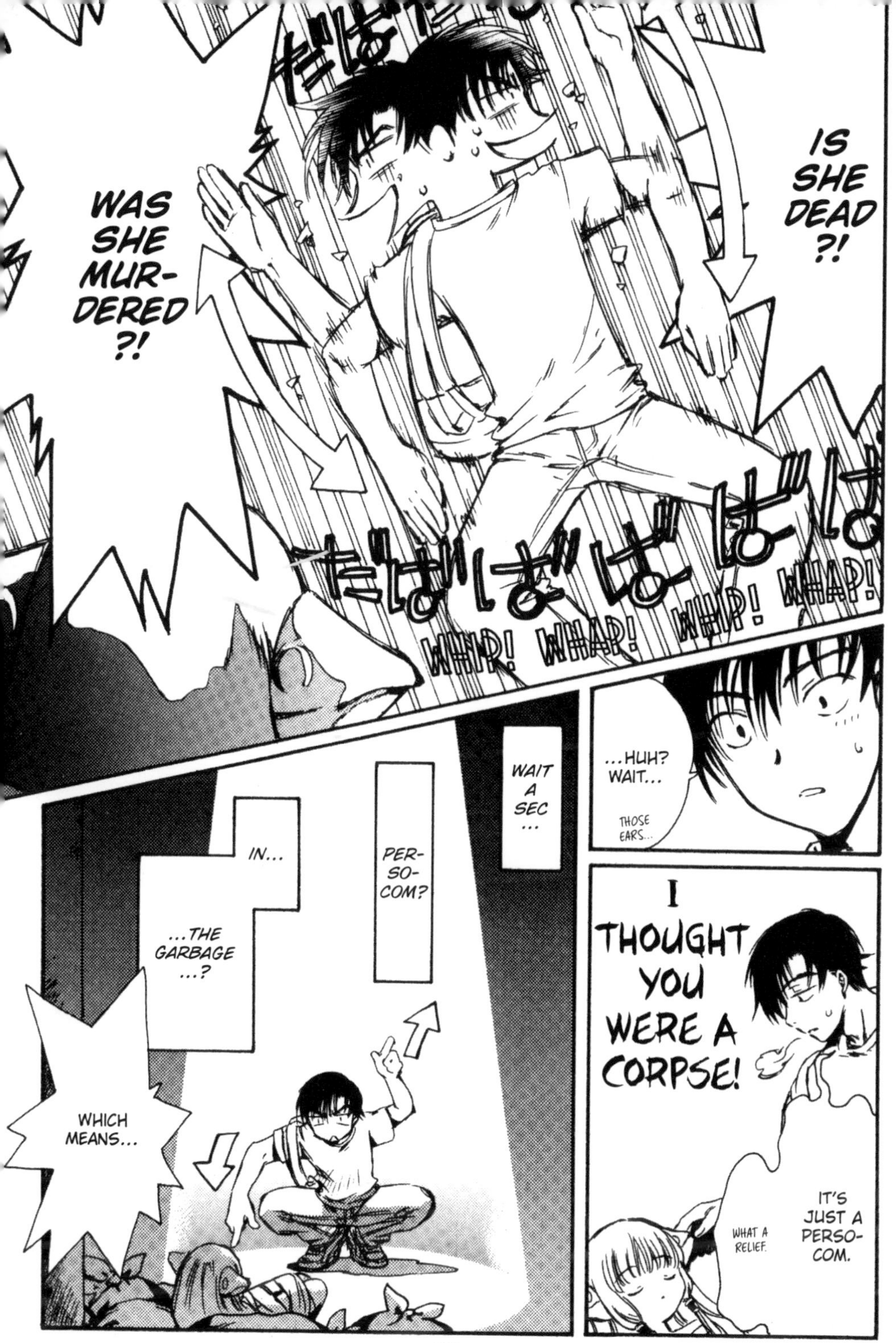

IS SHE DEAD?!
WAS SHE MURDERED?!
WHIP! WHAP! WHIP! WHAP!
...HUH? WAIT...
THOSE EARS...
I THOUGHT YOU WERE A CORPSE!
IT'S JUST A PERSOCOM.
WHAT A RELIEF.
WAIT A SEC...
PERSOCOM?
IN...
...THE GARBAGE...?
WHICH MEANS...

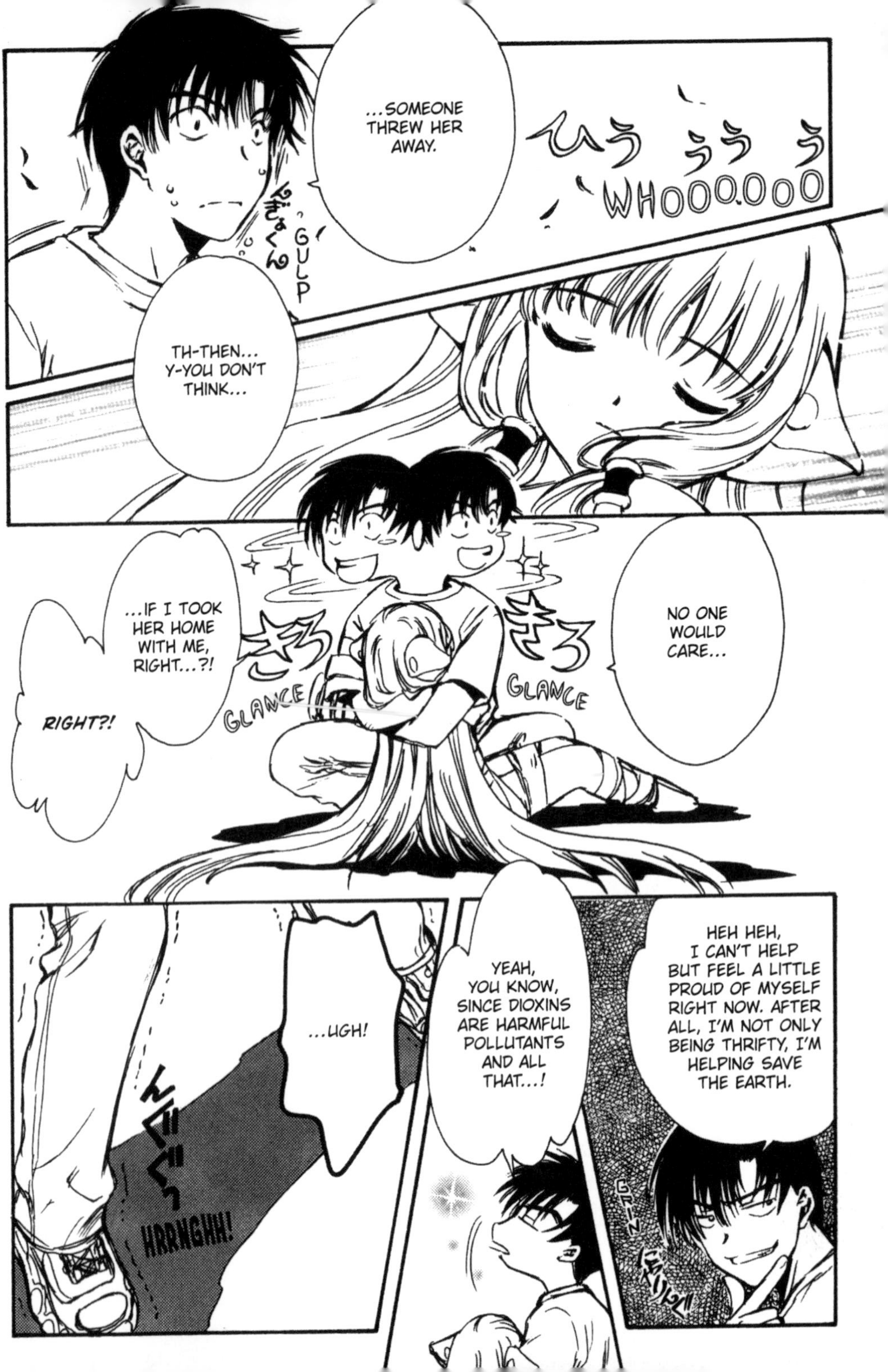
ひうううう
WHOOOOOOO
...SOMEONE THREW HER AWAY.
GULP
TH-THEN... Y-YOU DON'T THINK...
NO ONE WOULD CARE...
きろ
GLANCE
きろ
GLANCE
...IF I TOOK HER HOME WITH ME, RIGHT...?!
RIGHT?!
HEH HEH, I CAN'T HELP BUT FEEL A LITTLE PROUD OF MYSELF RIGHT NOW. AFTER ALL, I'M NOT ONLY BEING THRIFTY, I'M HELPING SAVE THE EARTH.
GRIN
YEAH, YOU KNOW, SINCE DIOXINS ARE HARMFUL POLLUTANTS AND ALL THAT...!
...UGH!
HRRNGHH!

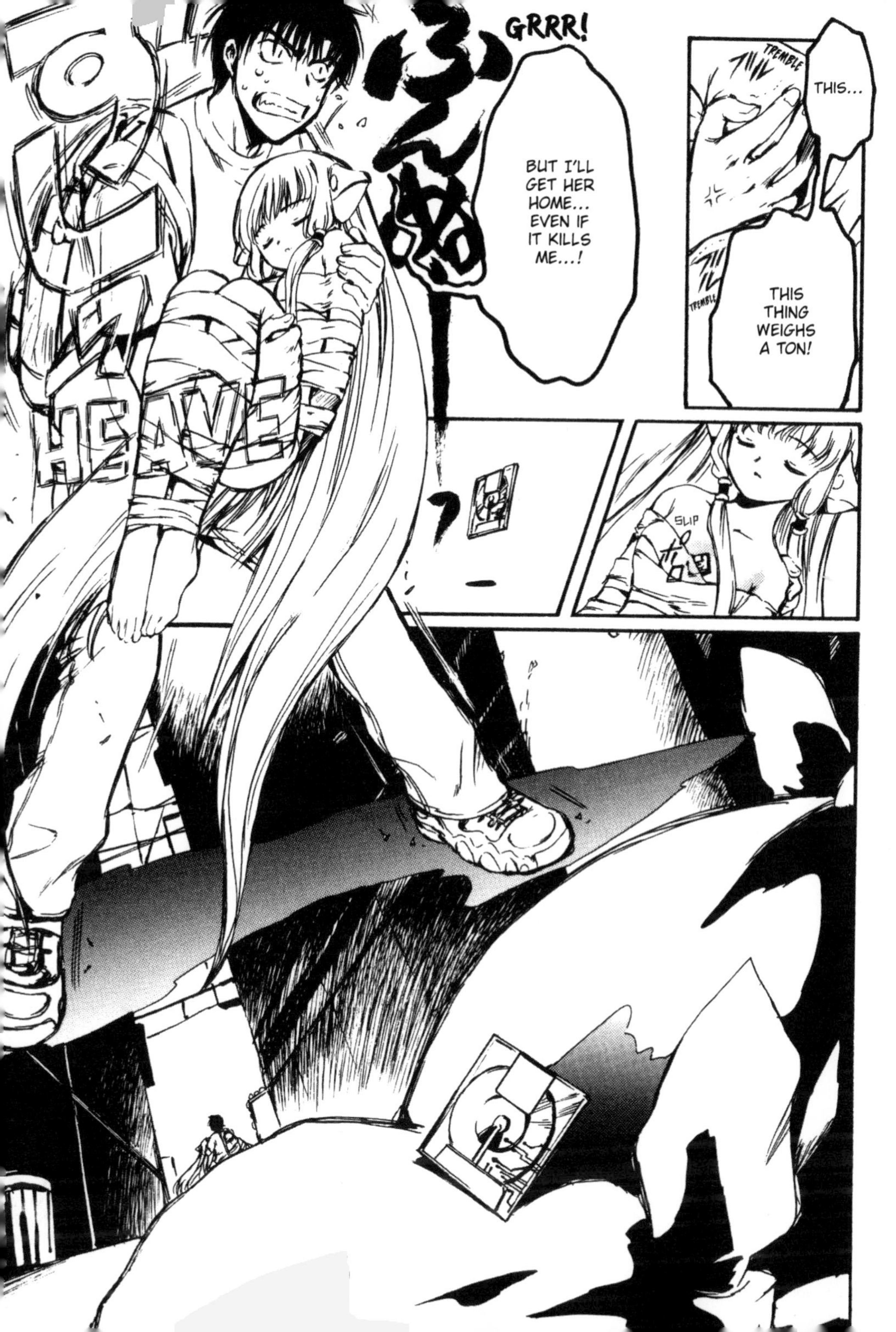
TREMBLE
THIS...
TREMBLE
THIS THING WEIGHS A TON!
SLIP
GRRR!
BUT I'LL GET HER HOME... EVEN IF IT KILLS ME...!
HEAVE

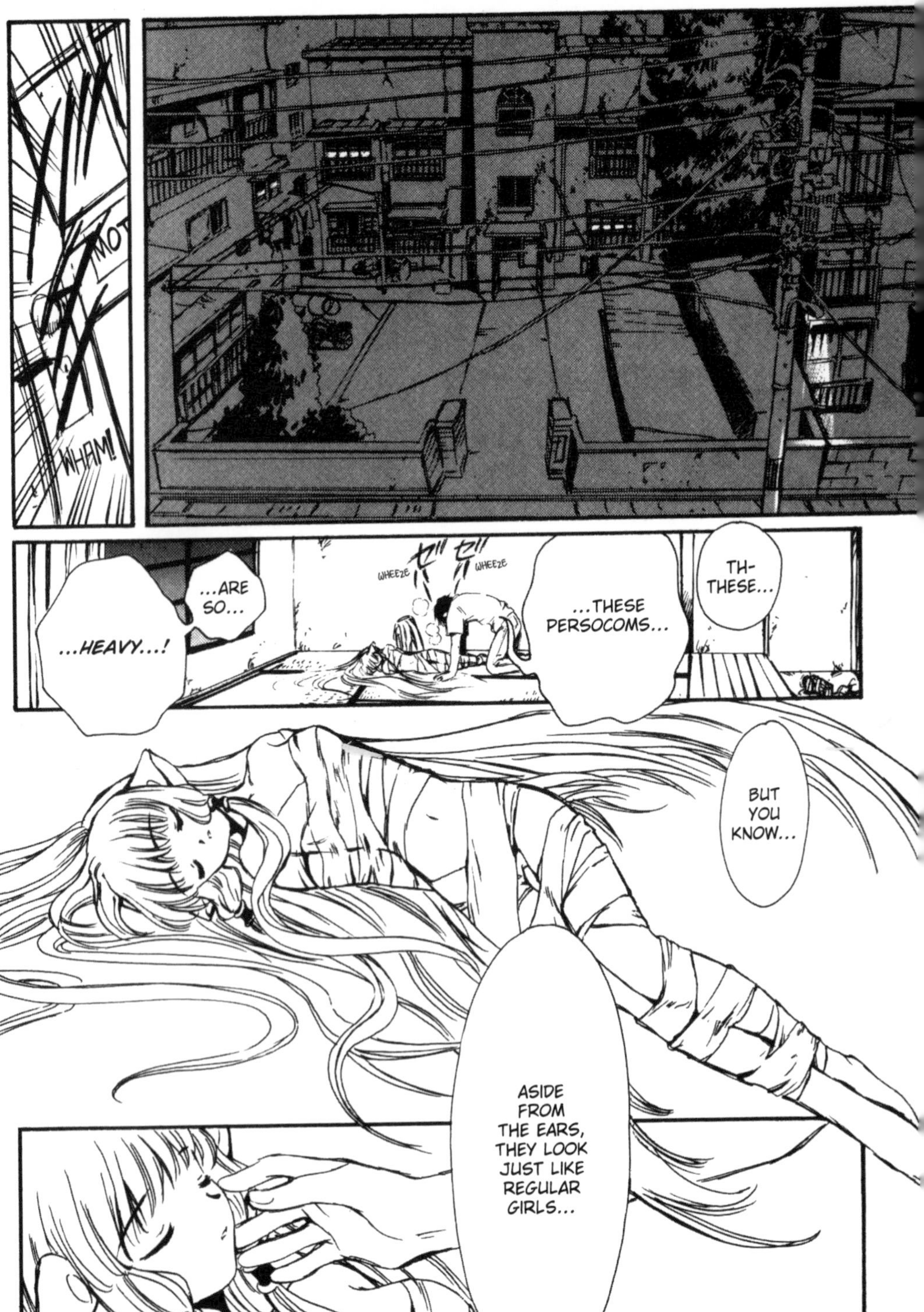
WHAM!
TH-THESE...
...THESE PERSOCOMS...
WHEEZE
WHEEZE
...ARE SO...
...HEAVY...!
BUT YOU KNOW...
ASIDE FROM THE EARS, THEY LOOK JUST LIKE REGULAR GIRLS...

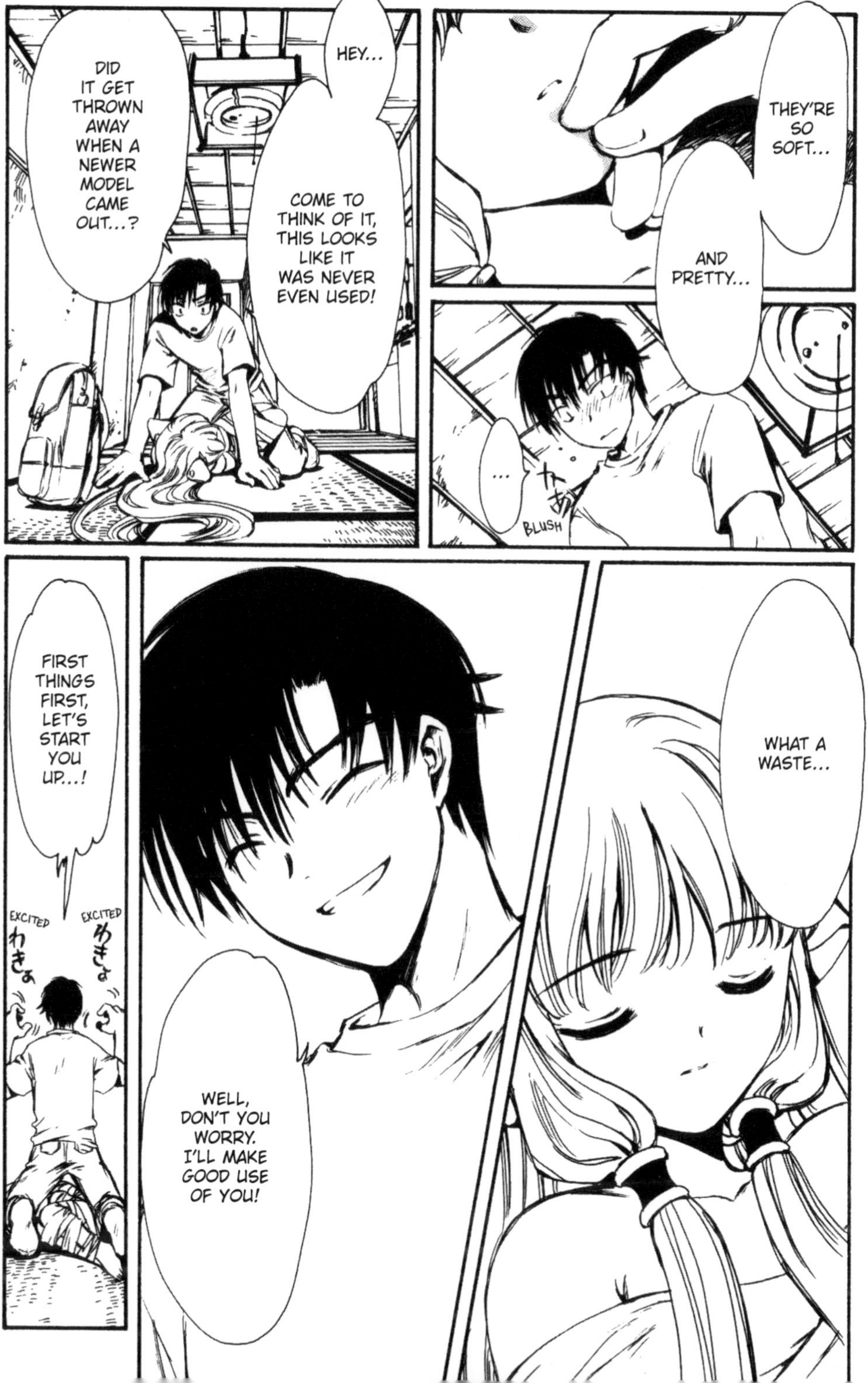
THEY'RE SO SOFT...
AND PRETTY...
...
BLUSH
HEY...
COME TO THINK OF IT, THIS LOOKS LIKE IT WAS NEVER EVEN USED!
DID IT GET THROWN AWAY WHEN A NEWER MODEL CAME OUT...?
WHAT A WASTE...
WELL, DON'T YOU WORRY. I'LL MAKE GOOD USE OF YOU!
FIRST THINGS FIRST, LET'S START YOU UP...!
EXCITED
EXCITED

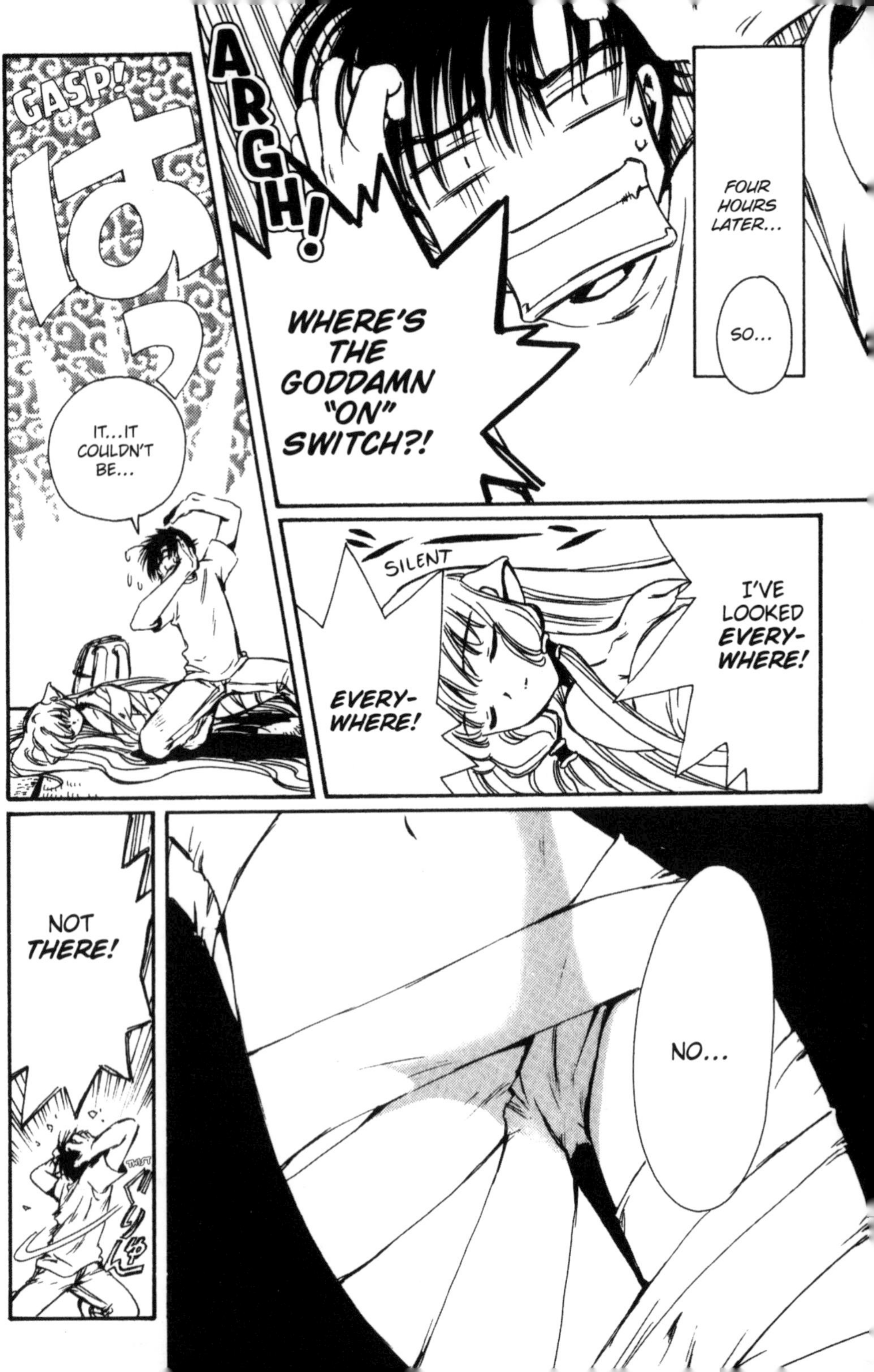
FOUR HOURS LATER...
SO...
ARGH!
WHERE'S THE GODDAMN "ON" SWITCH?!
I'VE LOOKED EVERY-WHERE!
SILENT
EVERY-WHERE!
GASP!
はっ
IT...IT COULDN'T BE...
NO...
NOT THERE!
TWIST

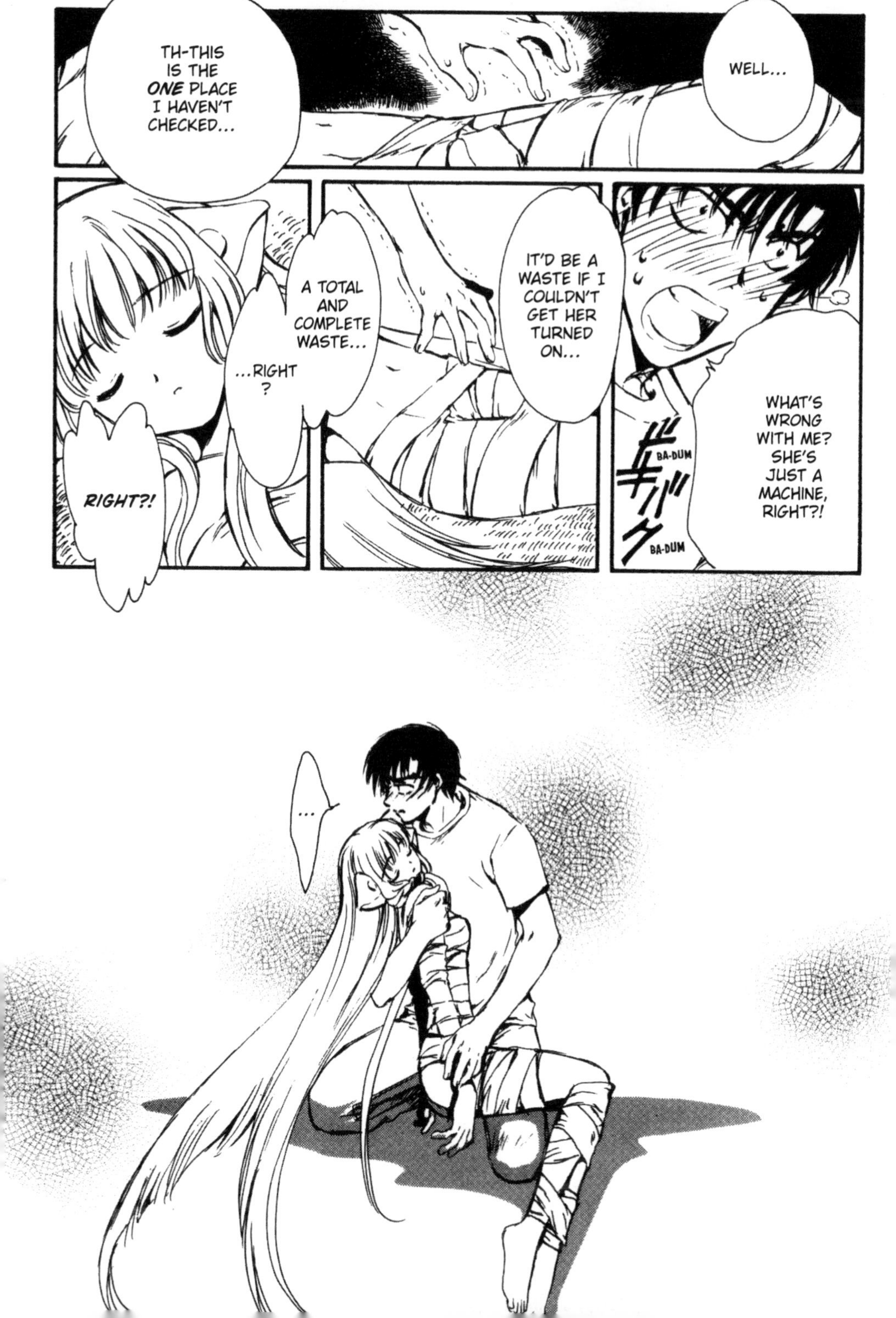
WELL...
TH-THIS IS THE *ONE* PLACE I HAVEN'T CHECKED...
WHAT'S WRONG WITH ME? SHE'S JUST A MACHINE, RIGHT?!
BA-DUM
BA-DUM
IT'D BE A WASTE IF I COULDN'T GET HER TURNED ON...
A TOTAL AND COMPLETE WASTE...
...RIGHT ?
RIGHT?!
...

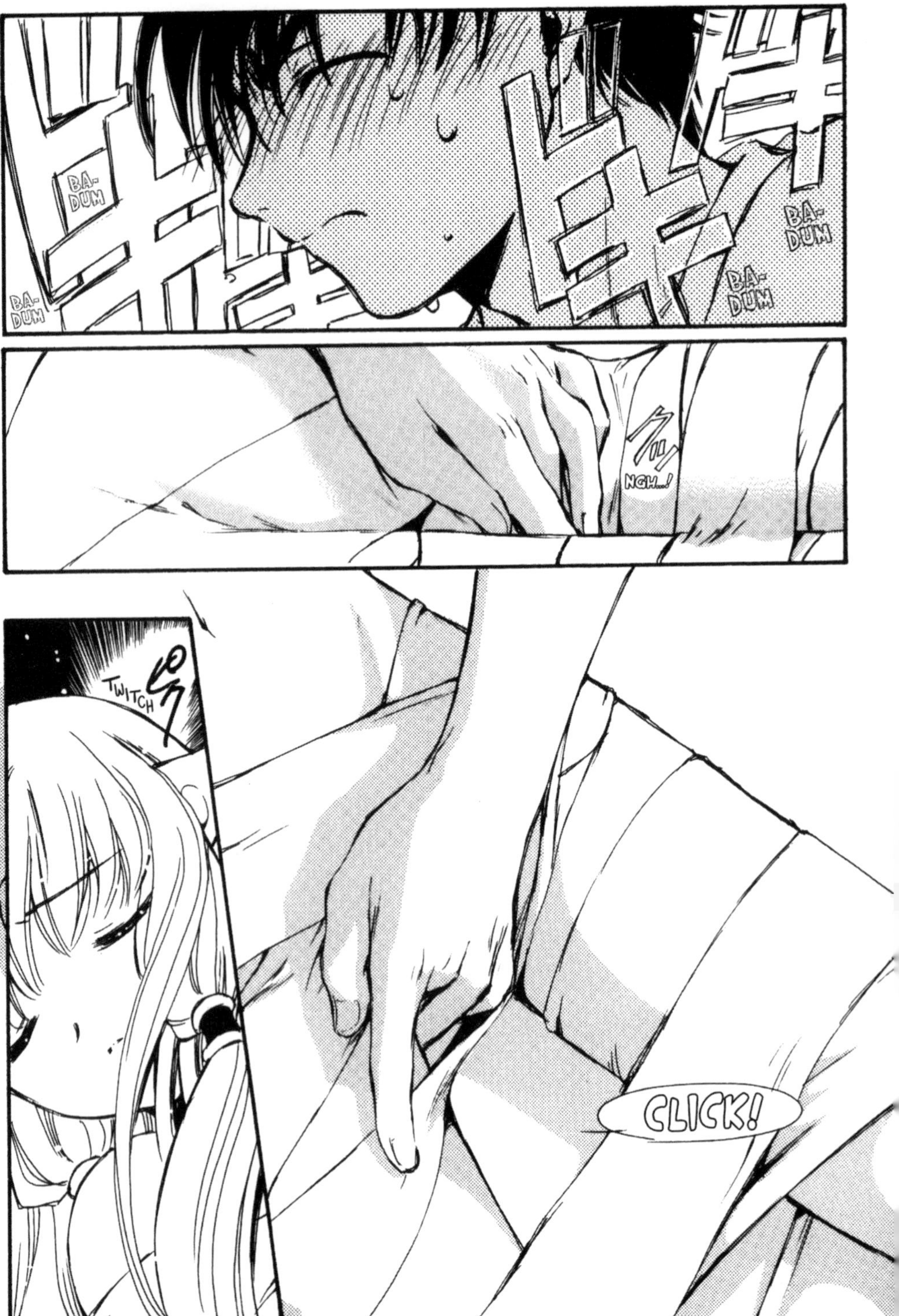
BA-DUM
BA-DUM
BA-DUM
BA-DUM
NGH...!
CLICK!
TWITCH

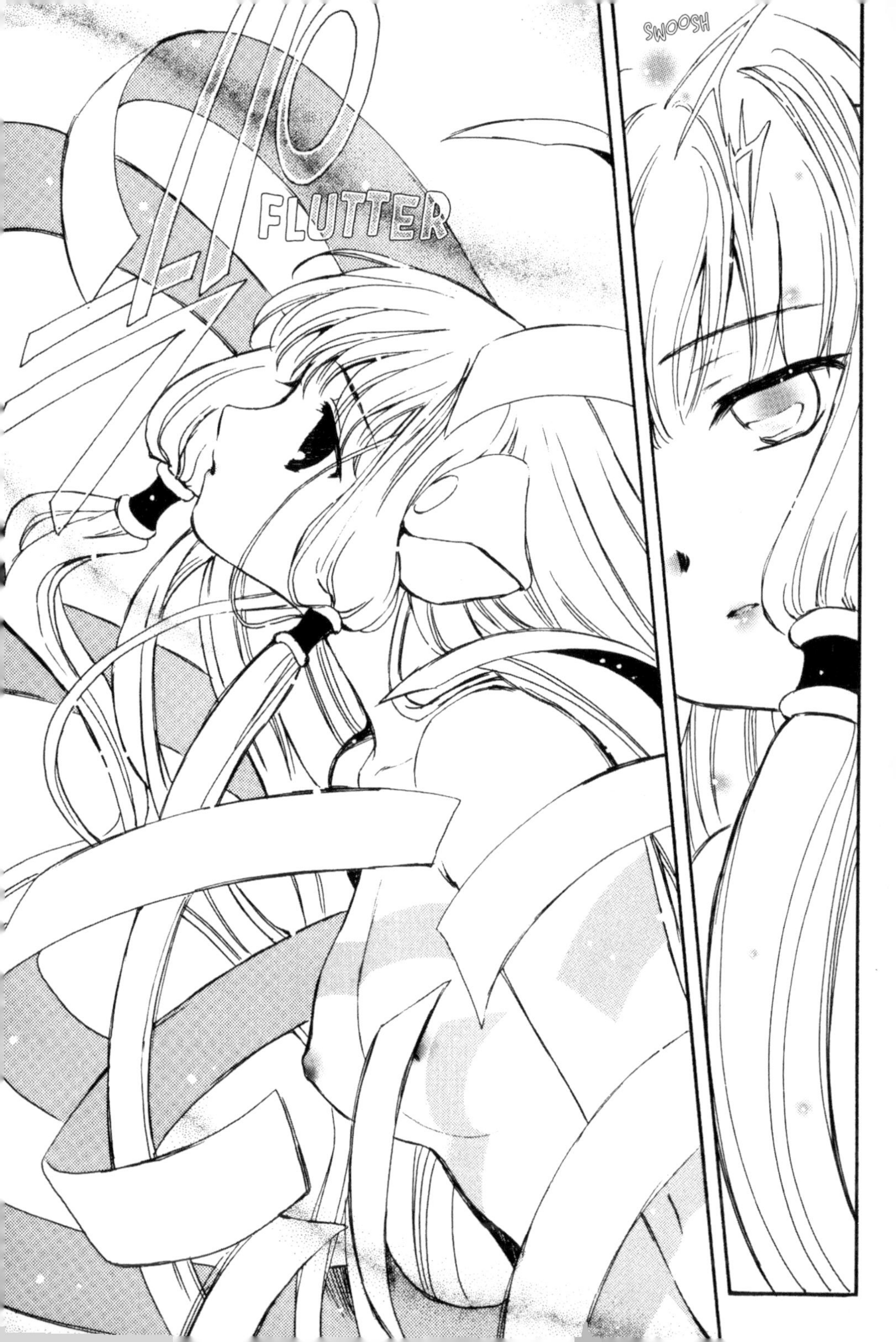
SWOOSH
FLUTTER

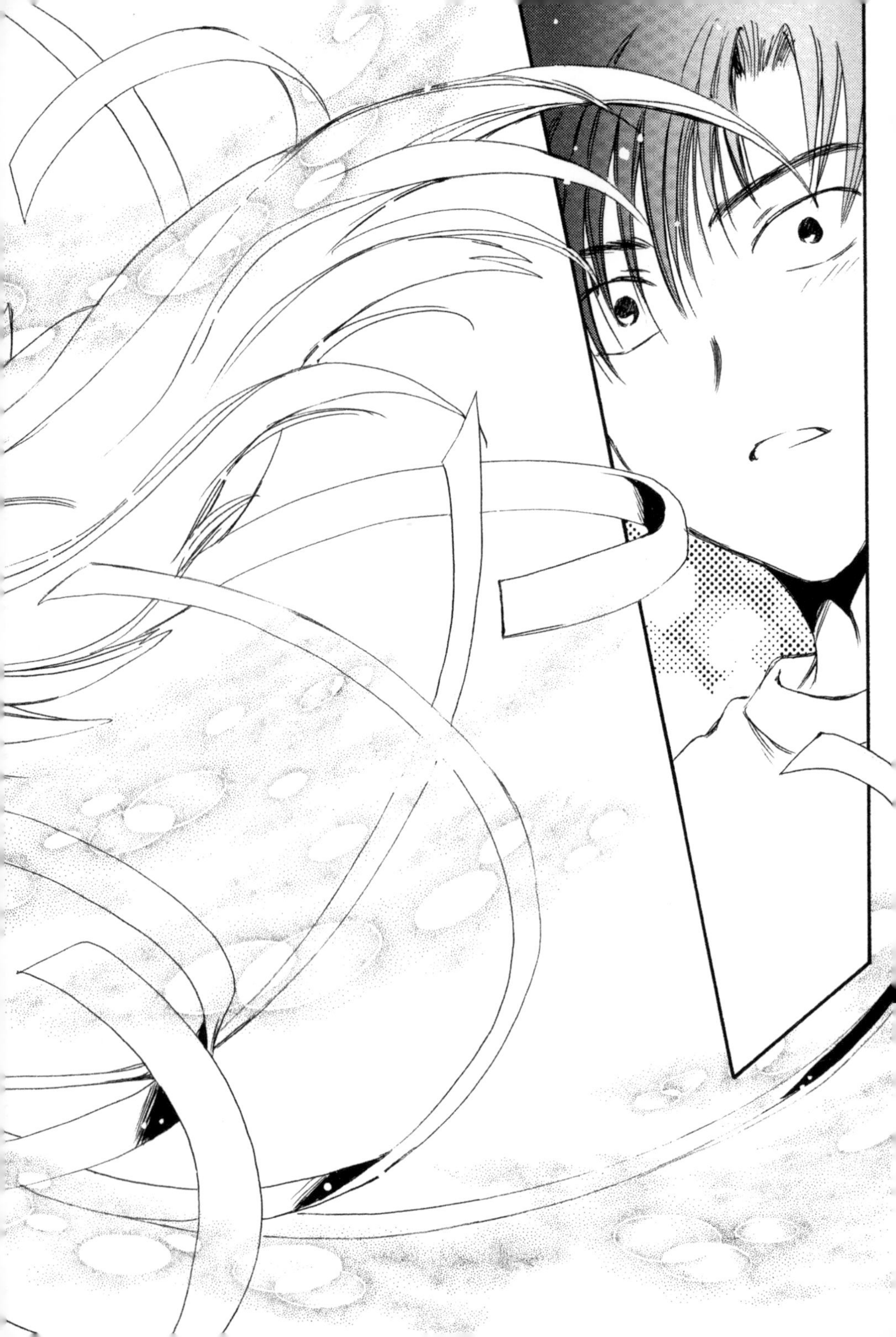

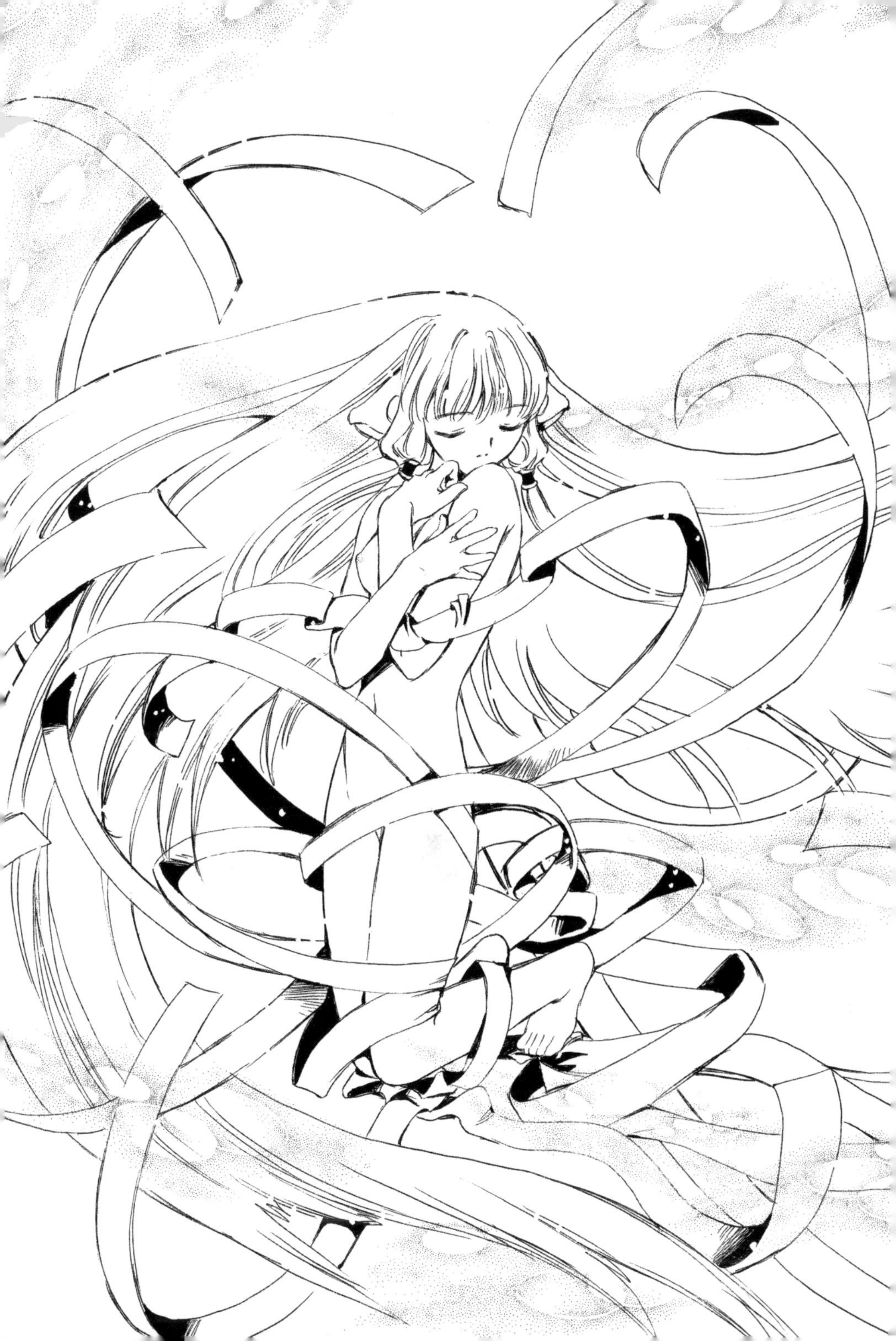

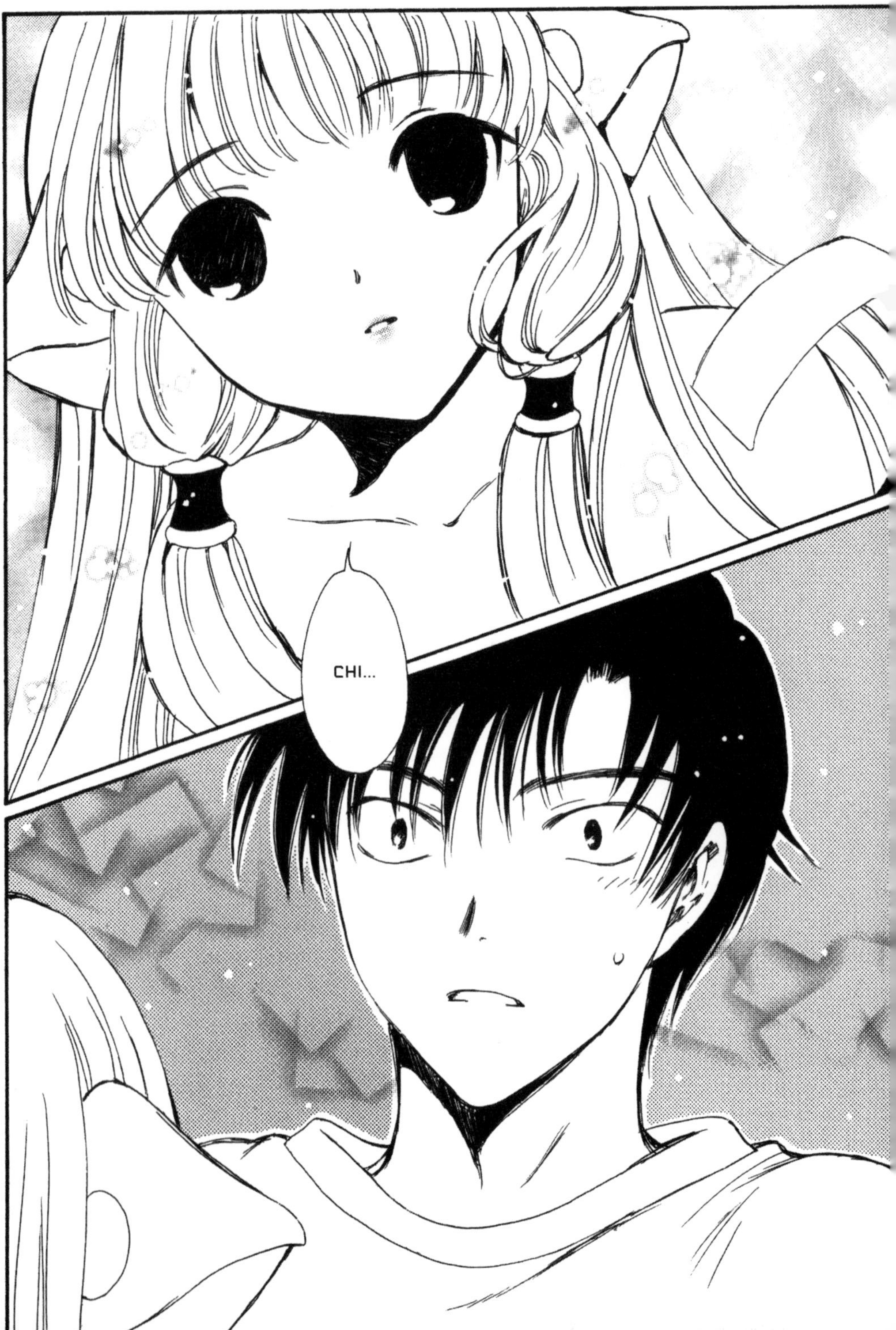
CHI...

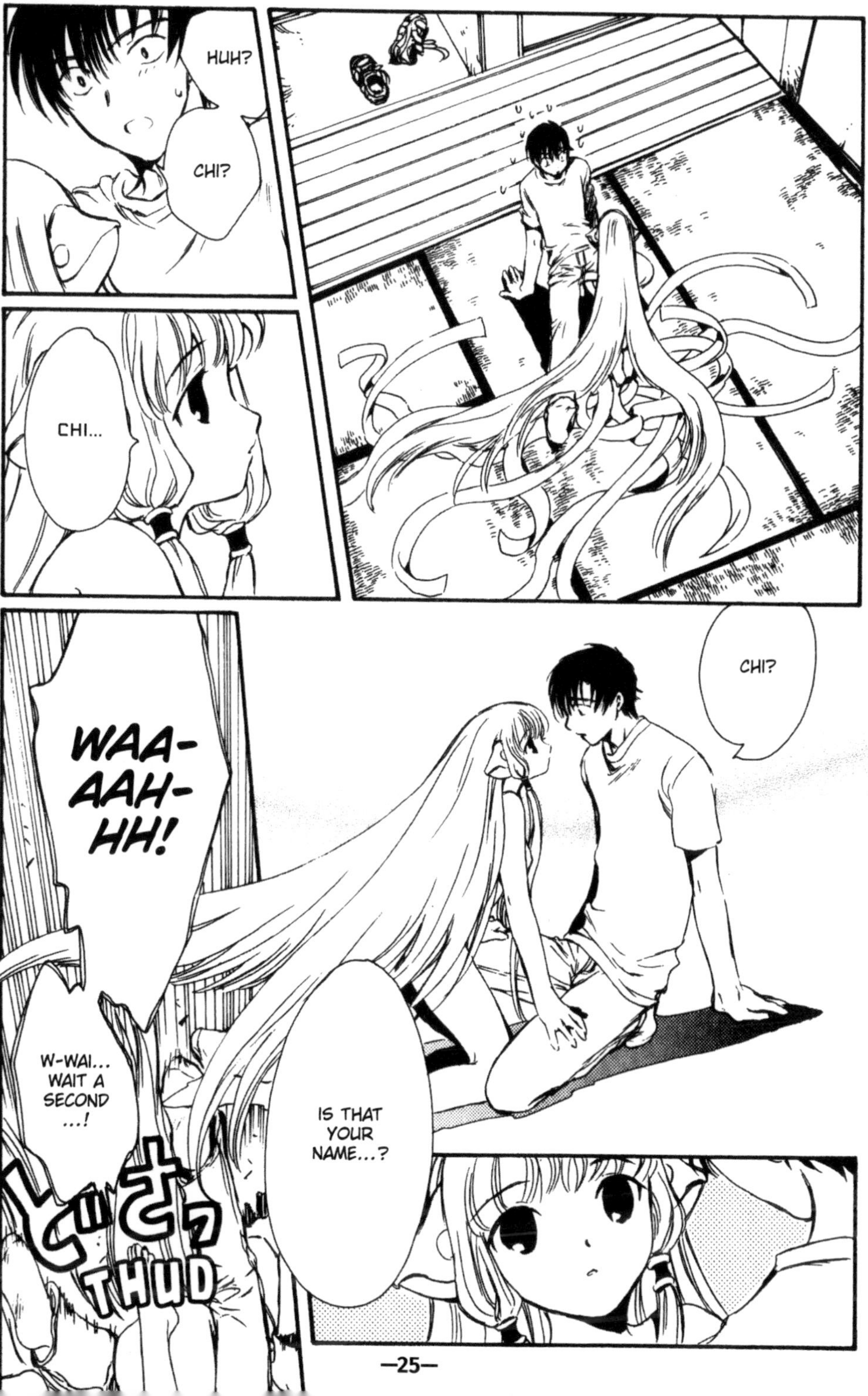
HUH?
CHI?
CHI...
CHI?
IS THAT YOUR NAME...?
WAA-AAH-HH!
W-WAI... WAIT A SECOND ...!
THUD

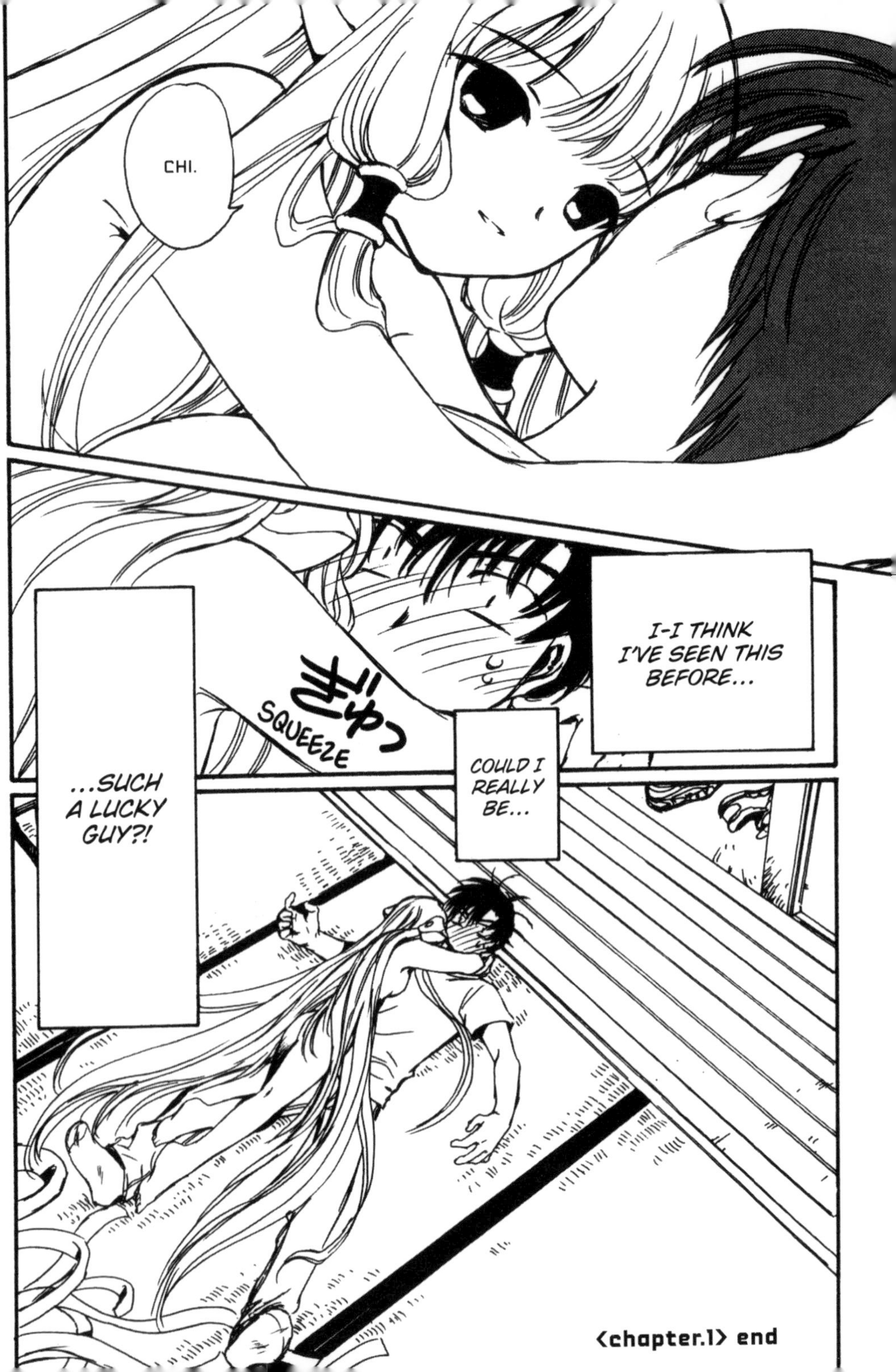
CHI.
I-I THINK I'VE SEEN THIS BEFORE...
ぎゅっ
SQUEEZE
COULD I REALLY BE...
...SUCH A LUCKY GUY?!
<chapter.1> end

⟨chapter.2⟩

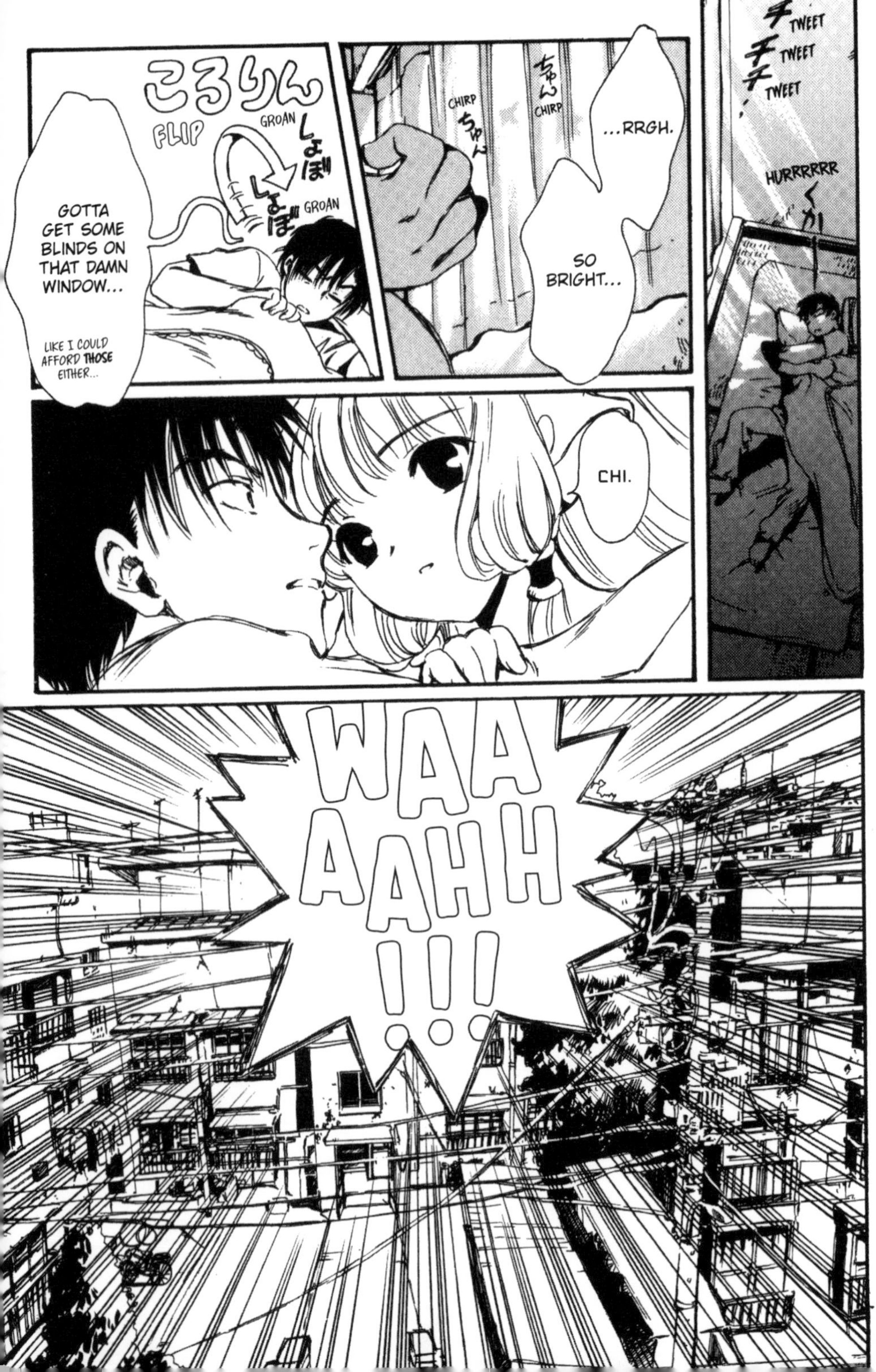
TWEET
TWEET
TWEET
HURRRRRR
CHIRP
CHIRP
...RRGH.
SO BRIGHT...
ころりん
FLIP
GROAN
GROAN
GOTTA GET SOME BLINDS ON THAT DAMN WINDOW...
LIKE I COULD AFFORD **THOSE** EITHER...
CHI.
WAAAAHH!!!

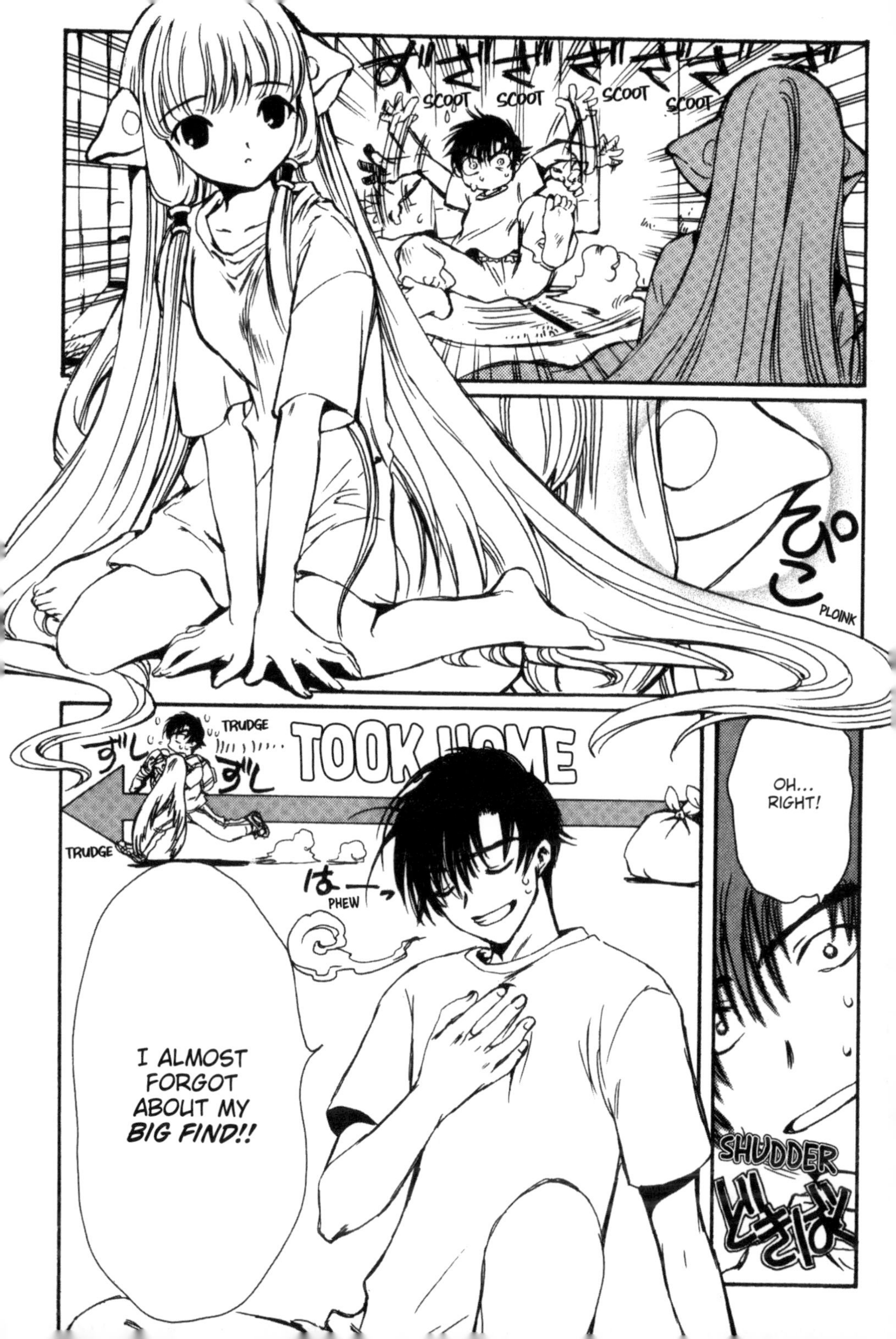

SCOOT
SCOOT
SCOOT
SCOOT
ぴこ
PLOINK
OH... RIGHT!
SHUDDER
TRUDGE
TRUDGE
TOOK HOME
はーっ
PHEW
I ALMOST FORGOT ABOUT MY BIG FIND!!

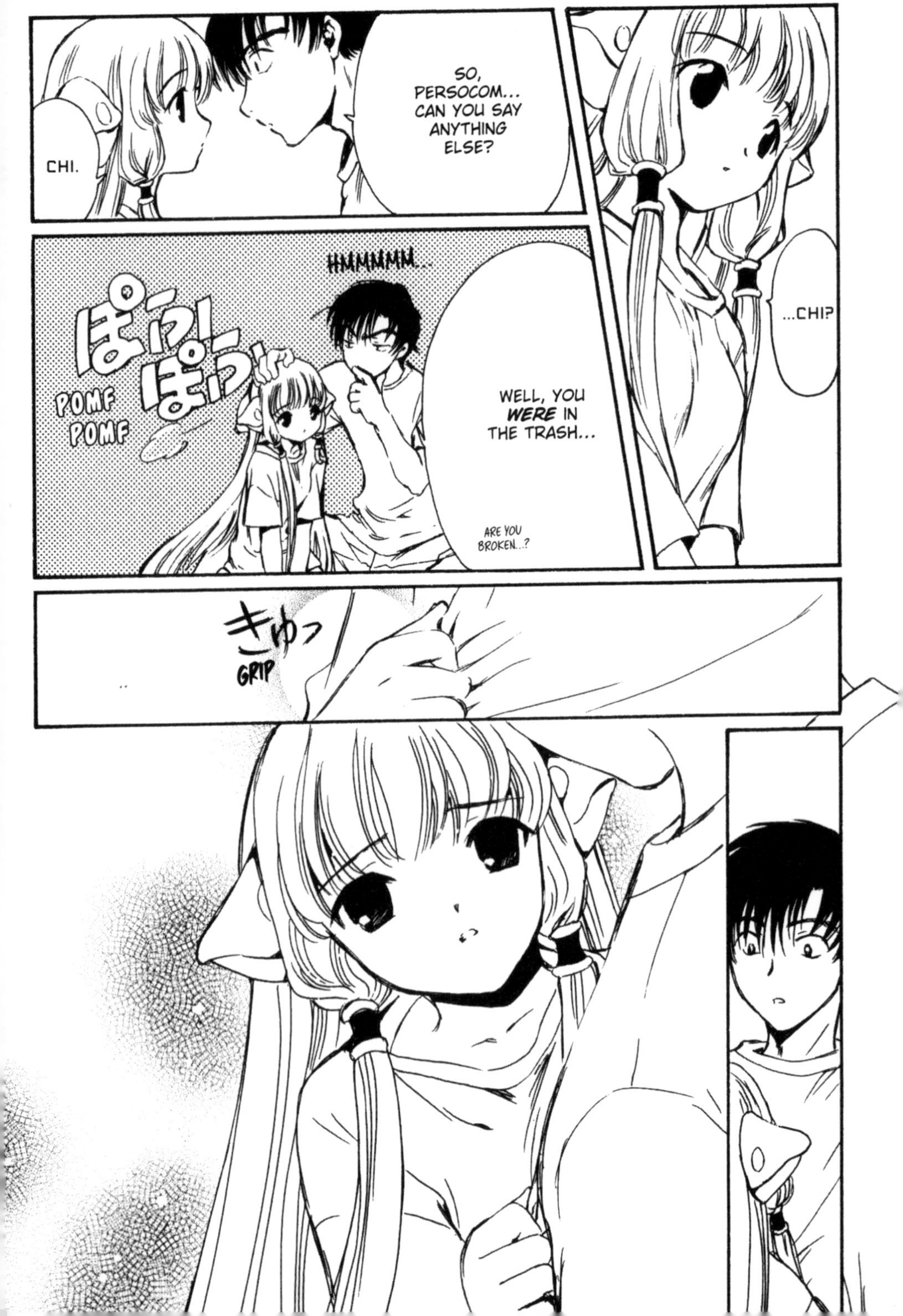

...CHI?
SO, PERSOCOM... CAN YOU SAY ANYTHING ELSE?
CHI.
HMMMMM...
WELL, YOU *WERE* IN THE TRASH...
ARE YOU BROKEN...?
ぽふっぽふっ
POMF POMF
きゅっ
GRIP

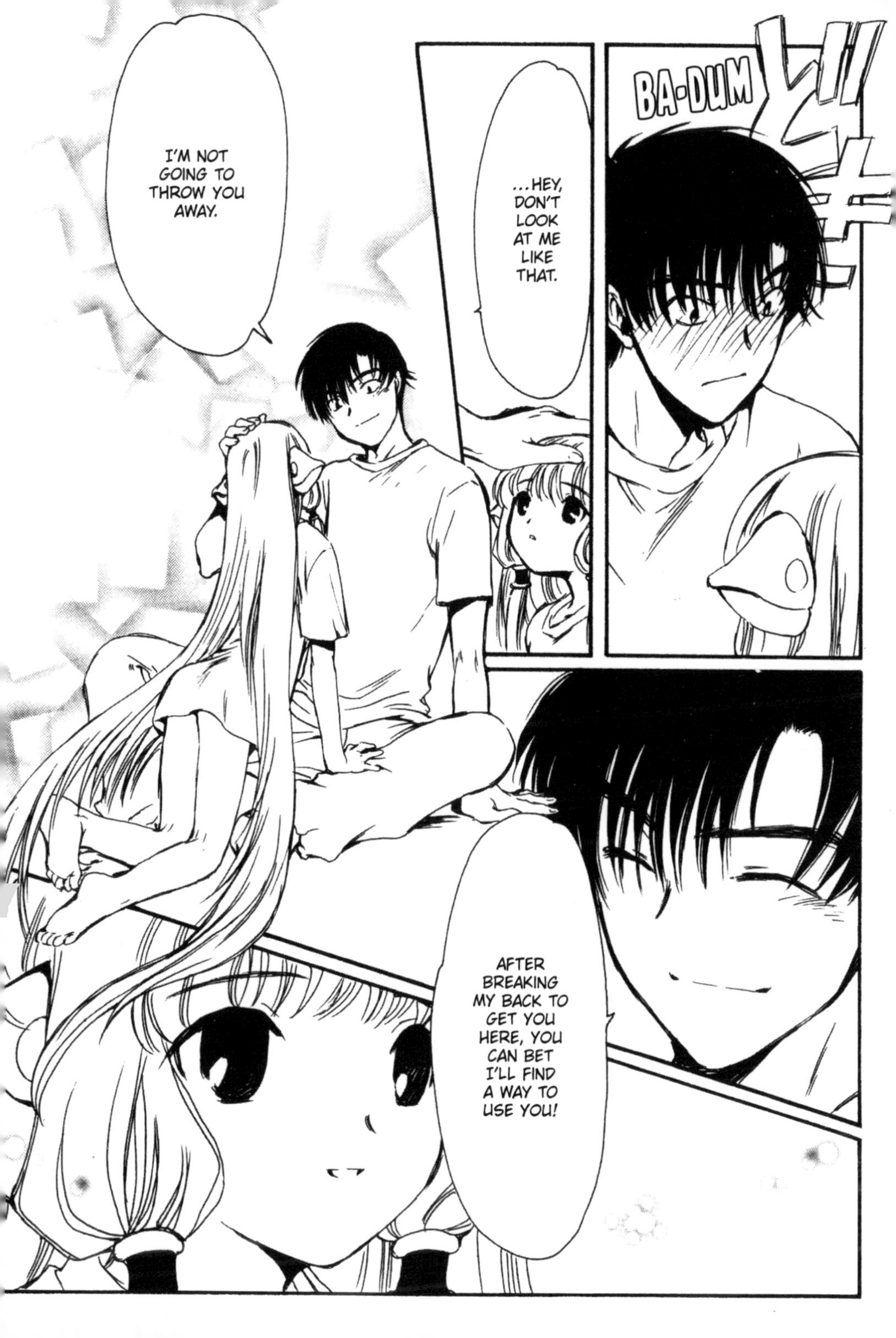
BA-DUM
...HEY, DON'T LOOK AT ME LIKE THAT.
AFTER BREAKING MY BACK TO GET YOU HERE, YOU CAN BET I'LL FIND A WAY TO USE YOU!
I'M NOT GOING TO THROW YOU AWAY.

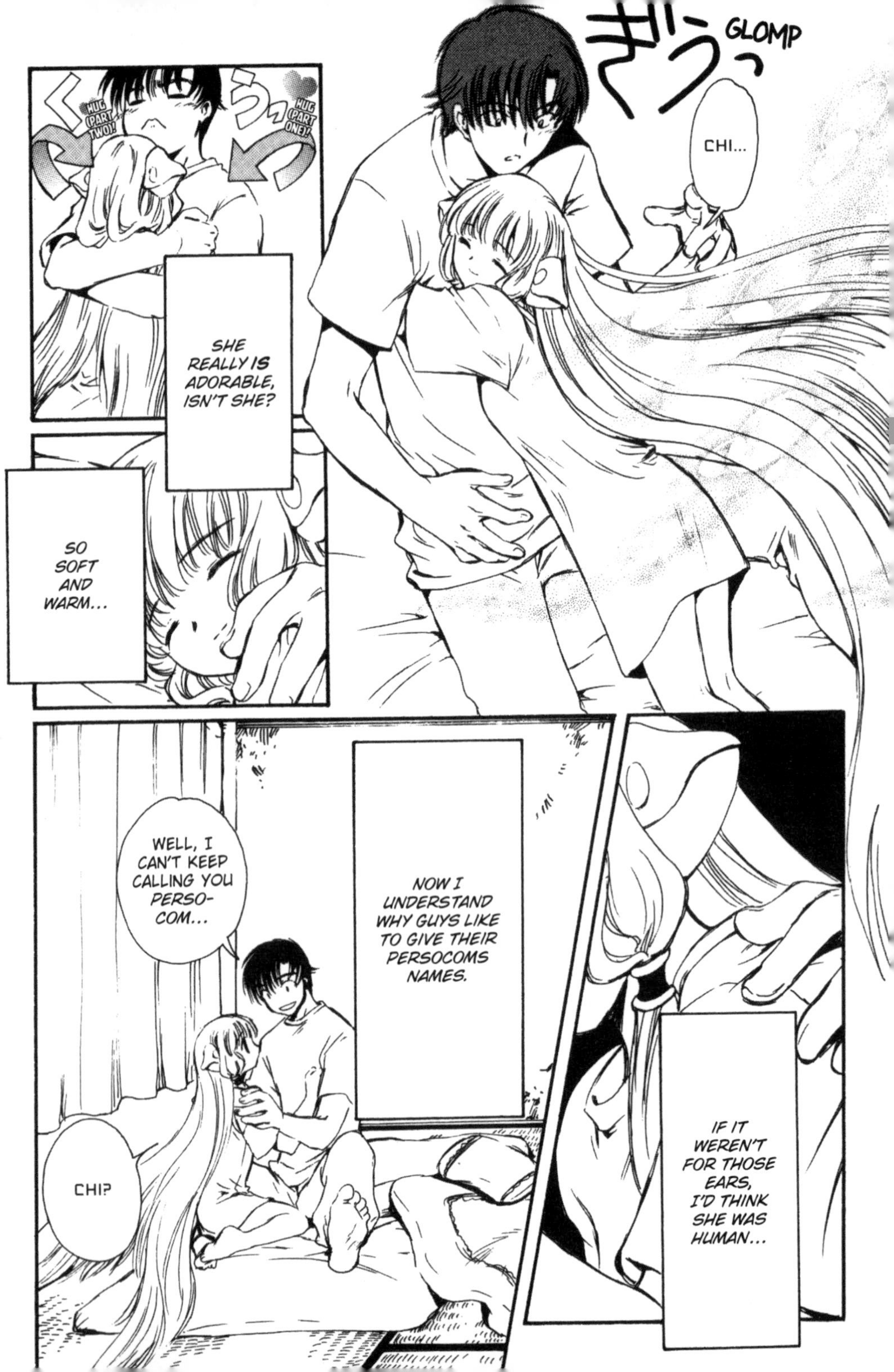
GLOMP
CHI...
HUG (PART ONE)!
HUG (PART TWO)!
SHE REALLY IS ADORABLE, ISN'T SHE?
SO SOFT AND WARM...
IF IT WEREN'T FOR THOSE EARS, I'D THINK SHE WAS HUMAN...
NOW I UNDERSTAND WHY GUYS LIKE TO GIVE THEIR PERSOCOMS NAMES.
WELL, I CAN'T KEEP CALLING YOU PERSO-COM...
CHI?

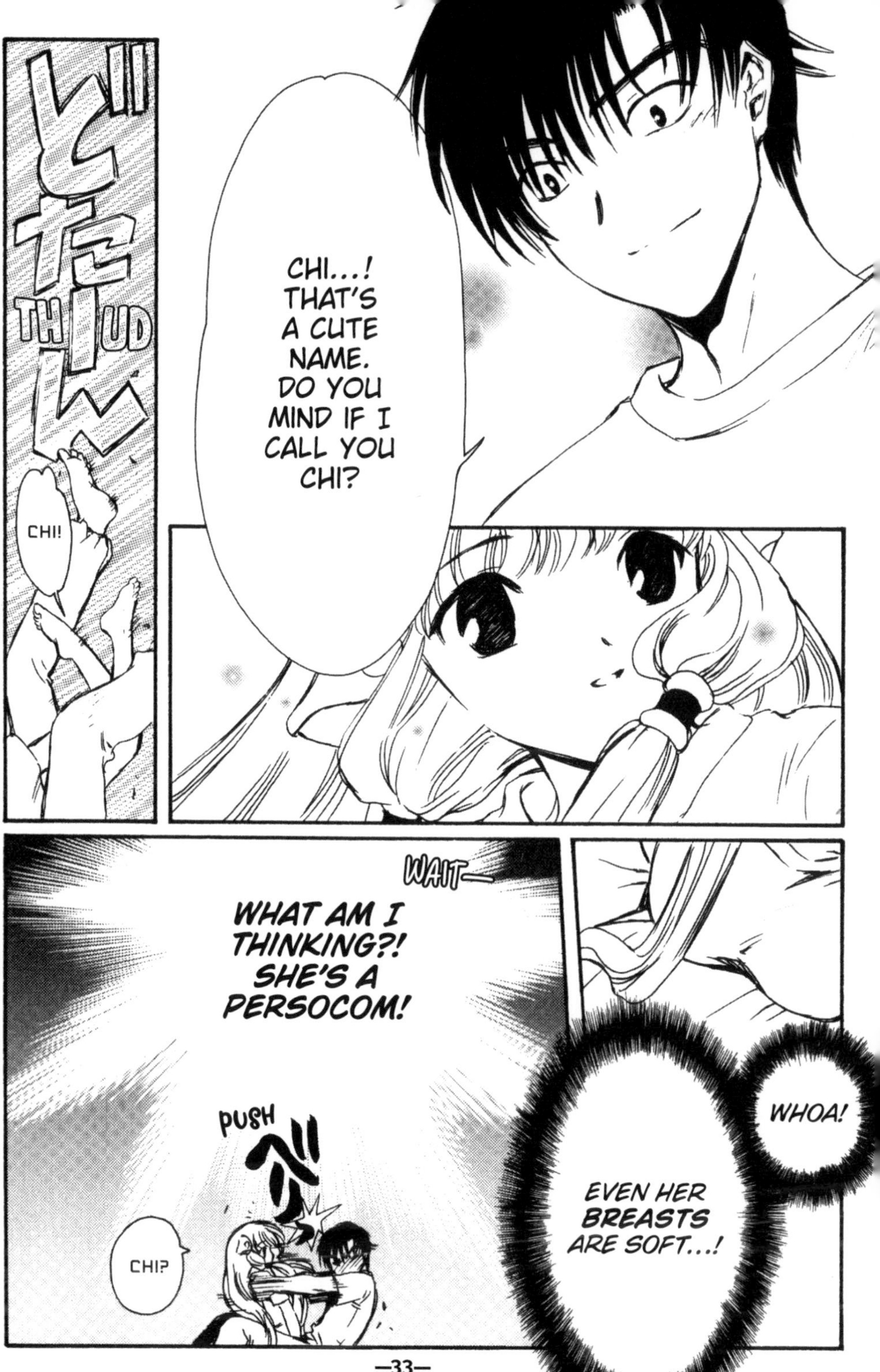

CHI...! THAT'S A CUTE NAME. DO YOU MIND IF I CALL YOU CHI?
THUD
CHI!
WHOA!
EVEN HER BREASTS ARE SOFT...!
WAIT—
WHAT AM I THINKING?! SHE'S A PERSOCOM!
PUSH
CHI?

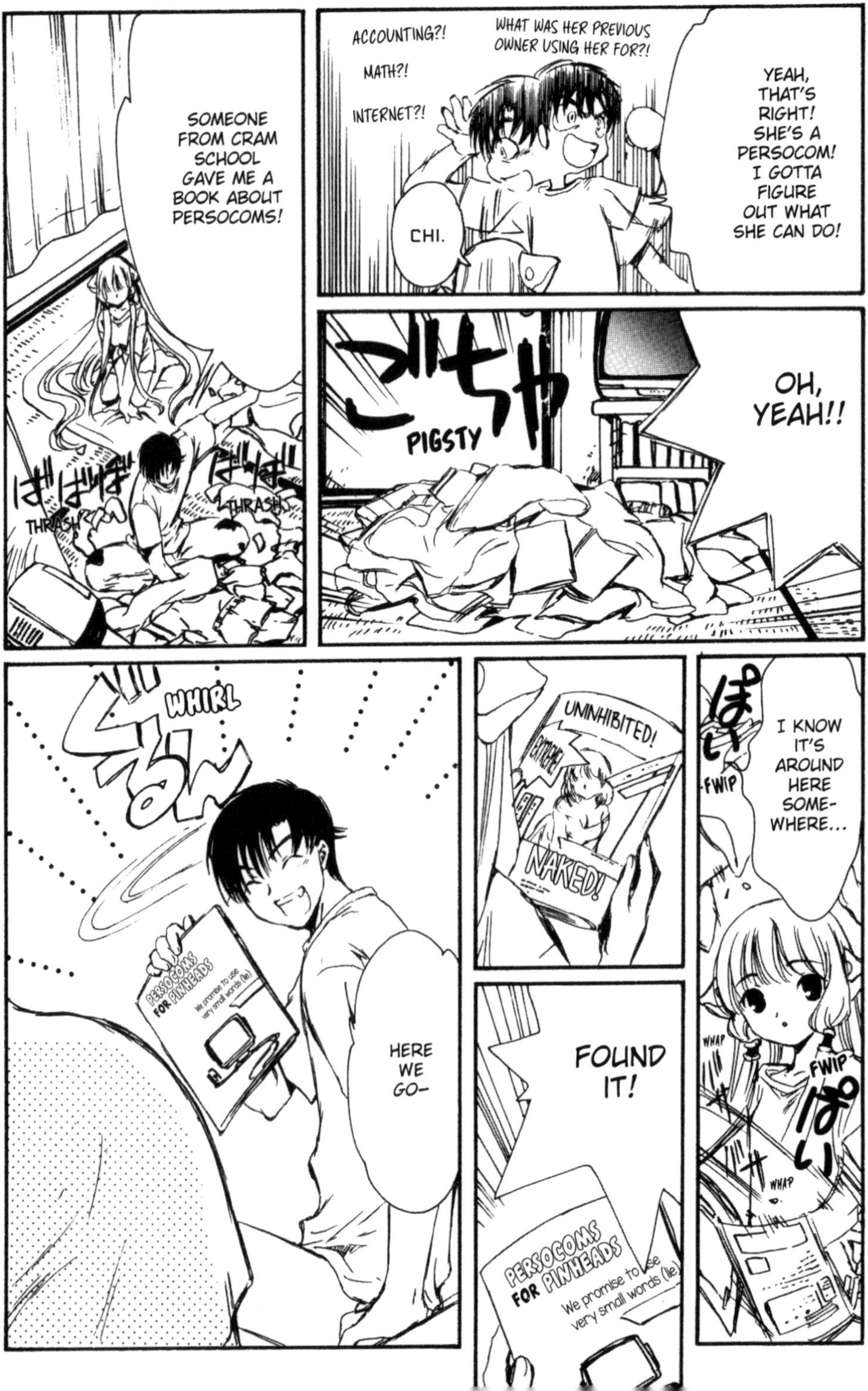

YEAH, THAT'S RIGHT! SHE'S A PERSOCOM! I GOTTA FIGURE OUT WHAT SHE CAN DO!
WHAT WAS HER PREVIOUS OWNER USING HER FOR?!
ACCOUNTING?!
MATH?!
INTERNET?!
CHI.
OH, YEAH!!
ごちゃ
PIGSTY
SOMEONE FROM CRAM SCHOOL GAVE ME A BOOK ABOUT PERSOCOMS!
ばばば
THRASH
ばば
THRASH
ぱい
FWIP
I KNOW IT'S AROUND HERE SOME-WHERE...
WHAP
FWIP
ぱい
WHAP
UNINHIBITED!
EXTREME!
NAKED!
FOUND IT!
PERSOCOMS FOR PINHEADS
We promise to use very small words (lie)
WHIRL
くるん
HERE WE GO-
PERSOCOMS FOR PINHEADS
We promise to use very small words (lie)

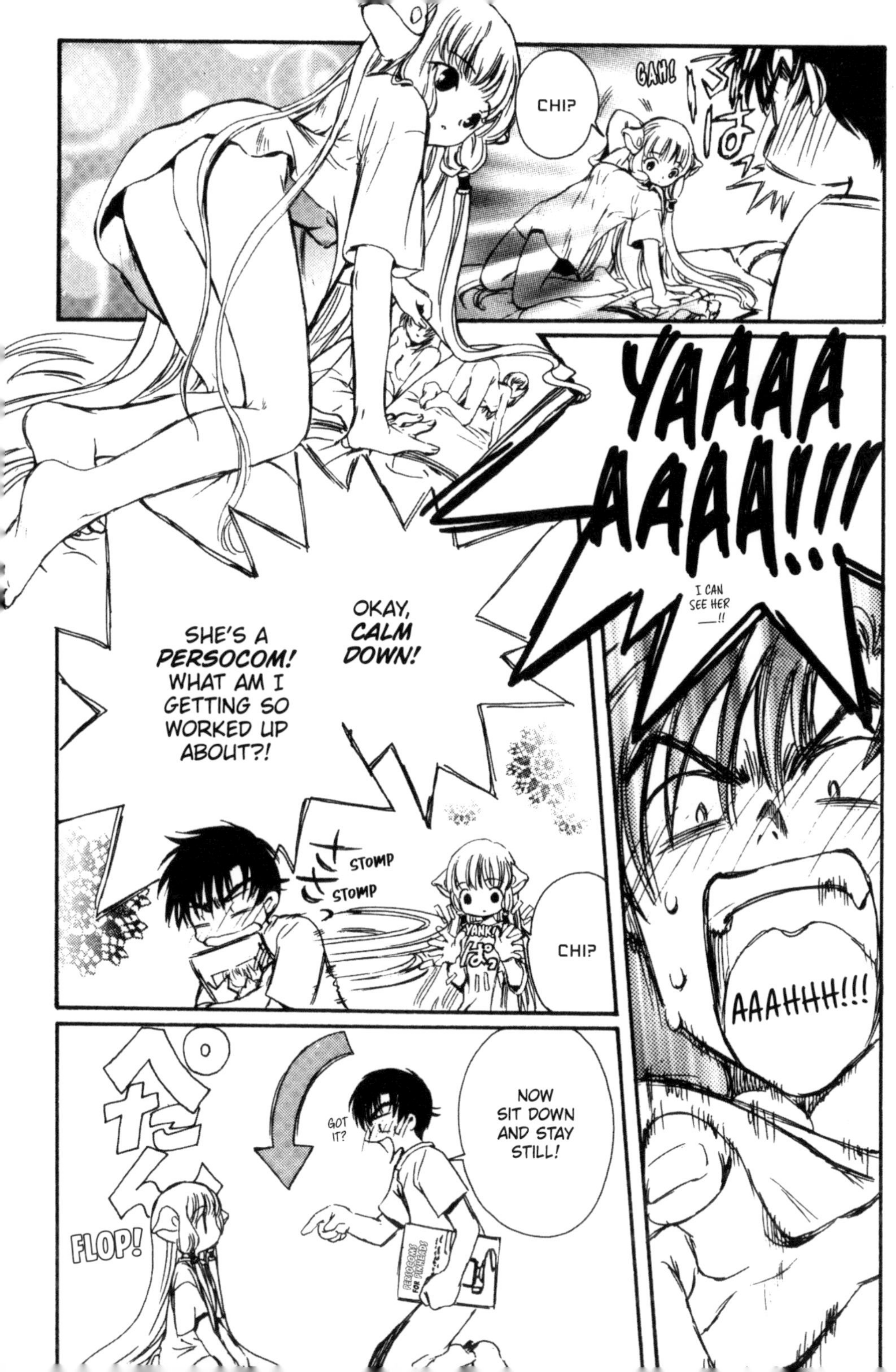
GAH!
ぶは
CHI?
YAAAAAAAAA!!!
I CAN SEE HER —!!
AAAHHH!!!
OKAY, CALM DOWN!
SHE'S A PERSOCOM! WHAT AM I GETTING SO WORKED UP ABOUT?!
CHI?
YANK!
STOMP
STOMP
NOW SIT DOWN AND STAY STILL!
GOT IT?
PERSOCOMS FOR PINHEADS
ぺたん
FLOP!

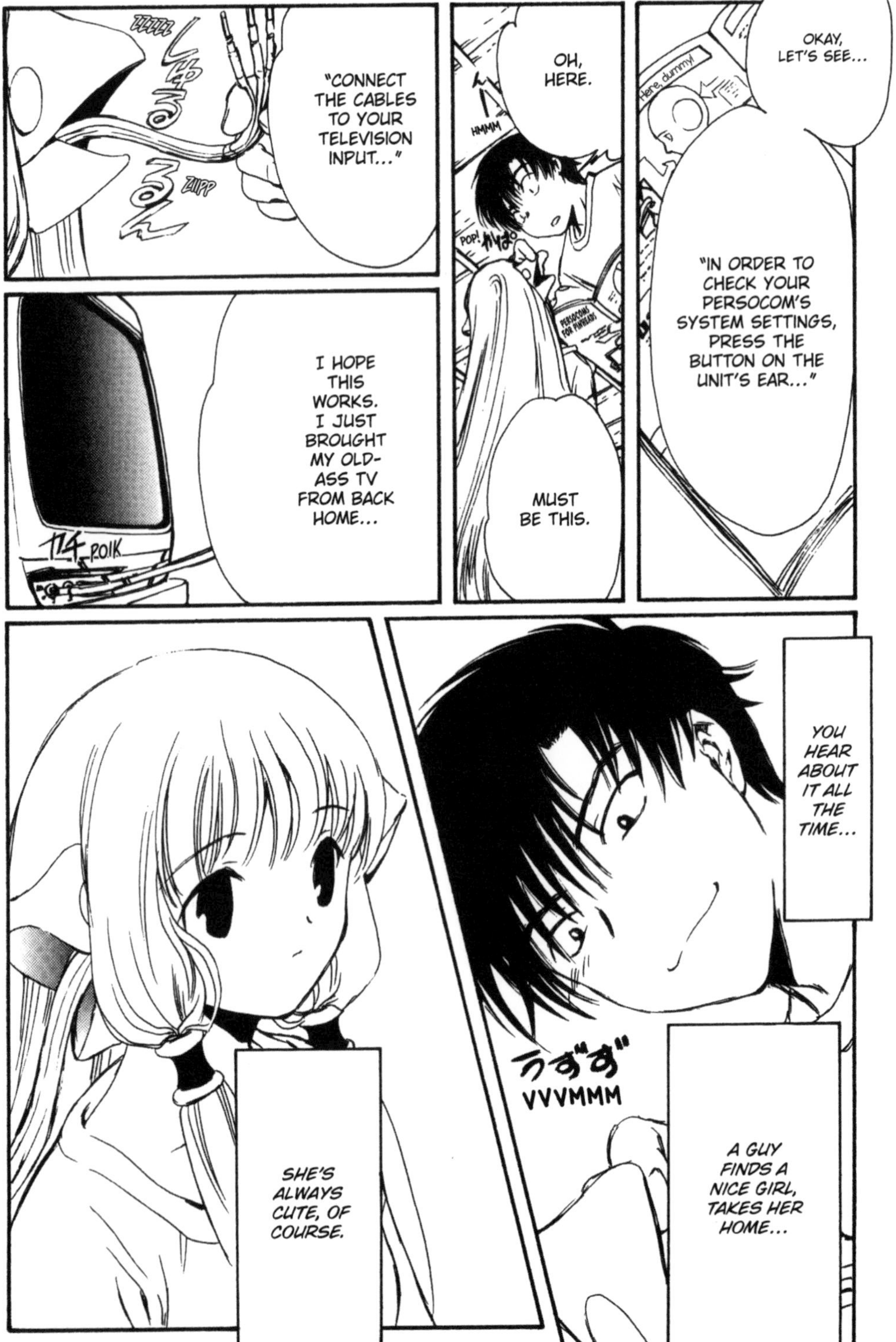
OKAY, LET'S SEE...
Here, dummy!
"IN ORDER TO CHECK YOUR PERSOCOM'S SYSTEM SETTINGS, PRESS THE BUTTON ON THE UNIT'S EAR..."
OH, HERE.
HMMM
POP!
PERSOCOMS FOR PINHEADS
MUST BE THIS.
ZZZZZ
"CONNECT THE CABLES TO YOUR TELEVISION INPUT..."
ZIIPP
I HOPE THIS WORKS. I JUST BROUGHT MY OLD-ASS TV FROM BACK HOME...
POIK
YOU HEAR ABOUT IT ALL THE TIME...
VVVMMM
A GUY FINDS A NICE GIRL, TAKES HER HOME...
SHE'S ALWAYS CUTE, OF COURSE.

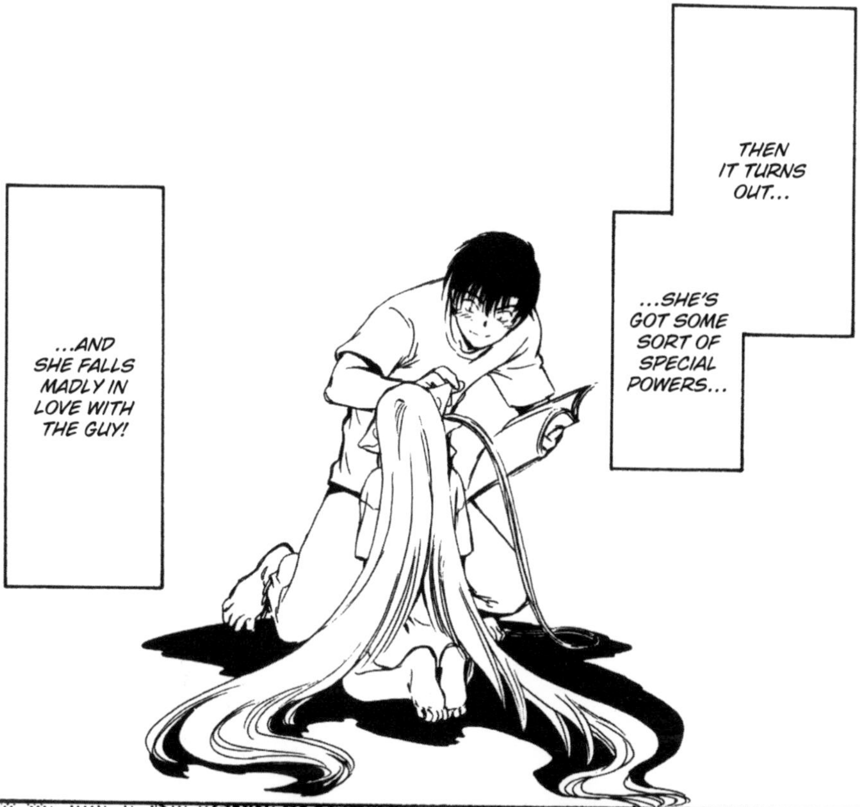
THEN IT TURNS OUT...
...SHE'S GOT SOME SORT OF SPECIAL POWERS...
...AND SHE FALLS MADLY IN LOVE WITH THE GUY!

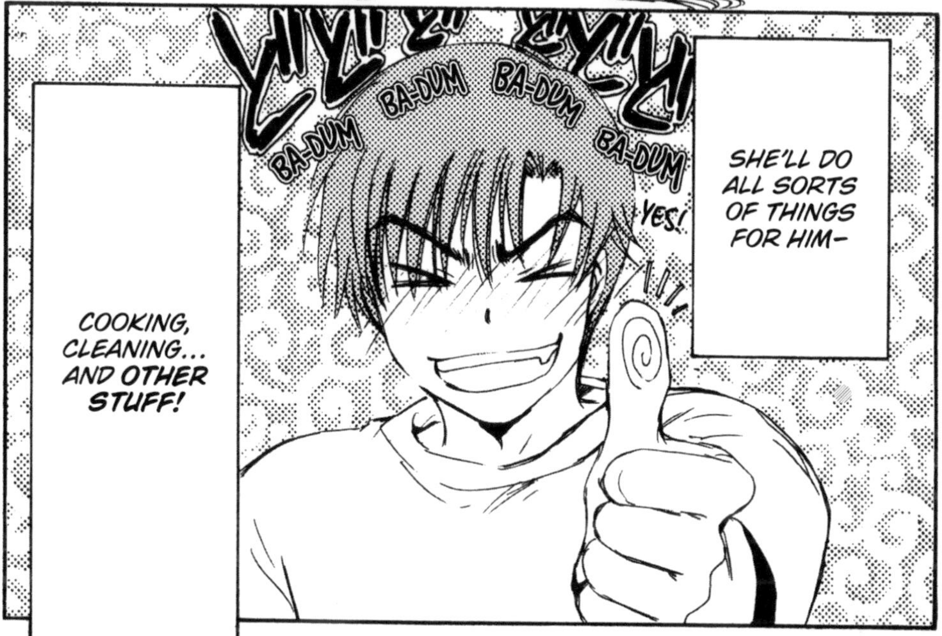
SHE'LL DO ALL SORTS OF THINGS FOR HIM-
BA-DUM BA-DUM BA-DUM BA-DUM BA-DUM
YES!
COOKING, CLEANING... AND OTHER STUFF!

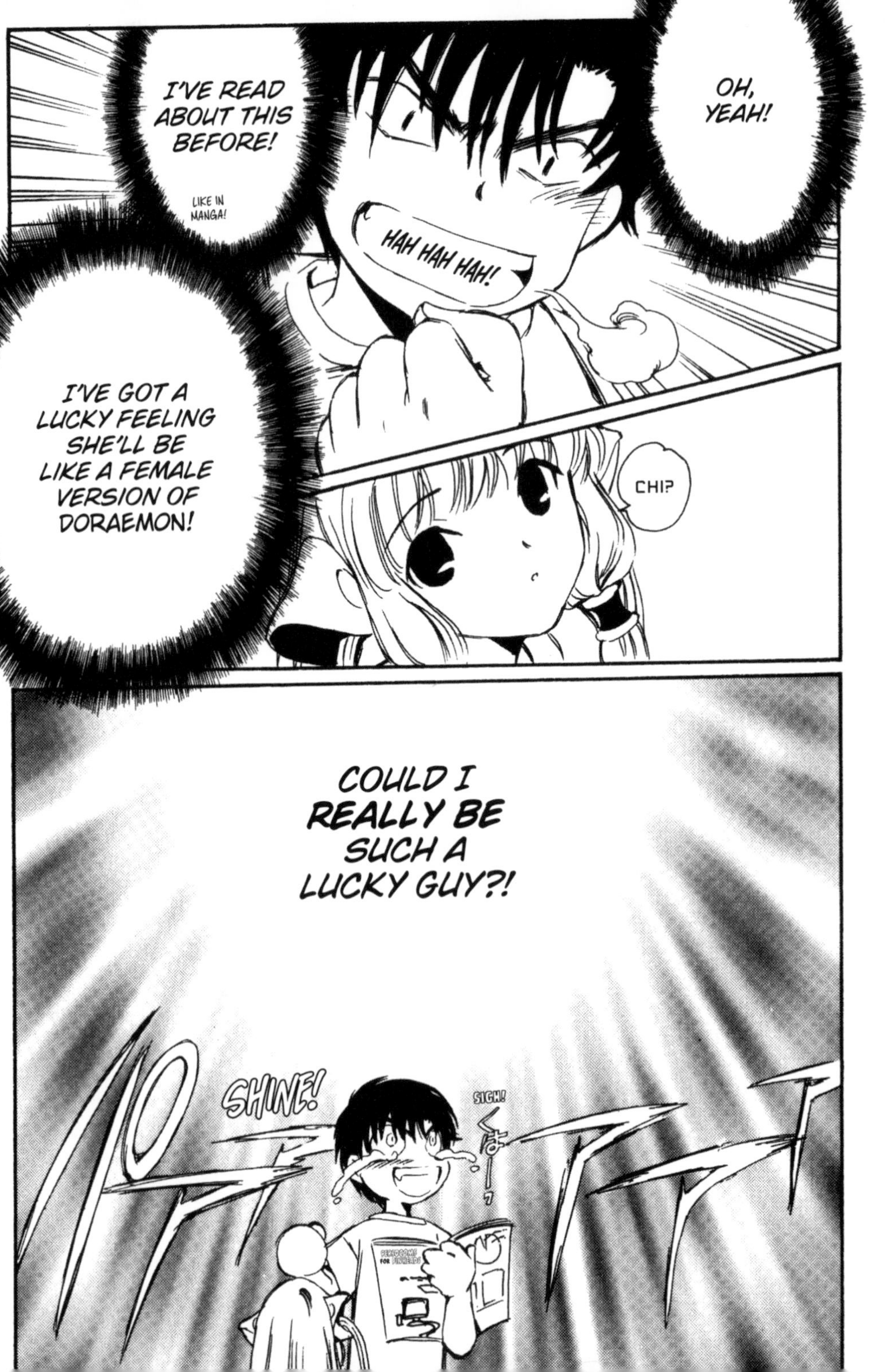
OH, YEAH!
I'VE READ ABOUT THIS BEFORE!
LIKE IN MANGA!
HAH HAH HAH!
I'VE GOT A LUCKY FEELING SHE'LL BE LIKE A FEMALE VERSION OF DORAEMON!
CHI?
COULD I REALLY BE SUCH A LUCKY GUY?!
SIGH!
SHINE!

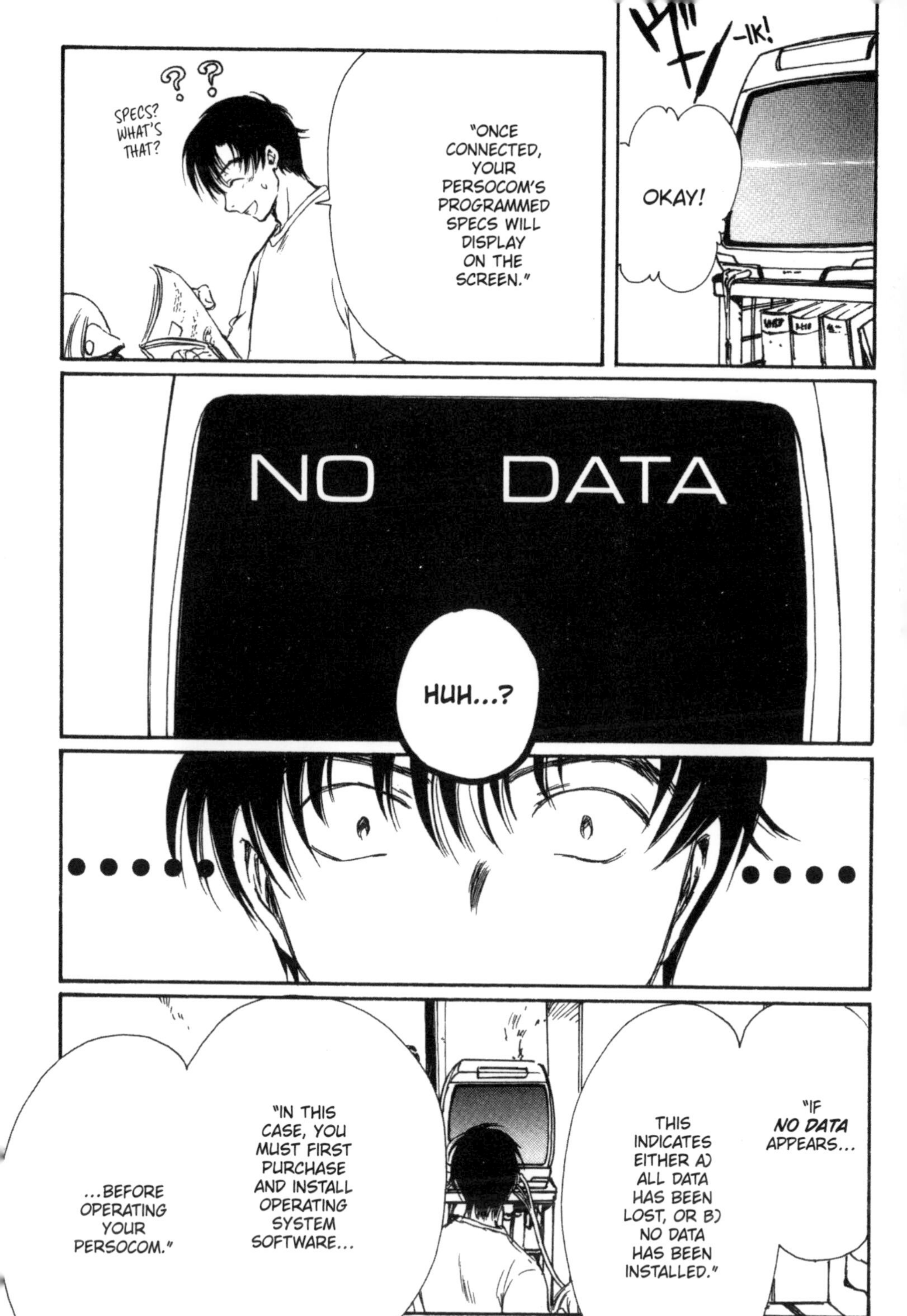
-IK!
OKAY!
"ONCE CONNECTED, YOUR PERSOCOM'S PROGRAMMED SPECS WILL DISPLAY ON THE SCREEN."
SPECS? WHAT'S THAT?
NO DATA
HUH...?
.....
....
"IF NO DATA APPEARS...
THIS INDICATES EITHER A) ALL DATA HAS BEEN LOST, OR B) NO DATA HAS BEEN INSTALLED."
"IN THIS CASE, YOU MUST FIRST PURCHASE AND INSTALL OPERATING SYSTEM SOFTWARE...
...BEFORE OPERATING YOUR PERSOCOM."

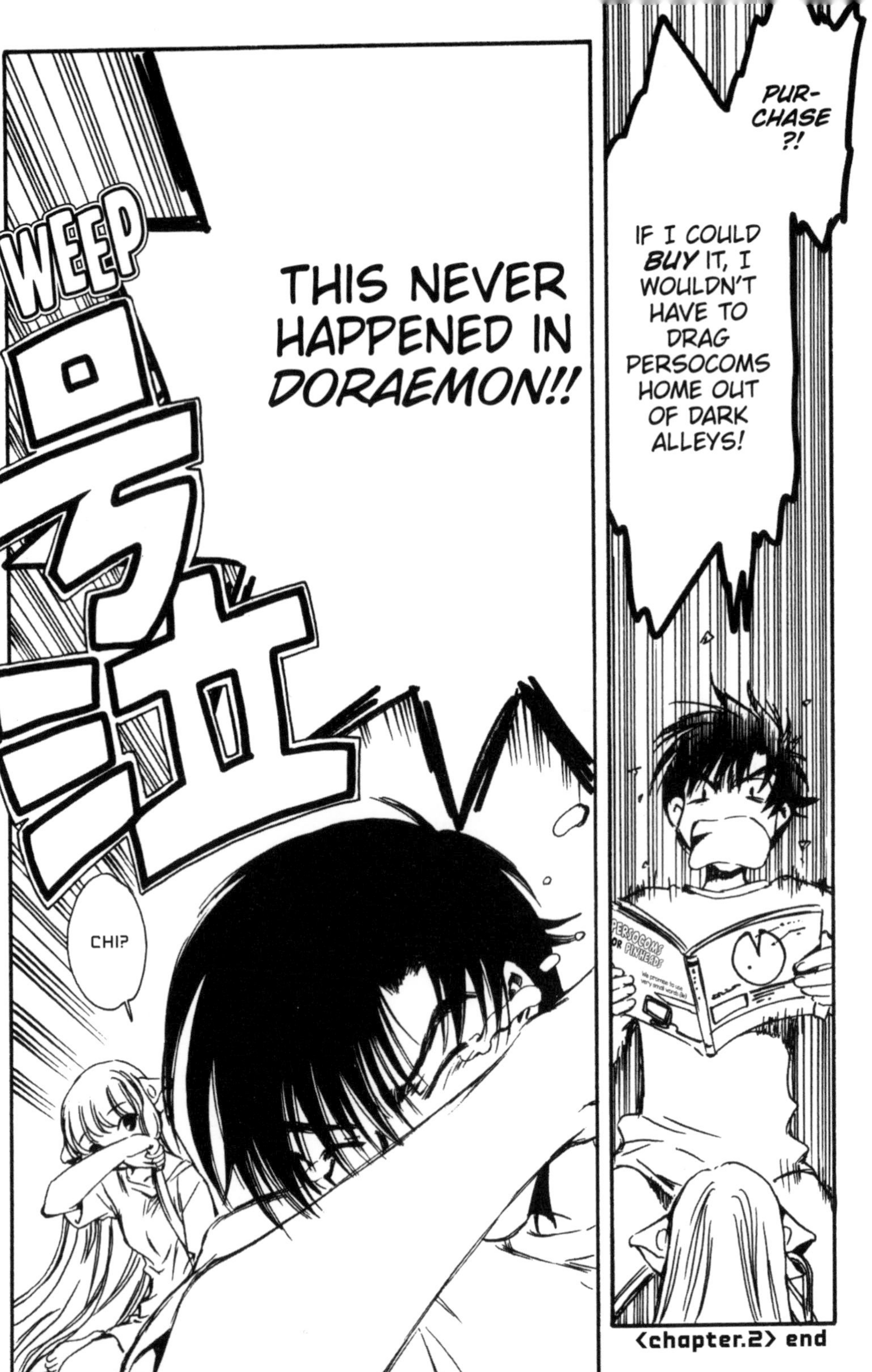
PUR-CHASE?!
IF I COULD BUY IT, I WOULDN'T HAVE TO DRAG PERSOCOMS HOME OUT OF DARK ALLEYS!
PERSOCOMS OR PINHEADS
WEEP
THIS NEVER HAPPENED IN DORAEMON!!
CHI?

<chapter.2> end

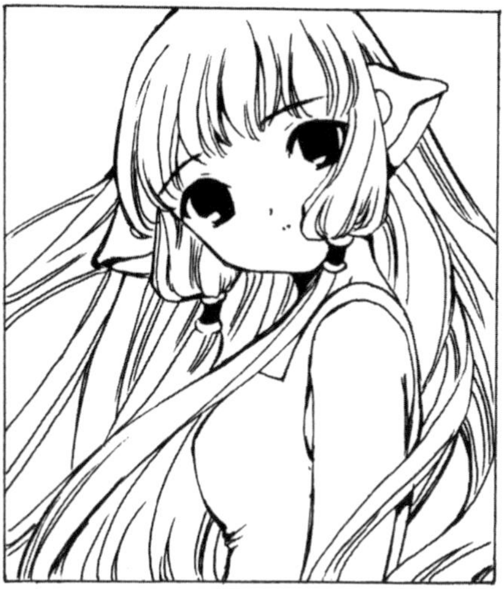
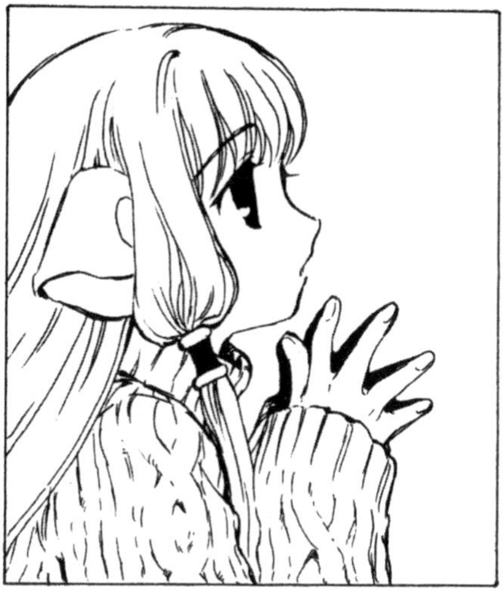
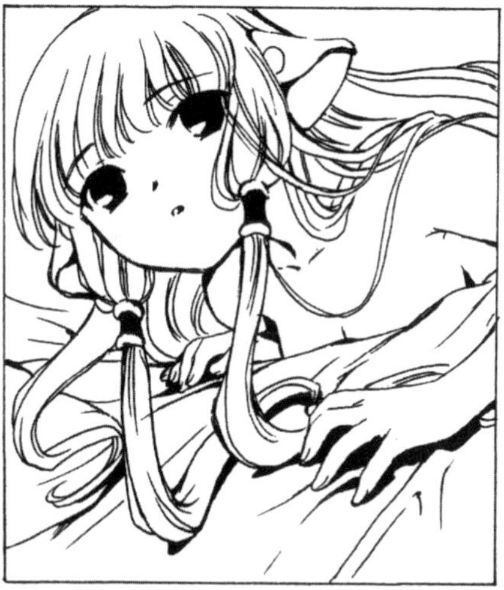
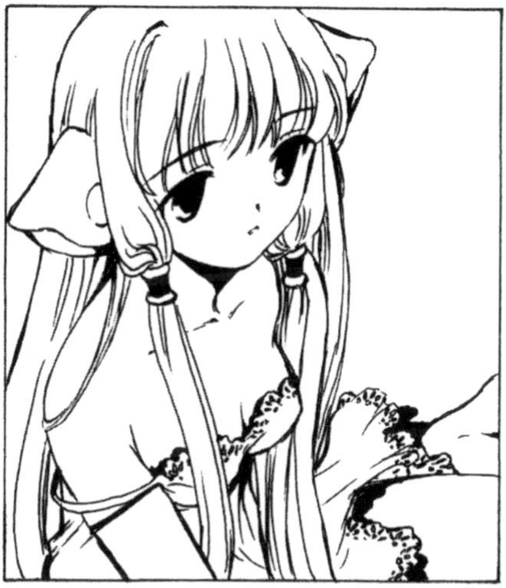

Chobits

<chapter.3>

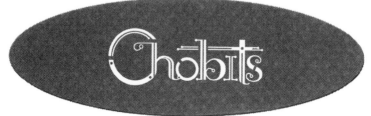

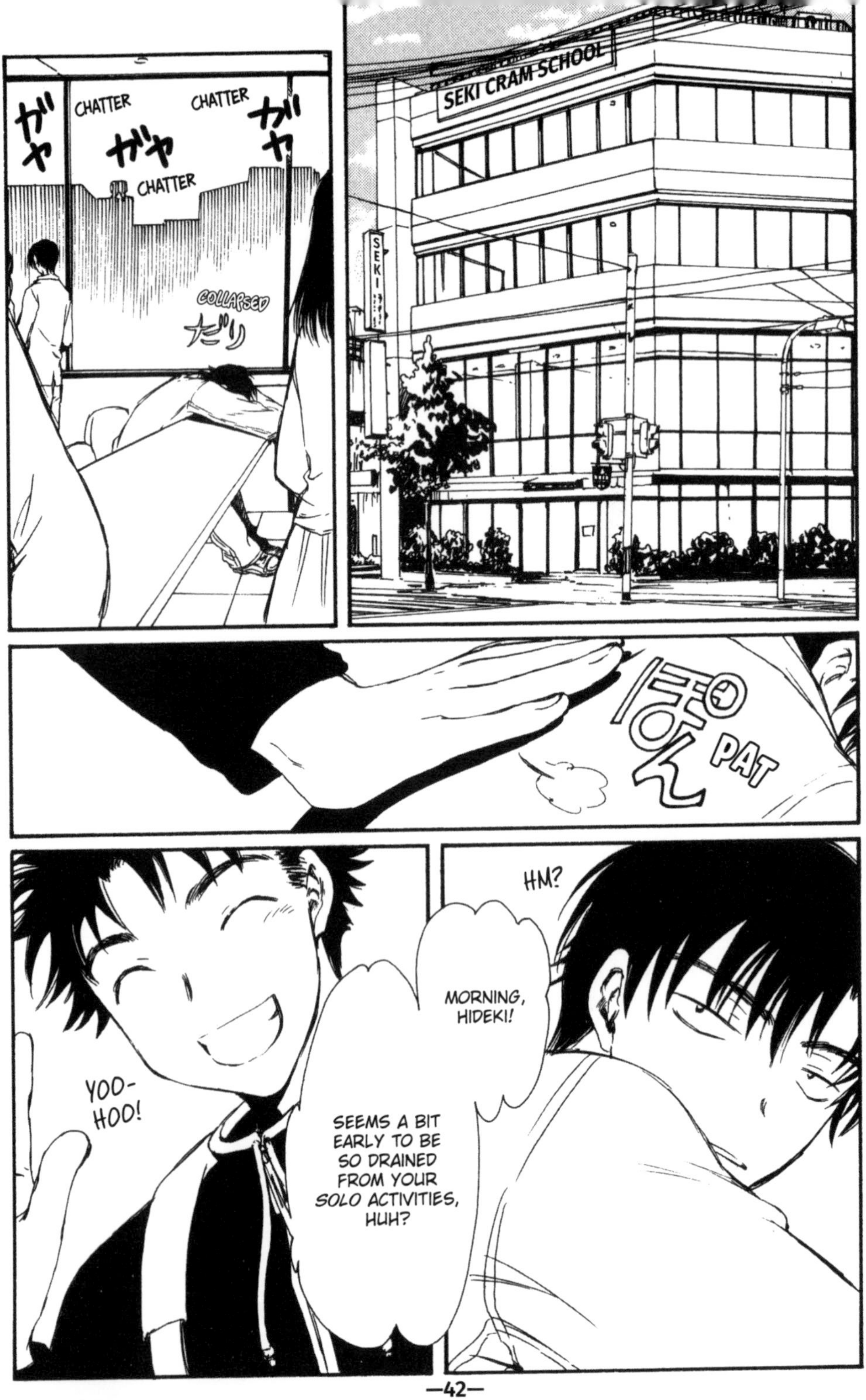

SEKI CRAM SCHOOL
SEKI
ガヤ
CHATTER
ガヤ
CHATTER
ガヤ
CHATTER
ダリ
COLLAPSED
ぽん
PAT
HM?
MORNING, HIDEKI!
SEEMS A BIT EARLY TO BE SO DRAINED FROM YOUR SOLO ACTIVITIES, HUH?
YOO-HOO!

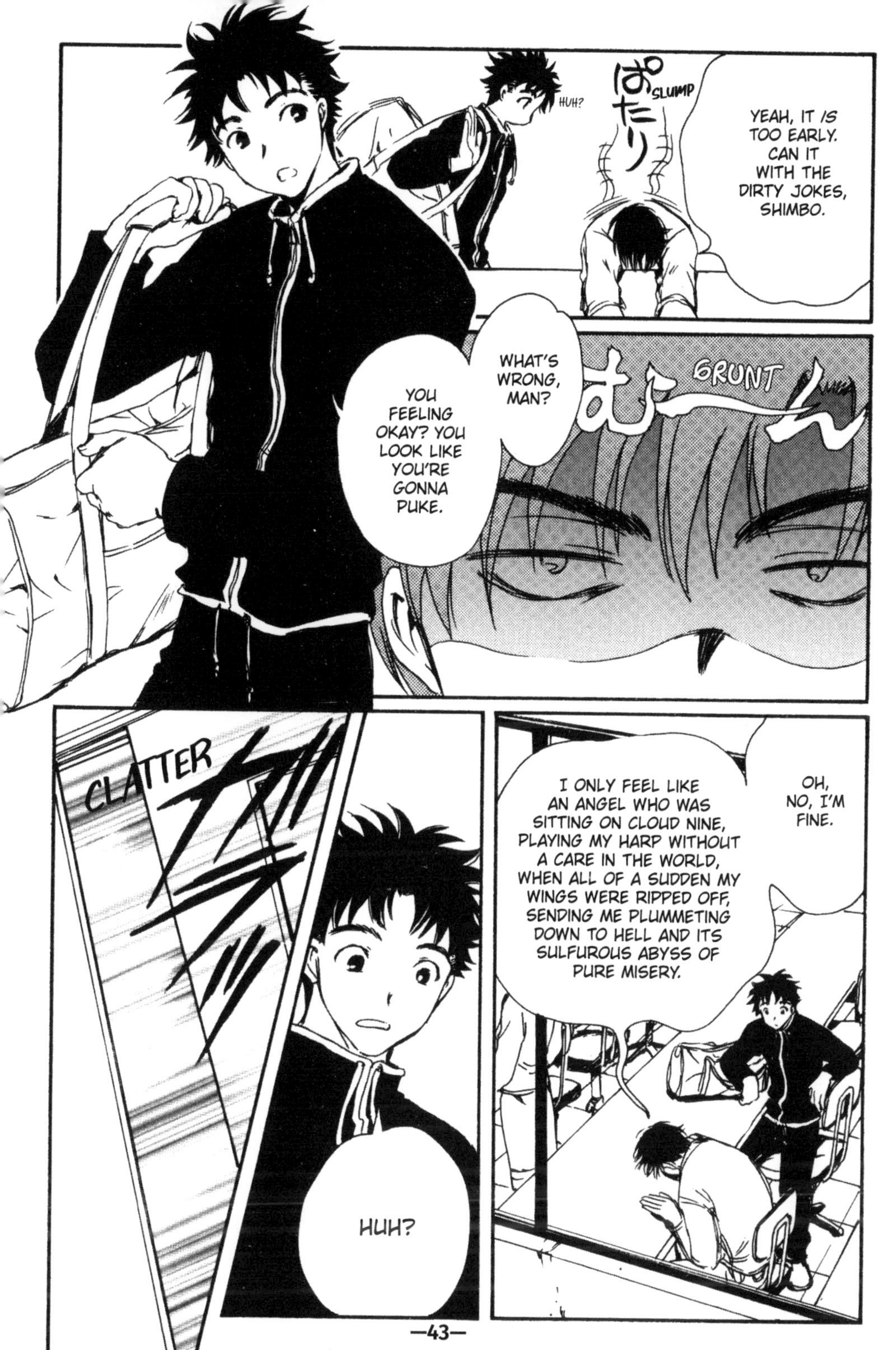
YEAH, IT IS TOO EARLY. CAN IT WITH THE DIRTY JOKES, SHIMBO.
ぱたり
SLUMP
HUH?
むーん
GRUNT
WHAT'S WRONG, MAN?
YOU FEELING OKAY? YOU LOOK LIKE YOU'RE GONNA PUKE.
OH, NO, I'M FINE.
I ONLY FEEL LIKE AN ANGEL WHO WAS SITTING ON CLOUD NINE, PLAYING MY HARP WITHOUT A CARE IN THE WORLD, WHEN ALL OF A SUDDEN MY WINGS WERE RIPPED OFF, SENDING ME PLUMMETING DOWN TO HELL AND ITS SULFUROUS ABYSS OF PURE MISERY.
CLATTER
HUH?

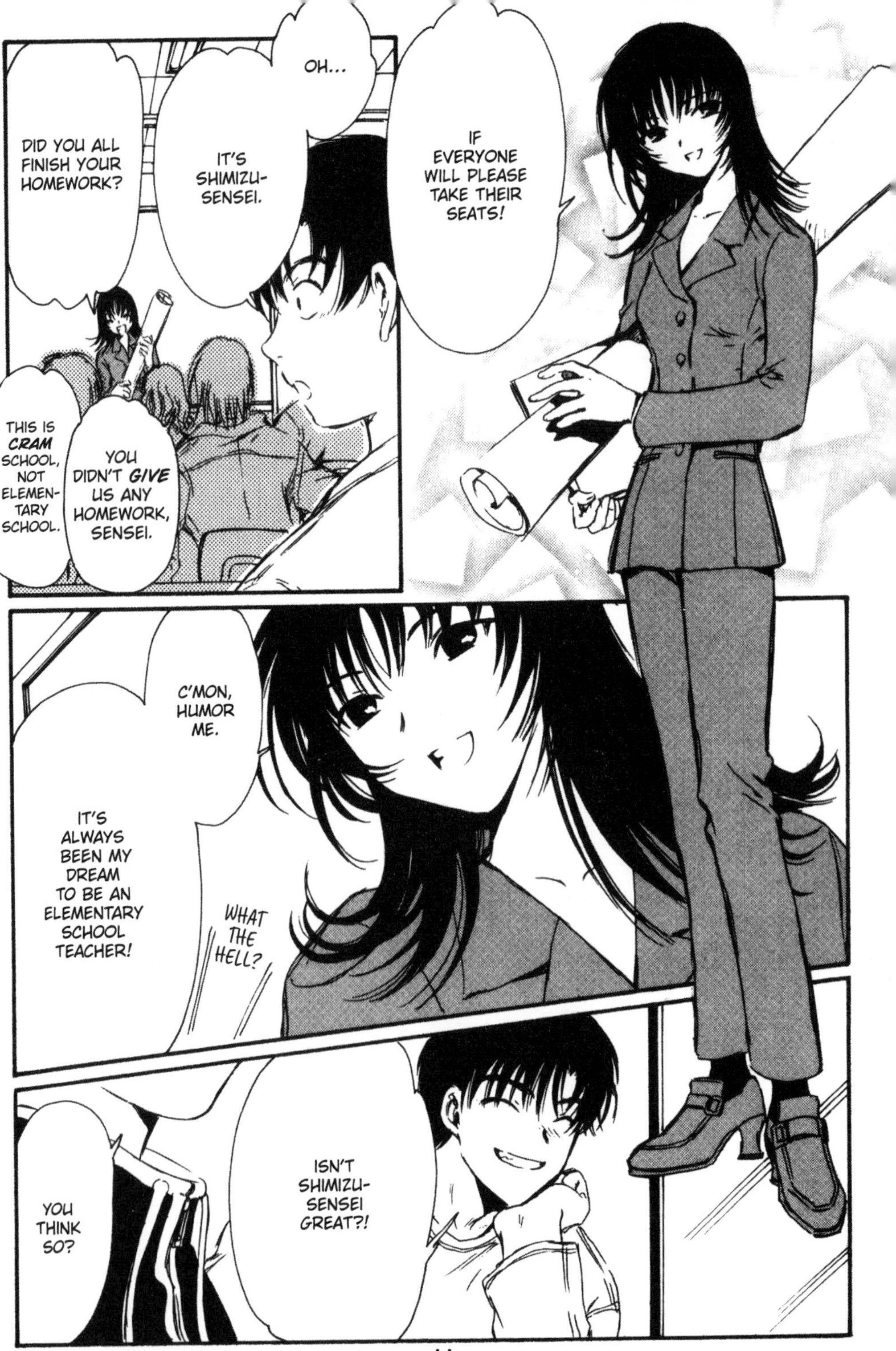
IF EVERYONE WILL PLEASE TAKE THEIR SEATS!
OH...
IT'S SHIMIZU-SENSEI.
DID YOU ALL FINISH YOUR HOMEWORK?
YOU DIDN'T *GIVE* US ANY HOMEWORK, SENSEI.
THIS IS *CRAM* SCHOOL, NOT ELEMENTARY SCHOOL.
C'MON, HUMOR ME.
IT'S ALWAYS BEEN MY DREAM TO BE AN ELEMENTARY SCHOOL TEACHER!
WHAT THE HELL?
ISN'T SHIMIZU-SENSEI GREAT?!
YOU THINK SO?

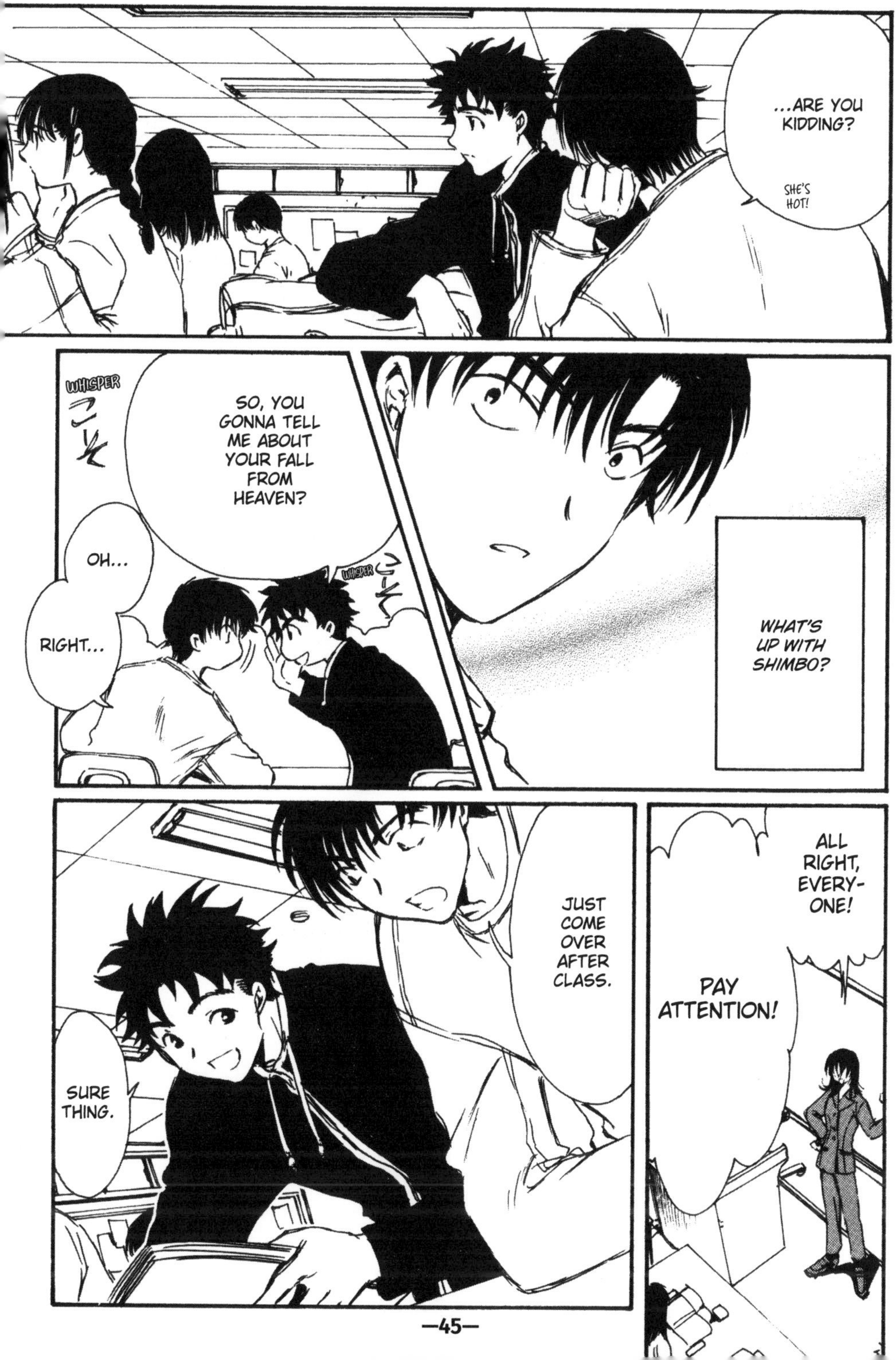
...ARE YOU KIDDING?
SHE'S HOT!
WHAT'S UP WITH SHIMBO?
WHISPER
SO, YOU GONNA TELL ME ABOUT YOUR FALL FROM HEAVEN?
WHISPER
OH...
RIGHT...
ALL RIGHT, EVERY-ONE!
PAY ATTENTION!
JUST COME OVER AFTER CLASS.
SURE THING.

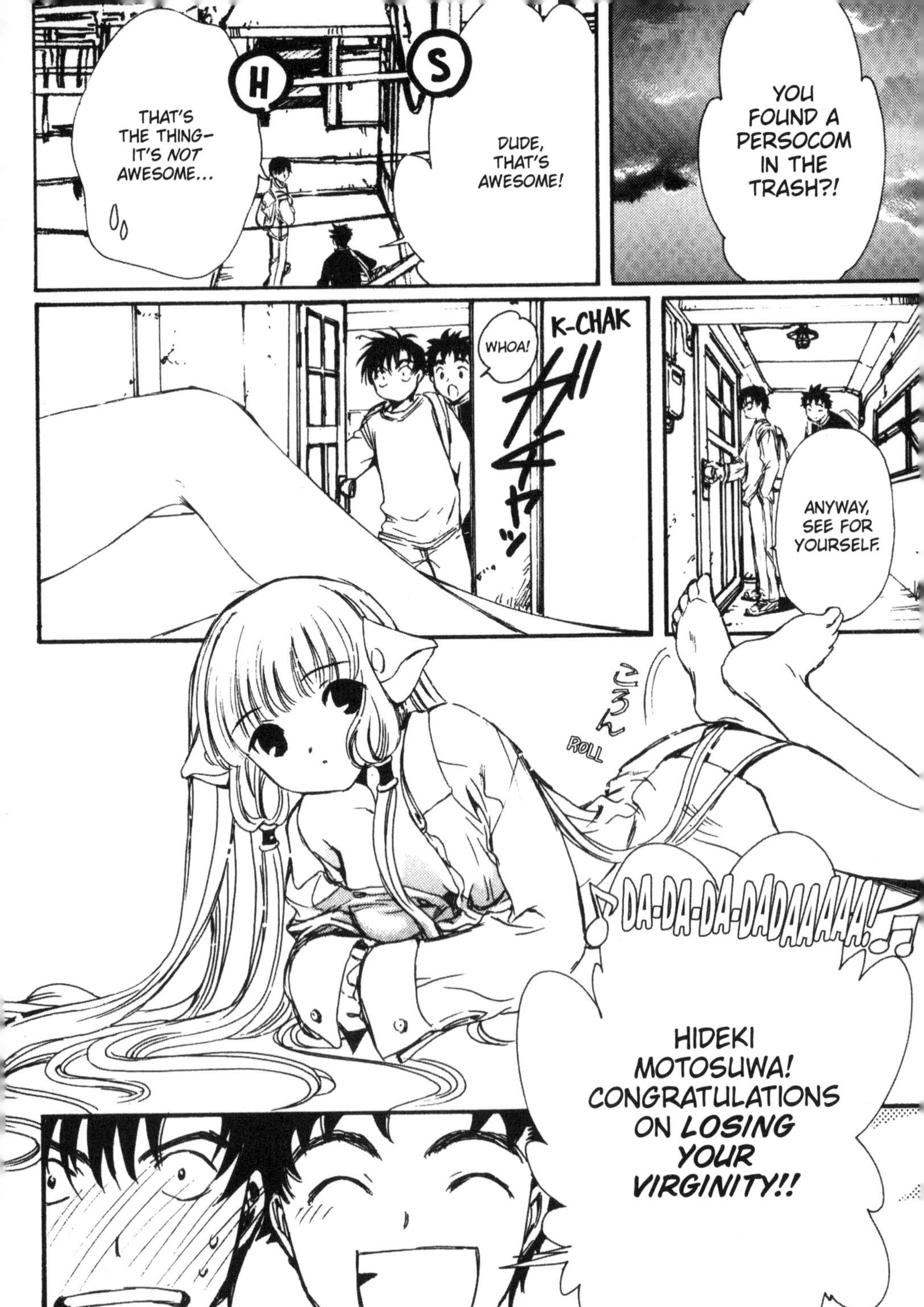
YOU FOUND A PERSOCOM IN THE TRASH?!
S
DUDE, THAT'S AWESOME!
H
THAT'S THE THING— IT'S *NOT* AWESOME...
ANYWAY, SEE FOR YOURSELF.
K-CHAK
ガチャッ
WHOA!
ころん
ROLL
DA-DA-DA-DADAAAAA!
HIDEKI MOTOSUWA! CONGRATULATIONS ON *LOSING YOUR VIRGINITY!!*

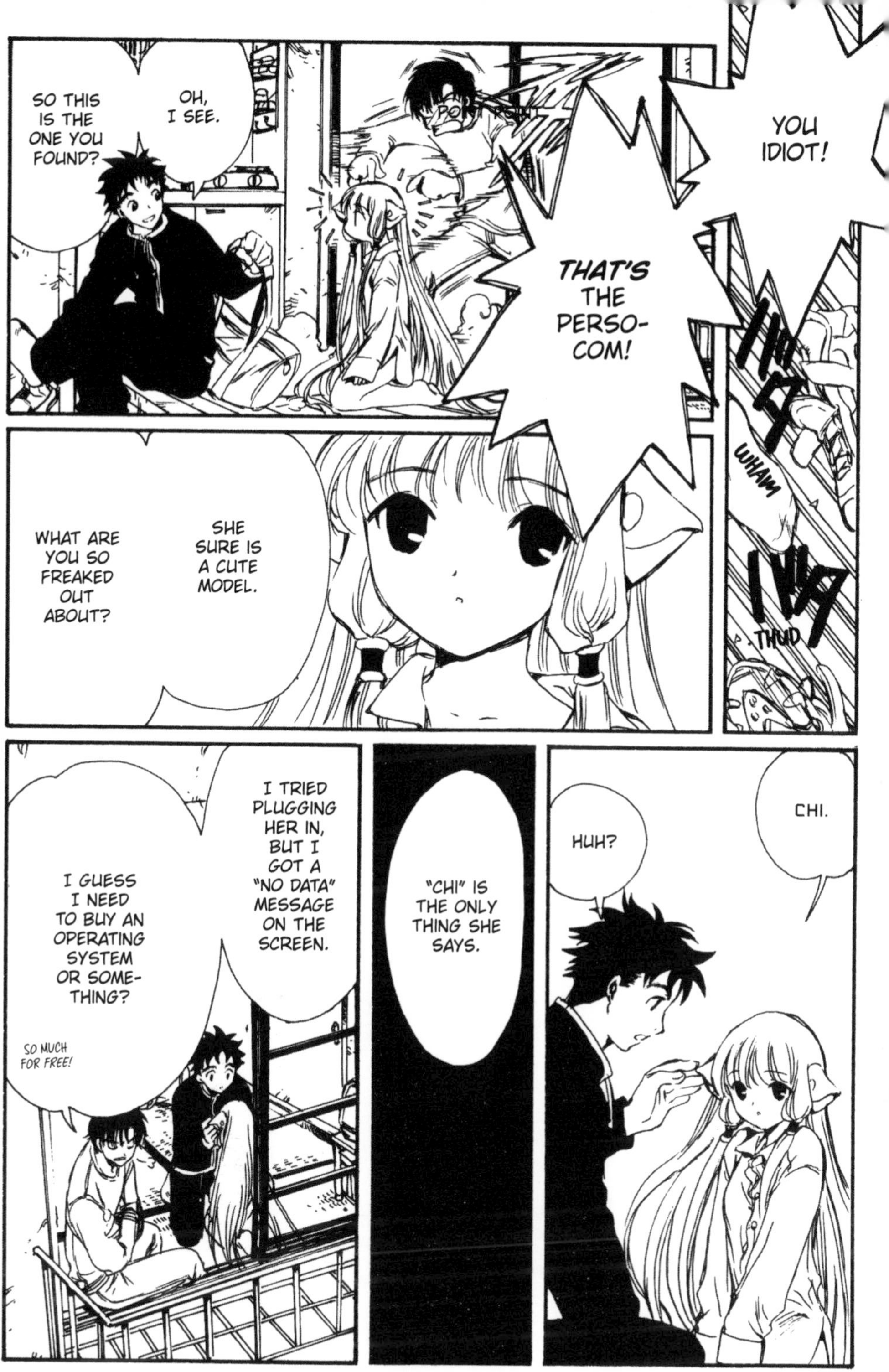
YOU IDIOT!
THAT'S THE PERSO-COM!
WHAM
THUD
OH, I SEE.
SO THIS IS THE ONE YOU FOUND?
SHE SURE IS A CUTE MODEL.
WHAT ARE YOU SO FREAKED OUT ABOUT?
CHI.
HUH?
"CHI" IS THE ONLY THING SHE SAYS.
I TRIED PLUGGING HER IN, BUT I GOT A "NO DATA" MESSAGE ON THE SCREEN.
I GUESS I NEED TO BUY AN OPERATING SYSTEM OR SOME-THING?
SO MUCH FOR FREE!

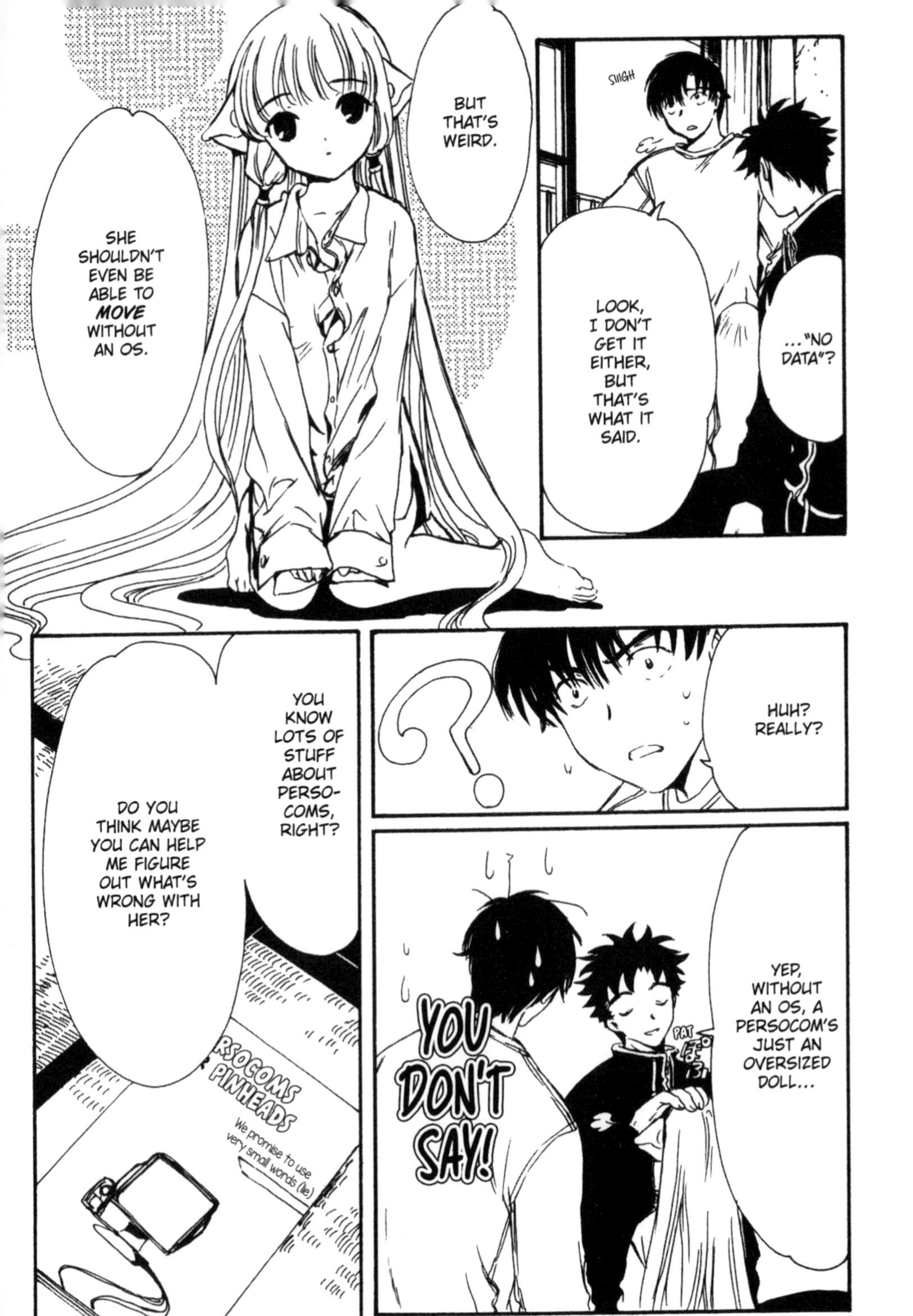
SIIGH
..."NO DATA"?
LOOK, I DON'T GET IT EITHER, BUT THAT'S WHAT IT SAID.
BUT THAT'S WEIRD.
SHE SHOULDN'T EVEN BE ABLE TO ***MOVE*** WITHOUT AN OS.
HUH? REALLY?
YEP, WITHOUT AN OS, A PERSOCOM'S JUST AN OVERSIZED DOLL...
PAT
YOU DON'T SAY!
YOU KNOW LOTS OF STUFF ABOUT PERSO-COMS, RIGHT?
DO YOU THINK MAYBE YOU CAN HELP ME FIGURE OUT WHAT'S WRONG WITH HER?
RSOCOMS PINHEADS
We promise to use very small words (lie)

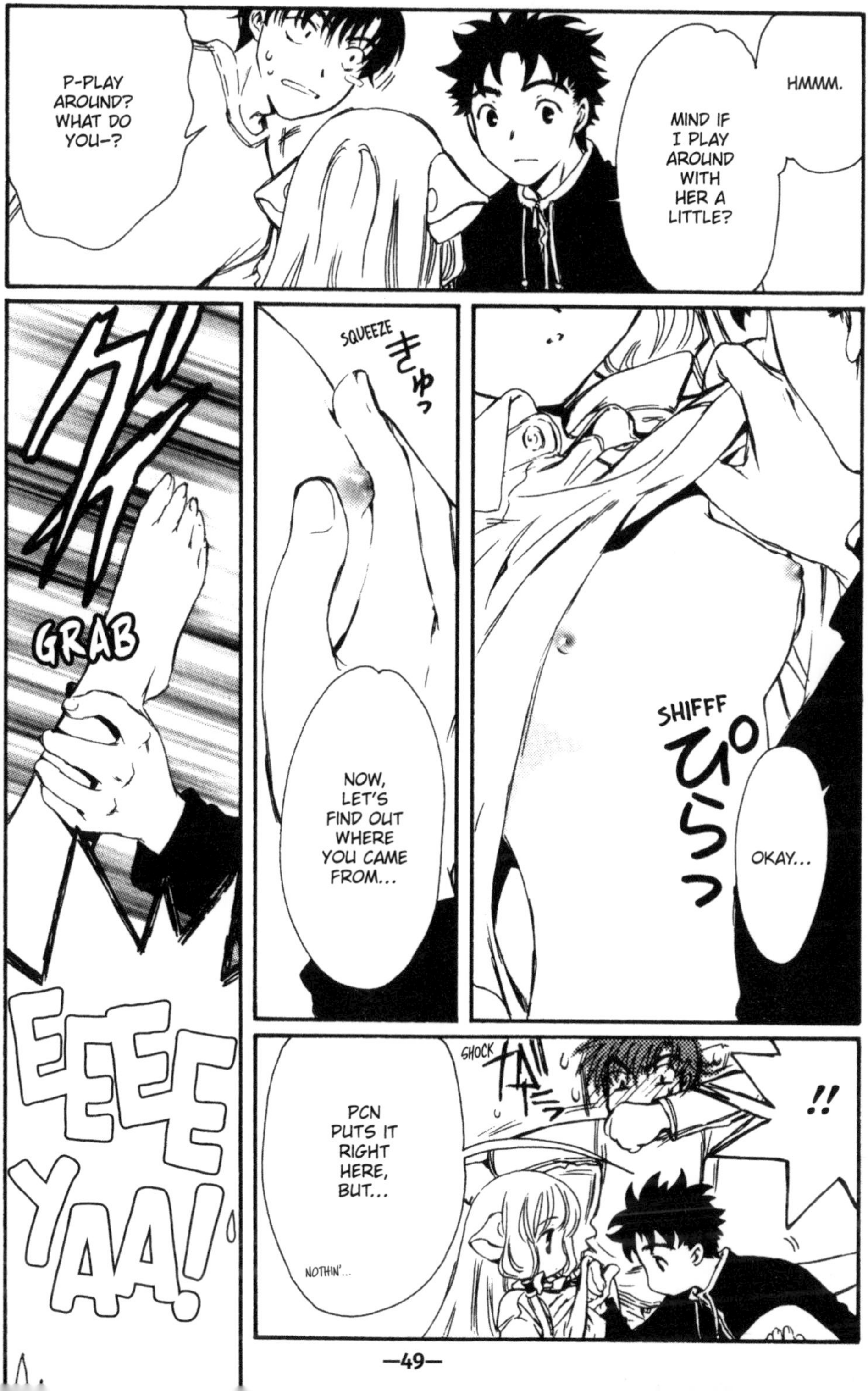
HMMM.
MIND IF I PLAY AROUND WITH HER A LITTLE?
P-PLAY AROUND? WHAT DO YOU-?
SHIFFF
ぴらっ
OKAY...
SQUEEZE
きゅっ
NOW, LET'S FIND OUT WHERE YOU CAME FROM...
!!
SHOCK
PCN PUTS IT RIGHT HERE, BUT...
NOTHIN'...
GRAB
EEEE YAA!

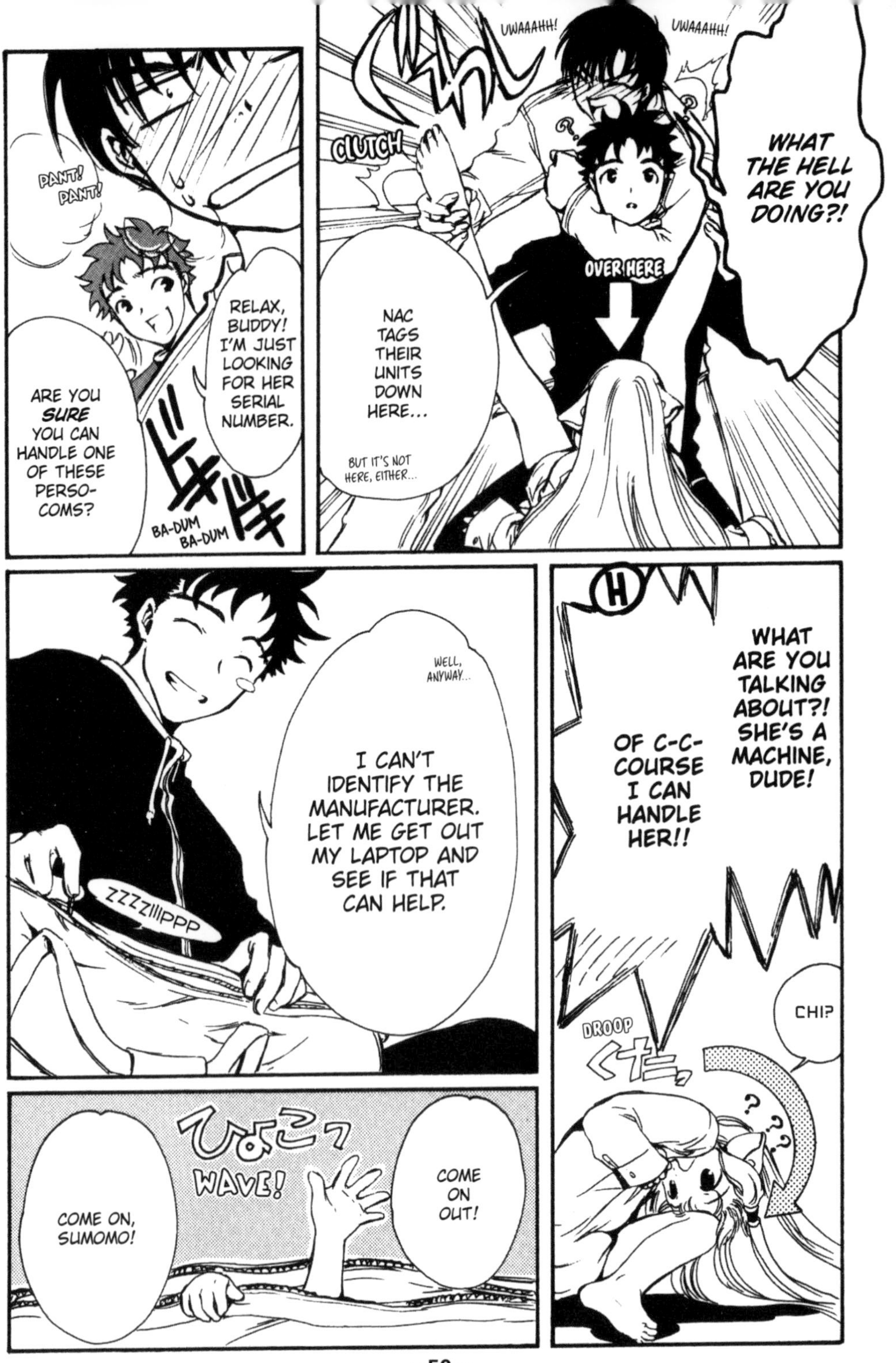
UWAAAHH!
UWAAAHH!
WHAT THE HELL ARE YOU DOING?!
CLUTCH
OVER HERE
NAC TAGS THEIR UNITS DOWN HERE...
BUT IT'S NOT HERE, EITHER...
RELAX, BUDDY! I'M JUST LOOKING FOR HER SERIAL NUMBER.
PANT! PANT!
ARE YOU *SURE* YOU CAN HANDLE ONE OF THESE PERSO-COMS?
BA-DUM BA-DUM
H
WHAT ARE YOU TALKING ABOUT?! SHE'S A MACHINE, DUDE!
OF C-C-COURSE I CAN HANDLE HER!!
CHI?
DROOP
WELL, ANYWAY...
I CAN'T IDENTIFY THE MANUFACTURER. LET ME GET OUT MY LAPTOP AND SEE IF THAT CAN HELP.
ZZZZIIIPPP
COME ON OUT!
WAVE!
COME ON, SUMOMO!

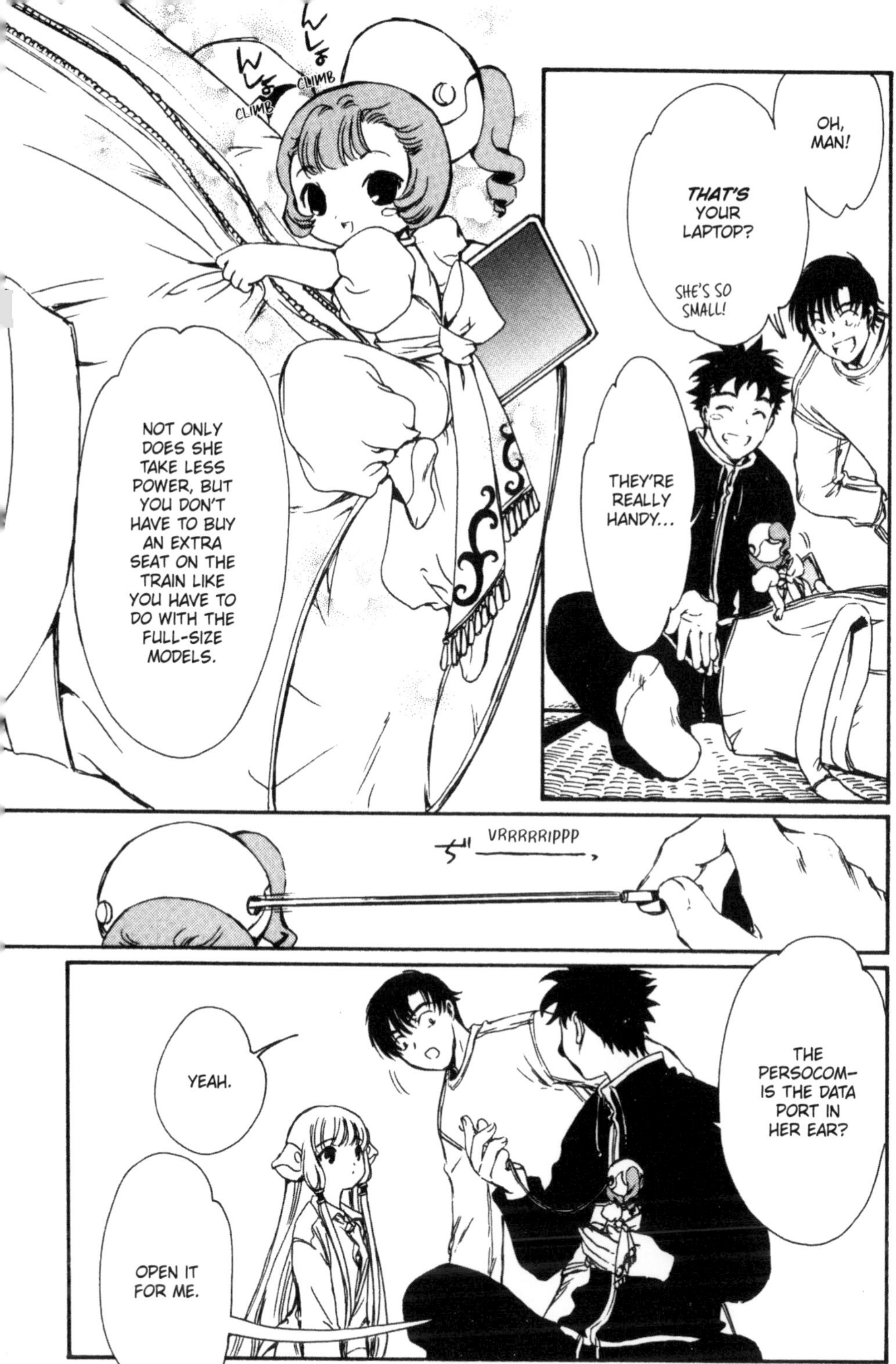
OH, MAN!
THAT'S YOUR LAPTOP?
SHE'S SO SMALL!
THEY'RE REALLY HANDY...
んしょ CLIMB
んしょ CLIMB
NOT ONLY DOES SHE TAKE LESS POWER, BUT YOU DON'T HAVE TO BUY AN EXTRA SEAT ON THE TRAIN LIKE YOU HAVE TO DO WITH THE FULL-SIZE MODELS.
VRRRRRIPPP
THE PERSOCOM–IS THE DATA PORT IN HER EAR?
YEAH.
OPEN IT FOR ME.

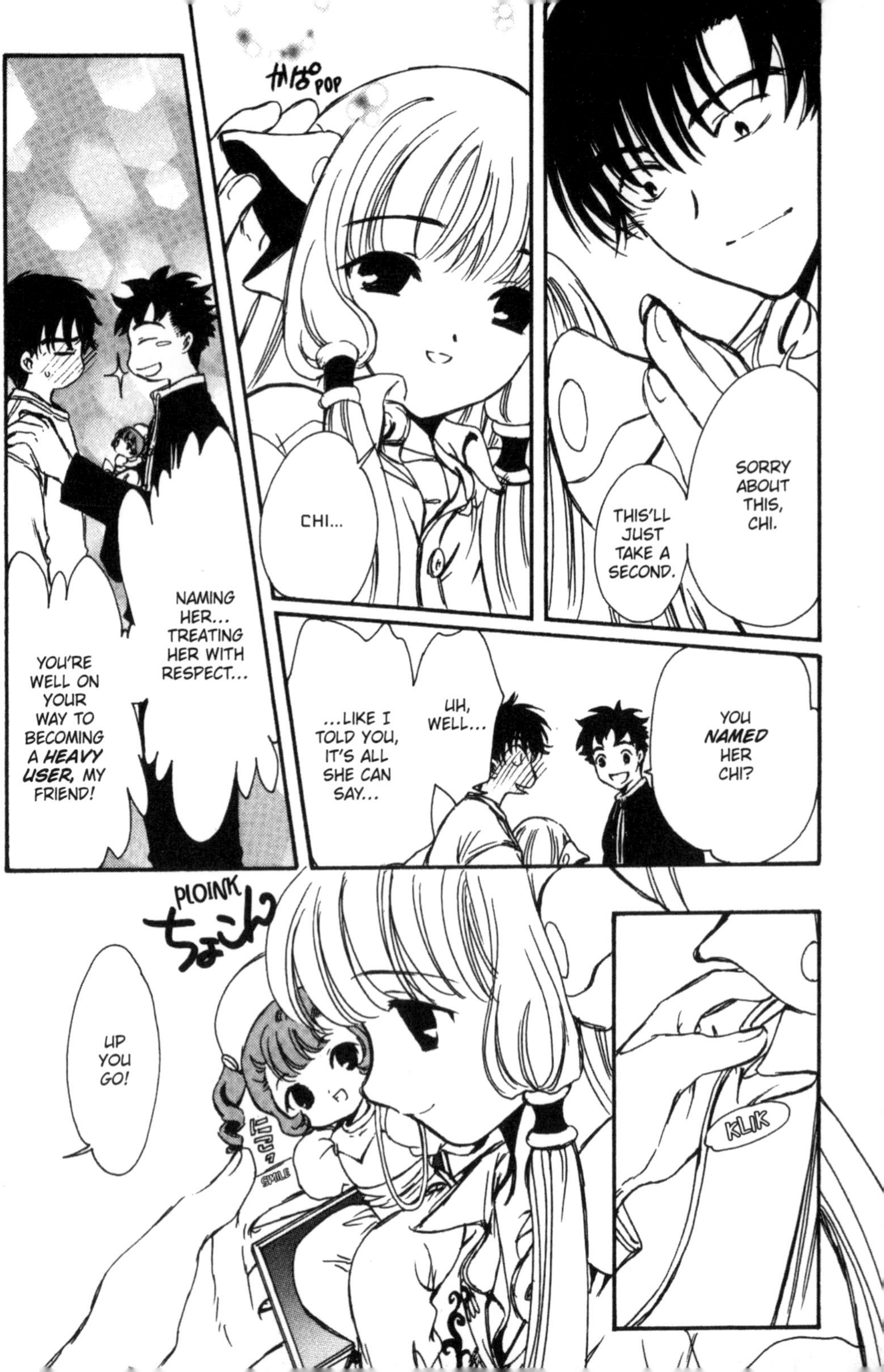
SORRY ABOUT THIS, CHI.
THIS'LL JUST TAKE A SECOND.
かぱ POP
CHI...
YOU **NAMED** HER CHI?
UH, WELL...
...LIKE I TOLD YOU, IT'S ALL SHE CAN SAY...
NAMING HER... TREATING HER WITH RESPECT...
YOU'RE WELL ON YOUR WAY TO BECOMING A **HEAVY USER**, MY FRIEND!
KLIK
PLOINK ちょこん
UP YOU GO!
ニコッ SMILE

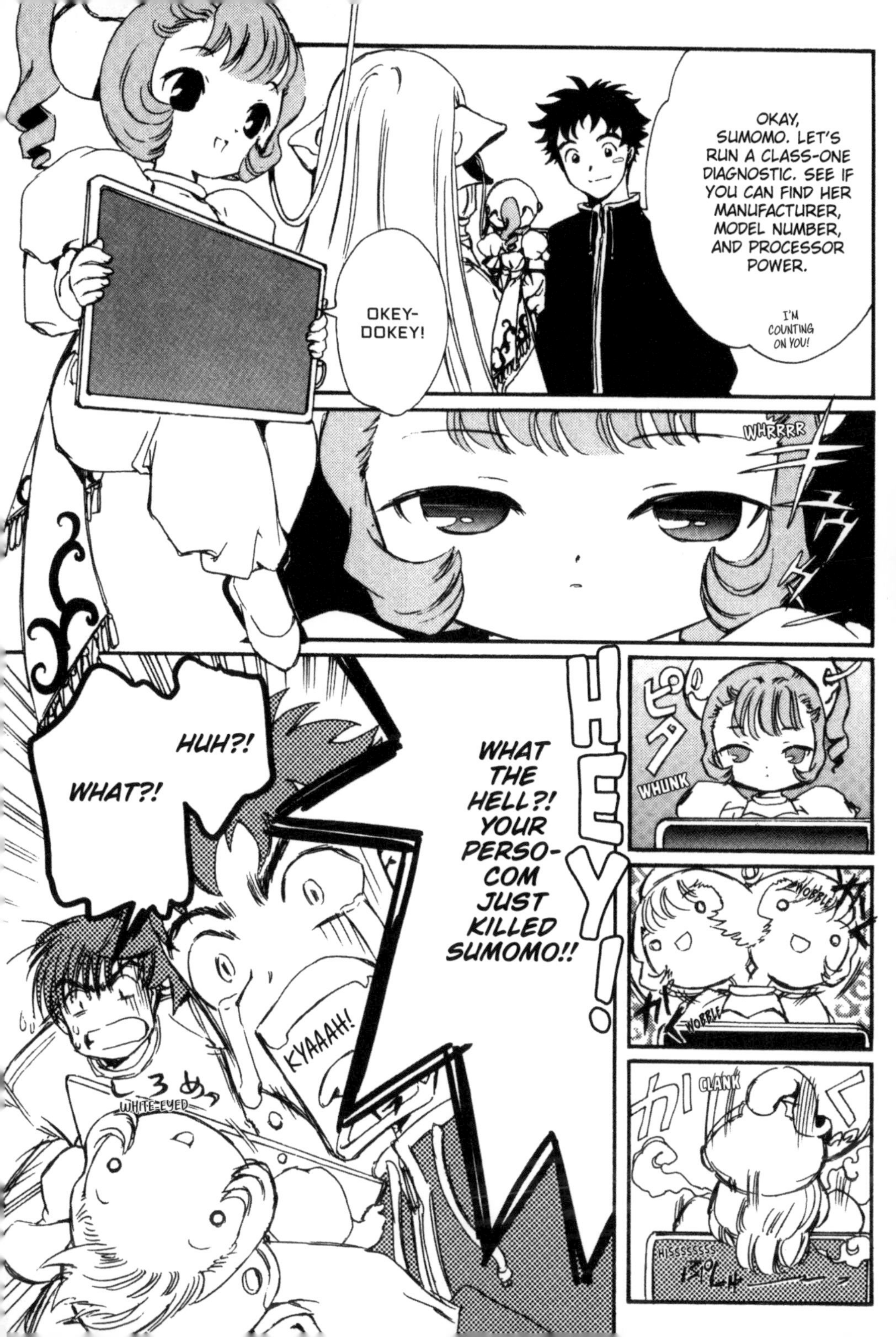
OKAY, SUMOMO. LET'S RUN A CLASS-ONE DIAGNOSTIC. SEE IF YOU CAN FIND HER MANUFACTURER, MODEL NUMBER, AND PROCESSOR POWER.
I'M COUNTING ON YOU!
OKEY-DOKEY!
WHRRRR
WHUNK
WOBBLE
WOBBLE
CLANK
HISSSSSSS
HEY!
WHAT THE HELL?! YOUR PERSO-COM JUST KILLED SUMOMO!!
HUH?!
WHAT?!
KYAAAH!
WHITE-EYED

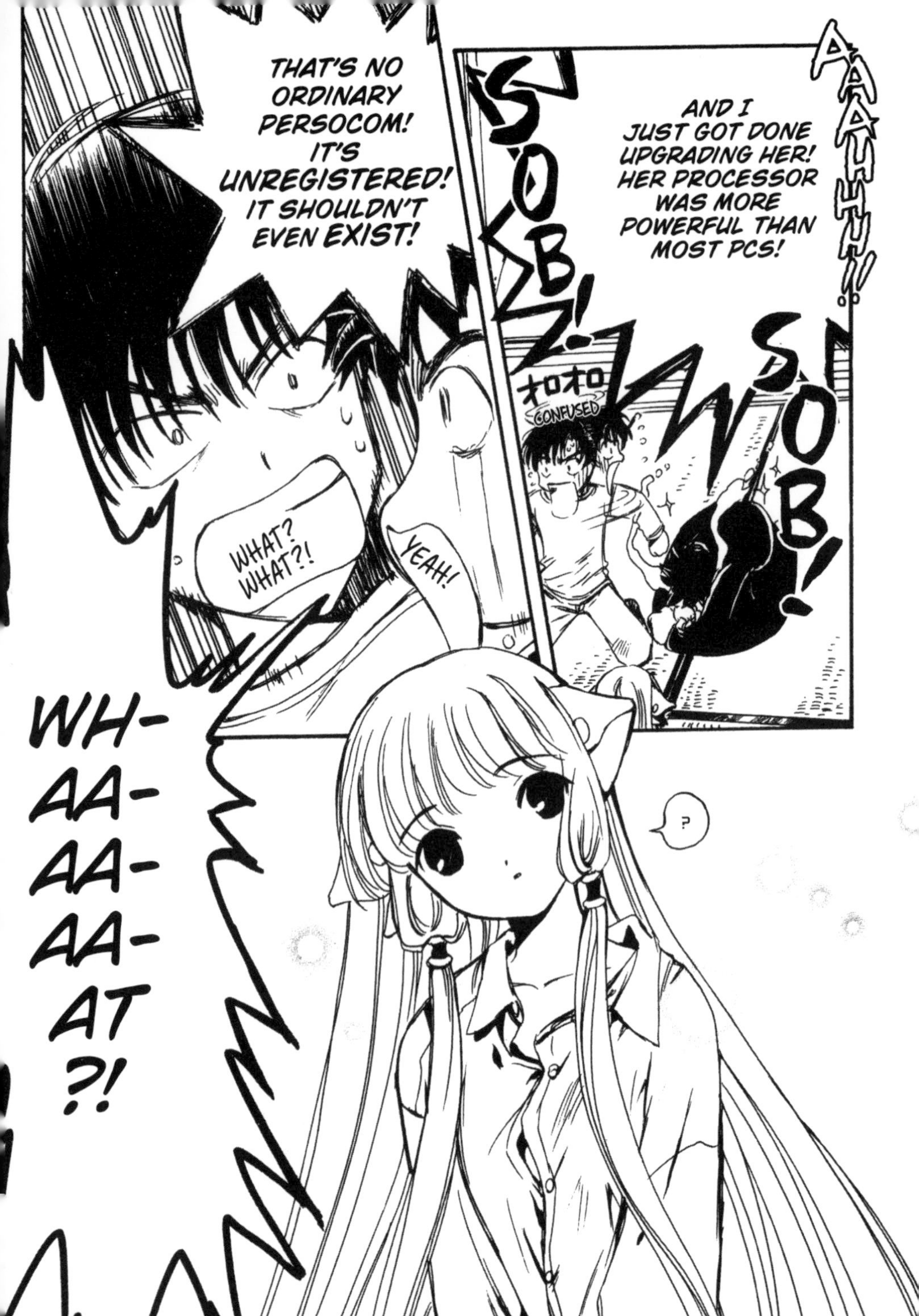
AAAUHH!!
AND I JUST GOT DONE UPGRADING HER! HER PROCESSOR WAS MORE POWERFUL THAN MOST PCS!
SOB!
SOB!
オロオロ CONFUSED
THAT'S NO ORDINARY PERSOCOM! IT'S UNREGISTERED! IT SHOULDN'T EVEN EXIST!
WHAT? WHAT?!
YEAH!
?
WH-AA-AA-AA-AT?!

<chapter.3> end

〈chapter.4〉

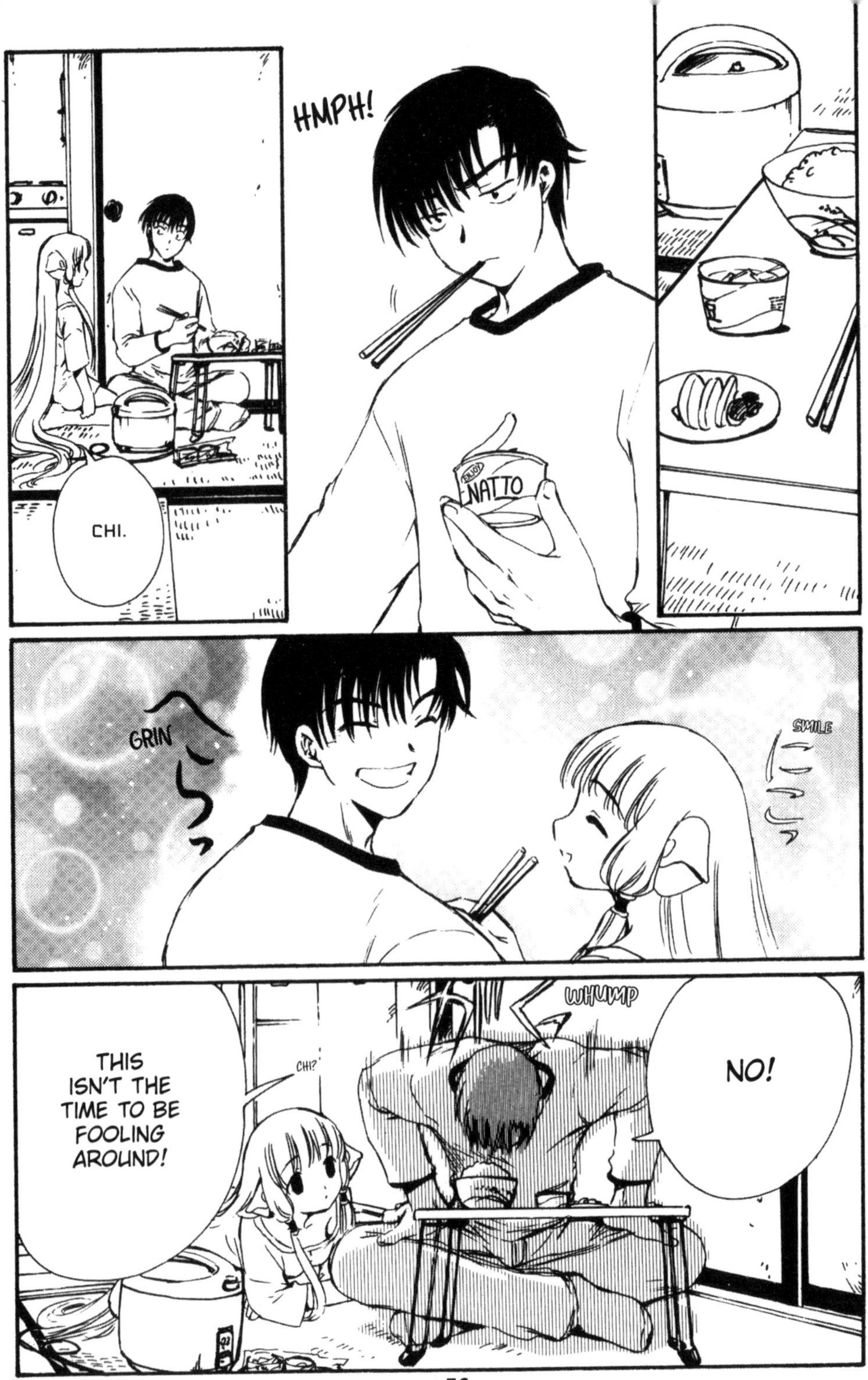
HMPH!
ENJOY
NATTO
CHI.
SMILE
GRIN
NO!
WHUMP
CHI?
THIS ISN'T THE TIME TO BE FOOLING AROUND!

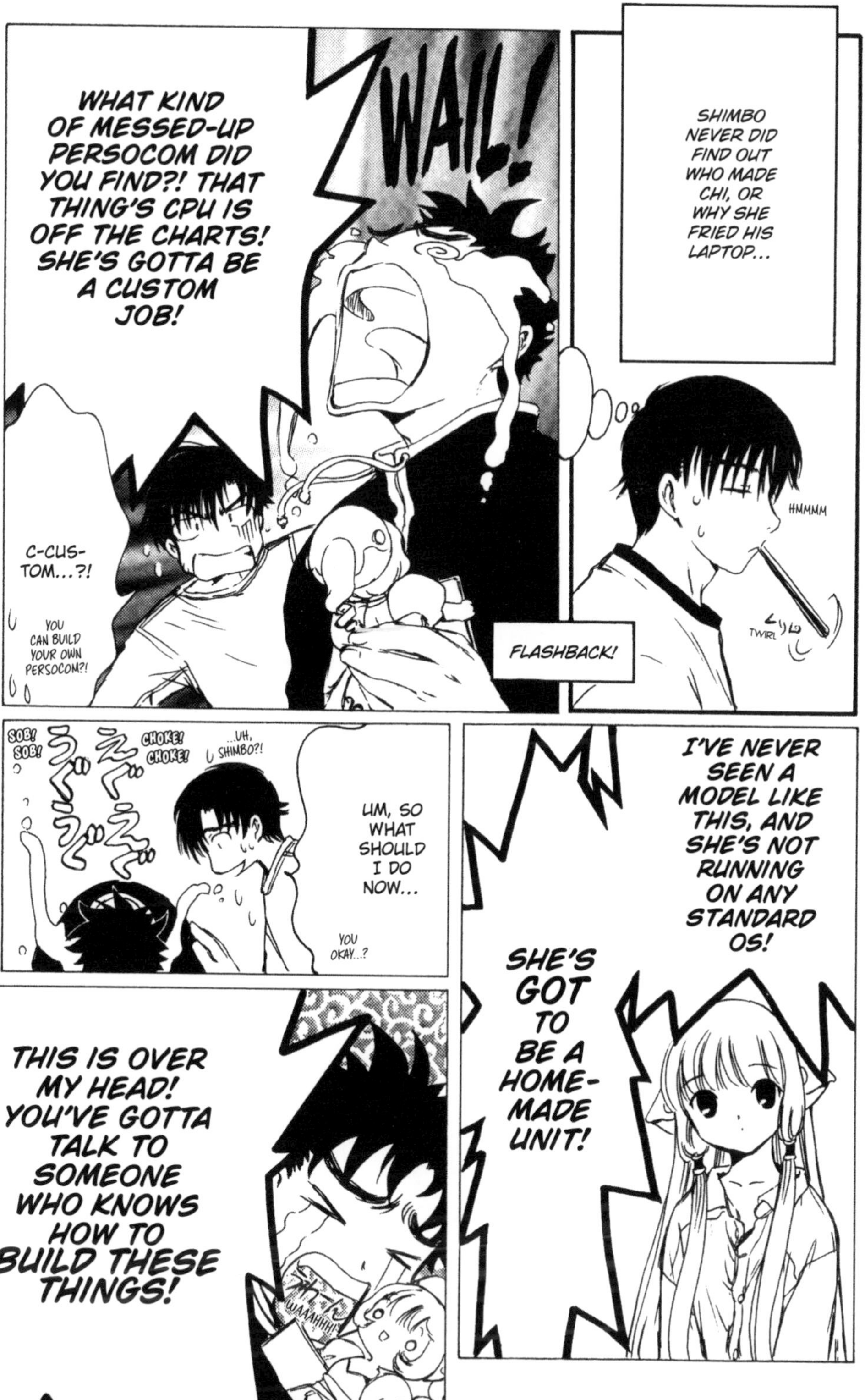
SHIMBO NEVER DID FIND OUT WHO MADE CHI, OR WHY SHE FRIED HIS LAPTOP...
HMMMM
TWIRL
FLASHBACK!
WAIL!
WHAT KIND OF MESSED-UP PERSOCOM DID YOU FIND?! THAT THING'S CPU IS OFF THE CHARTS! SHE'S GOTTA BE A CUSTOM JOB!
C-CUS-TOM...?!
YOU CAN BUILD YOUR OWN PERSOCOM?!
I'VE NEVER SEEN A MODEL LIKE THIS, AND SHE'S NOT RUNNING ON ANY STANDARD OS!
SHE'S GOT TO BE A HOME-MADE UNIT!
SOB! SOB!
CHOKE! CHOKE!
...UH, SHIMBO?!
UM, SO WHAT SHOULD I DO NOW...
YOU OKAY...?
THIS IS OVER MY HEAD! YOU'VE GOTTA TALK TO SOMEONE WHO KNOWS HOW TO BUILD THESE THINGS!
WAAAHHH!!

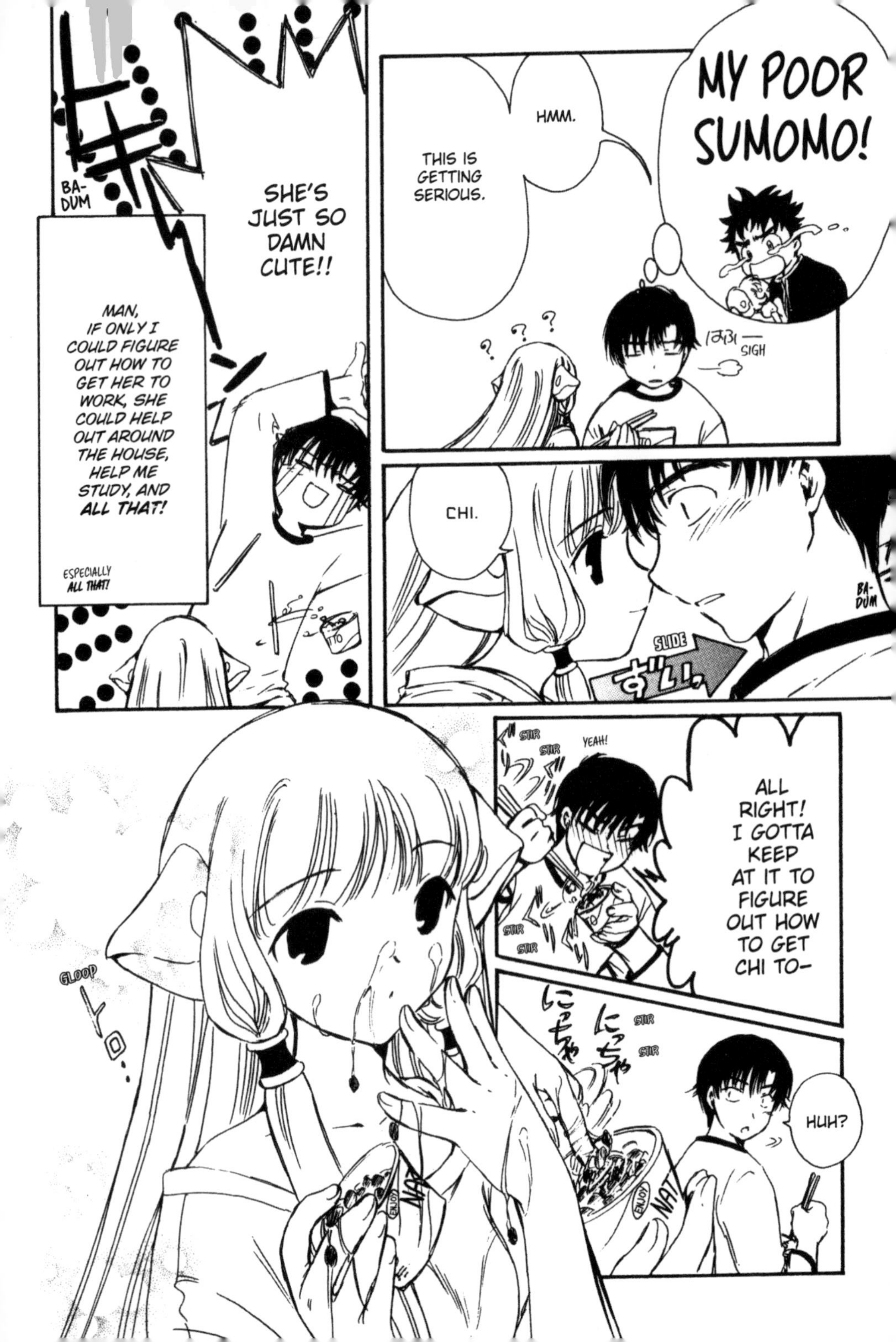
MY POOR SUMOMO!
HMM.
THIS IS GETTING SERIOUS.
SIGH
CHI.
BA-DUM
SLIDE
SHE'S JUST SO DAMN CUTE!!
BA-DUM
MAN, IF ONLY I COULD FIGURE OUT HOW TO GET HER TO WORK, SHE COULD HELP OUT AROUND THE HOUSE, HELP ME STUDY, AND ALL THAT!
ESPECIALLY ALL THAT!
ALL RIGHT! I GOTTA KEEP AT IT TO FIGURE OUT HOW TO GET CHI TO-
YEAH!
STIR
STIR
STIR
STIR
HUH?
STIR
STIR
ENJOY
NAT
GLOOP
ENJOY
NAT

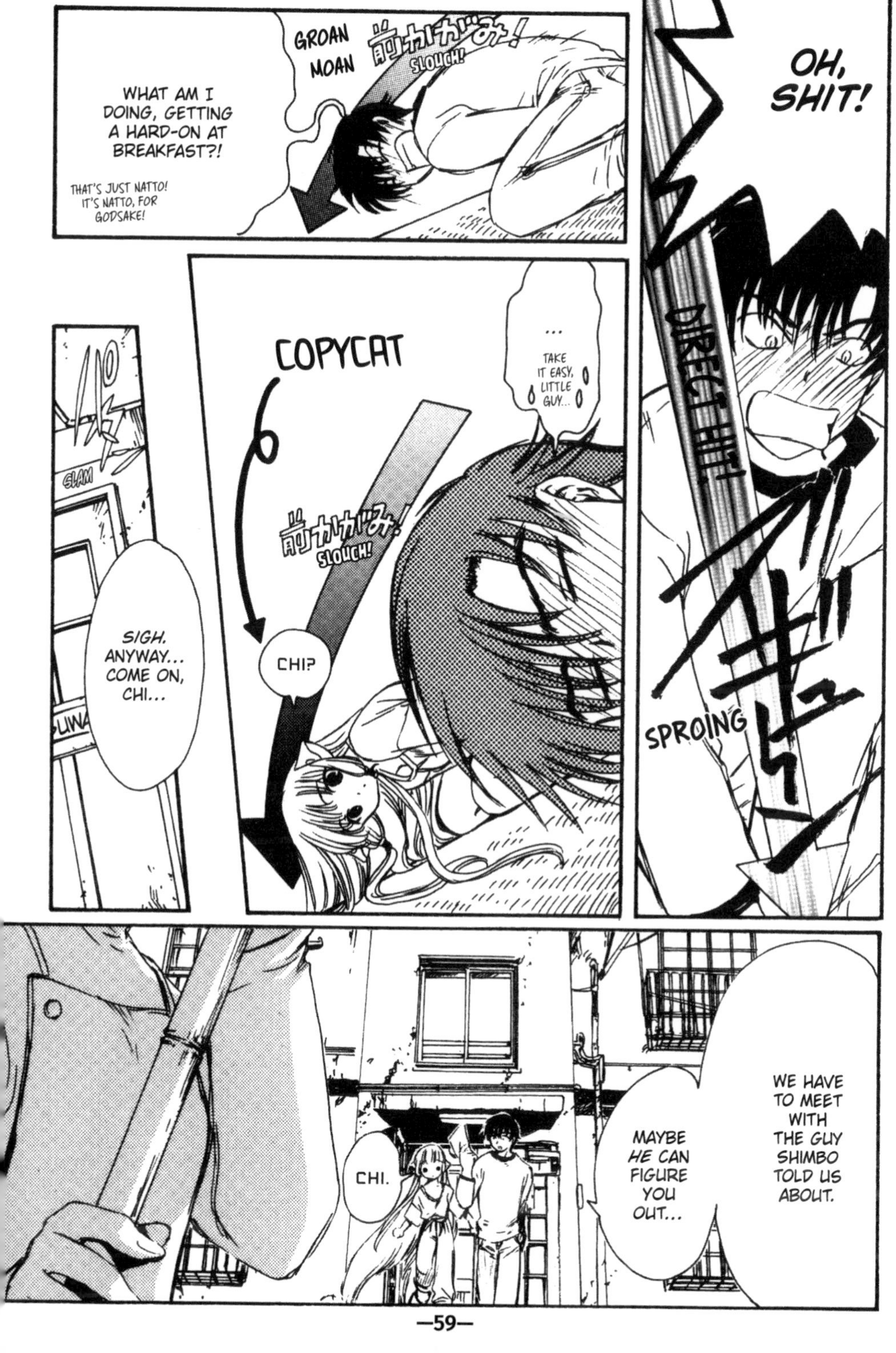
OH, SHIT!
DIRECT HIT!
SPROING
GROAN MOAN
前かがみ!
SLOUCH!
WHAT AM I DOING, GETTING A HARD-ON AT BREAKFAST?!
THAT'S JUST NATTO! IT'S NATTO, FOR GODSAKE!
...
TAKE IT EASY, LITTLE GUY...
COPYCAT
前かがみ!
SLOUCH!
CHI?
SLAM
SIGH. ANYWAY... COME ON, CHI...
WE HAVE TO MEET WITH THE GUY SHIMBO TOLD US ABOUT.
MAYBE HE CAN FIGURE YOU OUT...
CHI.

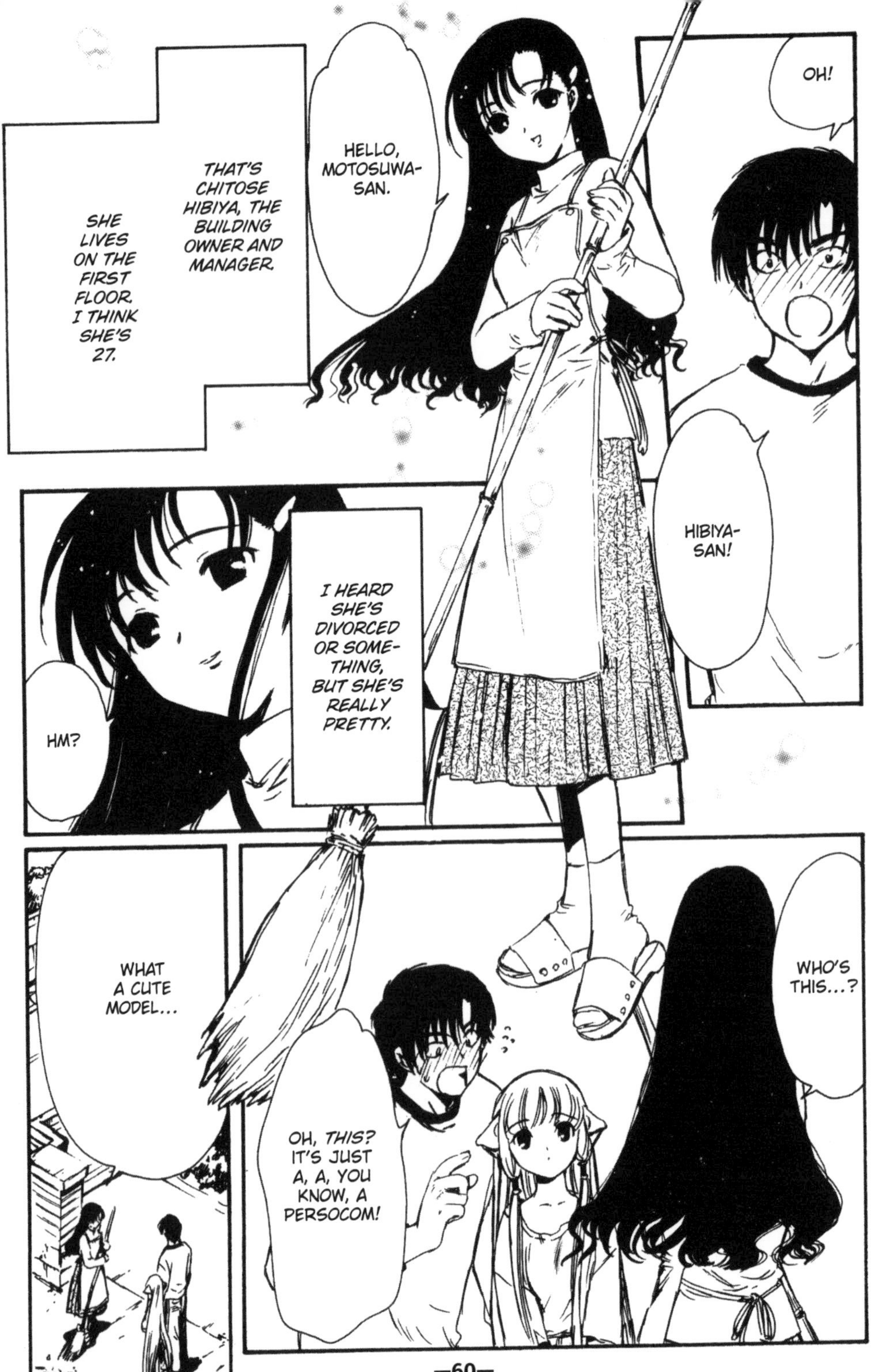

OH!
HIBIYA-SAN!
HELLO, MOTOSUWA-SAN.
THAT'S CHITOSE HIBIYA, THE BUILDING OWNER AND MANAGER.
SHE LIVES ON THE FIRST FLOOR. I THINK SHE'S 27.
I HEARD SHE'S DIVORCED OR SOMETHING, BUT SHE'S REALLY PRETTY.
HM?
WHO'S THIS...?
OH, *THIS?* IT'S JUST A, A, YOU KNOW, A PERSOCOM!
WHAT A CUTE MODEL...

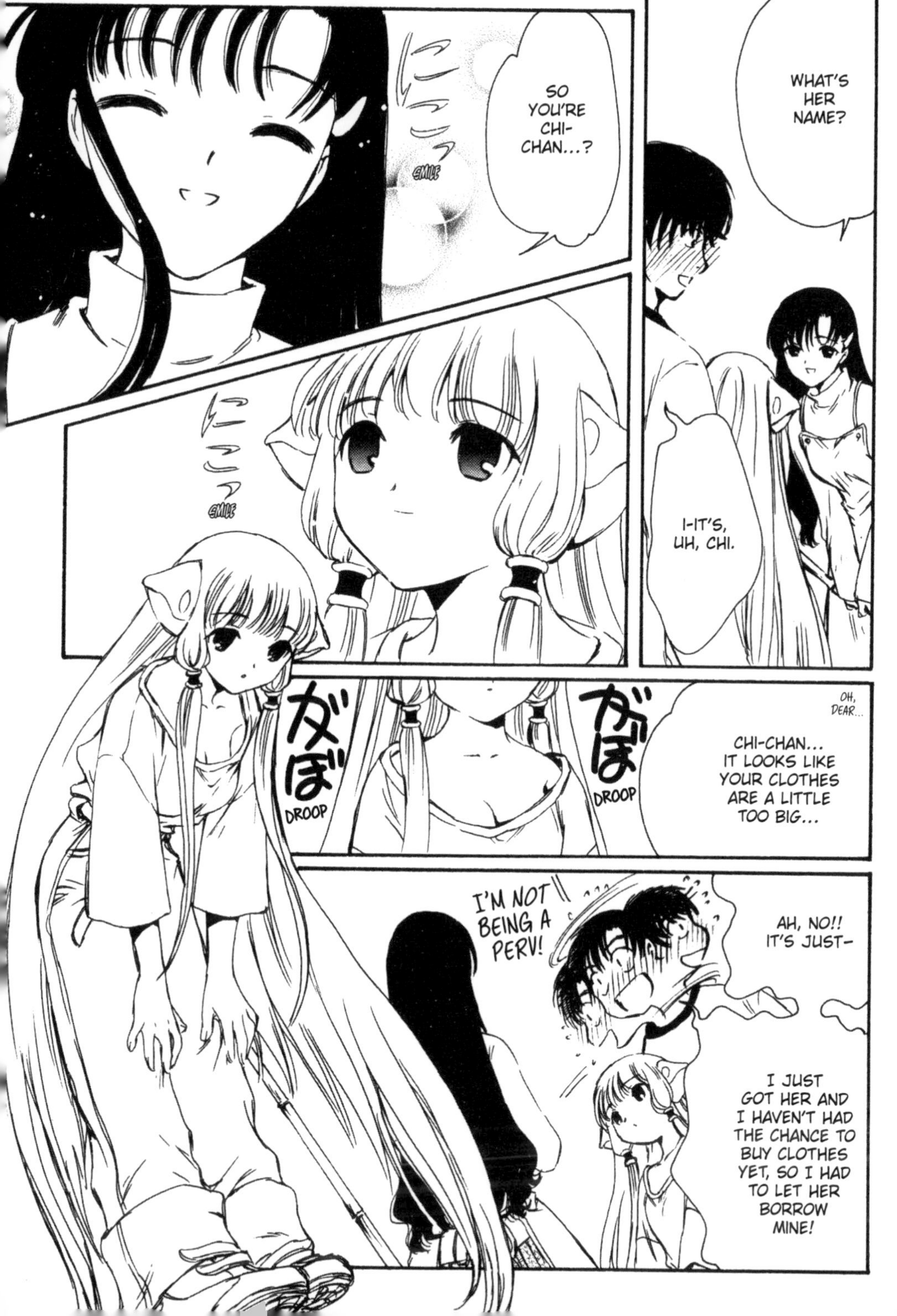
WHAT'S HER NAME?
I-IT'S, UH, CHI.
SO YOU'RE CHI-CHAN...?
にこっ
SMILE
にこっ
SMILE
OH, DEAR...
CHI-CHAN... IT LOOKS LIKE YOUR CLOTHES ARE A LITTLE TOO BIG...
がぼ
DROOP
がぼ
DROOP
AH, NO!! IT'S JUST-
I'M NOT BEING A PERV!
I JUST GOT HER AND I HAVEN'T HAD THE CHANCE TO BUY CLOTHES YET, SO I HAD TO LET HER BORROW MINE!

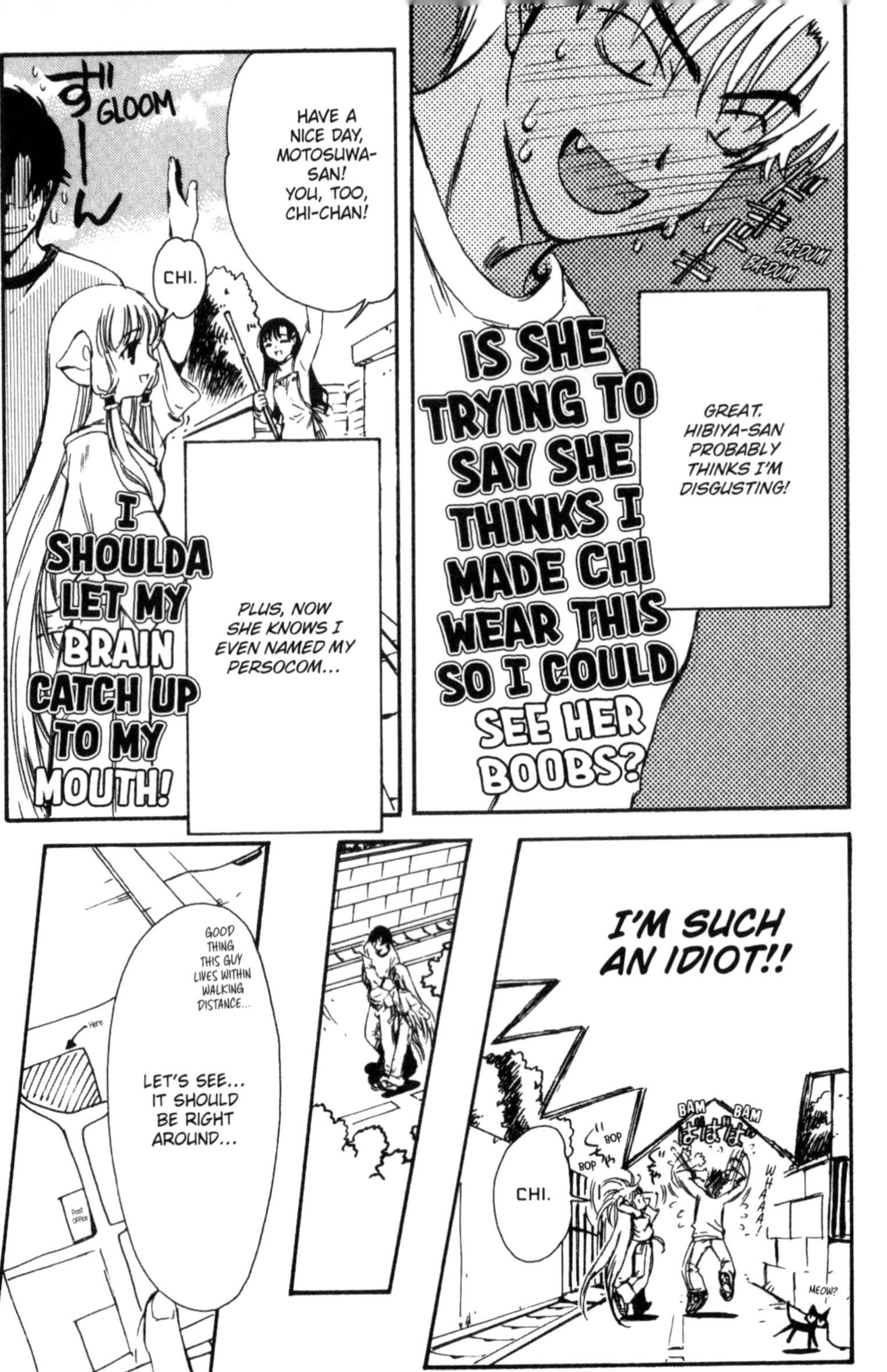
BA-DUM
BA-DUM
GREAT. HIBIYA-SAN PROBABLY THINKS I'M DISGUSTING!
IS SHE TRYING TO SAY SHE THINKS I MADE CHI WEAR THIS SO I COULD SEE HER BOOBS?
GLOOM
HAVE A NICE DAY, MOTOSUWA-SAN! YOU, TOO, CHI-CHAN!
CHI.
PLUS, NOW SHE KNOWS I EVEN NAMED MY PERSOCOM...
I SHOULDA LET MY BRAIN CATCH UP TO MY MOUTH!
I'M SUCH AN IDIOT!!
BAM BAM
WHAAAA!
BOP
BOP
CHI.
MEOW?
GOOD THING THIS GUY LIVES WITHIN WALKING DISTANCE...
LET'S SEE... IT SHOULD BE RIGHT AROUND...
Here
Post Office

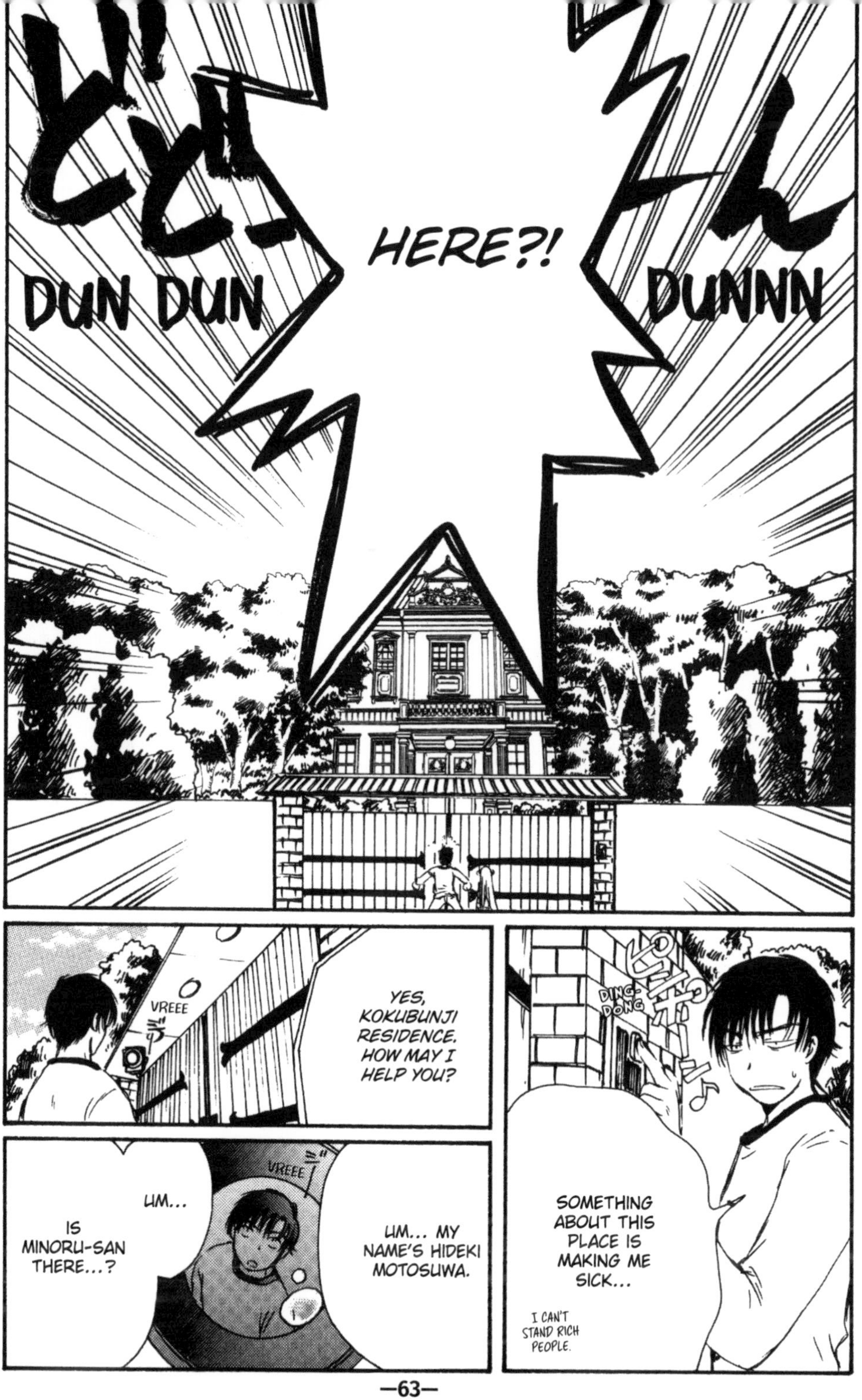
HERE?!
DUN DUN
DUNNN
DING-DONG
SOMETHING ABOUT THIS PLACE IS MAKING ME SICK...
I CAN'T STAND RICH PEOPLE.
YES, KOKUBUNJI RESIDENCE. HOW MAY I HELP YOU?
VREEE
UM... MY NAME'S HIDEKI MOTOSUWA.
VREEE
UM...
IS MINORU-SAN THERE...?

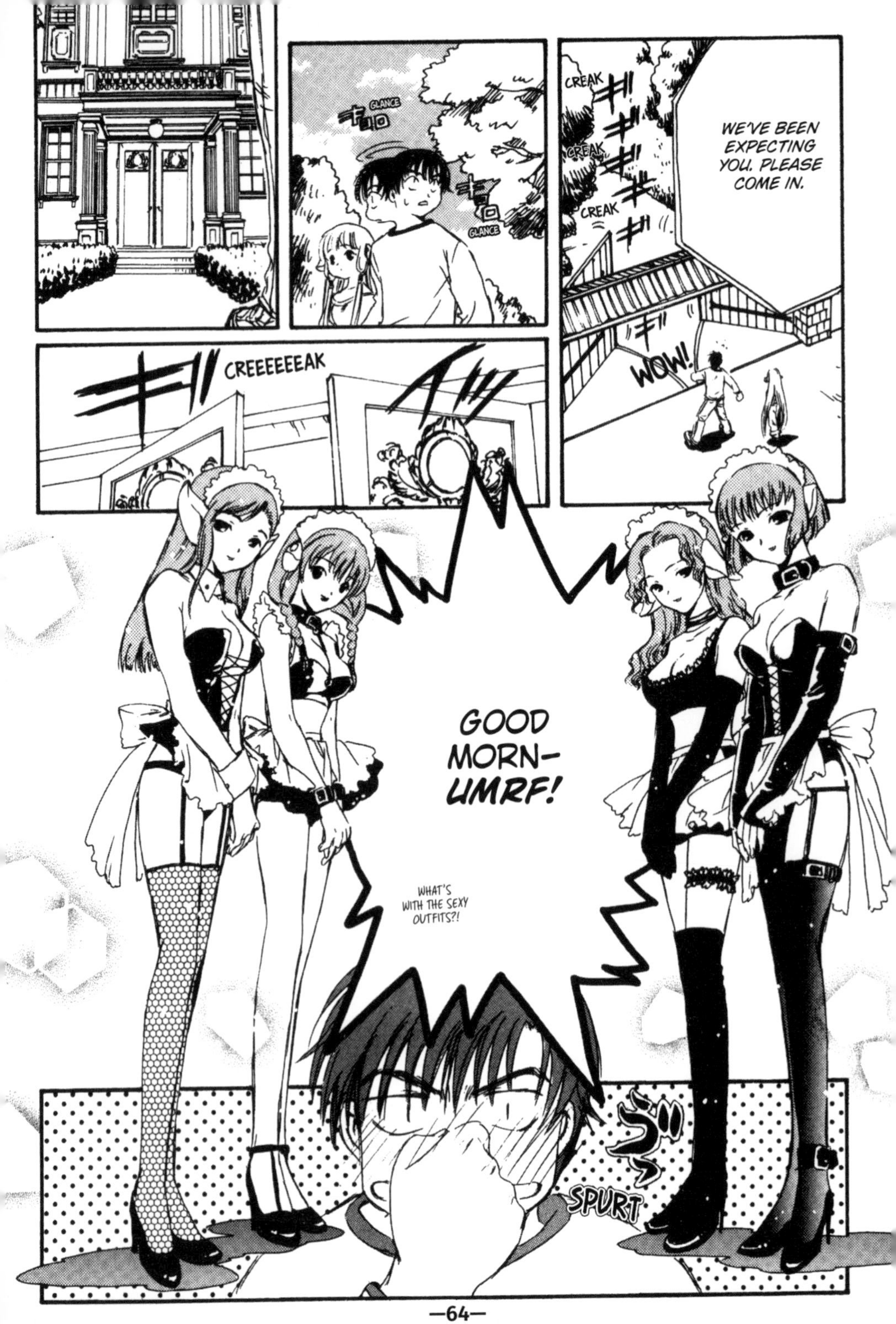
CREAK
CREAK
CREAK
WE'VE BEEN EXPECTING YOU. PLEASE COME IN.
WOW!
GLANCE
GLANCE
CREEEEEEAK
GOOD MORN-UMRF!
WHAT'S WITH THE SEXY OUTFITS?!
SPURT

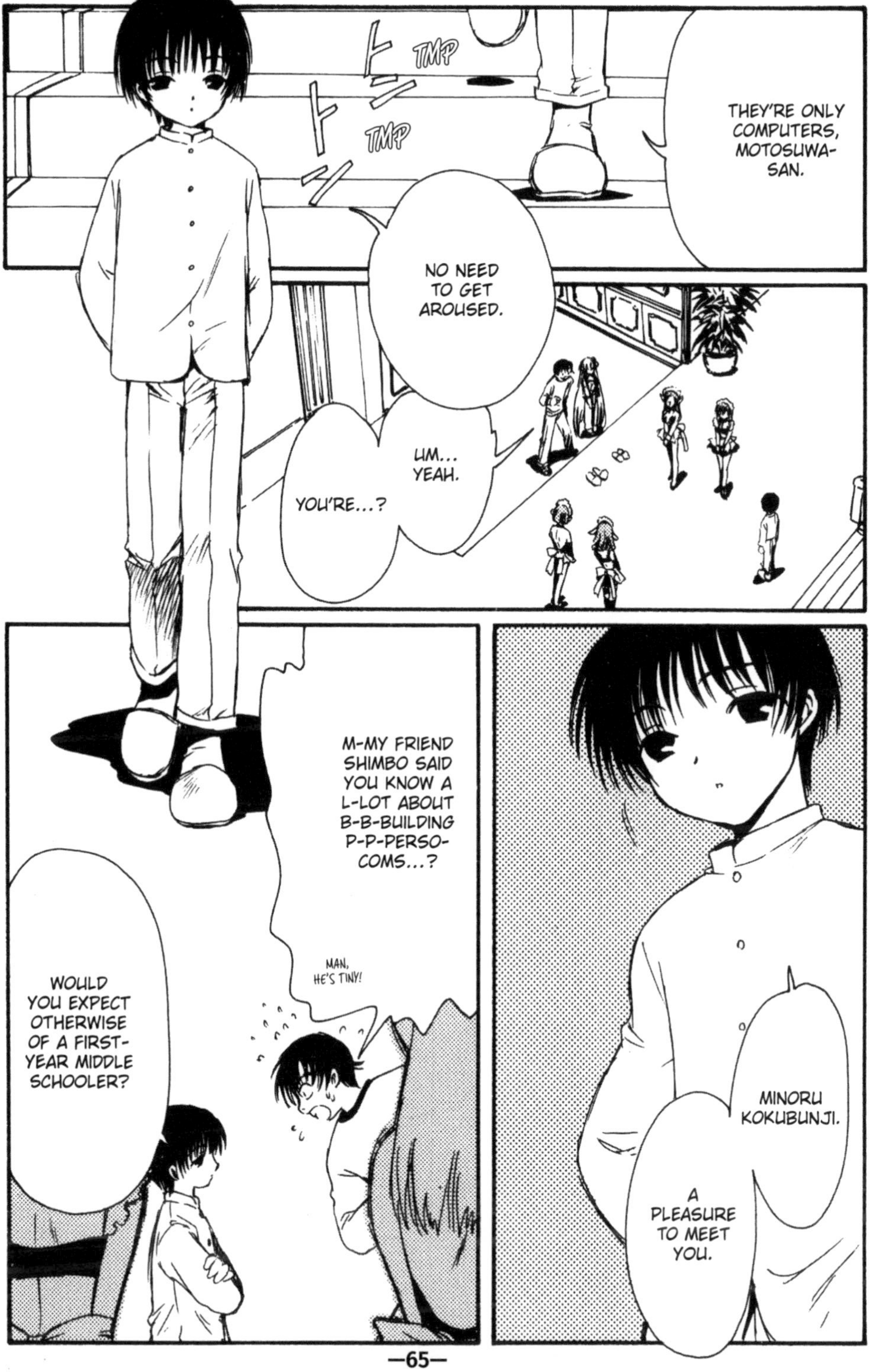
THEY'RE ONLY COMPUTERS, MOTOSUWA-SAN.
TMP
TMP
NO NEED TO GET AROUSED.
UM... YEAH.
YOU'RE...?
MINORU KOKUBUNJI.
A PLEASURE TO MEET YOU.
M-MY FRIEND SHIMBO SAID YOU KNOW A L-LOT ABOUT B-B-BUILDING P-P-PERSO-COMS...?
MAN, HE'S TINY!
WOULD YOU EXPECT OTHERWISE OF A FIRST-YEAR MIDDLE SCHOOLER?

EEEEE-EYAA-AA!!!

GLOMP

WELL, ANY-WAY...

DON'T JUST STAND THERE. COME IN.

WHA?

HEY!

OH, SHIT!

STAAARE

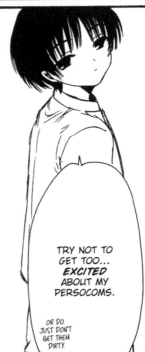

TRY NOT TO GET TOO... *EXCITED* ABOUT MY PERSOCOMS.

OR DO. JUST DON'T GET THEM DIRTY.

SQUEEZE

SQUEEZE

GET 'EM OFF OF ME!!

COPY-CAT

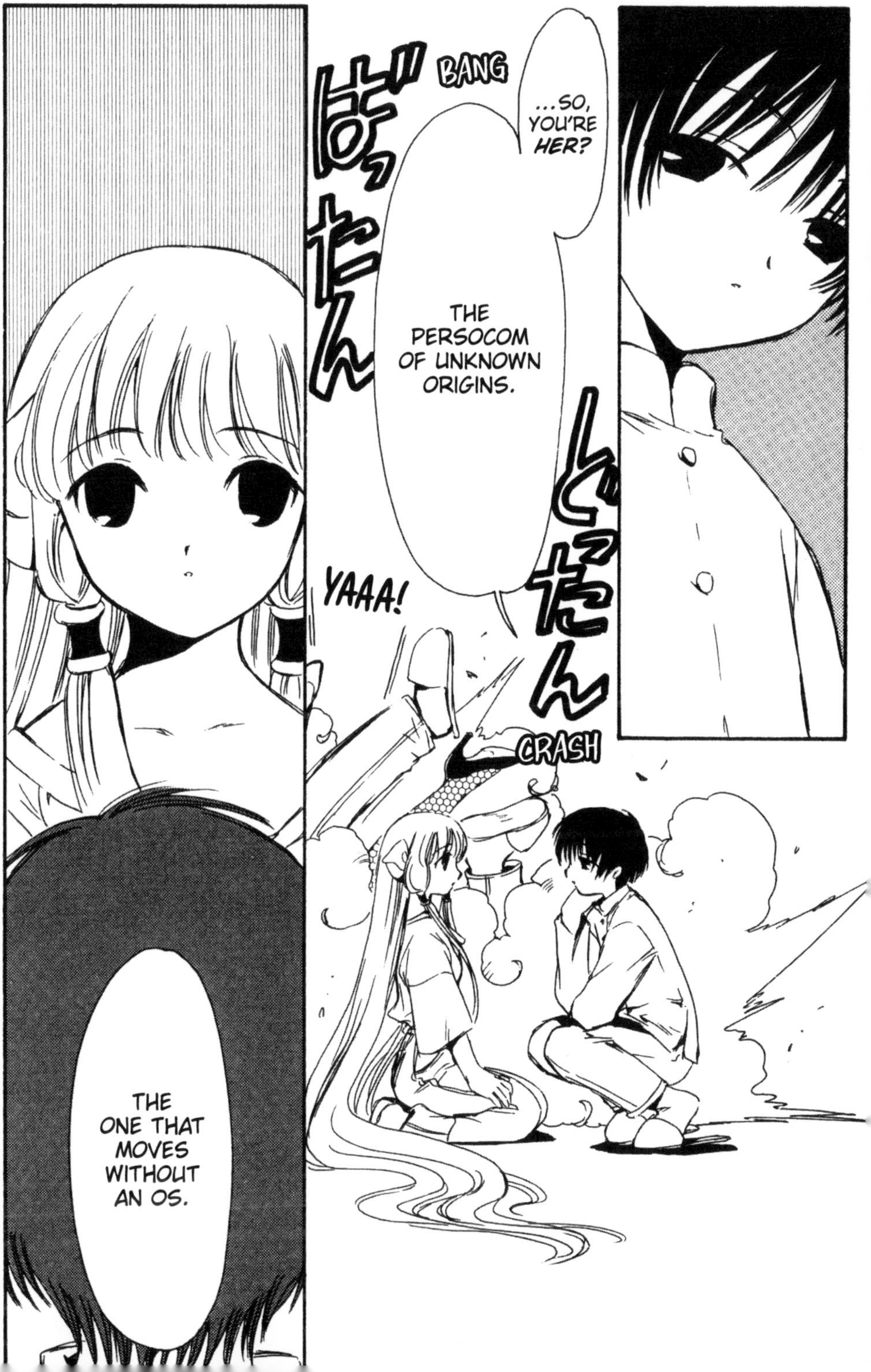

...SO, YOU'RE HER?
ばったん
BANG
THE PERSOCOM OF UNKNOWN ORIGINS.
どったん
YAAA!
CRASH
THE ONE THAT MOVES WITHOUT AN OS.

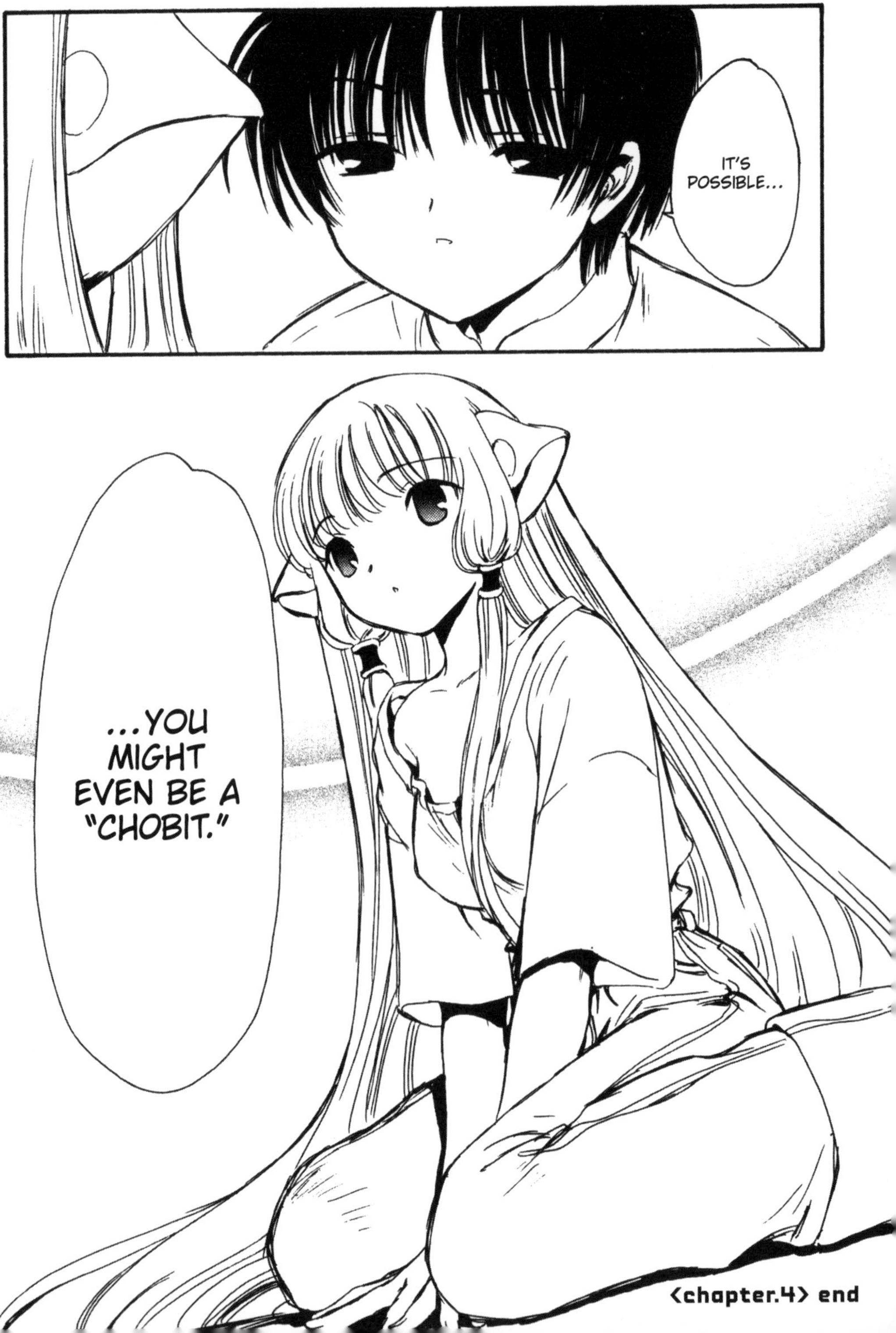
IT'S POSSIBLE...
...YOU MIGHT EVEN BE A "CHOBIT."
<chapter.4> end

⟨chapter.5⟩

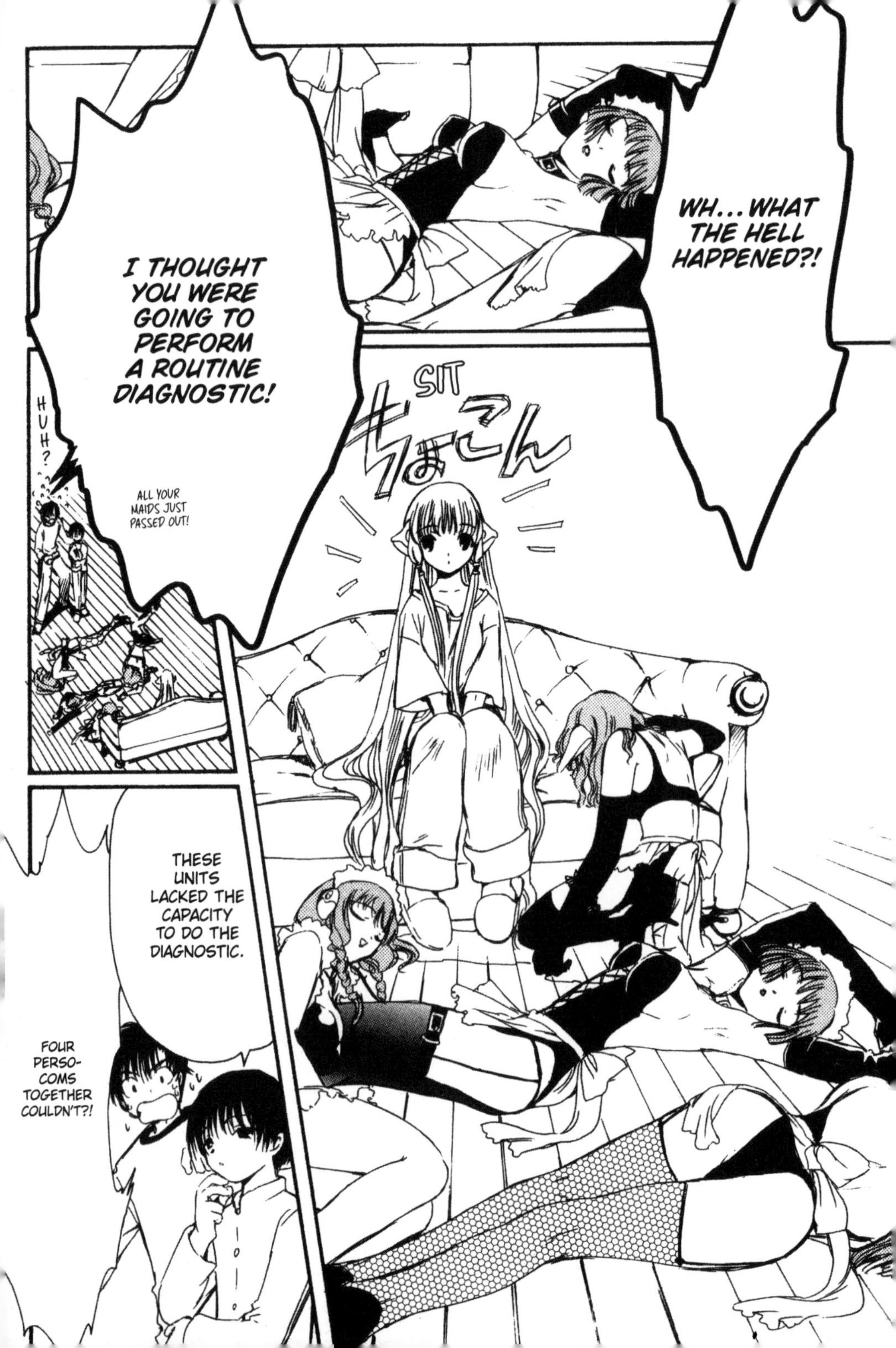
WH...WHAT THE HELL HAPPENED?!
I THOUGHT YOU WERE GOING TO PERFORM A ROUTINE DIAGNOSTIC!
SIT
ちょこん
HUH?
ALL YOUR MAIDS JUST PASSED OUT!
THESE UNITS LACKED THE CAPACITY TO DO THE DIAGNOSTIC.
FOUR PERSO-COMS TOGETHER COULDN'T?!

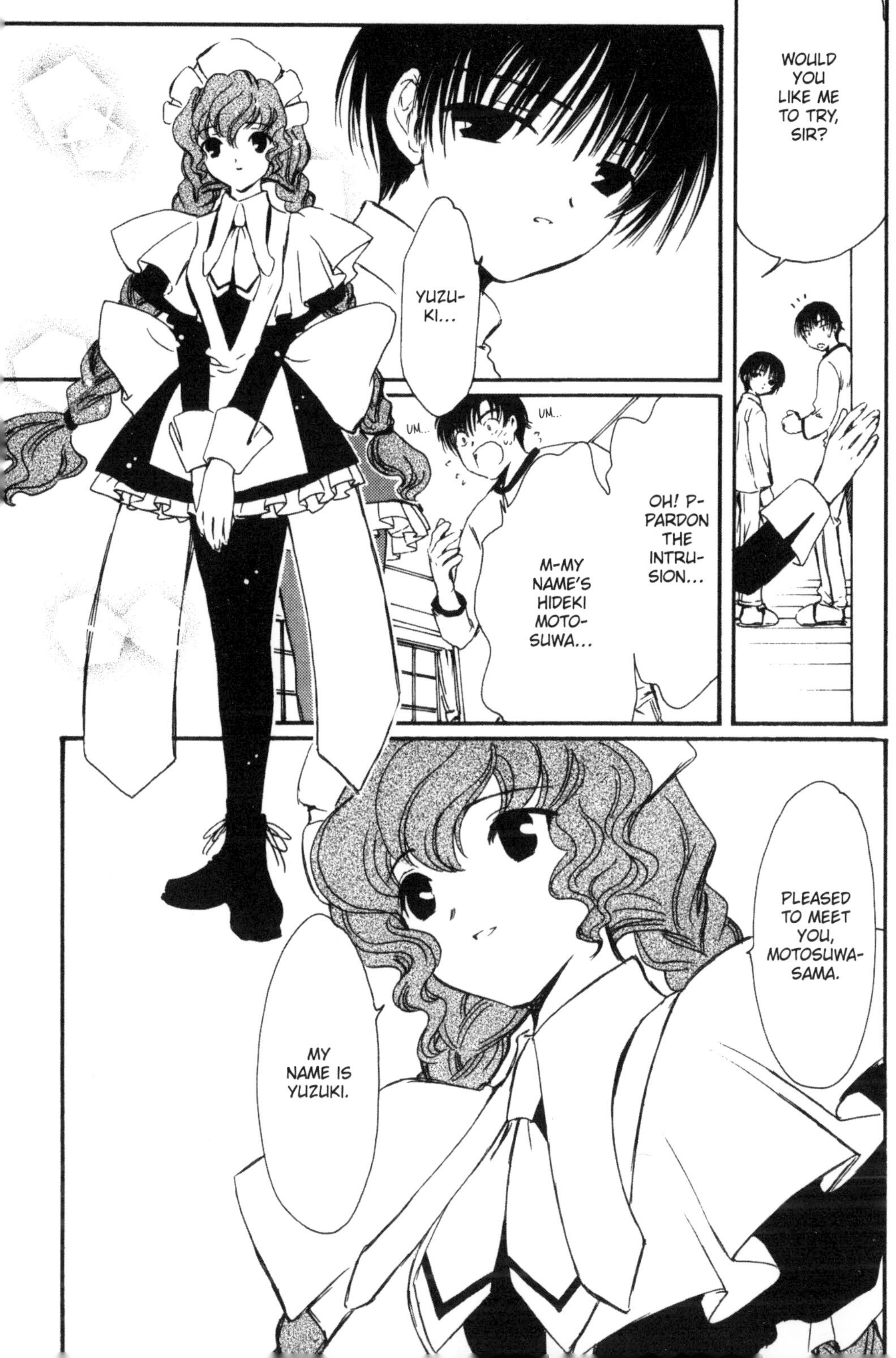
WOULD YOU LIKE ME TO TRY, SIR?
YUZU-KI...
UM...
UM...
OH! P-PARDON THE INTRUSION...
M-MY NAME'S HIDEKI MOTO-SUWA...
PLEASED TO MEET YOU, MOTOSUWA-SAMA.
MY NAME IS YUZUKI.

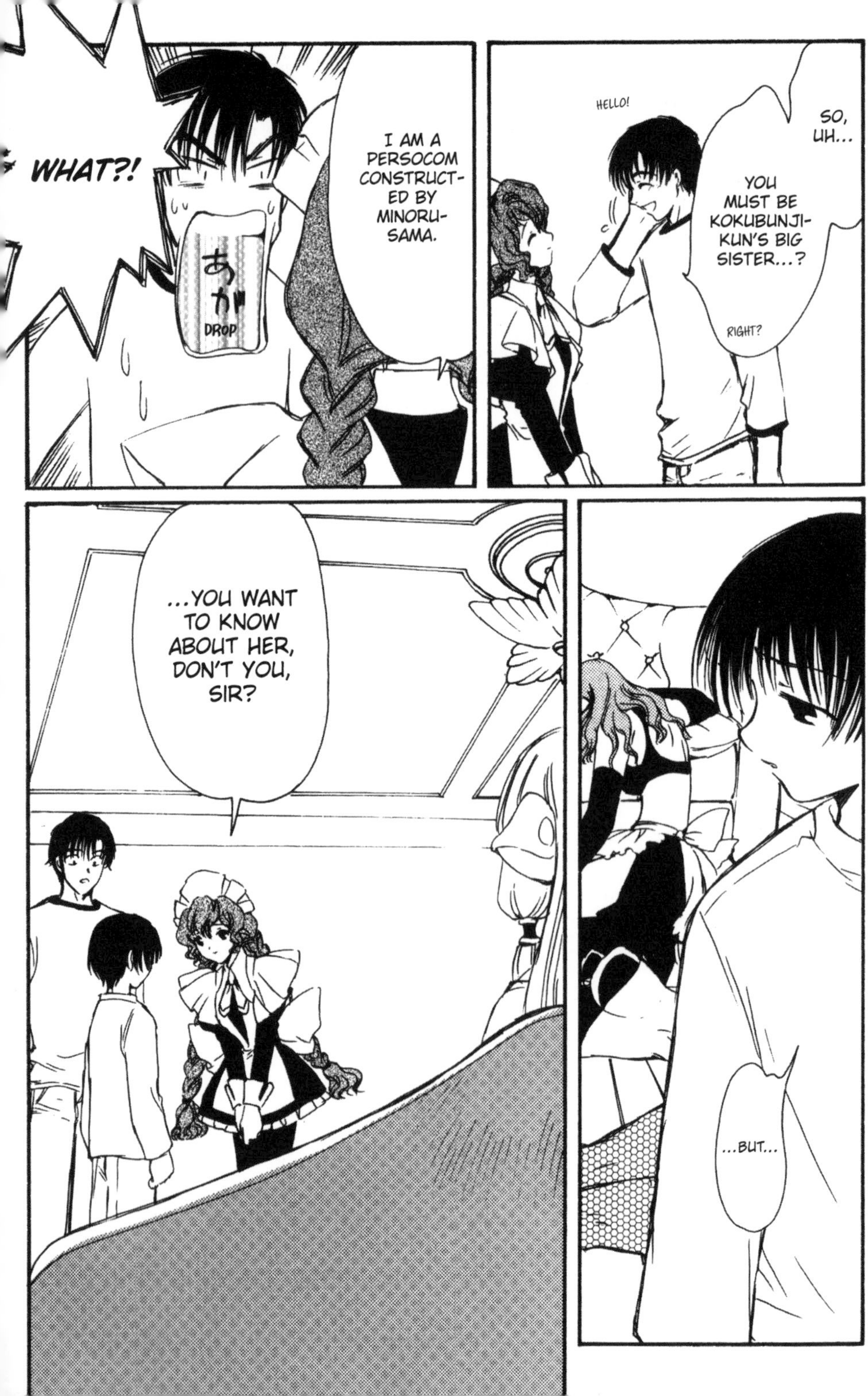
SO, UH…
HELLO!
YOU MUST BE KOKUBUNJI-KUN'S BIG SISTER…?
RIGHT?
I AM A PERSOCOM CONSTRUCTED BY MINORU-SAMA.
WHAT?!
あか
DROP
…BUT…
…YOU WANT TO KNOW ABOUT HER, DON'T YOU, SIR?

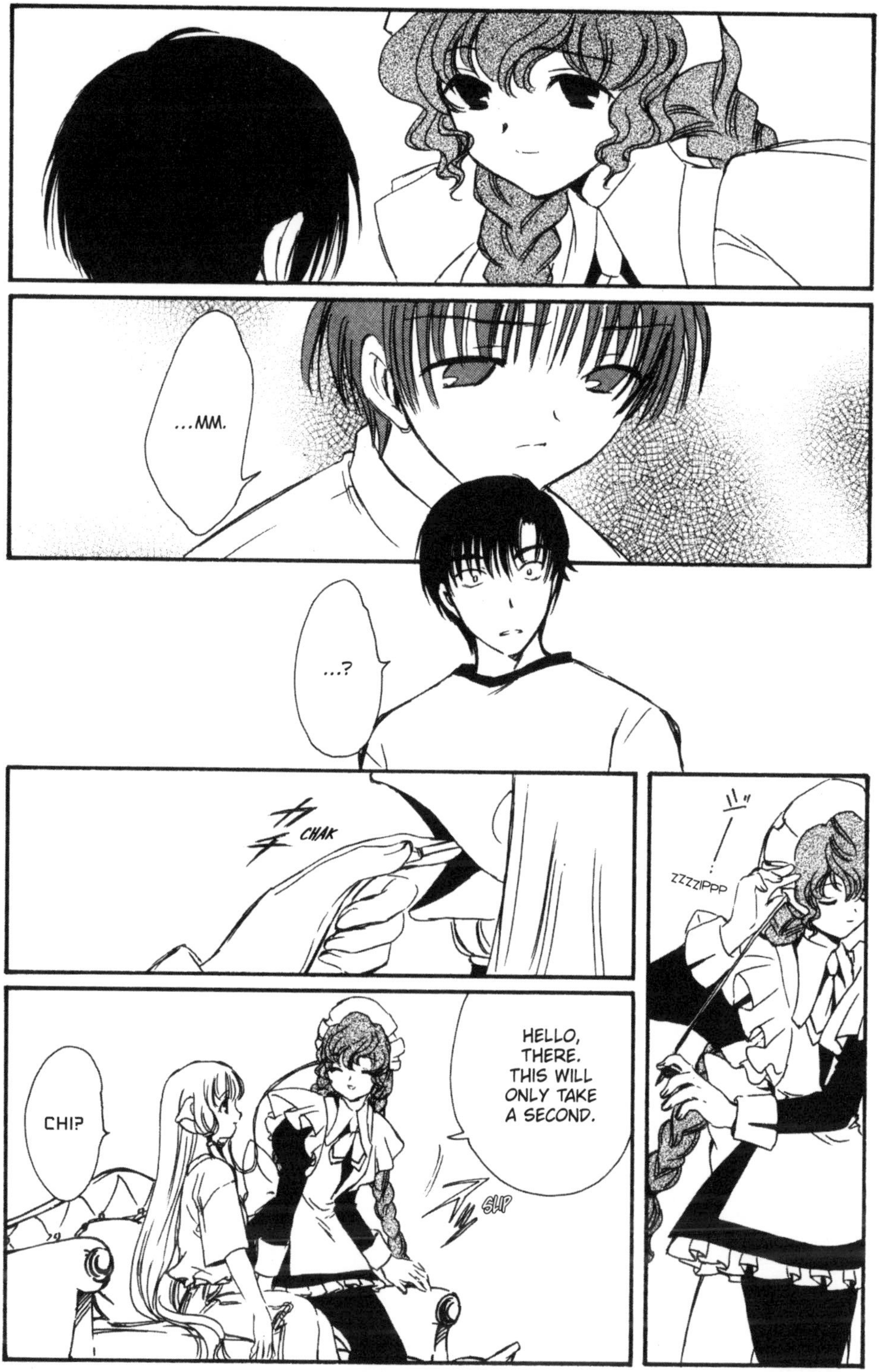

...MM.
...?
ZZZZIPPP
CHAK
HELLO, THERE. THIS WILL ONLY TAKE A SECOND.
SLIP
CHI?

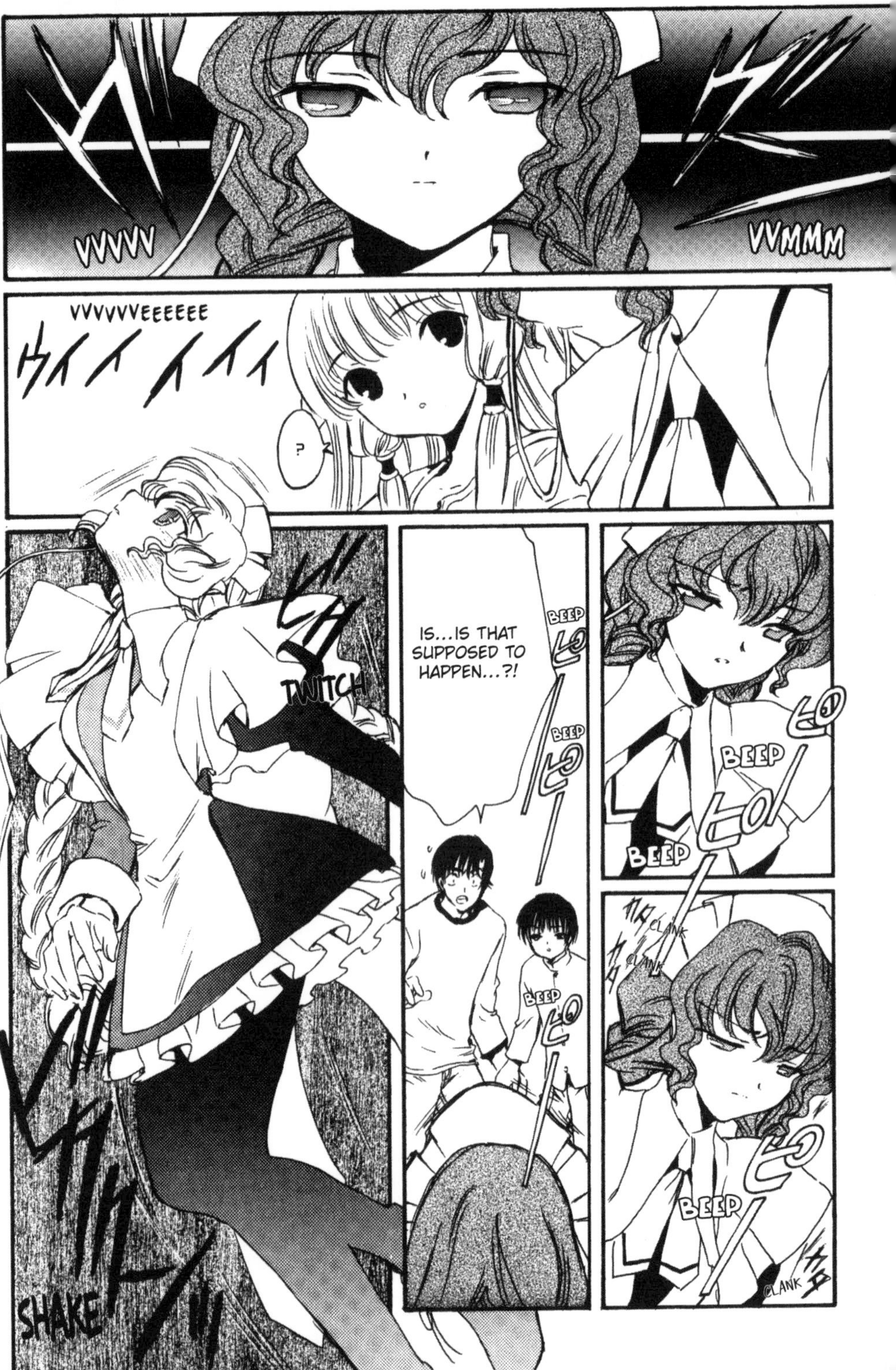

VVMMM
VVVVV
VVVVVVEEEEEE
ウィイ イイイ
?
BEEP
BEEP
CLANK
CLANK
BEEP
CLANK
BEEP
BEEP
IS...IS THAT SUPPOSED TO HAPPEN...?!
BEEP
TWITCH
SHAKE

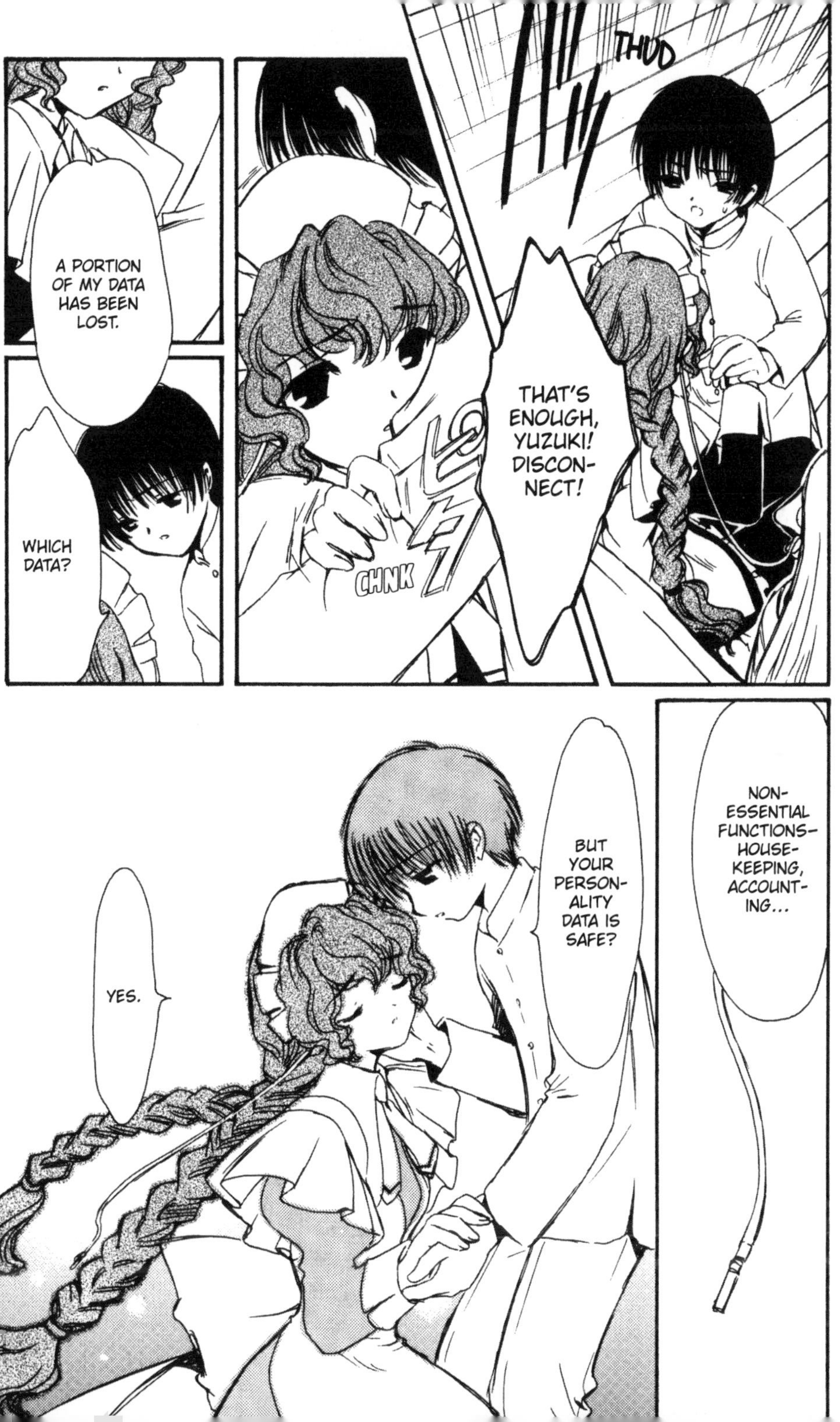
THUD
THAT'S ENOUGH, YUZUKI! DISCONNECT!
CHNK
A PORTION OF MY DATA HAS BEEN LOST.
WHICH DATA?
NON-ESSENTIAL FUNCTIONS—HOUSEKEEPING, ACCOUNTING...
BUT YOUR PERSONALITY DATA IS SAFE?
YES.

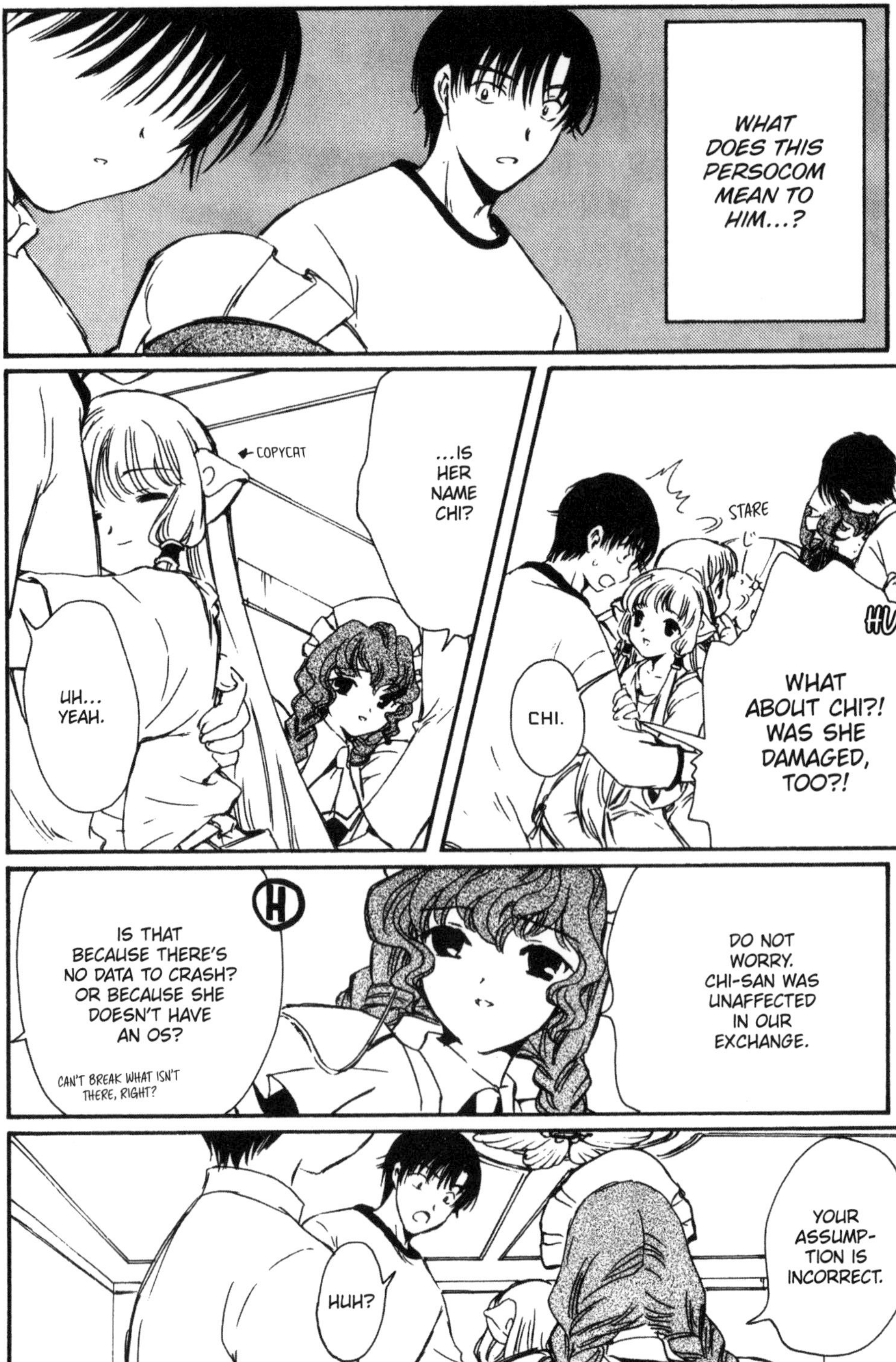
WHAT DOES THIS PERSOCOM MEAN TO HIM...?
HUH?
STARE
WHAT ABOUT CHI?! WAS SHE DAMAGED, TOO?!
CHI.
...IS HER NAME CHI?
COPYCAT
UH... YEAH.
DO NOT WORRY. CHI-SAN WAS UNAFFECTED IN OUR EXCHANGE.
IS THAT BECAUSE THERE'S NO DATA TO CRASH? OR BECAUSE SHE DOESN'T HAVE AN OS?
CAN'T BREAK WHAT ISN'T THERE, RIGHT?
YOUR ASSUMP-TION IS INCORRECT.
HUH?

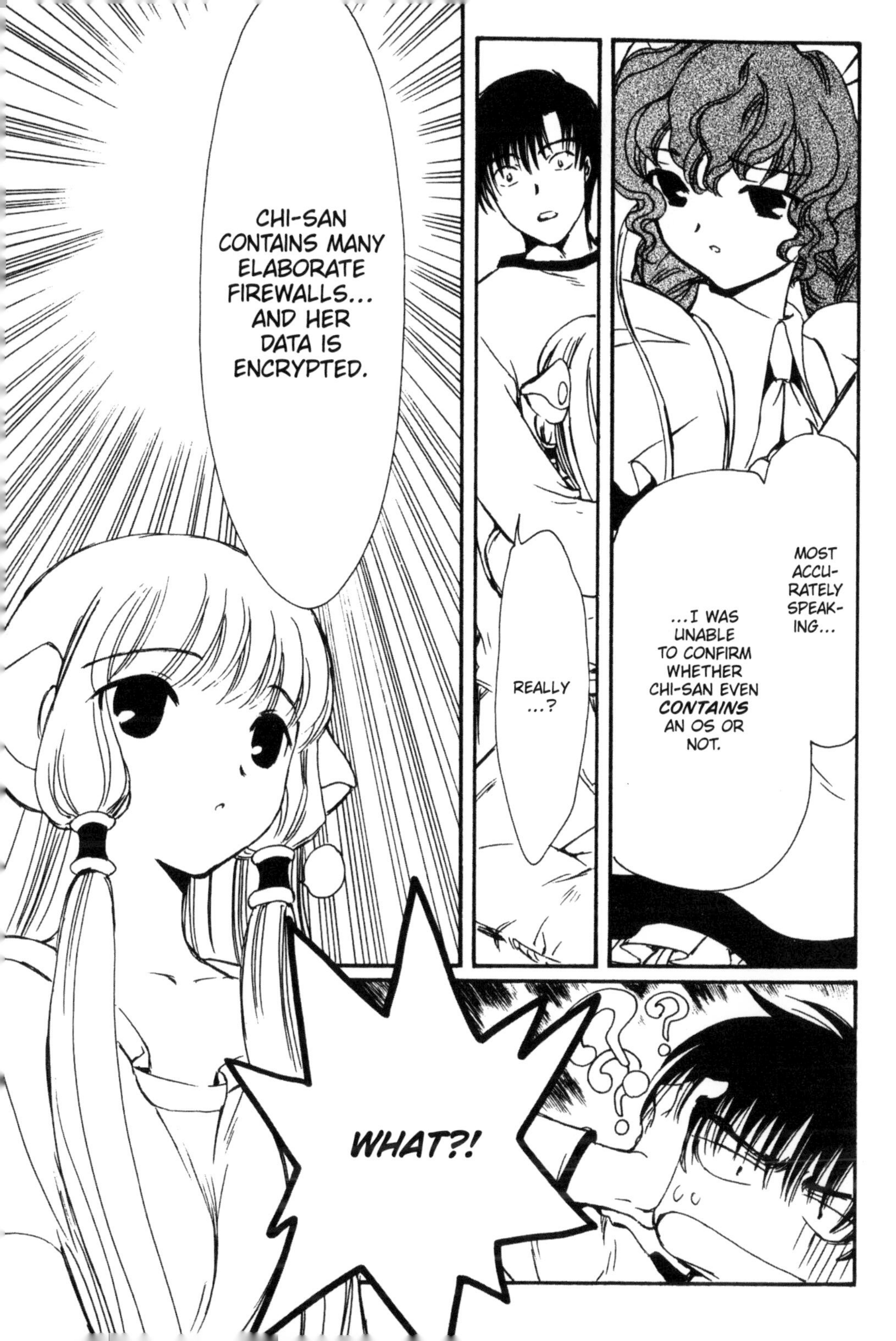
CHI-SAN CONTAINS MANY ELABORATE FIREWALLS... AND HER DATA IS ENCRYPTED.
REALLY ...?
MOST ACCU-RATELY SPEAK-ING...
...I WAS UNABLE TO CONFIRM WHETHER CHI-SAN EVEN CONTAINS AN OS OR NOT.
WHAT?!

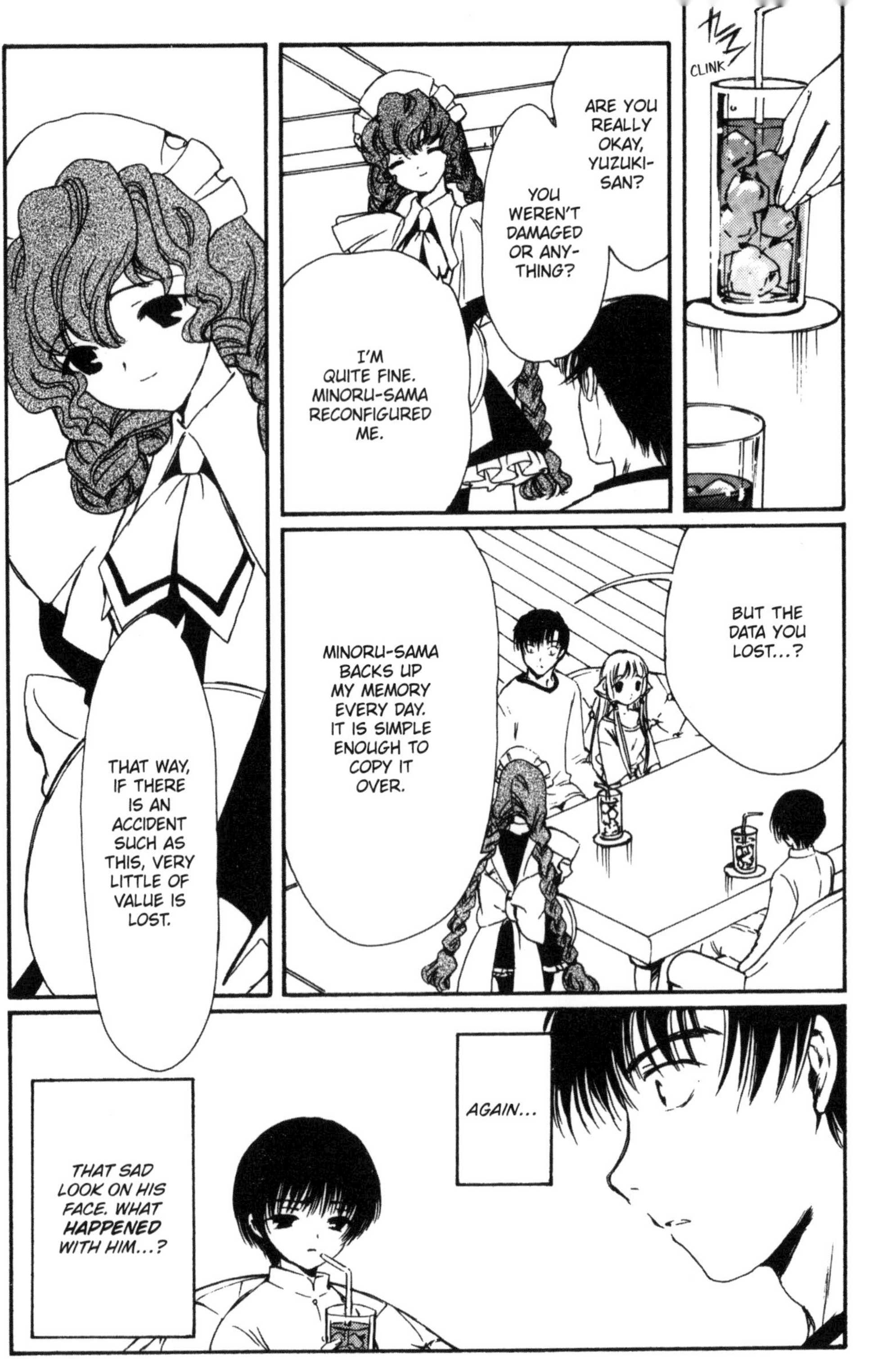
CLINK
ARE YOU REALLY OKAY, YUZUKI-SAN?
YOU WEREN'T DAMAGED OR ANY-THING?
I'M QUITE FINE. MINORU-SAMA RECONFIGURED ME.
BUT THE DATA YOU LOST...?
MINORU-SAMA BACKS UP MY MEMORY EVERY DAY. IT IS SIMPLE ENOUGH TO COPY IT OVER.
THAT WAY, IF THERE IS AN ACCIDENT SUCH AS THIS, VERY LITTLE OF VALUE IS LOST.
AGAIN...
THAT SAD LOOK ON HIS FACE. WHAT **HAPPENED** WITH HIM...?

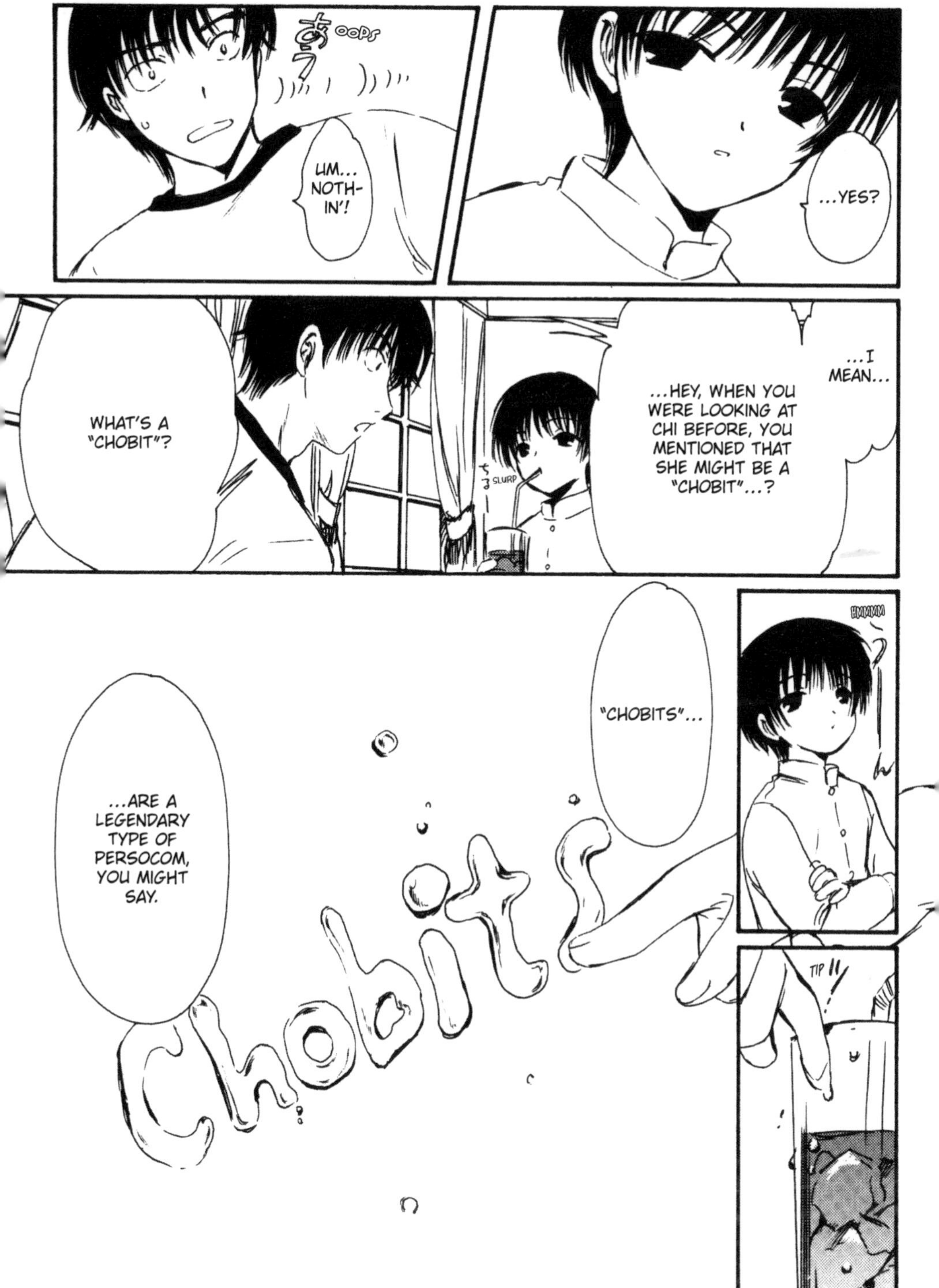
...YES?
あっ OOPS
UM... NOTHIN'!
...I MEAN...
...HEY, WHEN YOU WERE LOOKING AT CHI BEFORE, YOU MENTIONED THAT SHE MIGHT BE A "CHOBIT"...?
SLURP
WHAT'S A "CHOBIT"?
HMMMM
"CHOBITS"...
...ARE A LEGENDARY TYPE OF PERSOCOM, YOU MIGHT SAY.
Chobits
TIP

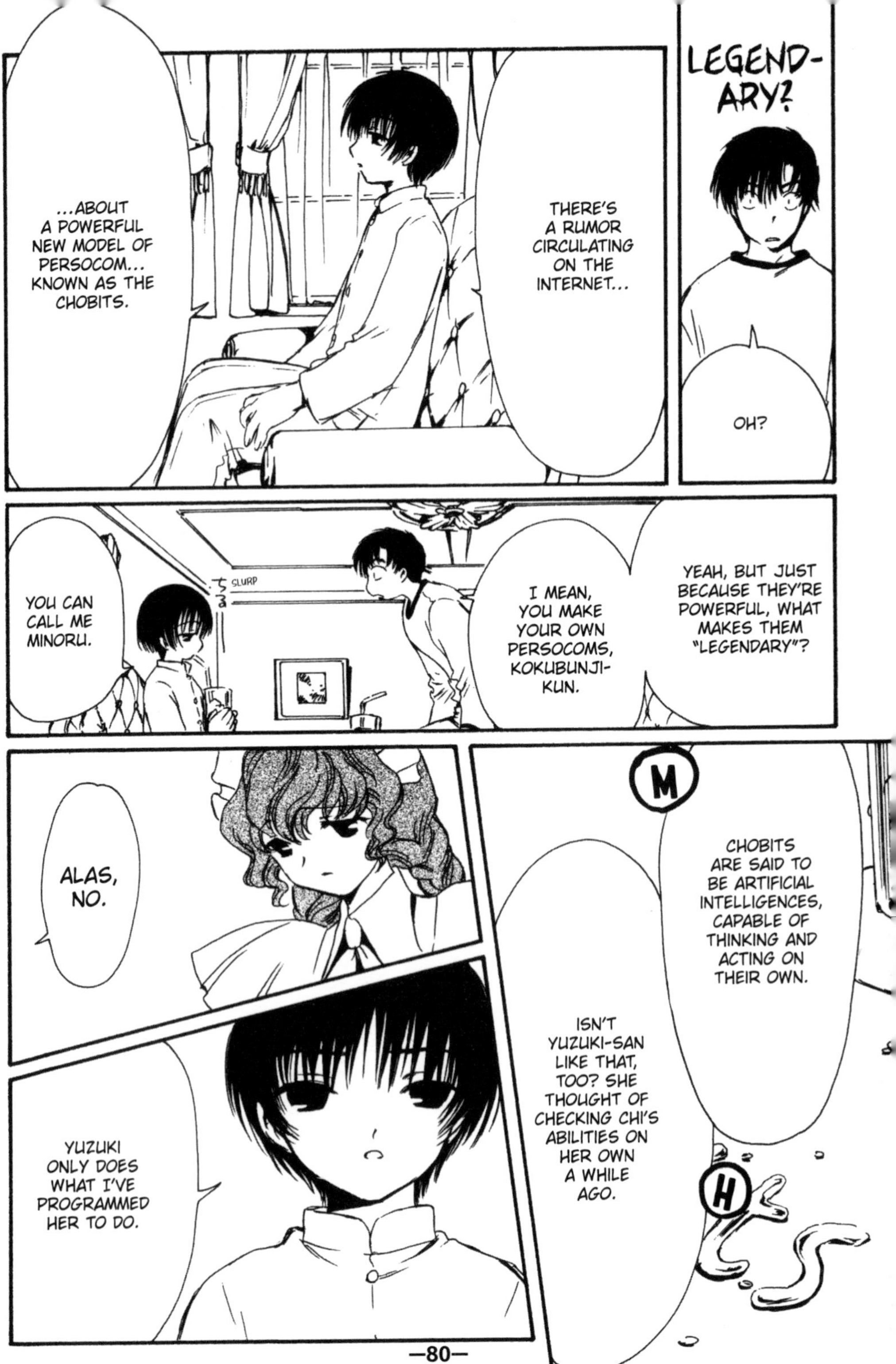
LEGEND-ARY?
OH?
THERE'S A RUMOR CIRCULATING ON THE INTERNET...
...ABOUT A POWERFUL NEW MODEL OF PERSOCOM... KNOWN AS THE CHOBITS.
YEAH, BUT JUST BECAUSE THEY'RE POWERFUL, WHAT MAKES THEM "LEGENDARY"?
I MEAN, YOU MAKE YOUR OWN PERSOCOMS, KOKUBUNJI-KUN.
SLURP
YOU CAN CALL ME MINORU.
CHOBITS ARE SAID TO BE ARTIFICIAL INTELLIGENCES, CAPABLE OF THINKING AND ACTING ON THEIR OWN.
ISN'T YUZUKI-SAN LIKE THAT, TOO? SHE THOUGHT OF CHECKING CHI'S ABILITIES ON HER OWN A WHILE AGO.
ALAS, NO.
YUZUKI ONLY DOES WHAT I'VE PROGRAMMED HER TO DO.

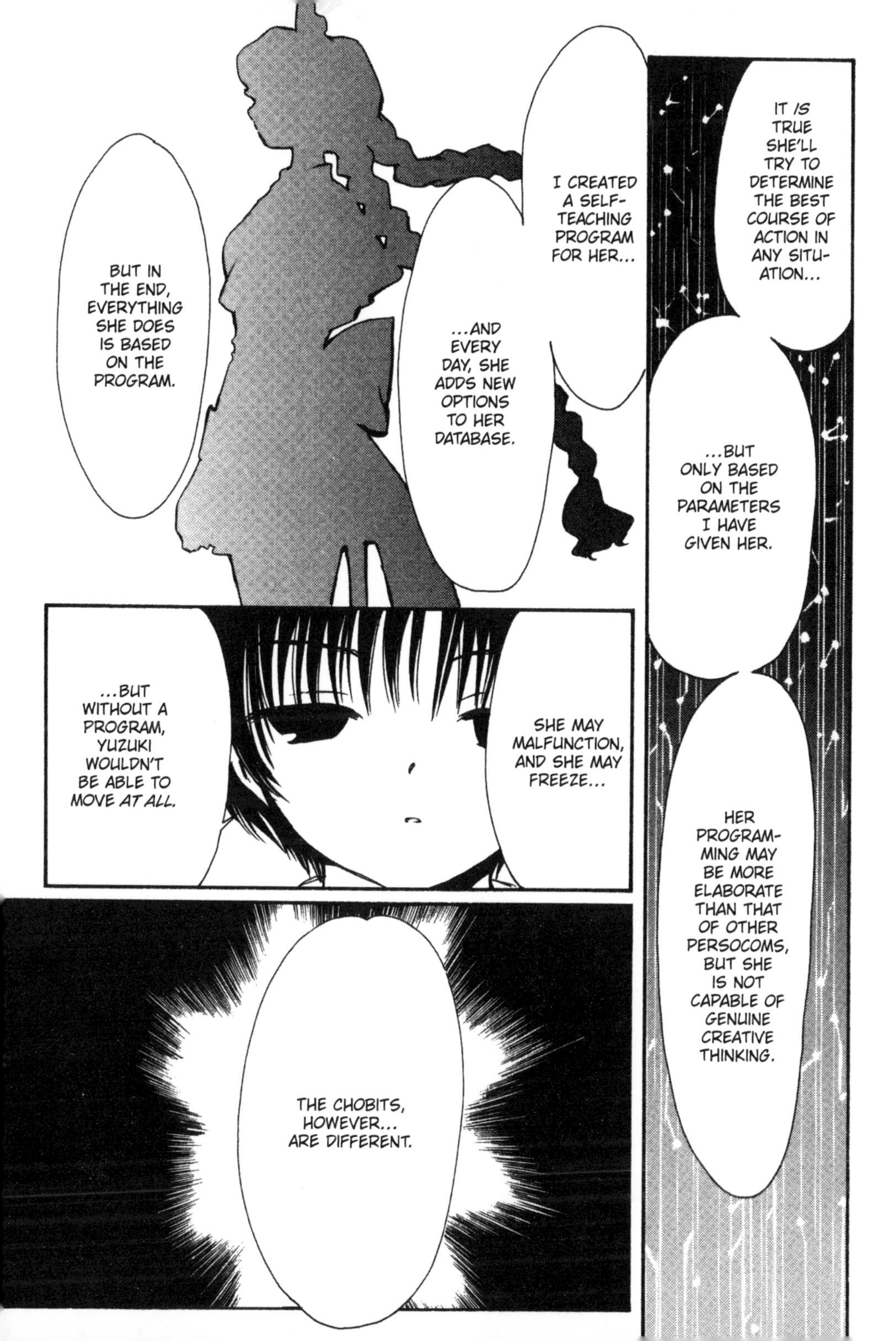
IT *IS* TRUE SHE'LL TRY TO DETERMINE THE BEST COURSE OF ACTION IN ANY SITU-ATION...
...BUT ONLY BASED ON THE PARAMETERS I HAVE GIVEN HER.
HER PROGRAM-MING MAY BE MORE ELABORATE THAN THAT OF OTHER PERSOCOMS, BUT SHE IS NOT CAPABLE OF GENUINE CREATIVE THINKING.
I CREATED A SELF-TEACHING PROGRAM FOR HER...
...AND EVERY DAY, SHE ADDS NEW OPTIONS TO HER DATABASE.
BUT IN THE END, EVERYTHING SHE DOES IS BASED ON THE PROGRAM.
SHE MAY MALFUNCTION, AND SHE MAY FREEZE...
...BUT WITHOUT A PROGRAM, YUZUKI WOULDN'T BE ABLE TO MOVE *AT ALL*.
THE CHOBITS, HOWEVER... ARE DIFFERENT.

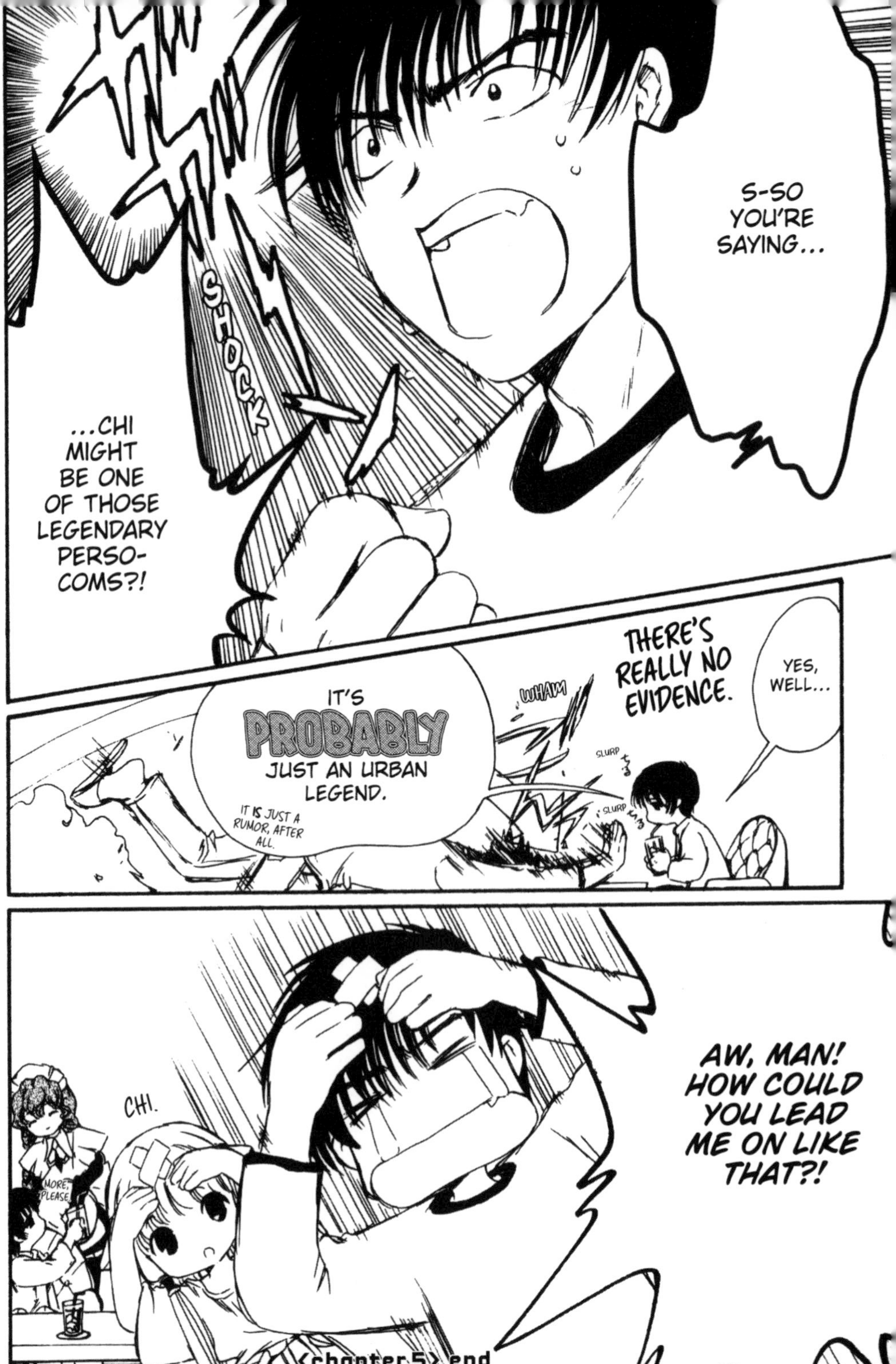
S-SO YOU'RE SAYING...
SHOCK
...CHI MIGHT BE ONE OF THOSE LEGENDARY PERSO-COMS?!
YES, WELL...
THERE'S REALLY NO EVIDENCE.
SLURP
SLURP
WHAM
IT'S PROBABLY JUST AN URBAN LEGEND.
IT IS JUST A RUMOR, AFTER ALL.
AW, MAN! HOW COULD YOU LEAD ME ON LIKE THAT?!
CHI.
MORE, PLEASE.

<chapter.5> end

〈chapter.6〉

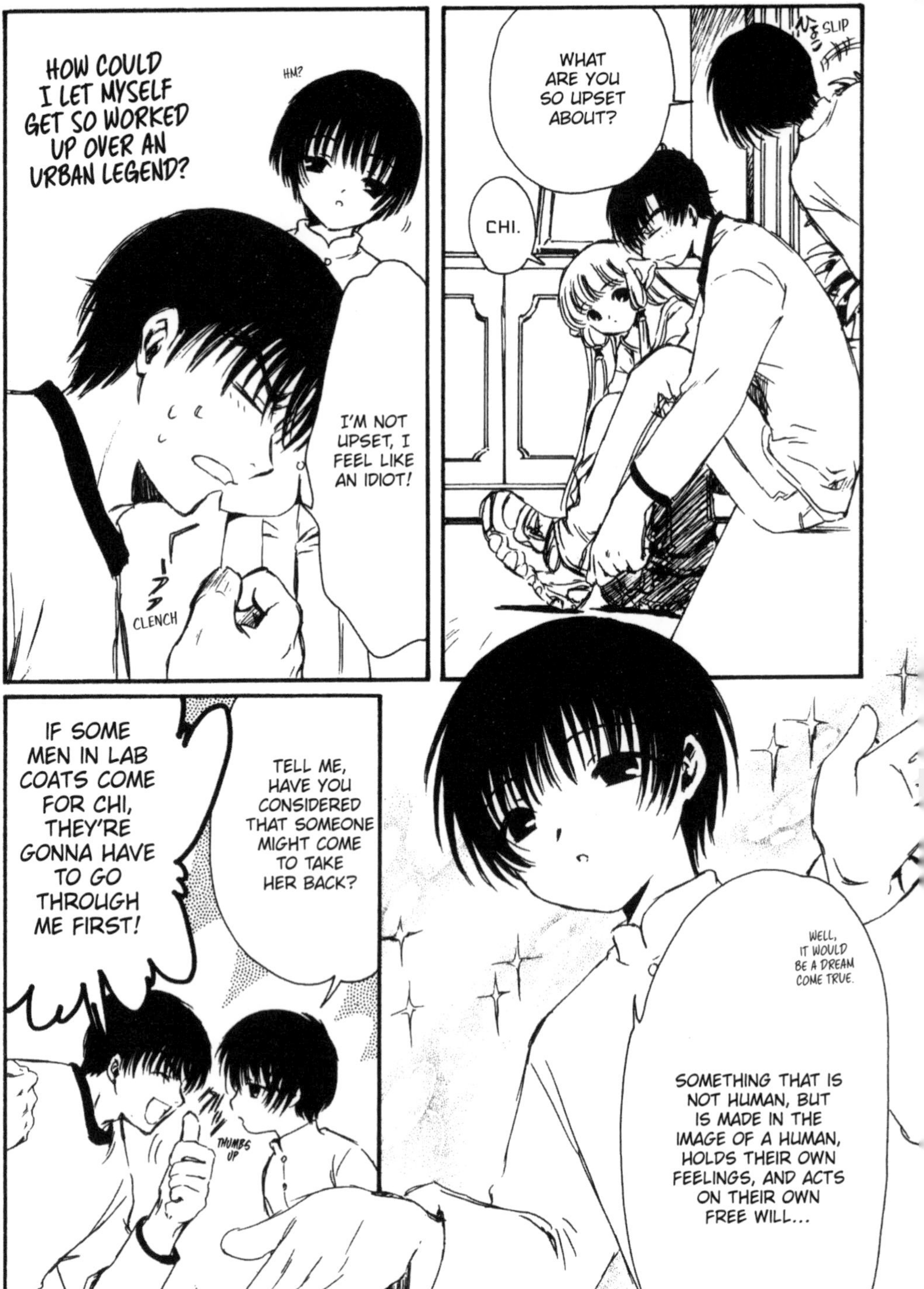
SLIP
WHAT ARE YOU SO UPSET ABOUT?
CHI.
HOW COULD I LET MYSELF GET SO WORKED UP OVER AN URBAN LEGEND?
HM?
I'M NOT UPSET, I FEEL LIKE AN IDIOT!
CLENCH
WELL, IT WOULD BE A DREAM COME TRUE.
SOMETHING THAT IS NOT HUMAN, BUT IS MADE IN THE IMAGE OF A HUMAN, HOLDS THEIR OWN FEELINGS, AND ACTS ON THEIR OWN FREE WILL...
TELL ME, HAVE YOU CONSIDERED THAT SOMEONE MIGHT COME TO TAKE HER BACK?
IF SOME MEN IN LAB COATS COME FOR CHI, THEY'RE GONNA HAVE TO GO THROUGH ME FIRST!
THUMBS UP

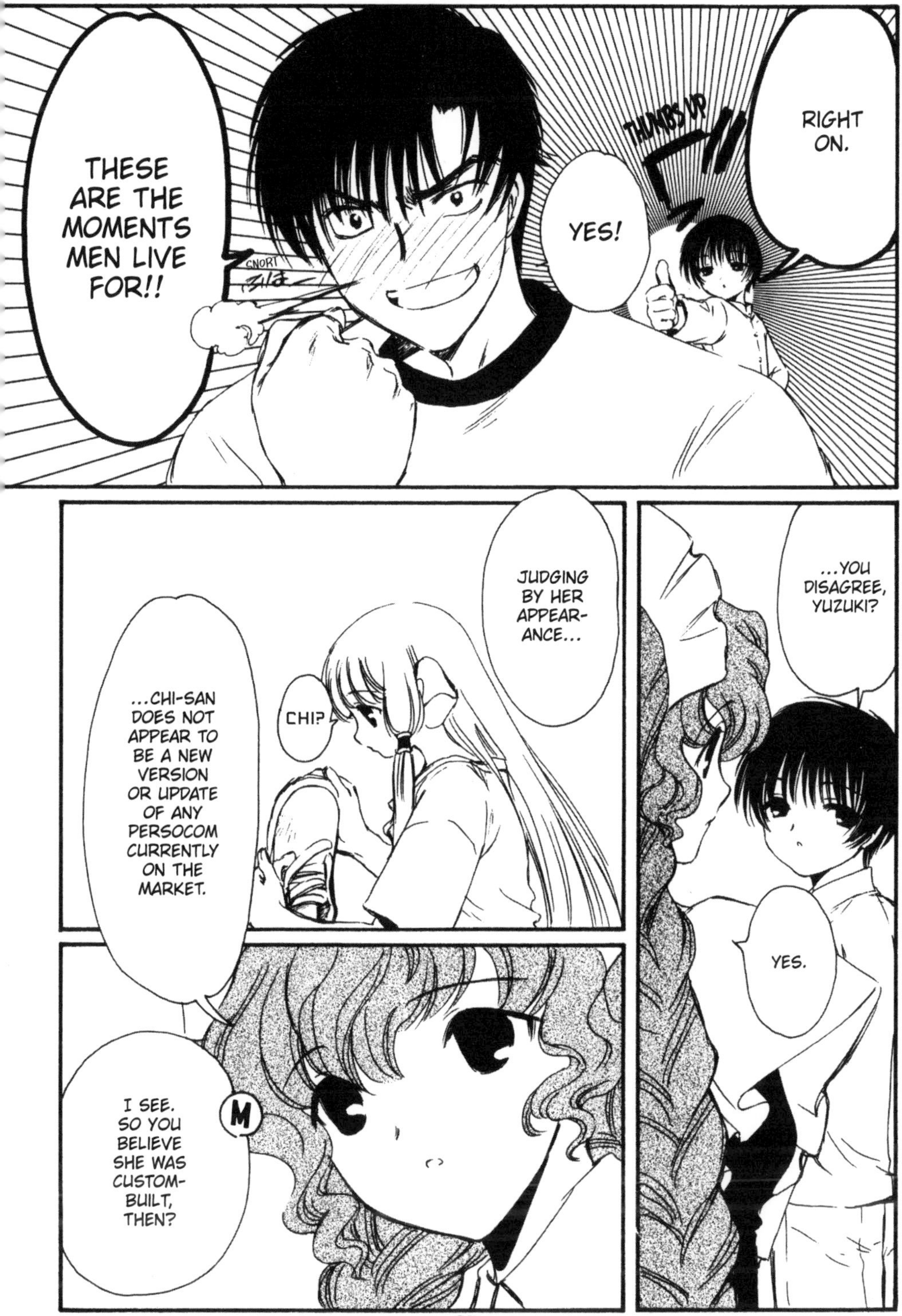
RIGHT ON.
THUMBS UP
YES!
CNORT
THESE ARE THE MOMENTS MEN LIVE FOR!!
...YOU DISAGREE, YUZUKI?
YES.
JUDGING BY HER APPEAR-ANCE...
CHI?
...CHI-SAN DOES NOT APPEAR TO BE A NEW VERSION OR UPDATE OF ANY PERSOCOM CURRENTLY ON THE MARKET.
I SEE. SO YOU BELIEVE SHE WAS CUSTOM-BUILT, THEN?
M

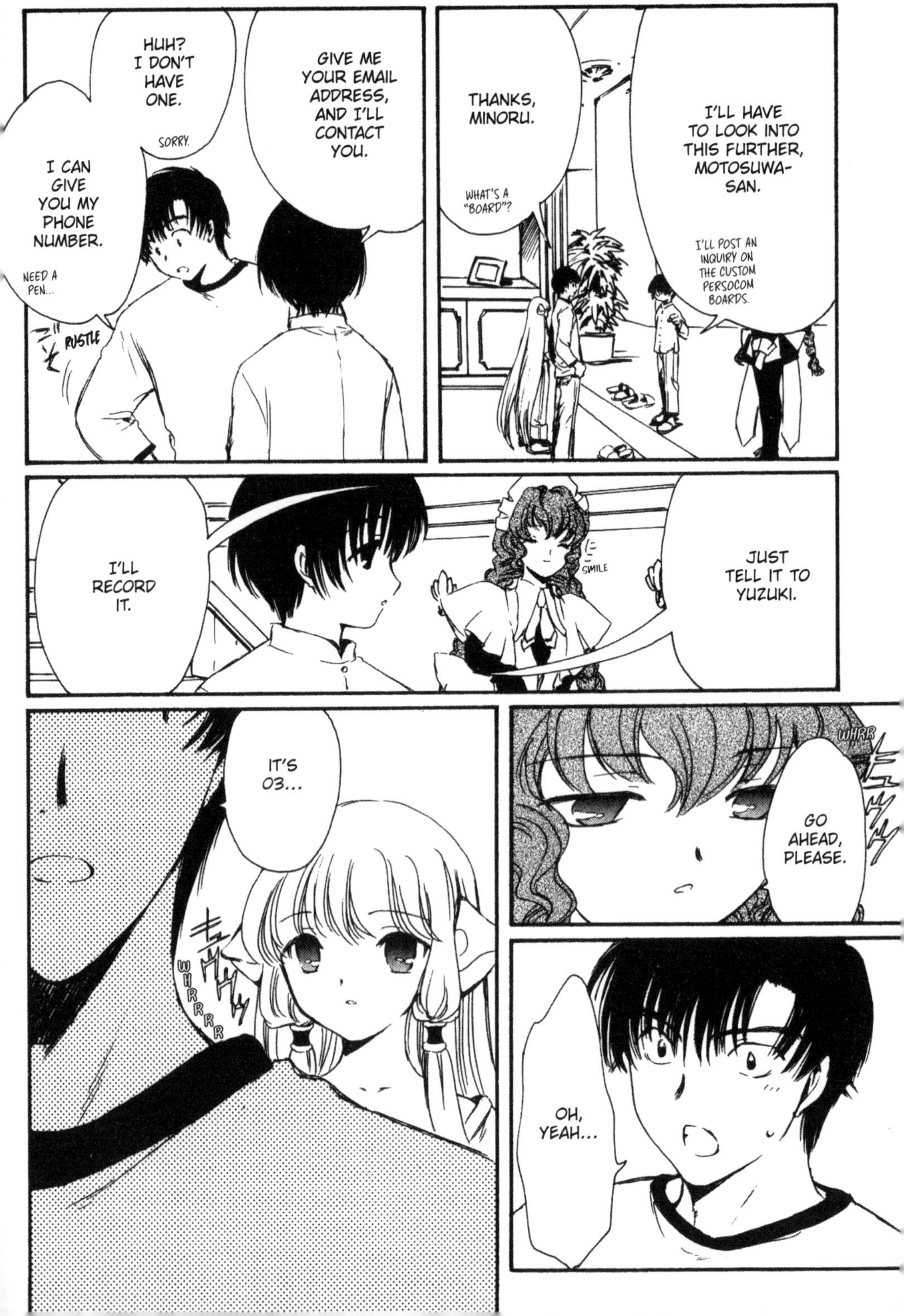
I'LL HAVE TO LOOK INTO THIS FURTHER, MOTOSUWA-SAN.
I'LL POST AN INQUIRY ON THE CUSTOM PERSOCOM BOARDS.
THANKS, MINORU.
WHAT'S A "BOARD"?
GIVE ME YOUR EMAIL ADDRESS, AND I'LL CONTACT YOU.
HUH? I DON'T HAVE ONE.
SORRY.
I CAN GIVE YOU MY PHONE NUMBER.
NEED A PEN...
RUSTLE
JUST TELL IT TO YUZUKI.
SMILE
I'LL RECORD IT.
WHRR
GO AHEAD, PLEASE.
OH, YEAH...
IT'S 03...
WHRRRR

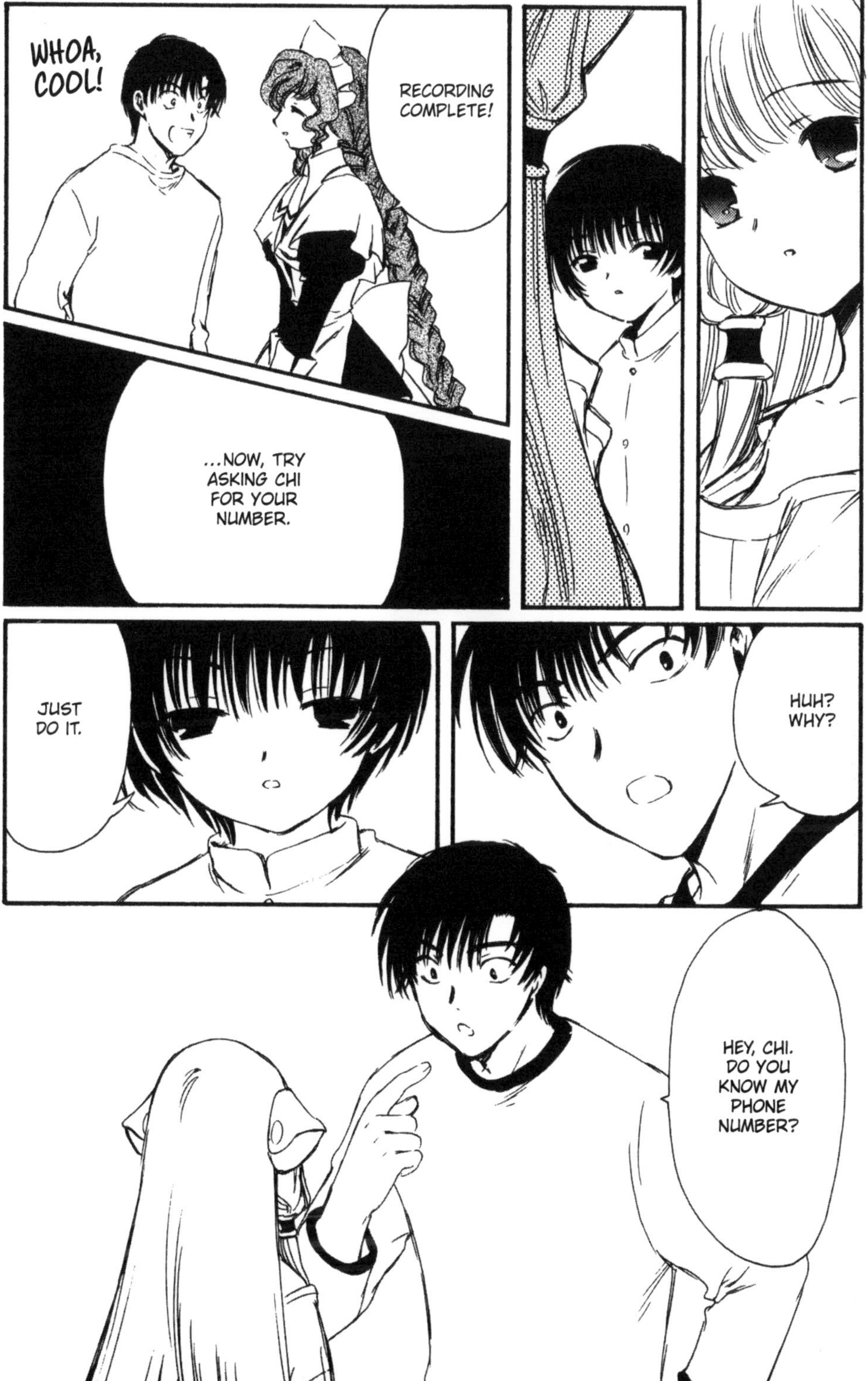
RECORDING COMPLETE!
WHOA, COOL!
...NOW, TRY ASKING CHI FOR YOUR NUMBER.
HUH? WHY?
JUST DO IT.
HEY, CHI. DO YOU KNOW MY PHONE NUMBER?

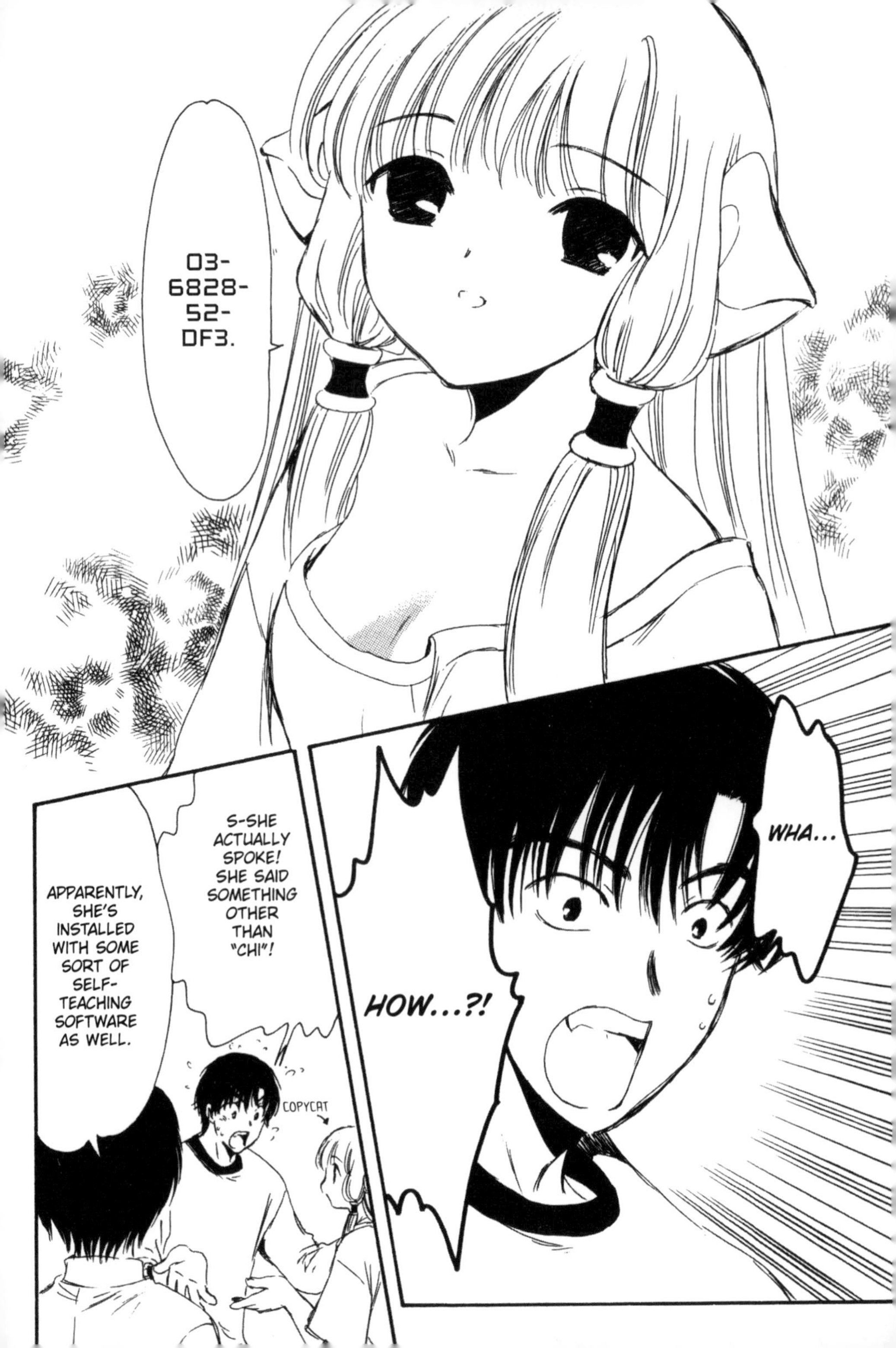
03-6828-52-DF3.
WHA...
HOW...?!
S-SHE ACTUALLY SPOKE! SHE SAID SOMETHING OTHER THAN "CHI"!
APPARENTLY, SHE'S INSTALLED WITH SOME SORT OF SELF-TEACHING SOFTWARE AS WELL.
COPYCAT

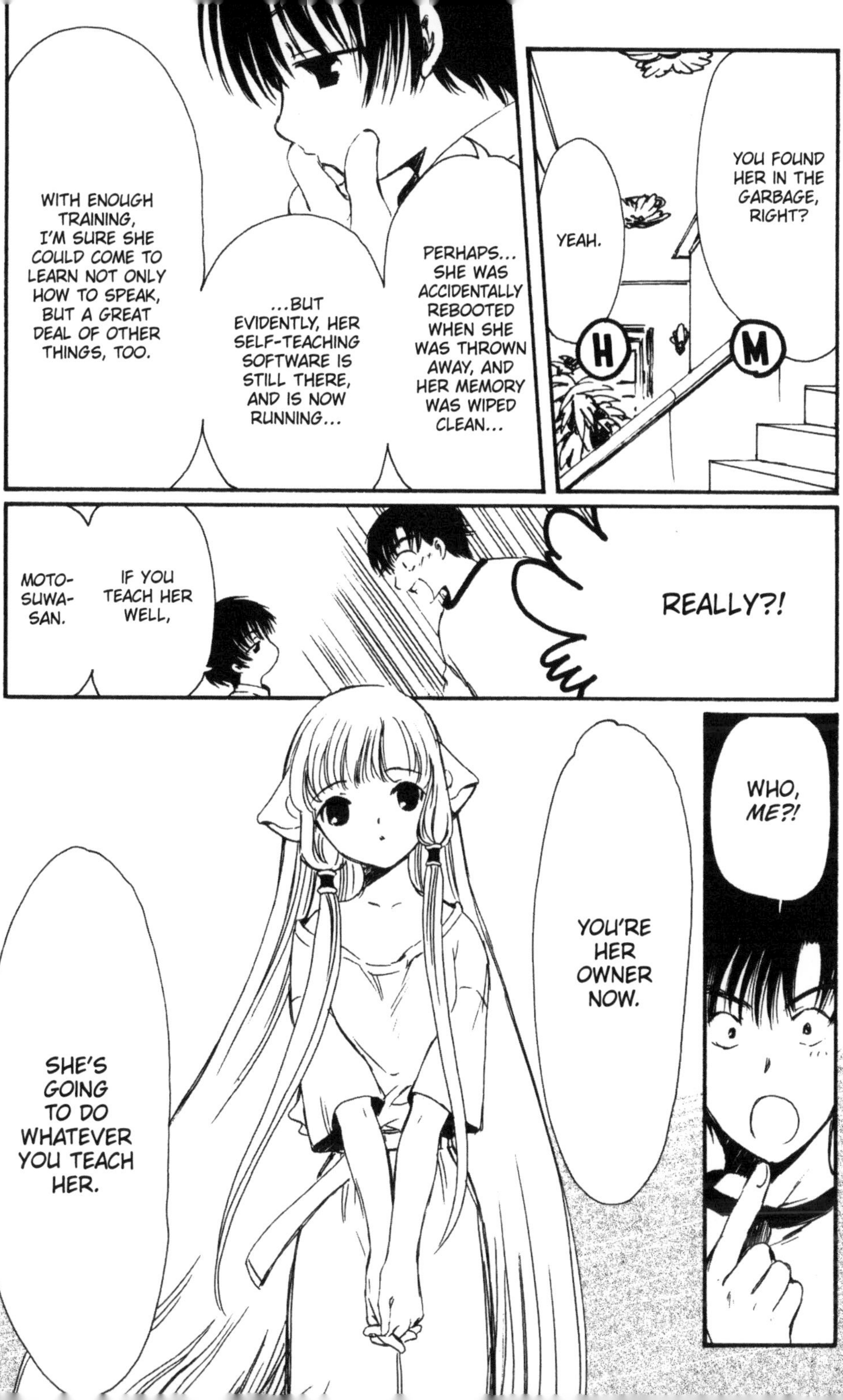

YOU FOUND HER IN THE GARBAGE, RIGHT?
YEAH.
HM
PERHAPS... SHE WAS ACCIDENTALLY REBOOTED WHEN SHE WAS THROWN AWAY, AND HER MEMORY WAS WIPED CLEAN...
...BUT EVIDENTLY, HER SELF-TEACHING SOFTWARE IS STILL THERE, AND IS NOW RUNNING...
WITH ENOUGH TRAINING, I'M SURE SHE COULD COME TO LEARN NOT ONLY HOW TO SPEAK, BUT A GREAT DEAL OF OTHER THINGS, TOO.
REALLY?!
MOTO-SUWA-SAN. IF YOU TEACH HER WELL,
WHO, *ME?!*
YOU'RE HER OWNER NOW.
SHE'S GOING TO DO WHATEVER YOU TEACH HER.

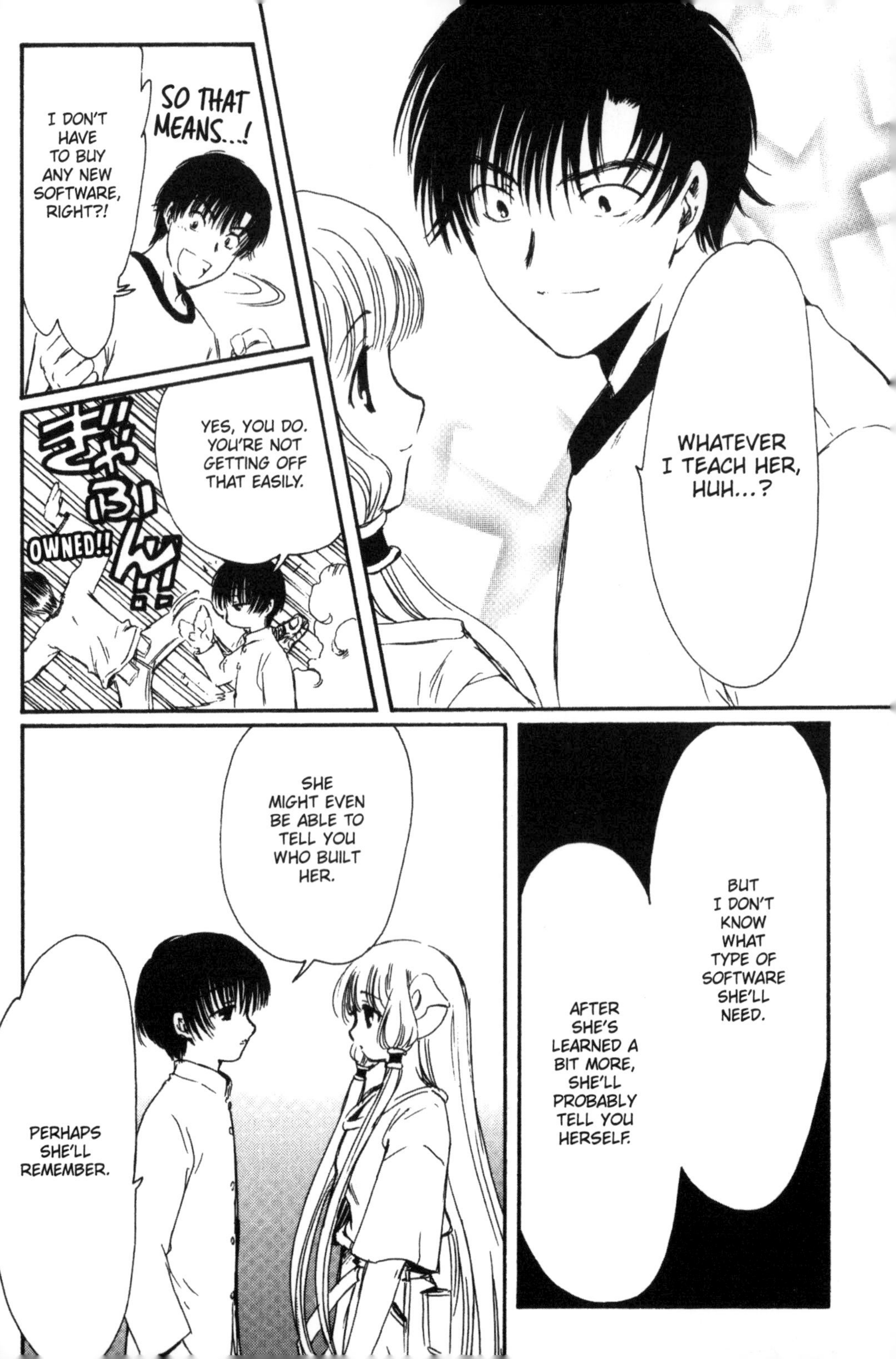
WHATEVER I TEACH HER, HUH...?
SO THAT MEANS...!
I DON'T HAVE TO BUY ANY NEW SOFTWARE, RIGHT?!
YES, YOU DO. YOU'RE NOT GETTING OFF THAT EASILY.
ぎゃふん!!
OWNED!!
BUT I DON'T KNOW WHAT TYPE OF SOFTWARE SHE'LL NEED.
AFTER SHE'S LEARNED A BIT MORE, SHE'LL PROBABLY TELL YOU HERSELF.
SHE MIGHT EVEN BE ABLE TO TELL YOU WHO BUILT HER.
PERHAPS SHE'LL REMEMBER.

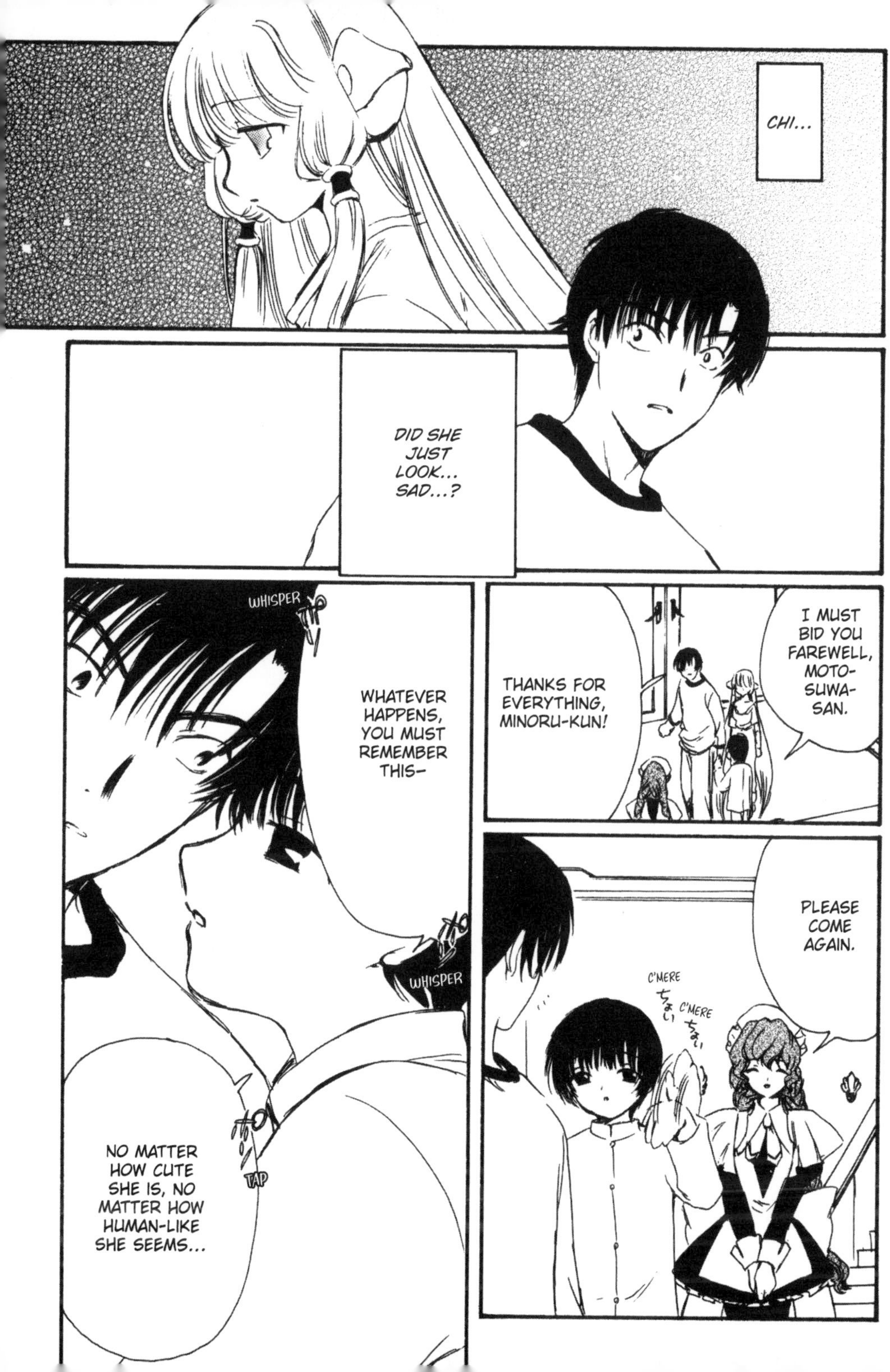
CHI...
DID SHE JUST LOOK... SAD...?
I MUST BID YOU FAREWELL, MOTO-SUWA-SAN.
THANKS FOR EVERYTHING, MINORU-KUN!
PLEASE COME AGAIN.
C'MERE
C'MERE
WHISPER
WHATEVER HAPPENS, YOU MUST REMEMBER THIS–
WHISPER
NO MATTER HOW CUTE SHE IS, NO MATTER HOW HUMAN-LIKE SHE SEEMS...
TAP

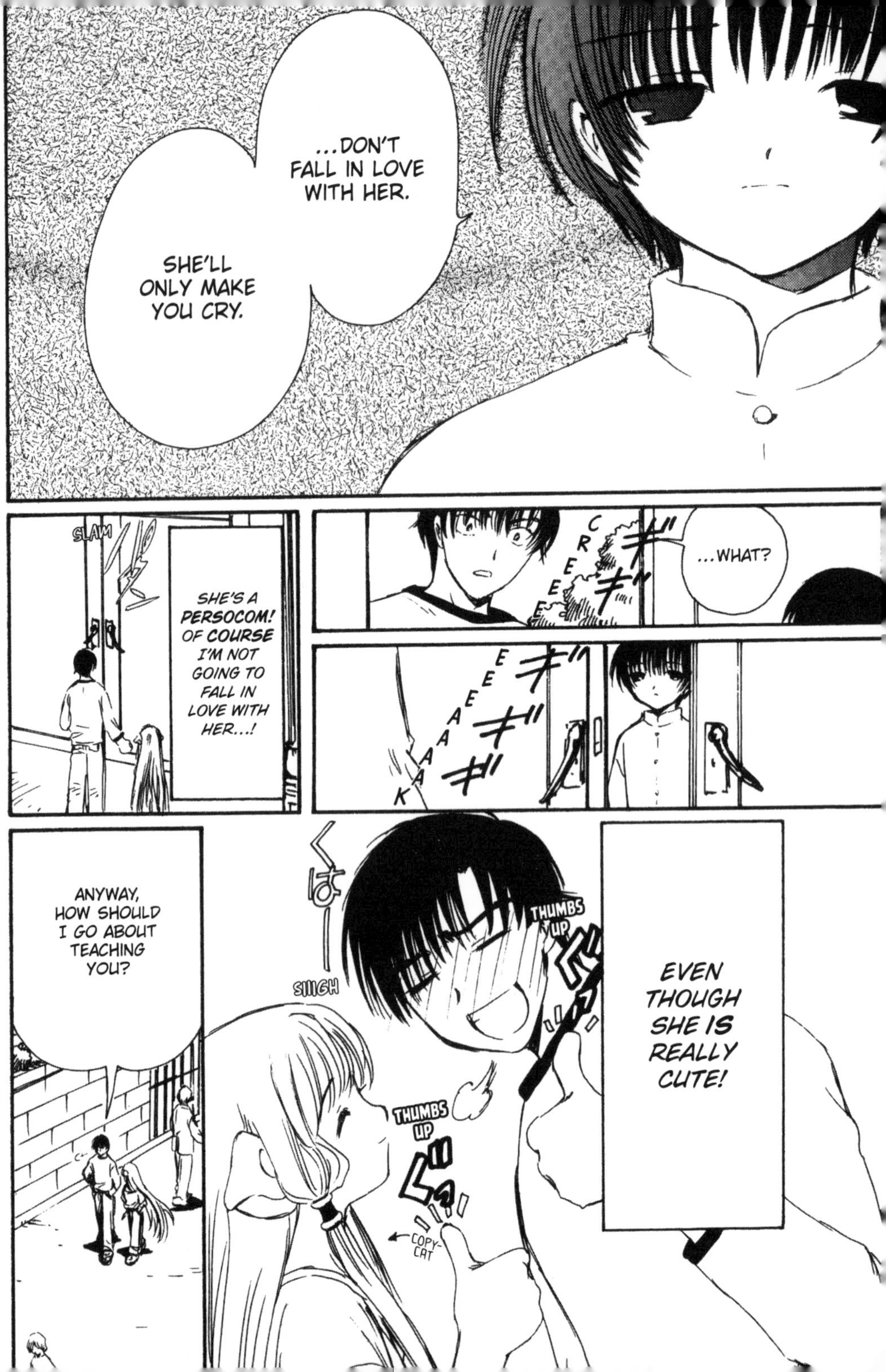
...DON'T FALL IN LOVE WITH HER.
SHE'LL ONLY MAKE YOU CRY.
...WHAT?
CREEEE
EEEAAAAK
SLAM
SHE'S A PERSOCOM! OF COURSE I'M NOT GOING TO FALL IN LOVE WITH HER...!
EVEN THOUGH SHE IS REALLY CUTE!
THUMBS UP
SIIIGH
THUMBS UP
COPY-CAT
ANYWAY, HOW SHOULD I GO ABOUT TEACHING YOU?

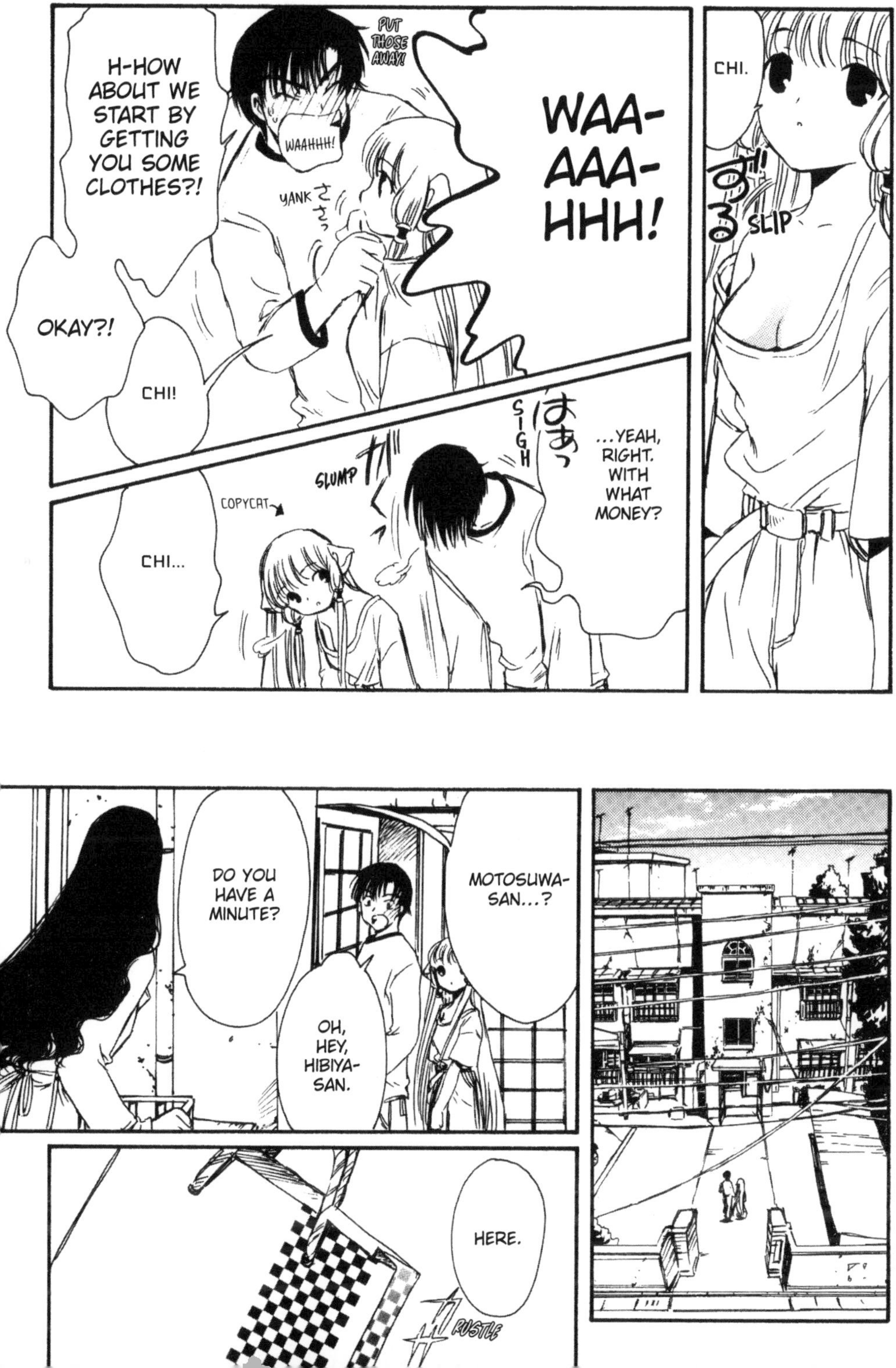
CHI.
SLIP
PUT THOSE AWAY!
WAA-AAA-HHH!
WAAHHH!
YANK
H-HOW ABOUT WE START BY GETTING YOU SOME CLOTHES?!
OKAY?!
CHI!
...YEAH, RIGHT. WITH WHAT MONEY?
SIGH
SLUMP
COPYCAT
CHI...
MOTOSUWA-SAN...?
OH, HEY, HIBIYA-SAN.
DO YOU HAVE A MINUTE?
HERE.
RUSTLE

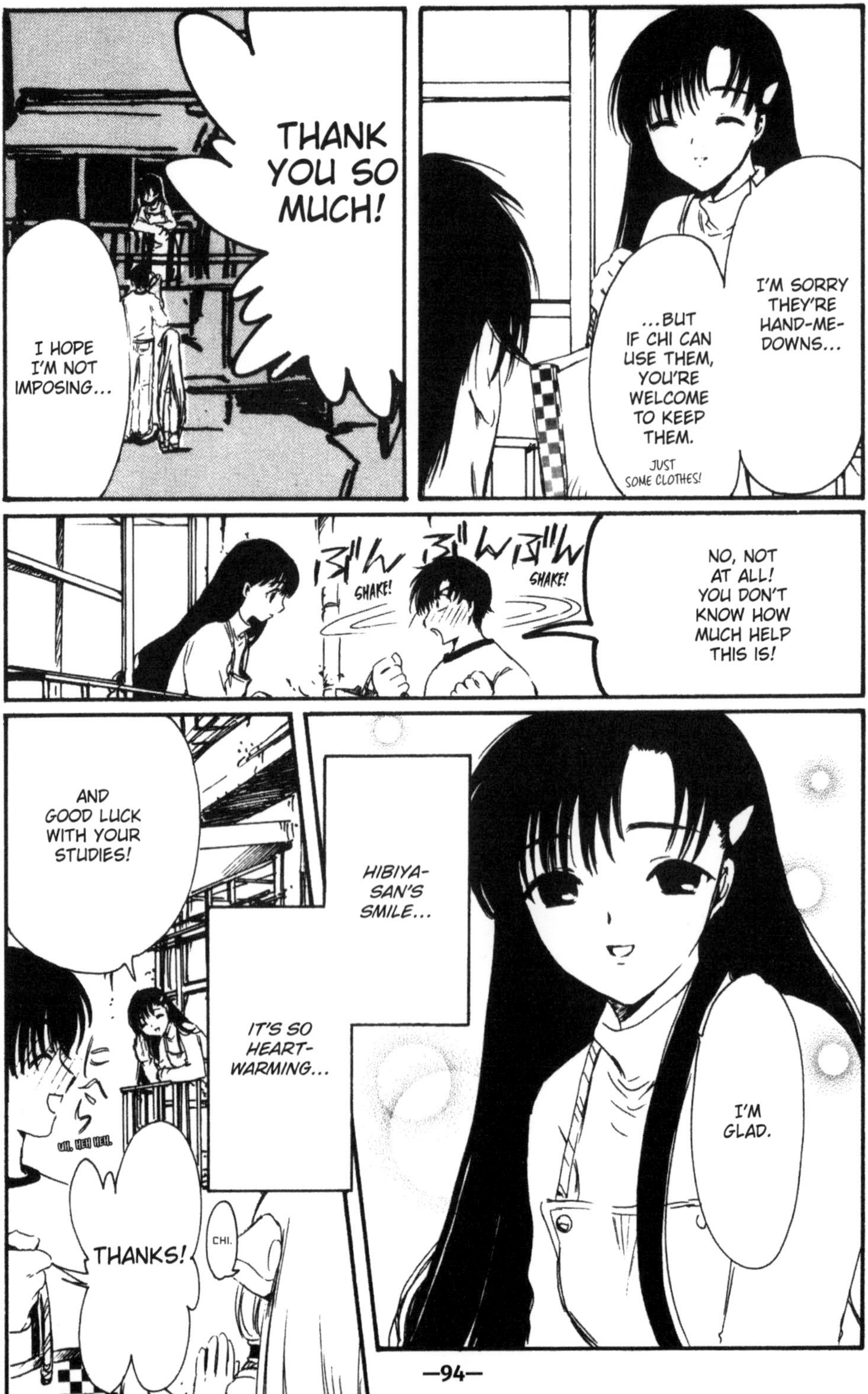
I'M SORRY THEY'RE HAND-ME-DOWNS...
...BUT IF CHI CAN USE THEM, YOU'RE WELCOME TO KEEP THEM.
JUST SOME CLOTHES!
THANK YOU SO MUCH!
I HOPE I'M NOT IMPOSING...
NO, NOT AT ALL! YOU DON'T KNOW HOW MUCH HELP THIS IS!
SHAKE!
SHAKE!
I'M GLAD.
HIBIYA-SAN'S SMILE...
IT'S SO HEART-WARMING...
AND GOOD LUCK WITH YOUR STUDIES!
UH, HEH HEH.
THANKS!
CHI.

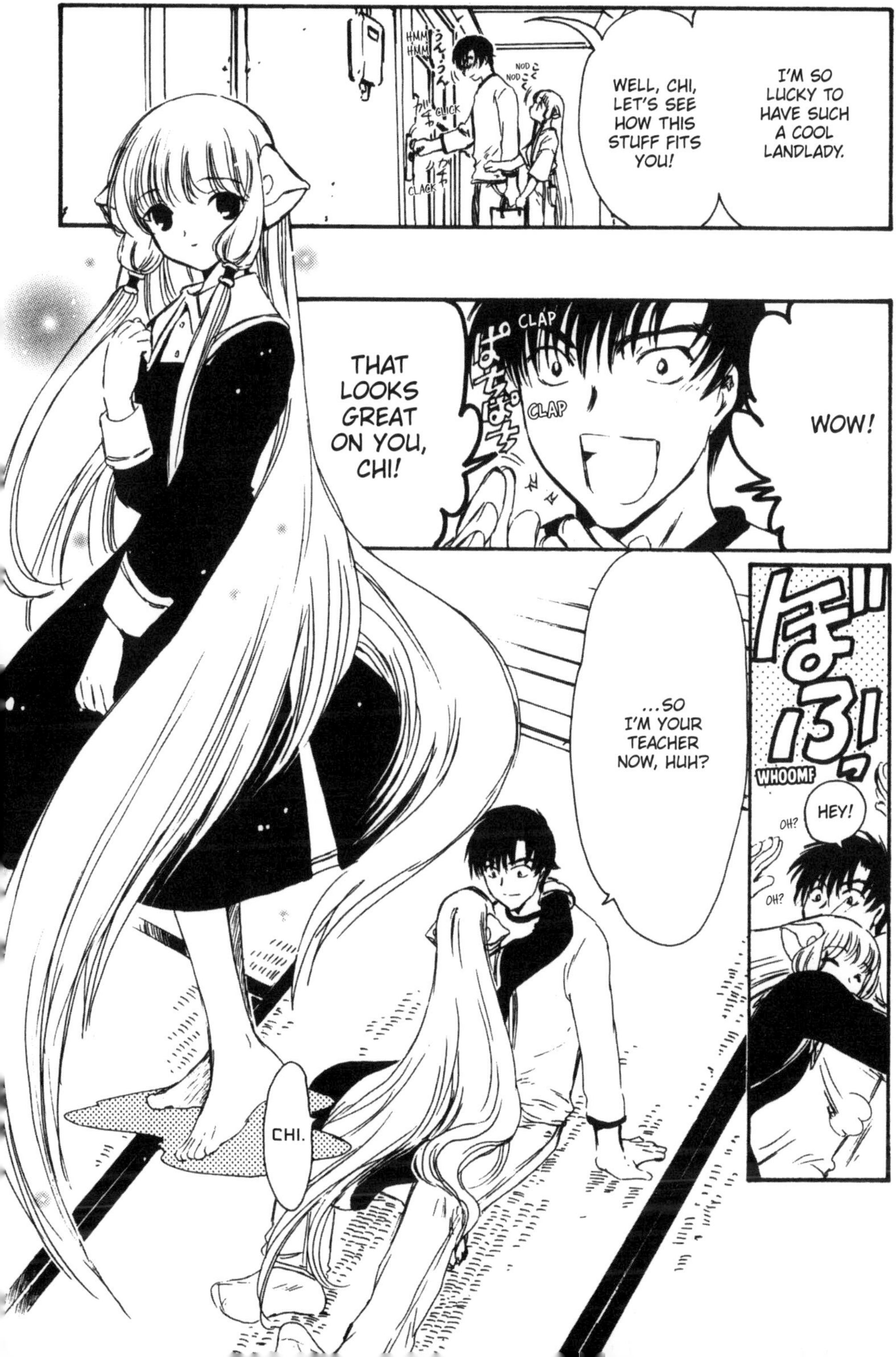
I'M SO LUCKY TO HAVE SUCH A COOL LANDLADY.
WELL, CHI, LET'S SEE HOW THIS STUFF FITS YOU!
NOD NOD
HMM HMM
CLICK
CLACK
WOW!
CLAP
CLAP
THAT LOOKS GREAT ON YOU, CHI!
WHOOMF
HEY!
OH?
OH?
...SO I'M YOUR TEACHER NOW, HUH?
CHI.

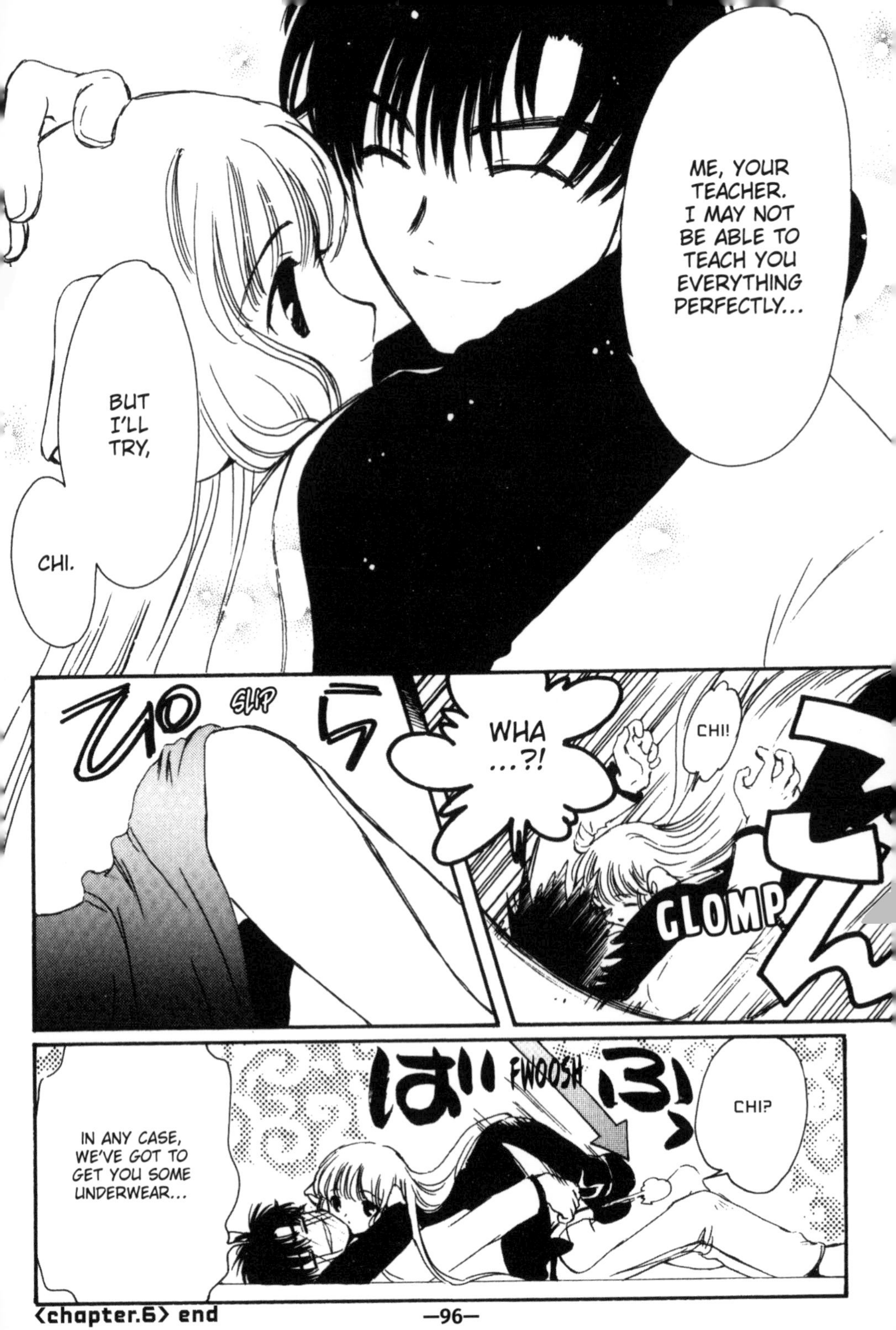
ME, YOUR TEACHER. I MAY NOT BE ABLE TO TEACH YOU EVERYTHING PERFECTLY...
BUT I'LL TRY,
CHI.
CHI!
GLOMP
WHA ...?!
SLIP
CHI?
FWOOSH
IN ANY CASE, WE'VE GOT TO GET YOU SOME UNDERWEAR...

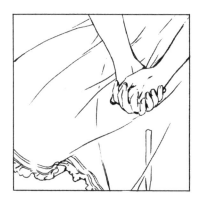

⟨chapter.7⟩

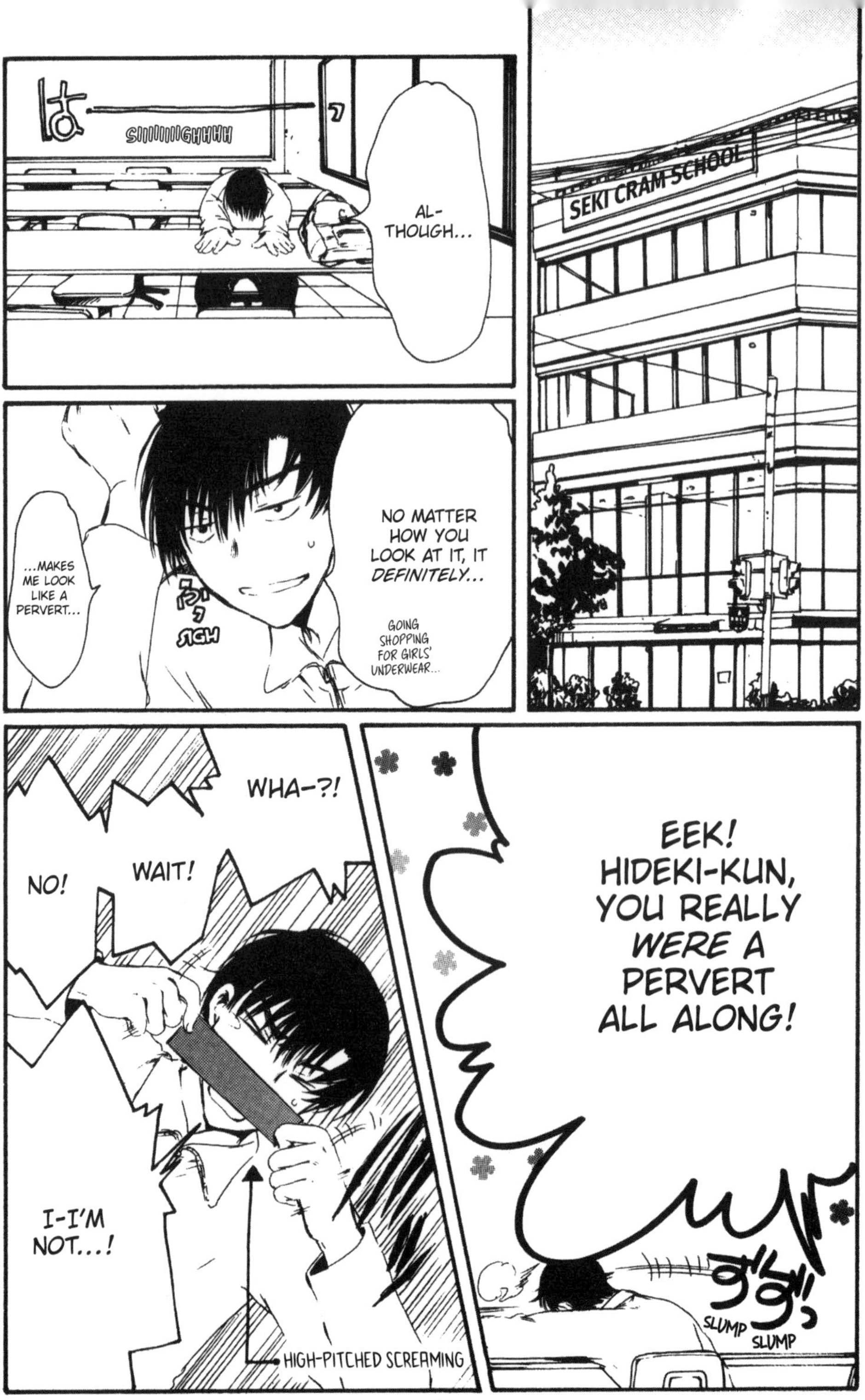
SEKI CRAM SCHOOL
は—ッ
SIIIIIIIGHHHH
AL-THOUGH...
NO MATTER HOW YOU LOOK AT IT, IT DEFINITELY...
GOING SHOPPING FOR GIRLS' UNDERWEAR...
SIGH
...MAKES ME LOOK LIKE A PERVERT...
EEK! HIDEKI-KUN, YOU REALLY WERE A PERVERT ALL ALONG!
SLUMP SLUMP
WHA-?!
WAIT!
NO!
I-I'M NOT...!
HIGH-PITCHED SCREAMING

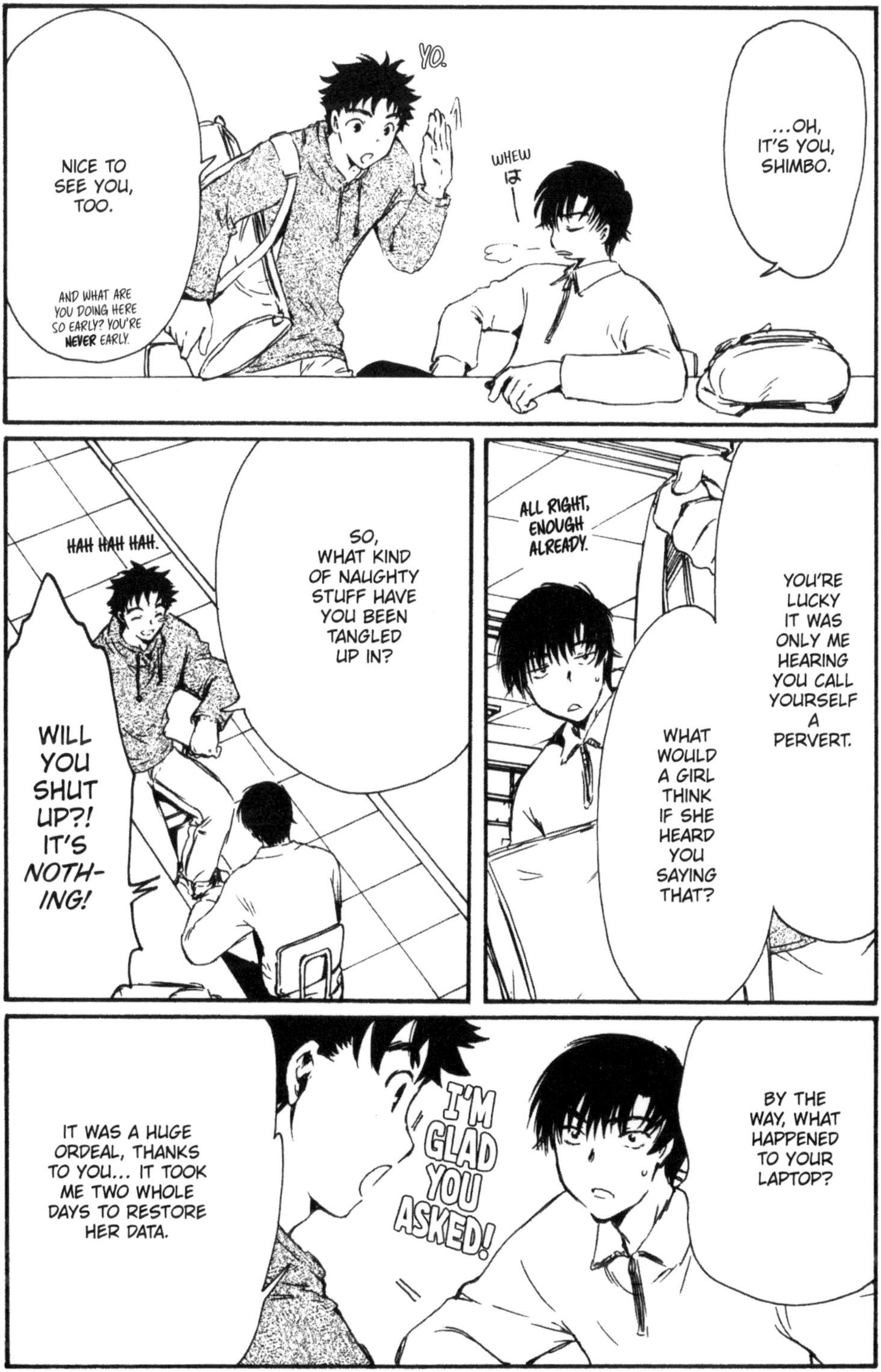
...OH, IT'S YOU, SHIMBO.
WHEW
は
YO.
NICE TO SEE YOU, TOO.
AND WHAT ARE YOU DOING HERE SO EARLY? YOU'RE NEVER EARLY.
YOU'RE LUCKY IT WAS ONLY ME HEARING YOU CALL YOURSELF A PERVERT.
WHAT WOULD A GIRL THINK IF SHE HEARD YOU SAYING THAT?
ALL RIGHT, ENOUGH ALREADY.
SO, WHAT KIND OF NAUGHTY STUFF HAVE YOU BEEN TANGLED UP IN?
HAH HAH HAH.
WILL YOU SHUT UP?! IT'S NOTHING!
BY THE WAY, WHAT HAPPENED TO YOUR LAPTOP?
I'M GLAD YOU ASKED!
IT WAS A HUGE ORDEAL, THANKS TO YOU... IT TOOK ME TWO WHOLE DAYS TO RESTORE HER DATA.

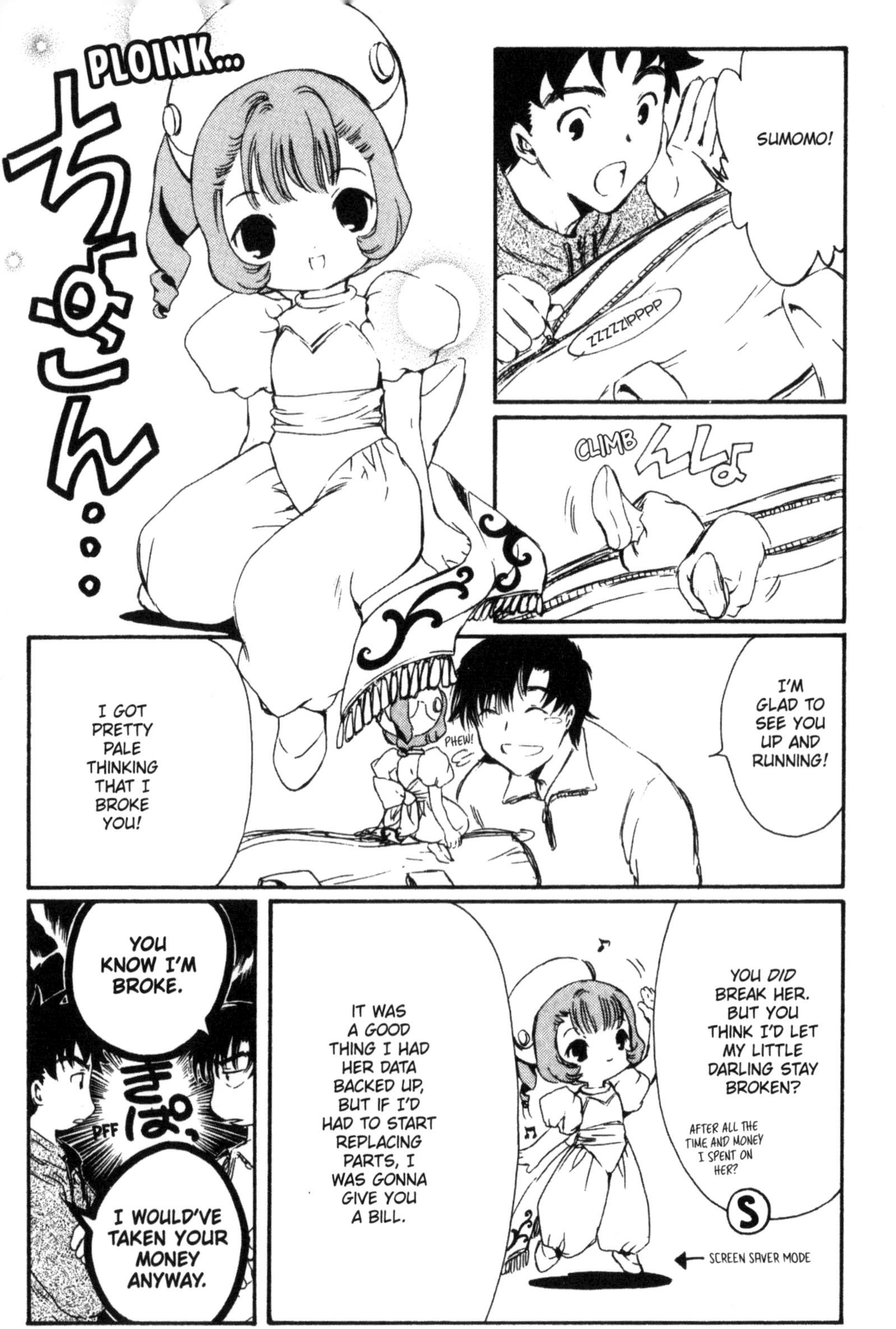

SUMOMO!
ZZZZIPPPP
CLIMB
PLOINK...
ちょこん…
I'M GLAD TO SEE YOU UP AND RUNNING!
PHEW!
I GOT PRETTY PALE THINKING THAT I BROKE YOU!
YOU *DID* BREAK HER. BUT YOU THINK I'D LET MY LITTLE DARLING STAY BROKEN?
AFTER ALL THE TIME AND MONEY I SPENT ON HER?
S
SCREEN SAVER MODE
IT WAS A GOOD THING I HAD HER DATA BACKED UP, BUT IF I'D HAD TO START REPLACING PARTS, I WAS GONNA GIVE YOU A BILL.
YOU KNOW I'M BROKE.
PFF
I WOULD'VE TAKEN YOUR MONEY ANYWAY.

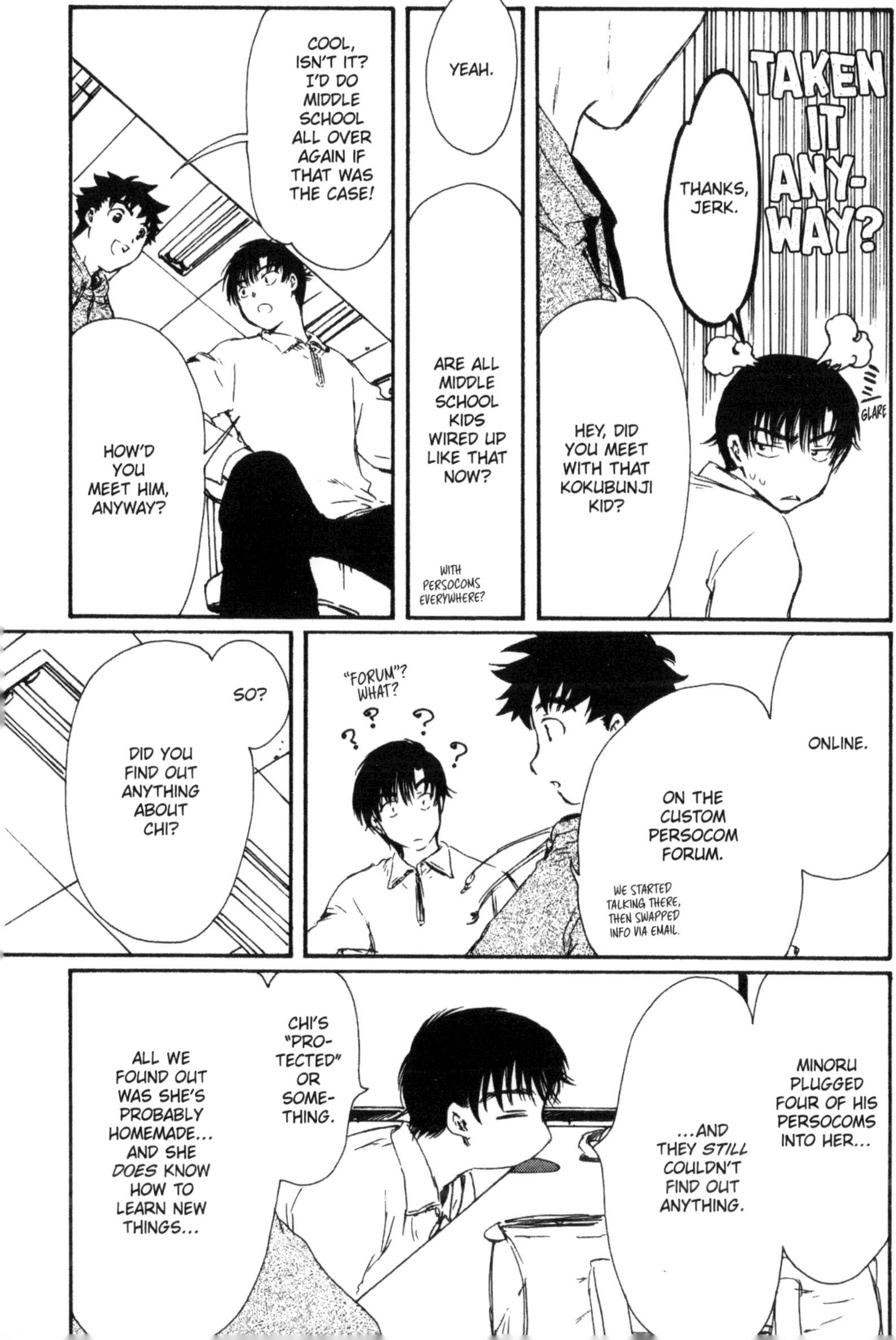

TAKEN IT ANY-WAY?
THANKS, JERK.
GLARE
HEY, DID YOU MEET WITH THAT KOKUBUNJI KID?
YEAH.
ARE ALL MIDDLE SCHOOL KIDS WIRED UP LIKE THAT NOW?
WITH PERSOCOMS EVERYWHERE?
COOL, ISN'T IT? I'D DO MIDDLE SCHOOL ALL OVER AGAIN IF THAT WAS THE CASE!
HOW'D YOU MEET HIM, ANYWAY?
ONLINE.
ON THE CUSTOM PERSOCOM FORUM.
WE STARTED TALKING THERE, THEN SWAPPED INFO VIA EMAIL.
"FORUM"? WHAT?
SO?
DID YOU FIND OUT ANYTHING ABOUT CHI?
MINORU PLUGGED FOUR OF HIS PERSOCOMS INTO HER...
...AND THEY *STILL* COULDN'T FIND OUT ANYTHING.
CHI'S "PRO-TECTED" OR SOME-THING.
ALL WE FOUND OUT WAS SHE'S PROBABLY HOMEMADE... AND SHE *DOES* KNOW HOW TO LEARN NEW THINGS...

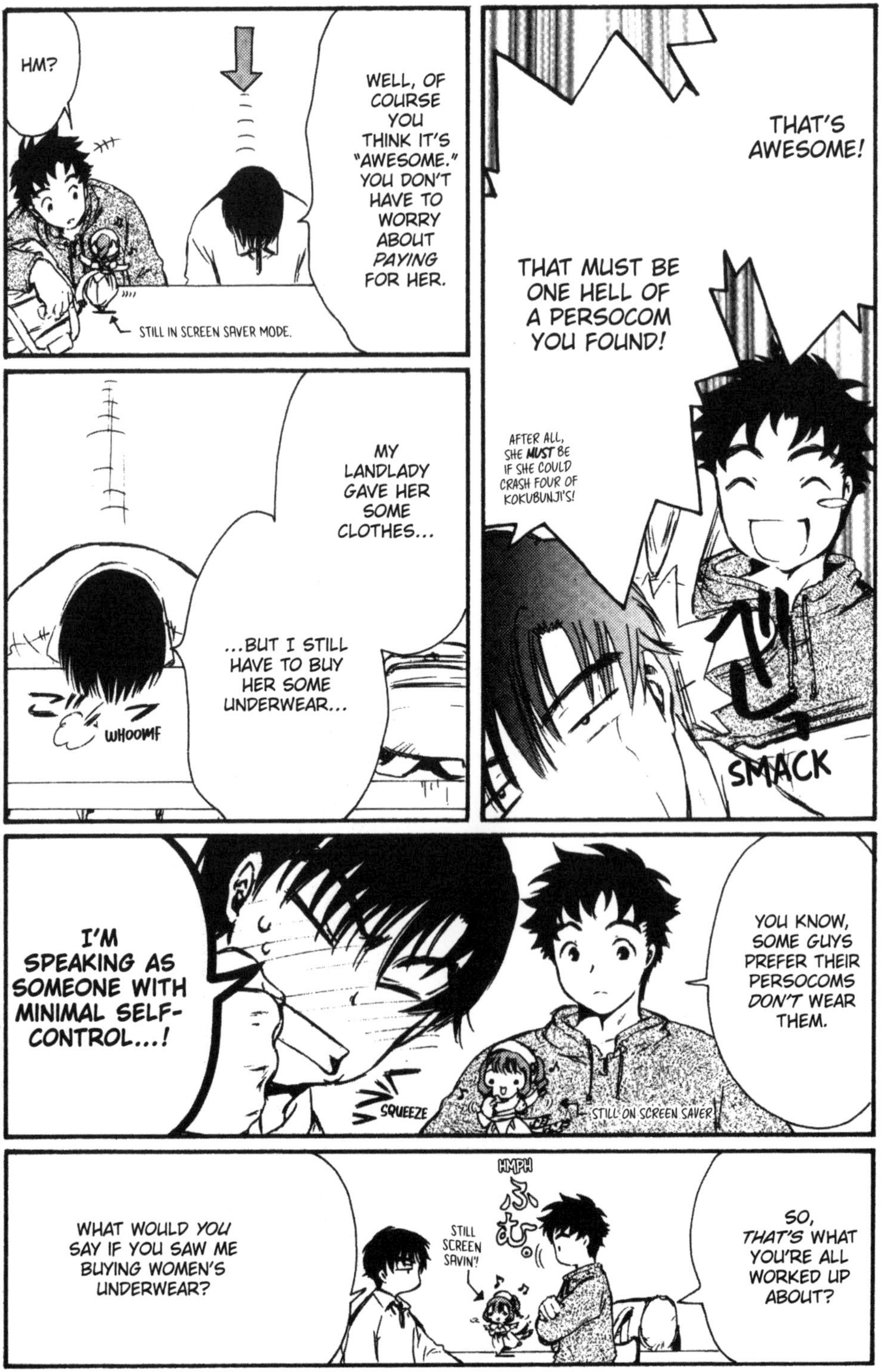
THAT'S AWESOME!
THAT MUST BE ONE HELL OF A PERSOCOM YOU FOUND!
AFTER ALL, SHE MUST BE IF SHE COULD CRASH FOUR OF KOKUBUNJI'S!
SMACK
WELL, OF COURSE YOU THINK IT'S "AWESOME." YOU DON'T HAVE TO WORRY ABOUT PAYING FOR HER.
HM?
STILL IN SCREEN SAVER MODE.
MY LANDLADY GAVE HER SOME CLOTHES...
...BUT I STILL HAVE TO BUY HER SOME UNDERWEAR...
WHOOMF
YOU KNOW, SOME GUYS PREFER THEIR PERSOCOMS DON'T WEAR THEM.
STILL ON SCREEN SAVER
SQUEEZE
I'M SPEAKING AS SOMEONE WITH MINIMAL SELF-CONTROL...!
SO, THAT'S WHAT YOU'RE ALL WORKED UP ABOUT?
HMPH
STILL SCREEN SAVIN'!
WHAT WOULD YOU SAY IF YOU SAW ME BUYING WOMEN'S UNDERWEAR?

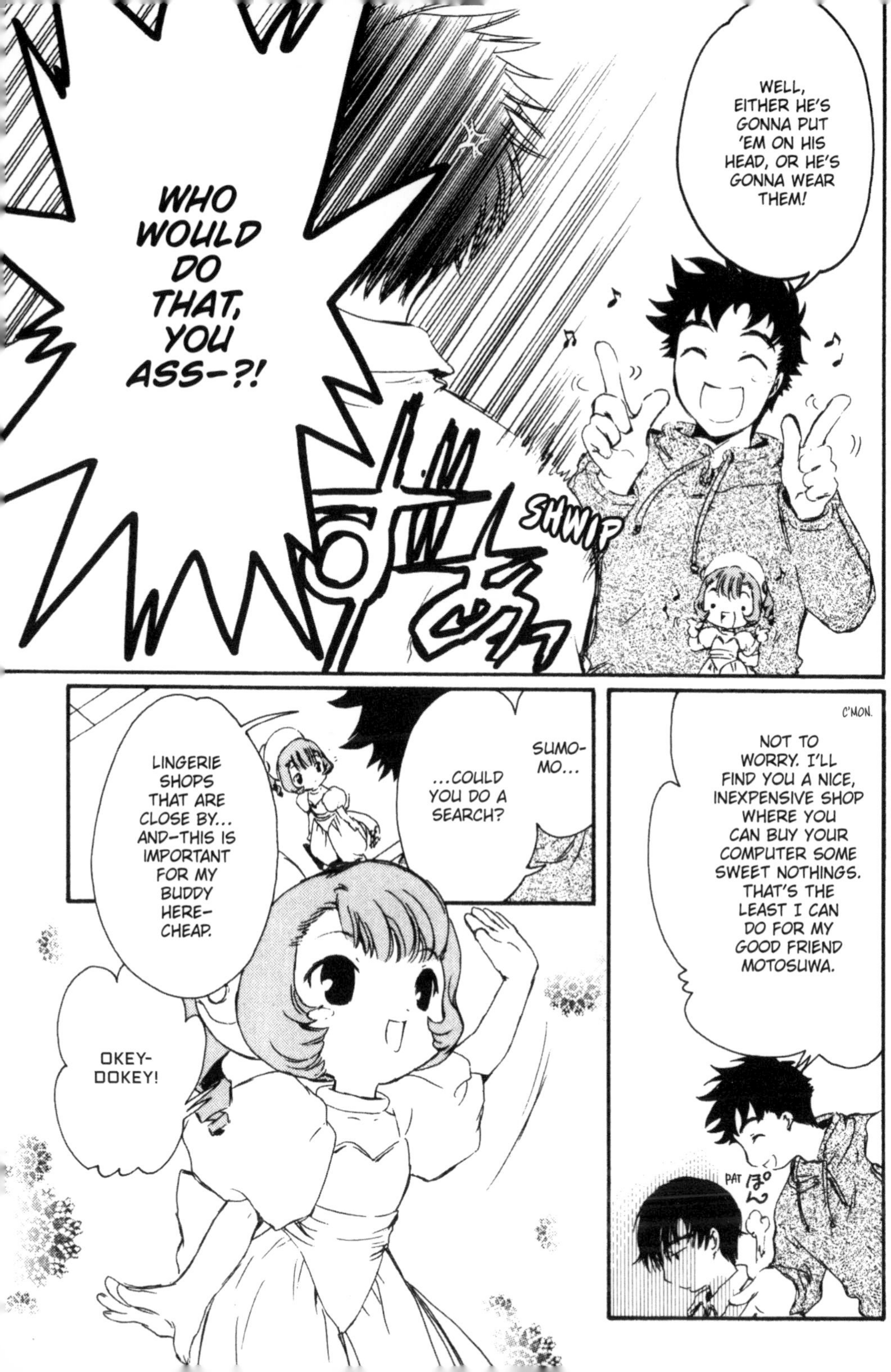
WELL, EITHER HE'S GONNA PUT 'EM ON HIS HEAD, OR HE'S GONNA WEAR THEM!
SHWIP
WHO WOULD DO THAT, YOU ASS-?!
C'MON.
NOT TO WORRY. I'LL FIND YOU A NICE, INEXPENSIVE SHOP WHERE YOU CAN BUY YOUR COMPUTER SOME SWEET NOTHINGS. THAT'S THE LEAST I CAN DO FOR MY GOOD FRIEND MOTOSUWA.
PAT
SUMO-MO...
...COULD YOU DO A SEARCH?
LINGERIE SHOPS THAT ARE CLOSE BY... AND–THIS IS IMPORTANT FOR MY BUDDY HERE–CHEAP.
OKEY-DOKEY!

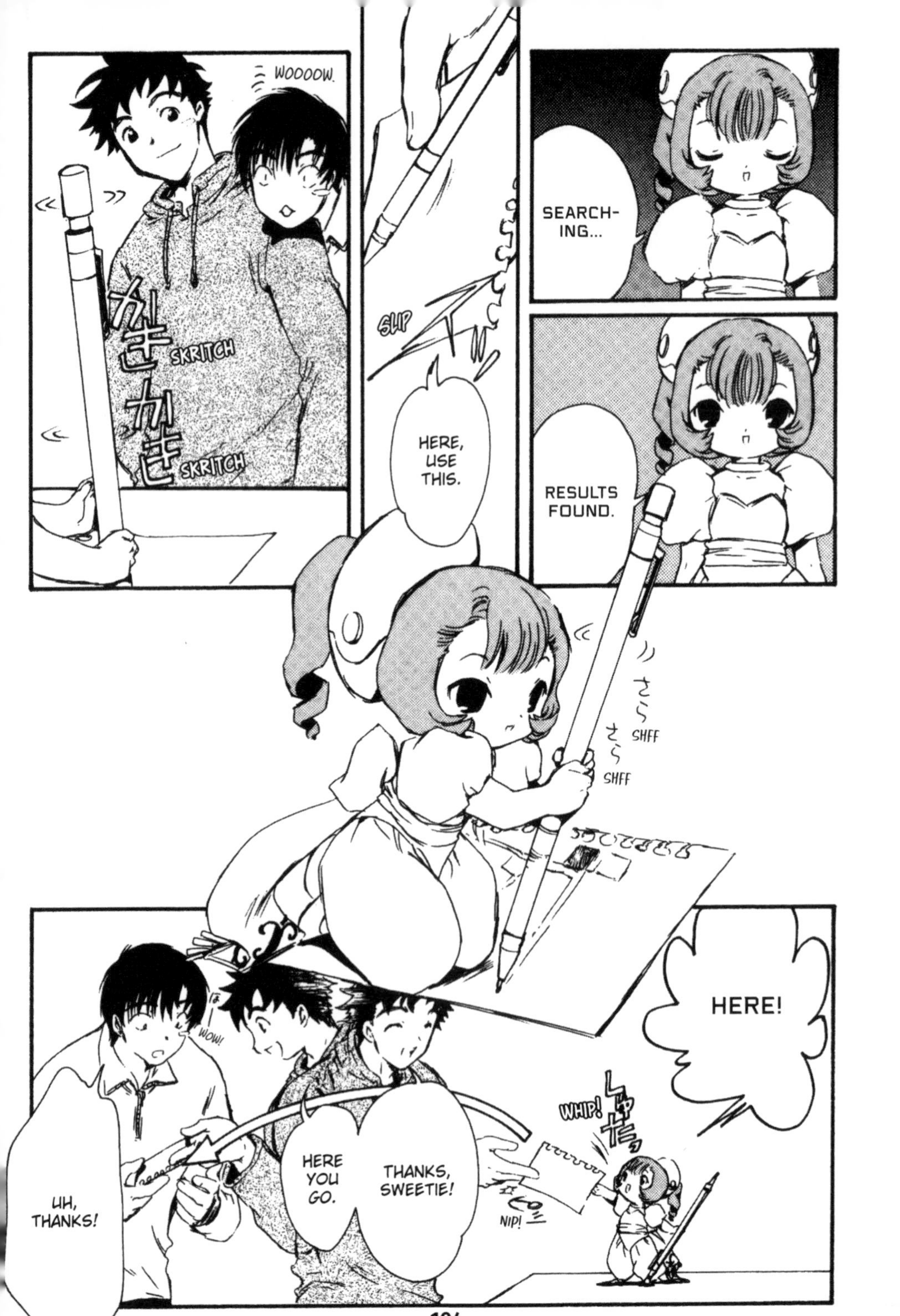
SEARCH-ING...
RESULTS FOUND.
SLIP
HERE, USE THIS.
WOOOOW.
SKRITCH
SKRITCH
SHFF
SHFF
HERE!
WHIP!
NIP!
THANKS, SWEETIE!
HERE YOU GO.
WOW!
UH, THANKS!

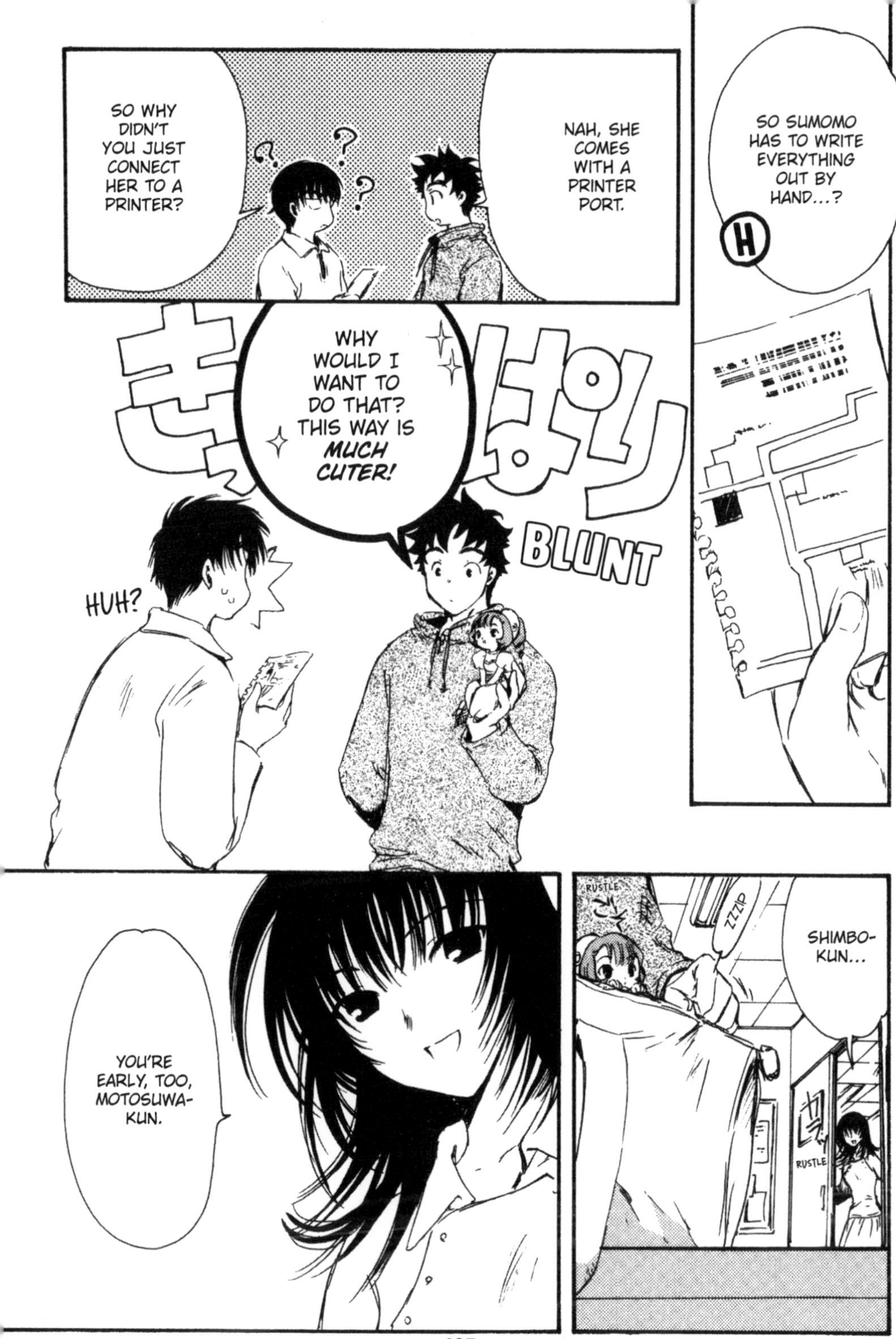
SO SUMOMO HAS TO WRITE EVERYTHING OUT BY HAND...?
H
NAH, SHE COMES WITH A PRINTER PORT.
SO WHY DIDN'T YOU JUST CONNECT HER TO A PRINTER?
WHY WOULD I WANT TO DO THAT? THIS WAY IS MUCH CUTER!
BLUNT
HUH?
RUSTLE
ZZZIP
SHIMBO-KUN...
RUSTLE
YOU'RE EARLY, TOO, MOTOSUWA-KUN.

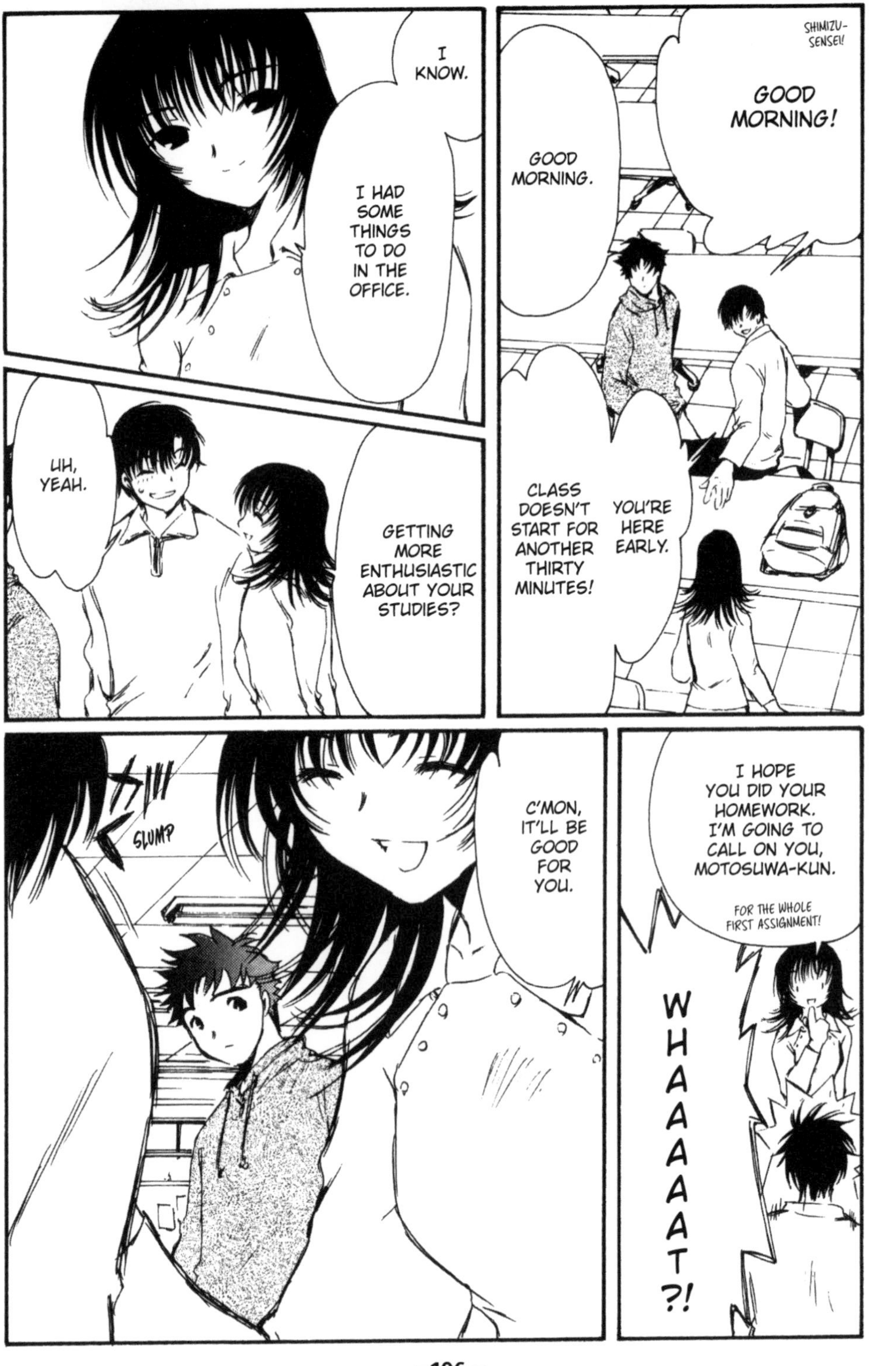
SHIMIZU-SENSEI!
GOOD MORNING!
GOOD MORNING.
YOU'RE HERE EARLY.
CLASS DOESN'T START FOR ANOTHER THIRTY MINUTES!
I KNOW.
I HAD SOME THINGS TO DO IN THE OFFICE.
GETTING MORE ENTHUSIASTIC ABOUT YOUR STUDIES?
UH, YEAH.
I HOPE YOU DID YOUR HOMEWORK. I'M GOING TO CALL ON YOU, MOTOSUWA-KUN.
FOR THE WHOLE FIRST ASSIGNMENT!
WHAAAAAAT?!
C'MON, IT'LL BE GOOD FOR YOU.
SLUMP

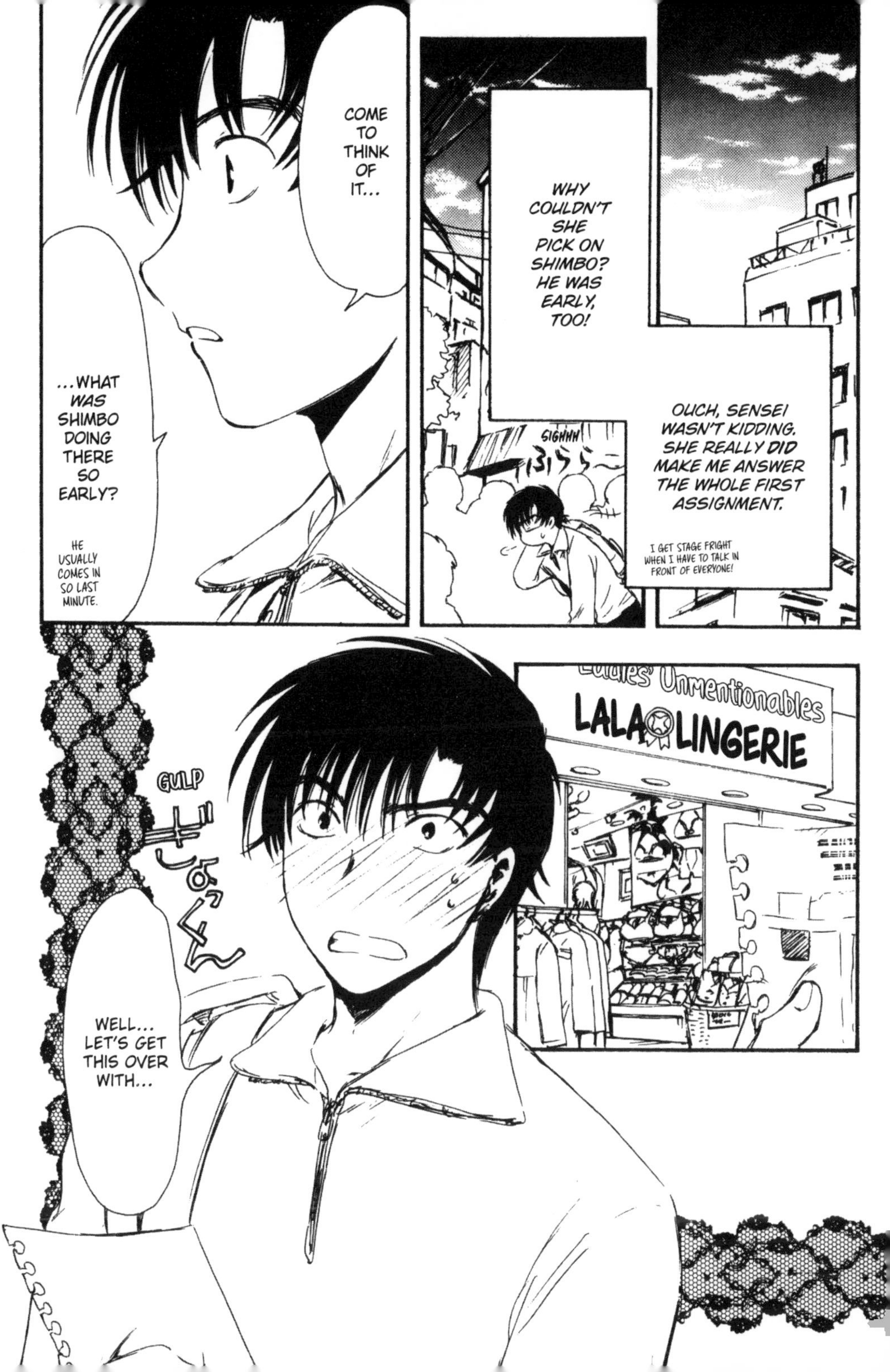
OUCH, SENSEI WASN'T KIDDING. SHE REALLY DID MAKE ME ANSWER THE WHOLE FIRST ASSIGNMENT.
I GET STAGE FRIGHT WHEN I HAVE TO TALK IN FRONT OF EVERYONE!
WHY COULDN'T SHE PICK ON SHIMBO? HE WAS EARLY, TOO!
SIGHHH
COME TO THINK OF IT...
...WHAT WAS SHIMBO DOING THERE SO EARLY?
HE USUALLY COMES IN SO LAST MINUTE.
Unmentionables
LALA LINGERIE
GULP
WELL... LET'S GET THIS OVER WITH...

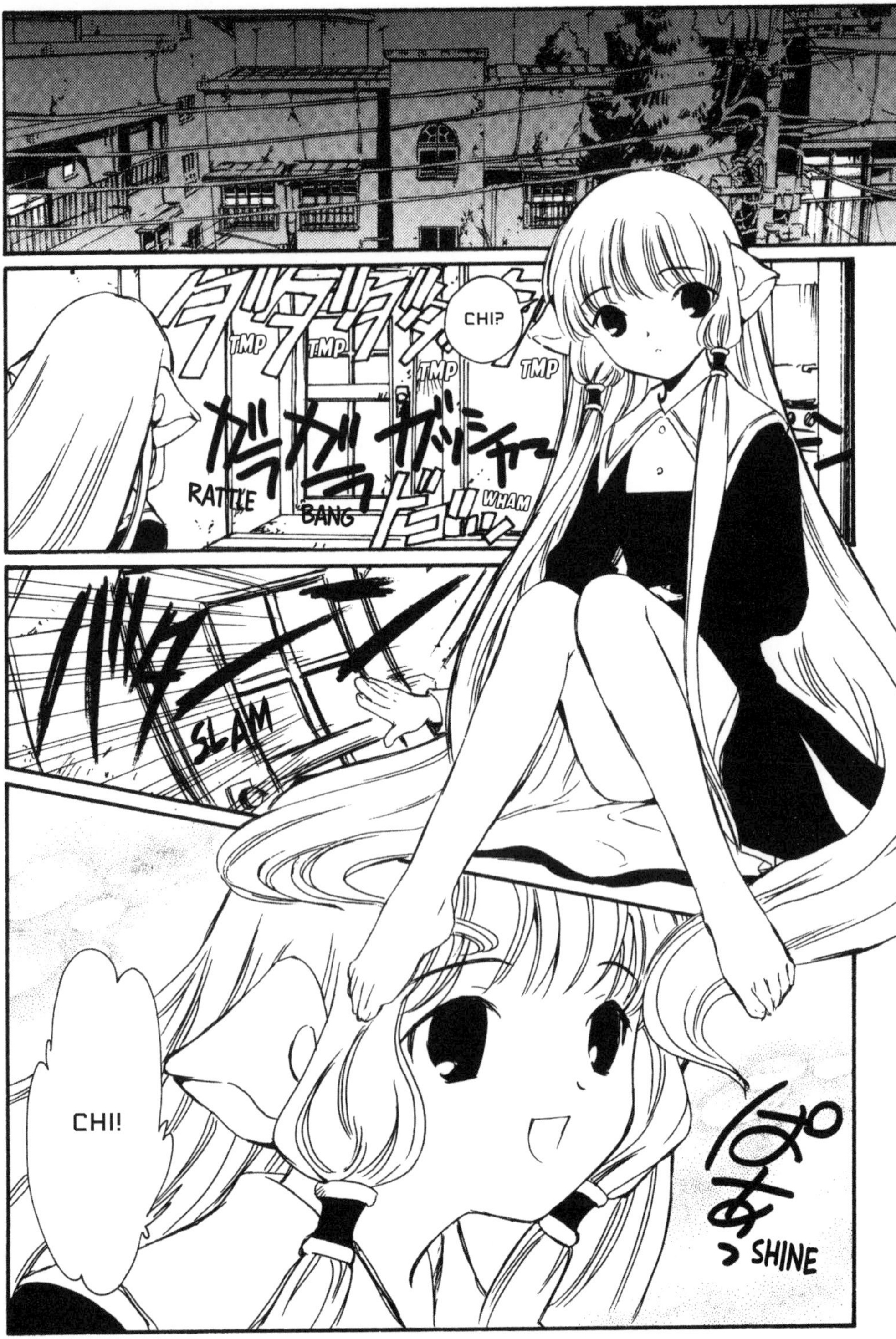
CHI?
TMP TMP TMP TMP
WHAM
BANG
RATTLE
SLAM
SHINE
CHI!

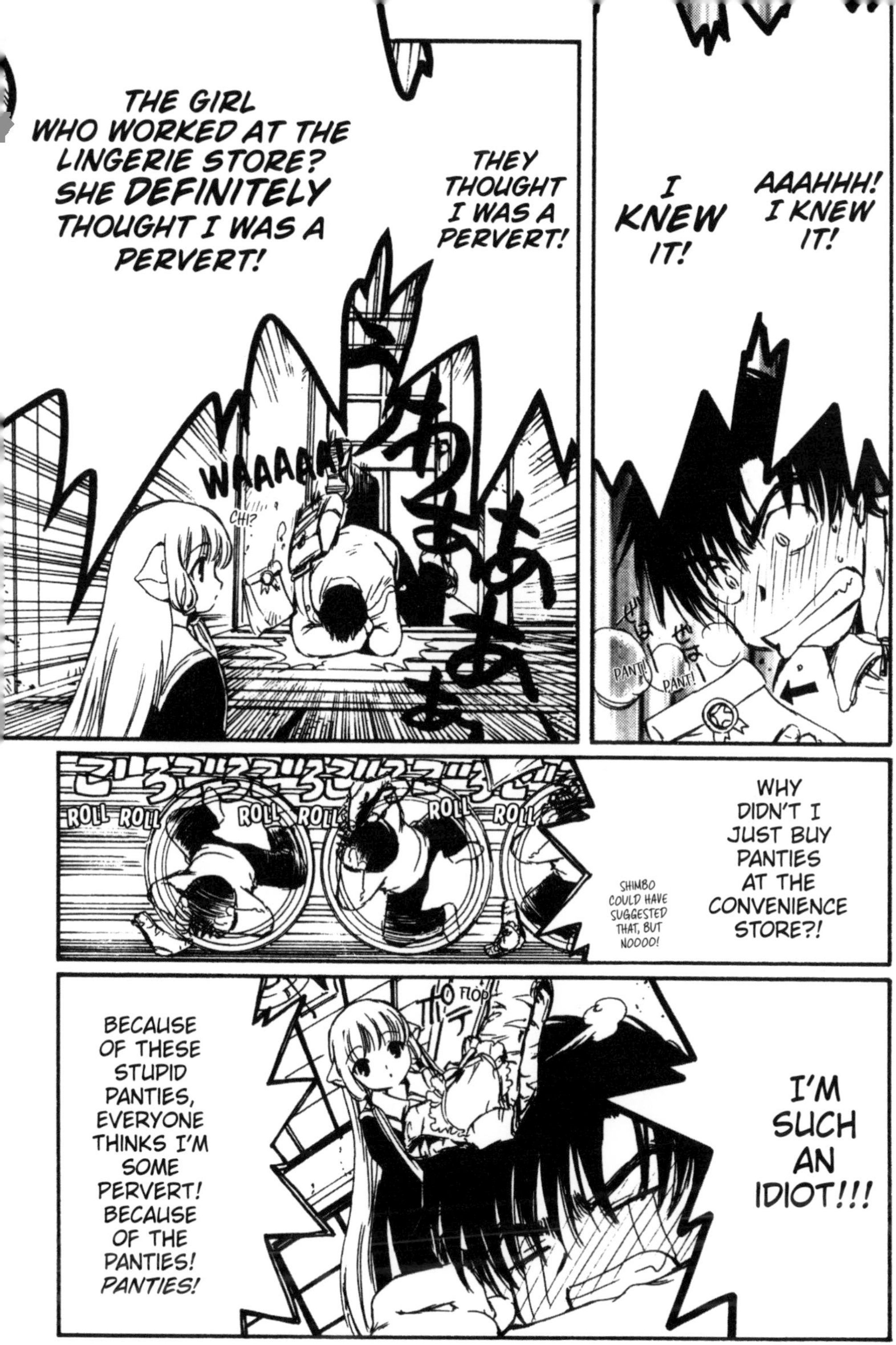
AAAHHH! I KNEW IT!
I KNEW IT!
PANT! PANT!
THEY THOUGHT I WAS A PERVERT!
THE GIRL WHO WORKED AT THE LINGERIE STORE? SHE DEFINITELY THOUGHT I WAS A PERVERT!
WAAAAA!
CHI?
WHY DIDN'T I JUST BUY PANTIES AT THE CONVENIENCE STORE?!
SHIMBO COULD HAVE SUGGESTED THAT, BUT NOOOO!
ROLL ROLL ROLL ROLL ROLL ROLL
I'M SUCH AN IDIOT!!!
FLOP
BECAUSE OF THESE STUPID PANTIES, EVERYONE THINKS I'M SOME PERVERT! BECAUSE OF THE PANTIES! PANTIES!

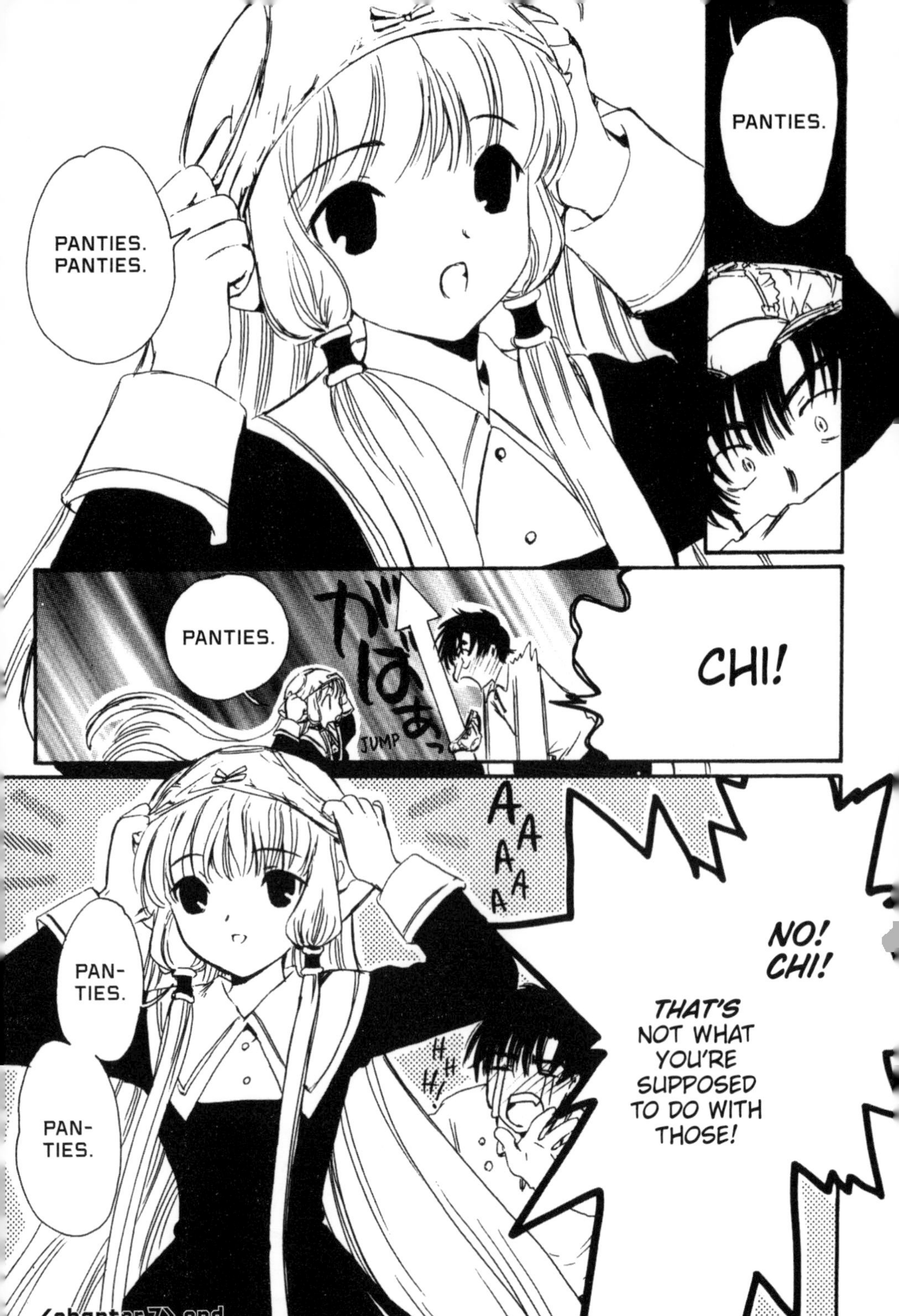
PANTIES.
PANTIES.
PANTIES.
CHI!
PANTIES.
JUMP
AAAAAA
NO! CHI!
THAT'S NOT WHAT YOU'RE SUPPOSED TO DO WITH THOSE!
HHH!
PAN-TIES.
PAN-TIES.

<chapter.7> end

⟨chapter.8⟩

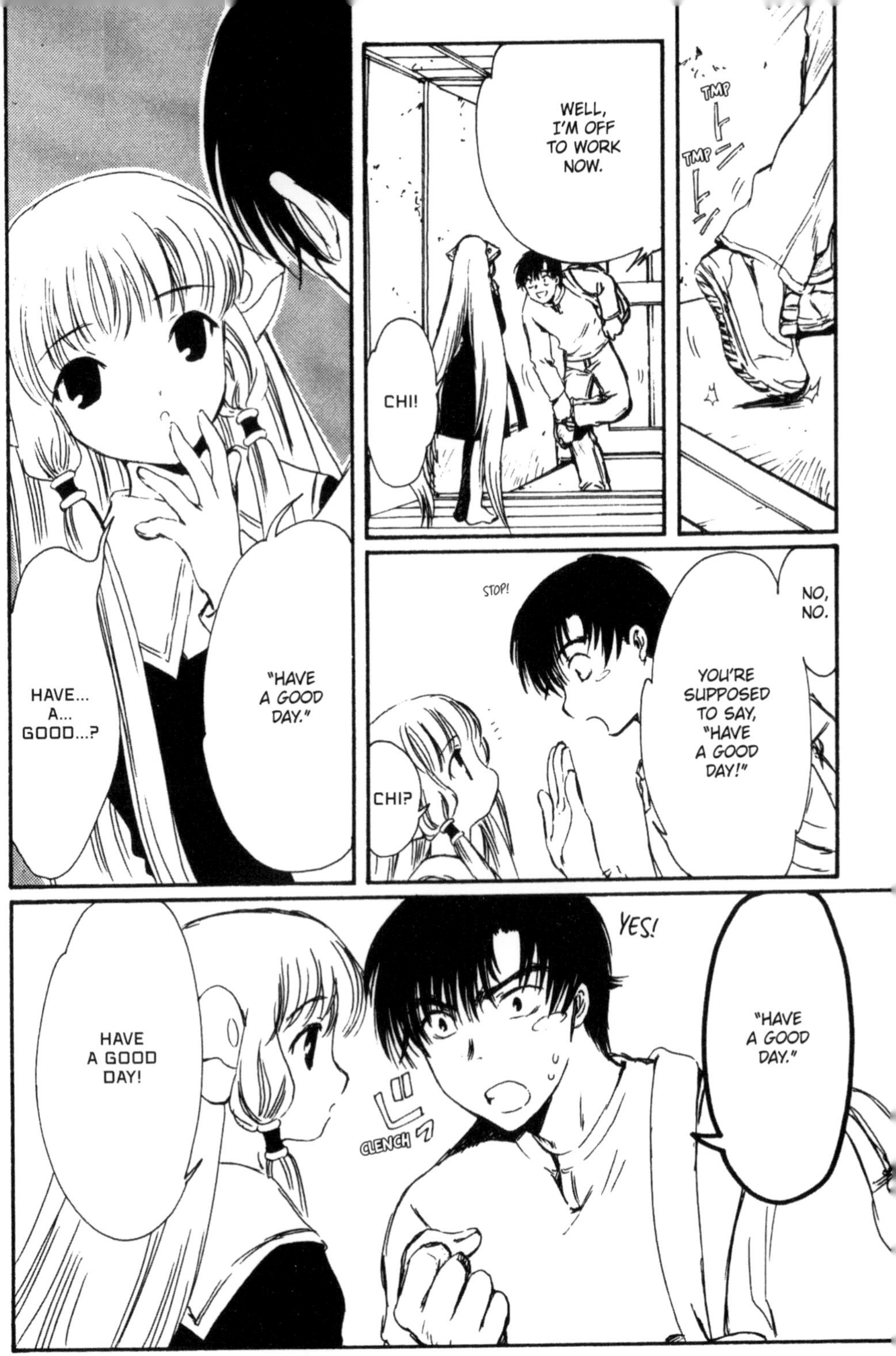
TMP
TMP
WELL, I'M OFF TO WORK NOW.
CHI!
NO, NO.
YOU'RE SUPPOSED TO SAY, "HAVE A GOOD DAY!"
STOP!
CHI?
"HAVE A GOOD DAY."
HAVE... A... GOOD...?
YES!
"HAVE A GOOD DAY."
CLENCH
HAVE A GOOD DAY!

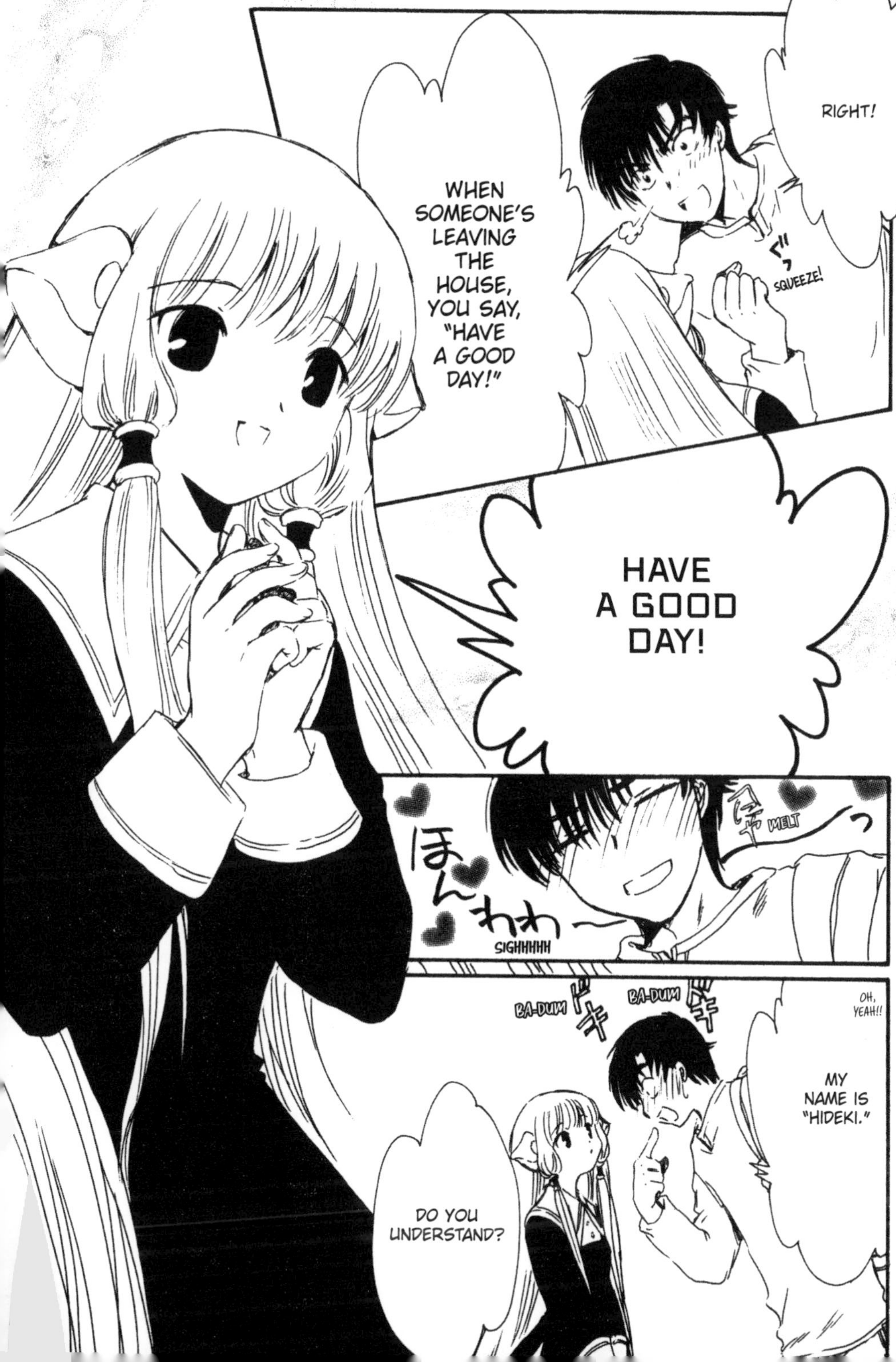
RIGHT!
WHEN SOMEONE'S LEAVING THE HOUSE, YOU SAY, "HAVE A GOOD DAY!"
SQUEEZE!
HAVE A GOOD DAY!
MELT
ほんわわ~
SIGHHHHH
OH, YEAH!!
BA-DUM
BA-DUM
MY NAME IS "HIDEKI."
DO YOU UNDERSTAND?

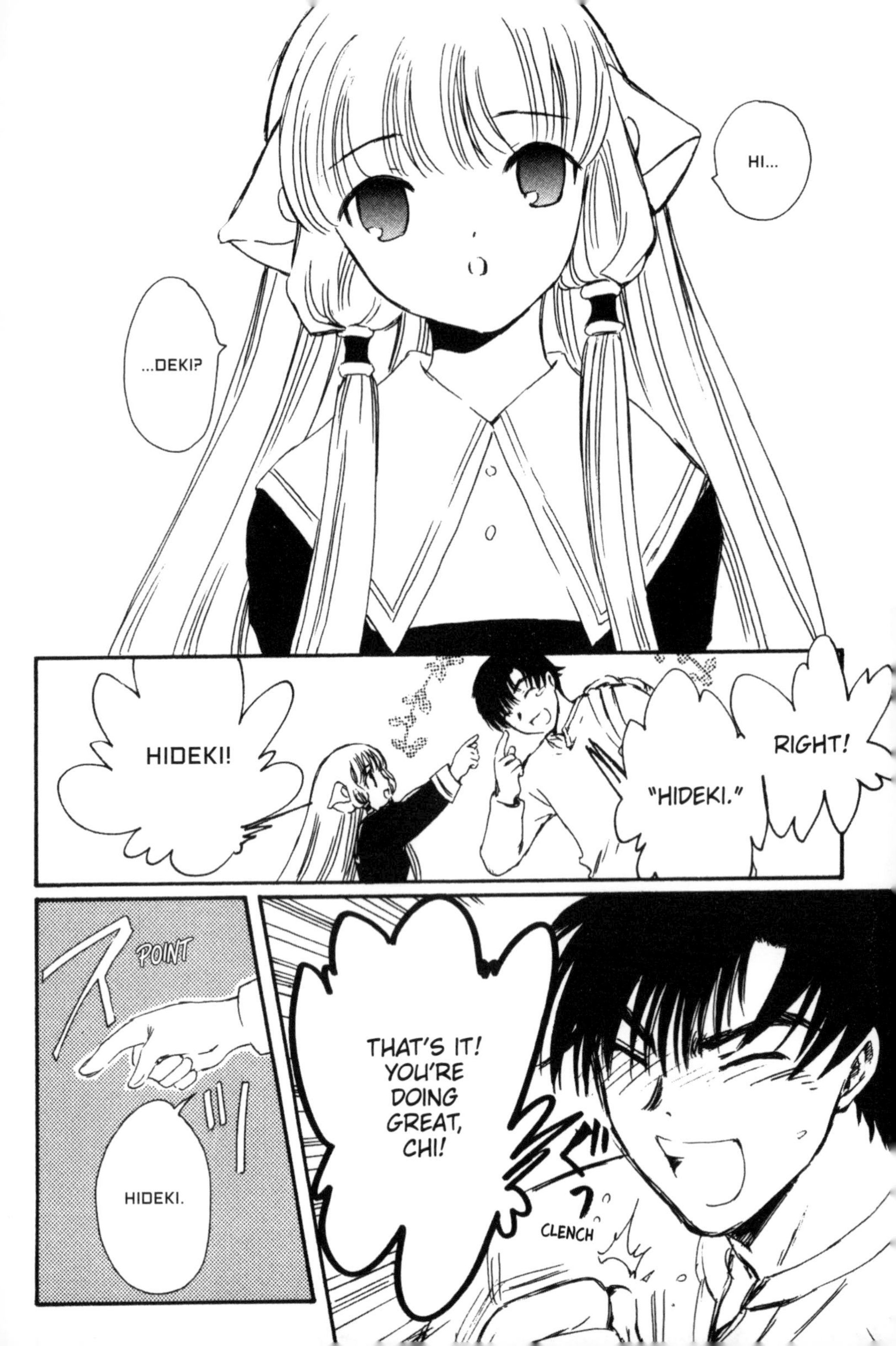
HI...
...DEKI?
RIGHT!
"HIDEKI."
HIDEKI!
THAT'S IT! YOU'RE DOING GREAT, CHI!
CLENCH
POINT
HIDEKI.

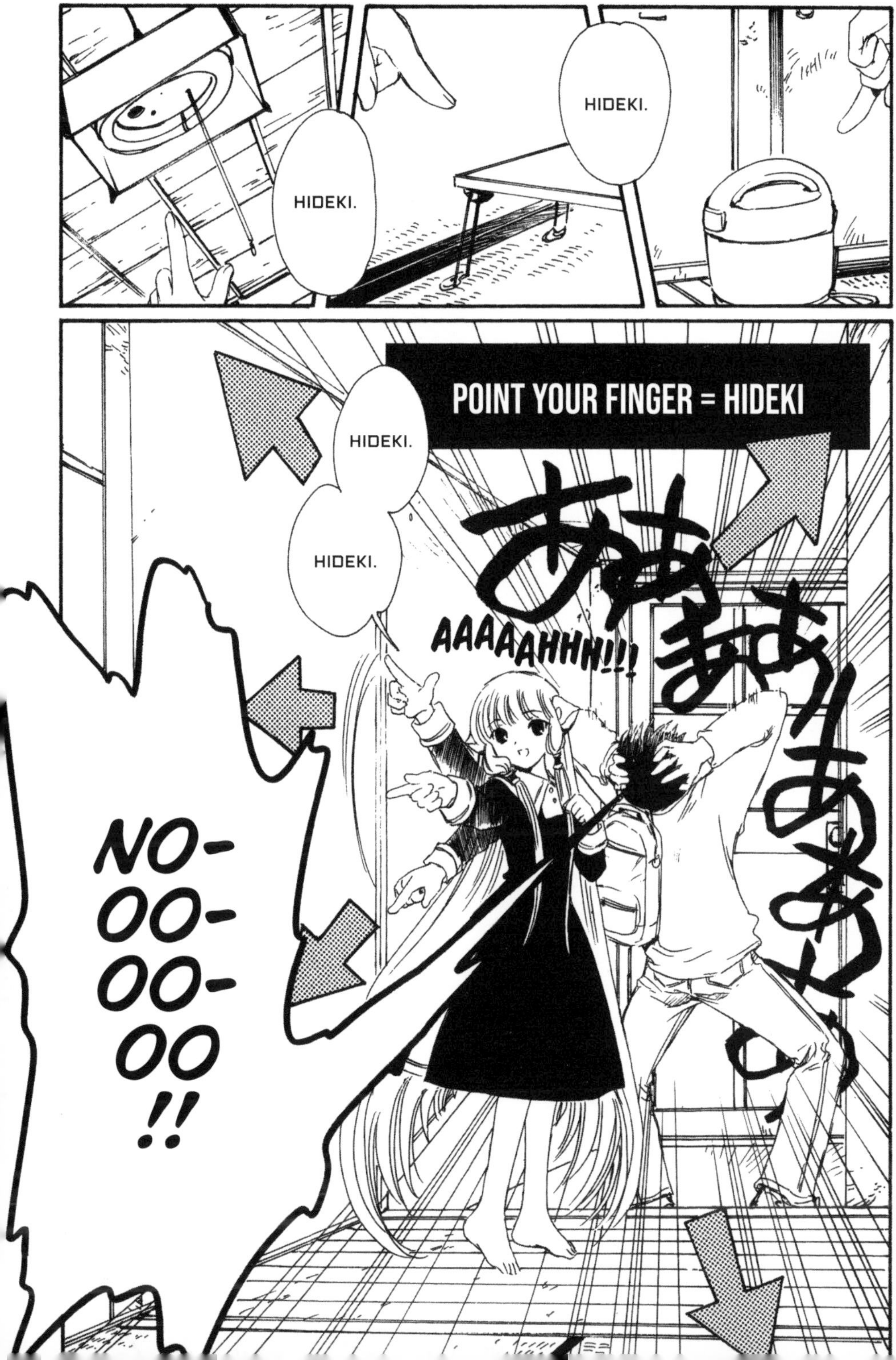

HIDEKI.
HIDEKI.
POINT YOUR FINGER = HIDEKI
HIDEKI.
HIDEKI.
AAAAAHHH!!!
NO-OO-OO-OO!!

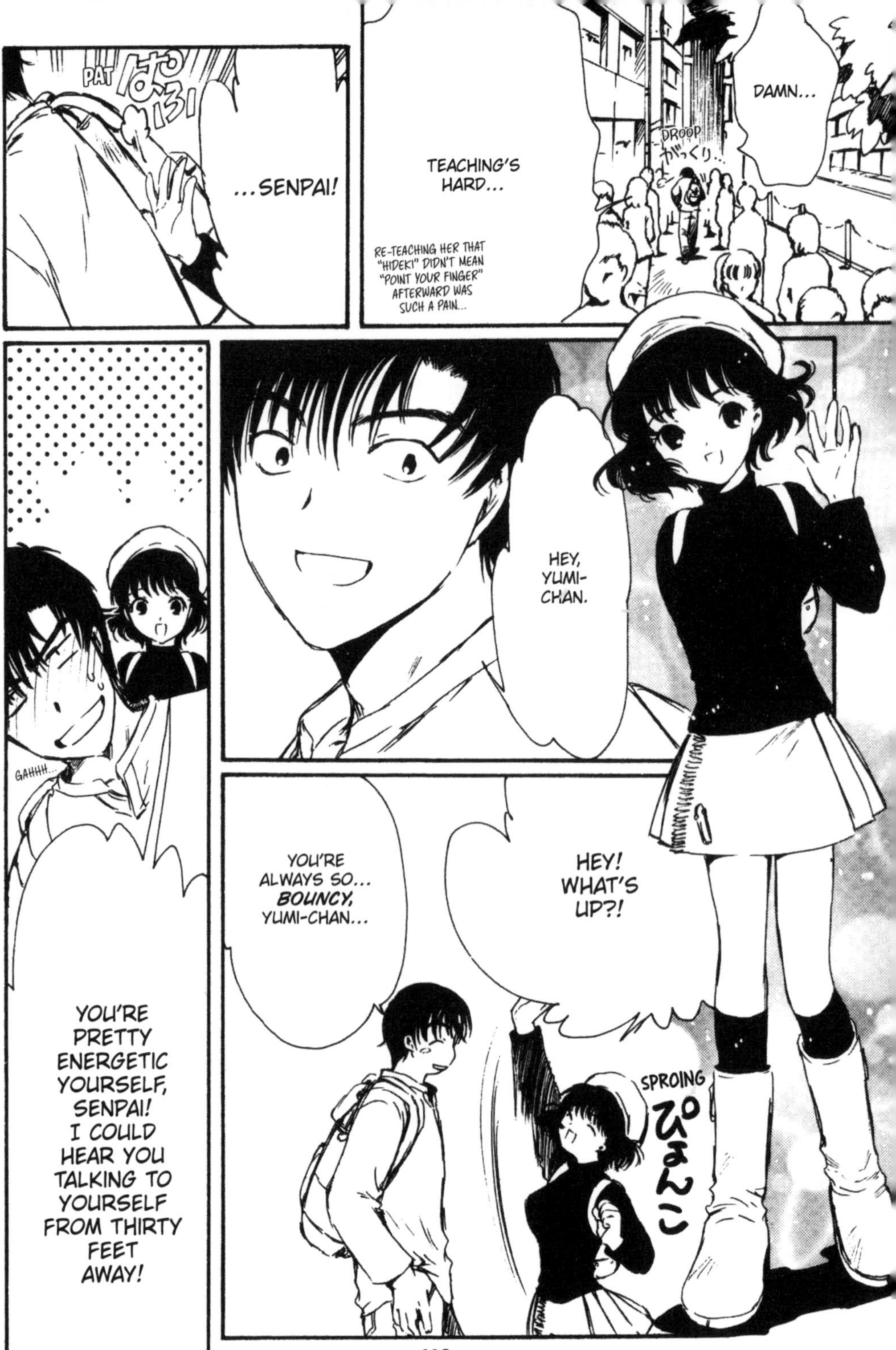
DAMN...
DROOP
がっくり...
TEACHING'S HARD...
RE-TEACHING HER THAT "HIDEKI" DIDN'T MEAN "POINT YOUR FINGER" AFTERWARD WAS SUCH A PAIN...
PAT
ぽふ
...SENPAI!
HEY, YUMI-CHAN.
HEY! WHAT'S UP?!
YOU'RE ALWAYS SO... *BOUNCY*, YUMI-CHAN...
SPROING
ぴょんこ
GAHHH...
YOU'RE PRETTY ENERGETIC YOURSELF, SENPAI! I COULD HEAR YOU TALKING TO YOURSELF FROM THIRTY FEET AWAY!

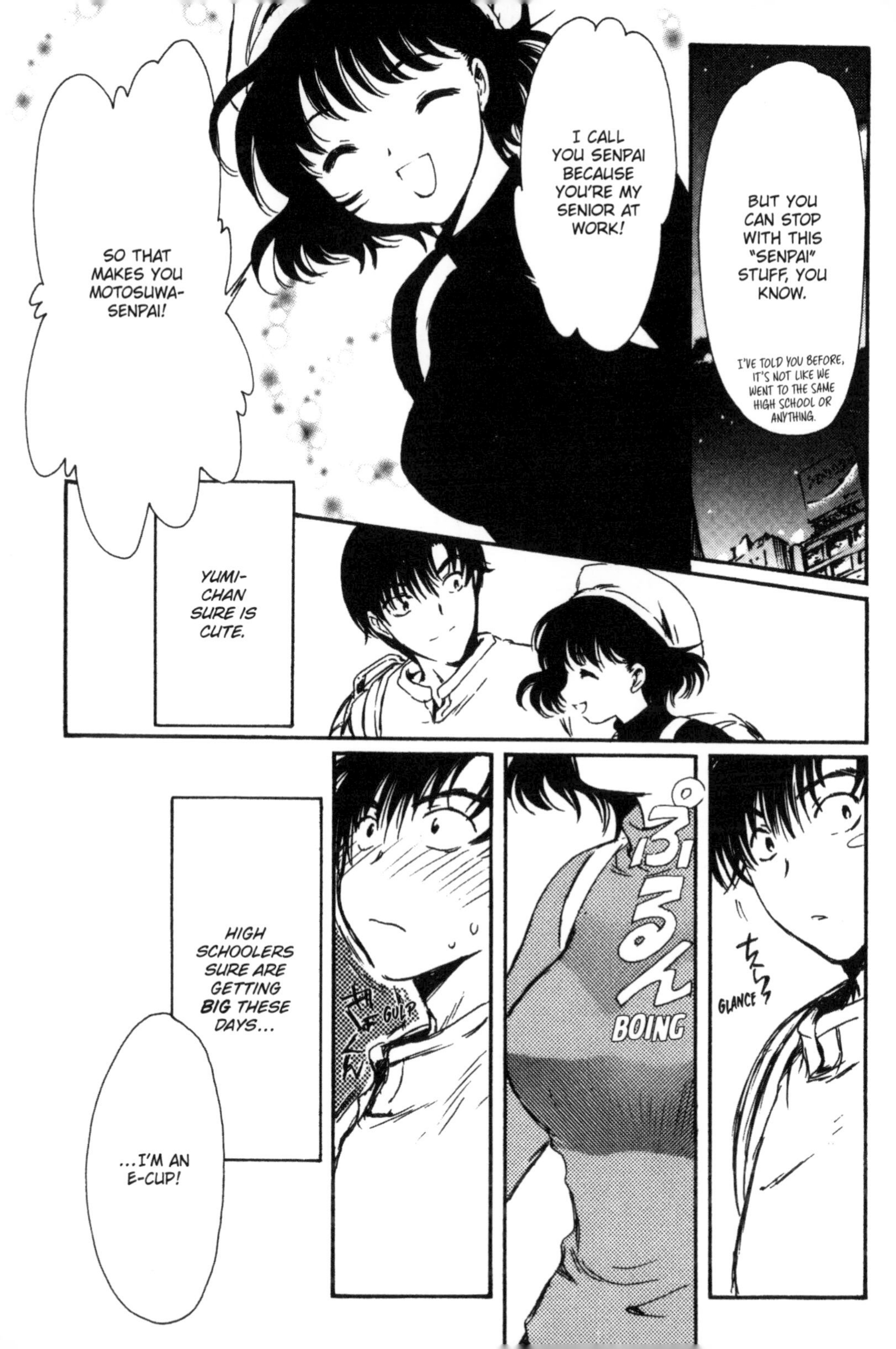
BUT YOU CAN STOP WITH THIS "SENPAI" STUFF, YOU KNOW.
I'VE TOLD YOU BEFORE, IT'S NOT LIKE WE WENT TO THE SAME HIGH SCHOOL OR ANYTHING.
I CALL YOU SENPAI BECAUSE YOU'RE MY SENIOR AT WORK!
SO THAT MAKES YOU MOTOSUWA-SENPAI!
YUMI-CHAN SURE IS CUTE.
GLANCE
ぷるん
BOING
GULP
HIGH SCHOOLERS SURE ARE GETTING BIG THESE DAYS...
...I'M AN E-CUP!

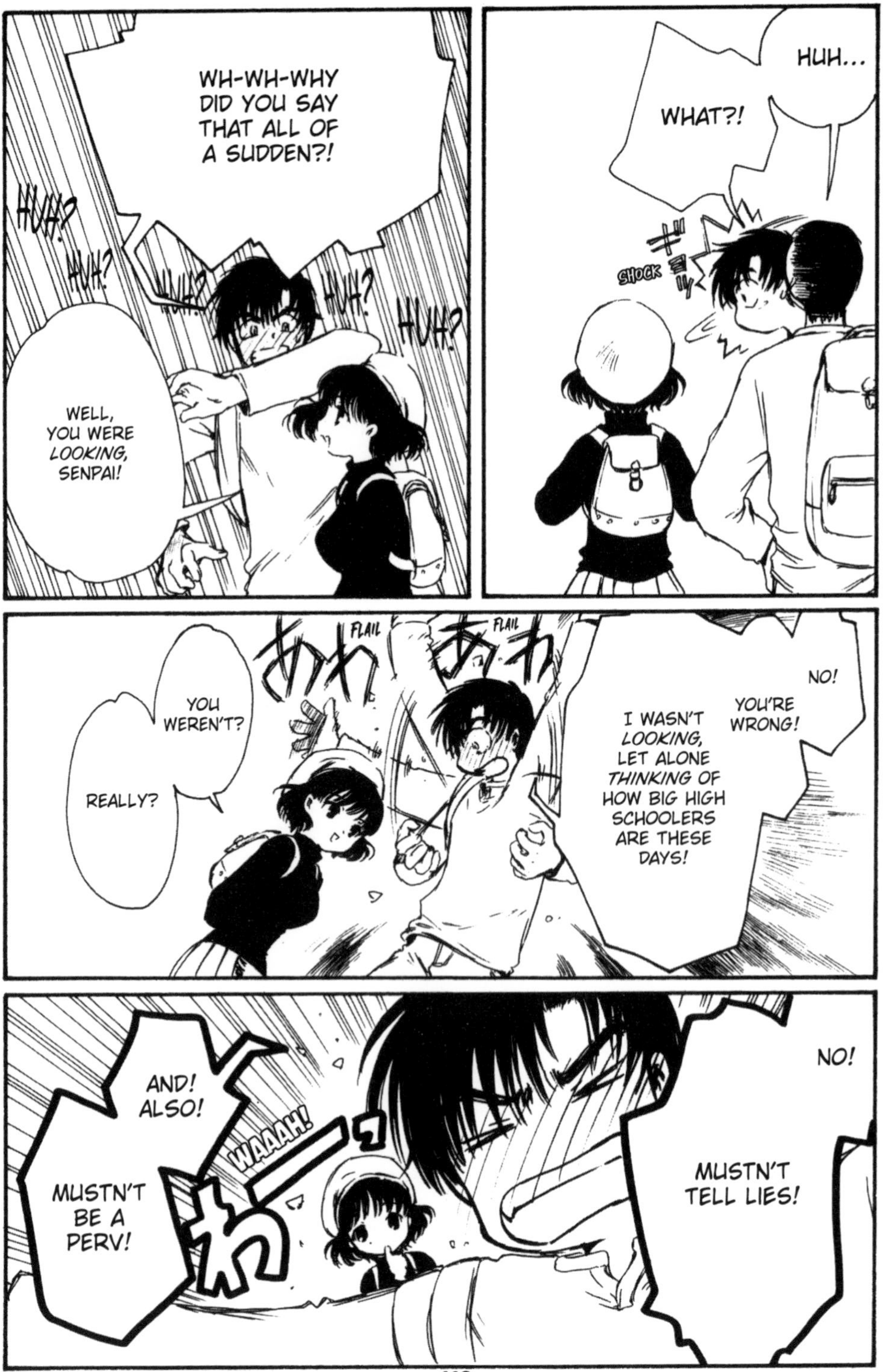
HUH...
WHAT?!
SHOCK
WH-WH-WHY DID YOU SAY THAT ALL OF A SUDDEN?!
HUH? HUH? HUH? HUH? HUH?
WELL, YOU WERE *LOOKING*, SENPAI!
NO!
YOU'RE WRONG!
I WASN'T *LOOKING*, LET ALONE *THINKING* OF HOW BIG HIGH SCHOOLERS ARE THESE DAYS!
FLAIL
FLAIL
YOU WEREN'T?
REALLY?
NO!
MUSTN'T TELL LIES!
WAAAH!
AND! ALSO!
MUSTN'T BE A PERV!

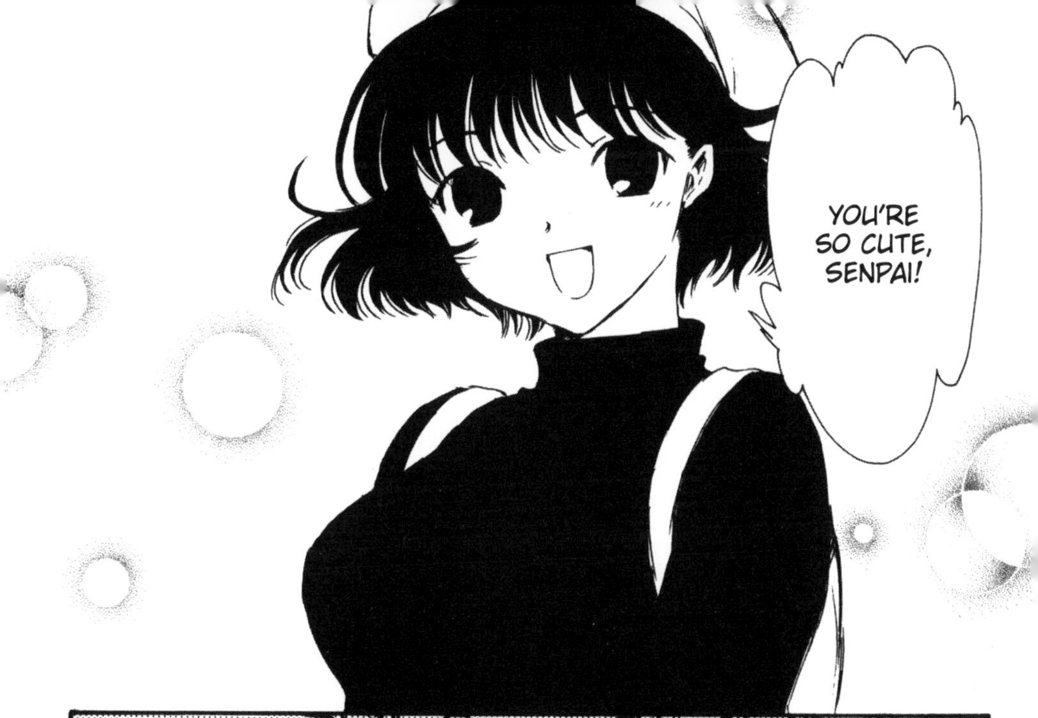
YOU'RE SO CUTE, SENPAI!

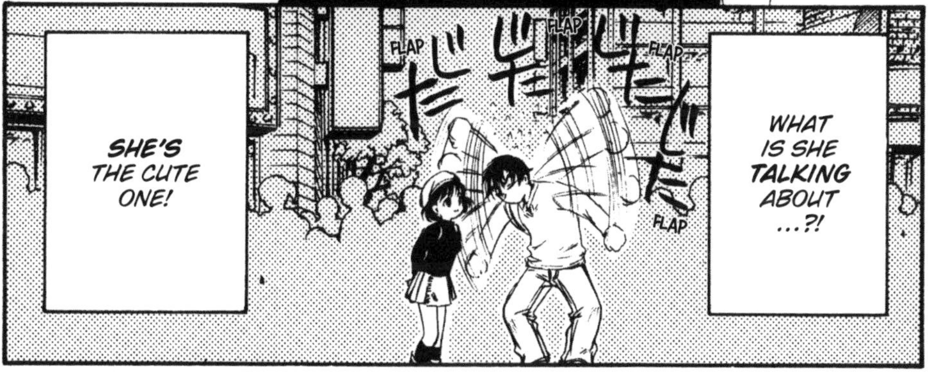
WHAT IS SHE TALKING ABOUT ...?!
FLAP
FLAP
FLAP
FLAP
SHE'S THE CUTE ONE!

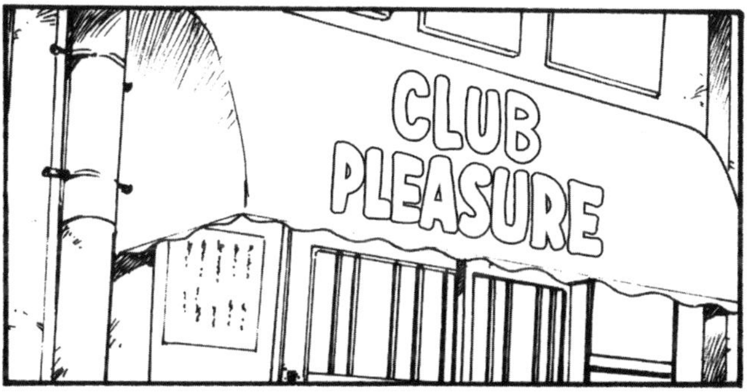
CLUB PLEASURE

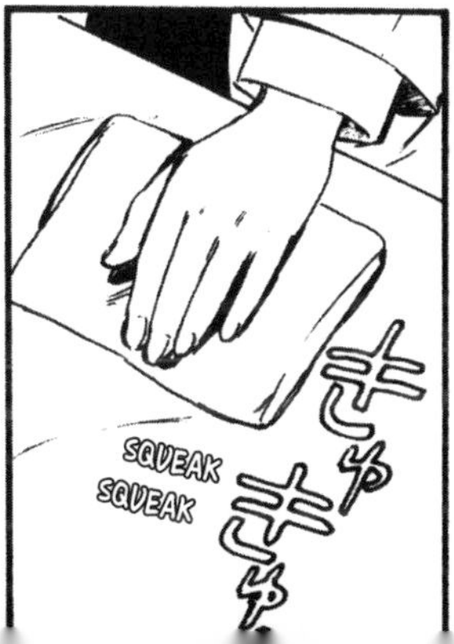
SQUEAK
SQUEAK

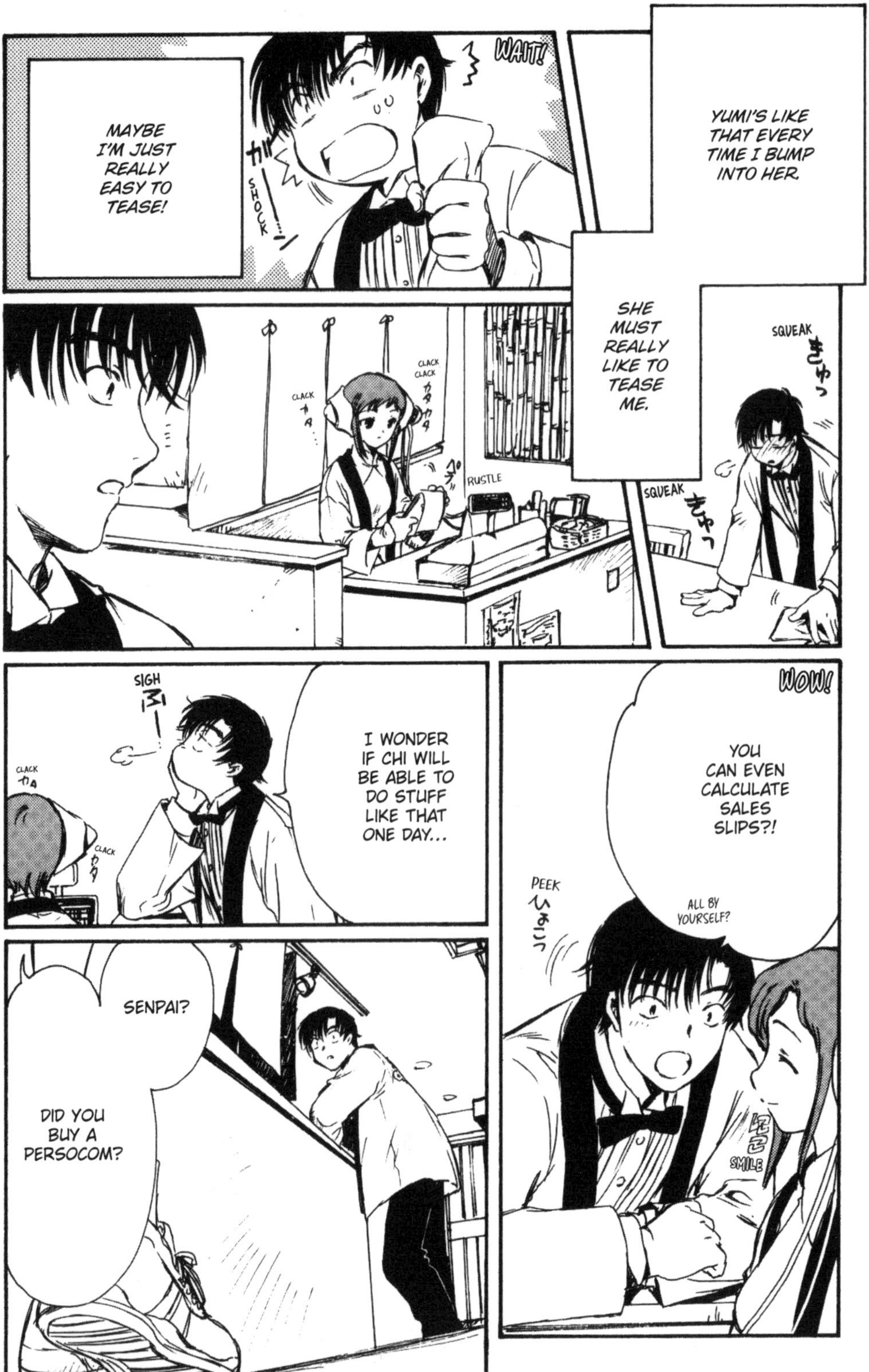
YUMI'S LIKE THAT EVERY TIME I BUMP INTO HER.
WAIT!
SHOCK
MAYBE I'M JUST REALLY EASY TO TEASE!
SHE MUST REALLY LIKE TO TEASE ME.
SQUEAK
SQUEAK
CLACK CLACK
RUSTLE
CLACK
WOW!
YOU CAN EVEN CALCULATE SALES SLIPS?!
PEEK
ALL BY YOURSELF?
SMILE
SIGH
I WONDER IF CHI WILL BE ABLE TO DO STUFF LIKE THAT ONE DAY...
CLACK
CLACK
SENPAI?
DID YOU BUY A PERSOCOM?

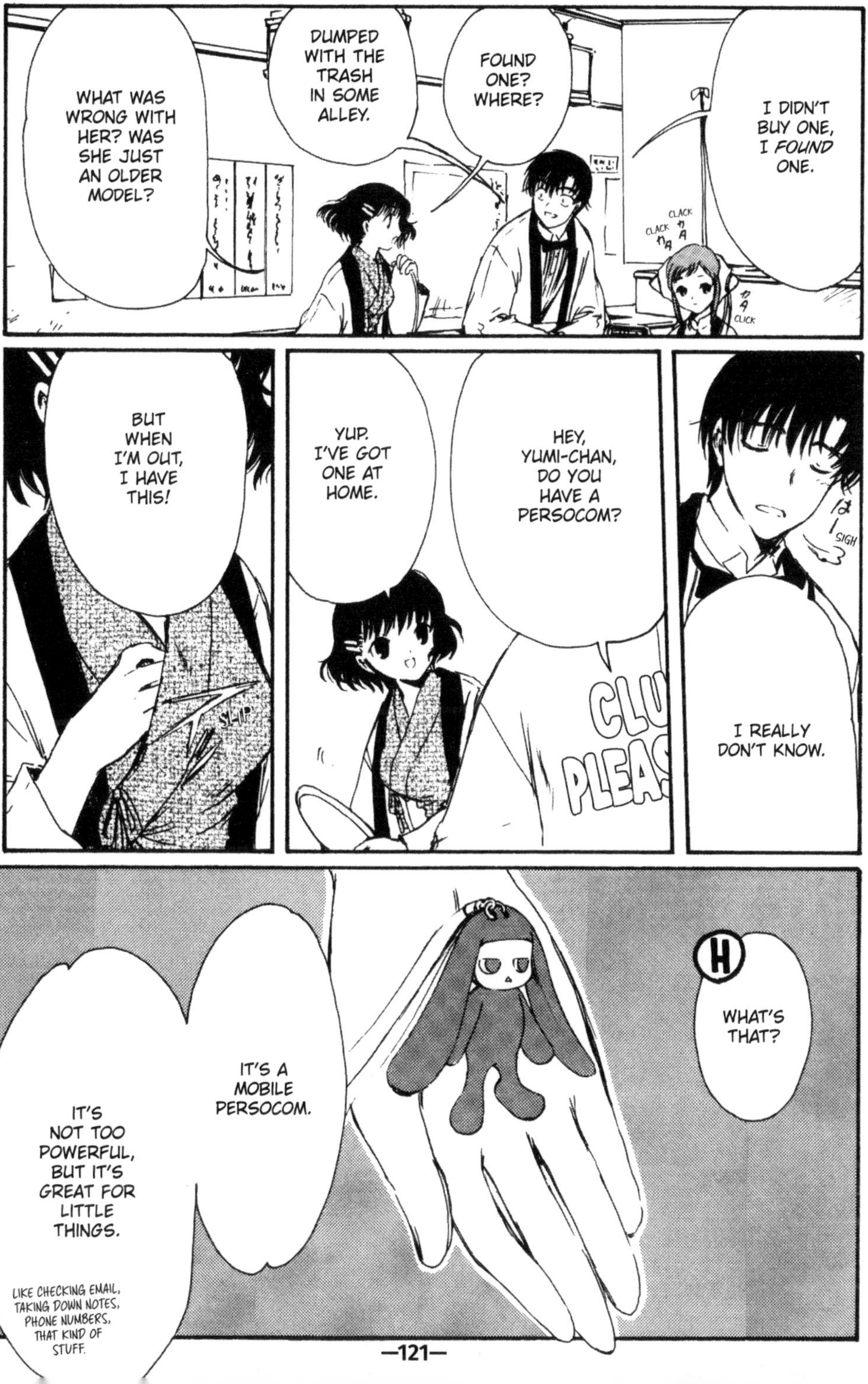
I DIDN'T BUY ONE, I *FOUND* ONE.
CLACK
CLACK
CLACK
FOUND ONE? WHERE?
DUMPED WITH THE TRASH IN SOME ALLEY.
WHAT WAS WRONG WITH HER? WAS SHE JUST AN OLDER MODEL?
SIGH
I REALLY DON'T KNOW.
HEY, YUMI-CHAN, DO YOU HAVE A PERSOCOM?
YUP. I'VE GOT ONE AT HOME.
BUT WHEN I'M OUT, I HAVE THIS!
SLIP
H
WHAT'S THAT?
IT'S A MOBILE PERSOCOM.
IT'S NOT TOO POWERFUL, BUT IT'S GREAT FOR LITTLE THINGS.
LIKE CHECKING EMAIL, TAKING DOWN NOTES, PHONE NUMBERS, THAT KIND OF STUFF.

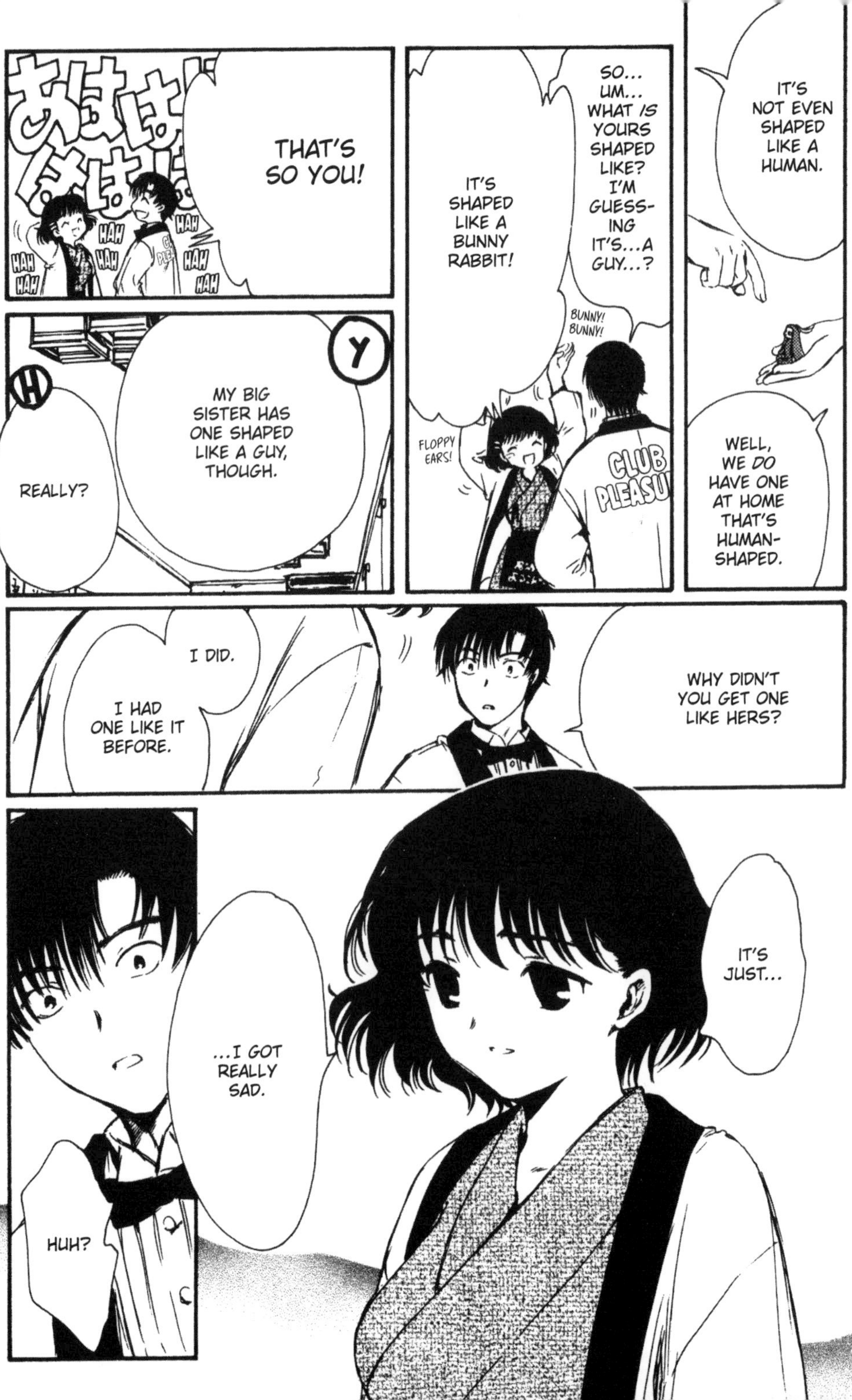
IT'S NOT EVEN SHAPED LIKE A HUMAN.
WELL, WE *DO* HAVE ONE AT HOME THAT'S HUMAN-SHAPED.
SO... UM... WHAT *IS* YOURS SHAPED LIKE? I'M GUESSING IT'S...A GUY...?
IT'S SHAPED LIKE A BUNNY RABBIT!
BUNNY! BUNNY!
FLOPPY EARS!
THAT'S SO YOU!
HAH HAH
HAH HAH
HAH
HAH
HAH HAH
MY BIG SISTER HAS ONE SHAPED LIKE A GUY, THOUGH.
REALLY?
WHY DIDN'T YOU GET ONE LIKE HERS?
I DID.
I HAD ONE LIKE IT BEFORE.
IT'S JUST...
...I GOT REALLY SAD.
HUH?

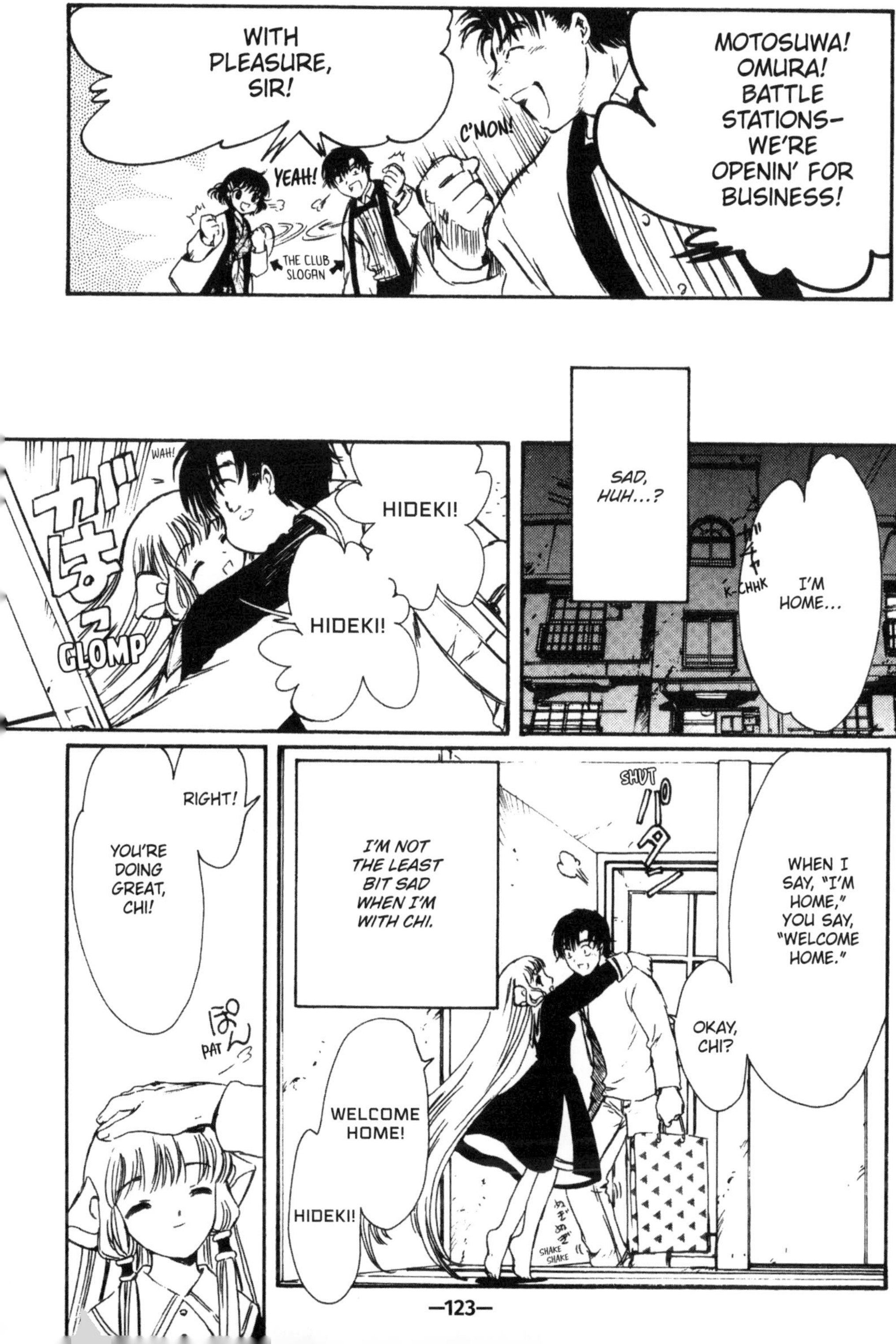
MOTOSUWA! OMURA! BATTLE STATIONS— WE'RE OPENIN' FOR BUSINESS!
C'MON!
WITH PLEASURE, SIR!
YEAH!
THE CLUB SLOGAN
SAD, HUH...?
K-CHHK
I'M HOME...
HIDEKI!
HIDEKI!
WAH!
GLOMP
WHEN I SAY, "I'M HOME," YOU SAY, "WELCOME HOME."
OKAY, CHI?
SHUT
I'M NOT THE LEAST BIT SAD WHEN I'M WITH CHI.
WELCOME HOME!
HIDEKI!
SHAKE SHAKE
RIGHT!
YOU'RE DOING GREAT, CHI!
PAT

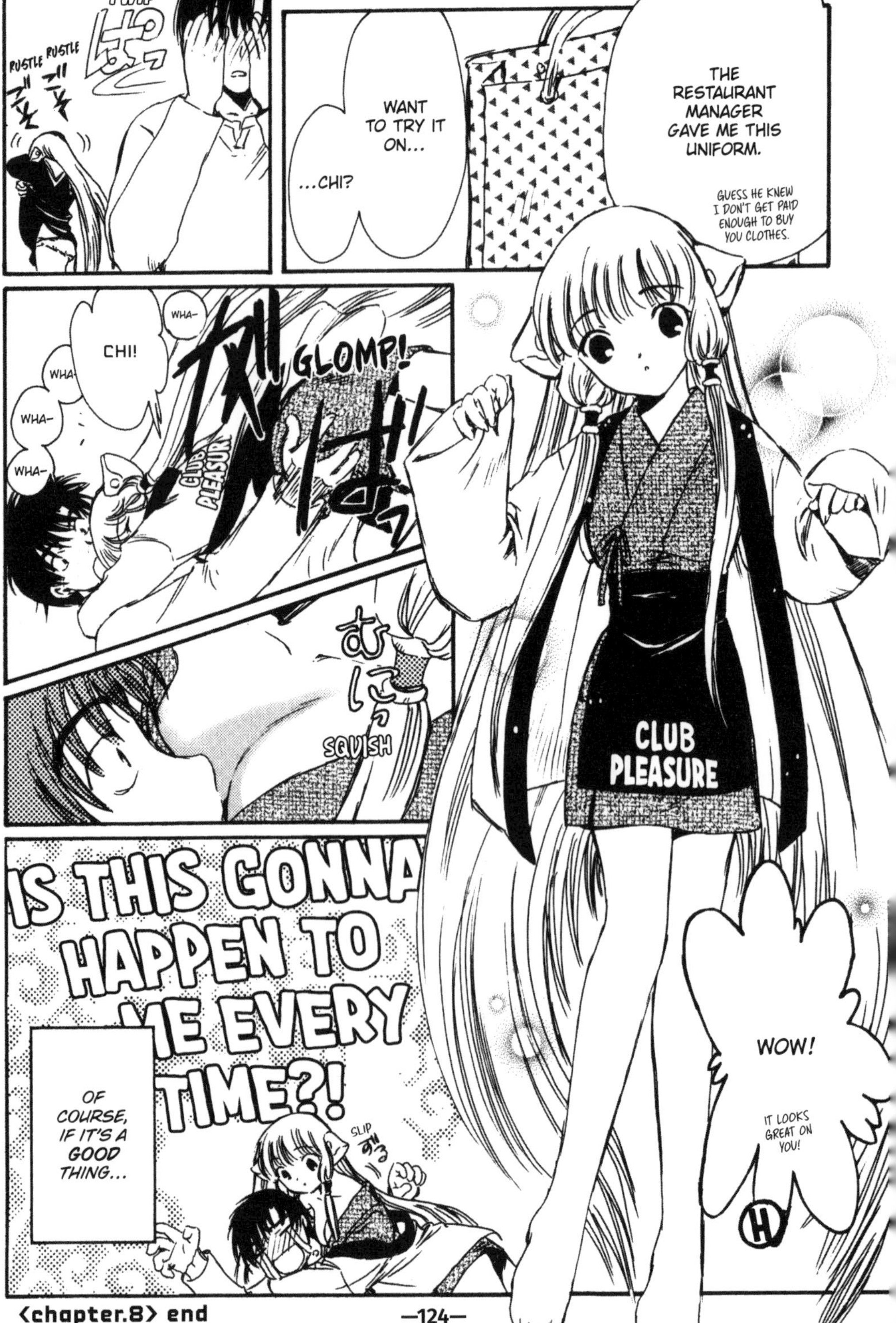

THE RESTAURANT MANAGER GAVE ME THIS UNIFORM.
GUESS HE KNEW I DON'T GET PAID ENOUGH TO BUY YOU CLOTHES.
WANT TO TRY IT ON...
...CHI?
FWIP
RUSTLE RUSTLE
CLUB PLEASURE
WOW!
IT LOOKS GREAT ON YOU!
WHA-
CHI!
WHA-
WHA-
WHA-
GLOMP!
CLUB PLEASURE
SQUISH
IS THIS GONNA HAPPEN TO ME EVERY TIME?!
OF COURSE, IF IT'S A GOOD THING...
SLIP

⟨chapter.9⟩

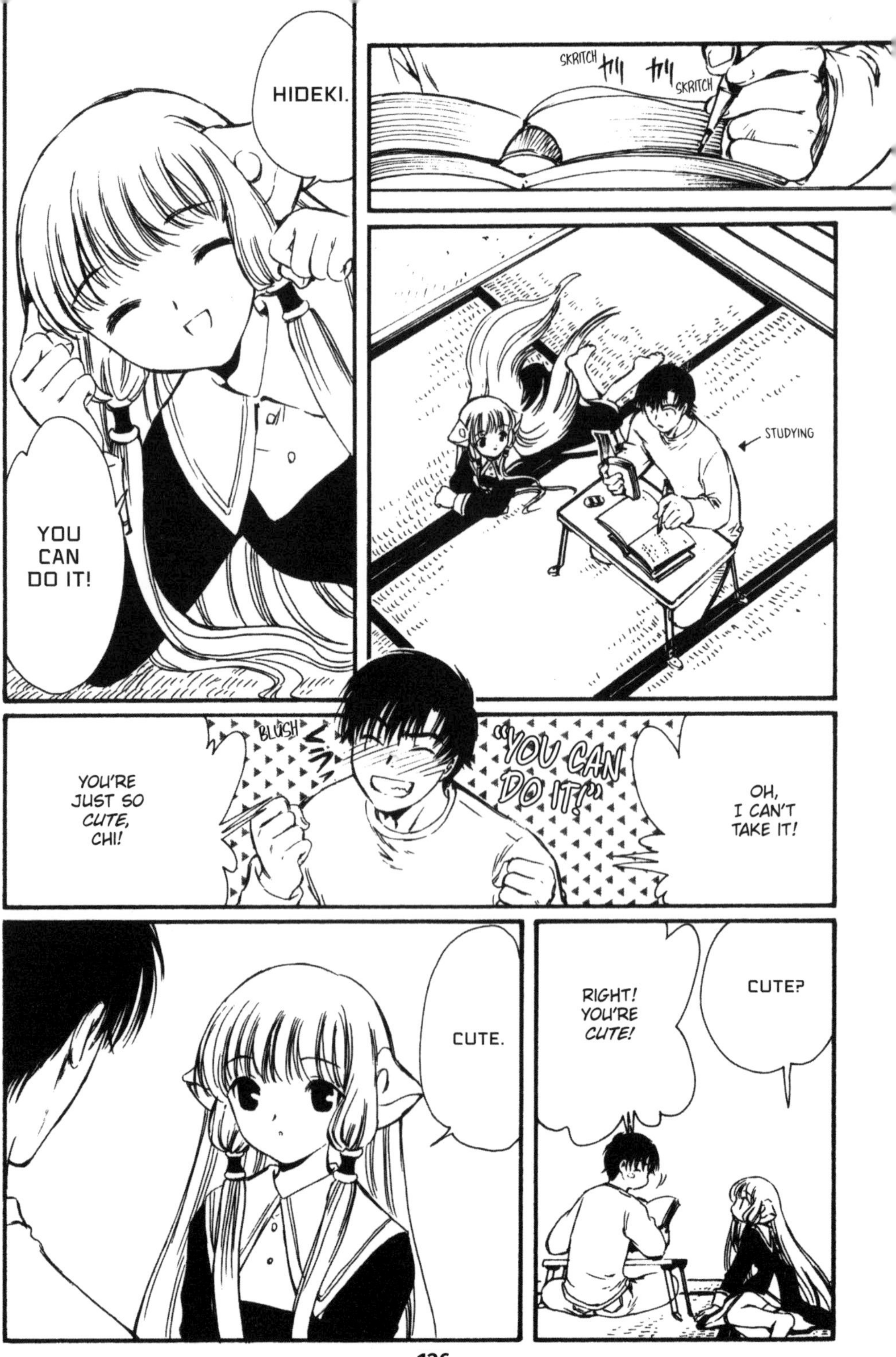
SKRITCH
カリ
カリ
SKRITCH
STUDYING
HIDEKI.
YOU CAN DO IT!
OH, I CAN'T TAKE IT!
"YOU CAN DO IT!"
BLUSH
YOU'RE JUST SO CUTE, CHI!
CUTE?
RIGHT! YOU'RE CUTE!
CUTE.

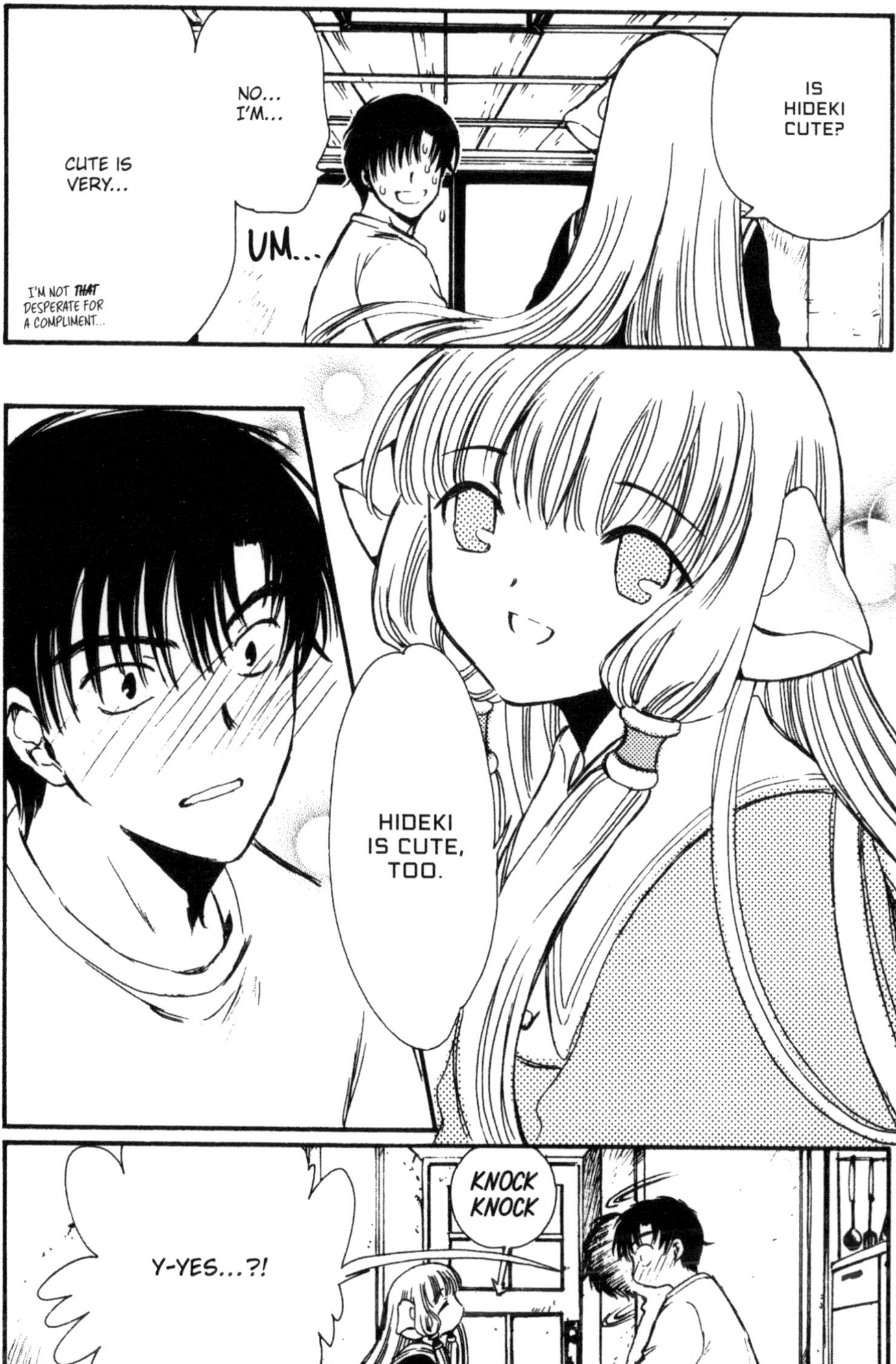
IS HIDEKI CUTE?
NO... I'M...
CUTE IS VERY...
UM...
I'M NOT *THAT* DESPERATE FOR A COMPLIMENT...
HIDEKI IS CUTE, TOO.
KNOCK KNOCK
Y-YES...?!

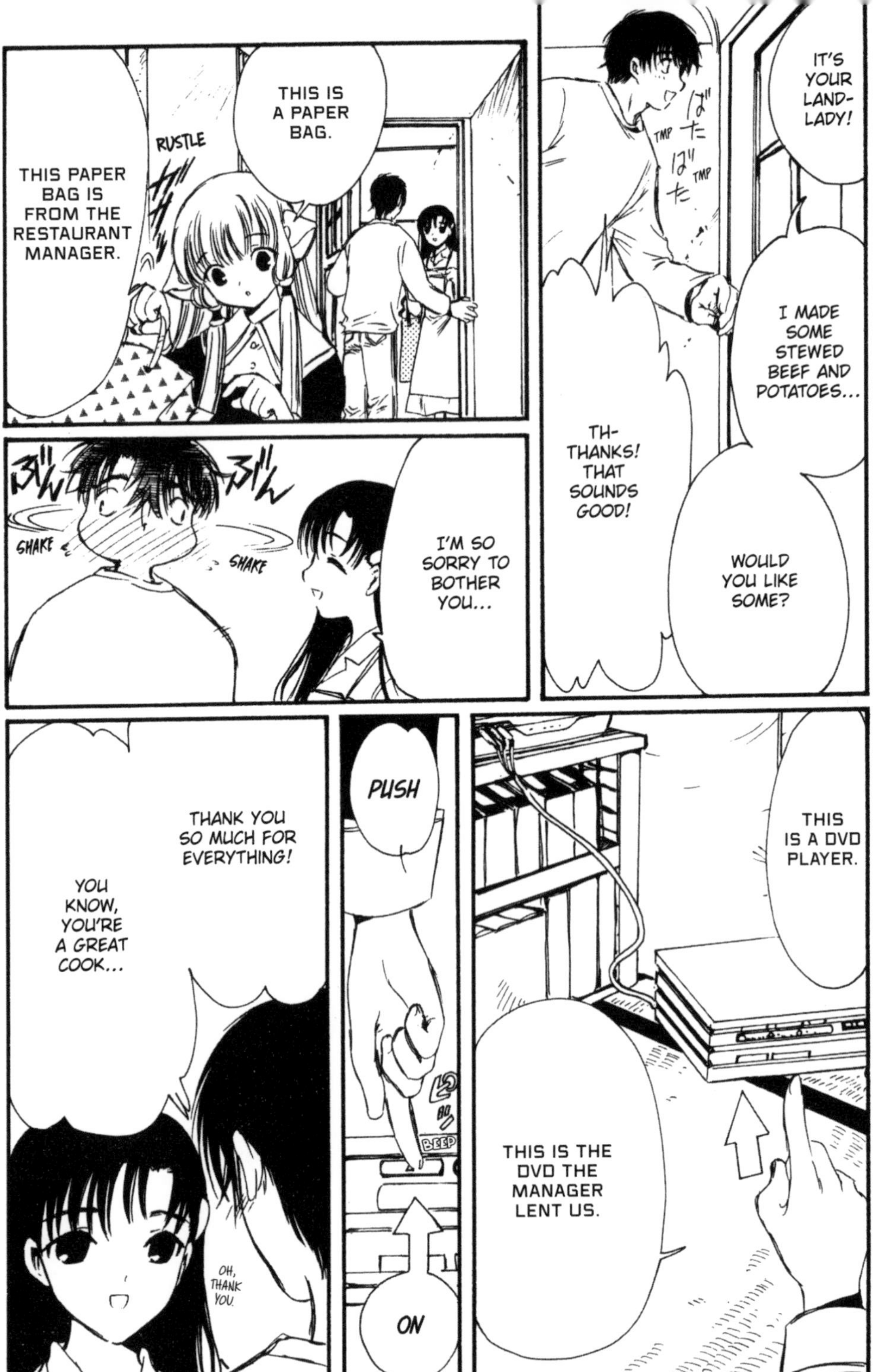
IT'S YOUR LANDLADY!
TMP TMP
I MADE SOME STEWED BEEF AND POTATOES...
TH- THANKS! THAT SOUNDS GOOD!
WOULD YOU LIKE SOME?
THIS IS A PAPER BAG.
RUSTLE
THIS PAPER BAG IS FROM THE RESTAURANT MANAGER.
I'M SO SORRY TO BOTHER YOU...
SHAKE
SHAKE
THIS IS A DVD PLAYER.
THIS IS THE DVD THE MANAGER LENT US.
PUSH
BEEP
ON
THANK YOU SO MUCH FOR EVERYTHING!
YOU KNOW, YOU'RE A GREAT COOK...
OH, THANK YOU.

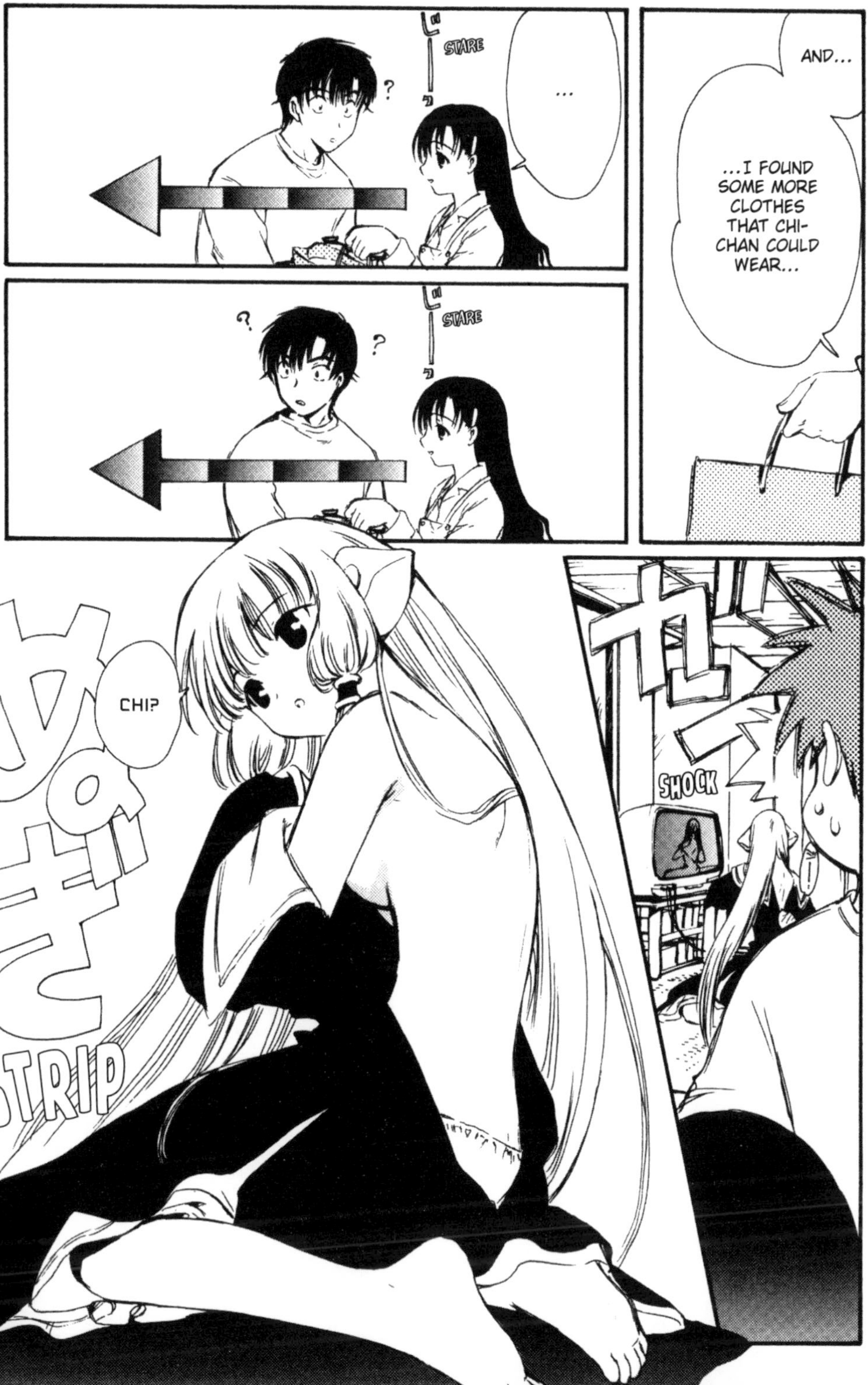
AND...
...I FOUND SOME MORE CLOTHES THAT CHI-CHAN COULD WEAR...
STARE
...
STARE
SHOCK
CHI?
STRIP

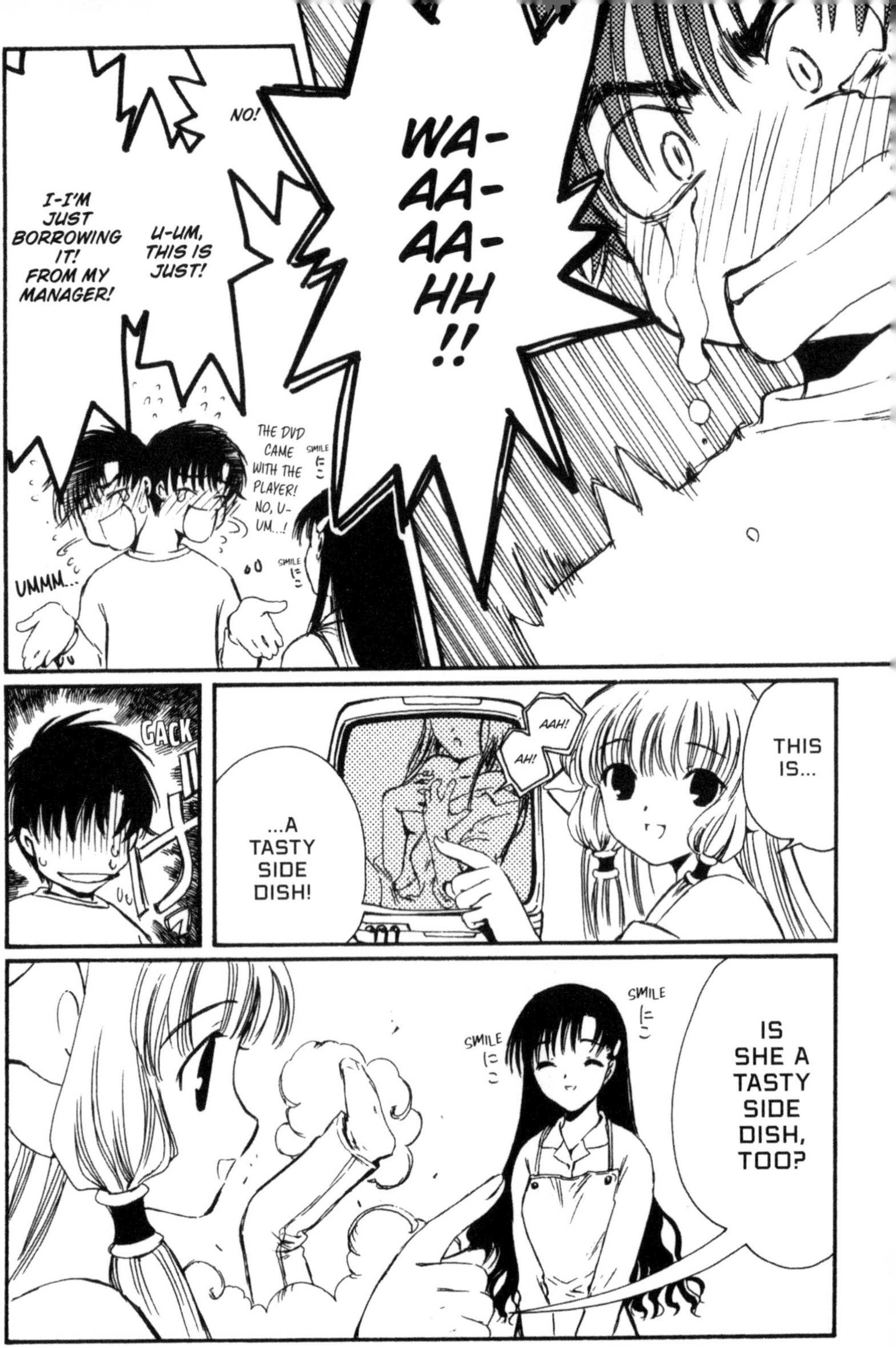

WA-AA-AA-AHH!!
NO!
U-UM, THIS IS JUST!
I-I'M JUST BORROWING IT! FROM MY MANAGER!
THE DVD CAME WITH THE PLAYER! NO, U-UM...!
SMILE
SMILE
UMMM...
THIS IS...
AAH!
AH!
...A TASTY SIDE DISH!
GACK
IS SHE A TASTY SIDE DISH, TOO?
SMILE
SMILE

GAAHHHH!!!

AAA-RRR-RRGH!!!

OH, IT'S JUST TYPICAL GUY STUFF.

DON'T WORRY ABOUT IT.

CREAK

CREAK

GOOD LUCK!

CREAK

CREAK

CREAK

CREAK

CREAK

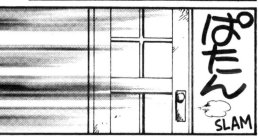

SLAM

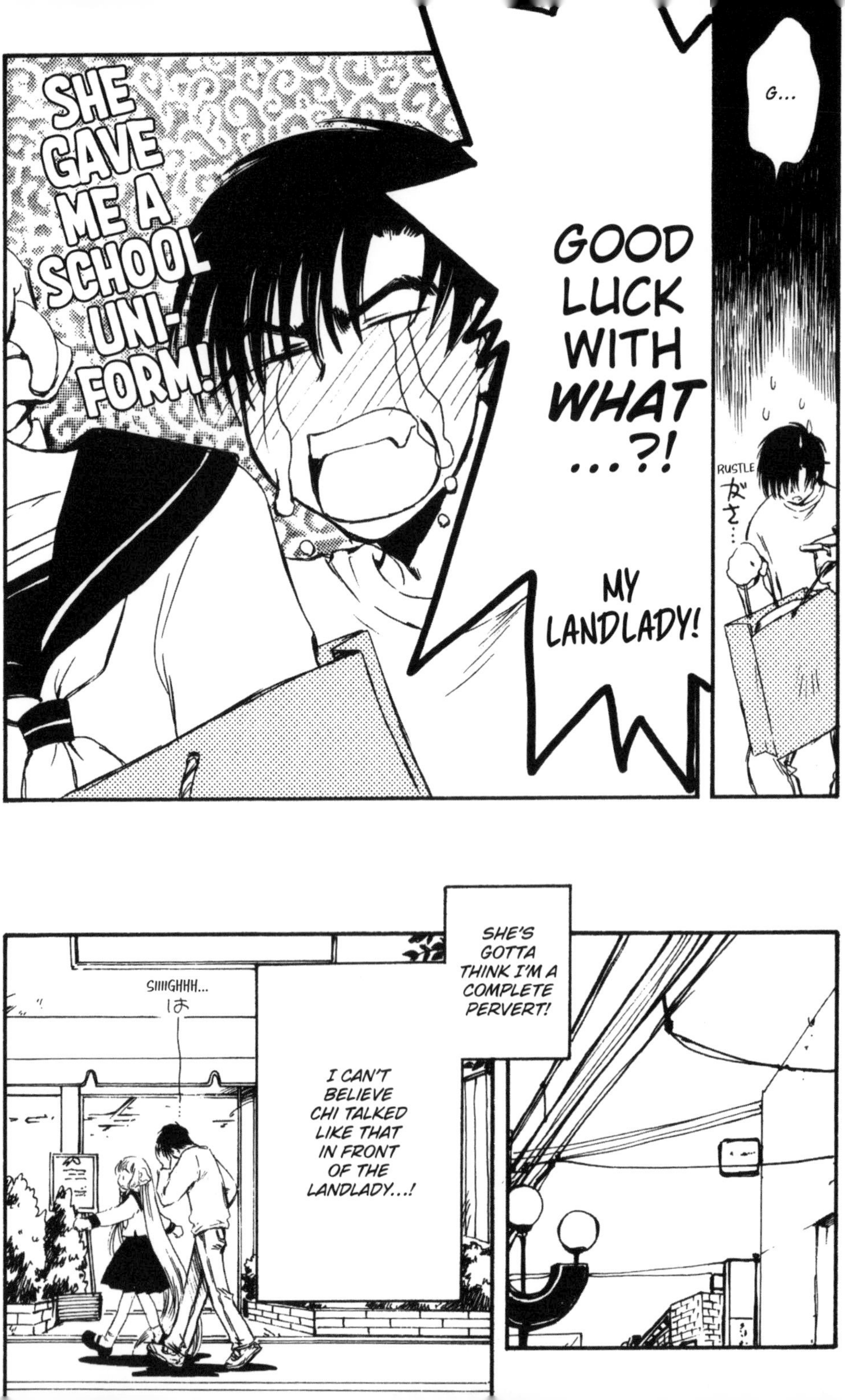
G...
RUSTLE
がさ...
GOOD LUCK WITH WHAT...?!
MY LANDLADY!
SHE GAVE ME A SCHOOL UNI-FORM!
SIIIGHHH...
は
I CAN'T BELIEVE CHI TALKED LIKE THAT IN FRONT OF THE LANDLADY...!
SHE'S GOTTA THINK I'M A COMPLETE PERVERT!

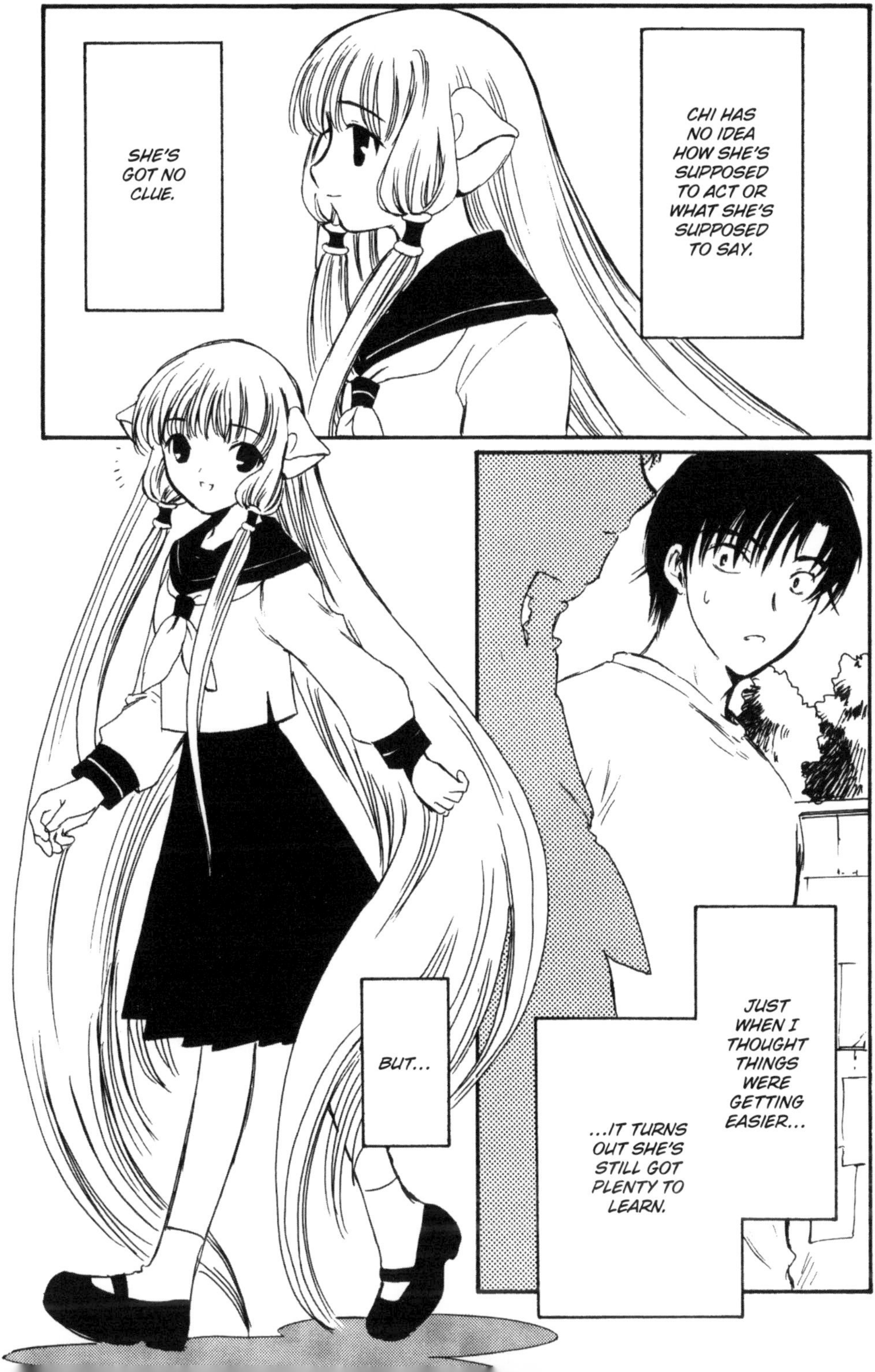
CHI HAS NO IDEA HOW SHE'S SUPPOSED TO ACT OR WHAT SHE'S SUPPOSED TO SAY.
SHE'S GOT NO CLUE.
BUT...
JUST WHEN I THOUGHT THINGS WERE GETTING EASIER...
...IT TURNS OUT SHE'S STILL GOT PLENTY TO LEARN.

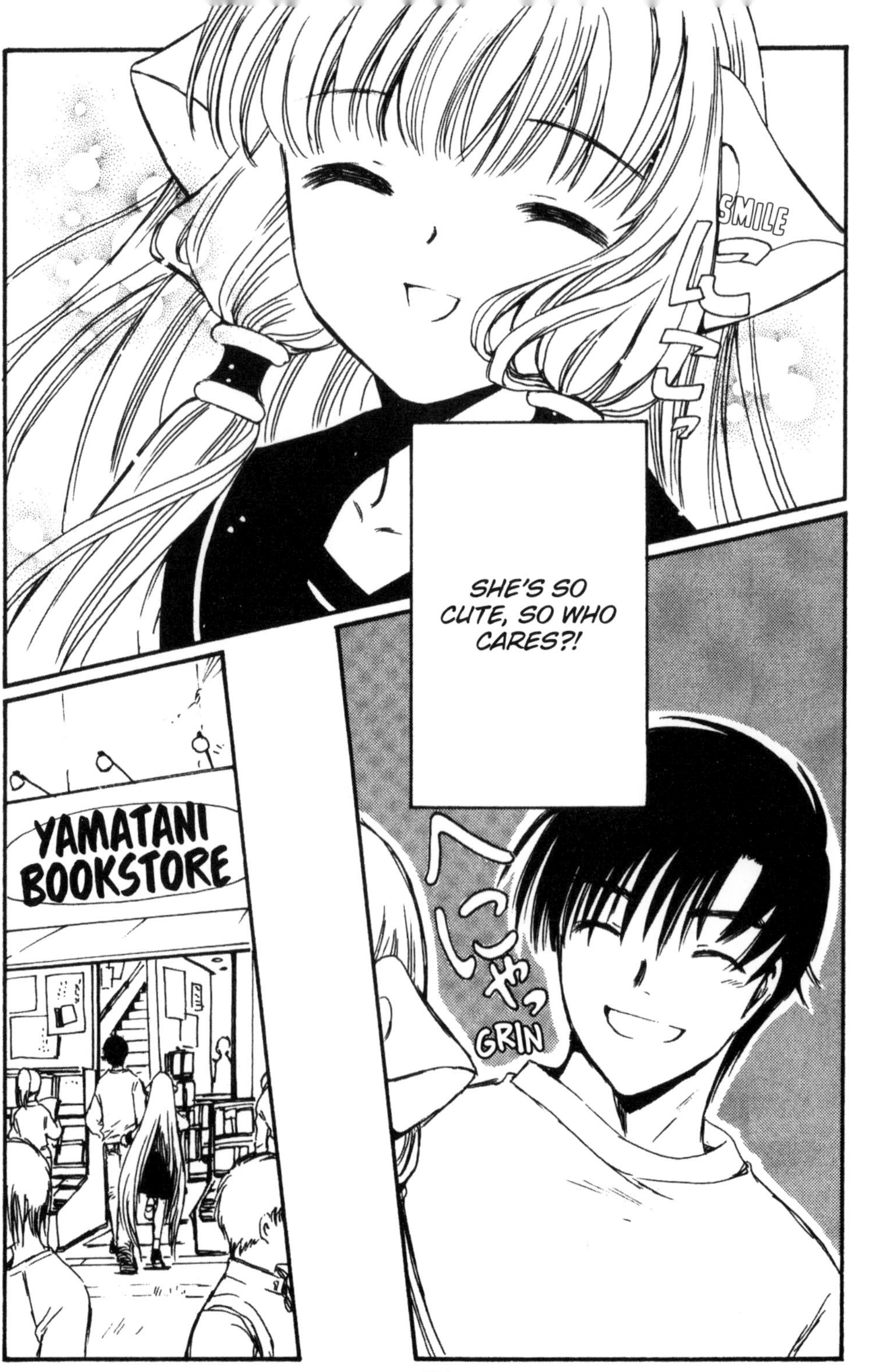
SMILE
SHE'S SO CUTE, SO WHO CARES?!
GRIN
YAMATANI BOOKSTORE

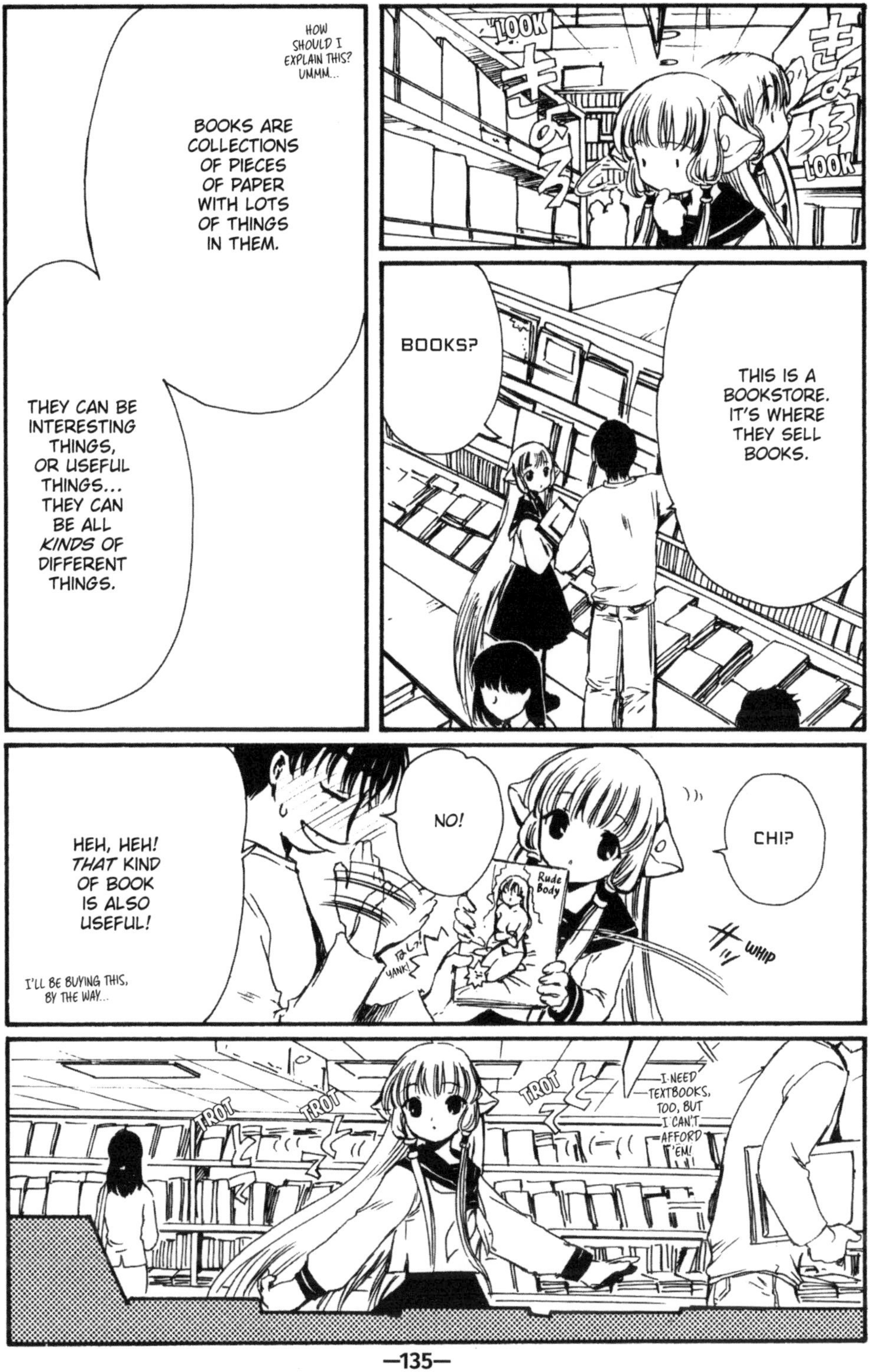
LOOK
LOOK
THIS IS A BOOKSTORE. IT'S WHERE THEY SELL BOOKS.
BOOKS?
HOW SHOULD I EXPLAIN THIS? UMMM...
BOOKS ARE COLLECTIONS OF PIECES OF PAPER WITH LOTS OF THINGS IN THEM.
THEY CAN BE INTERESTING THINGS, OR USEFUL THINGS... THEY CAN BE ALL *KINDS* OF DIFFERENT THINGS.
CHI?
WHIP
Rude Body
NO!
YANK!
HEH, HEH! *THAT* KIND OF BOOK IS ALSO USEFUL!
I'LL BE BUYING THIS, BY THE WAY...
I NEED TEXTBOOKS, TOO, BUT I CAN'T AFFORD 'EM!
TROT
TROT
TROT

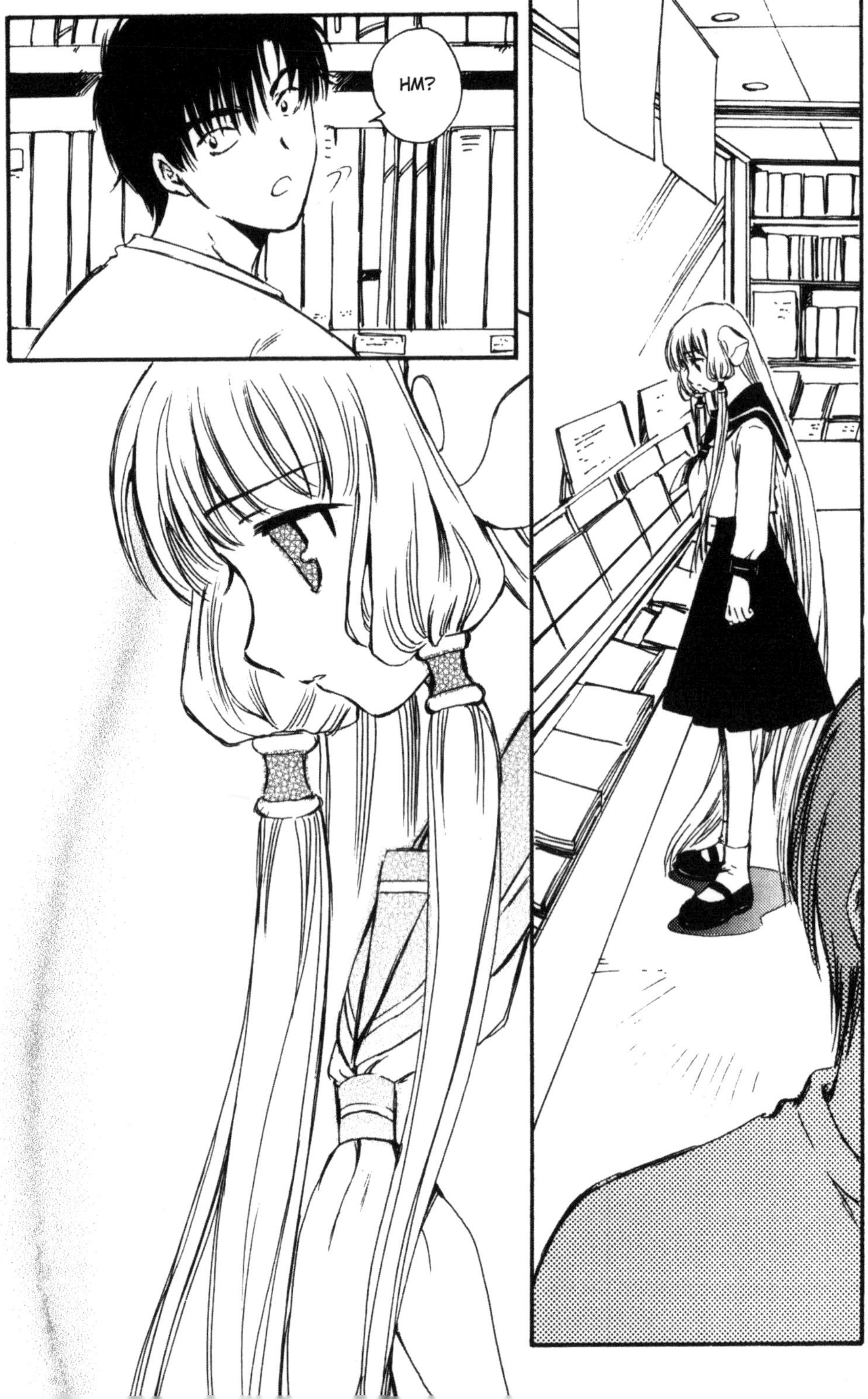
HM?

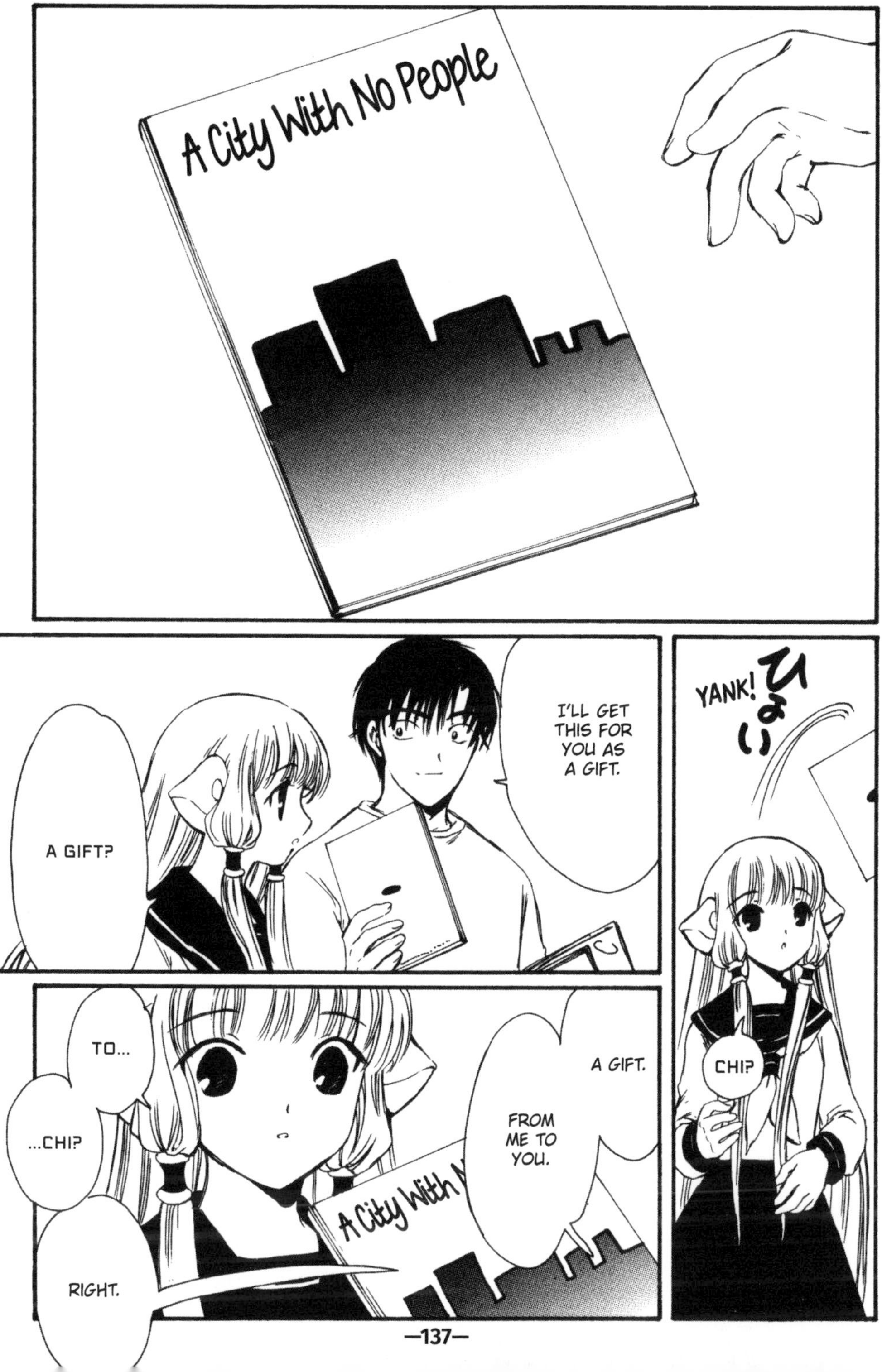
A City With No People
YANK! ひょい
CHI?
I'LL GET THIS FOR YOU AS A GIFT.
A GIFT?
A GIFT.
FROM ME TO YOU.
TO...
...CHI?
RIGHT.
A City With N

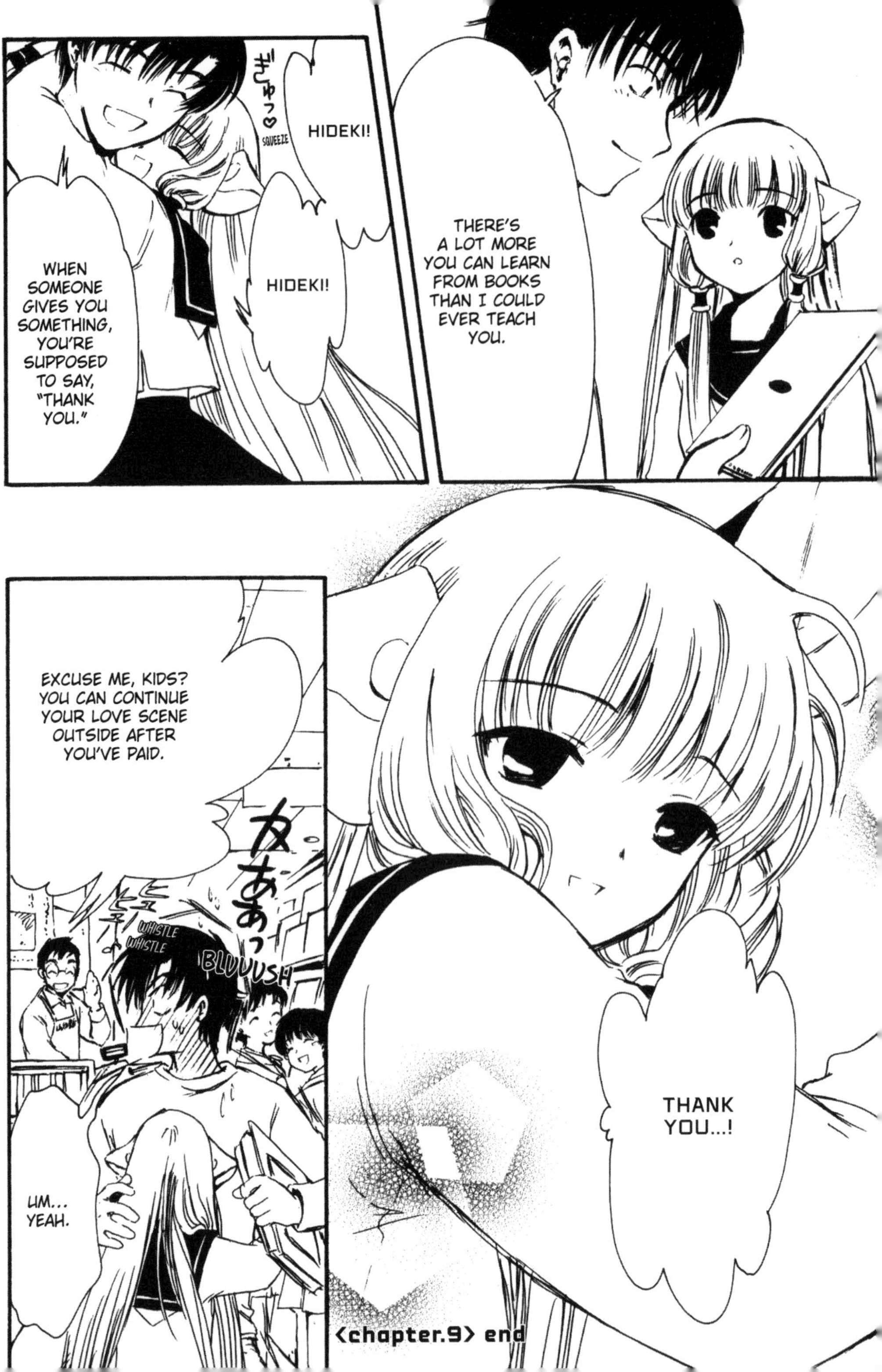
THERE'S A LOT MORE YOU CAN LEARN FROM BOOKS THAN I COULD EVER TEACH YOU.
HIDEKI!
ぎゅっ♡
SQUEEZE
HIDEKI!
WHEN SOMEONE GIVES YOU SOMETHING, YOU'RE SUPPOSED TO SAY, "THANK YOU."
THANK YOU...!
<chapter.9> end
EXCUSE ME, KIDS? YOU CAN CONTINUE YOUR LOVE SCENE OUTSIDE AFTER YOU'VE PAID.
かあっ
BLUUUSH
WHISTLE WHISTLE
UM... YEAH.

〈chapter.10〉

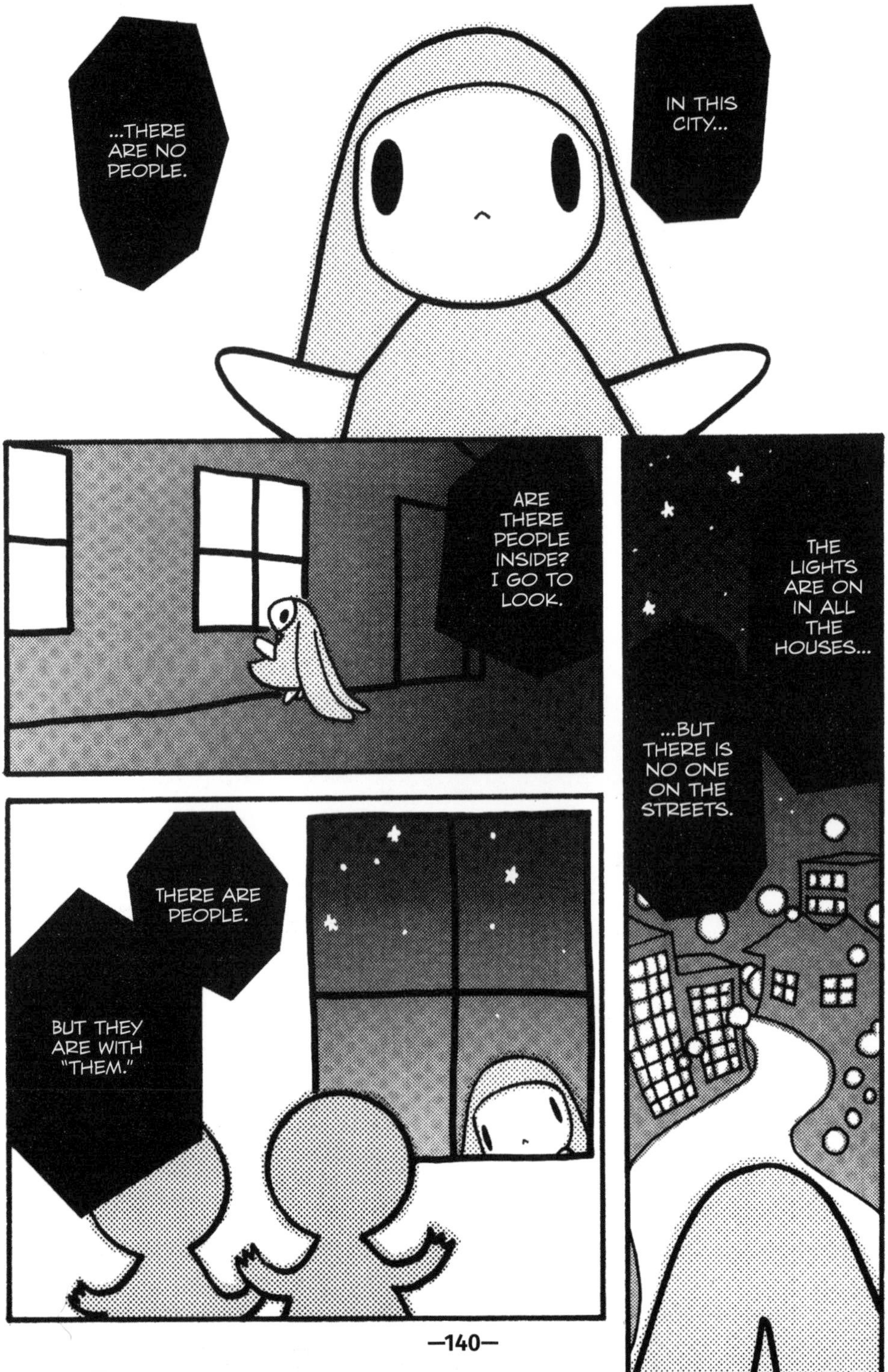
IN THIS CITY...
...THERE ARE NO PEOPLE.
THE LIGHTS ARE ON IN ALL THE HOUSES...
...BUT THERE IS NO ONE ON THE STREETS.
ARE THERE PEOPLE INSIDE? I GO TO LOOK.
THERE ARE PEOPLE.
BUT THEY ARE WITH "THEM."

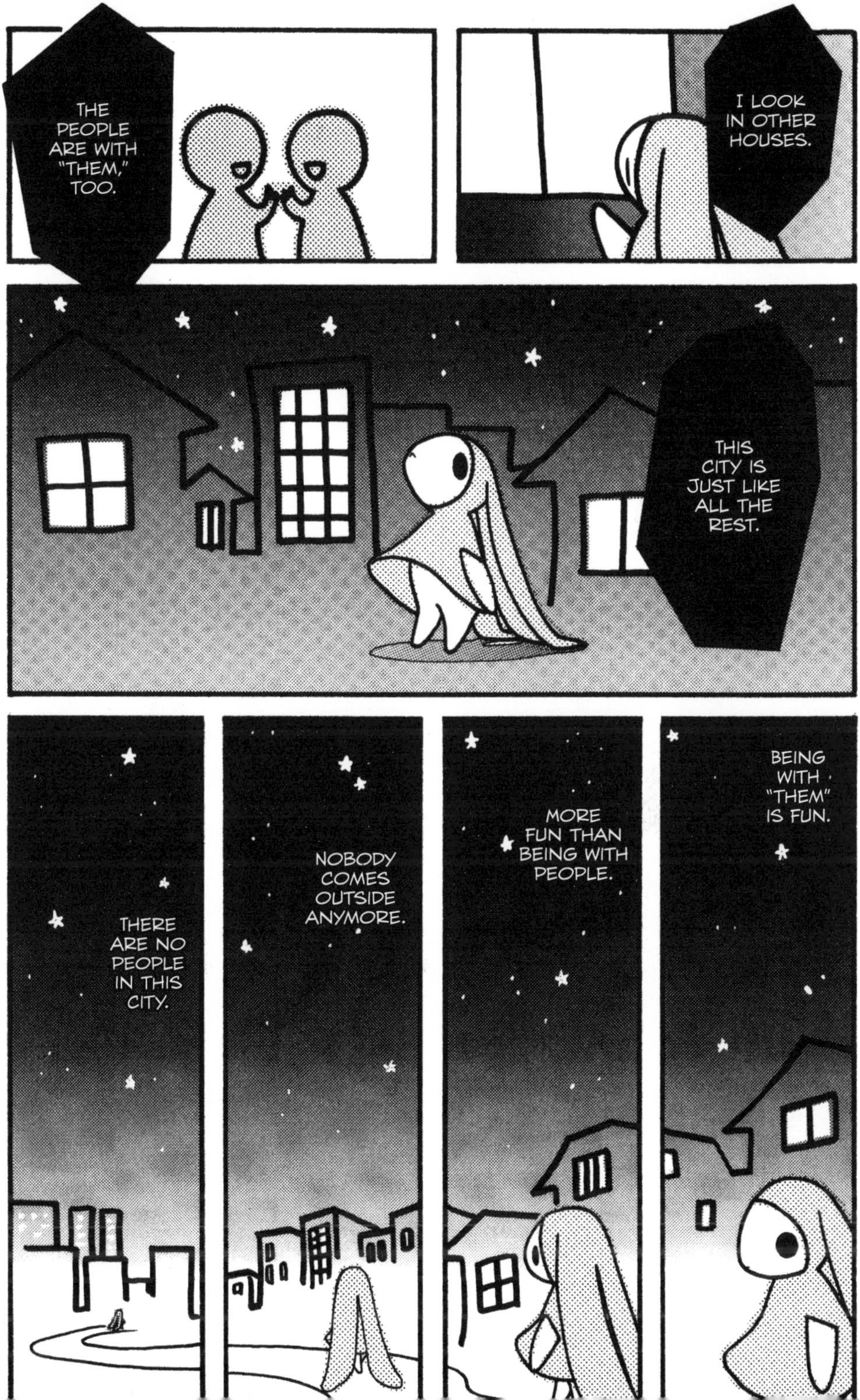
I LOOK IN OTHER HOUSES.
THE PEOPLE ARE WITH "THEM," TOO.
THIS CITY IS JUST LIKE ALL THE REST.
BEING WITH "THEM" IS FUN.
MORE FUN THAN BEING WITH PEOPLE.
NOBODY COMES OUTSIDE ANYMORE.
THERE ARE NO PEOPLE IN THIS CITY.

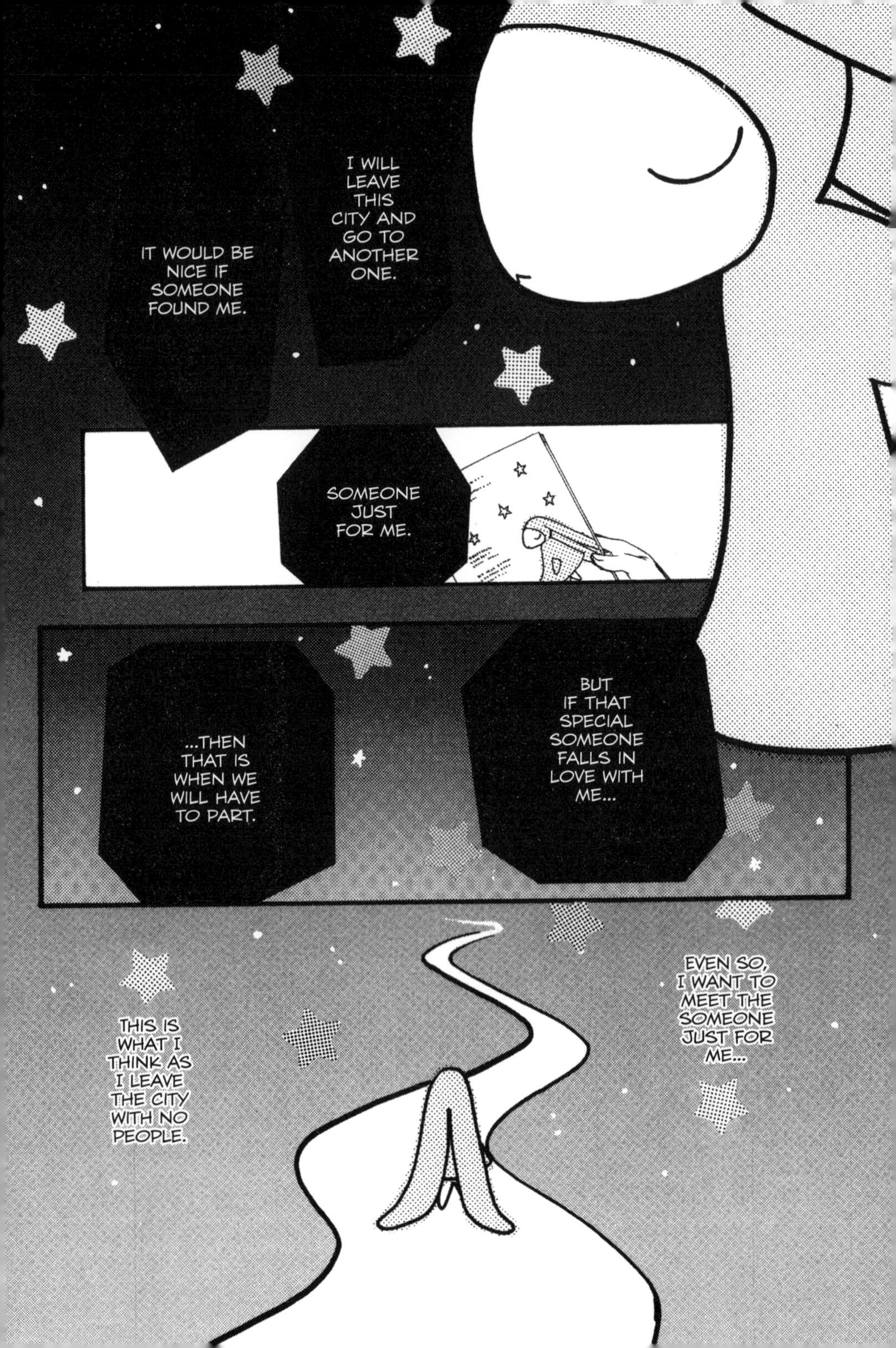
I WILL LEAVE THIS CITY AND GO TO ANOTHER ONE.
IT WOULD BE NICE IF SOMEONE FOUND ME.
SOMEONE JUST FOR ME.
BUT IF THAT SPECIAL SOMEONE FALLS IN LOVE WITH ME...
...THEN THAT IS WHEN WE WILL HAVE TO PART.
EVEN SO, I WANT TO MEET THE SOMEONE JUST FOR ME...
THIS IS WHAT I THINK AS I LEAVE THE CITY WITH NO PEOPLE.

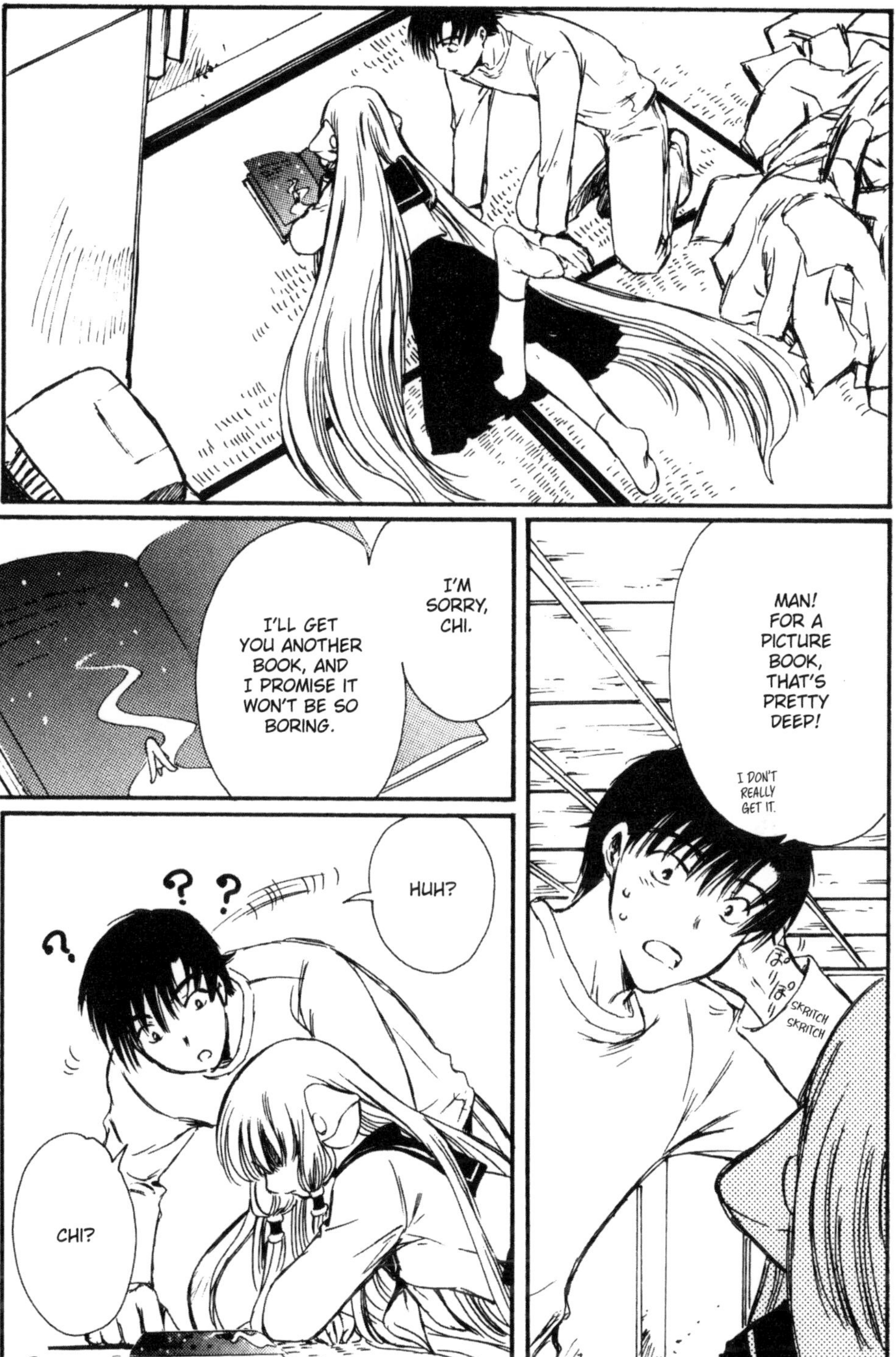
MAN! FOR A PICTURE BOOK, THAT'S PRETTY DEEP!
I DON'T REALLY GET IT.
ぽりぽり
SKRITCH SKRITCH
I'M SORRY, CHI.
I'LL GET YOU ANOTHER BOOK, AND I PROMISE IT WON'T BE SO BORING.
HUH?
CHI?

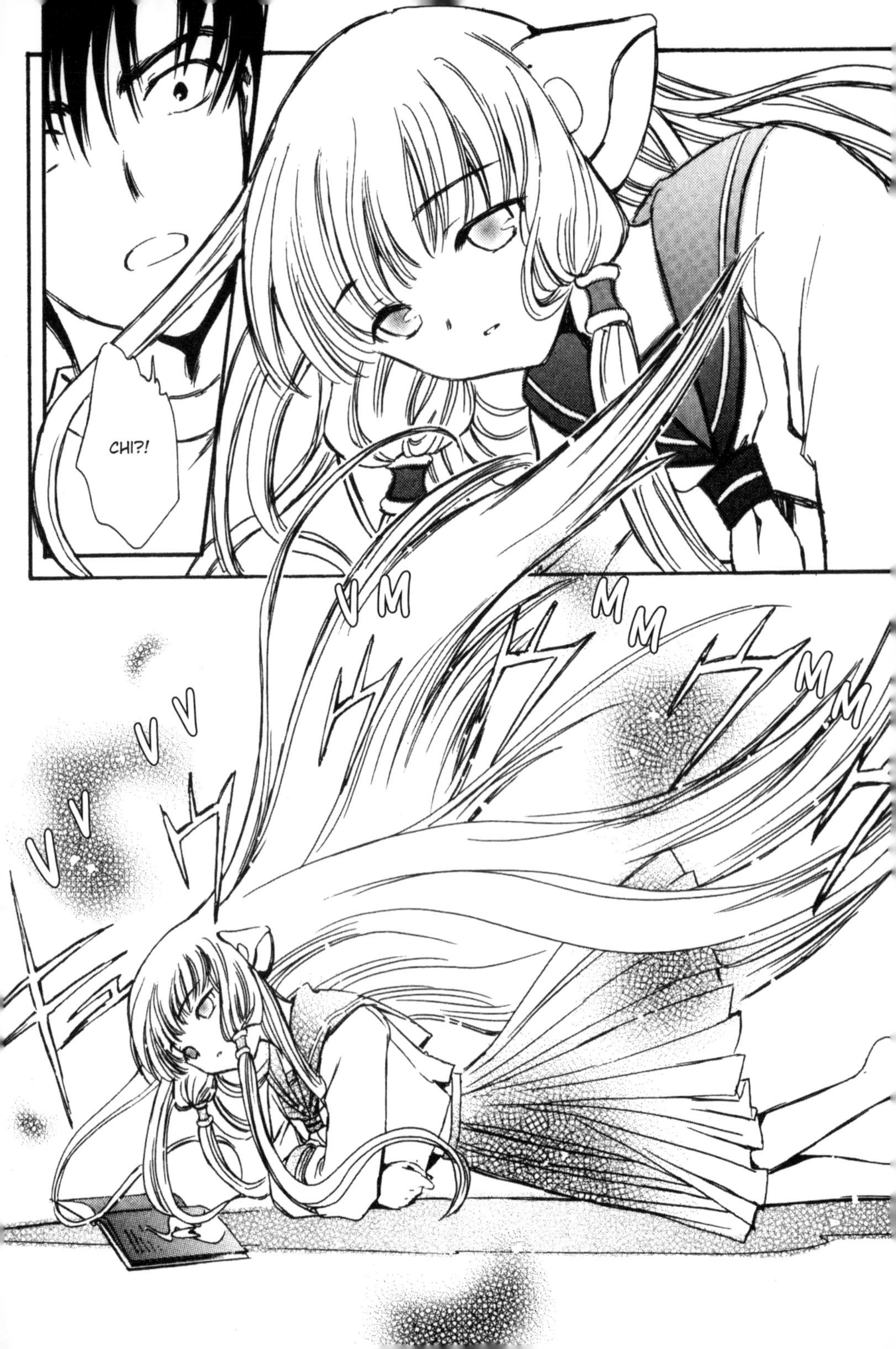
CHI?!
VV
VV
VM
MM
MM
MM

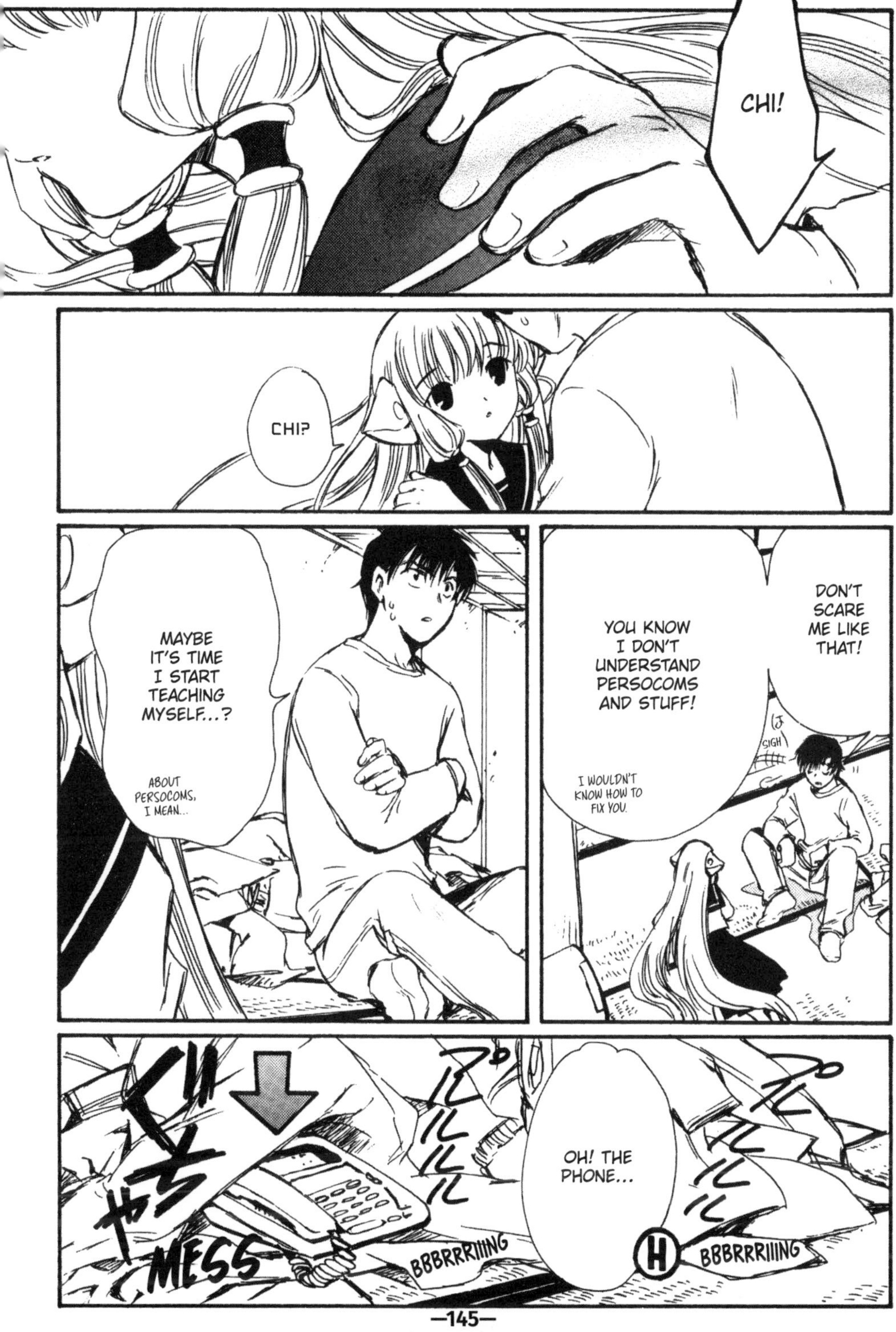
CHI!
CHI?
DON'T SCARE ME LIKE THAT!
YOU KNOW I DON'T UNDERSTAND PERSOCOMS AND STUFF!
I WOULDN'T KNOW HOW TO FIX YOU.
SIGH
MAYBE IT'S TIME I START TEACHING MYSELF...?
ABOUT PERSOCOMS, I MEAN...
BBBRRRIIING
OH! THE PHONE...
BBBRRRIIING
MESS

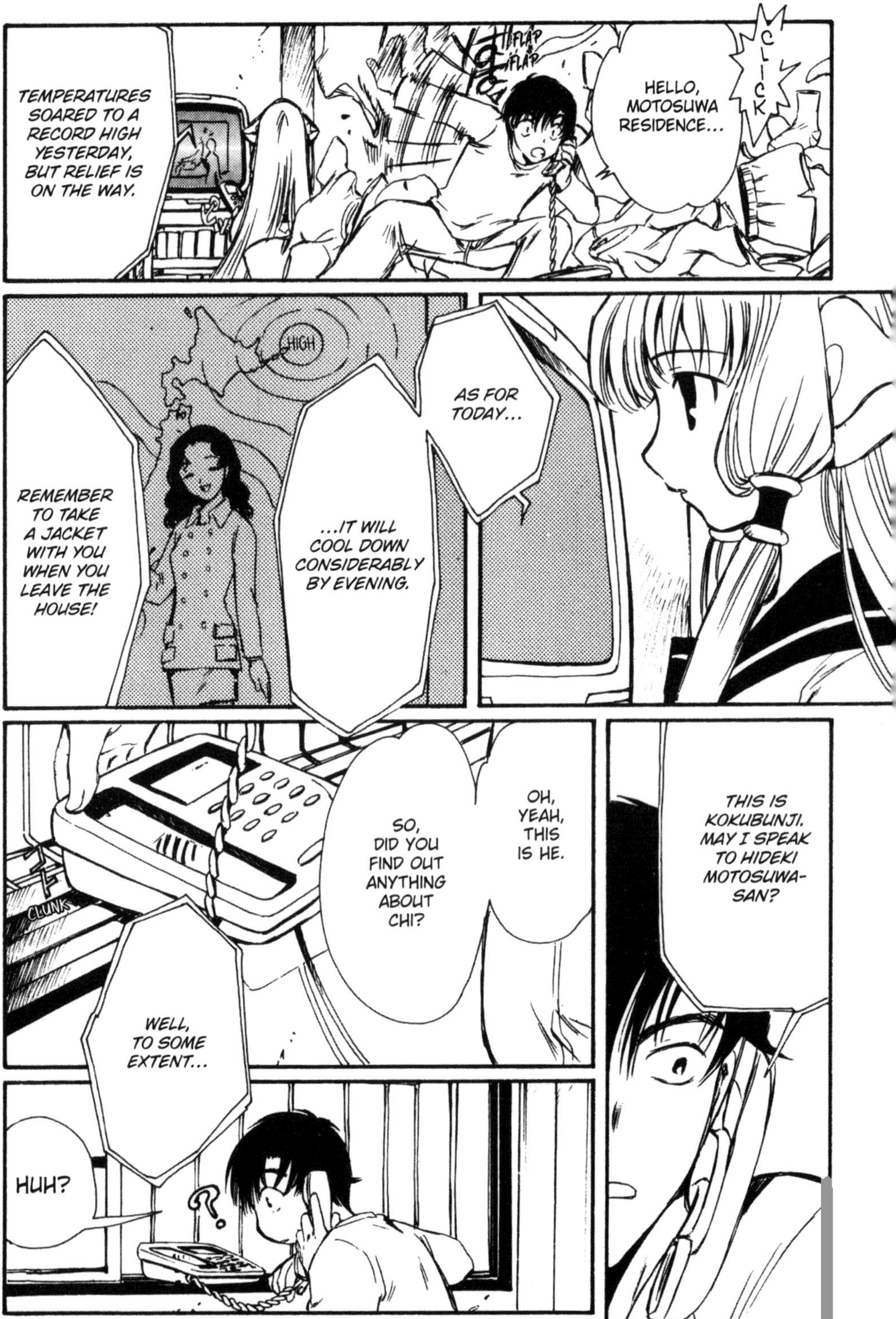
CLICK
HELLO, MOTOSUWA RESIDENCE...
FLAP FLAP
TEMPERATURES SOARED TO A RECORD HIGH YESTERDAY, BUT RELIEF IS ON THE WAY.
AS FOR TODAY...
HIGH
...IT WILL COOL DOWN CONSIDERABLY BY EVENING.
REMEMBER TO TAKE A JACKET WITH YOU WHEN YOU LEAVE THE HOUSE!
THIS IS KOKUBUNJI. MAY I SPEAK TO HIDEKI MOTOSUWA-SAN?
OH, YEAH, THIS IS HE.
SO, DID YOU FIND OUT ANYTHING ABOUT CHI?
CLUNK
WELL, TO SOME EXTENT...
HUH?

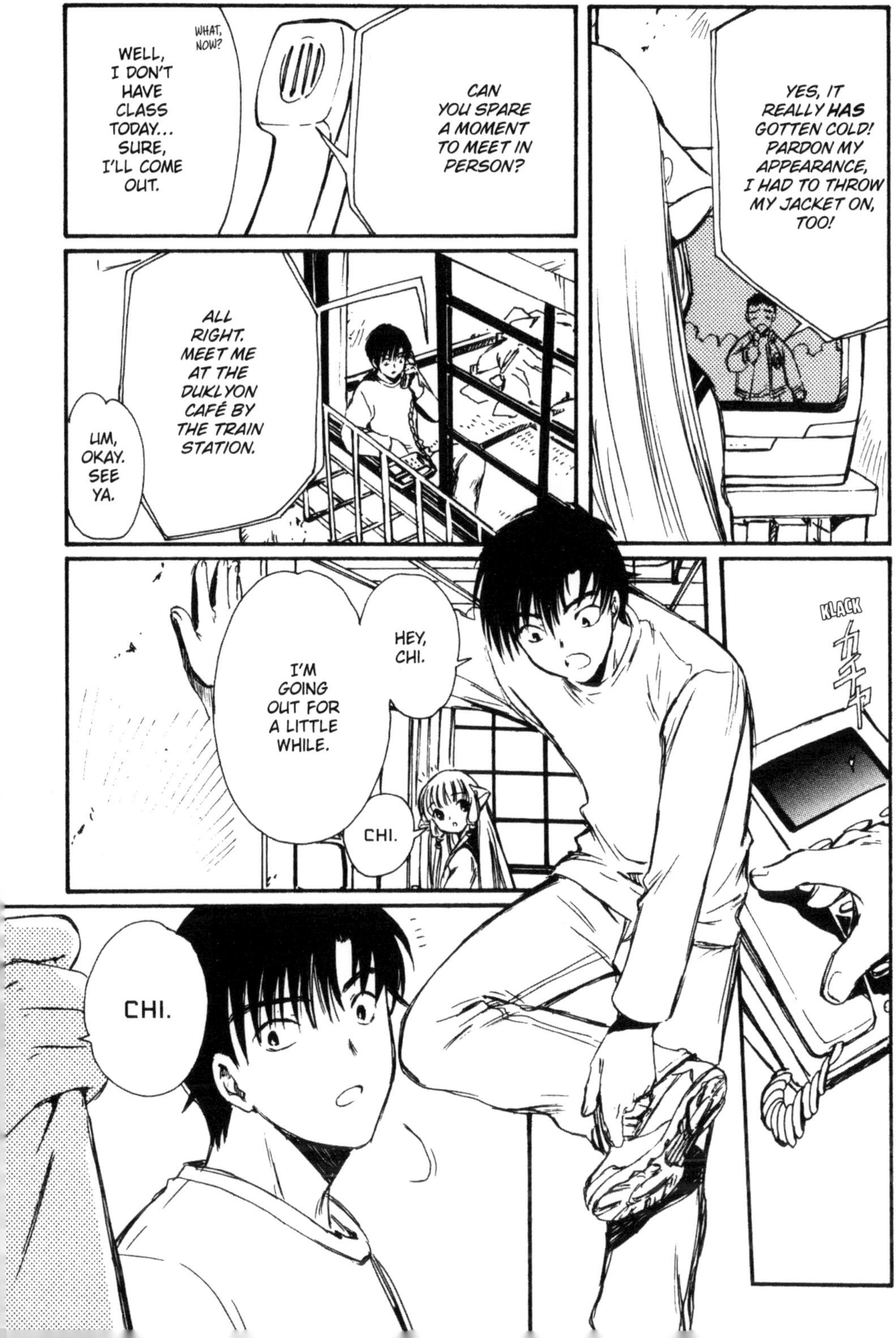
YES, IT REALLY **HAS** GOTTEN COLD! PARDON MY APPEARANCE, I HAD TO THROW MY JACKET ON, TOO!
CAN YOU SPARE A MOMENT TO MEET IN PERSON?
WHAT, NOW?
WELL, I DON'T HAVE CLASS TODAY... SURE, I'LL COME OUT.
ALL RIGHT. MEET ME AT THE DUKLYON CAFÉ BY THE TRAIN STATION.
UM, OKAY. SEE YA.
KLACK
カチャ
HEY, CHI.
I'M GOING OUT FOR A LITTLE WHILE.
CHI.
CHI.

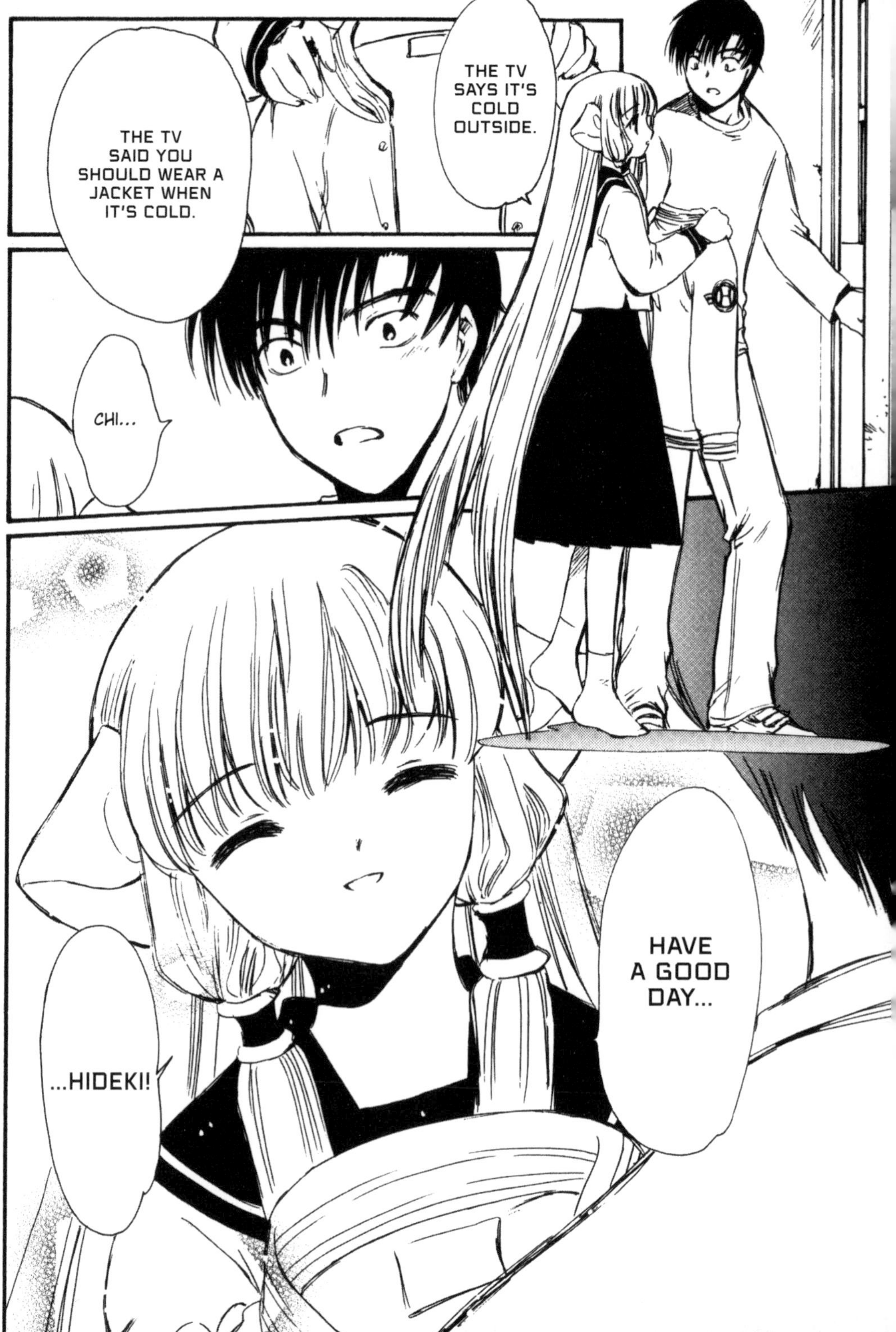
THE TV SAYS IT'S COLD OUTSIDE.
THE TV SAID YOU SHOULD WEAR A JACKET WHEN IT'S COLD.
CHI...
HAVE A GOOD DAY...
...HIDEKI!

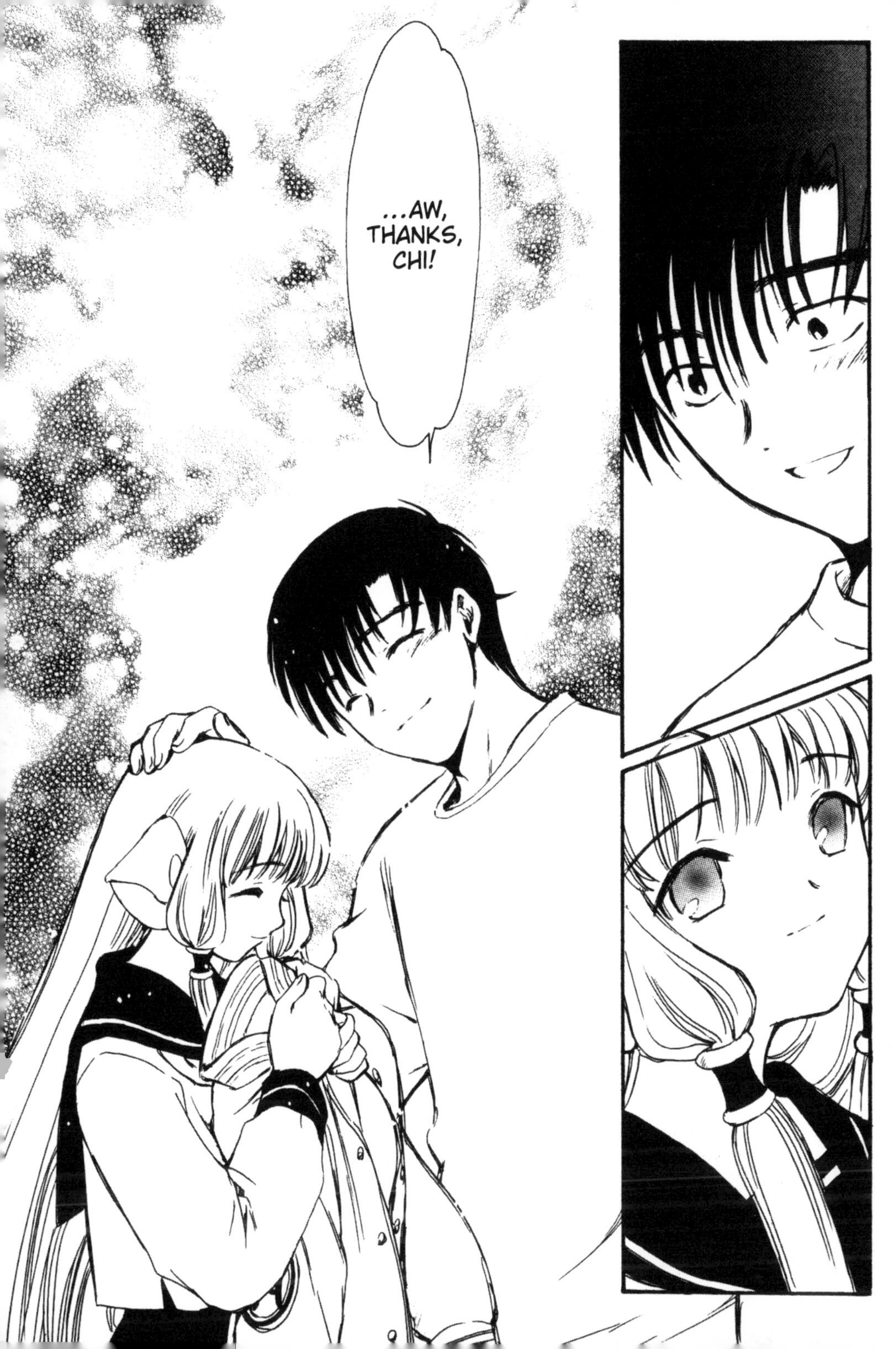
...AW, THANKS, CHI!

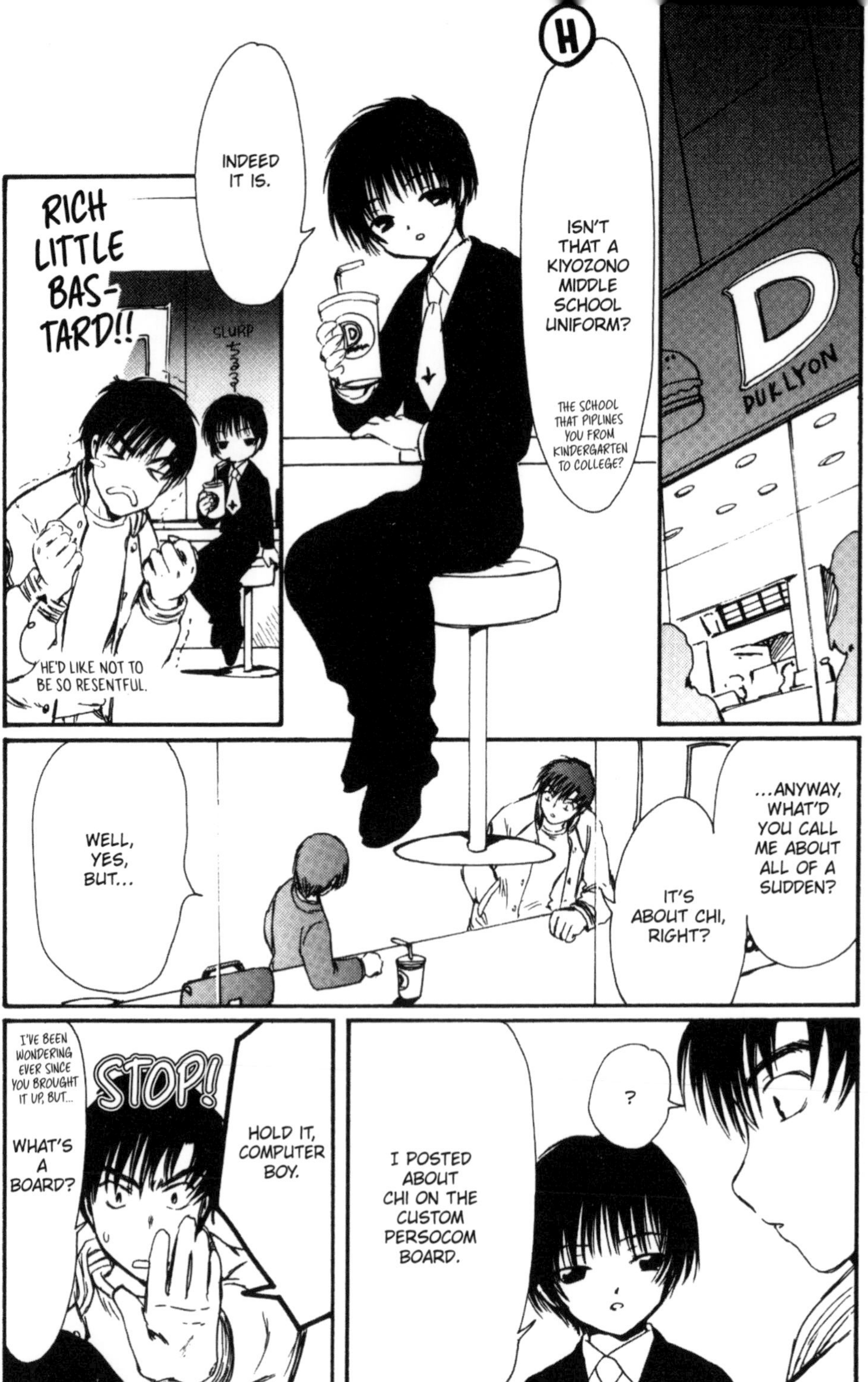
H
DUKLYON
ISN'T THAT A KIYOZONO MIDDLE SCHOOL UNIFORM?
THE SCHOOL THAT PIPLINES YOU FROM KINDERGARTEN TO COLLEGE?
INDEED IT IS.
SLURP
RICH LITTLE BAS-TARD!!
HE'D LIKE NOT TO BE SO RESENTFUL.
...ANYWAY, WHAT'D YOU CALL ME ABOUT ALL OF A SUDDEN?
IT'S ABOUT CHI, RIGHT?
WELL, YES, BUT...
?
I POSTED ABOUT CHI ON THE CUSTOM PERSOCOM BOARD.
HOLD IT, COMPUTER BOY.
STOP!
I'VE BEEN WONDERING EVER SINCE YOU BROUGHT IT UP, BUT...
WHAT'S A BOARD?

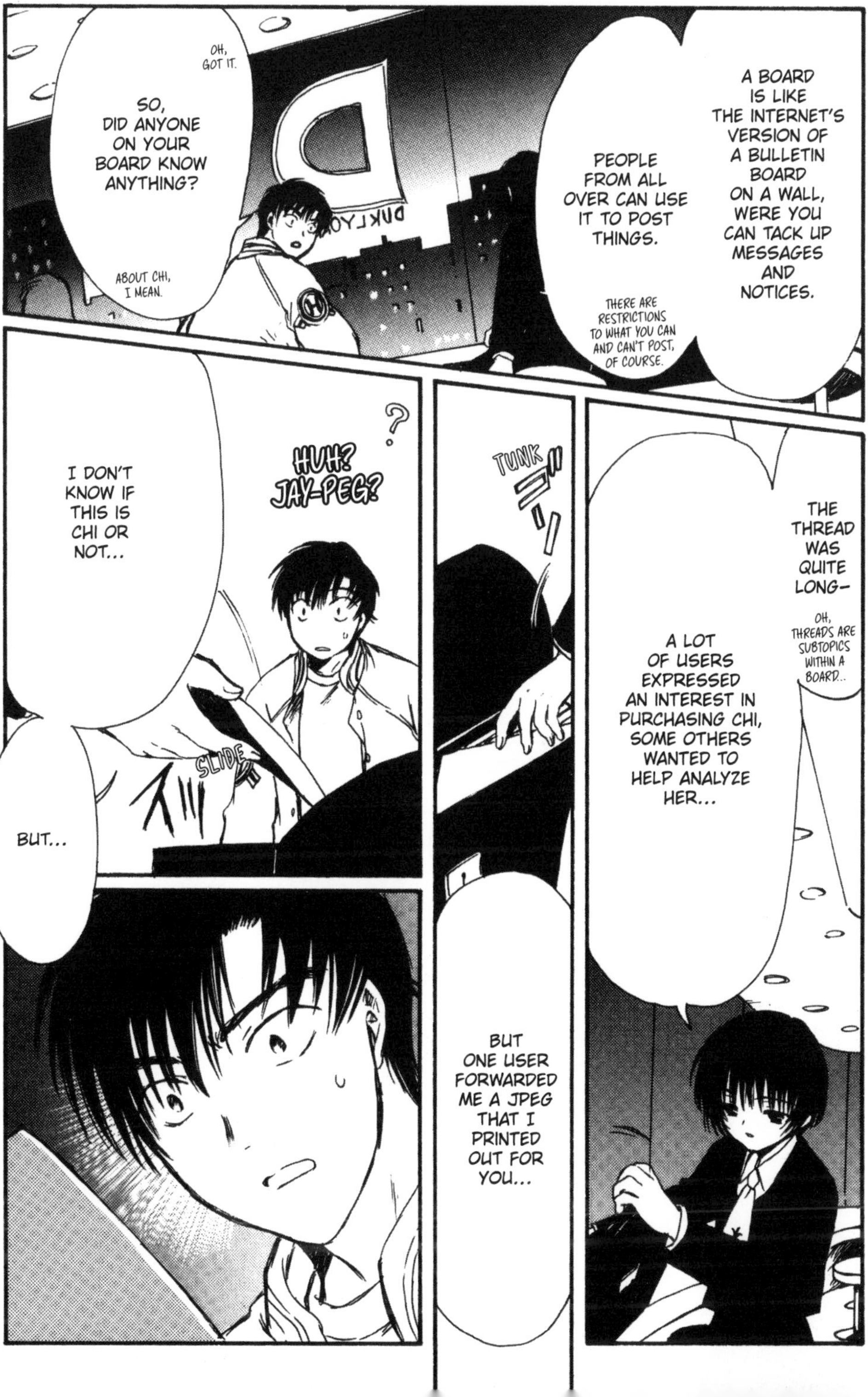
A BOARD IS LIKE THE INTERNET'S VERSION OF A BULLETIN BOARD ON A WALL, WERE YOU CAN TACK UP MESSAGES AND NOTICES.
PEOPLE FROM ALL OVER CAN USE IT TO POST THINGS.
THERE ARE RESTRICTIONS TO WHAT YOU CAN AND CAN'T POST, OF COURSE.
OH, GOT IT.
SO, DID ANYONE ON YOUR BOARD KNOW ANYTHING?
ABOUT CHI, I MEAN.
THE THREAD WAS QUITE LONG-
OH, THREADS ARE SUBTOPICS WITHIN A BOARD...
A LOT OF USERS EXPRESSED AN INTEREST IN PURCHASING CHI, SOME OTHERS WANTED TO HELP ANALYZE HER...
TUNK
BUT ONE USER FORWARDED ME A JPEG THAT I PRINTED OUT FOR YOU...
I DON'T KNOW IF THIS IS CHI OR NOT...
?
HUH? JAY-PEG?
SLIDE
BUT...

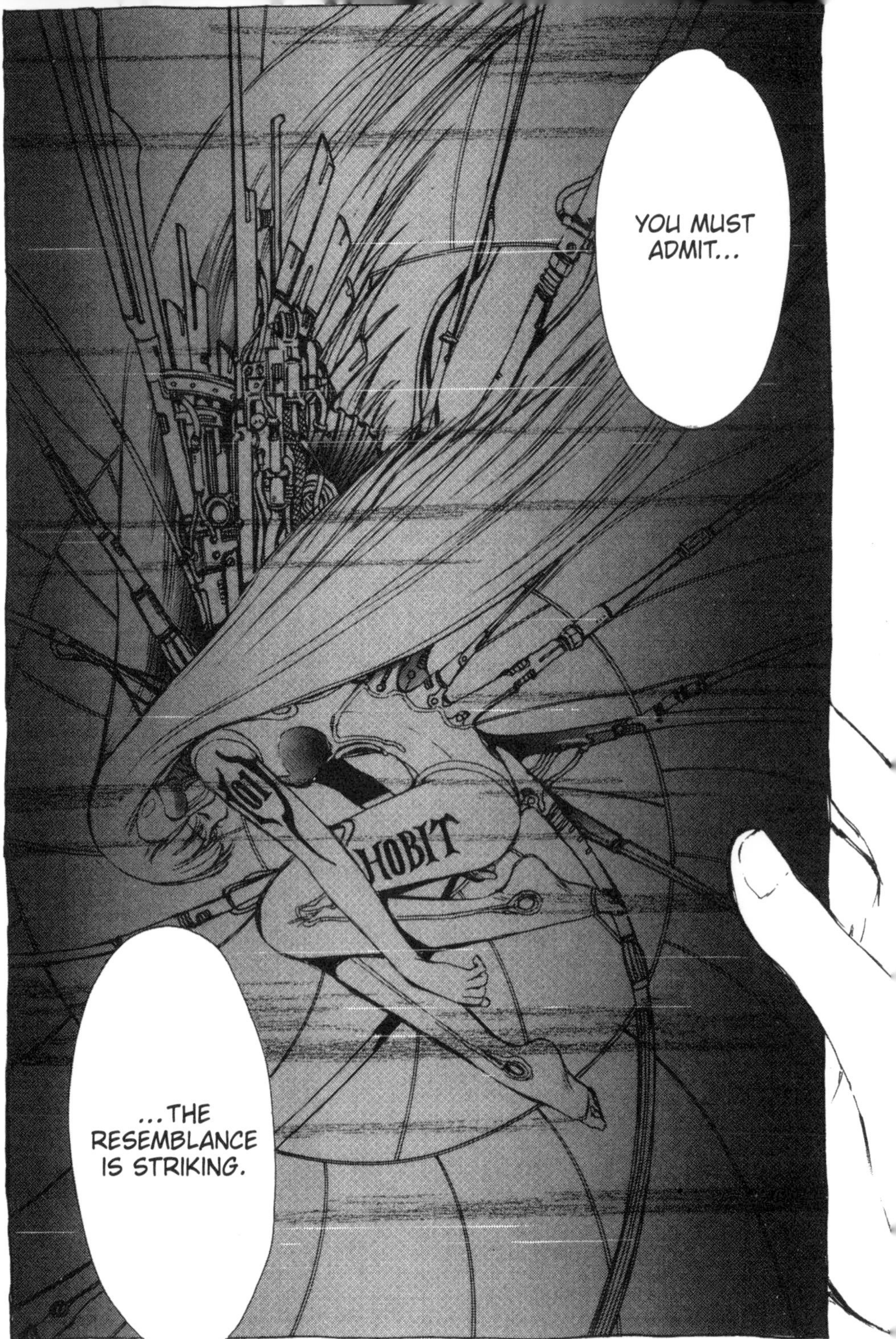
YOU MUST ADMIT...
HOBIT
...THE RESEMBLANCE IS STRIKING.

<chapter.10> end

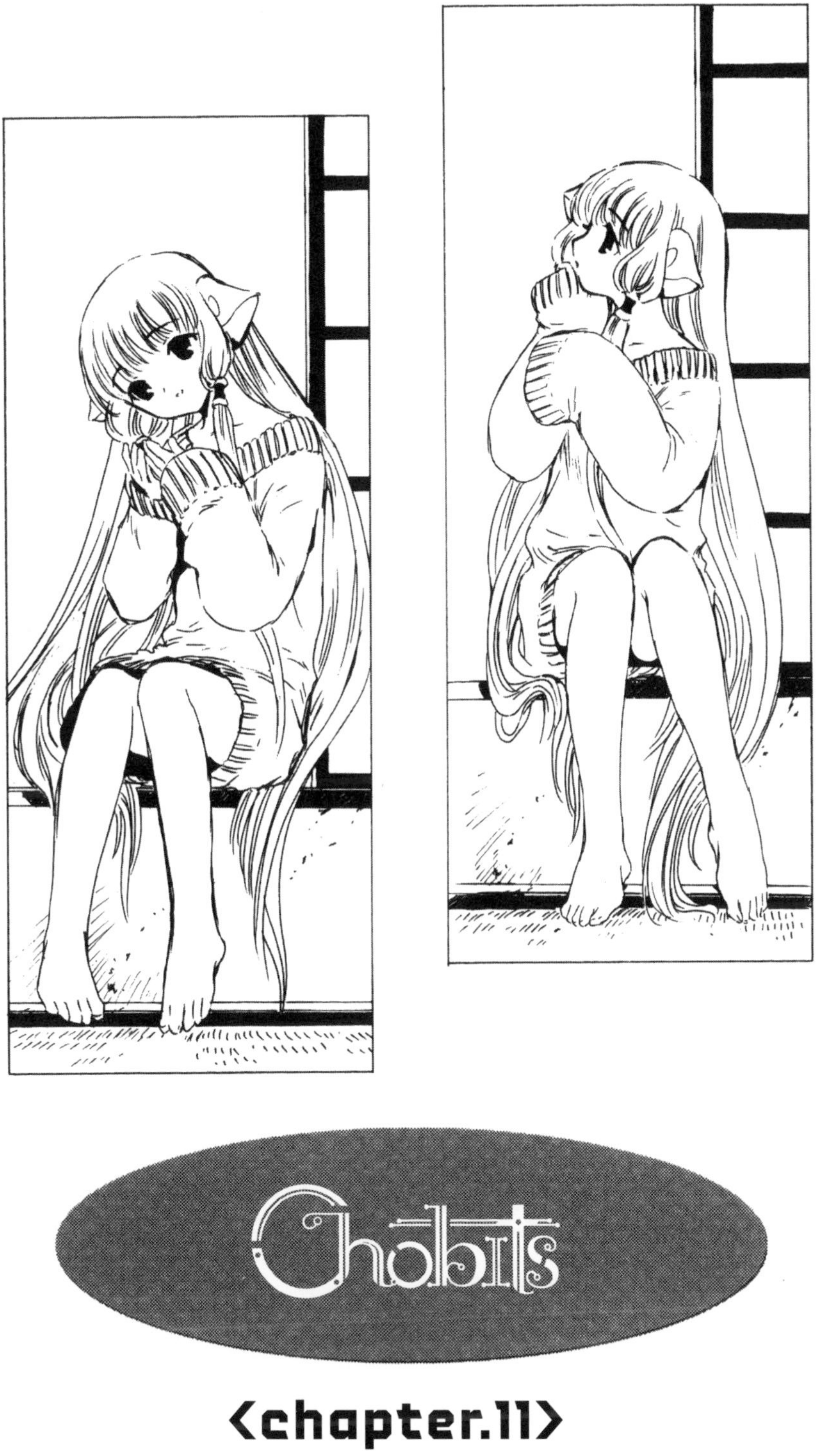

Chobits

<chapter.11>

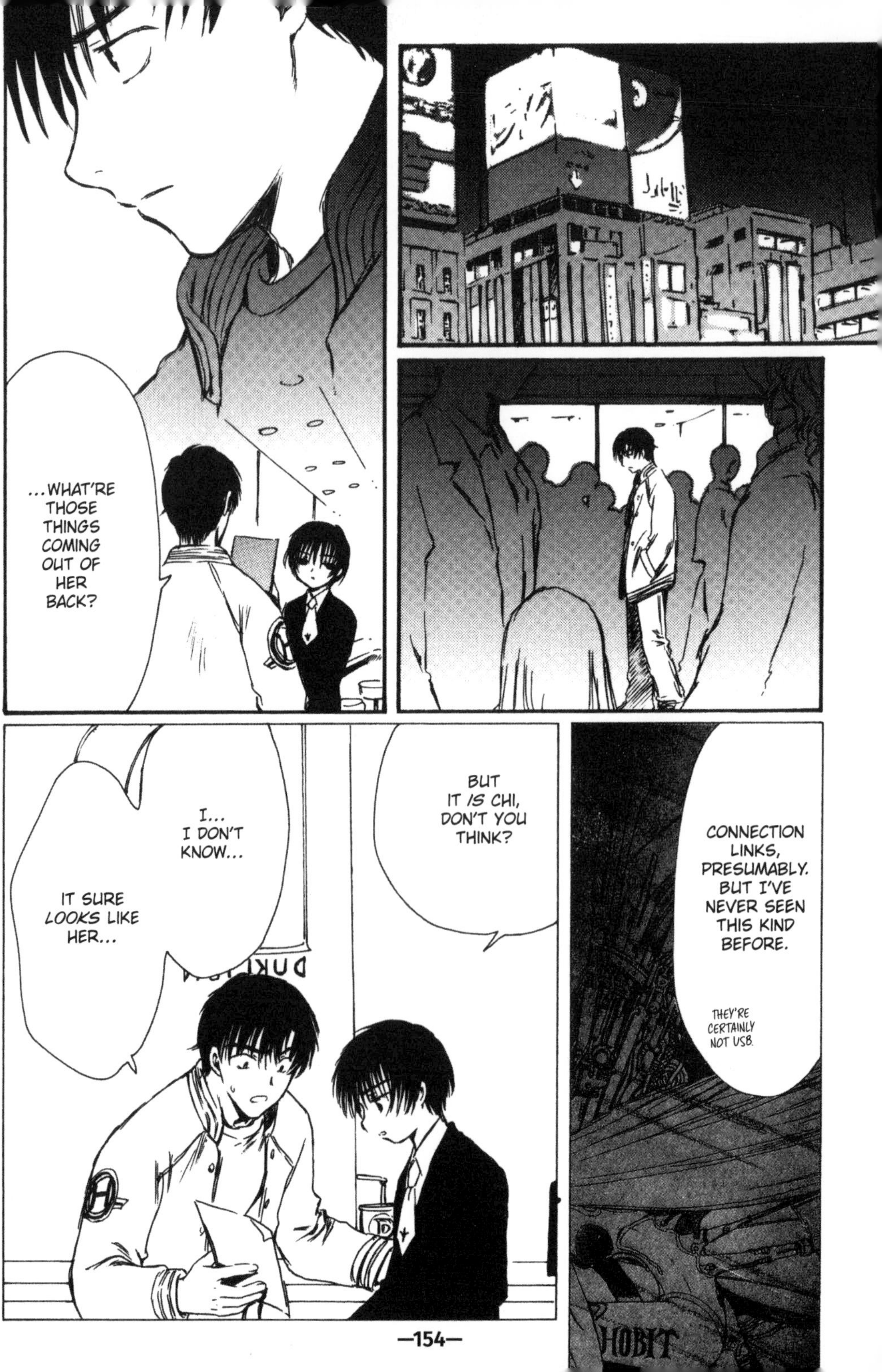
...WHAT'RE THOSE THINGS COMING OUT OF HER BACK?
CONNECTION LINKS, PRESUMABLY. BUT I'VE NEVER SEEN THIS KIND BEFORE.
THEY'RE CERTAINLY NOT USB.
HOBIT
BUT IT *IS* CHI, DON'T YOU THINK?
I... I DON'T KNOW...
IT SURE *LOOKS* LIKE HER...

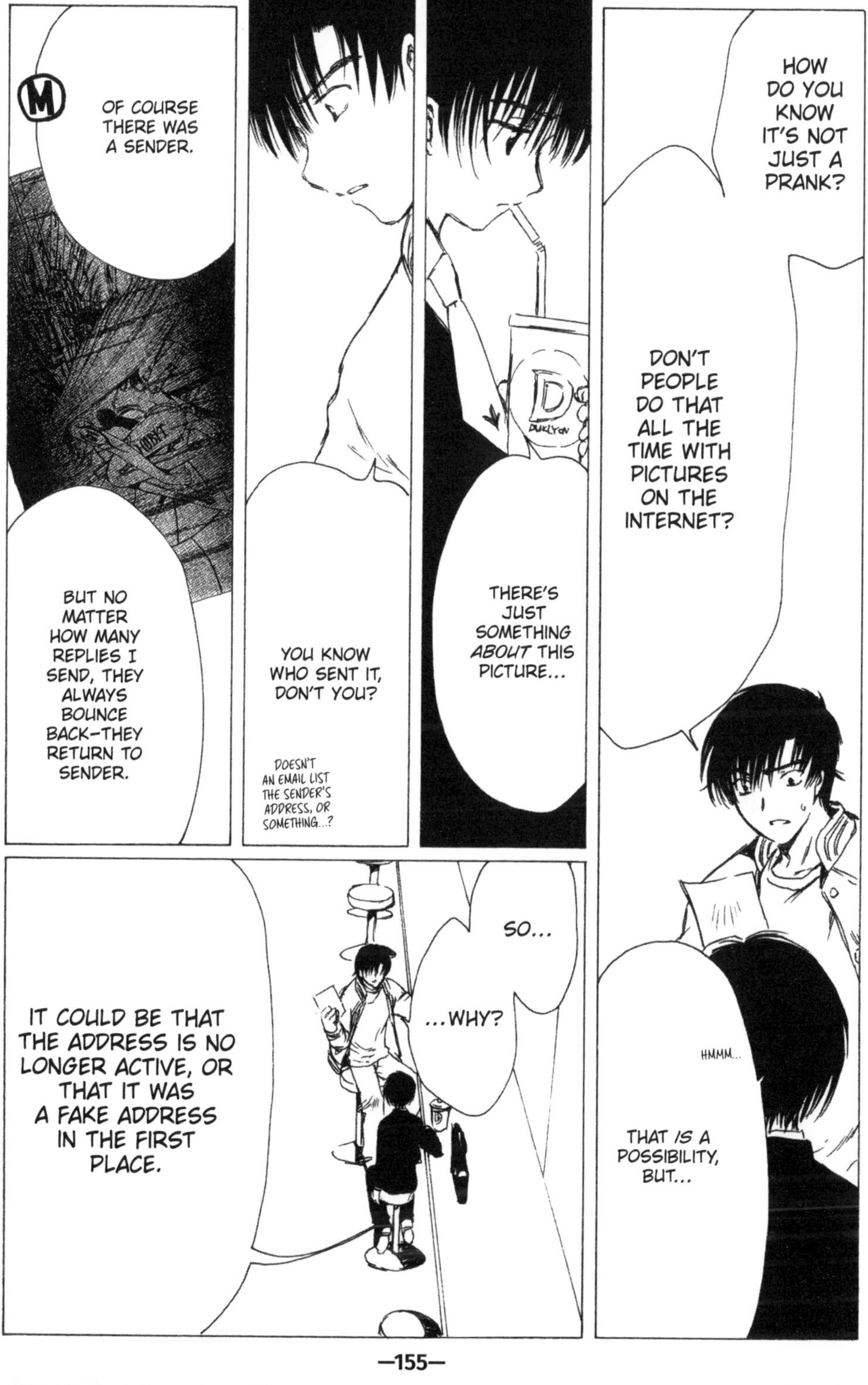
HOW DO YOU KNOW IT'S NOT JUST A PRANK?
DON'T PEOPLE DO THAT ALL THE TIME WITH PICTURES ON THE INTERNET?
HMMM...
THAT *IS* A POSSIBILITY, BUT...
THERE'S JUST SOMETHING *ABOUT* THIS PICTURE...
YOU KNOW WHO SENT IT, DON'T YOU?
DOESN'T AN EMAIL LIST THE SENDER'S ADDRESS, OR SOMETHING...?
OF COURSE THERE WAS A SENDER.
BUT NO MATTER HOW MANY REPLIES I SEND, THEY ALWAYS BOUNCE BACK–THEY RETURN TO SENDER.
SO...
...WHY?
IT COULD BE THAT THE ADDRESS IS NO LONGER ACTIVE, OR THAT IT WAS A FAKE ADDRESS IN THE FIRST PLACE.

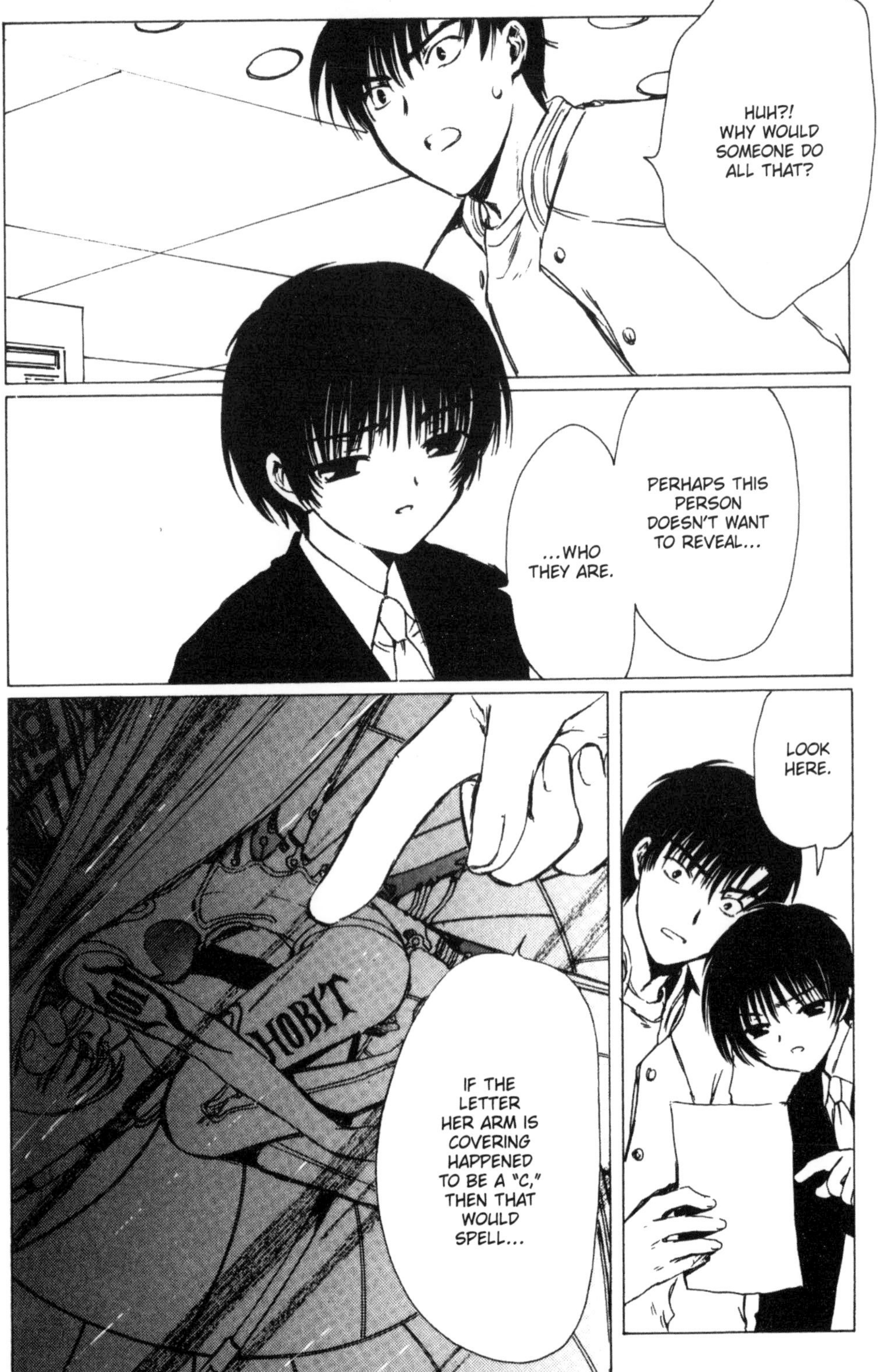
HUH?! WHY WOULD SOMEONE DO ALL THAT?
PERHAPS THIS PERSON DOESN'T WANT TO REVEAL...
...WHO THEY ARE.
LOOK HERE.
HOBIT
IF THE LETTER HER ARM IS COVERING HAPPENED TO BE A "C," THEN THAT WOULD SPELL...

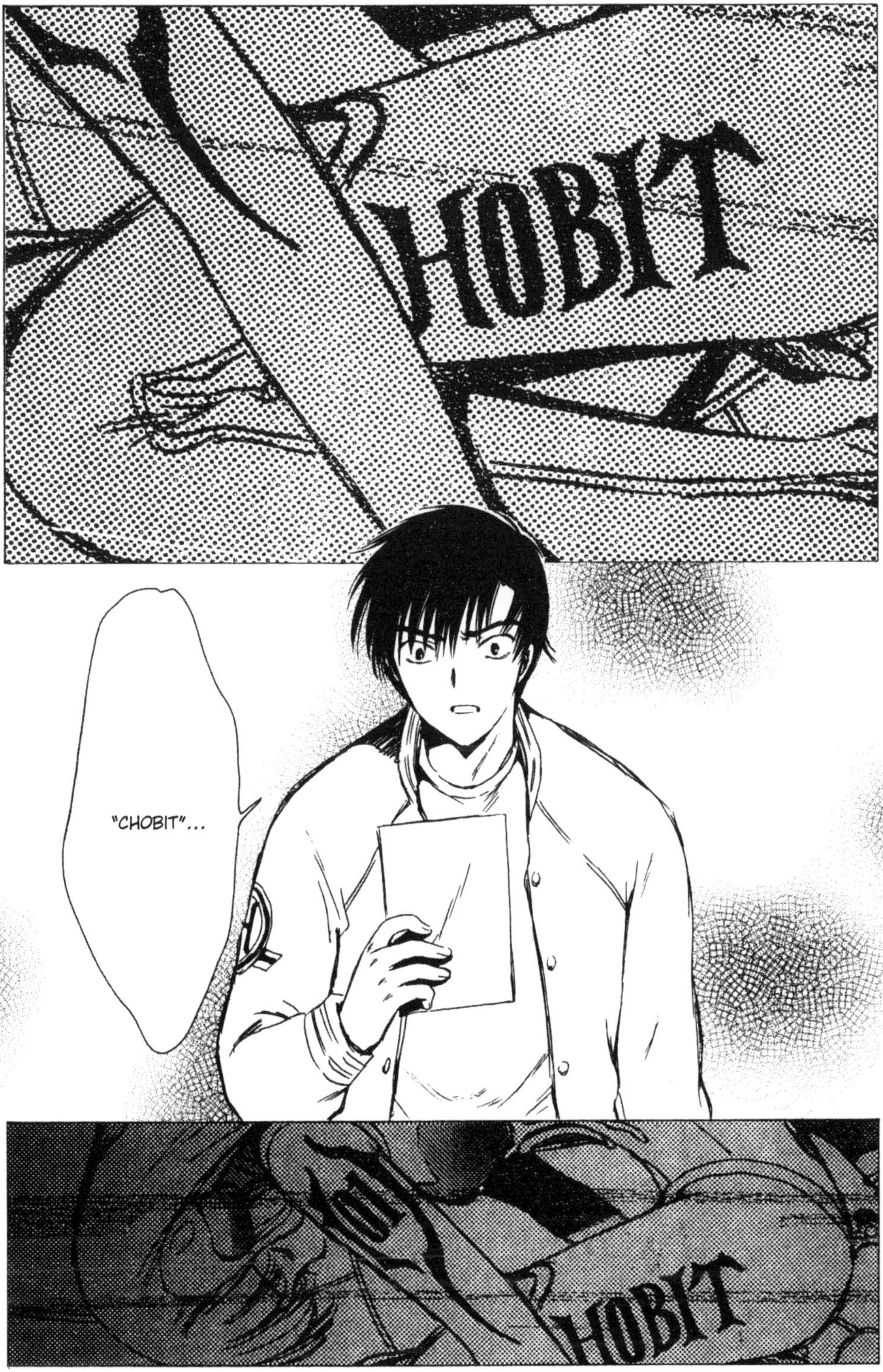
HOBIT
"CHOBIT"...
HOBIT

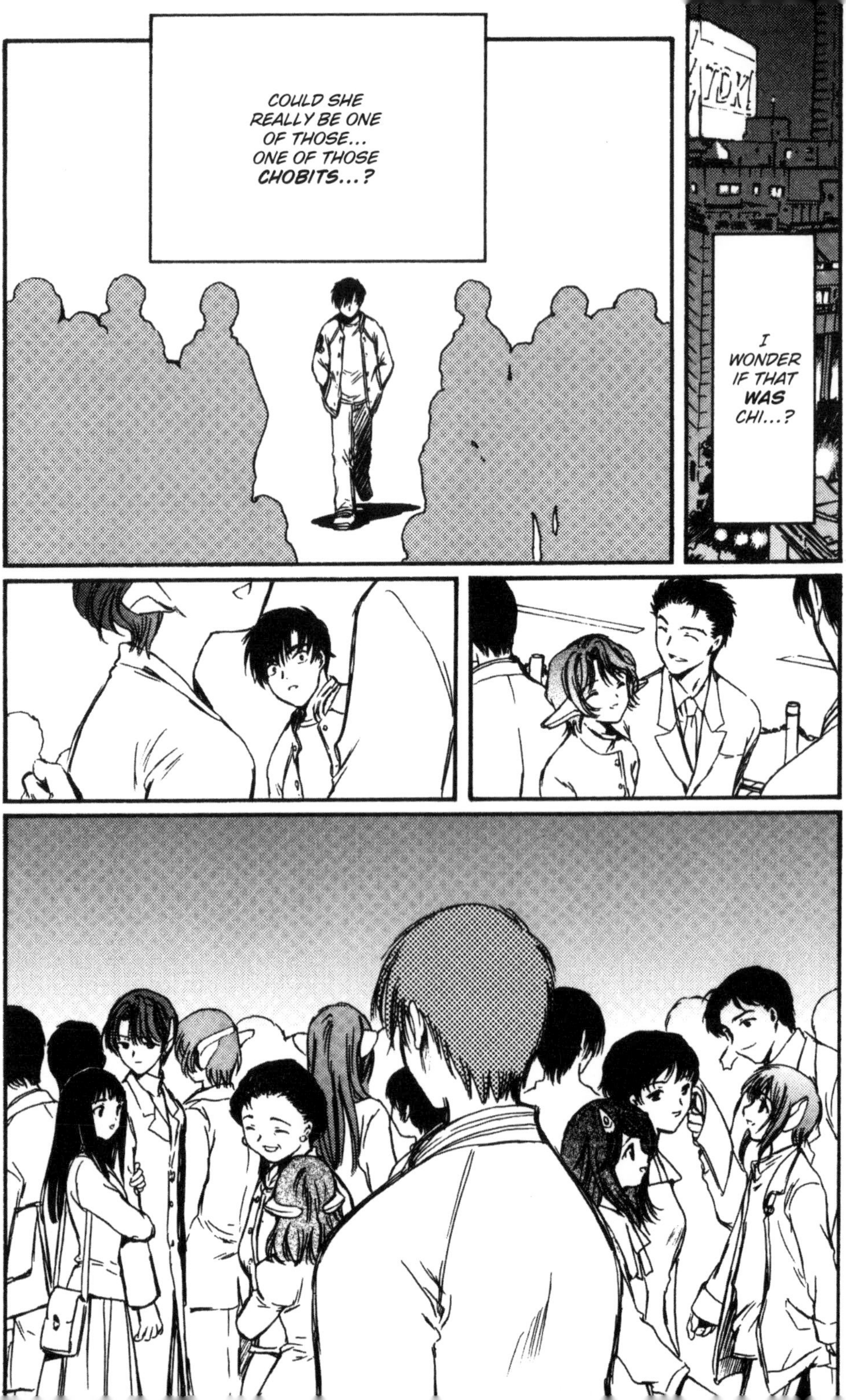
TDK
I WONDER IF THAT WAS CHI...?
COULD SHE REALLY BE ONE OF THOSE... ONE OF THOSE CHOBITS...?

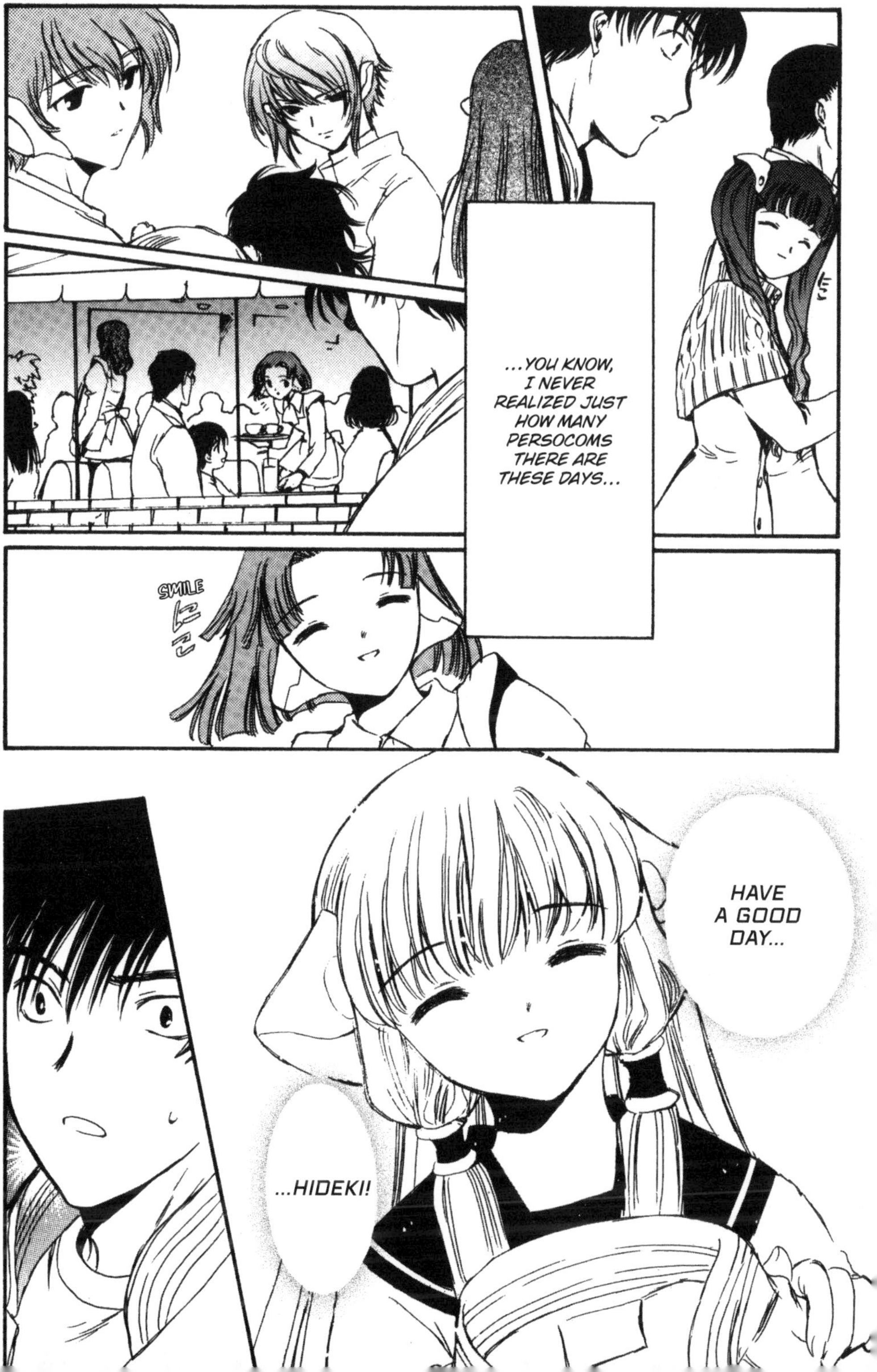
...YOU KNOW, I NEVER REALIZED JUST HOW MANY PERSOCOMS THERE ARE THESE DAYS...
SMILE
にこ
HAVE A GOOD DAY...
...HIDEKI!

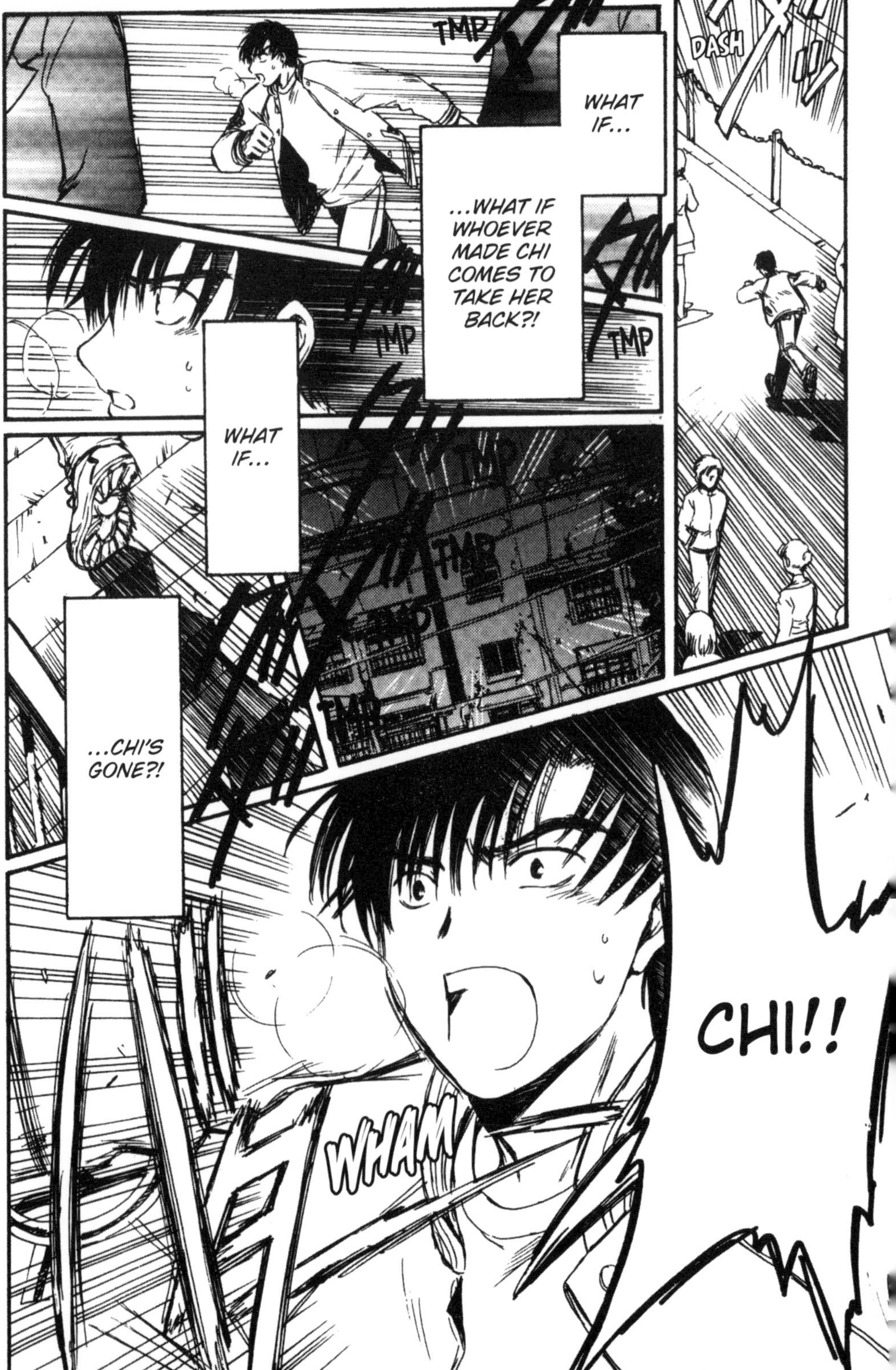
DASH
TMP
WHAT IF...
...WHAT IF WHOEVER MADE CHI COMES TO TAKE HER BACK?!
TMP
TMP
WHAT IF...
TMP
TMP
TMP
...CHI'S GONE?!
CHI!!
WHAM

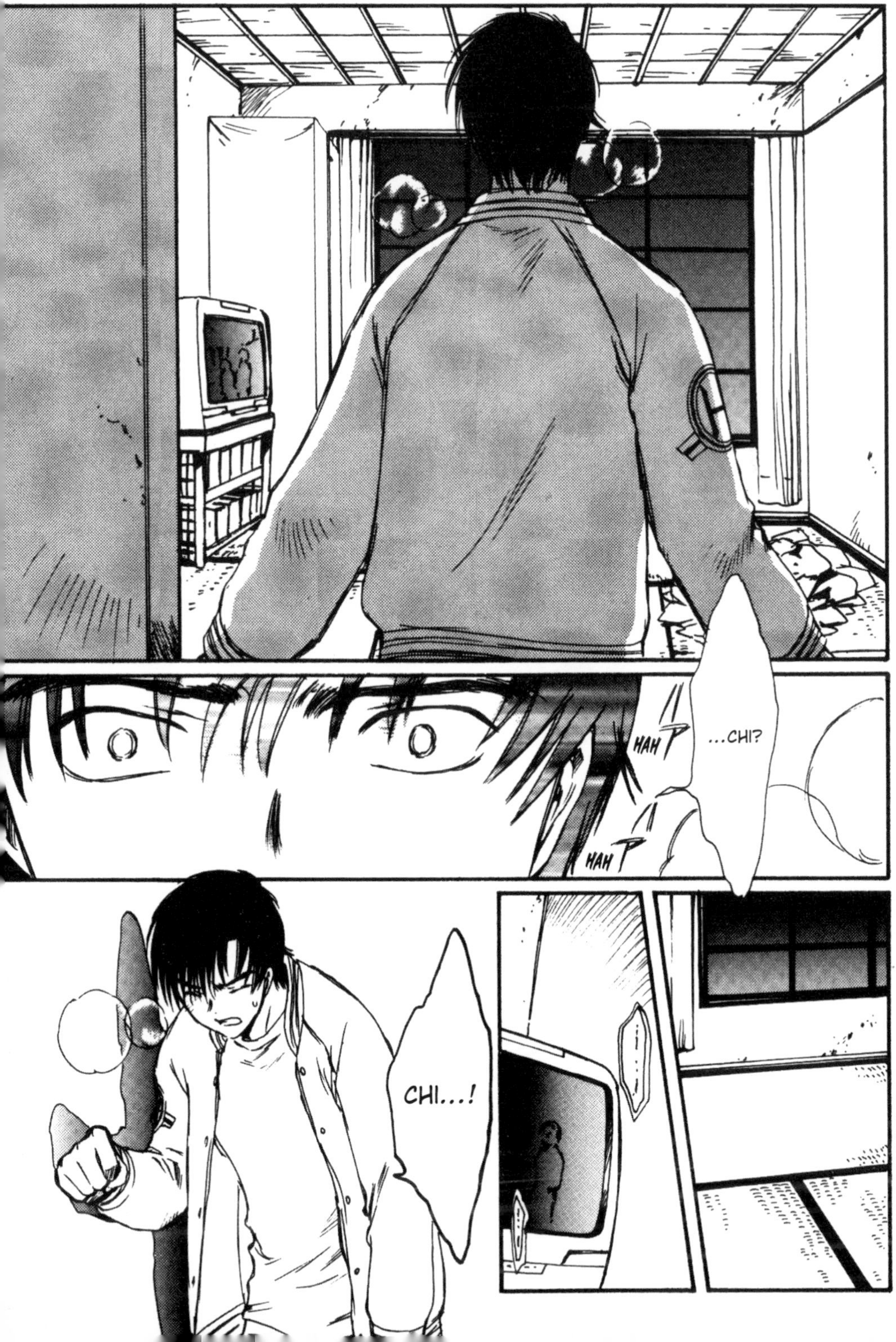
...CHI?
HAH
HAH
CHI...!

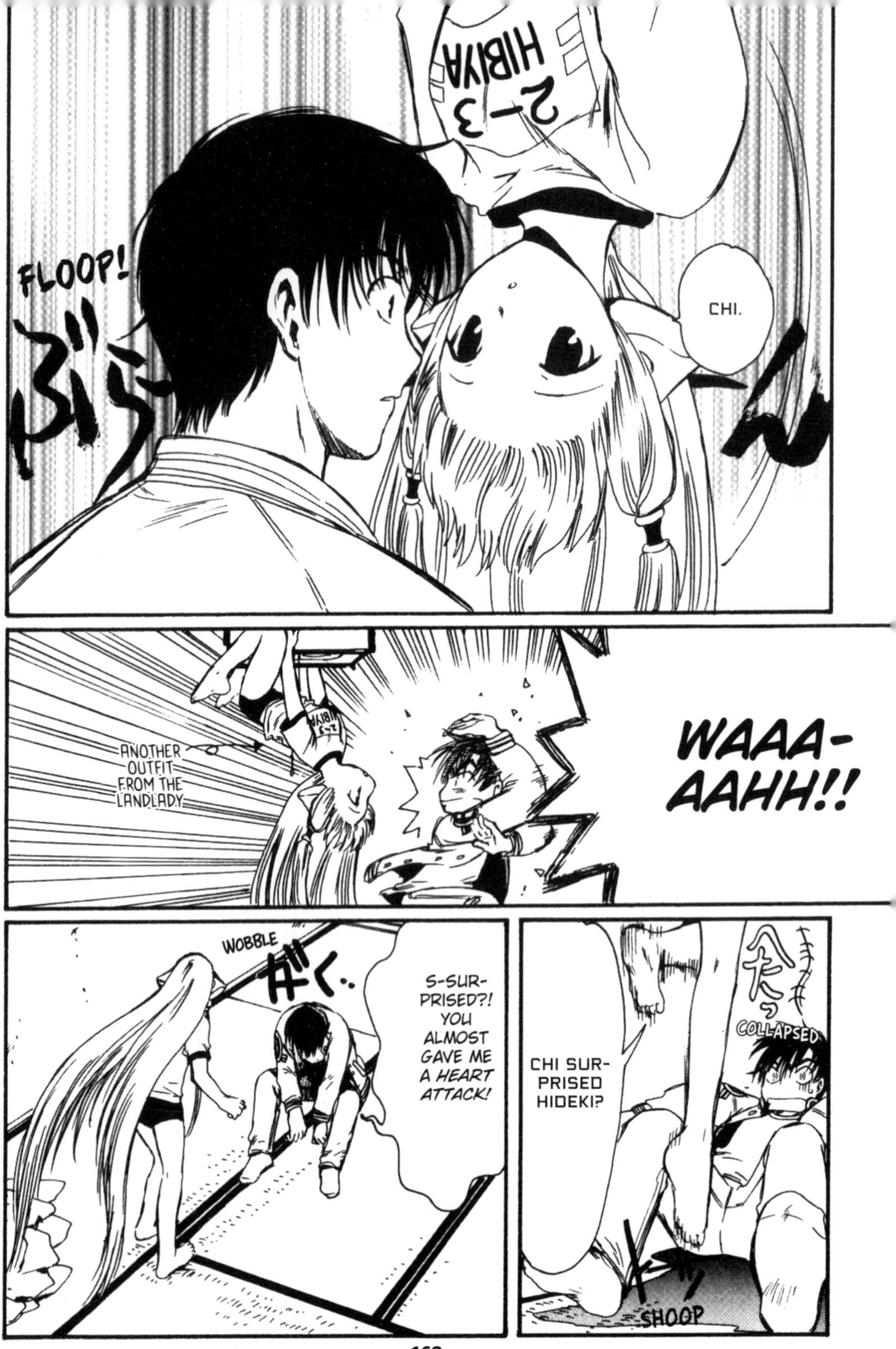
2-3 HIBIYA
FLOOP!
CHI.
ANOTHER OUTFIT FROM THE LANDLADY
WAAA-AAHH!!
COLLAPSED
CHI SURPRISED HIDEKI?
SHOOP
WOBBLE
S-SURPRISED?! YOU ALMOST GAVE ME A *HEART ATTACK!*

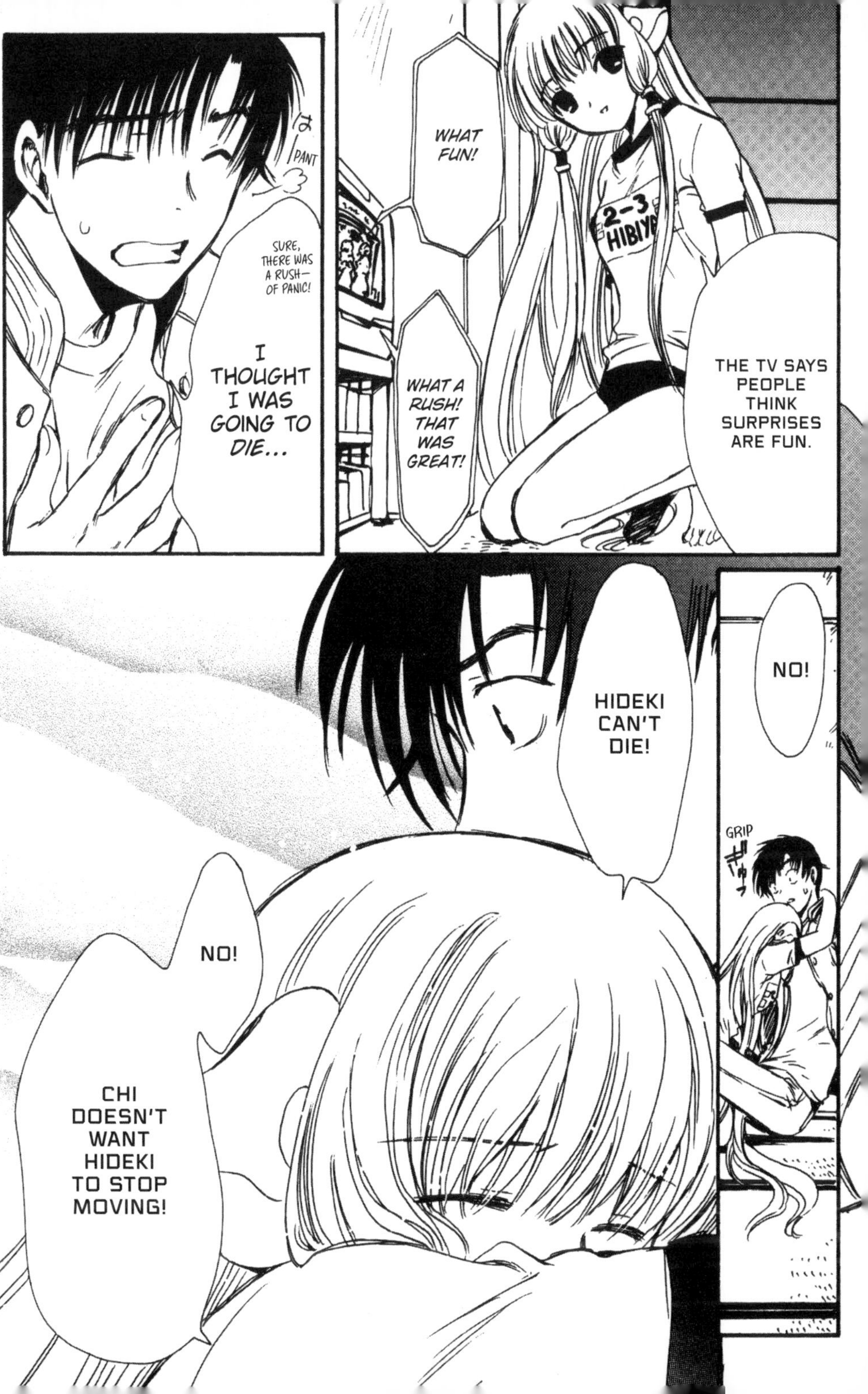
THE TV SAYS PEOPLE THINK SURPRISES ARE FUN.
WHAT FUN!
WHAT A RUSH! THAT WAS GREAT!
PANT
SURE, THERE WAS A RUSH— OF PANIC!
I THOUGHT I WAS GOING TO DIE...
NO!
GRIP
HIDEKI CAN'T DIE!
NO!
CHI DOESN'T WANT HIDEKI TO STOP MOVING!

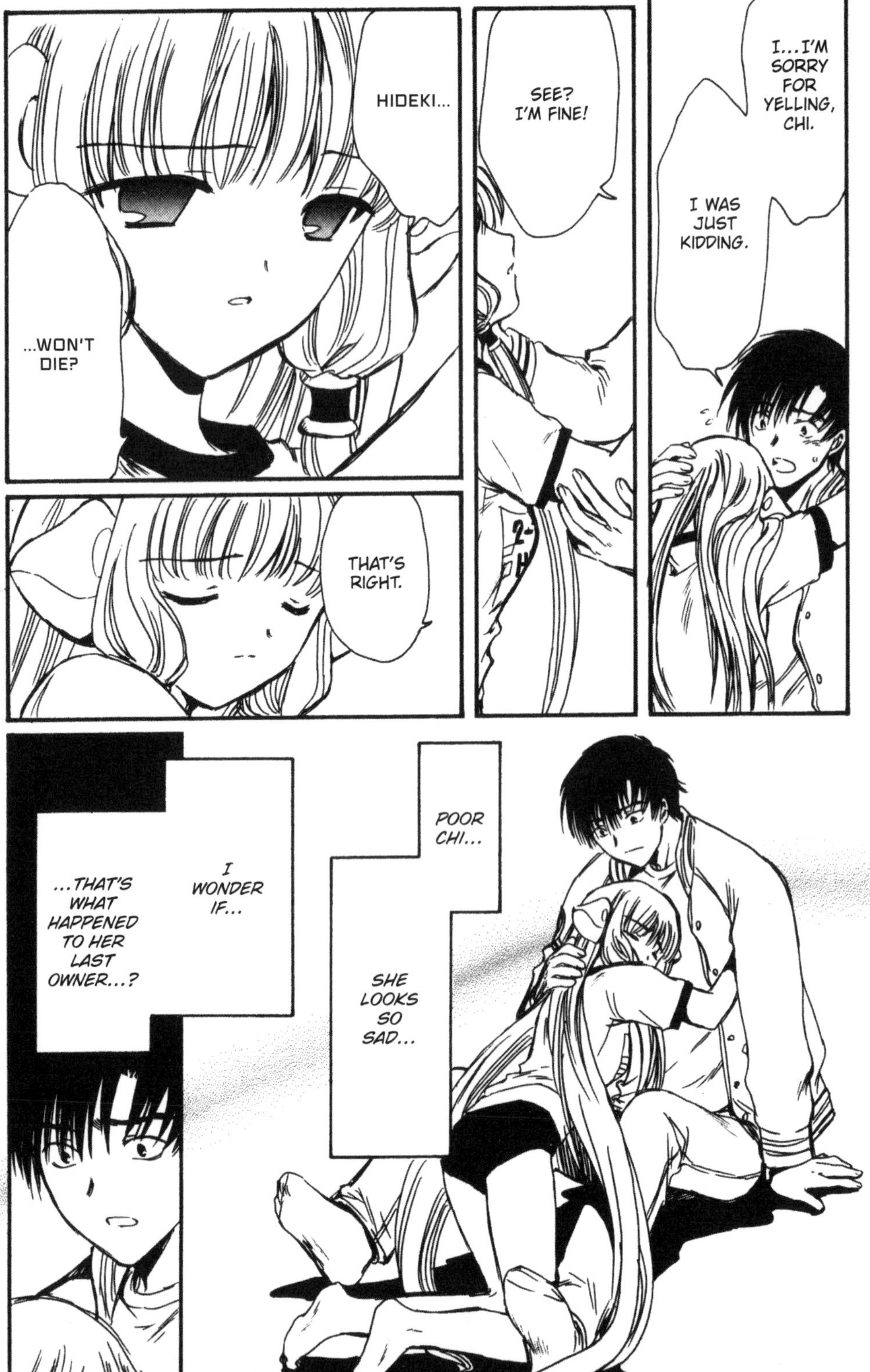
I...I'M SORRY FOR YELLING, CHI.
I WAS JUST KIDDING.
SEE? I'M FINE!
HIDEKI...
...WON'T DIE?
THAT'S RIGHT.
POOR CHI...
SHE LOOKS SO SAD...
I WONDER IF...
...THAT'S WHAT HAPPENED TO HER LAST OWNER...?

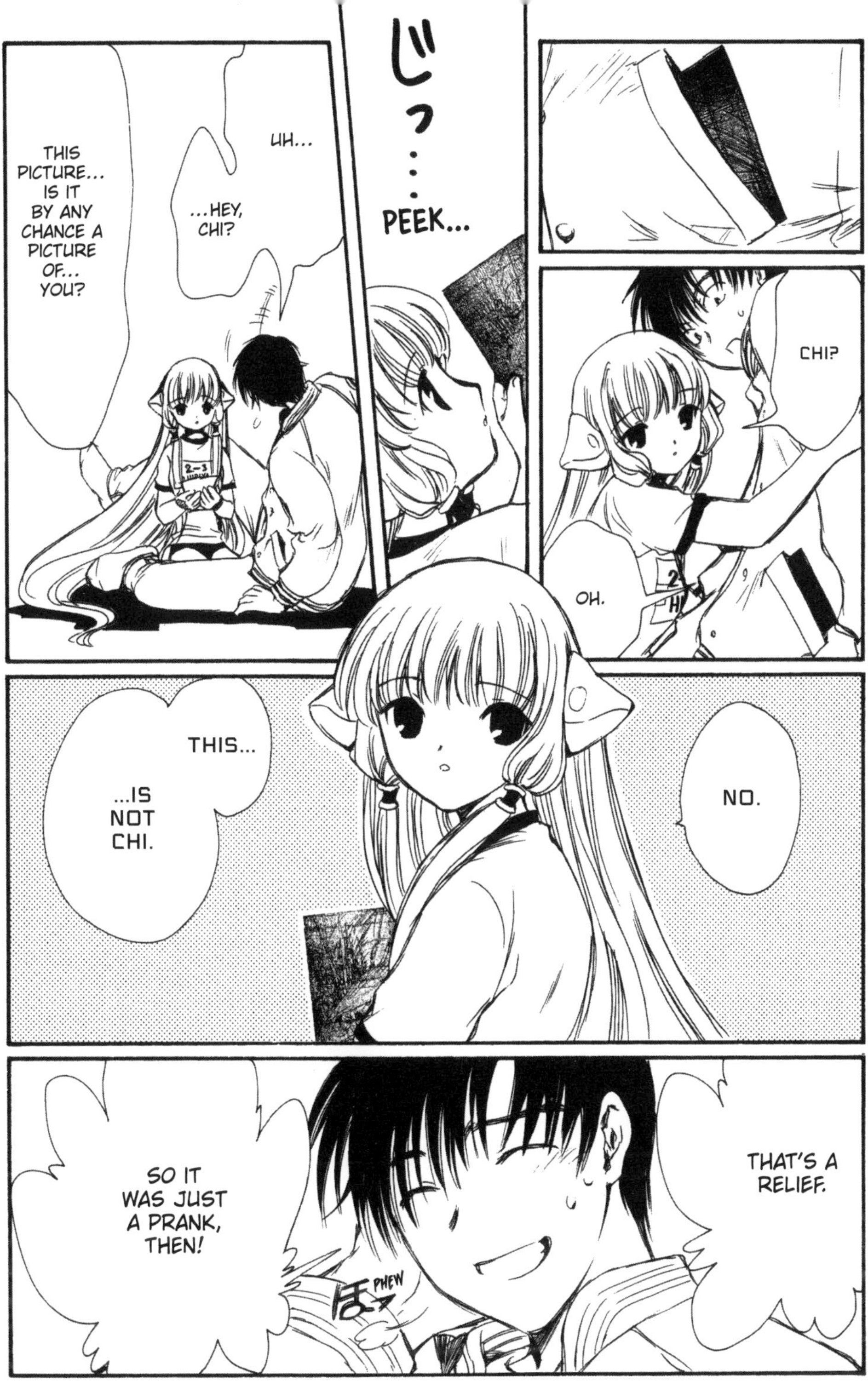

CHI?
OH.
じっ…
PEEK...
UH...
...HEY, CHI?
THIS PICTURE... IS IT BY ANY CHANCE A PICTURE OF... YOU?
NO.
THIS...
...IS NOT CHI.
THAT'S A RELIEF.
SO IT WAS JUST A PRANK, THEN!
ほーっ
PHEW

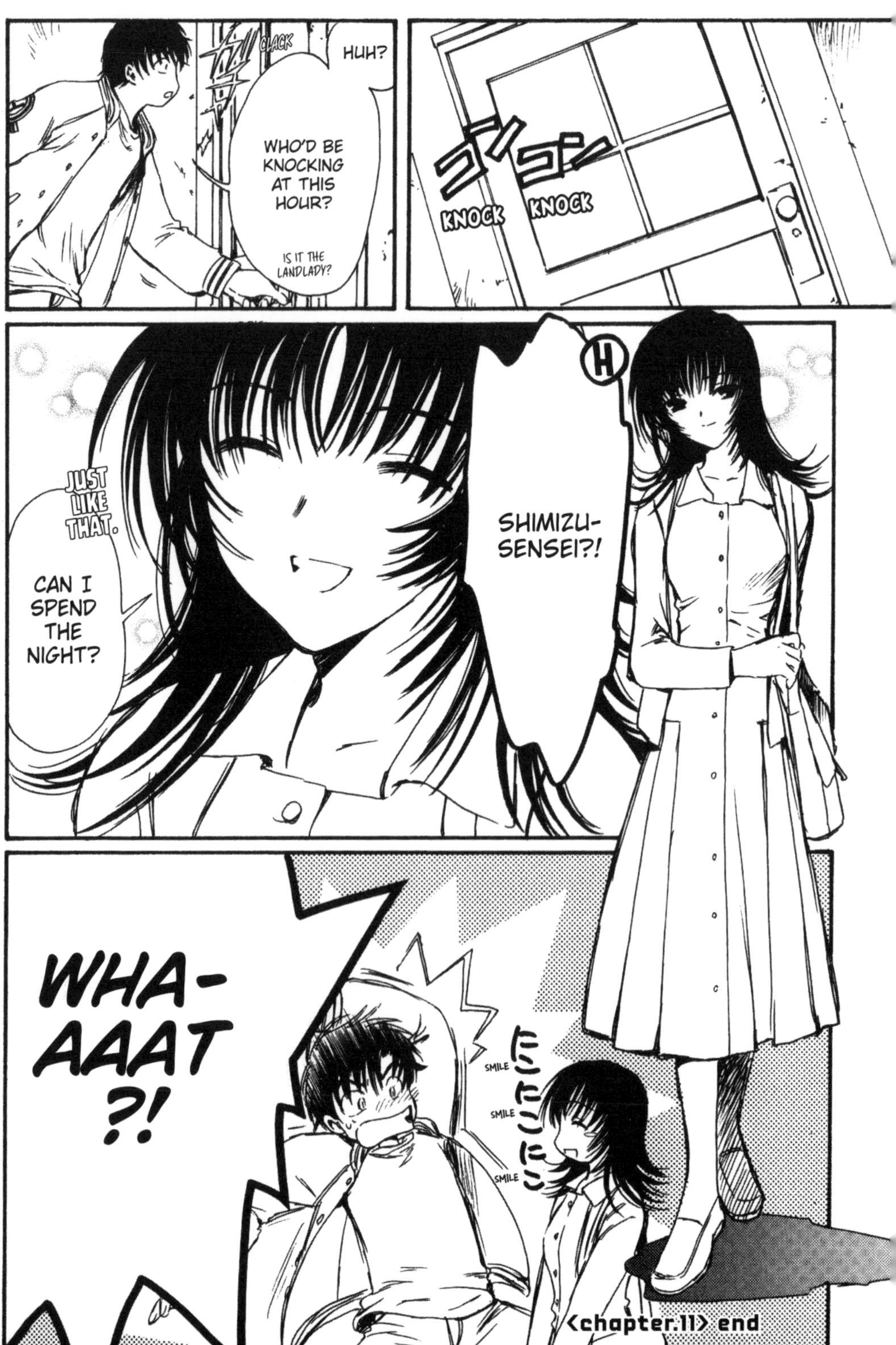
KNOCK KNOCK
CLACK
HUH?
WHO'D BE KNOCKING AT THIS HOUR?
IS IT THE LANDLADY?
H
SHIMIZU-SENSEI?!
JUST LIKE THAT.
CAN I SPEND THE NIGHT?
WHA-AAAT?!
SMILE
SMILE
SMILE
<chapter.11> end

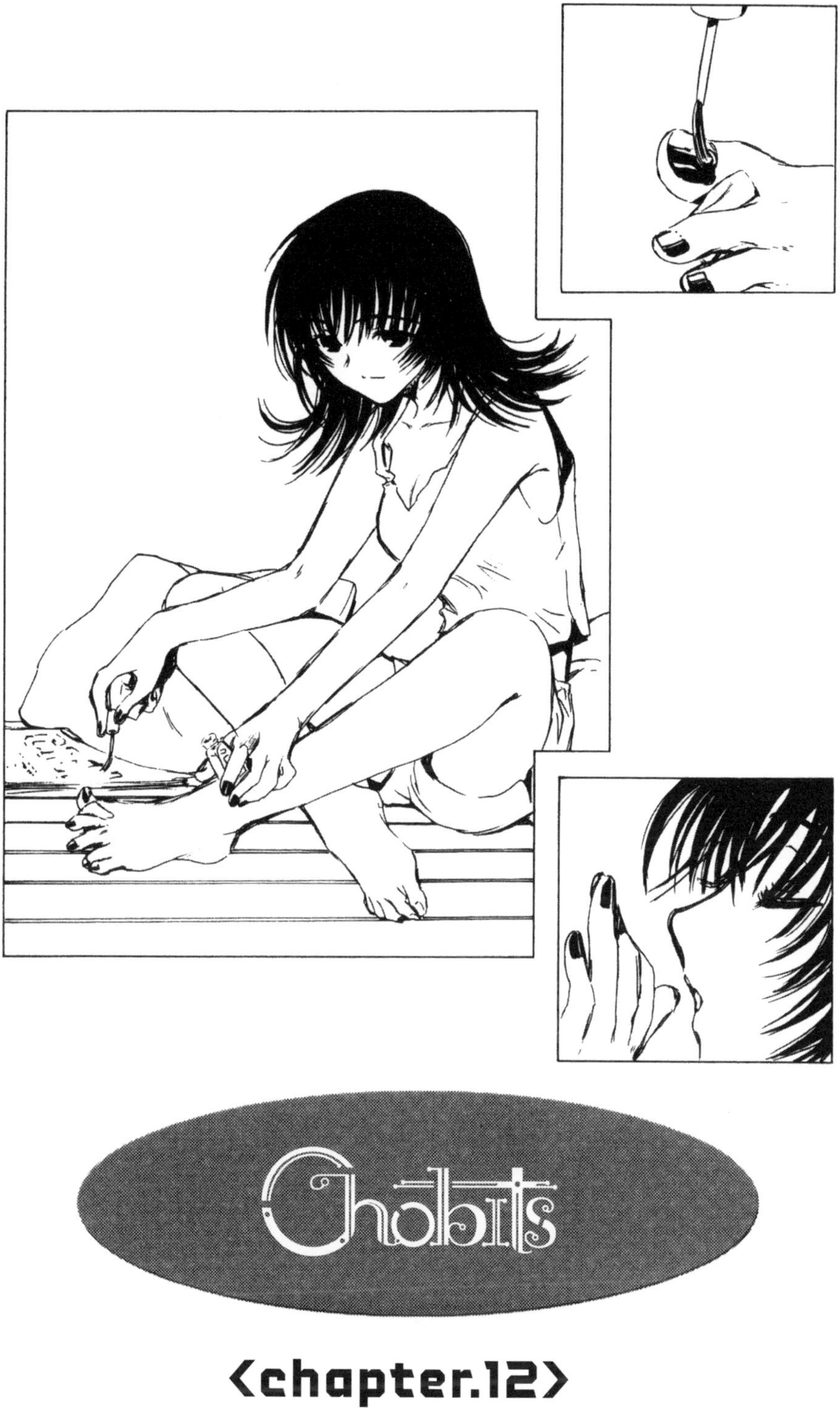

Chobits

<chapter.12>

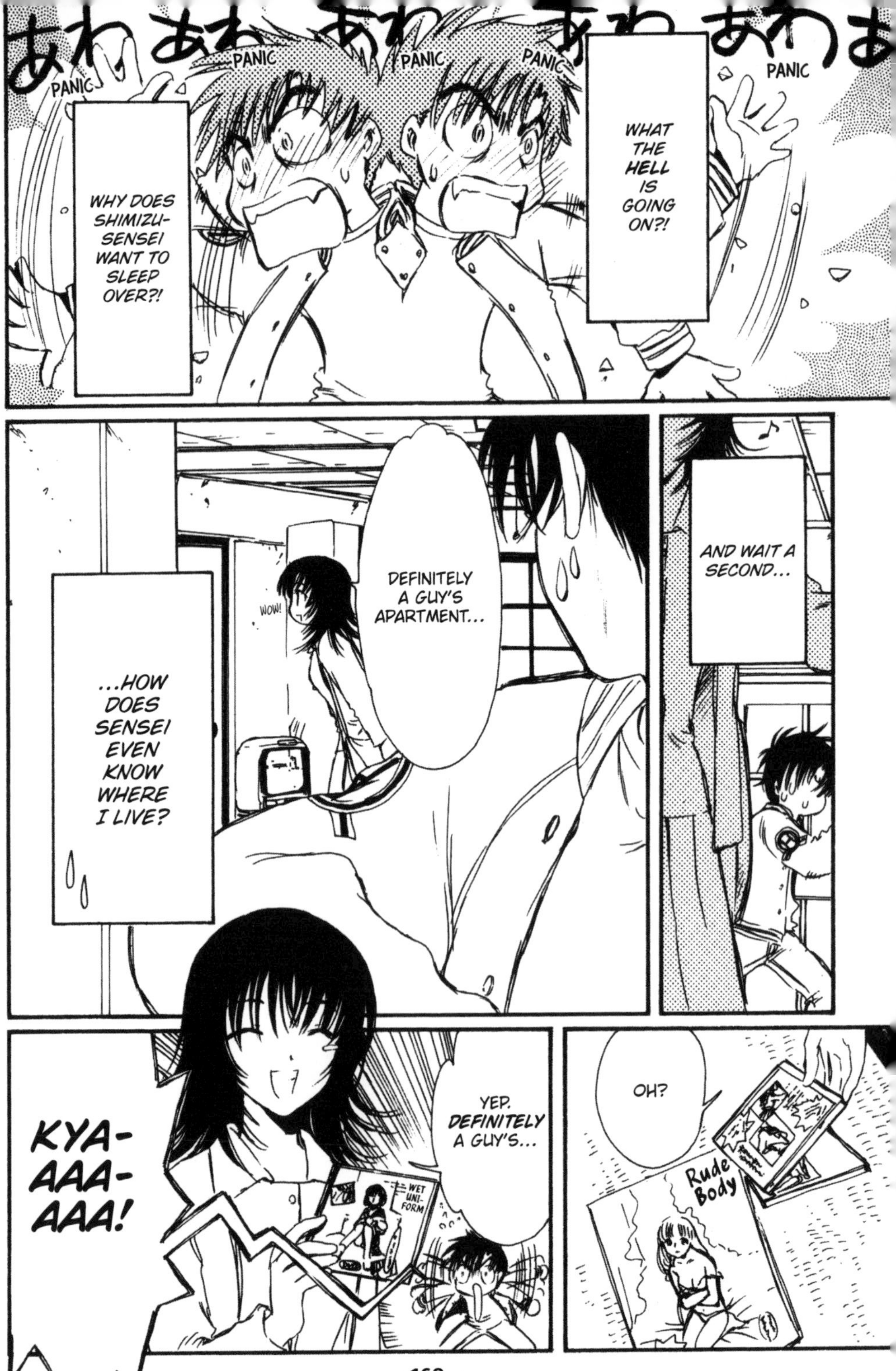
あわ あわ あわ あわ あわ
PANIC
PANIC
PANIC
PANIC
WHAT THE HELL IS GOING ON?!
WHY DOES SHIMIZU-SENSEI WANT TO SLEEP OVER?!
AND WAIT A SECOND...
DEFINITELY A GUY'S APARTMENT...
WOW!
...HOW DOES SENSEI EVEN KNOW WHERE I LIVE?
OH?
Rude Body
YEP. DEFINITELY A GUY'S...
WET UNI-FORM
KYA-AAA-AAA!

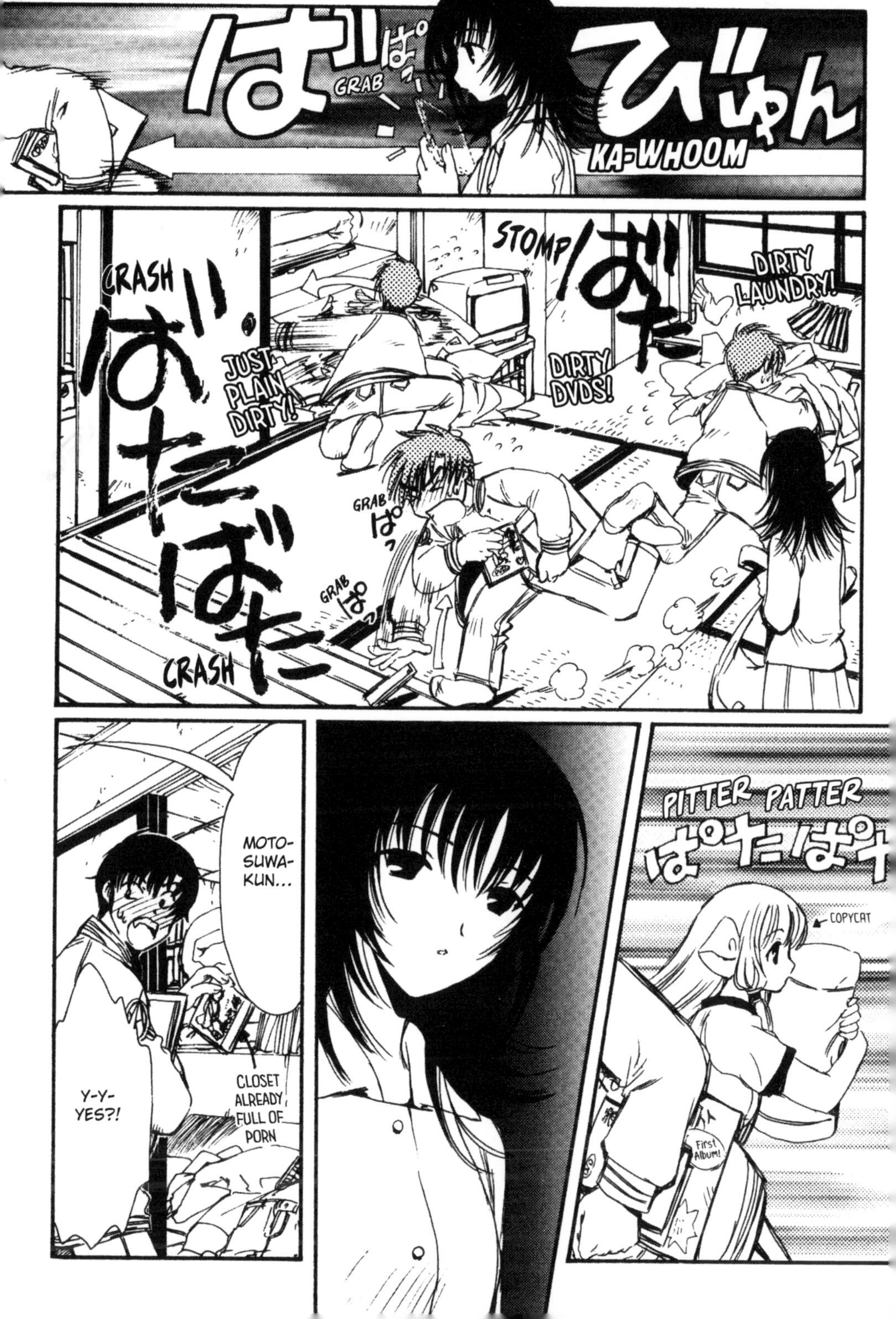

KA-WHOOM
GRAB
DIRTY LAUNDRY!
STOMP
DIRTY DVDS!
JUST PLAIN DIRTY!
CRASH
GRAB
GRAB
CRASH
PITTER PATTER
COPYCAT
First Album!
MOTO-SUWA-KUN...
CLOSET ALREADY FULL OF PORN
Y-Y-YES?!

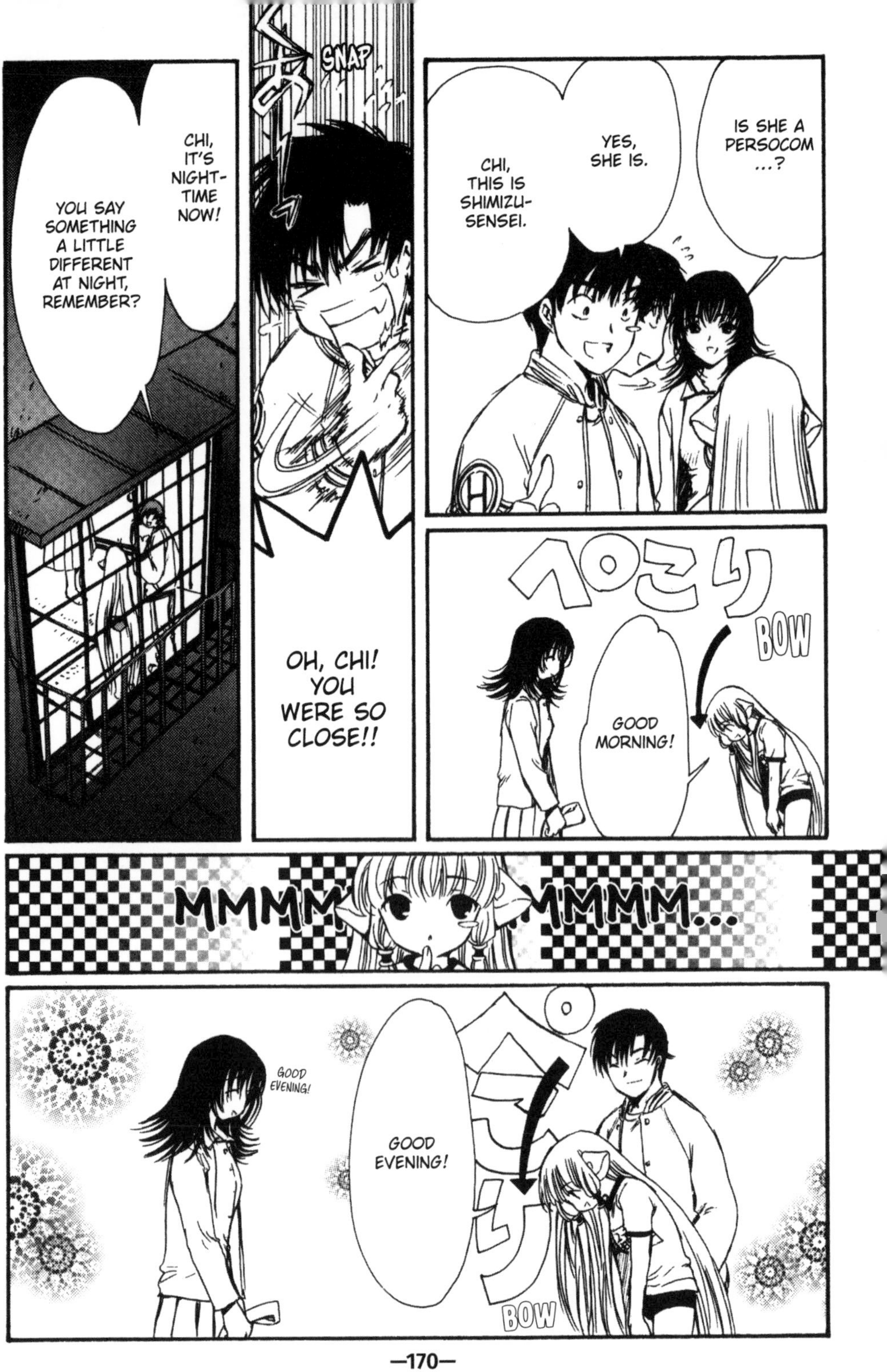
IS SHE A PERSOCOM ...?
YES, SHE IS.
CHI, THIS IS SHIMIZU-SENSEI.
ぺこり
BOW
GOOD MORNING!
SNAP
OH, CHI! YOU WERE SO CLOSE!!
CHI, IT'S NIGHT-TIME NOW!
YOU SAY SOMETHING A LITTLE DIFFERENT AT NIGHT, REMEMBER?
MMMM...MMMMM...
BOW
GOOD EVENING!
GOOD EVENING!

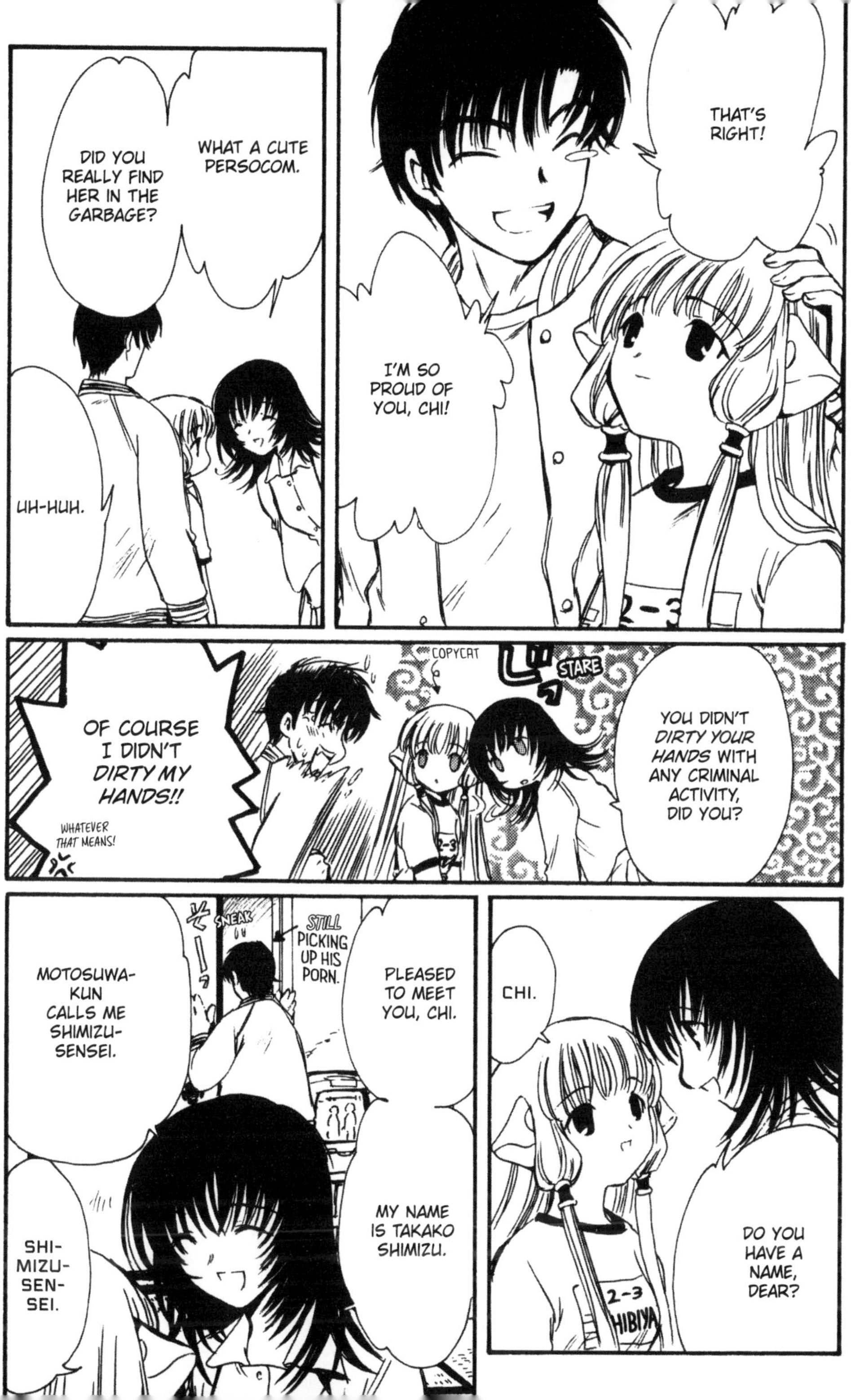
THAT'S RIGHT!
I'M SO PROUD OF YOU, CHI!
WHAT A CUTE PERSOCOM.
DID YOU REALLY FIND HER IN THE GARBAGE?
UH-HUH.
STARE
COPYCAT
YOU DIDN'T DIRTY YOUR HANDS WITH ANY CRIMINAL ACTIVITY, DID YOU?
OF COURSE I DIDN'T DIRTY MY HANDS!!
WHATEVER THAT MEANS!
CHI.
DO YOU HAVE A NAME, DEAR?
PLEASED TO MEET YOU, CHI.
MY NAME IS TAKAKO SHIMIZU.
STILL PICKING UP HIS PORN.
SNEAK
MOTOSUWA-KUN CALLS ME SHIMIZU-SENSEI.
SHIMI-ZU-SEN-SEI.

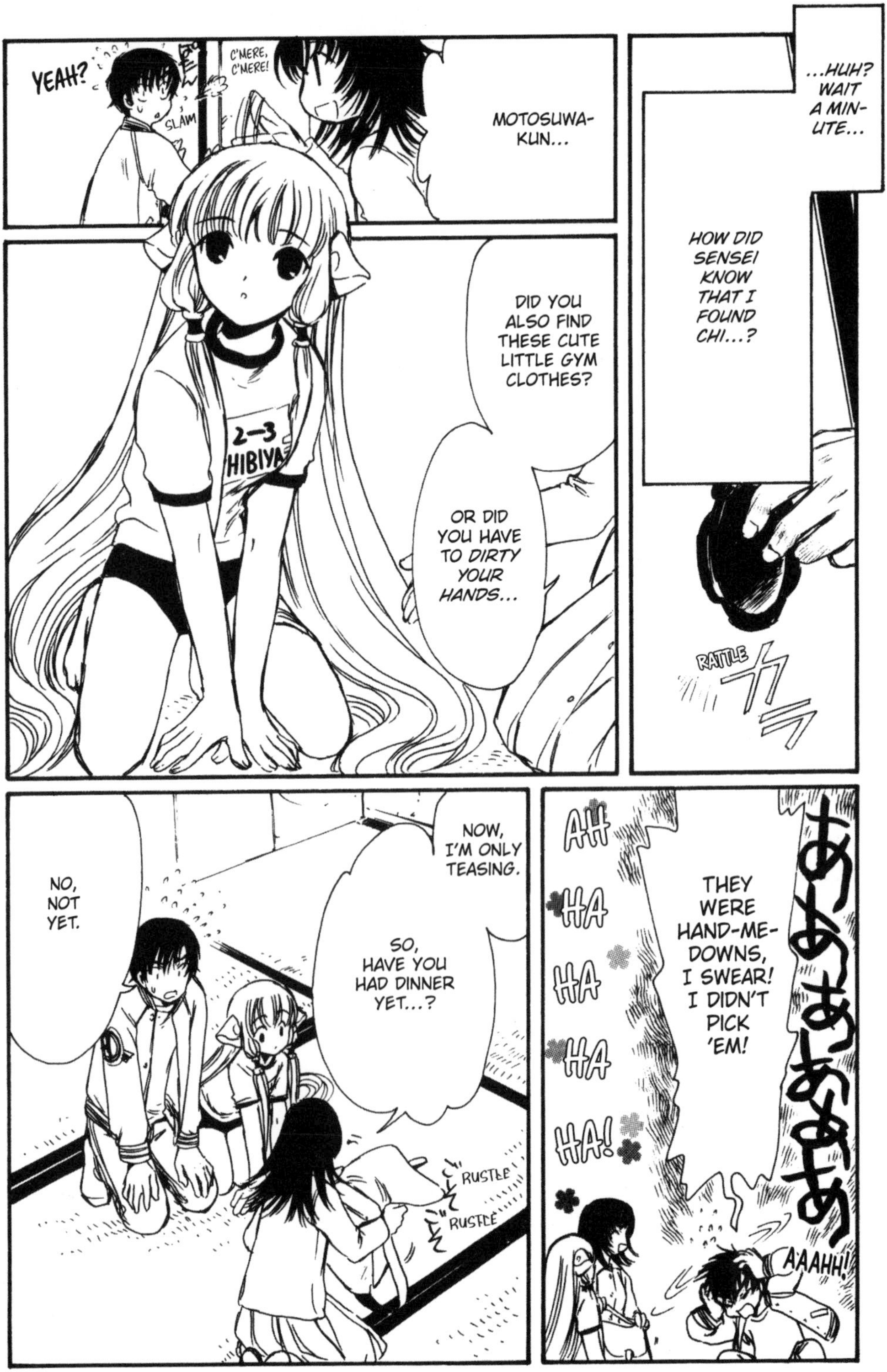
...HUH? WAIT A MIN-UTE...
HOW DID SENSEI KNOW THAT I FOUND CHI...?
RATTLE
MOTOSUWA-KUN...
C'MERE, C'MERE!
YEAH?
SLAM
DID YOU ALSO FIND THESE CUTE LITTLE GYM CLOTHES?
OR DID YOU HAVE TO *DIRTY* YOUR HANDS...
2-3 HIBIYA
あああああ
AAAHH!
THEY WERE HAND-ME-DOWNS, I SWEAR! I DIDN'T PICK 'EM!
AH HA HA HA HA!
NOW, I'M ONLY TEASING.
SO, HAVE YOU HAD DINNER YET...?
NO, NOT YET.
RUSTLE
RUSTLE

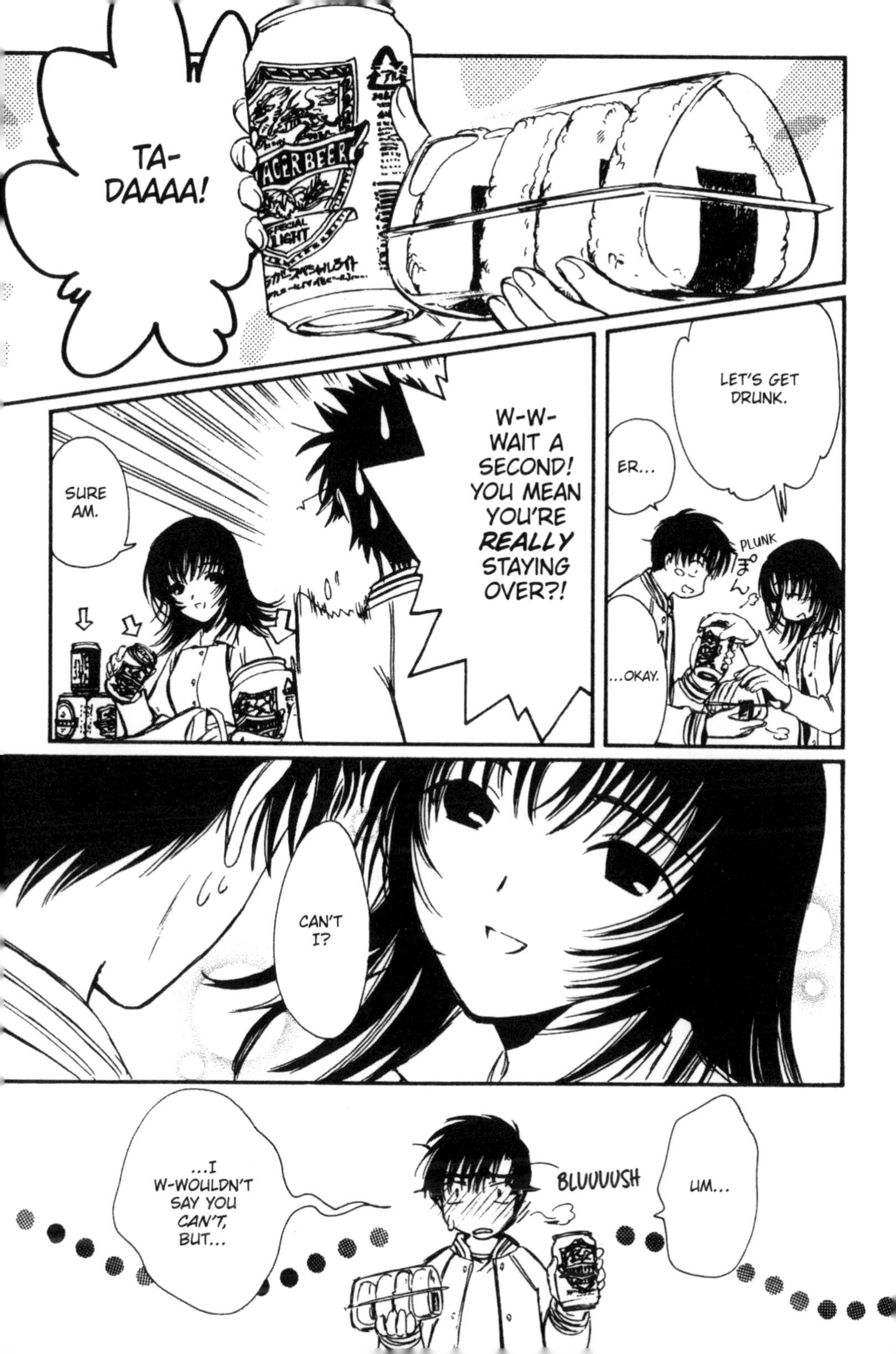
TA-DAAAA!
LET'S GET DRUNK.
ER...
PLUNK
ぽん
...OKAY.
W-W-WAIT A SECOND! YOU MEAN YOU'RE *REALLY* STAYING OVER?!
SURE AM.
CAN'T I?
UM...
BLUUUUSH
...I W-WOULDN'T SAY YOU *CAN'T*, BUT...

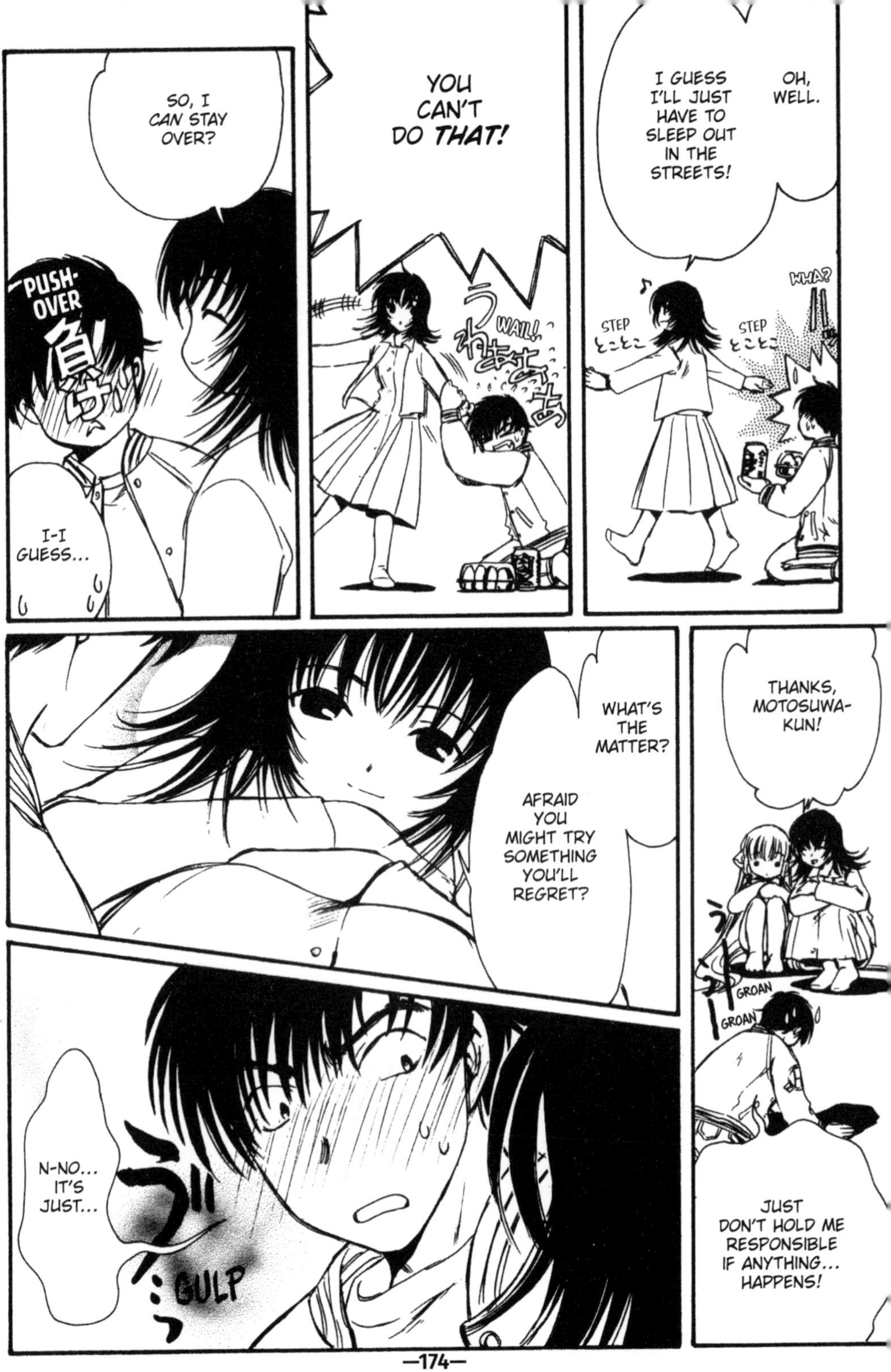
OH, WELL.
I GUESS I'LL JUST HAVE TO SLEEP OUT IN THE STREETS!
STEP とことこ
STEP とことこ
WHA?
YOU CAN'T DO *THAT!*
WAIL!
SO, I CAN STAY OVER?
PUSH-OVER
I-I GUESS...
THANKS, MOTOSUWA-KUN!
GROAN
GROAN
JUST DON'T HOLD ME RESPONSIBLE IF ANYTHING... HAPPENS!
WHAT'S THE MATTER?
AFRAID YOU MIGHT TRY SOMETHING YOU'LL REGRET?
N-NO... IT'S JUST...
GULP

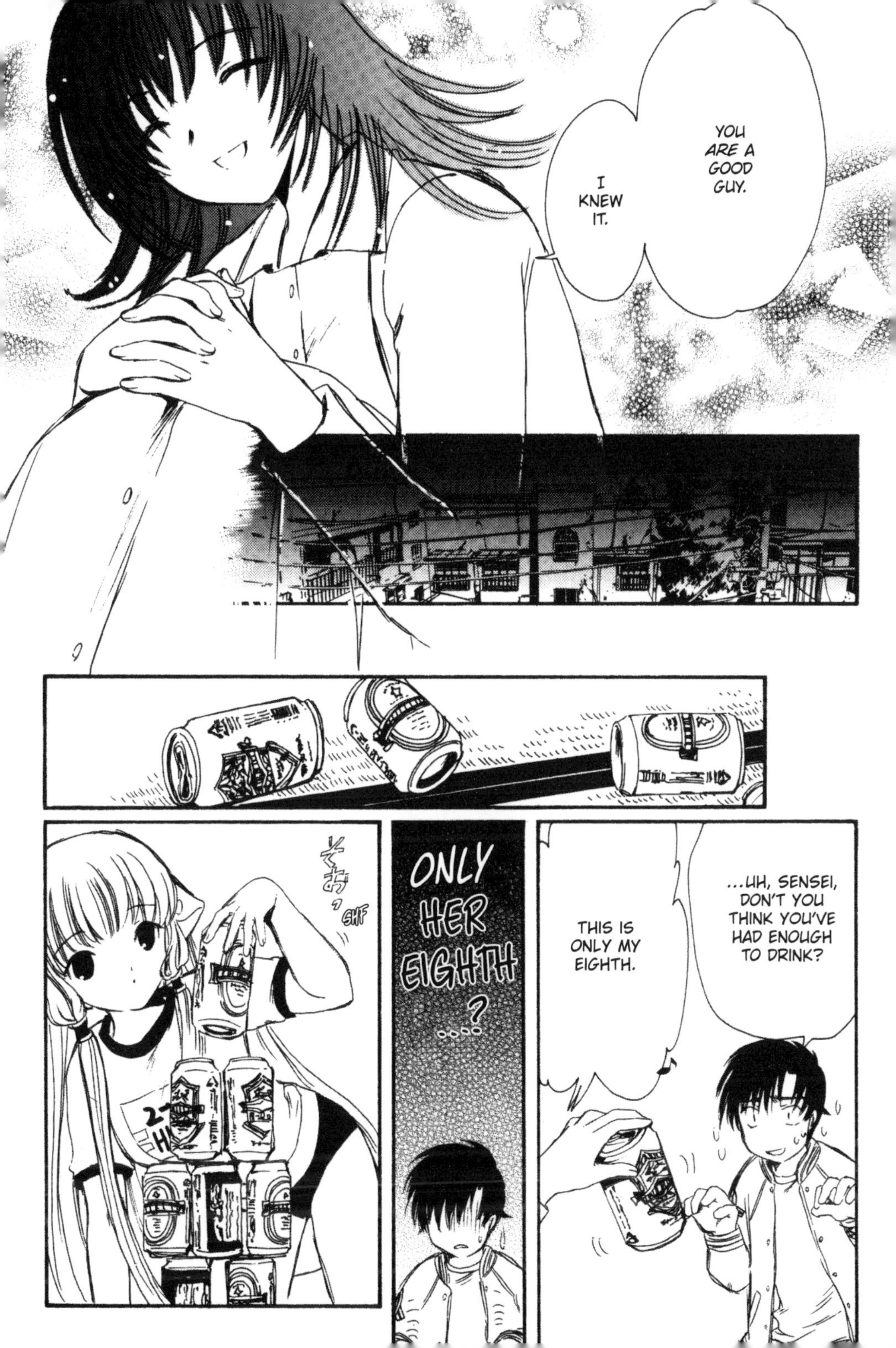

YOU ARE A GOOD GUY.
I KNEW IT.
...UH, SENSEI, DON'T YOU THINK YOU'VE HAD ENOUGH TO DRINK?
THIS IS ONLY MY EIGHTH.
ONLY HER EIGHTH ...?
そおっ
SHF

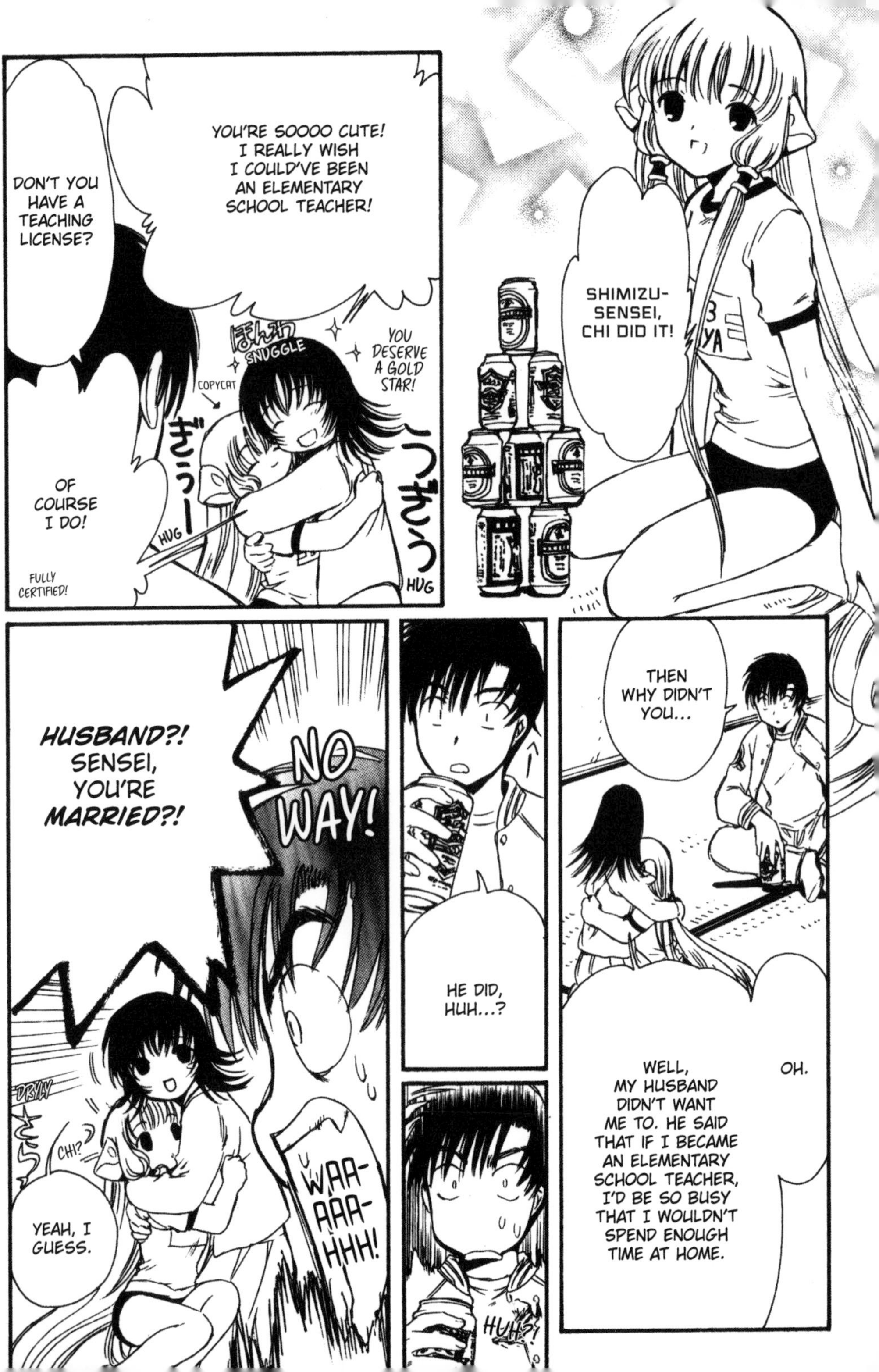

SHIMIZU-SENSEI, CHI DID IT!
YOU DESERVE A GOLD STAR!
SNUGGLE
YOU'RE SOOOO CUTE! I REALLY WISH I COULD'VE BEEN AN ELEMENTARY SCHOOL TEACHER!
DON'T YOU HAVE A TEACHING LICENSE?
HUG
COPYCAT
HUG
OF COURSE I DO!
FULLY CERTIFIED!
THEN WHY DIDN'T YOU...
OH.
WELL, MY HUSBAND DIDN'T WANT ME TO. HE SAID THAT IF I BECAME AN ELEMENTARY SCHOOL TEACHER, I'D BE SO BUSY THAT I WOULDN'T SPEND ENOUGH TIME AT HOME.
HE DID, HUH...?
HUH?!
NO WAY!
HUSBAND?! SENSEI, YOU'RE MARRIED?!
WAAAAAAHHH!
CHI?
DRYLY
YEAH, I GUESS.

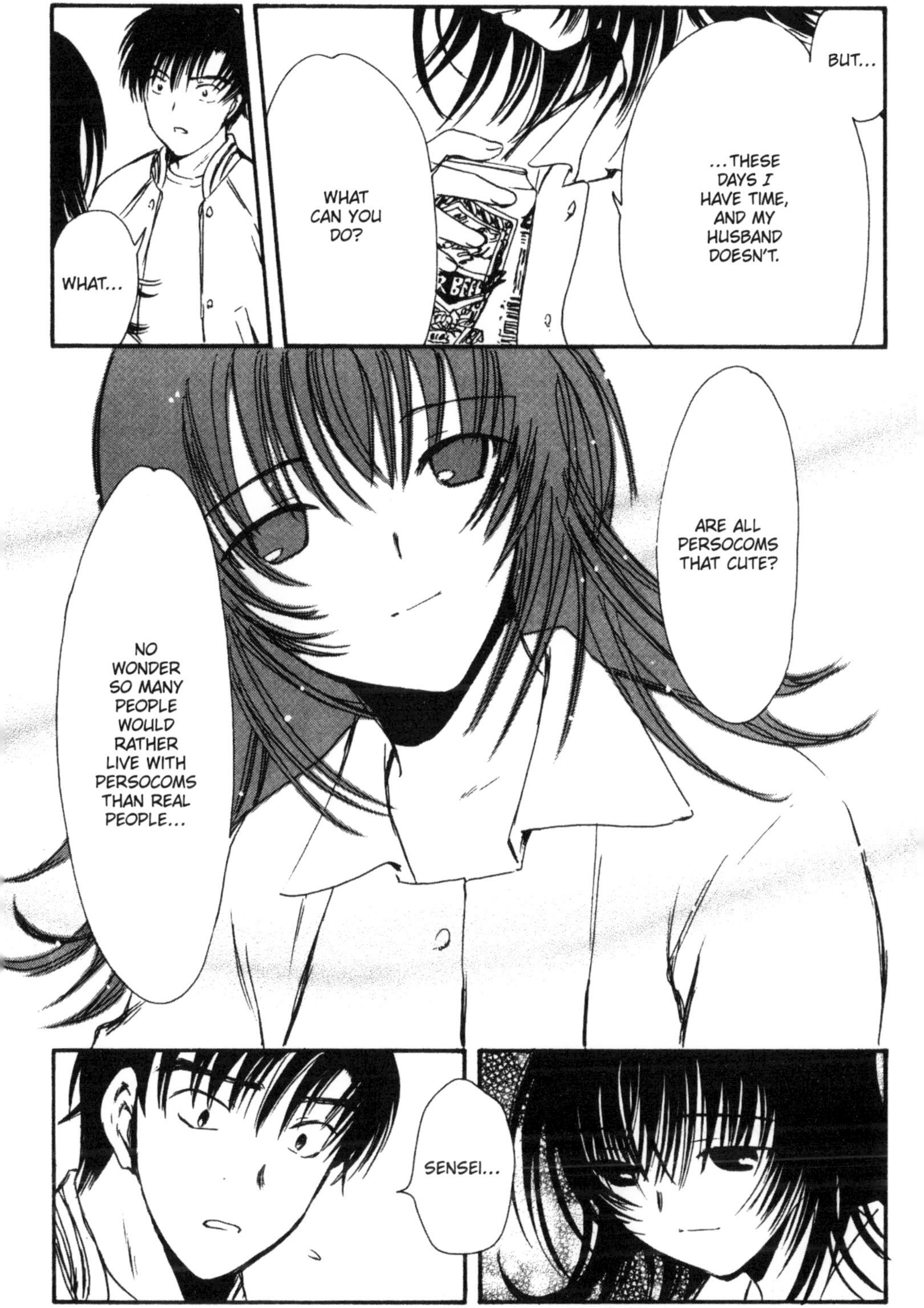
BUT...
...THESE DAYS I HAVE TIME, AND MY HUSBAND DOESN'T.
WHAT CAN YOU DO?
WHAT...
ARE ALL PERSOCOMS THAT CUTE?
NO WONDER SO MANY PEOPLE WOULD RATHER LIVE WITH PERSOCOMS THAN REAL PEOPLE...
SENSEI...

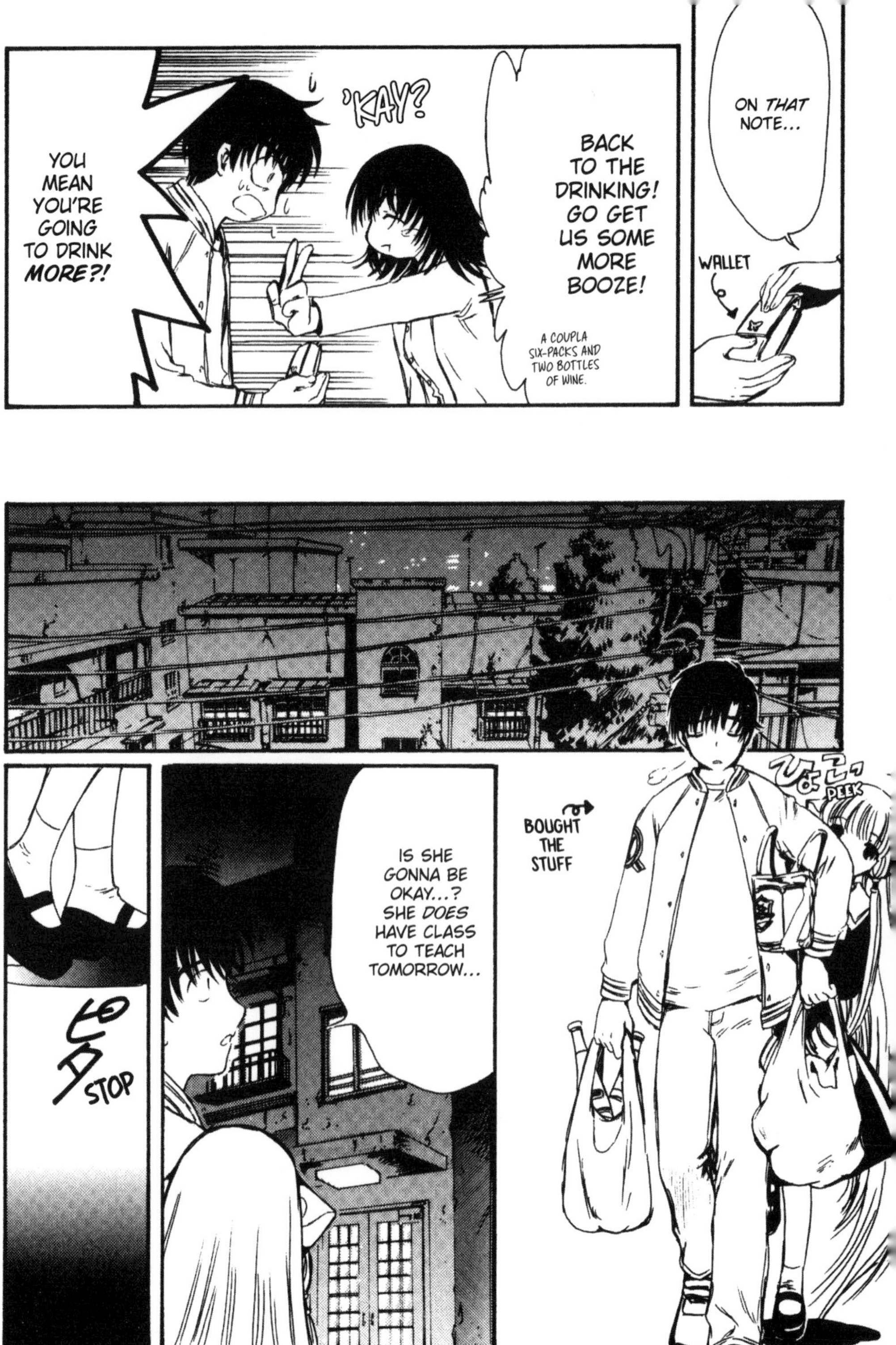
ON THAT NOTE...
WALLET
BACK TO THE DRINKING! GO GET US SOME MORE BOOZE!
A COUPLA SIX-PACKS AND TWO BOTTLES OF WINE.
'KAY?
YOU MEAN YOU'RE GOING TO DRINK MORE?!
ひょこっ
PEEK
BOUGHT THE STUFF
IS SHE GONNA BE OKAY...? SHE DOES HAVE CLASS TO TEACH TOMORROW...
ピタ
STOP

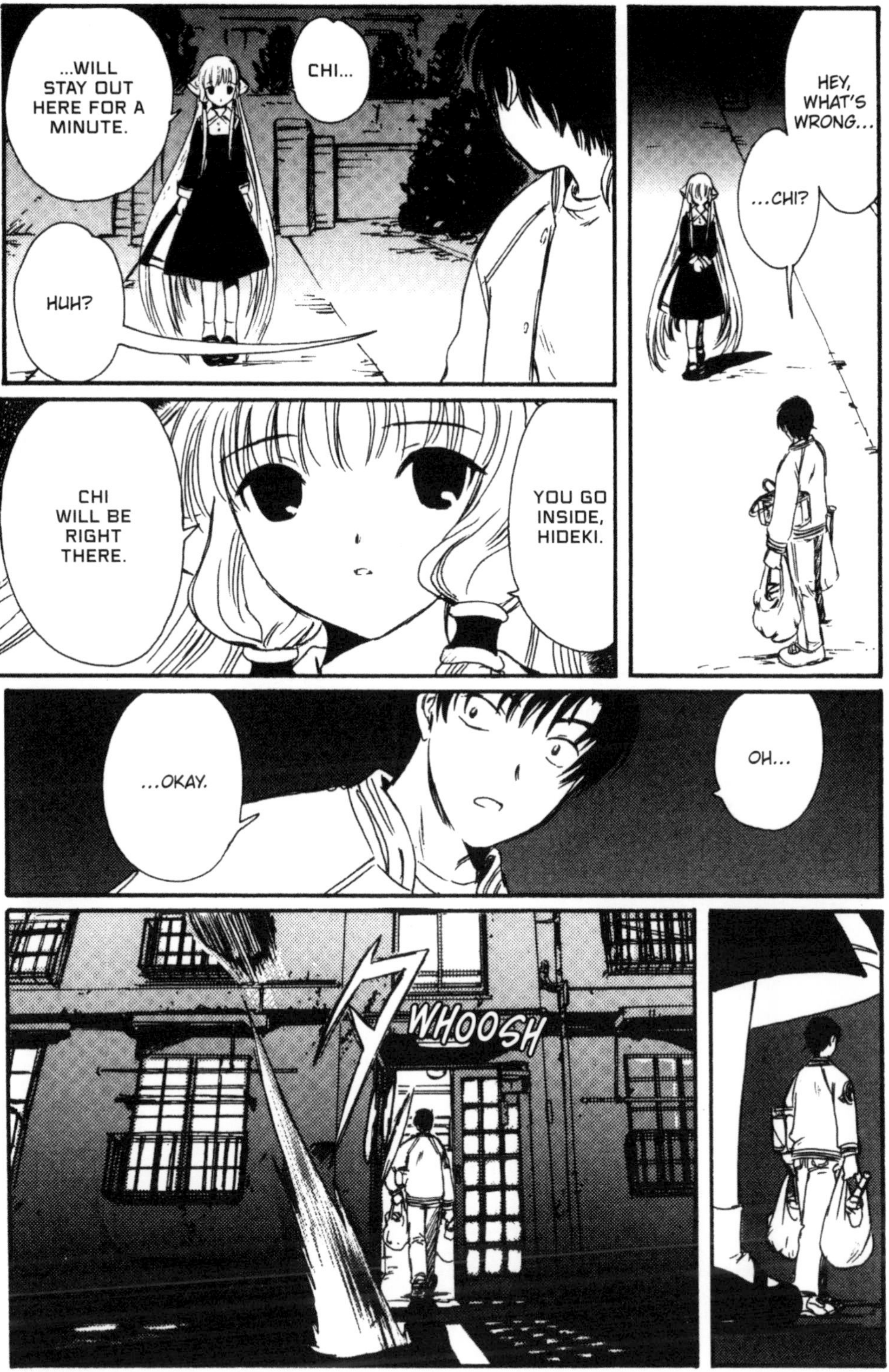
HEY, WHAT'S WRONG...
...CHI?
CHI...
...WILL STAY OUT HERE FOR A MINUTE.
HUH?
YOU GO INSIDE, HIDEKI.
CHI WILL BE RIGHT THERE.
OH...
...OKAY.
WHOOSH

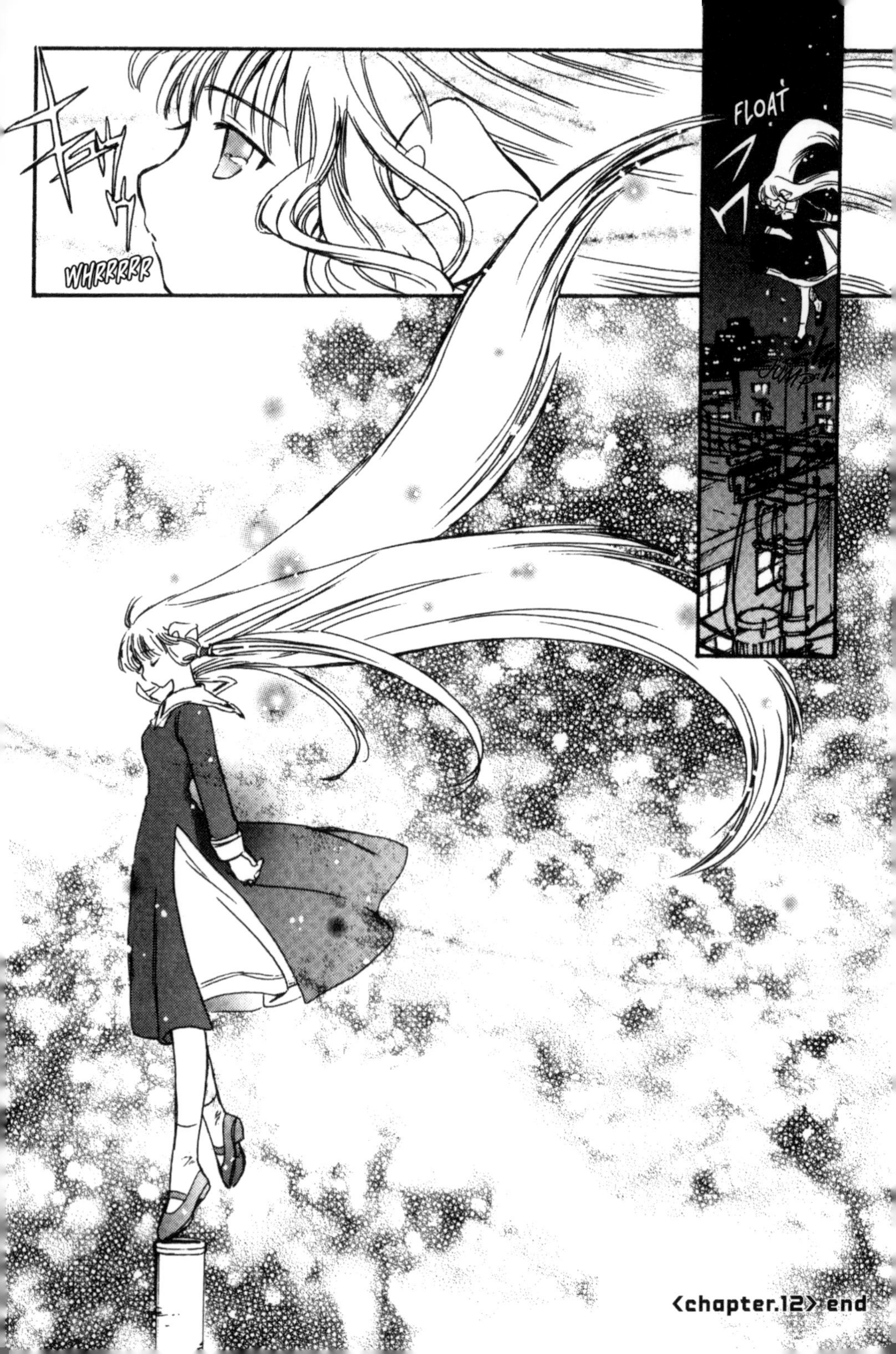
FLOAT
JUMP
WHRRRRR

<chapter.12> end

Chobits

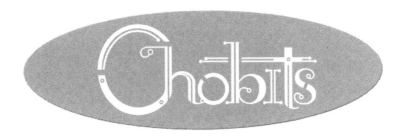

Chobits

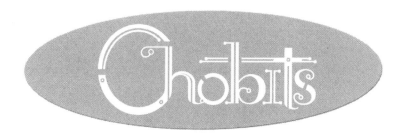

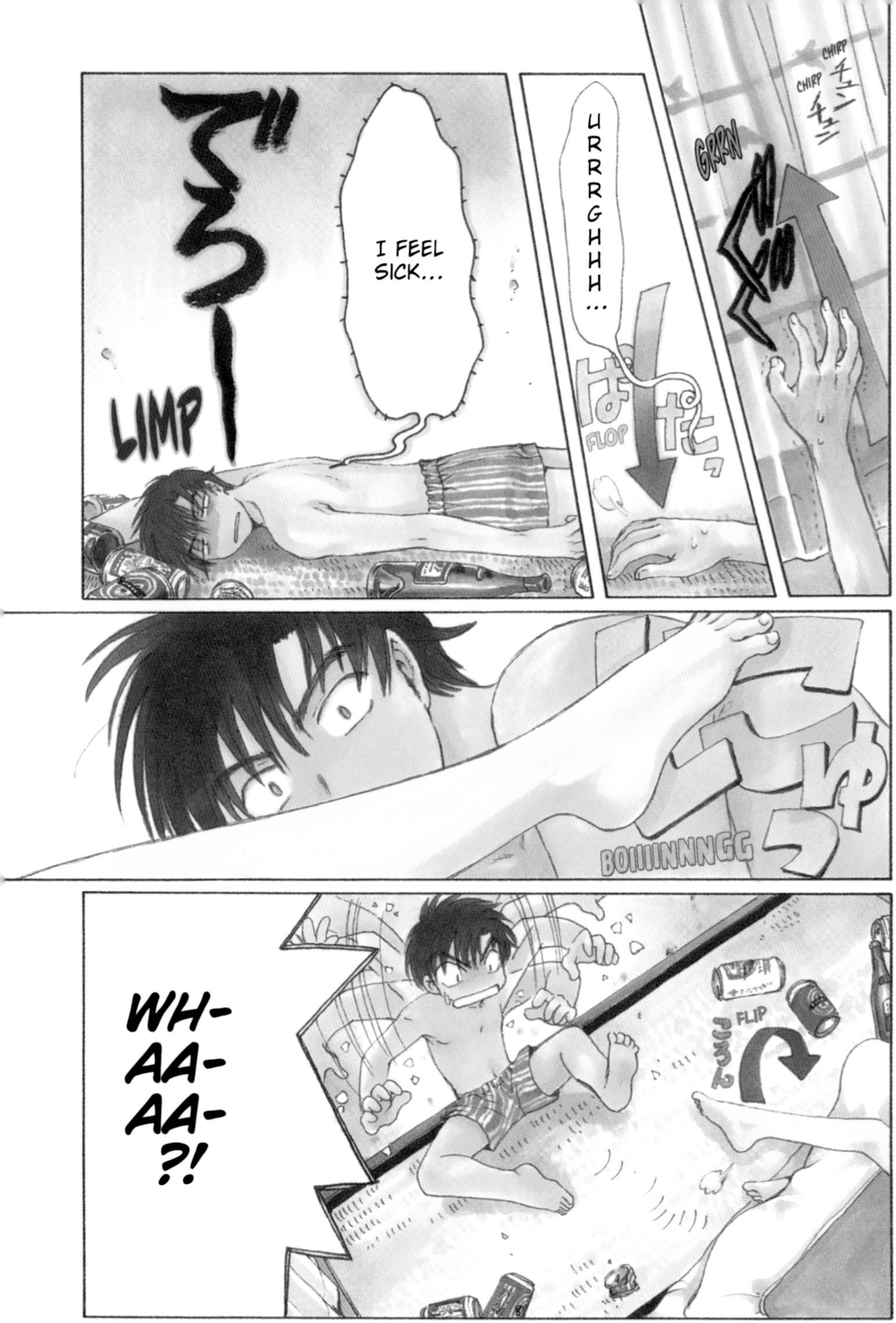
CHIRP
CHIRP
GRRN
URRRGHHH...
FLOP
I FEEL SICK...
LIMP
BOIIIINNNGG
WH-AA-AA-?!
FLIP

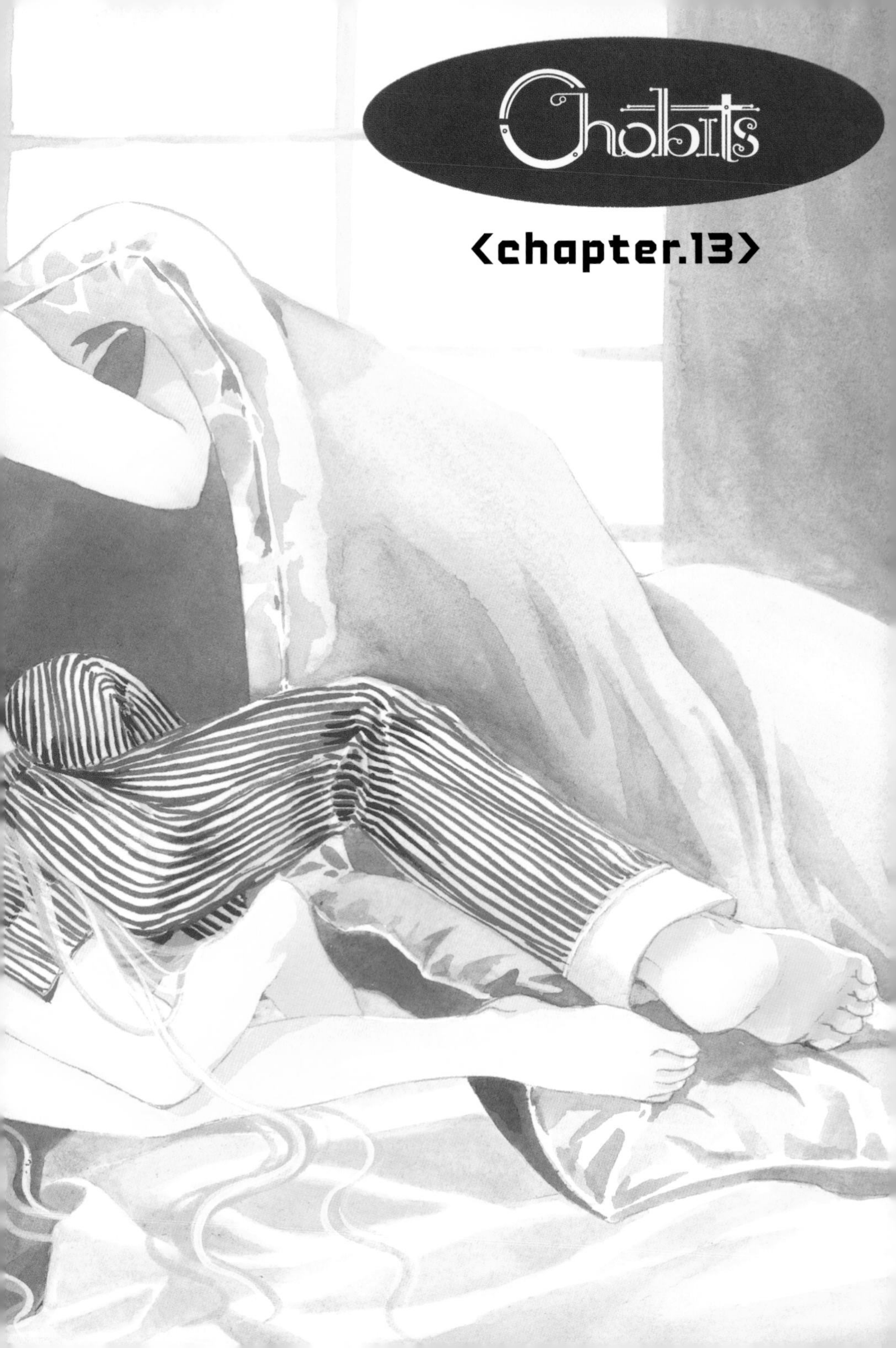
Chobits
<chapter.13>

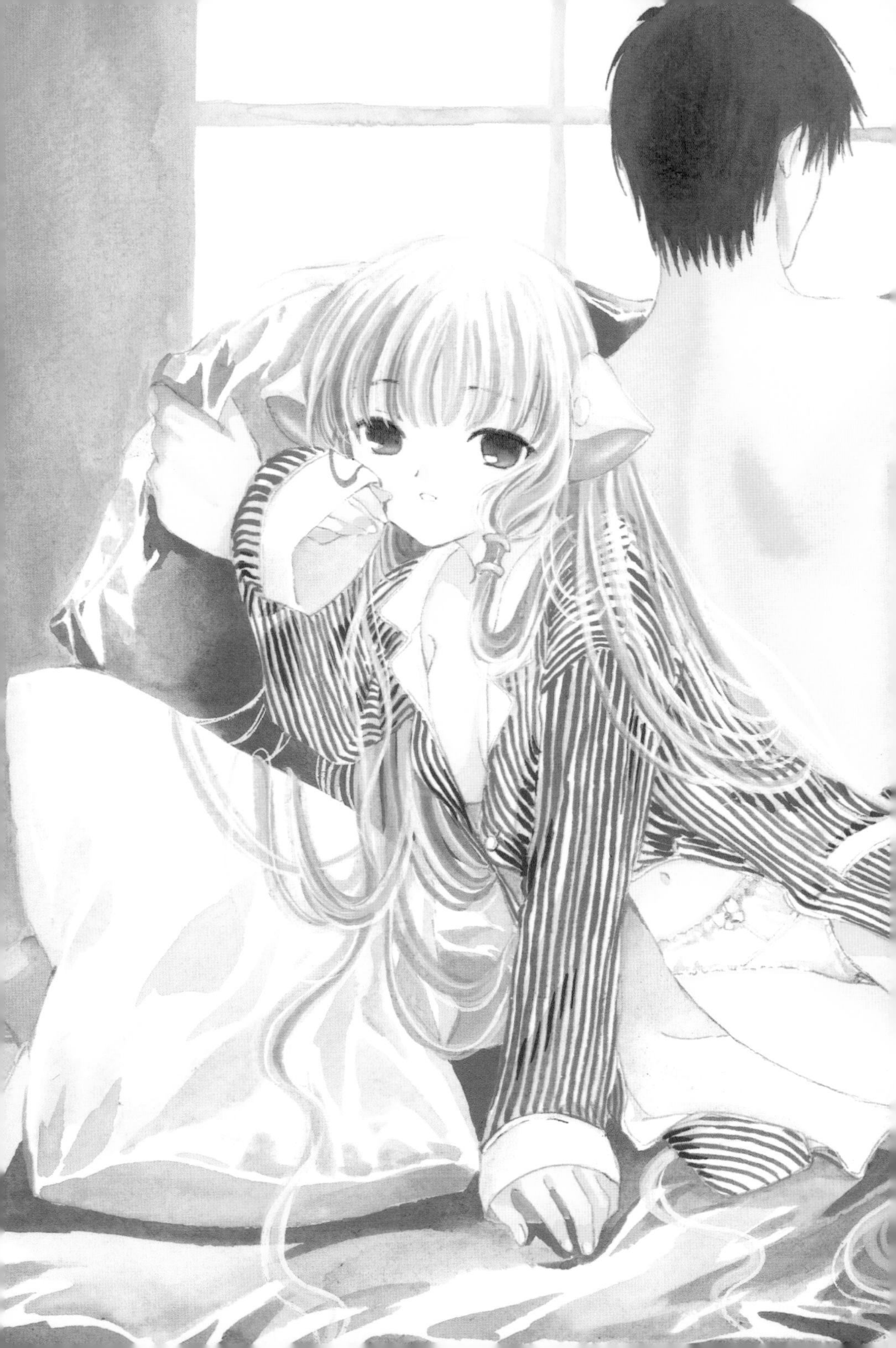

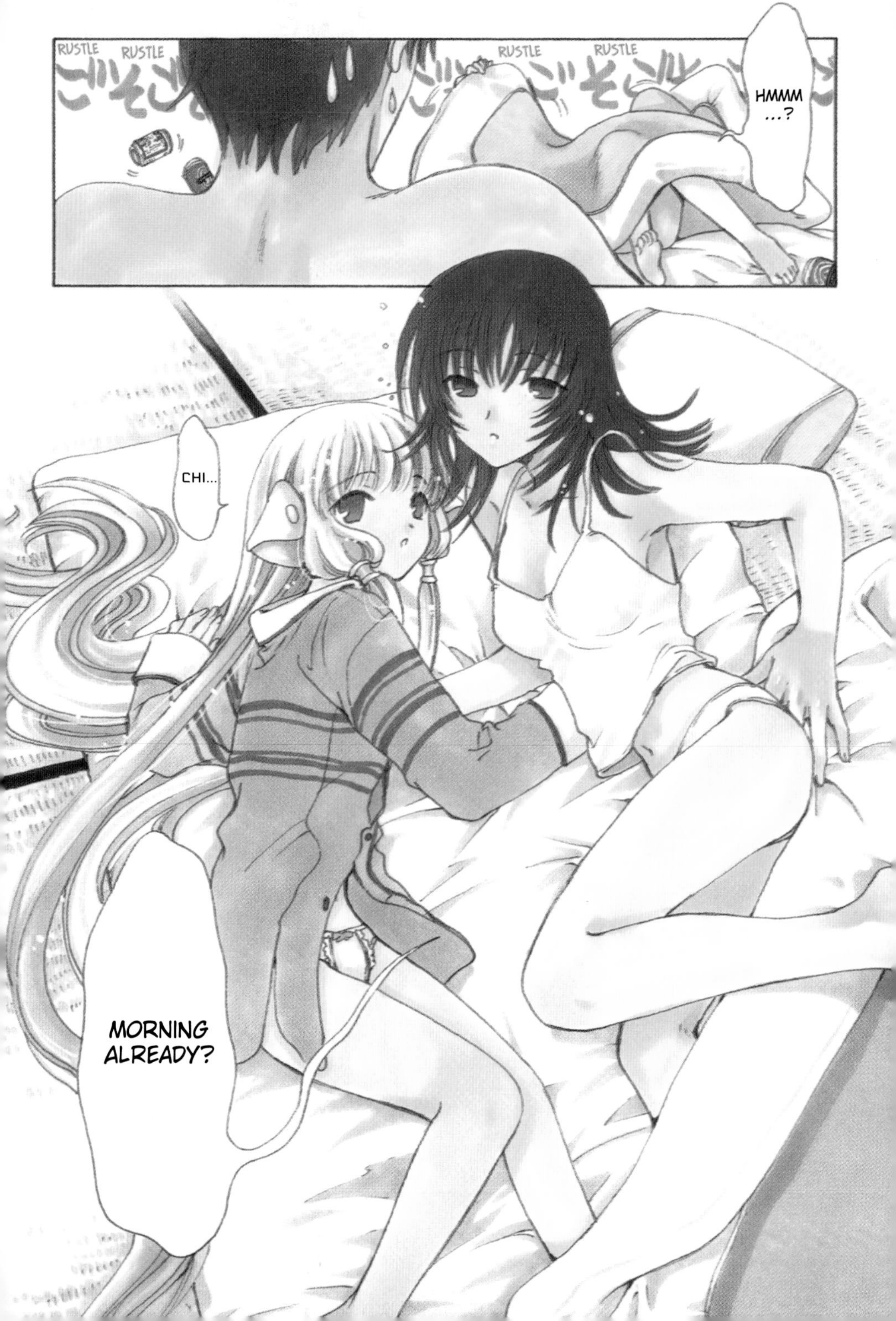
HMMM ...?
RUSTLE
RUSTLE
RUSTLE
RUSTLE
CHI...
MORNING ALREADY?

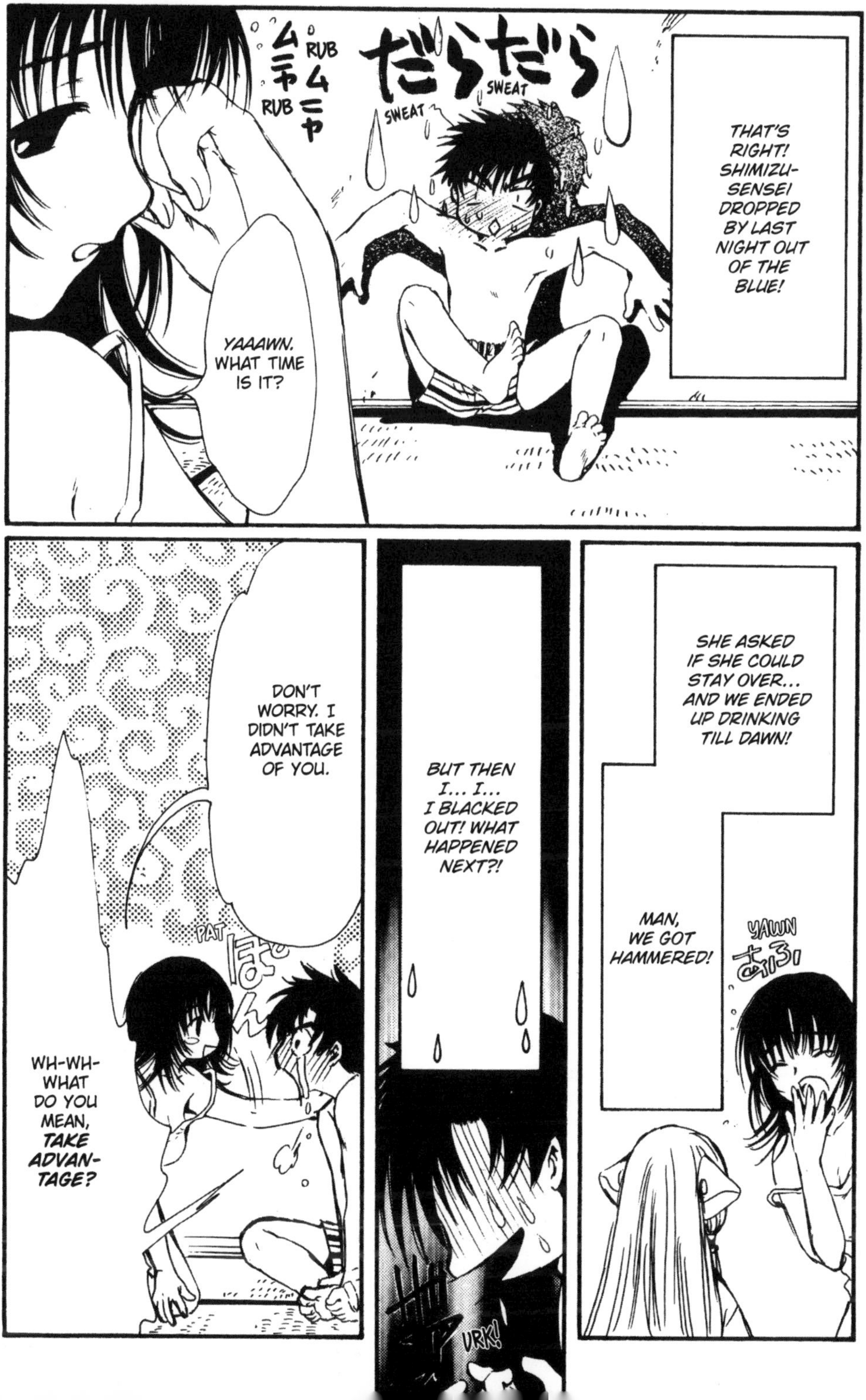
THAT'S RIGHT! SHIMIZU-SENSEI DROPPED BY LAST NIGHT OUT OF THE BLUE!
だらだら
SWEAT
SWEAT
ムニャムニャ
RUB
RUB
YAAAWN. WHAT TIME IS IT?
SHE ASKED IF SHE COULD STAY OVER... AND WE ENDED UP DRINKING TILL DAWN!
YAWN
MAN, WE GOT HAMMERED!
BUT THEN I... I... I BLACKED OUT! WHAT HAPPENED NEXT?!
URK!
DON'T WORRY. I DIDN'T TAKE ADVANTAGE OF YOU.
PAT
ぽん
WH-WH-WHAT DO YOU MEAN, TAKE ADVANTAGE?

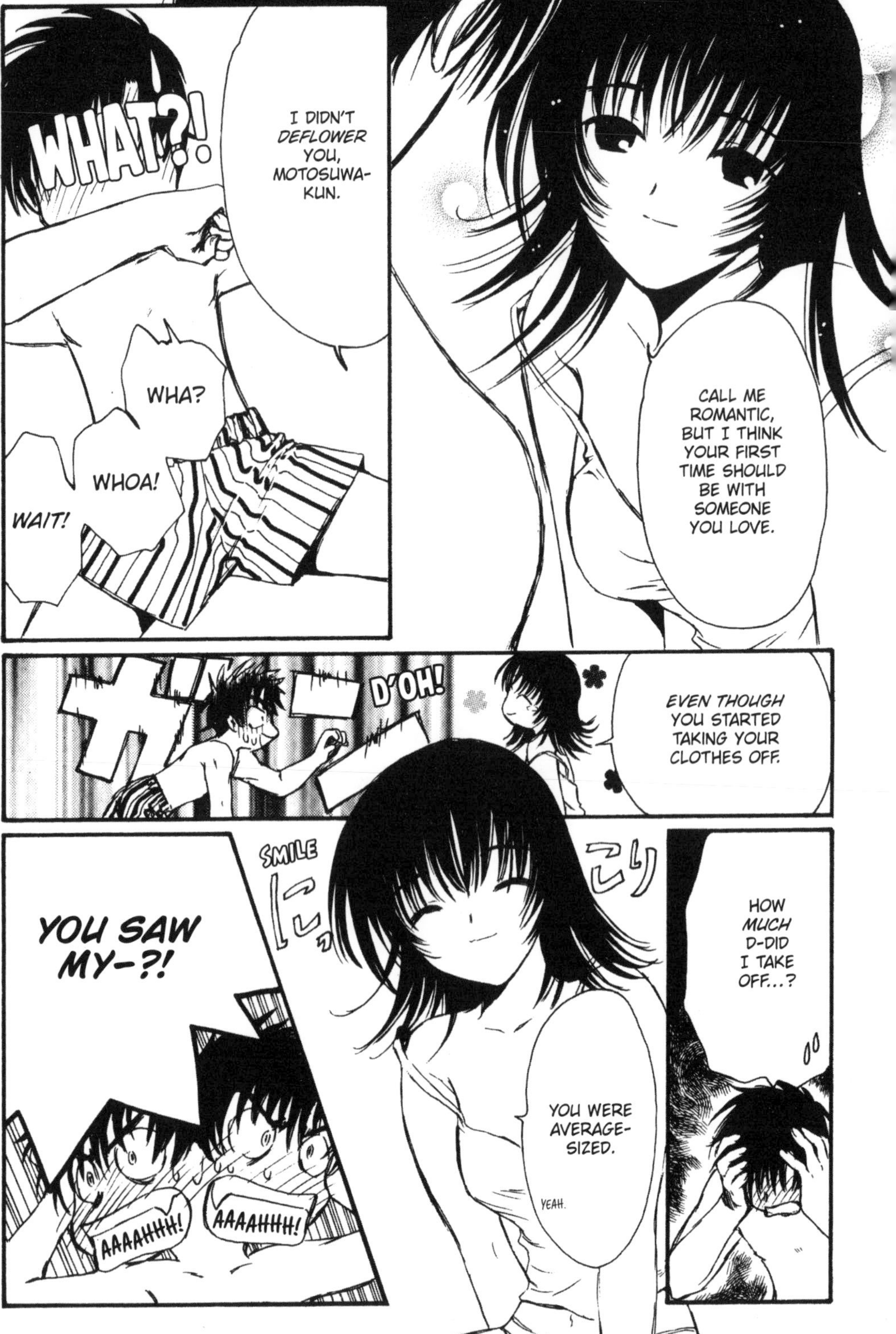
CALL ME ROMANTIC, BUT I THINK YOUR FIRST TIME SHOULD BE WITH SOMEONE YOU LOVE.
I DIDN'T DEFLOWER YOU, MOTOSUWA-KUN.
WHAT?!
WHA?
WHOA!
WAIT!
EVEN THOUGH YOU STARTED TAKING YOUR CLOTHES OFF.
D'OH!
HOW MUCH D-DID I TAKE OFF...?
SMILE
YOU WERE AVERAGE-SIZED.
YEAH.
YOU SAW MY-?!
AAAAHHHH!
AAAAHHH!

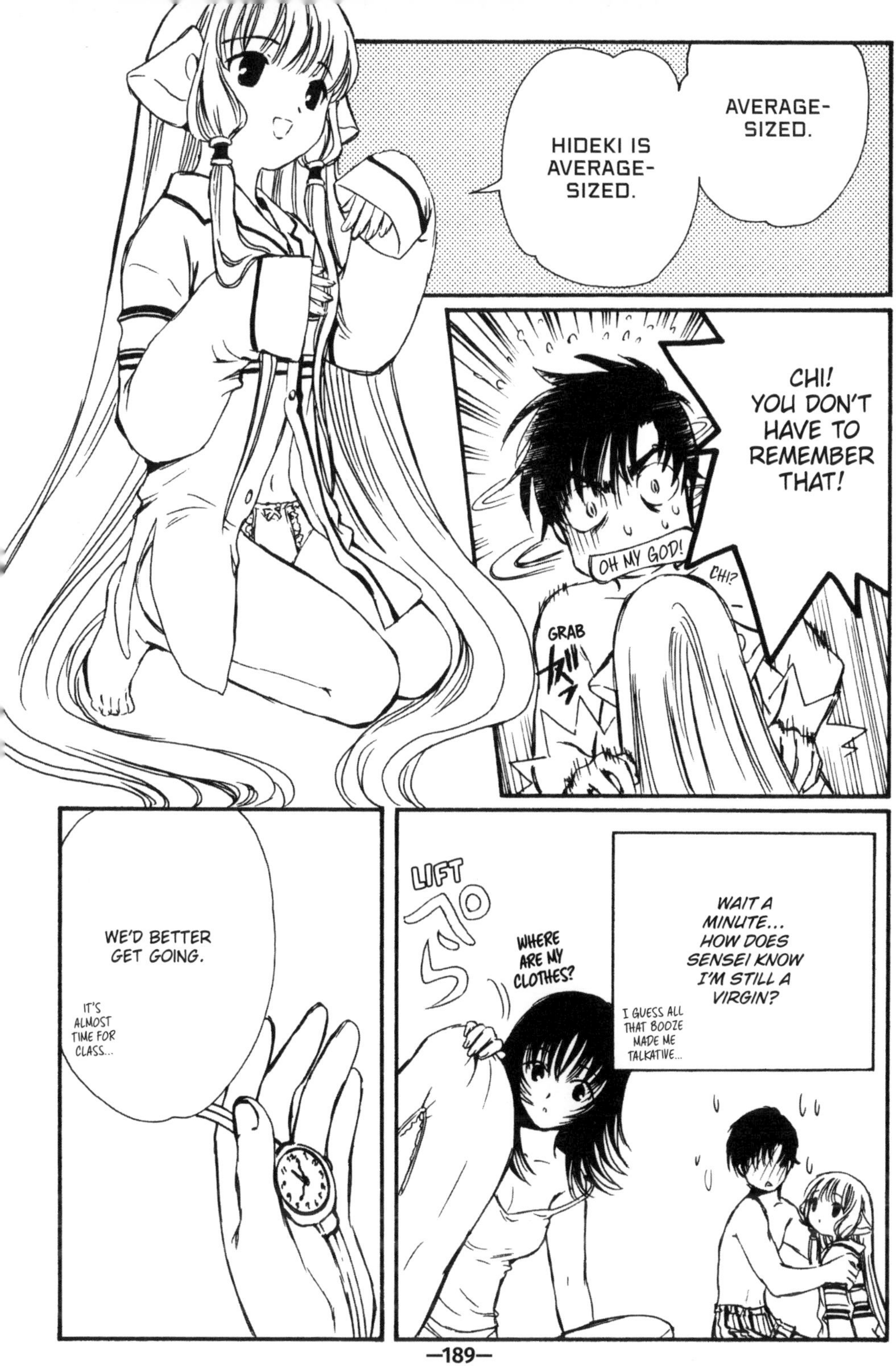
AVERAGE-SIZED.
HIDEKI IS AVERAGE-SIZED.
CHI! YOU DON'T HAVE TO REMEMBER THAT!
OH MY GOD!
CHI?
GRAB
WAIT A MINUTE... HOW DOES SENSEI KNOW I'M STILL A VIRGIN?
I GUESS ALL THAT BOOZE MADE ME TALKATIVE...
WHERE ARE MY CLOTHES?
LIFT
WE'D BETTER GET GOING.
IT'S ALMOST TIME FOR CLASS...

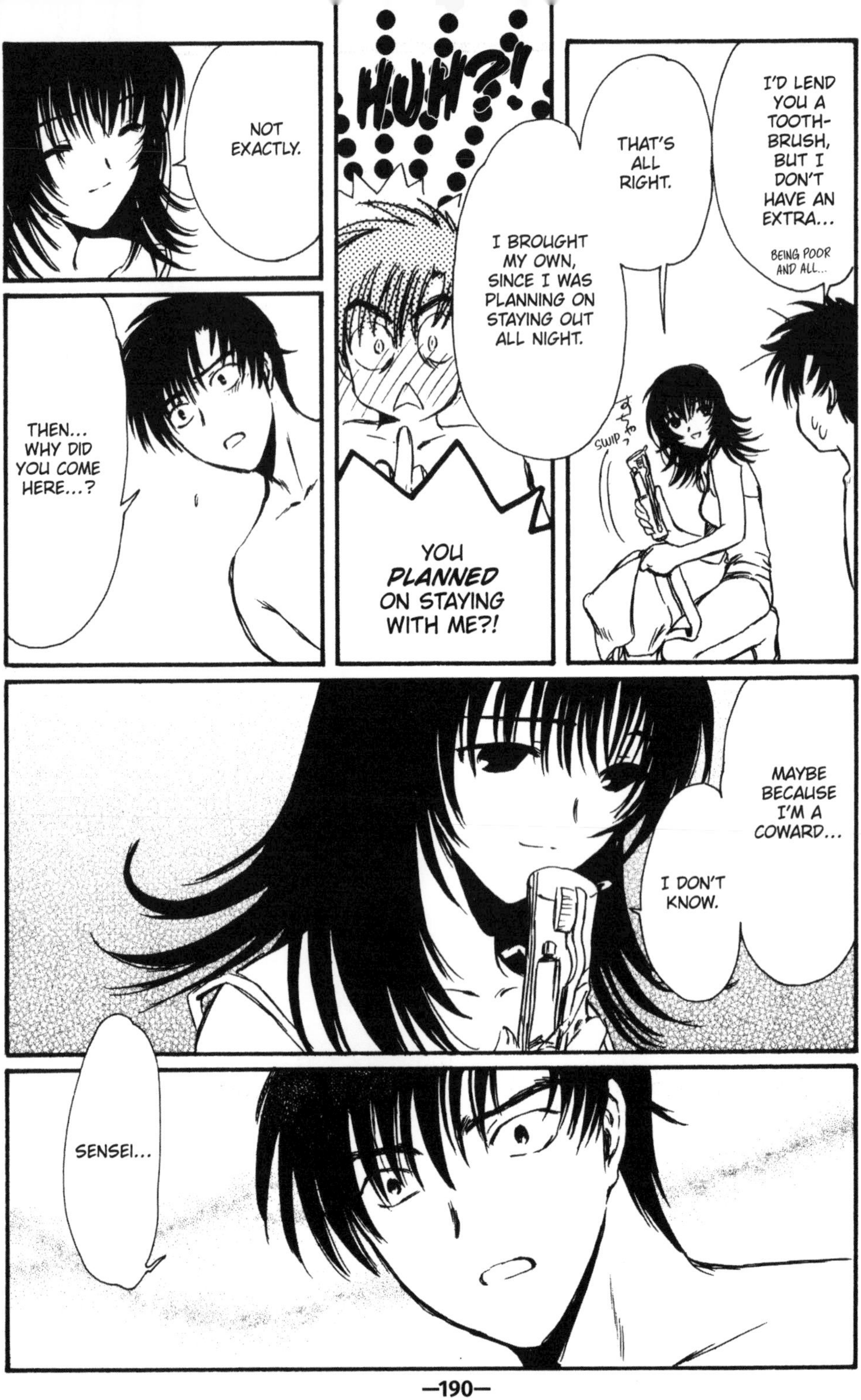
I'D LEND YOU A TOOTH-BRUSH, BUT I DON'T HAVE AN EXTRA...
BEING POOR AND ALL...
THAT'S ALL RIGHT.
I BROUGHT MY OWN, SINCE I WAS PLANNING ON STAYING OUT ALL NIGHT.
SWIP
HUH?!
YOU PLANNED ON STAYING WITH ME?!
NOT EXACTLY.
THEN... WHY DID YOU COME HERE...?
MAYBE BECAUSE I'M A COWARD...
I DON'T KNOW.
SENSEI...

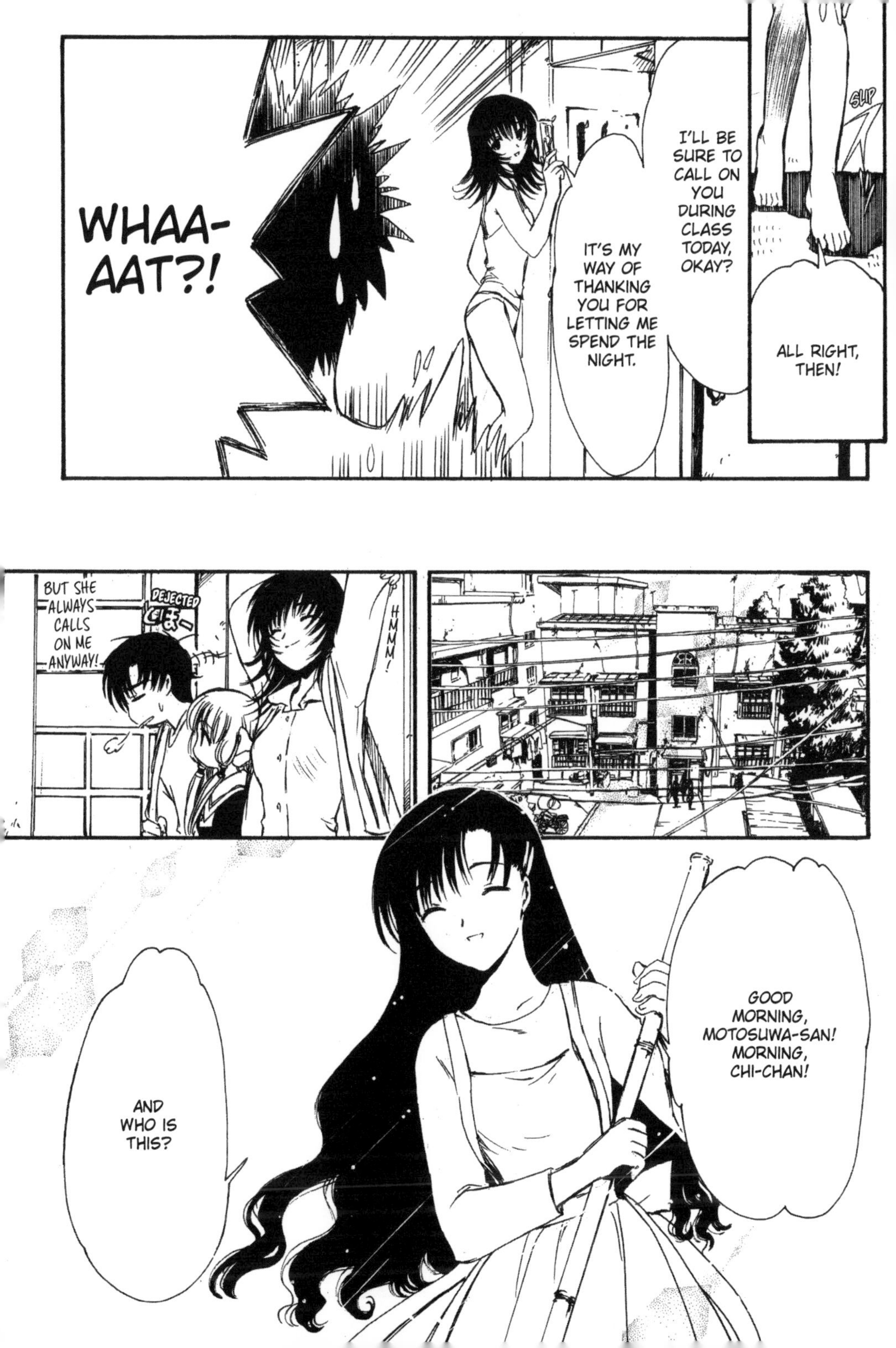
SLIP
ALL RIGHT, THEN!
I'LL BE SURE TO CALL ON YOU DURING CLASS TODAY, OKAY?
IT'S MY WAY OF THANKING YOU FOR LETTING ME SPEND THE NIGHT.
WHAA-AAT?!
HMMM!
DEJECTED
BUT SHE ALWAYS CALLS ON ME ANYWAY!
GOOD MORNING, MOTOSUWA-SAN! MORNING, CHI-CHAN!
AND WHO IS THIS?

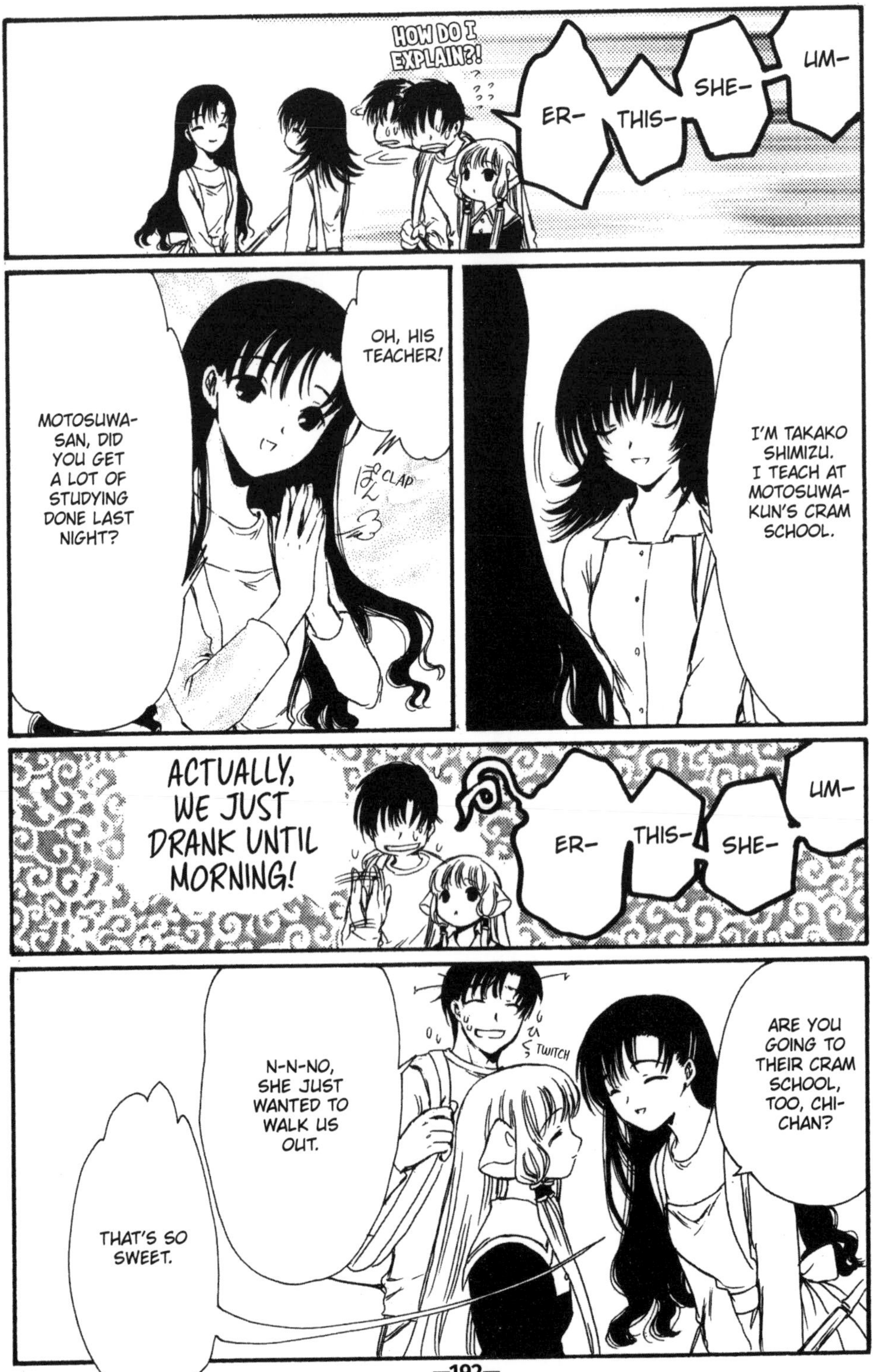

UM—
SHE—
THIS—
ER—
HOW DO I EXPLAIN?!
I'M TAKAKO SHIMIZU. I TEACH AT MOTOSUWA-KUN'S CRAM SCHOOL.
OH, HIS TEACHER!
CLAP
MOTOSUWA-SAN, DID YOU GET A LOT OF STUDYING DONE LAST NIGHT?
UM—
SHE—
THIS—
ER—
ACTUALLY, WE JUST DRANK UNTIL MORNING!
ARE YOU GOING TO THEIR CRAM SCHOOL, TOO, CHI-CHAN?
TWITCH
N-N-NO, SHE JUST WANTED TO WALK US OUT.
THAT'S SO SWEET.

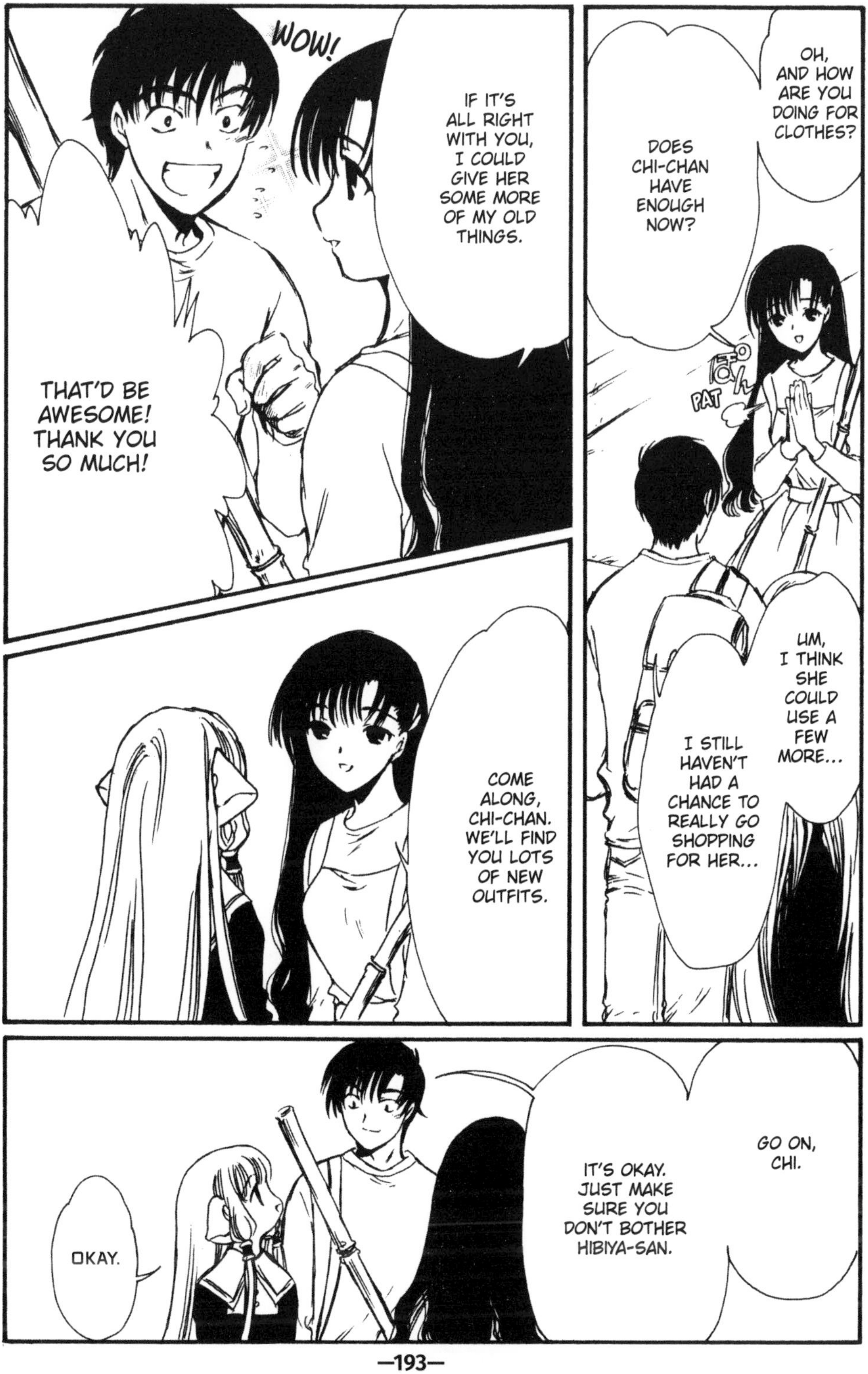
OH, AND HOW ARE YOU DOING FOR CLOTHES?
DOES CHI-CHAN HAVE ENOUGH NOW?
PAT
UM, I THINK SHE COULD USE A FEW MORE...
I STILL HAVEN'T HAD A CHANCE TO REALLY GO SHOPPING FOR HER...
IF IT'S ALL RIGHT WITH YOU, I COULD GIVE HER SOME MORE OF MY OLD THINGS.
WOW!
THAT'D BE AWESOME! THANK YOU SO MUCH!
COME ALONG, CHI-CHAN. WE'LL FIND YOU LOTS OF NEW OUTFITS.
GO ON, CHI.
IT'S OKAY. JUST MAKE SURE YOU DON'T BOTHER HIBIYA-SAN.
OKAY.

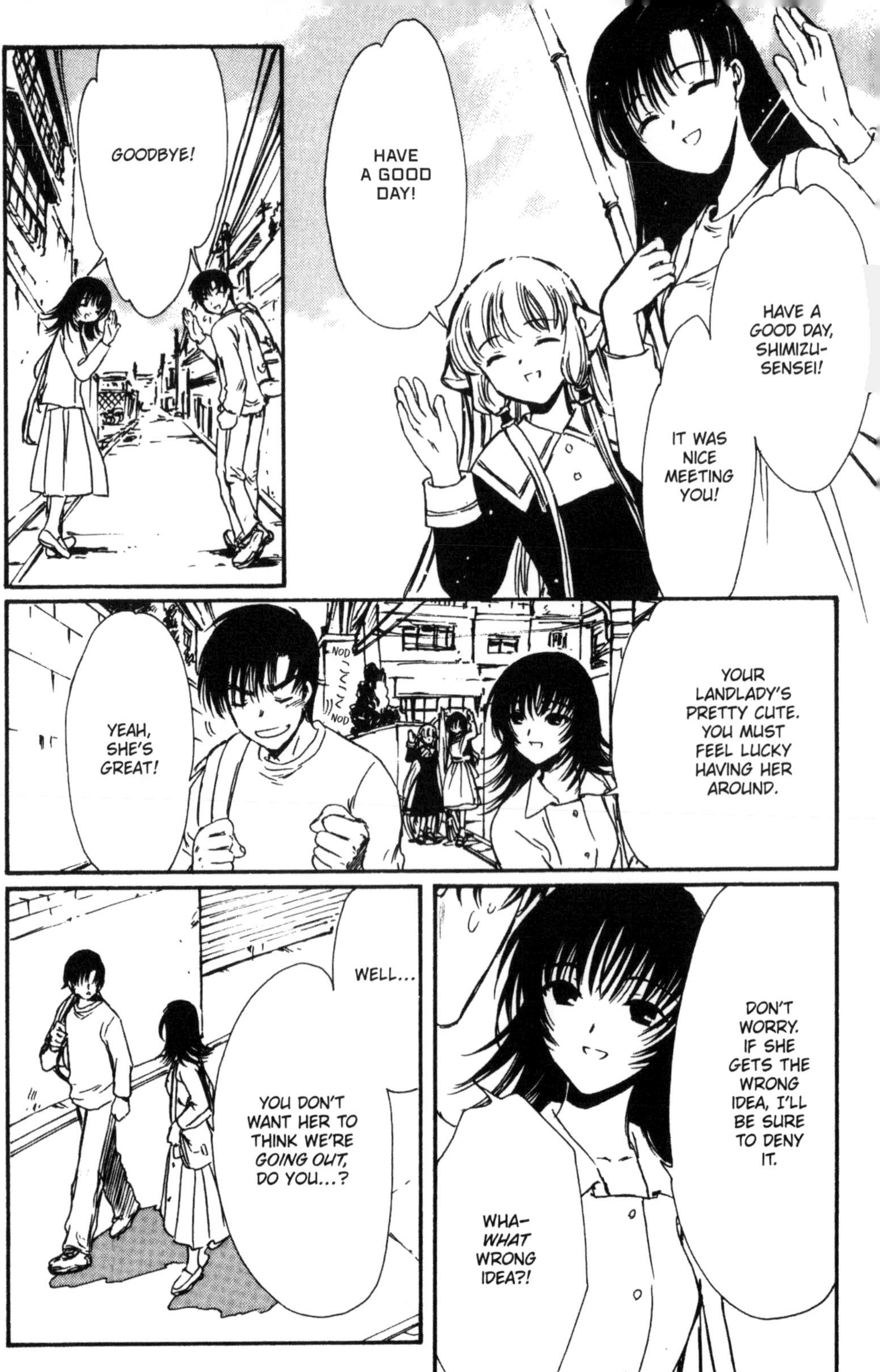
HAVE A GOOD DAY, SHIMIZU-SENSEI!
IT WAS NICE MEETING YOU!
HAVE A GOOD DAY!
GOODBYE!
YOUR LANDLADY'S PRETTY CUTE. YOU MUST FEEL LUCKY HAVING HER AROUND.
NOD
NOD
YEAH, SHE'S GREAT!
DON'T WORRY. IF SHE GETS THE WRONG IDEA, I'LL BE SURE TO DENY IT.
WHA-*WHAT* WRONG IDEA?!
WELL...
YOU DON'T WANT HER TO THINK WE'RE *GOING OUT*, DO YOU...?

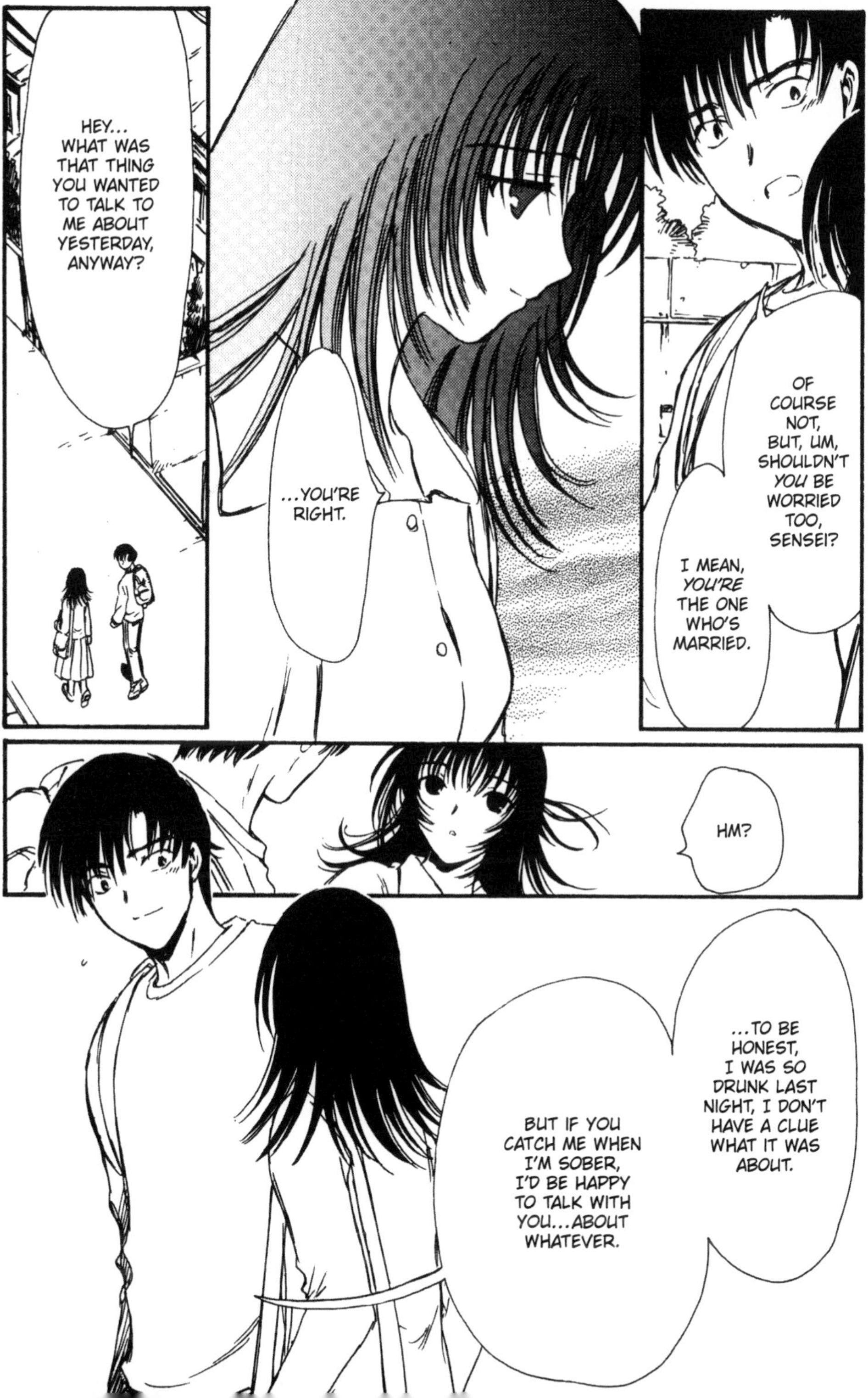
OF COURSE NOT, BUT, UM, SHOULDN'T *YOU* BE WORRIED TOO, SENSEI?
I MEAN, *YOU'RE* THE ONE WHO'S MARRIED.
...YOU'RE RIGHT.
HEY... WHAT WAS THAT THING YOU WANTED TO TALK TO ME ABOUT YESTERDAY, ANYWAY?
HM?
...TO BE HONEST, I WAS SO DRUNK LAST NIGHT, I DON'T HAVE A CLUE WHAT IT WAS ABOUT.
BUT IF YOU CATCH ME WHEN I'M SOBER, I'D BE HAPPY TO TALK WITH YOU...ABOUT WHATEVER.

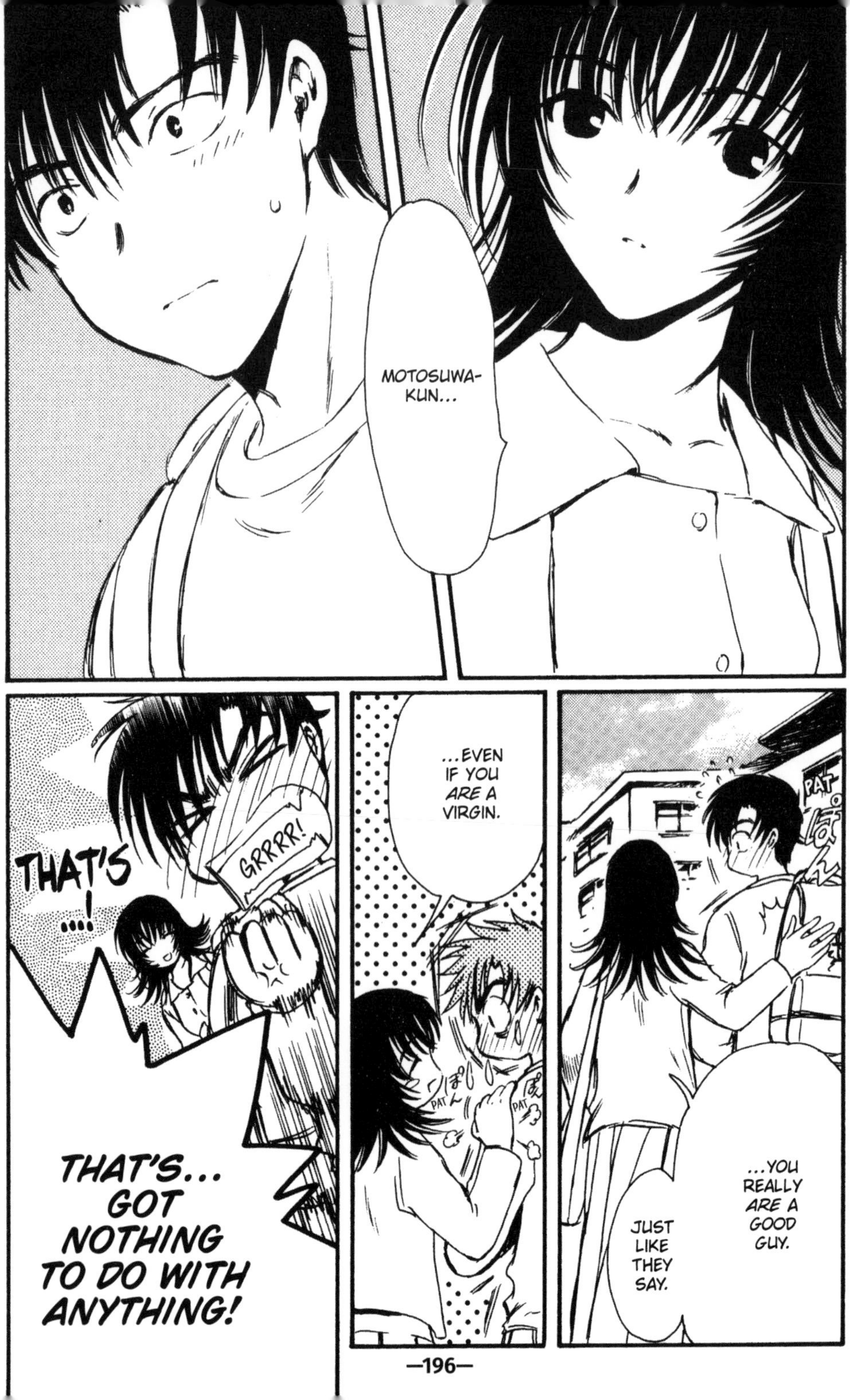
MOTOSUWA-KUN...
PAT
...YOU REALLY ARE A GOOD GUY.
JUST LIKE THEY SAY.
...EVEN IF YOU ARE A VIRGIN.
PAT
PAT
GRRRR!
THAT'S ...!
THAT'S... GOT NOTHING TO DO WITH ANYTHING!

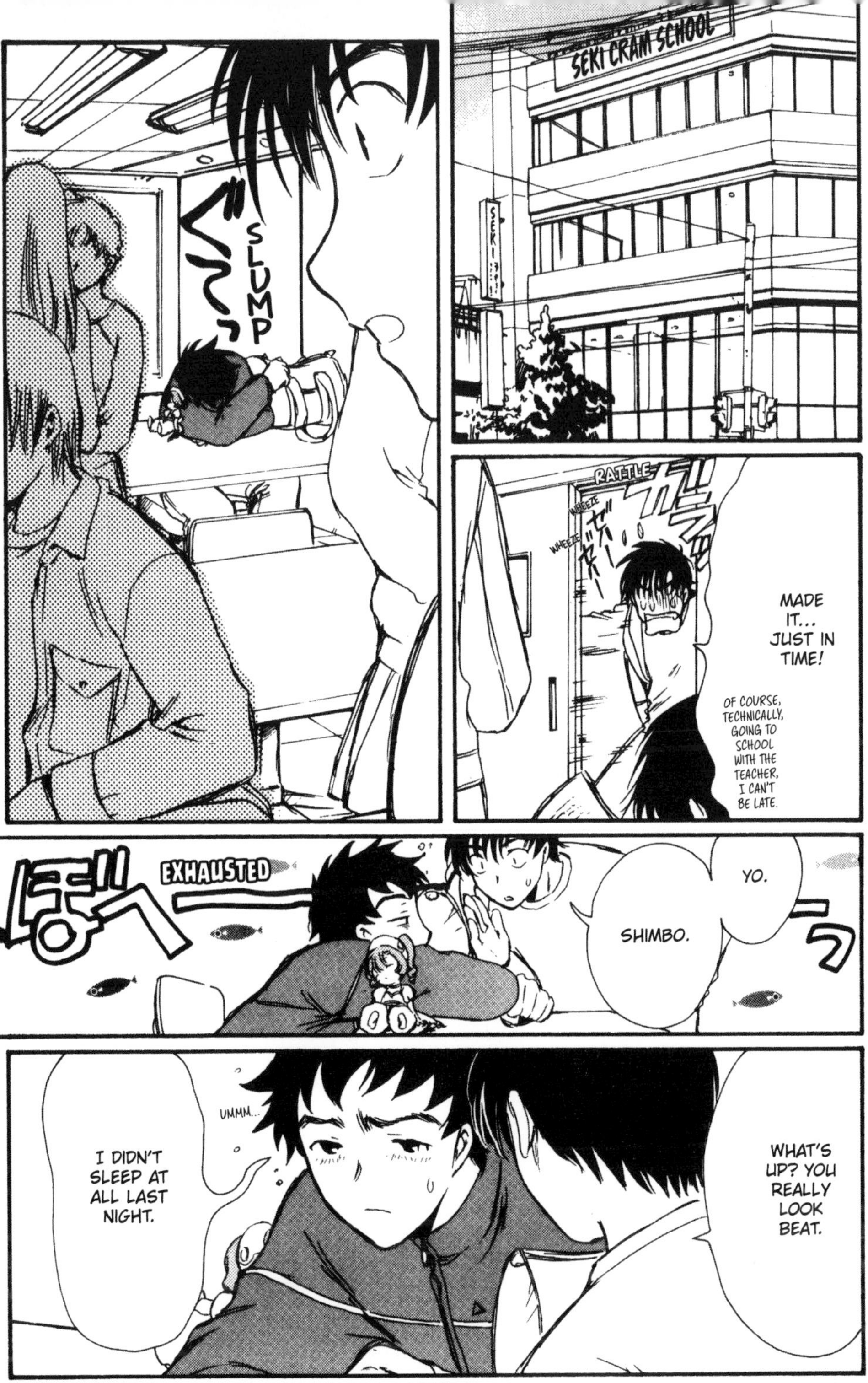

SEKI CRAM SCHOOL
SEKI
RATTLE
WHEEZE
WHEEZE
MADE IT... JUST IN TIME!
OF COURSE, TECHNICALLY, GOING TO SCHOOL WITH THE TEACHER, I CAN'T BE LATE.
SLUMP
YO.
SHIMBO.
EXHAUSTED
WHAT'S UP? YOU REALLY LOOK BEAT.
UMMM...
I DIDN'T SLEEP AT ALL LAST NIGHT.

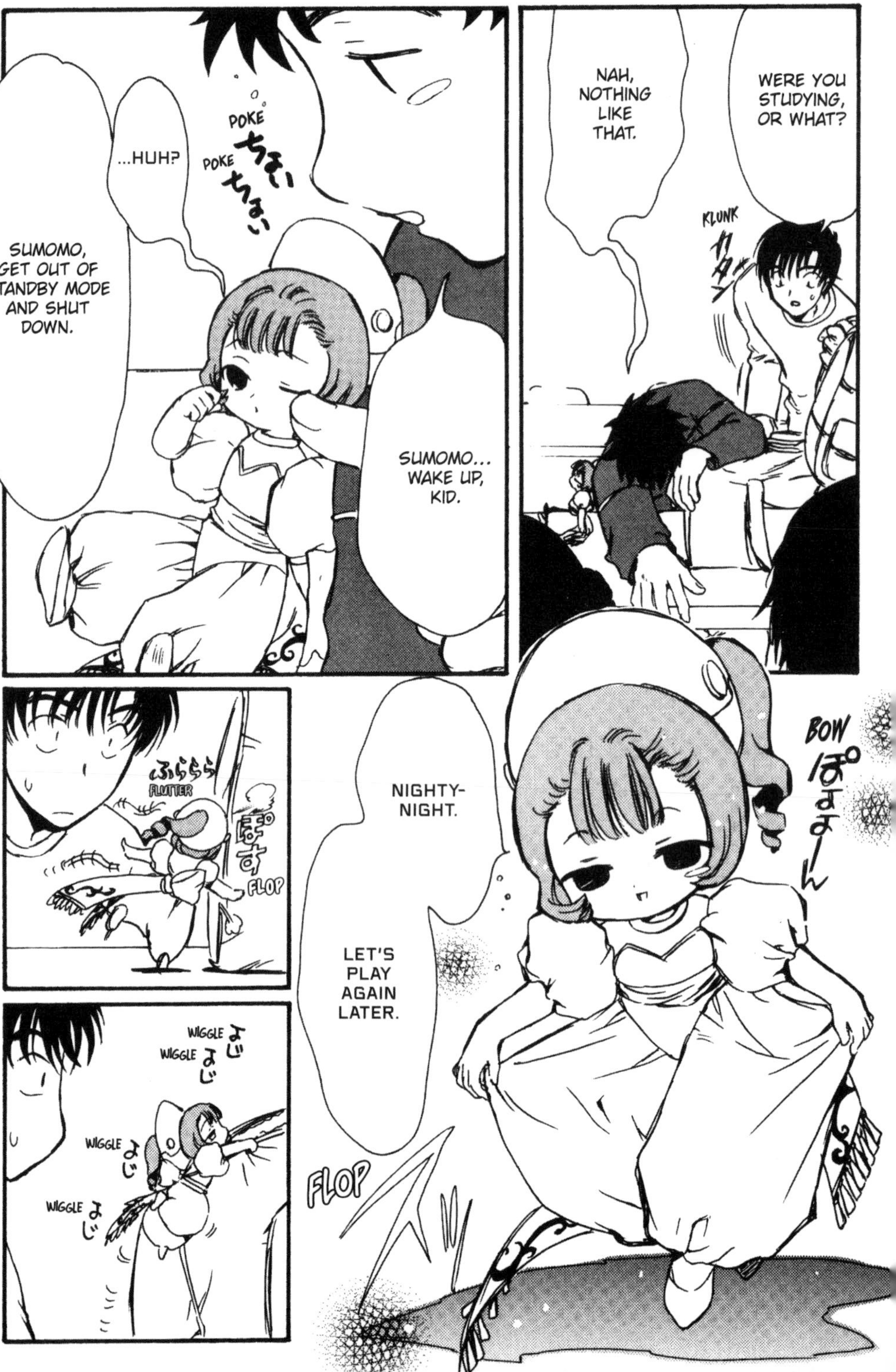
WERE YOU STUDYING, OR WHAT?
KLUNK
ガタッ
NAH, NOTHING LIKE THAT.
POKE
ちょい
POKE
ちょい
SUMOMO... WAKE UP, KID.
...HUH?
SUMOMO, GET OUT OF STANDBY MODE AND SHUT DOWN.
BOW
ぽよよーん
NIGHTY-NIGHT.
LET'S PLAY AGAIN LATER.
FLOP
ふららら
FLUTTER
ぽす
FLOP
WIGGLE よじ
WIGGLE よじ
WIGGLE よじ
WIGGLE よじ

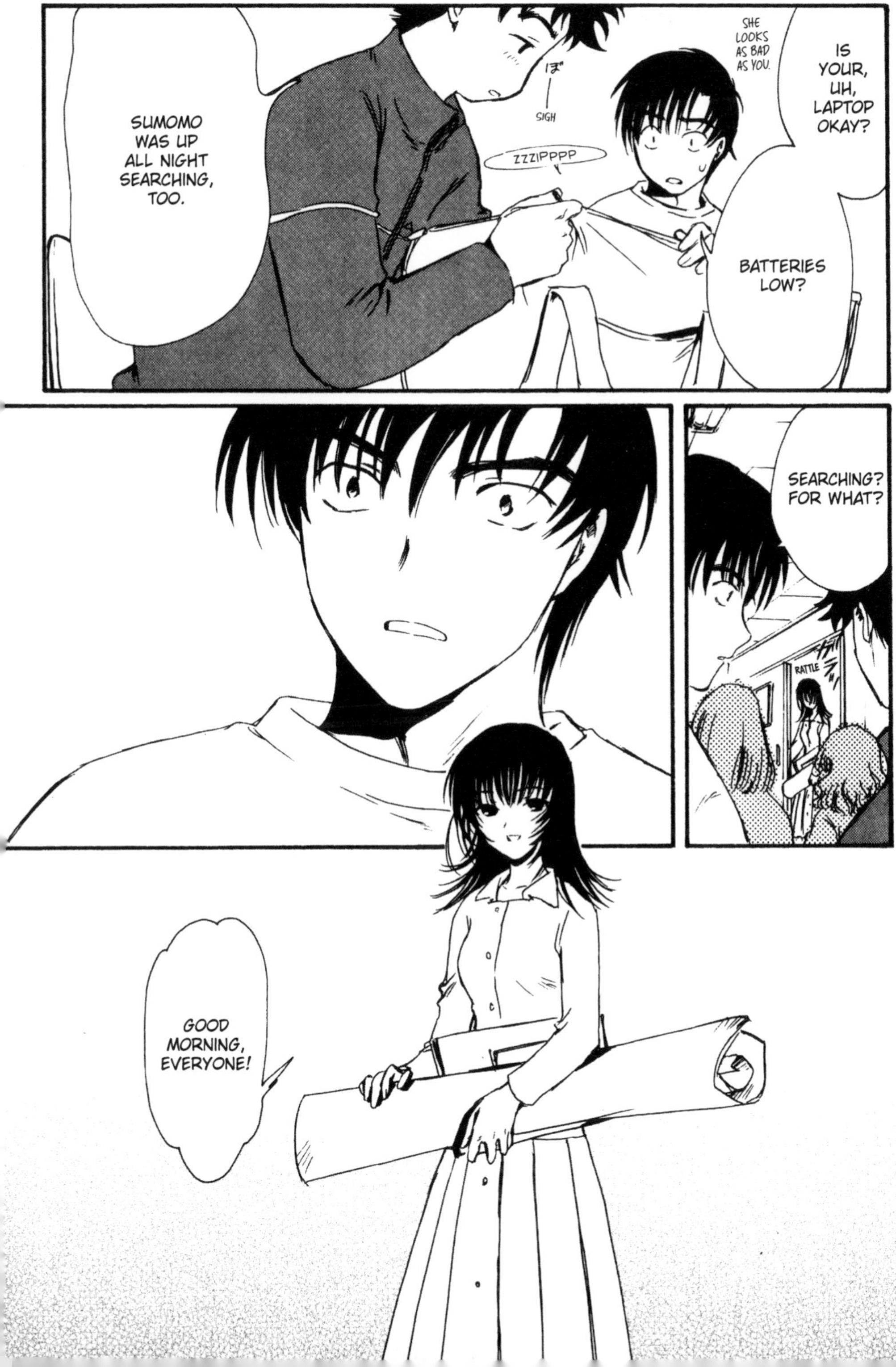
IS YOUR, UH, LAPTOP OKAY?
BATTERIES LOW?
SHE LOOKS AS BAD AS YOU.
ぼ
SIGH
ZZZIPPPP
SUMOMO WAS UP ALL NIGHT SEARCHING, TOO.
SEARCHING? FOR WHAT?
RATTLE
GOOD MORNING, EVERYONE!

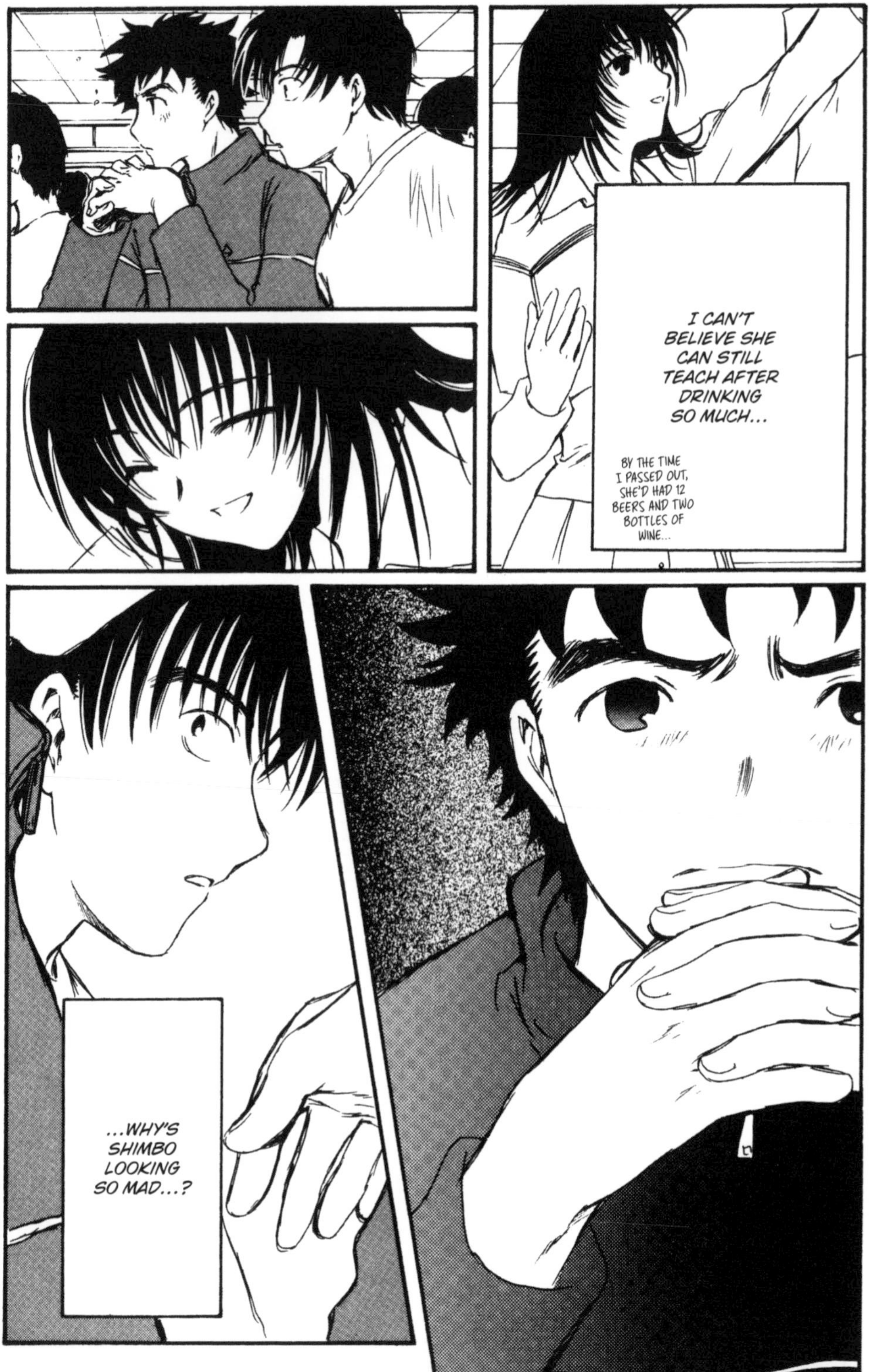
I CAN'T BELIEVE SHE CAN STILL TEACH AFTER DRINKING SO MUCH...
BY THE TIME I PASSED OUT, SHE'D HAD 12 BEERS AND TWO BOTTLES OF WINE...
...WHY'S SHIMBO LOOKING SO MAD...?

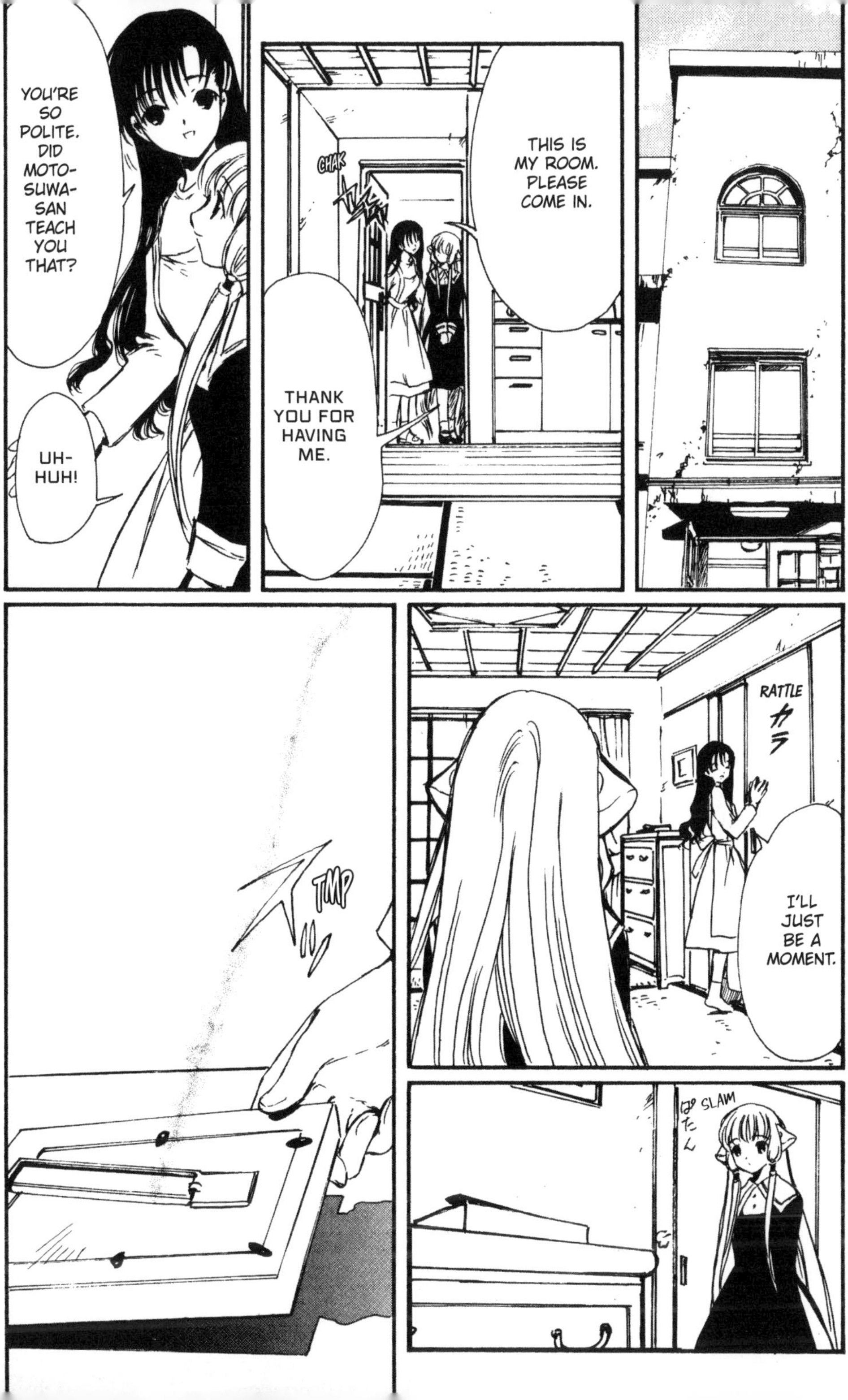
CHAK
THIS IS MY ROOM. PLEASE COME IN.
THANK YOU FOR HAVING ME.
YOU'RE SO POLITE. DID MOTO-SUWA-SAN TEACH YOU THAT?
UH-HUH!
RATTLE
カラ
I'LL JUST BE A MOMENT.
ぱたん
SLAM
TMP

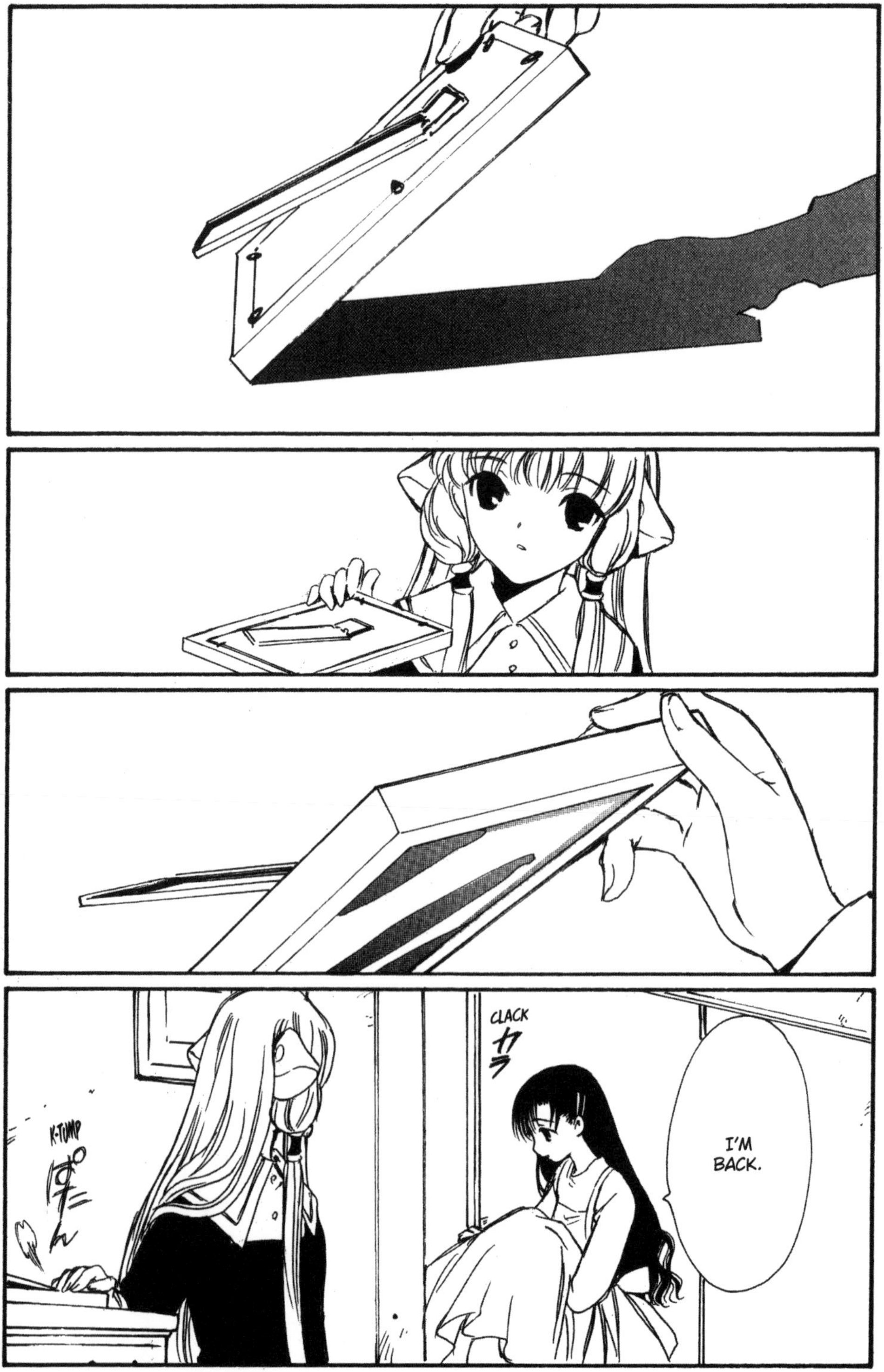

I'M BACK.
CLACK
K-TUMP

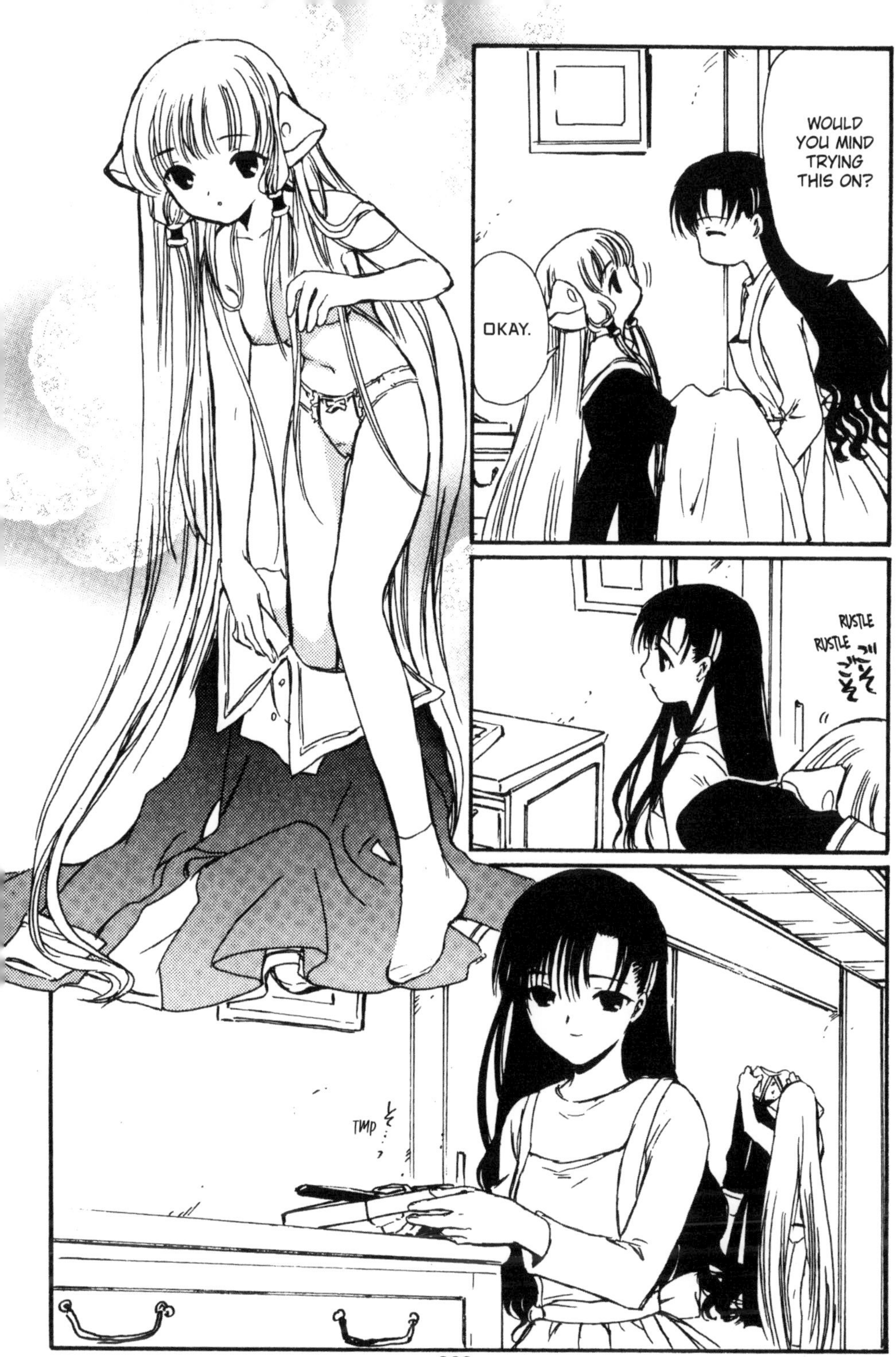
WOULD YOU MIND TRYING THIS ON?
OKAY.
RUSTLE
RUSTLE
TMP

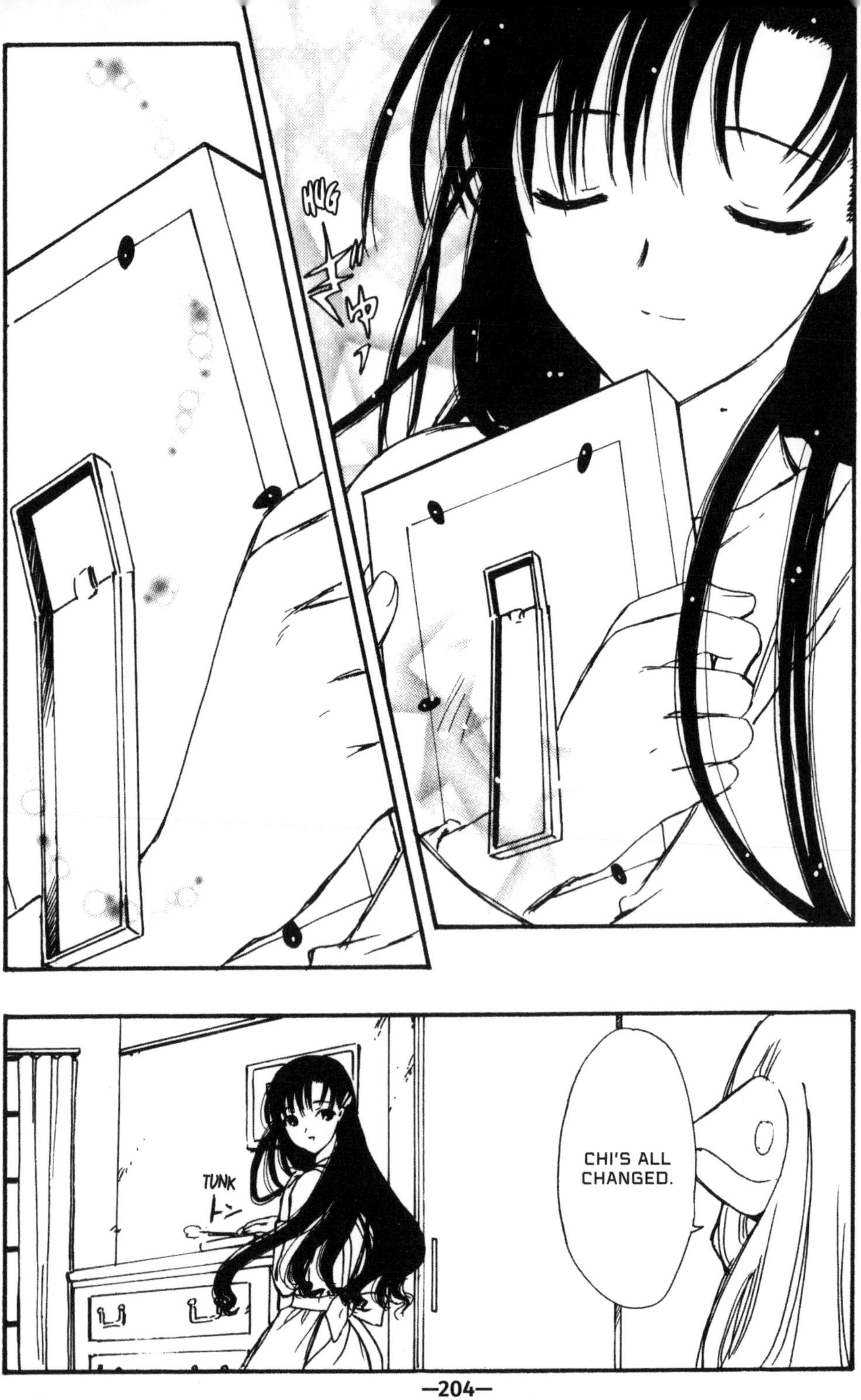
HUG
ぎゅっ
CHI'S ALL CHANGED.
TUNK
トン

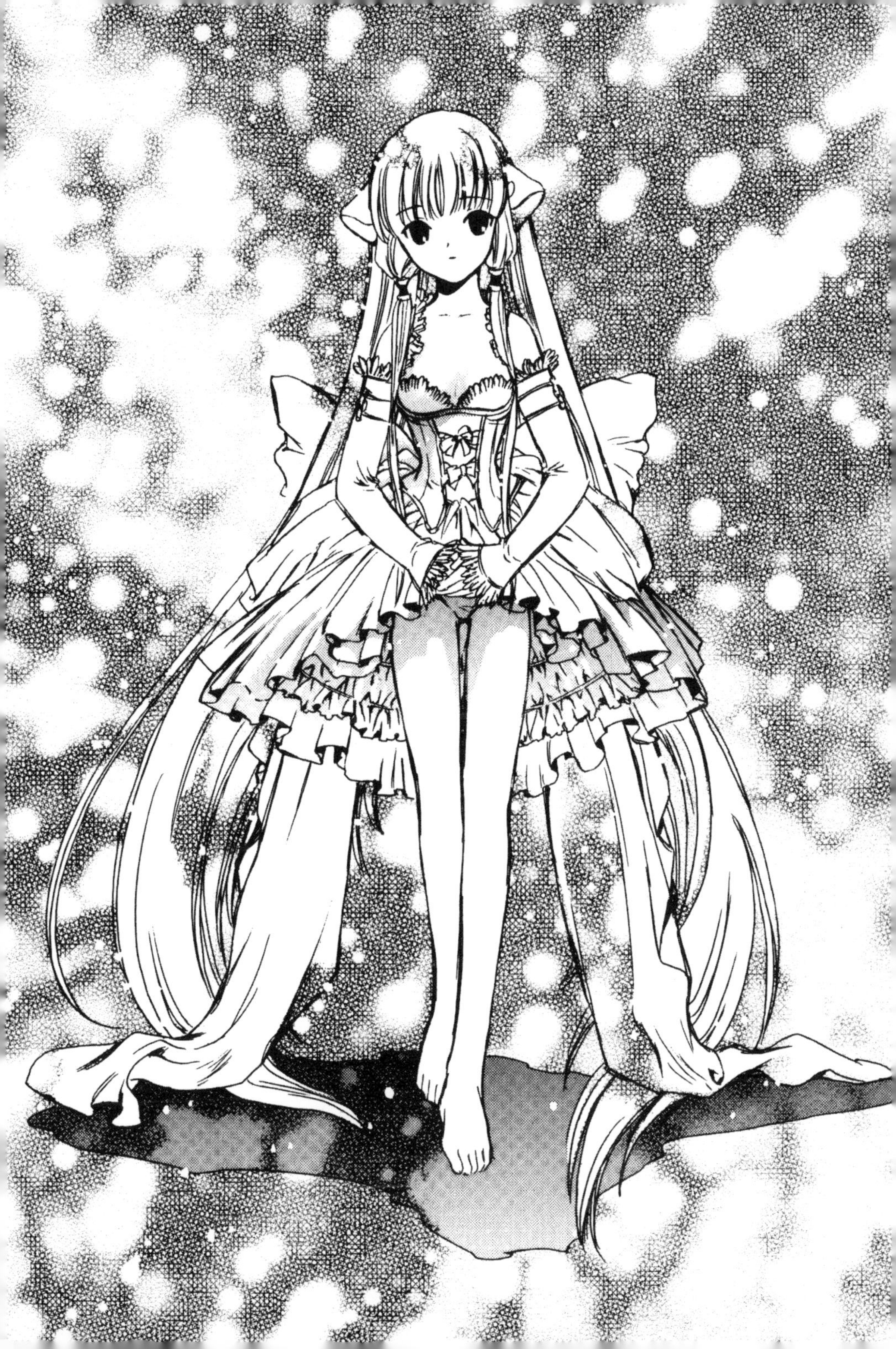

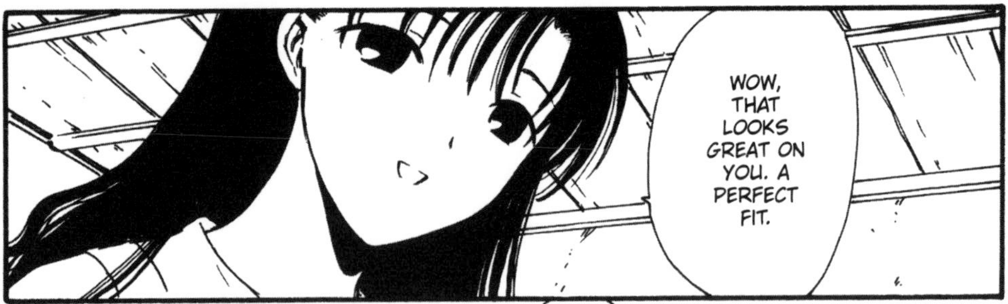
WOW, THAT LOOKS GREAT ON YOU. A PERFECT FIT.

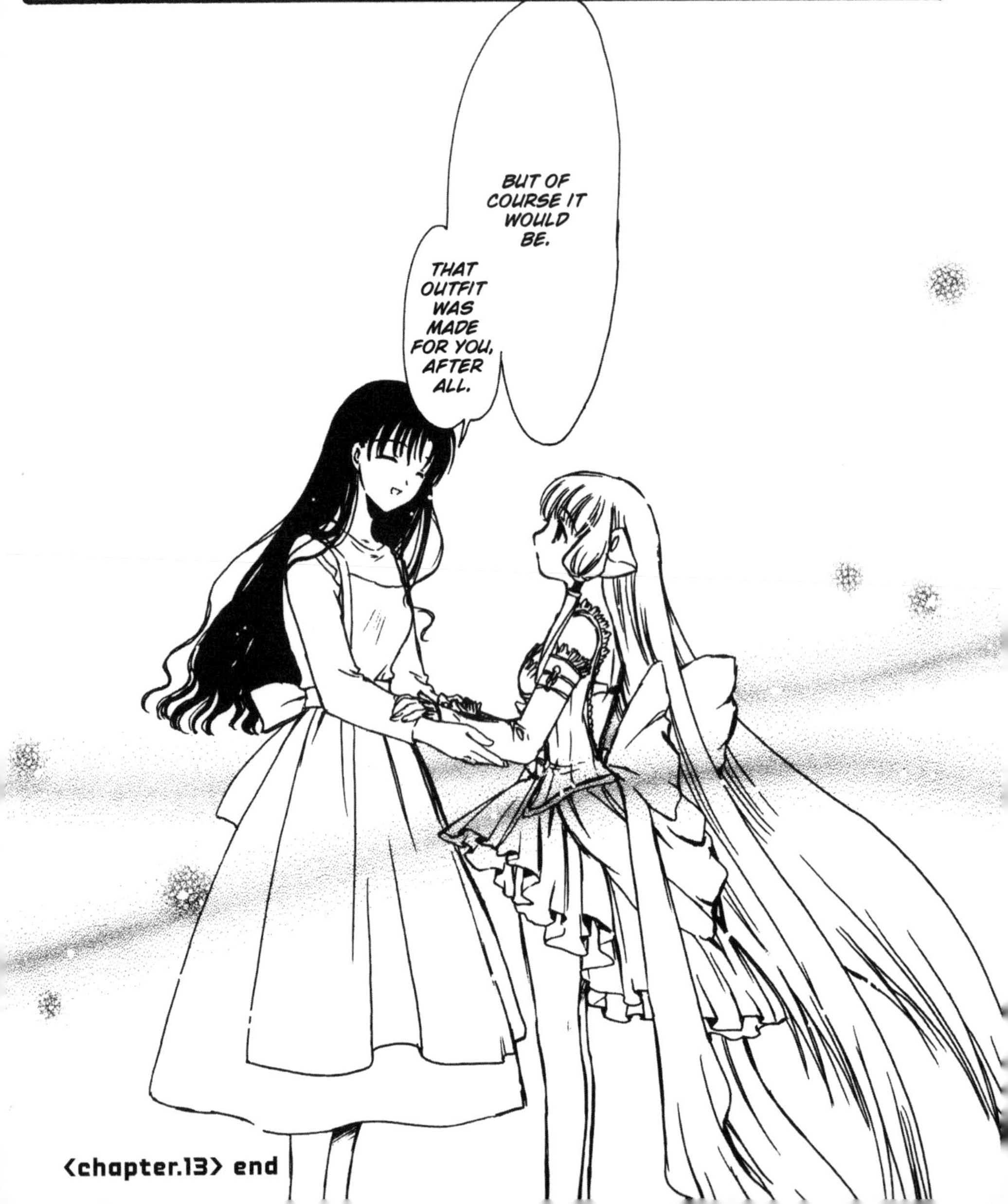
BUT OF COURSE IT WOULD BE.
THAT OUTFIT WAS MADE FOR YOU, AFTER ALL.

<chapter.13> end

〈chapter.14〉

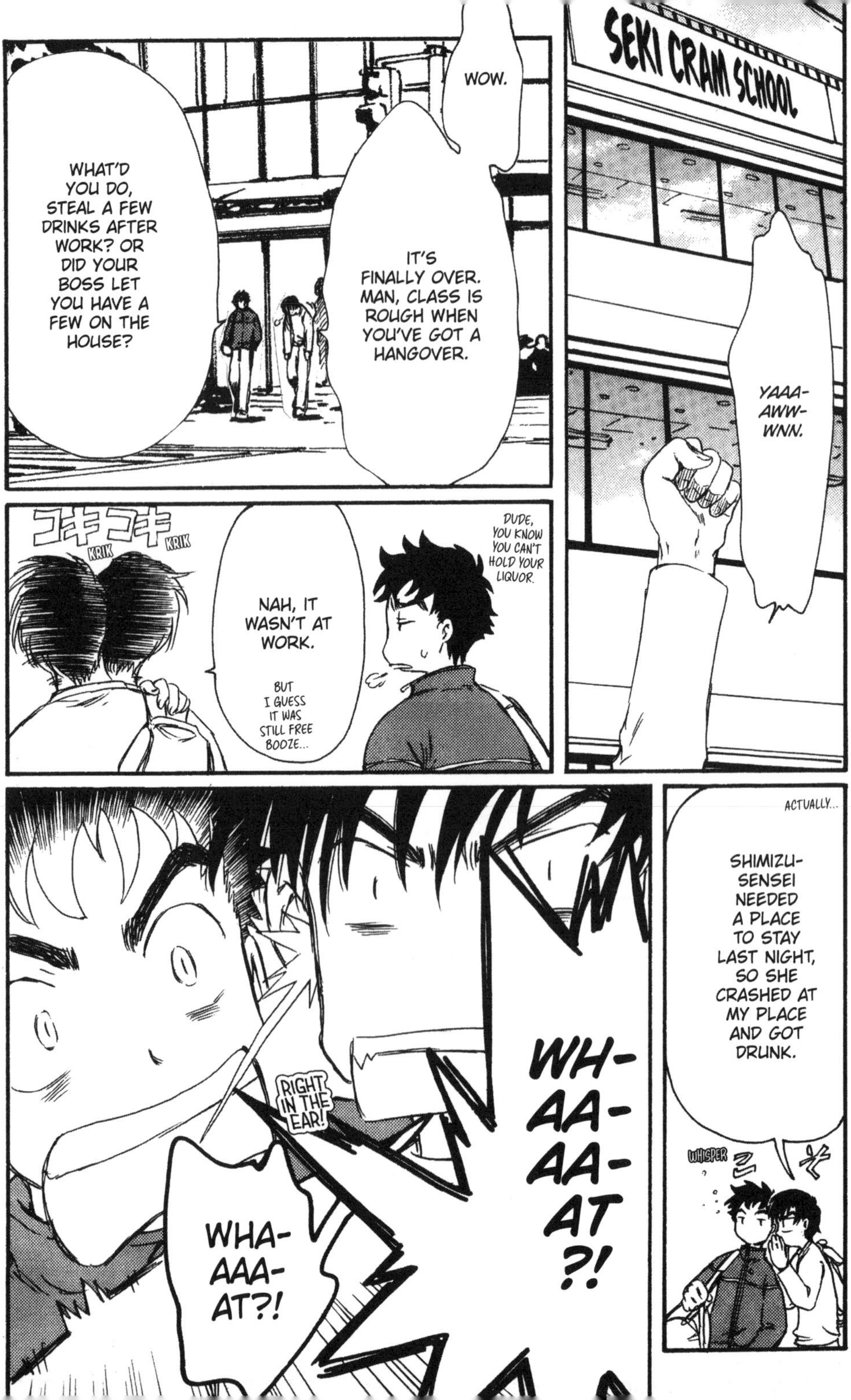
SEKI CRAM SCHOOL
YAAA-AWW-WNN.
WOW.
IT'S FINALLY OVER. MAN, CLASS IS ROUGH WHEN YOU'VE GOT A HANGOVER.
WHAT'D YOU DO, STEAL A FEW DRINKS AFTER WORK? OR DID YOUR BOSS LET YOU HAVE A FEW ON THE HOUSE?
DUDE, YOU KNOW YOU CAN'T HOLD YOUR LIQUOR.
NAH, IT WASN'T AT WORK.
BUT I GUESS IT WAS STILL FREE BOOZE...
コキコキ
KRIK KRIK
ACTUALLY...
SHIMIZU-SENSEI NEEDED A PLACE TO STAY LAST NIGHT, SO SHE CRASHED AT MY PLACE AND GOT DRUNK.
WHISPER
WH-AA-AA-AT?!
RIGHT IN THE EAR!
WHA-AAA-AT?!

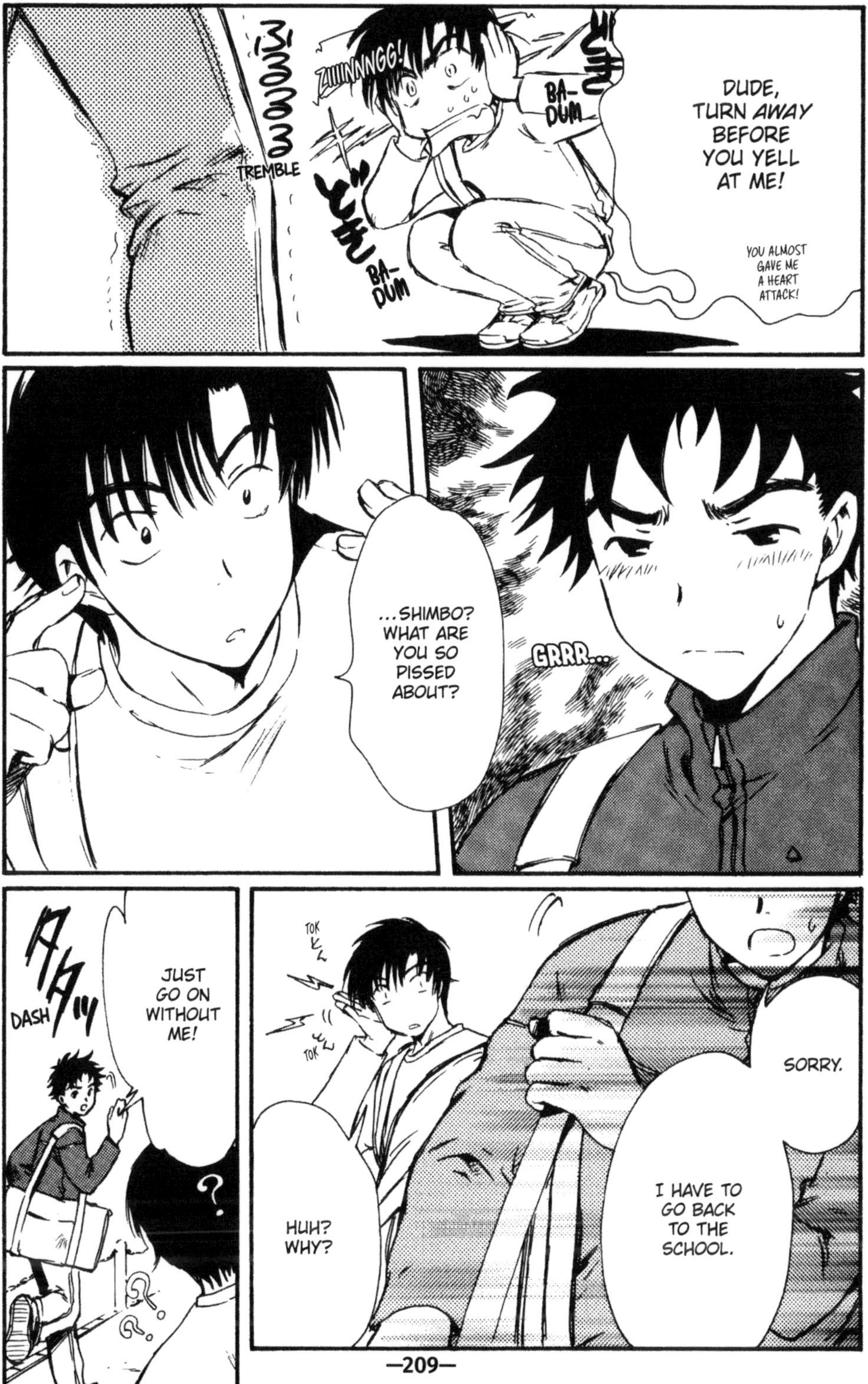
DUDE, TURN AWAY BEFORE YOU YELL AT ME!
YOU ALMOST GAVE ME A HEART ATTACK!
BA-DUM
ZIIIINNNGG!
TREMBLE
BA-DUM
GRRR...
...SHIMBO? WHAT ARE YOU SO PISSED ABOUT?
SORRY.
I HAVE TO GO BACK TO THE SCHOOL.
HUH? WHY?
TOK
TOK
JUST GO ON WITHOUT ME!
DASH

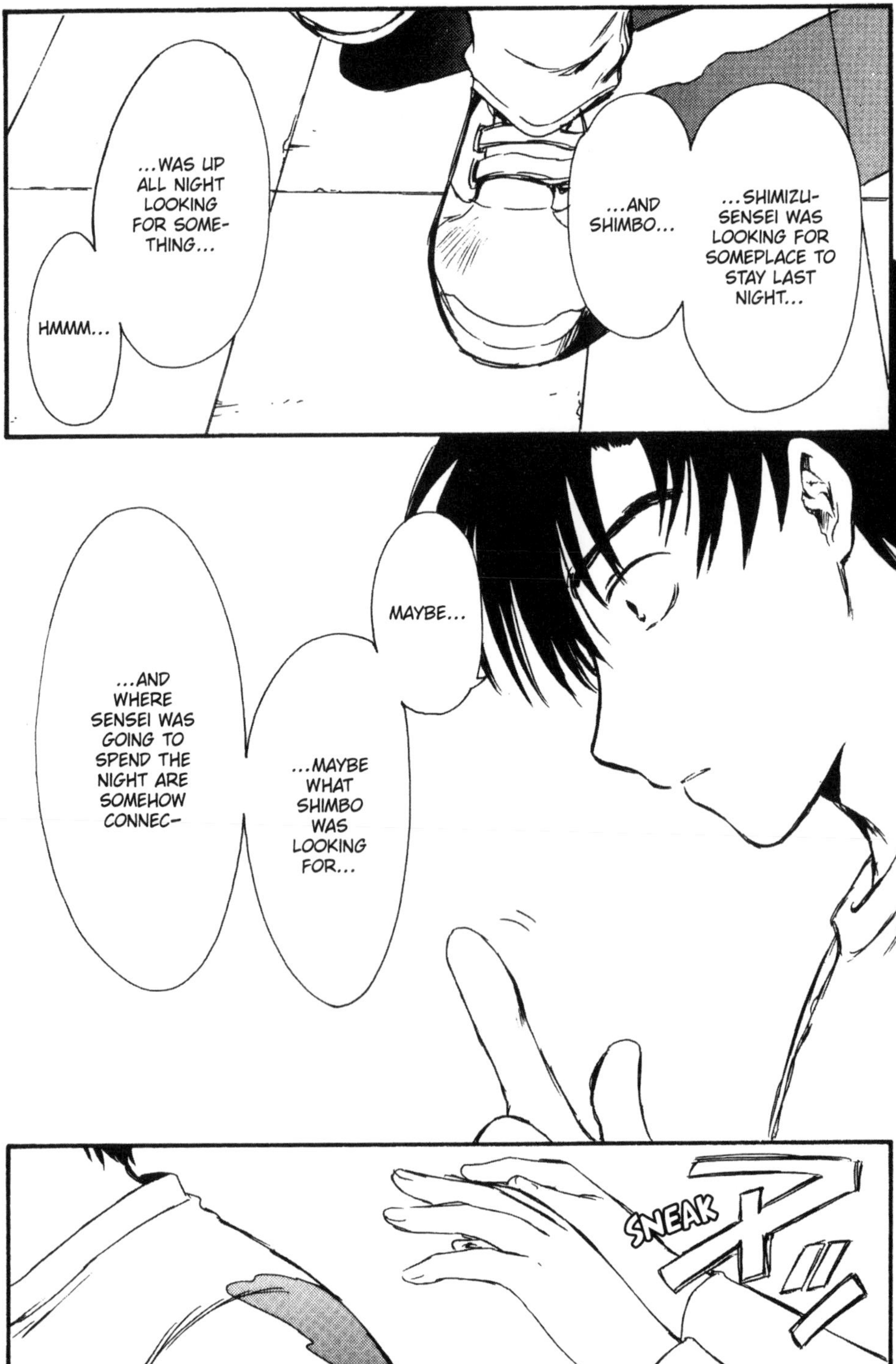
...SHIMIZU-SENSEI WAS LOOKING FOR SOMEPLACE TO STAY LAST NIGHT...
...AND SHIMBO...
...WAS UP ALL NIGHT LOOKING FOR SOME-THING...
HMMM...
MAYBE...
...MAYBE WHAT SHIMBO WAS LOOKING FOR...
...AND WHERE SENSEI WAS GOING TO SPEND THE NIGHT ARE SOMEHOW CONNEC-
SNEAK

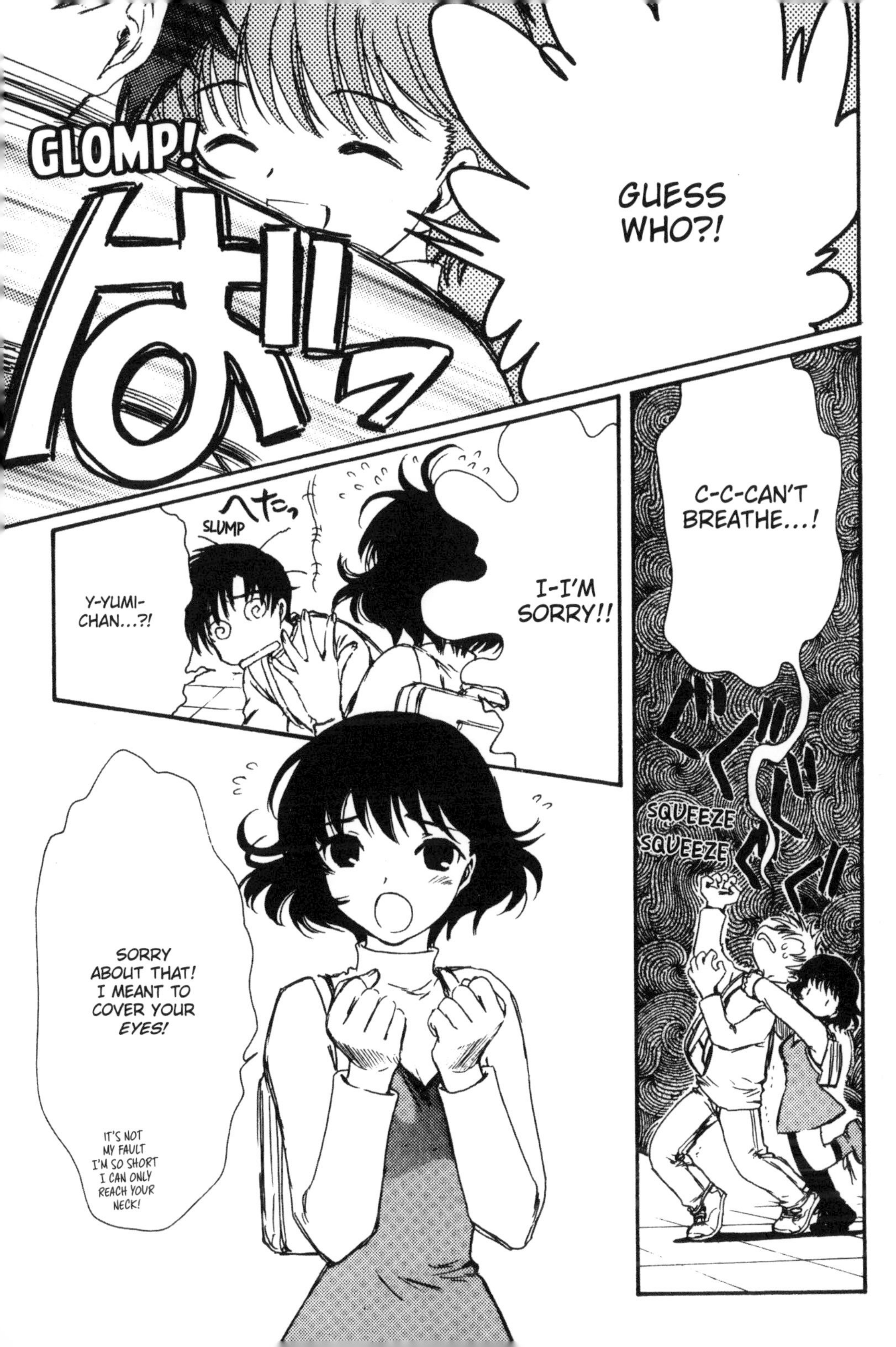
GUESS WHO?!
GLOMP!
C-C-CAN'T BREATHE...!
SQUEEZE SQUEEZE
I-I'M SORRY!!
SLUMP
Y-YUMI-CHAN...?!
SORRY ABOUT THAT! I MEANT TO COVER YOUR *EYES!*
IT'S NOT MY FAULT I'M SO SHORT I CAN ONLY REACH YOUR NECK!

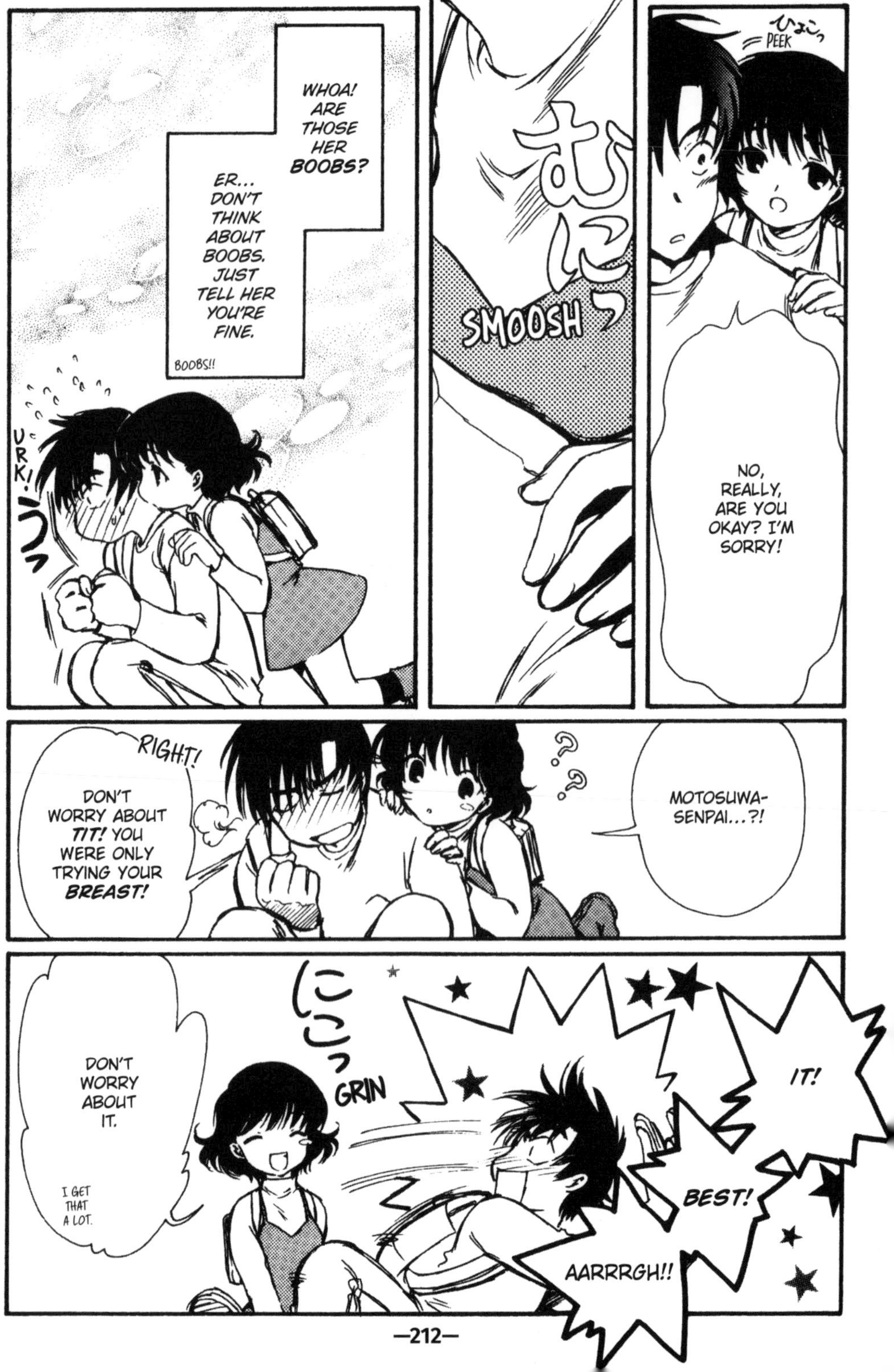
ひょこっ
PEEK
NO, REALLY, ARE YOU OKAY? I'M SORRY!
むにっ
SMOOSH
WHOA! ARE THOSE HER BOOBS?
ER... DON'T THINK ABOUT BOOBS. JUST TELL HER YOU'RE FINE.
BOOBS!!
URK!
うっ
MOTOSUWA-SENPAI...?!
RIGHT!
DON'T WORRY ABOUT TIT! YOU WERE ONLY TRYING YOUR BREAST!
IT!
BEST!
AARRRGH!!
にこっ
GRIN
DON'T WORRY ABOUT IT.
I GET THAT A LOT.

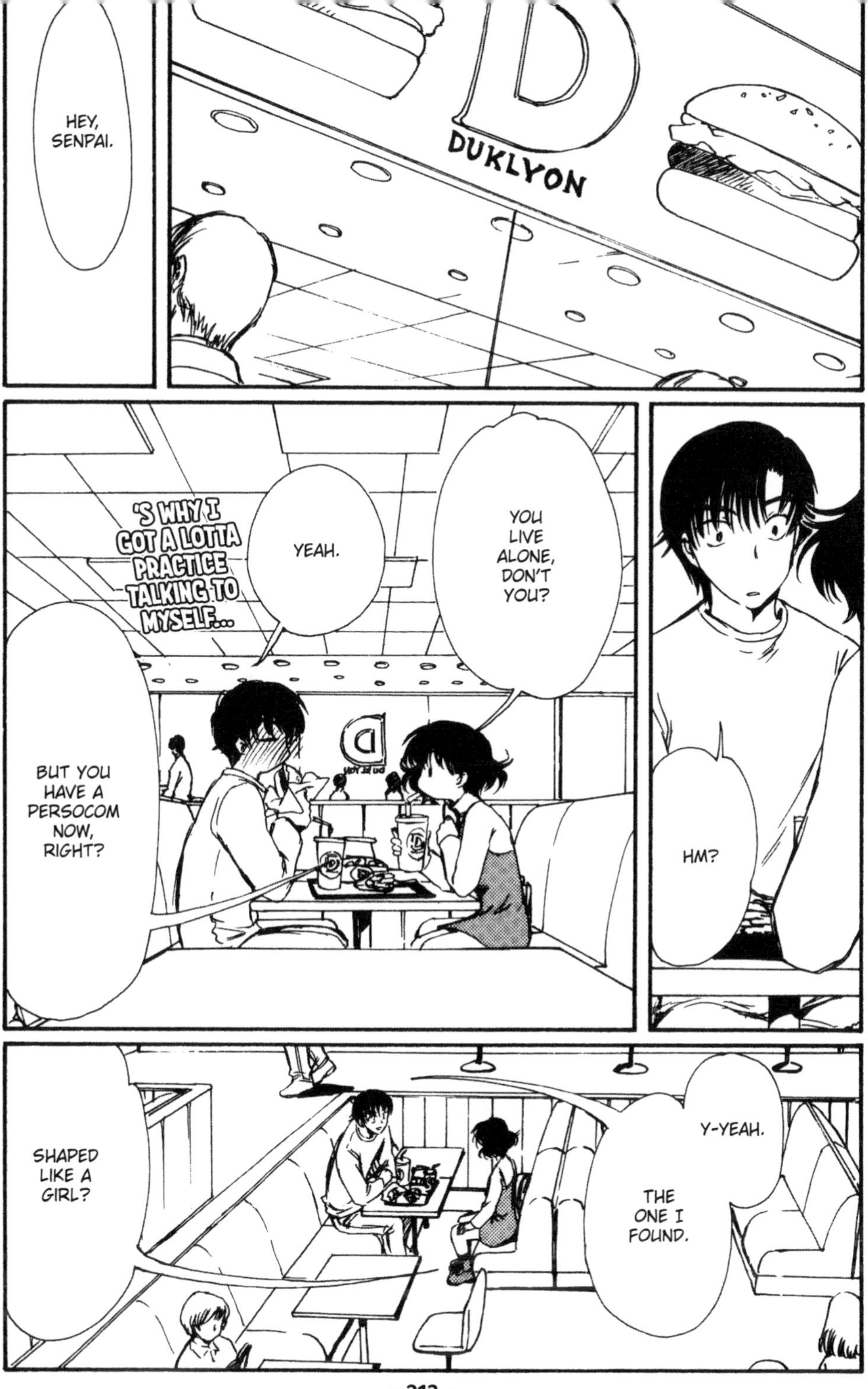
DUKLYON
HEY, SENPAI.
HM?
YOU LIVE ALONE, DON'T YOU?
YEAH.
'S WHY I GOT A LOTTA PRACTICE TALKING TO MYSELF...
BUT YOU HAVE A PERSOCOM NOW, RIGHT?
Y-YEAH.
THE ONE I FOUND.
SHAPED LIKE A GIRL?

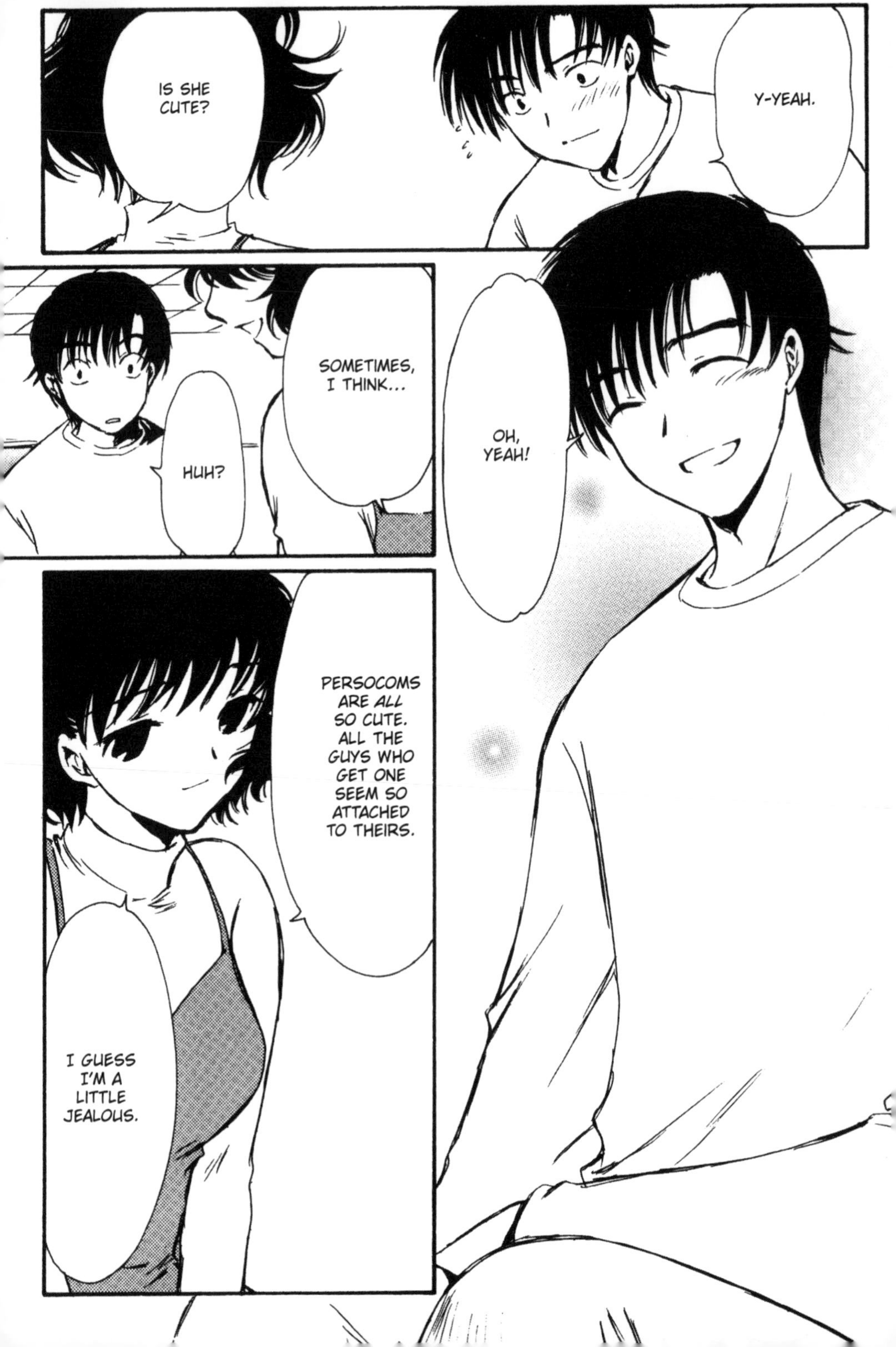
Y-YEAH.
IS SHE CUTE?
OH, YEAH!
SOMETIMES, I THINK...
HUH?
PERSOCOMS ARE *ALL* SO CUTE. ALL THE GUYS WHO GET ONE SEEM SO ATTACHED TO THEIRS.
I GUESS I'M A LITTLE JEALOUS.

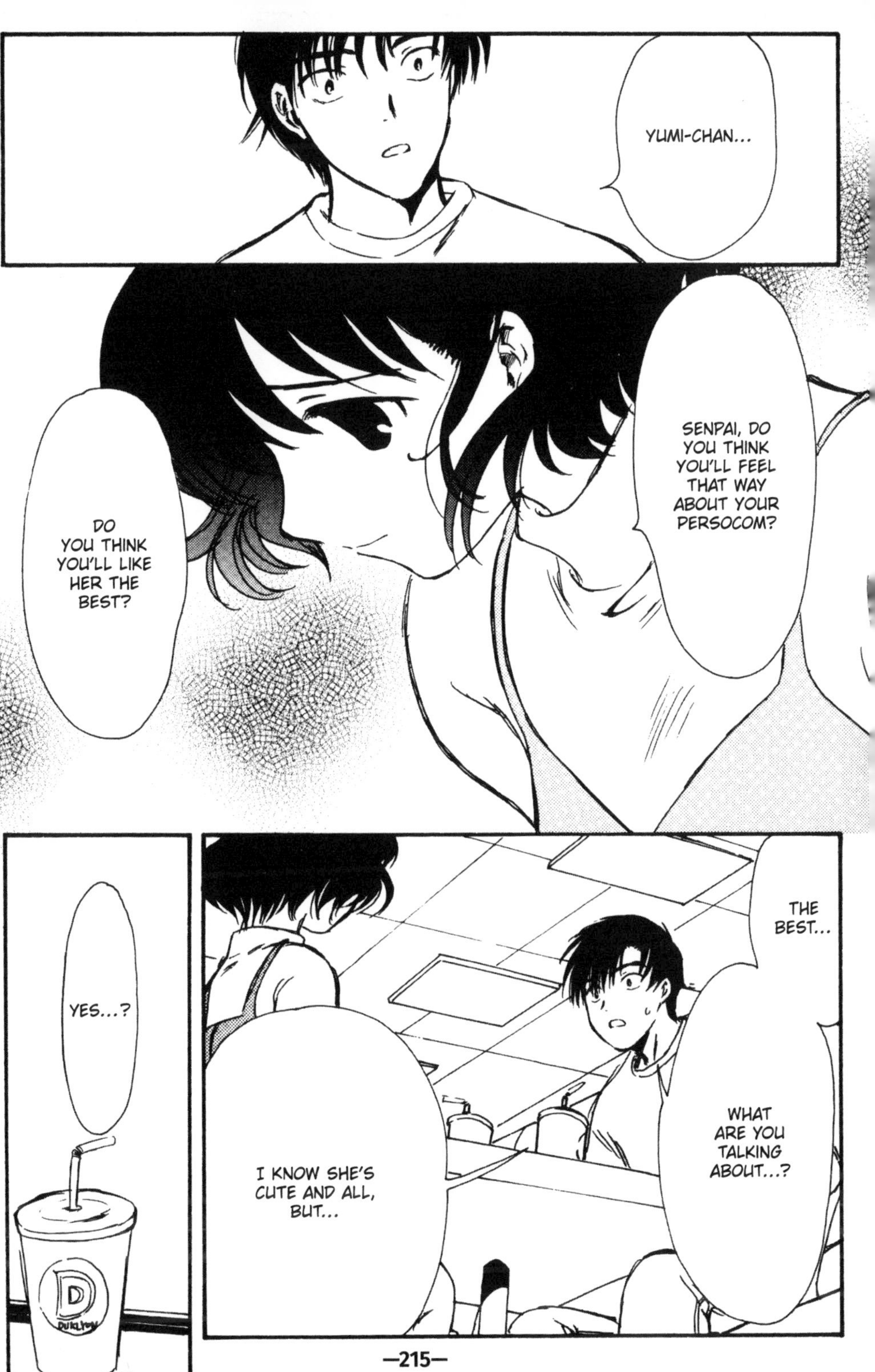
YUMI-CHAN...
SENPAI, DO YOU THINK YOU'LL FEEL THAT WAY ABOUT YOUR PERSOCOM?
DO YOU THINK YOU'LL LIKE HER THE BEST?
THE BEST...
WHAT ARE YOU TALKING ABOUT...?
I KNOW SHE'S CUTE AND ALL, BUT...
YES...?

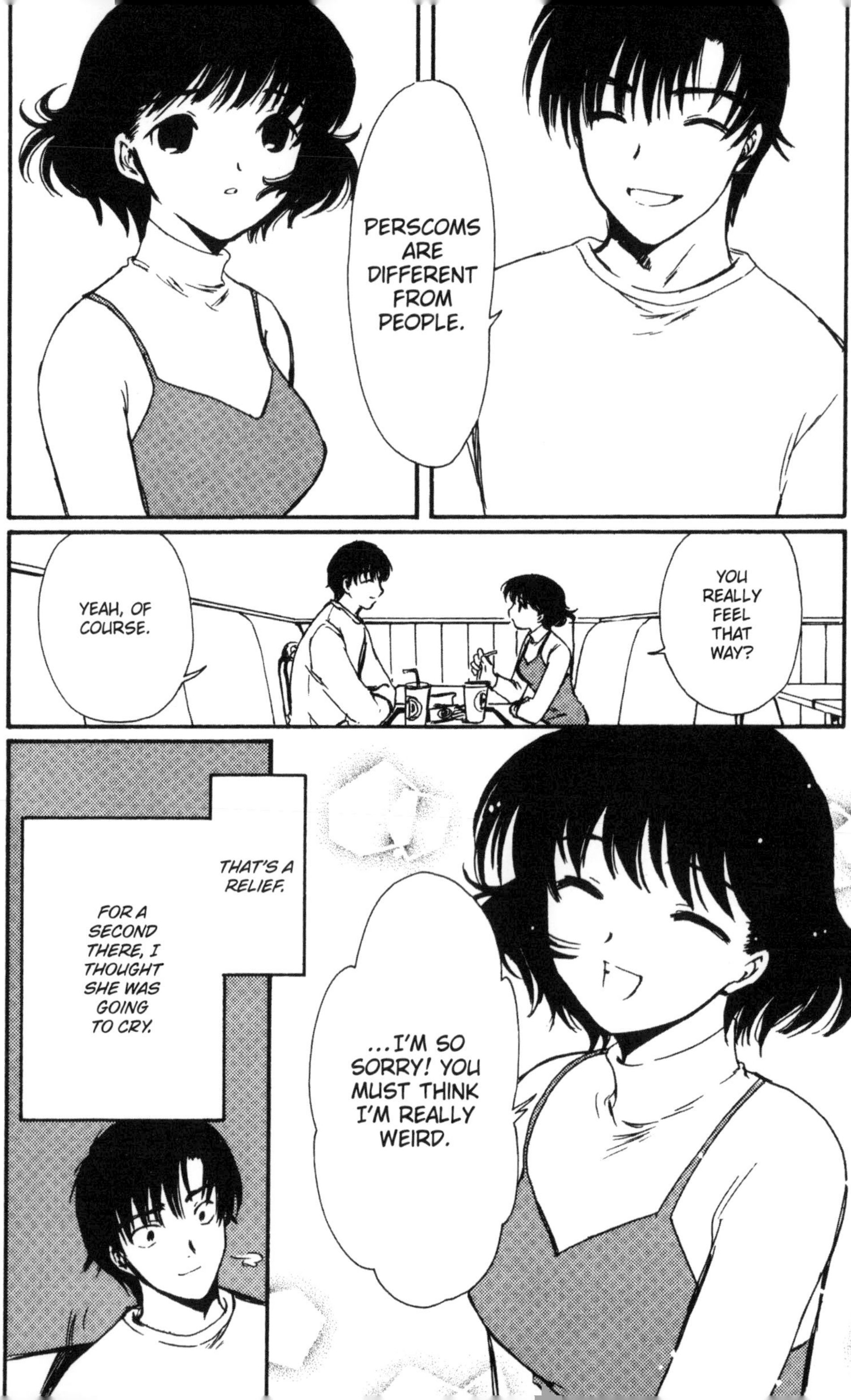
PERSCOMS ARE DIFFERENT FROM PEOPLE.
YOU REALLY FEEL THAT WAY?
YEAH, OF COURSE.
...I'M SO SORRY! YOU MUST THINK I'M REALLY WEIRD.
THAT'S A RELIEF.
FOR A SECOND THERE, I THOUGHT SHE WAS GOING TO CRY.

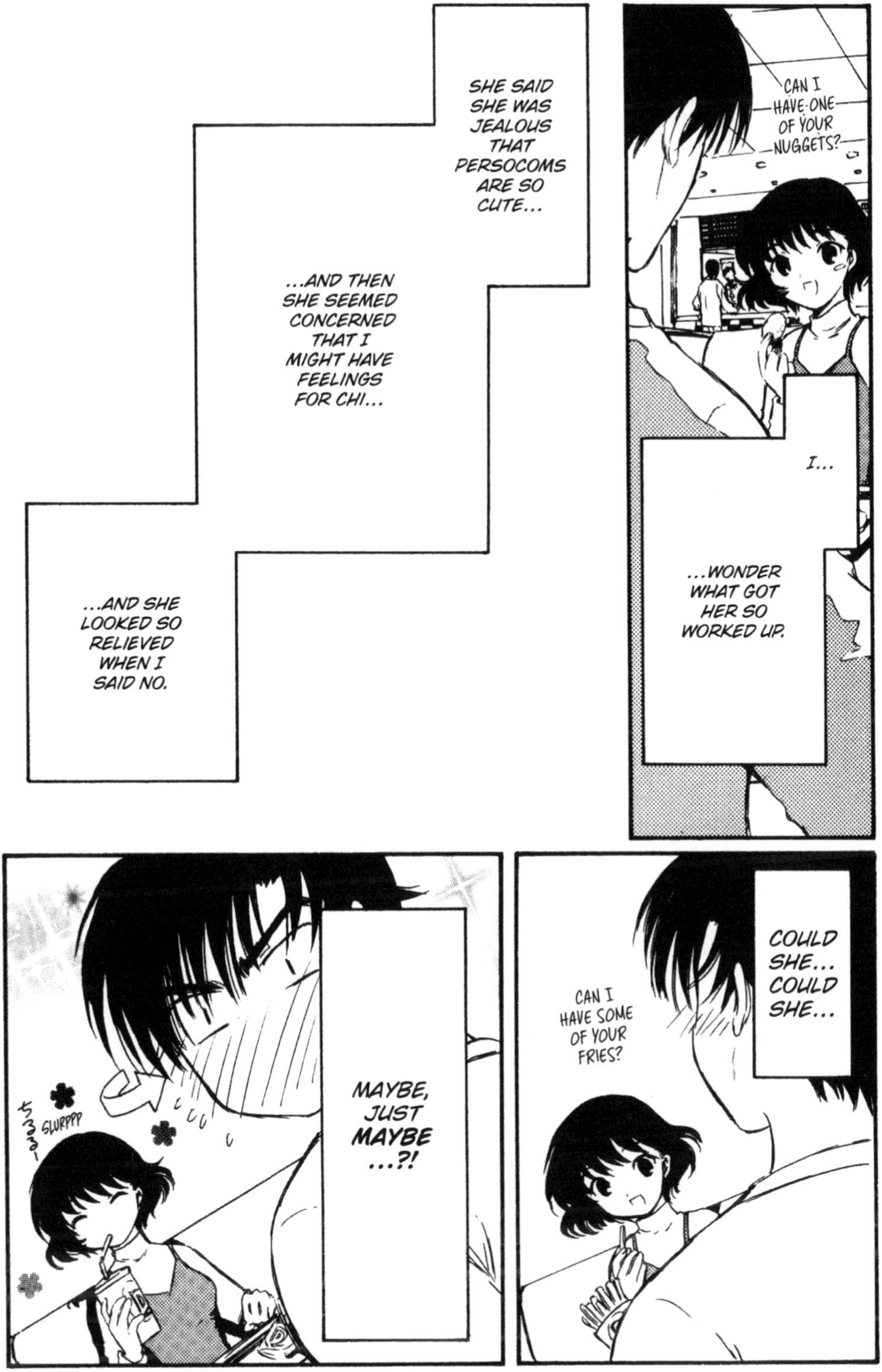
CAN I HAVE ONE OF YOUR NUGGETS?
I...
...WONDER WHAT GOT HER SO WORKED UP.
SHE SAID SHE WAS JEALOUS THAT PERSOCOMS ARE SO CUTE...
...AND THEN SHE SEEMED CONCERNED THAT I MIGHT HAVE FEELINGS FOR CHI...
...AND SHE LOOKED SO RELIEVED WHEN I SAID NO.
COULD SHE... COULD SHE...
CAN I HAVE SOME OF YOUR FRIES?
MAYBE, JUST **MAYBE** ...?!
SLURPPP

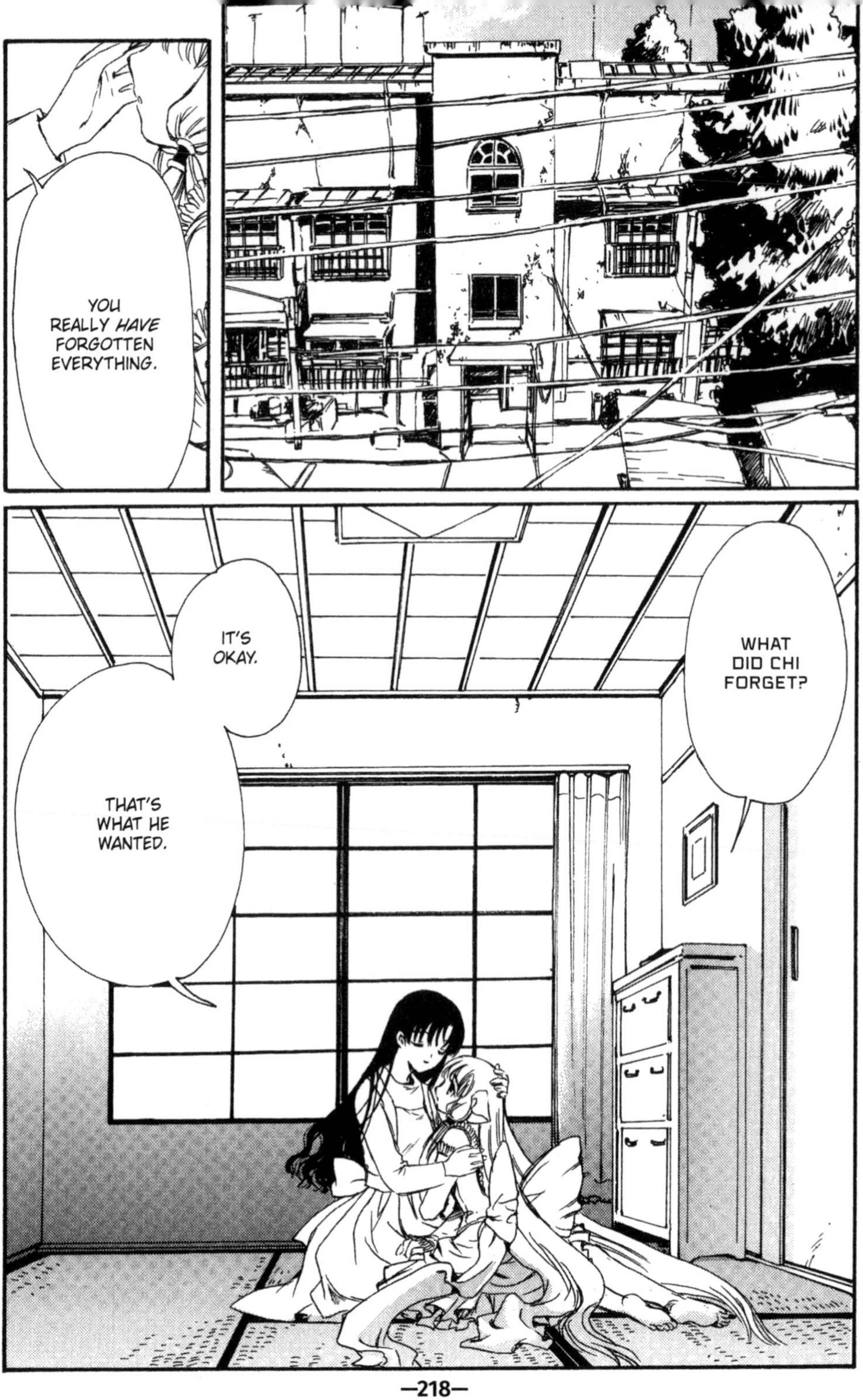
YOU REALLY *HAVE* FORGOTTEN EVERYTHING.
WHAT DID CHI FORGET?
IT'S OKAY.
THAT'S WHAT HE WANTED.

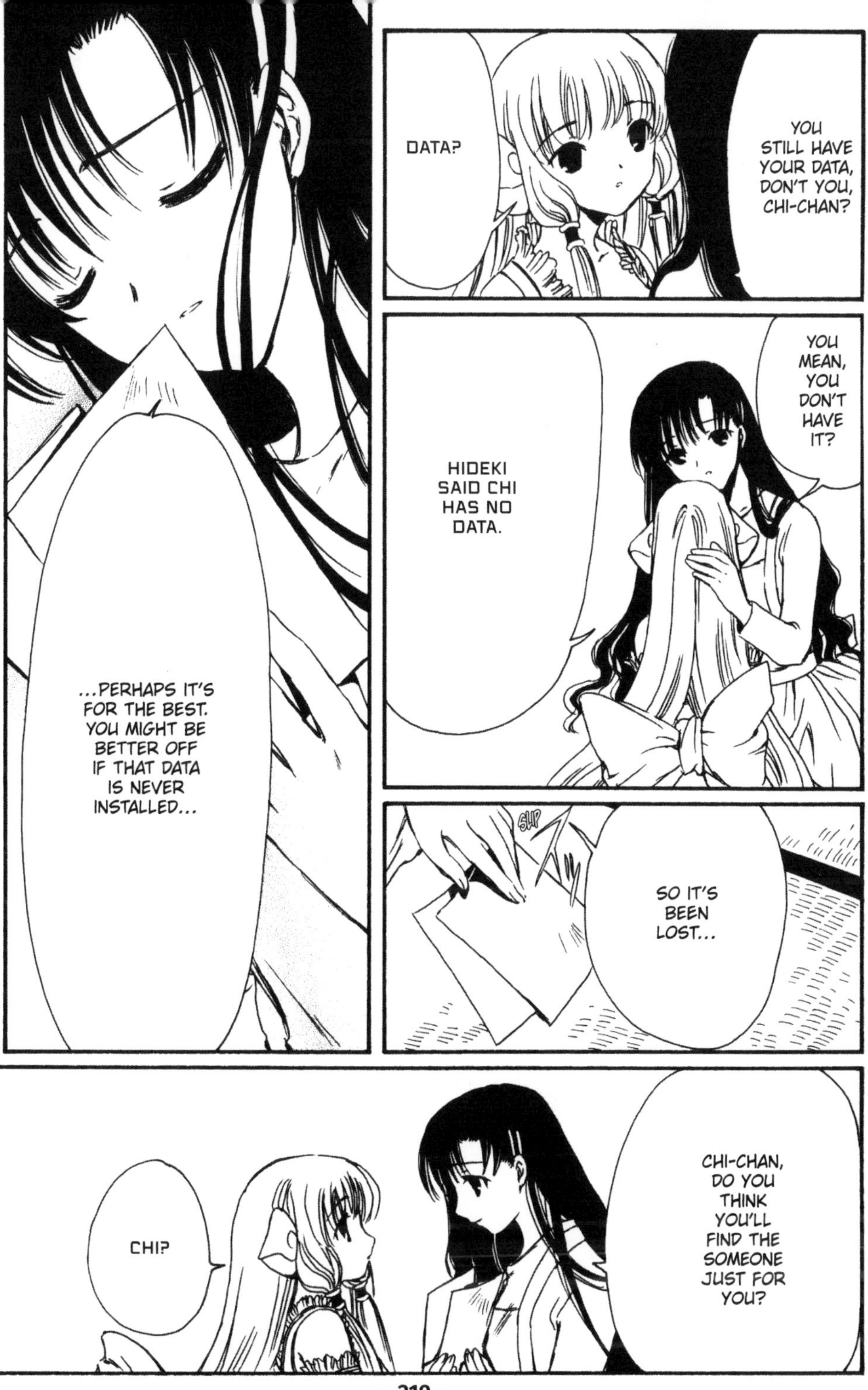
YOU STILL HAVE YOUR DATA, DON'T YOU, CHI-CHAN?
DATA?
YOU MEAN, YOU DON'T HAVE IT?
HIDEKI SAID CHI HAS NO DATA.
SLIP
SO IT'S BEEN LOST...
...PERHAPS IT'S FOR THE BEST. YOU MIGHT BE BETTER OFF IF THAT DATA IS NEVER INSTALLED...
CHI-CHAN, DO YOU THINK YOU'LL FIND THE SOMEONE JUST FOR YOU?
CHI?

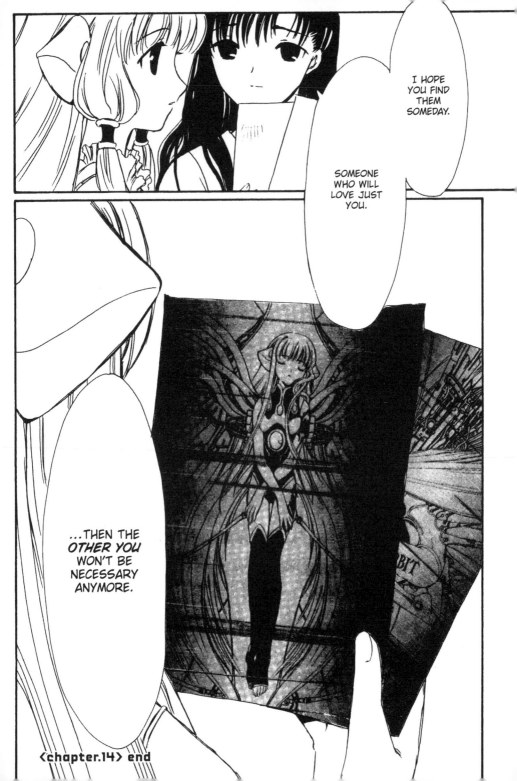

I HOPE YOU FIND THEM SOMEDAY.

SOMEONE WHO WILL LOVE JUST YOU.

...THEN THE *OTHER YOU* WON'T BE NECESSARY ANYMORE.

⟨chapter.14⟩ end

Chobits

〈chapter.15〉

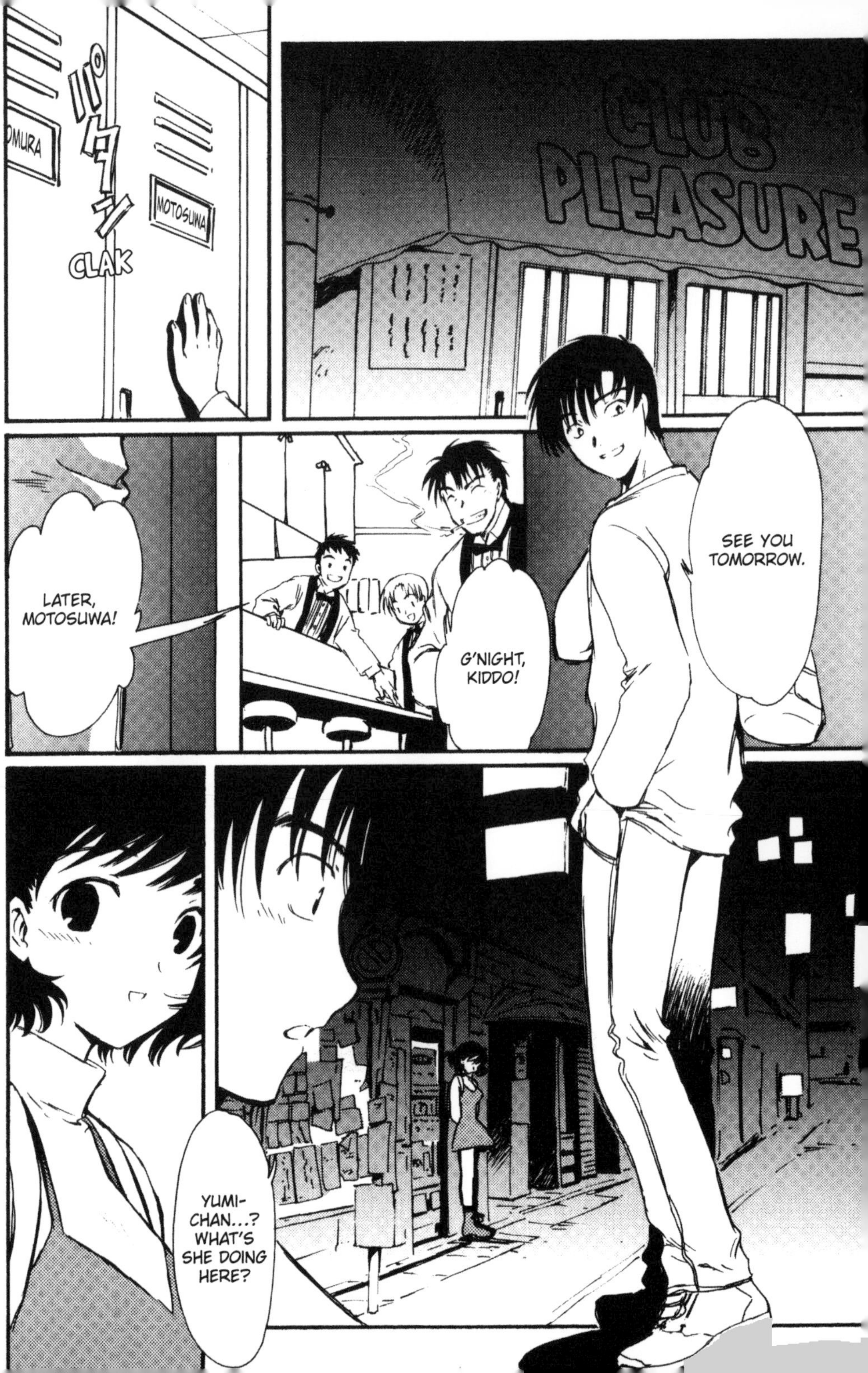
CLUB PLEASURE
MOTOSUWA
OMURA
パタン
CLAK
SEE YOU TOMORROW.
G'NIGHT, KIDDO!
LATER, MOTOSUWA!
YUMI-CHAN...? WHAT'S SHE DOING HERE?

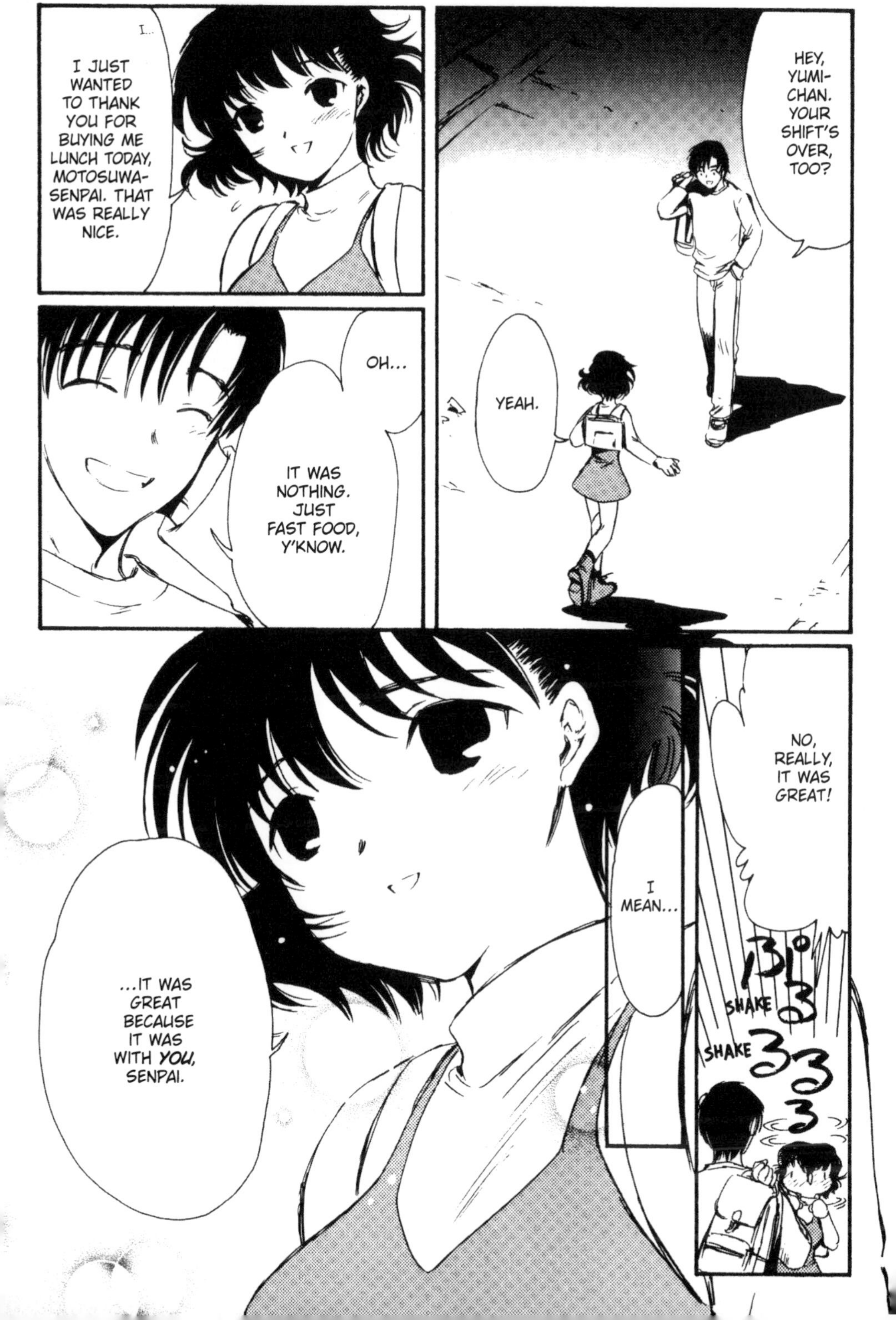
HEY, YUMI-CHAN. YOUR SHIFT'S OVER, TOO?
YEAH.
I...
I JUST WANTED TO THANK YOU FOR BUYING ME LUNCH TODAY, MOTOSUWA-SENPAI. THAT WAS REALLY NICE.
OH...
IT WAS NOTHING. JUST FAST FOOD, Y'KNOW.
NO, REALLY, IT WAS GREAT!
SHAKE
SHAKE
I MEAN...
...IT WAS GREAT BECAUSE IT WAS WITH *YOU*, SENPAI.

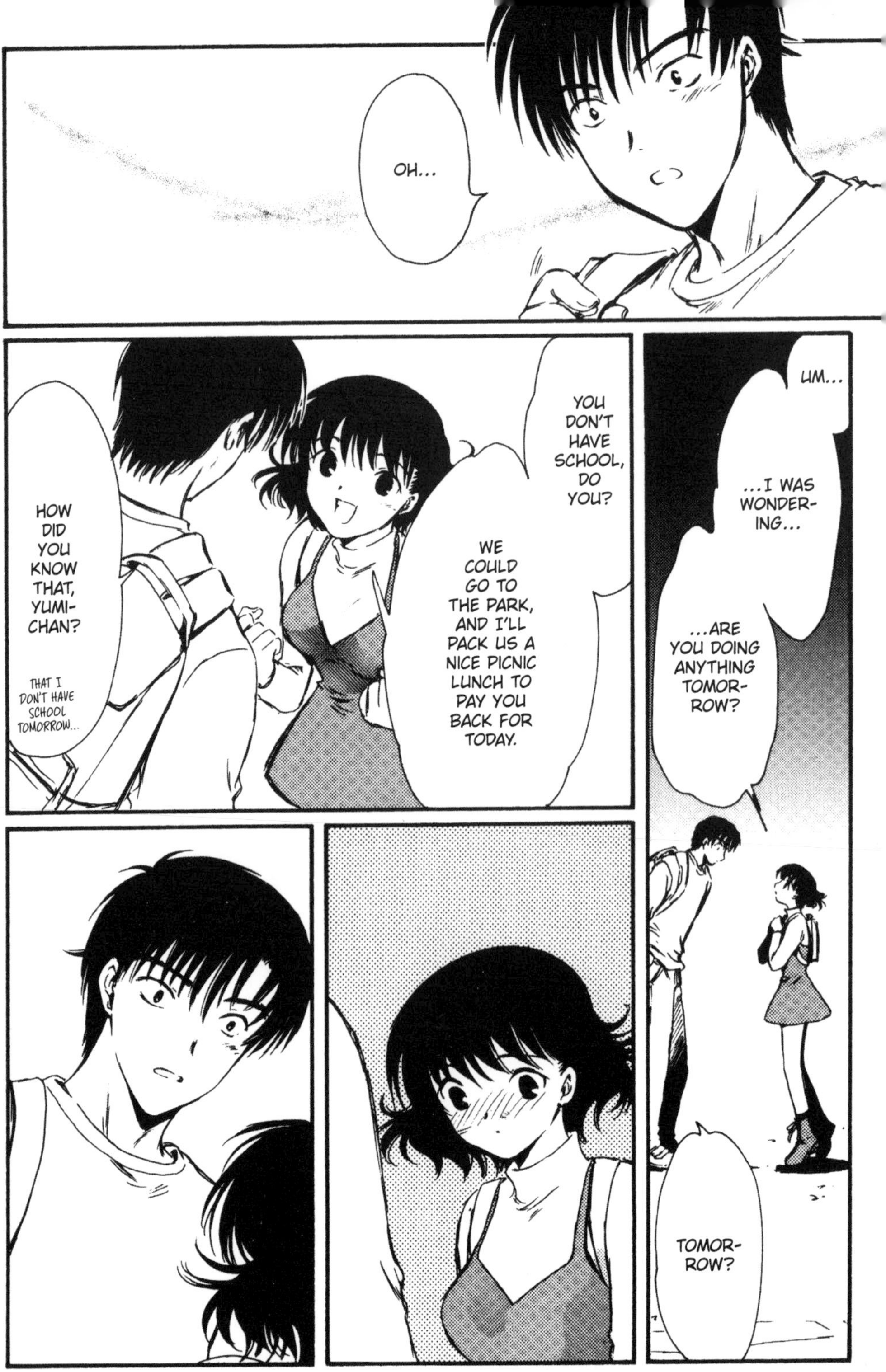
OH...
UM...
...I WAS WONDER-ING...
...ARE YOU DOING ANYTHING TOMOR-ROW?
TOMOR-ROW?
YOU DON'T HAVE SCHOOL, DO YOU?
WE COULD GO TO THE PARK, AND I'LL PACK US A NICE PICNIC LUNCH TO PAY YOU BACK FOR TODAY.
HOW DID YOU KNOW THAT, YUMI-CHAN?
THAT I DON'T HAVE SCHOOL TOMORROW...

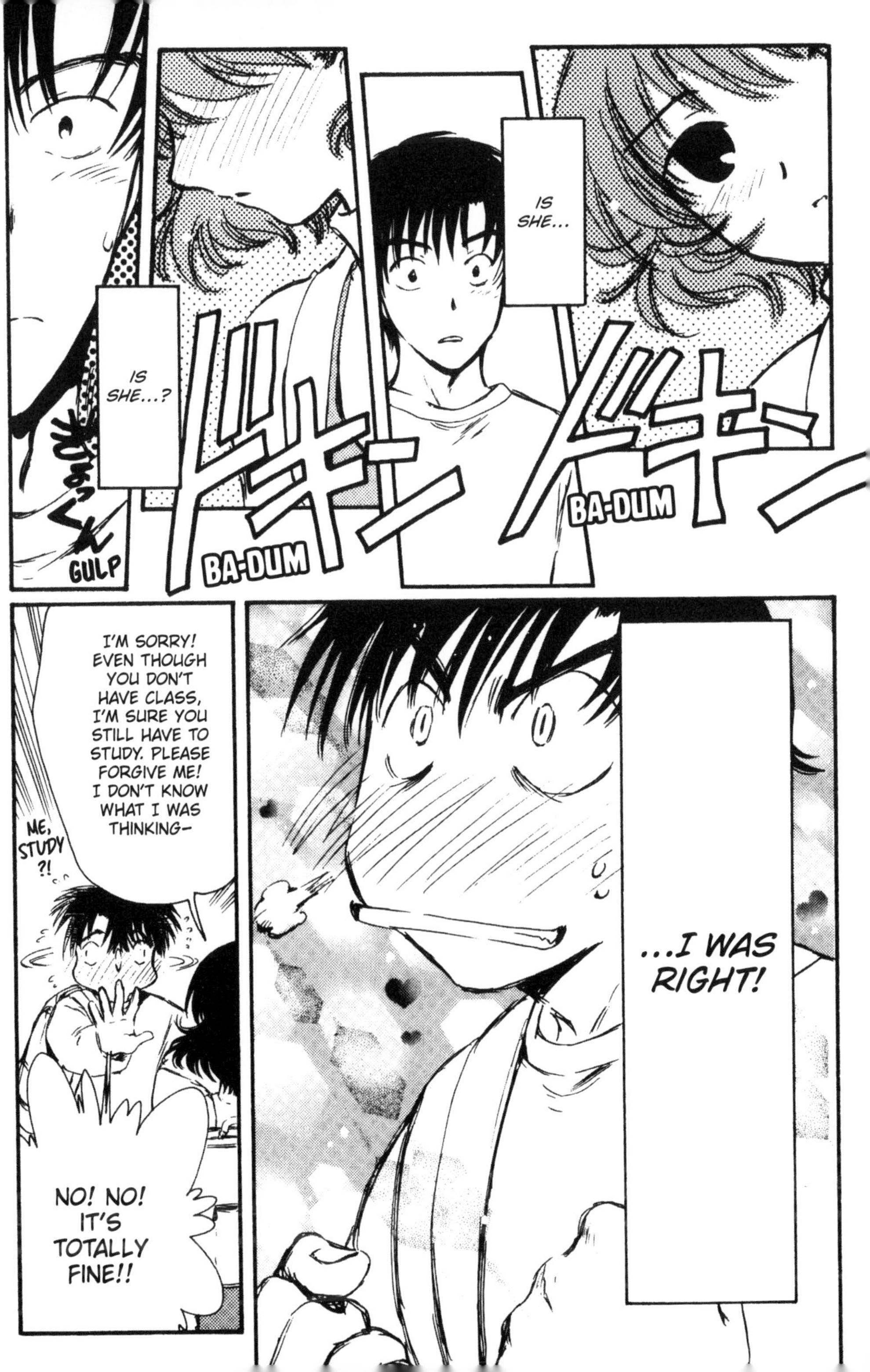
IS SHE...
BA-DUM
IS SHE...?
BA-DUM
GULP
...I WAS RIGHT!
I'M SORRY! EVEN THOUGH YOU DON'T HAVE CLASS, I'M SURE YOU STILL HAVE TO STUDY. PLEASE FORGIVE ME! I DON'T KNOW WHAT I WAS THINKING–
ME, STUDY ?!
NO! NO! IT'S TOTALLY FINE!!

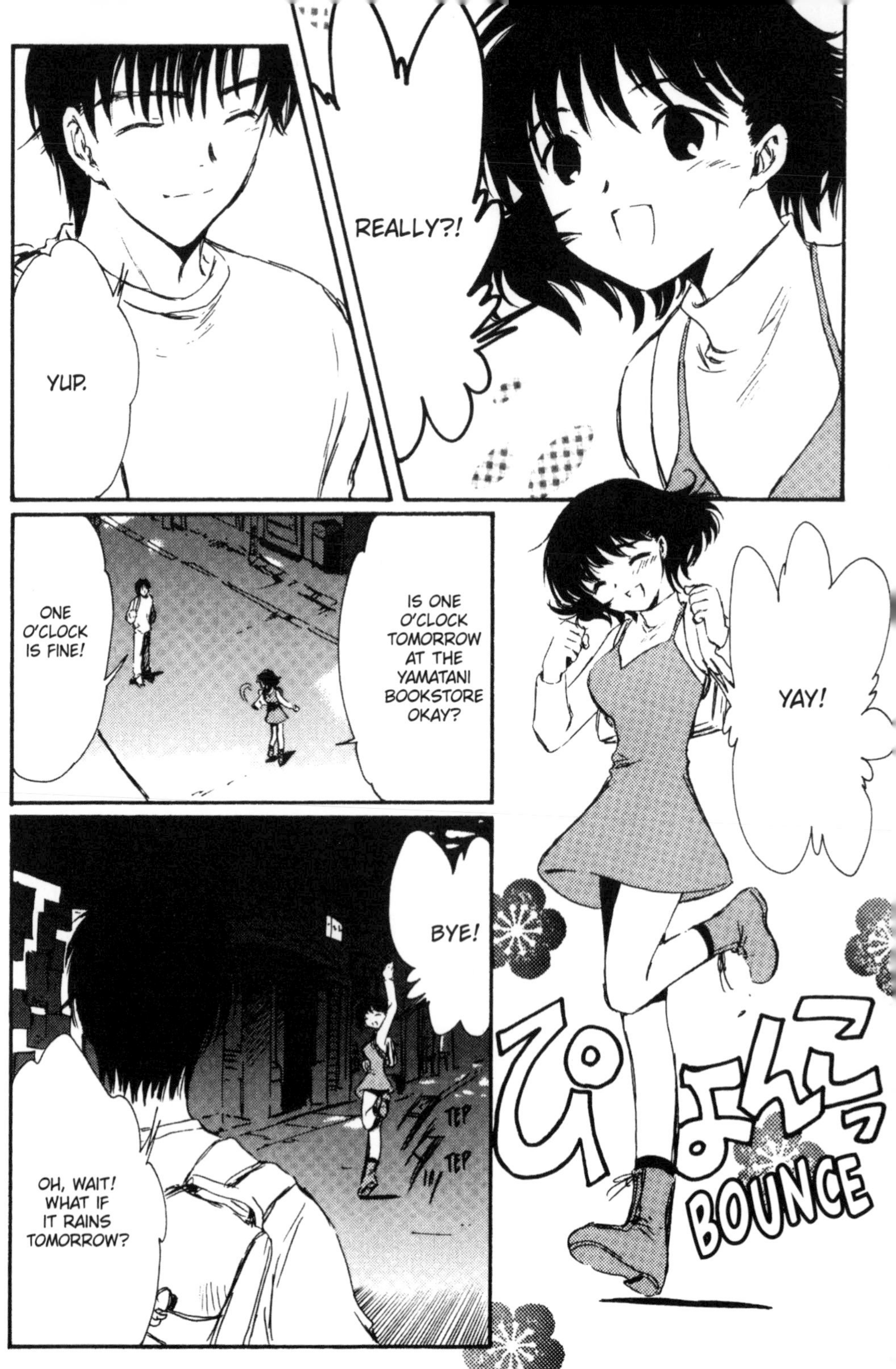
REALLY?!
YUP.
YAY!
ぴょんこ
BOUNCE
IS ONE O'CLOCK TOMORROW AT THE YAMATANI BOOKSTORE OKAY?
ONE O'CLOCK IS FINE!
BYE!
TEP
TEP
OH, WAIT! WHAT IF IT RAINS TOMORROW?

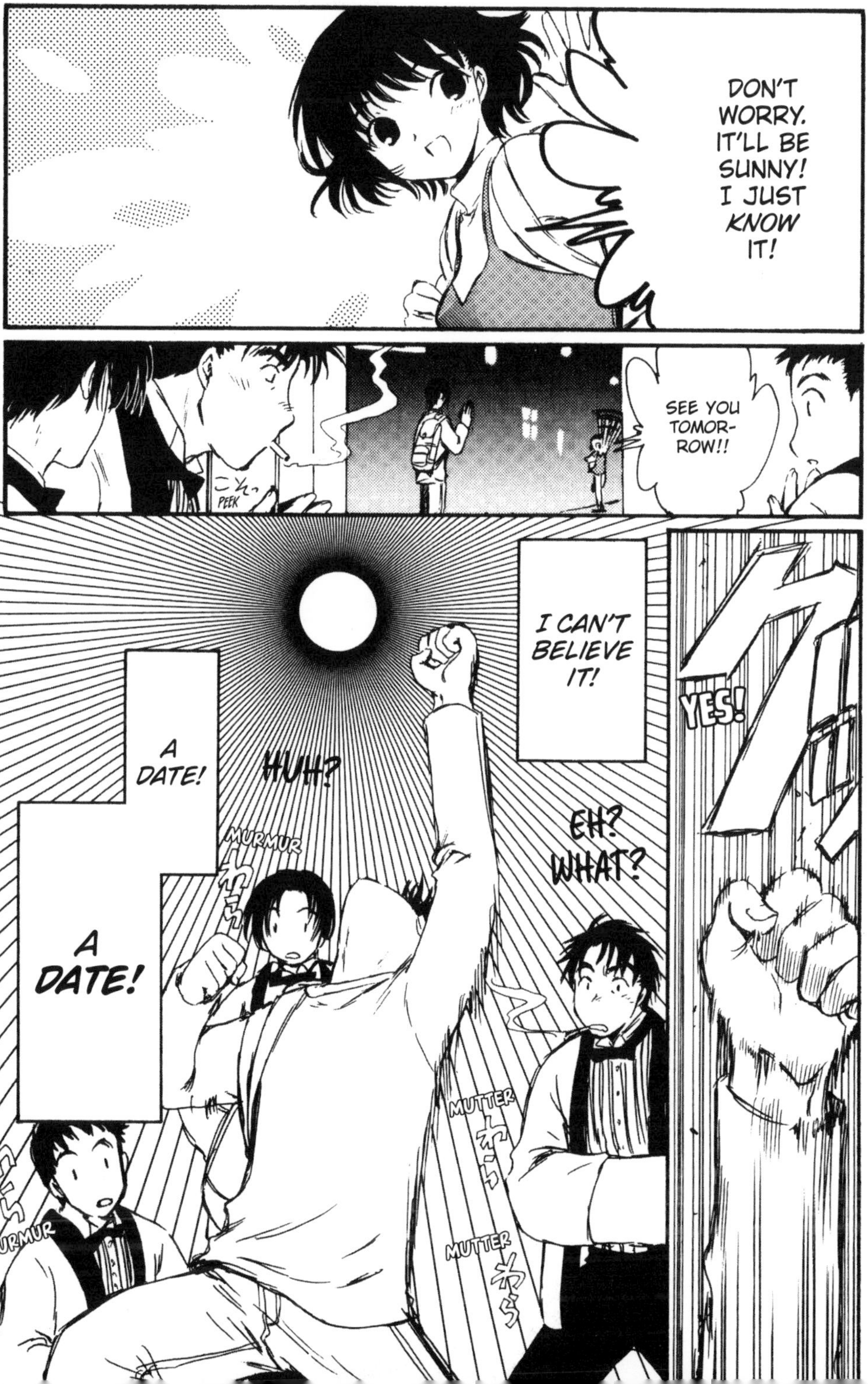
DON'T WORRY. IT'LL BE SUNNY! I JUST KNOW IT!
SEE YOU TOMORROW!!
こそっ PEEK
YES!
I CAN'T BELIEVE IT!
EH? WHAT?
HUH?
A DATE!
A DATE!
MURMUR
MUTTER
MUTTER
MURMUR

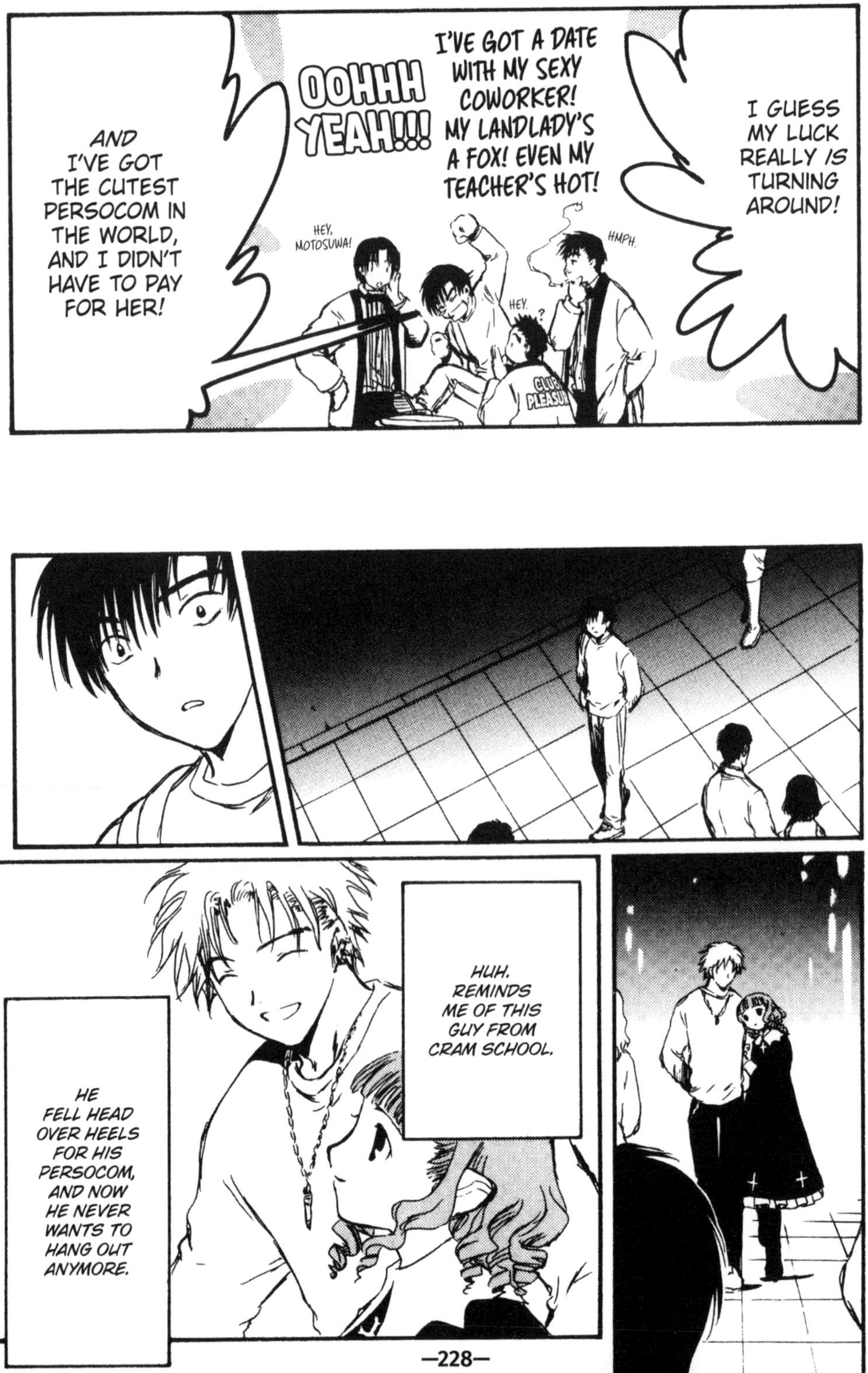
I GUESS MY LUCK REALLY IS TURNING AROUND!
I'VE GOT A DATE WITH MY SEXY COWORKER! MY LANDLADY'S A FOX! EVEN MY TEACHER'S HOT!
OOHHH YEAH!!!
AND I'VE GOT THE CUTEST PERSOCOM IN THE WORLD, AND I DIDN'T HAVE TO PAY FOR HER!
HMPH.
HEY. ?
HEY, MOTOSUWA!
CLUB PLEASU
HUH. REMINDS ME OF THIS GUY FROM CRAM SCHOOL.
HE FELL HEAD OVER HEELS FOR HIS PERSOCOM, AND NOW HE NEVER WANTS TO HANG OUT ANYMORE.

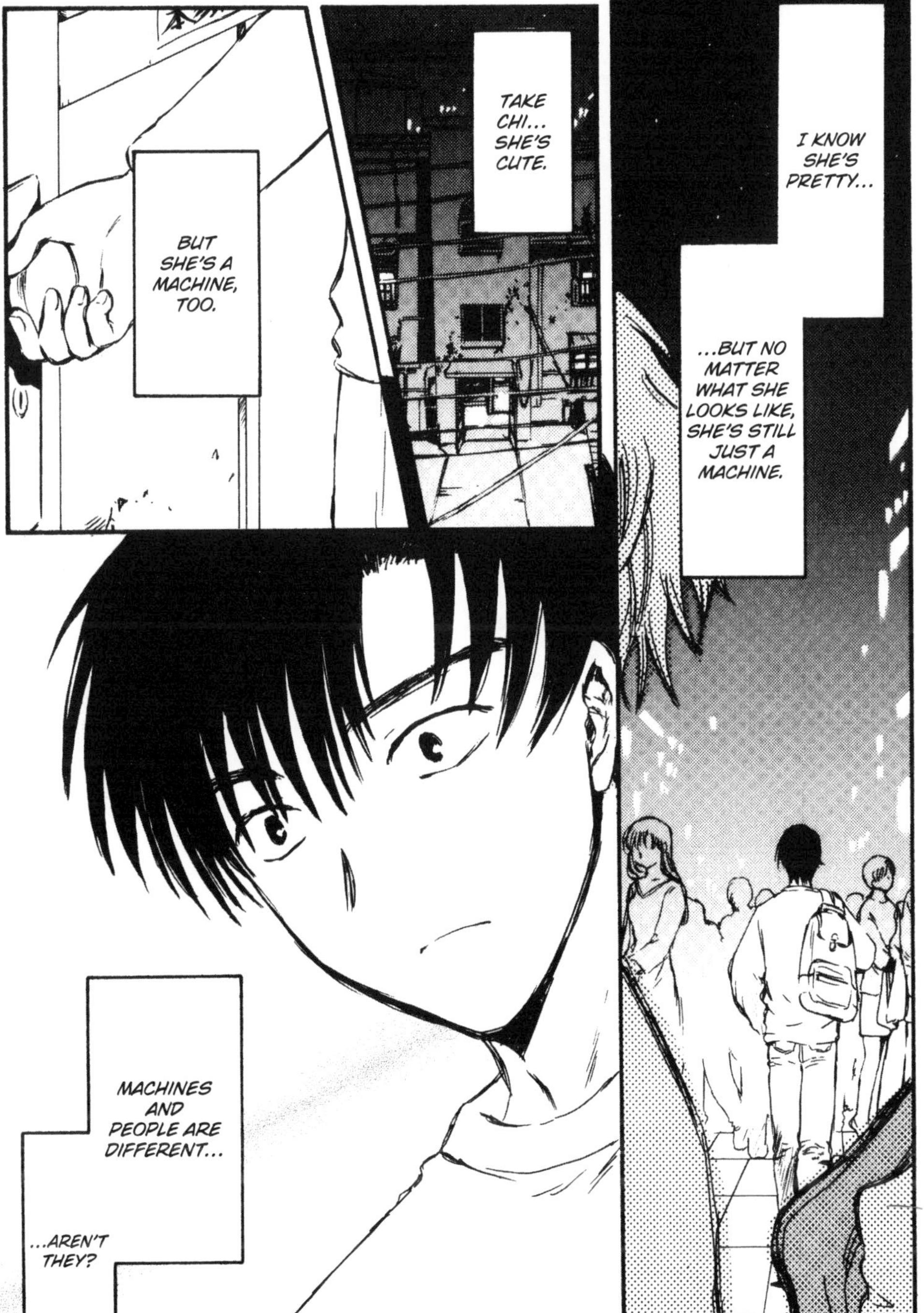
I KNOW SHE'S PRETTY...
...BUT NO MATTER WHAT SHE LOOKS LIKE, SHE'S STILL JUST A MACHINE.
TAKE CHI... SHE'S CUTE.
BUT SHE'S A MACHINE, TOO.
MACHINES AND PEOPLE ARE DIFFERENT...
...AREN'T THEY?

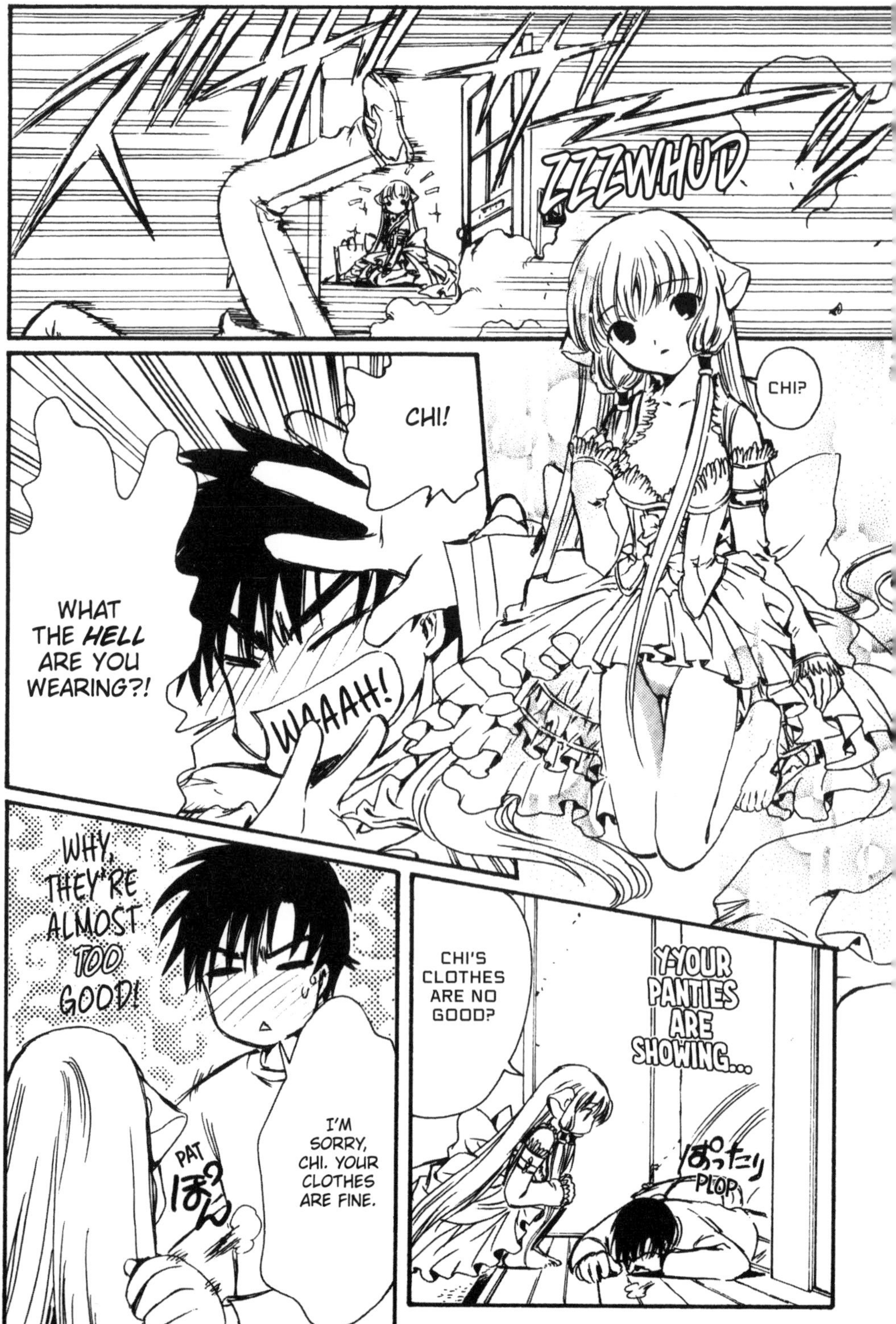

ZZZWHUD
CHI?
CHI!
WAAAH!
WHAT THE HELL ARE YOU WEARING?!
Y-YOUR PANTIES ARE SHOWING...
CHI'S CLOTHES ARE NO GOOD?
ぽったり
PLOP
I'M SORRY, CHI. YOUR CLOTHES ARE FINE.
PAT
ぽん
WHY, THEY'RE ALMOST TOO GOOD!

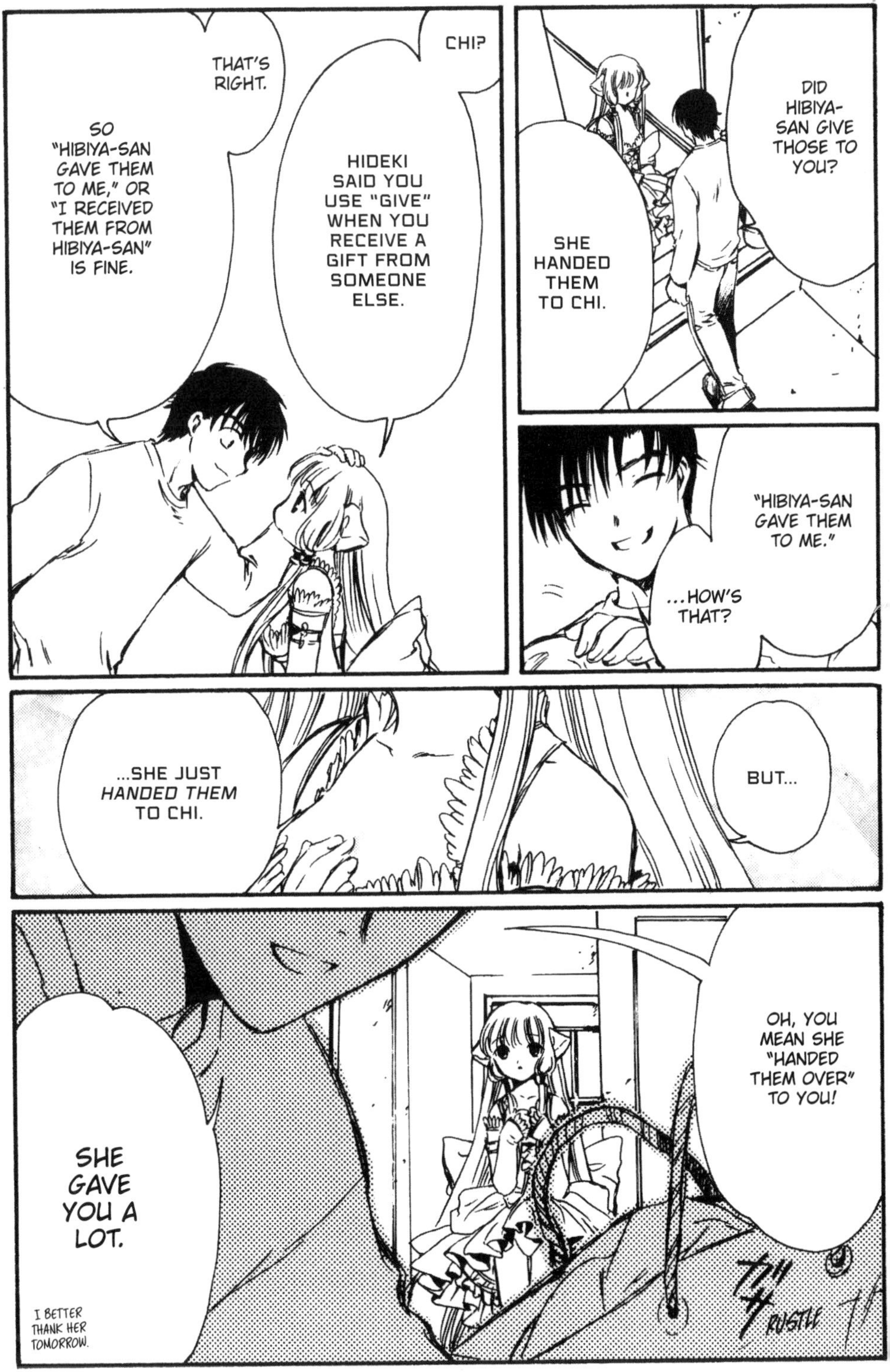

DID HIBIYA-SAN GIVE THOSE TO YOU?
SHE HANDED THEM TO CHI.
"HIBIYA-SAN GAVE THEM TO ME."
...HOW'S THAT?
CHI?
HIDEKI SAID YOU USE "GIVE" WHEN YOU RECEIVE A GIFT FROM SOMEONE ELSE.
THAT'S RIGHT.
SO "HIBIYA-SAN GAVE THEM TO ME," OR "I RECEIVED THEM FROM HIBIYA-SAN" IS FINE.
BUT...
...SHE JUST *HANDED THEM* TO CHI.
OH, YOU MEAN SHE "HANDED THEM OVER" TO YOU!
RUSTLE
SHE GAVE YOU A LOT.
I BETTER THANK HER TOMORROW.

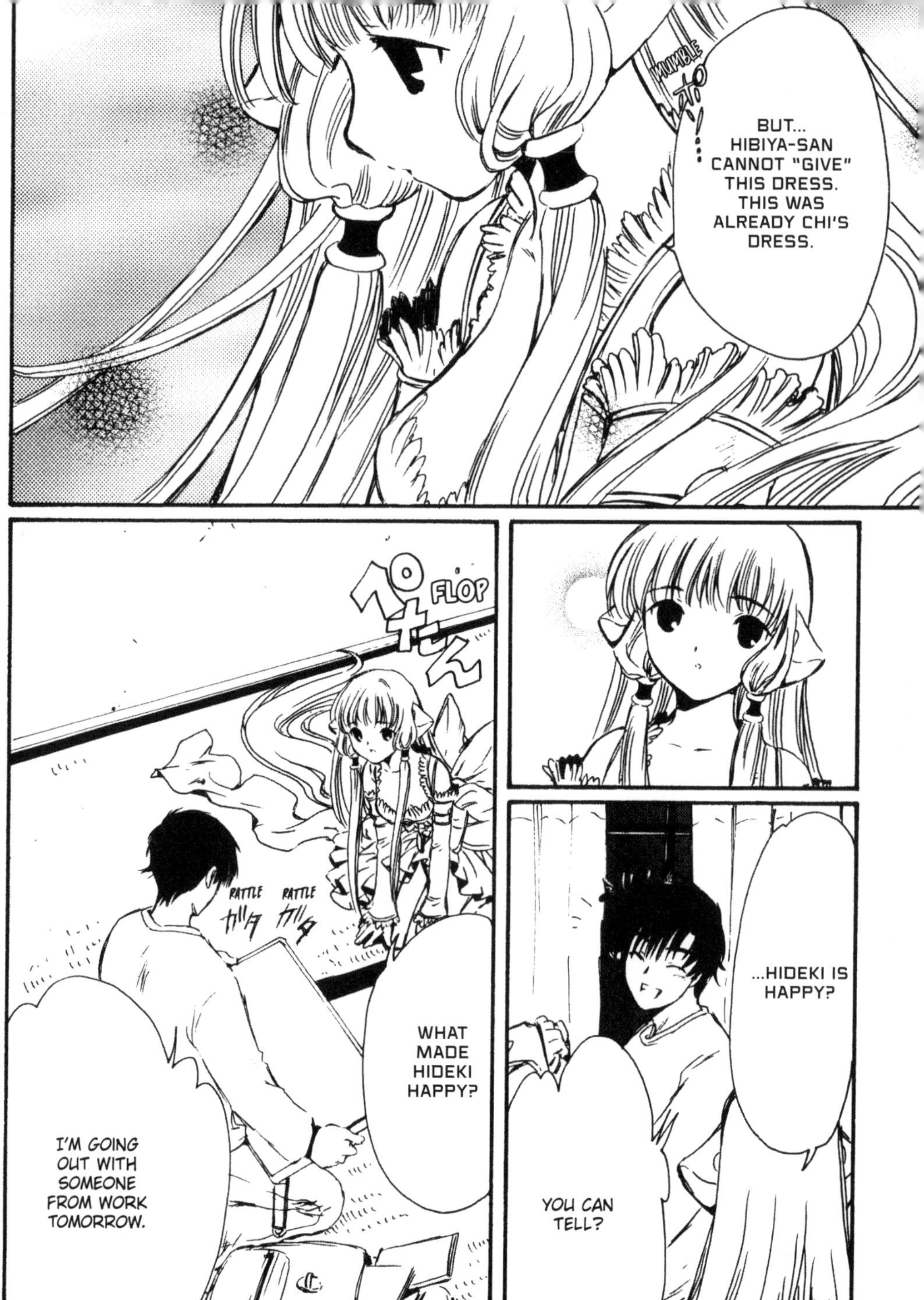
MUMBLE
BUT... HIBIYA-SAN CANNOT "GIVE" THIS DRESS. THIS WAS ALREADY CHI'S DRESS.
...HIDEKI IS HAPPY?
YOU CAN TELL?
I GUESS MY FACE SAYS IT ALL.
FLOP
RATTLE RATTLE
WHAT MADE HIDEKI HAPPY?
I'M GOING OUT WITH SOMEONE FROM WORK TOMORROW.

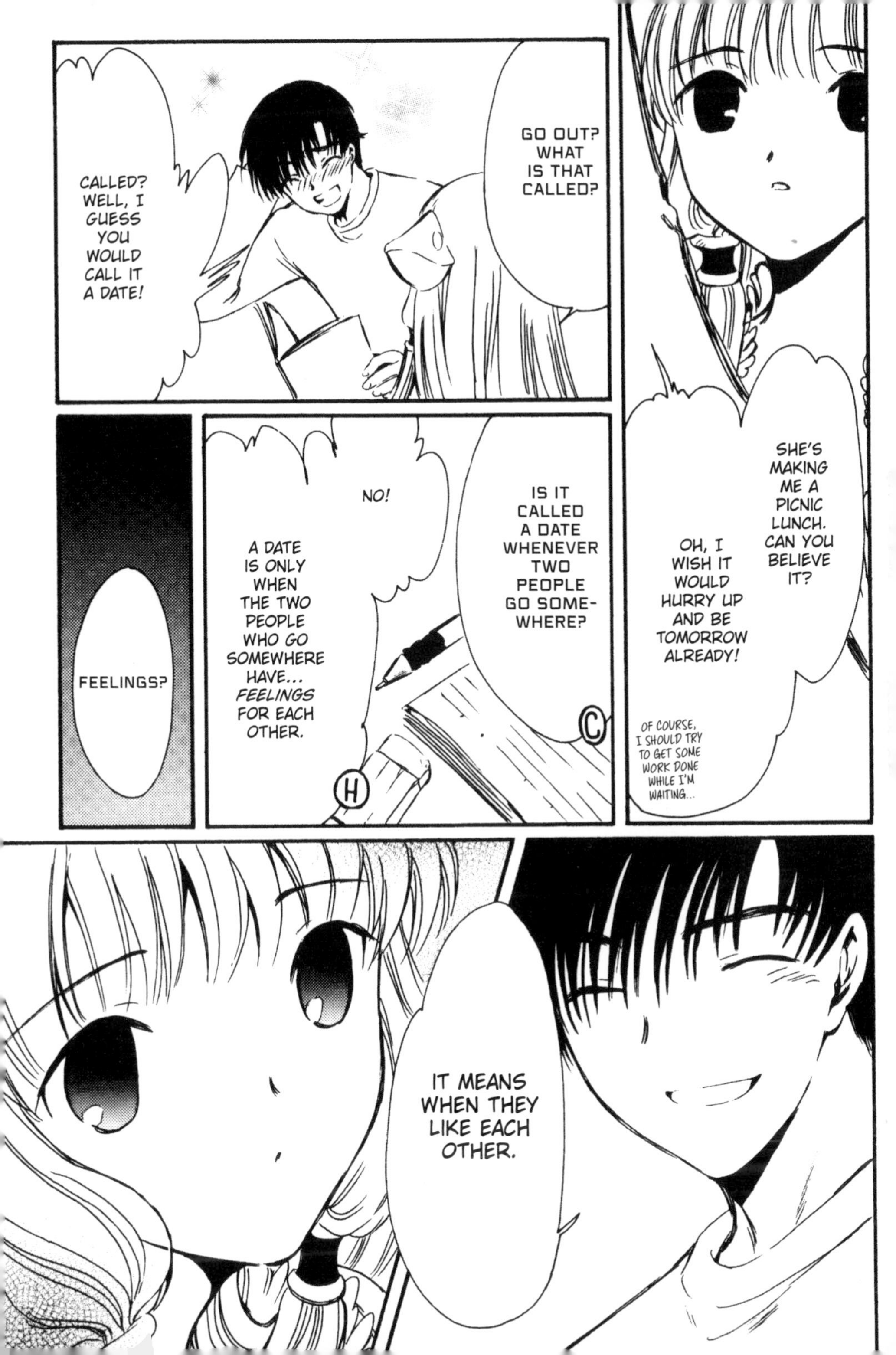
SHE'S MAKING ME A PICNIC LUNCH. CAN YOU BELIEVE IT?
OH, I WISH IT WOULD HURRY UP AND BE TOMORROW ALREADY!
OF COURSE, I SHOULD TRY TO GET SOME WORK DONE WHILE I'M WAITING...
GO OUT? WHAT IS THAT CALLED?
CALLED? WELL, I GUESS YOU WOULD CALL IT A DATE!
IS IT CALLED A DATE WHENEVER TWO PEOPLE GO SOME-WHERE?
NO!
A DATE IS ONLY WHEN THE TWO PEOPLE WHO GO SOMEWHERE HAVE... *FEELINGS* FOR EACH OTHER.
C
H
FEELINGS?
IT MEANS WHEN THEY LIKE EACH OTHER.

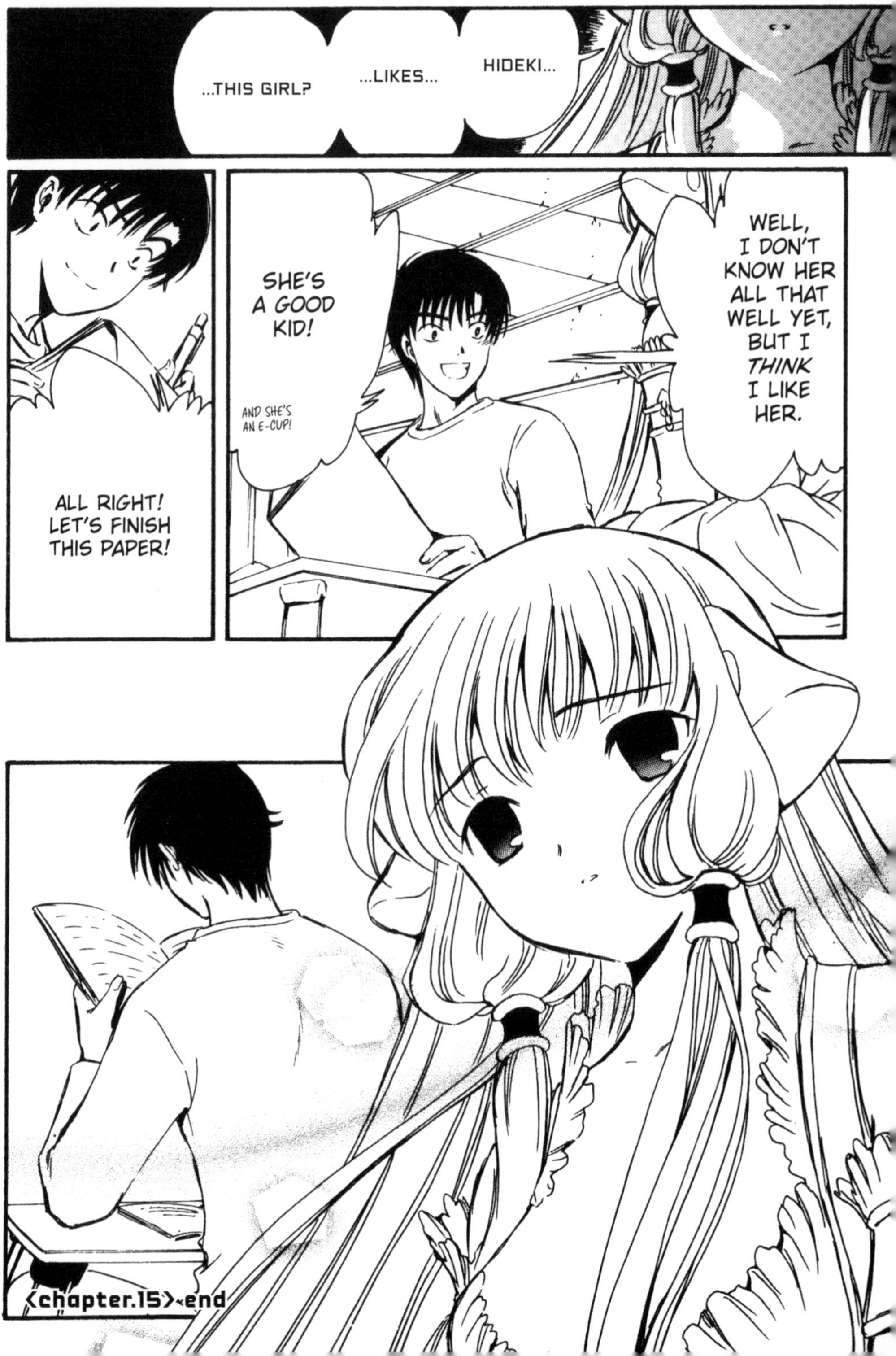
HIDEKI...
...LIKES...
...THIS GIRL?
WELL, I DON'T KNOW HER ALL THAT WELL YET, BUT I *THINK* I LIKE HER.
SHE'S A GOOD KID!
AND SHE'S AN E-CUP!
ALL RIGHT! LET'S FINISH THIS PAPER!
<chapter.15>-end

〈chapter.16〉

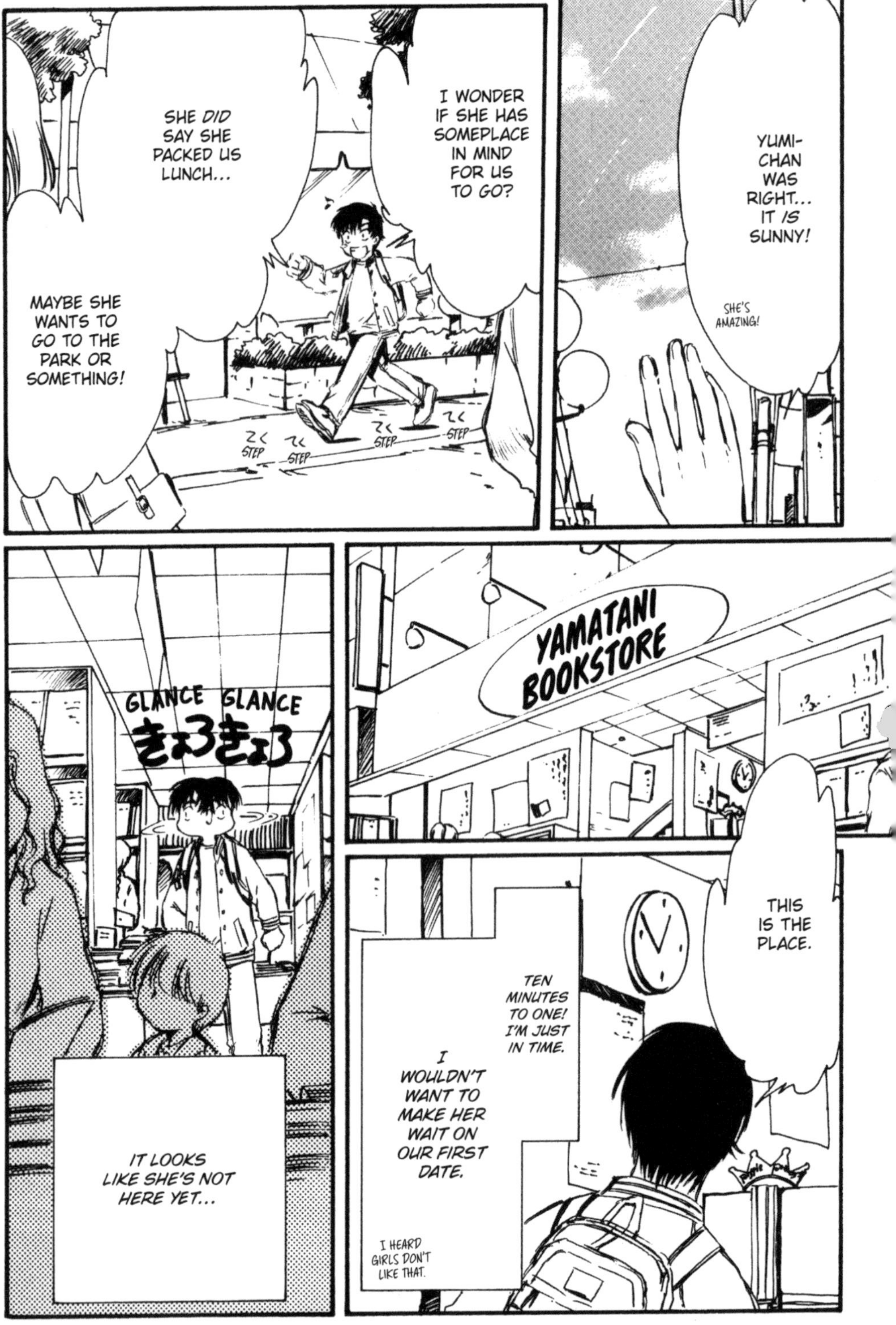
YUMI-CHAN WAS RIGHT... IT *IS* SUNNY!
SHE'S AMAZING!
I WONDER IF SHE HAS SOMEPLACE IN MIND FOR US TO GO?
SHE *DID* SAY SHE PACKED US LUNCH...
MAYBE SHE WANTS TO GO TO THE PARK OR SOMETHING!
てく STEP てく STEP てく STEP てく STEP
YAMATANI BOOKSTORE
THIS IS THE PLACE.
TEN MINUTES TO ONE! I'M JUST IN TIME.
I WOULDN'T WANT TO MAKE HER WAIT ON OUR FIRST DATE.
I HEARD GIRLS DON'T LIKE THAT.
GLANCE GLANCE
きょろきょろ
IT LOOKS LIKE SHE'S NOT HERE YET...

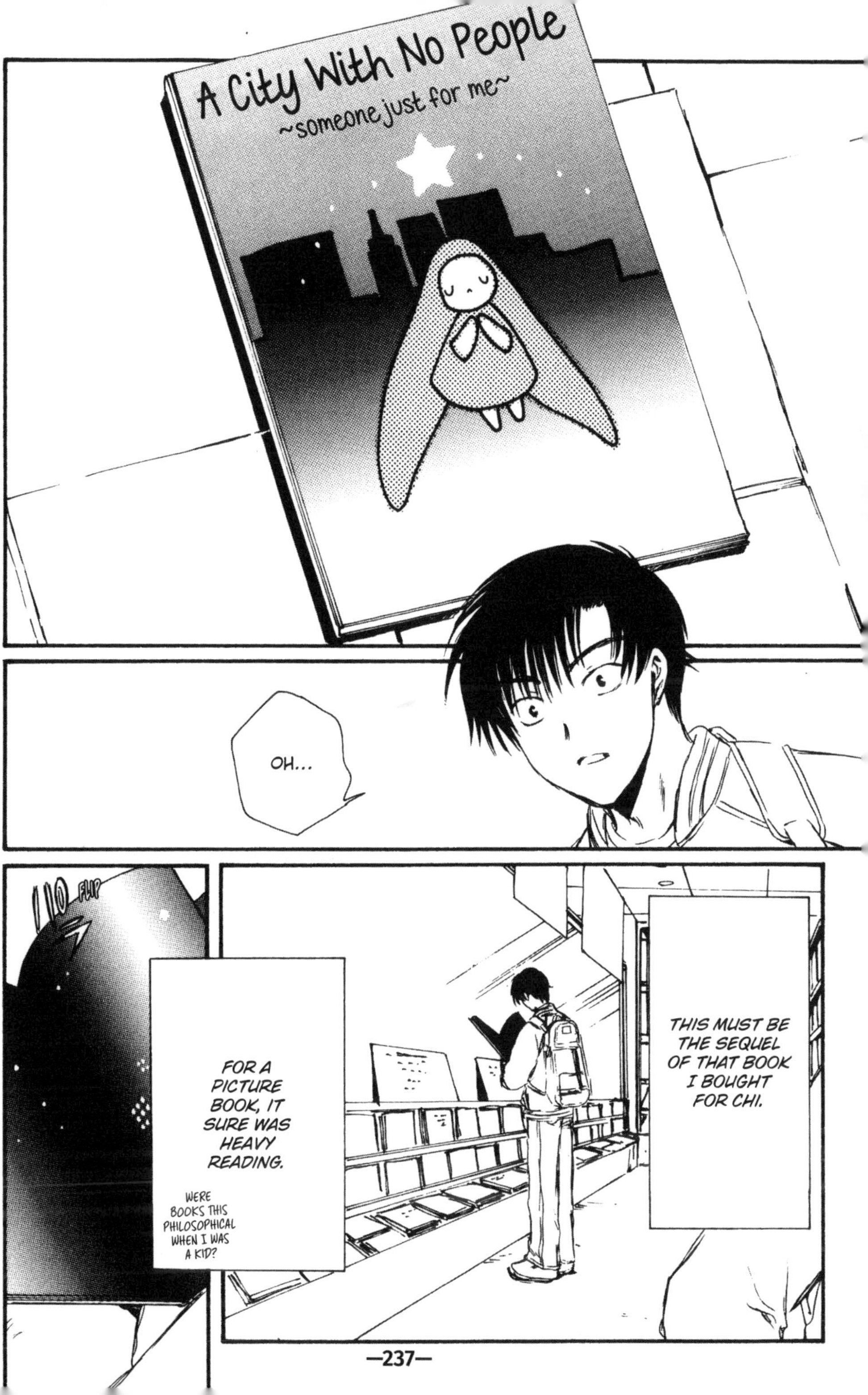
A City With No People
~someone just for me~
OH...
THIS MUST BE THE SEQUEL OF THAT BOOK I BOUGHT FOR CHI.
FOR A PICTURE BOOK, IT SURE WAS HEAVY READING.
WERE BOOKS THIS PHILOSOPHICAL WHEN I WAS A KID?
FLIP

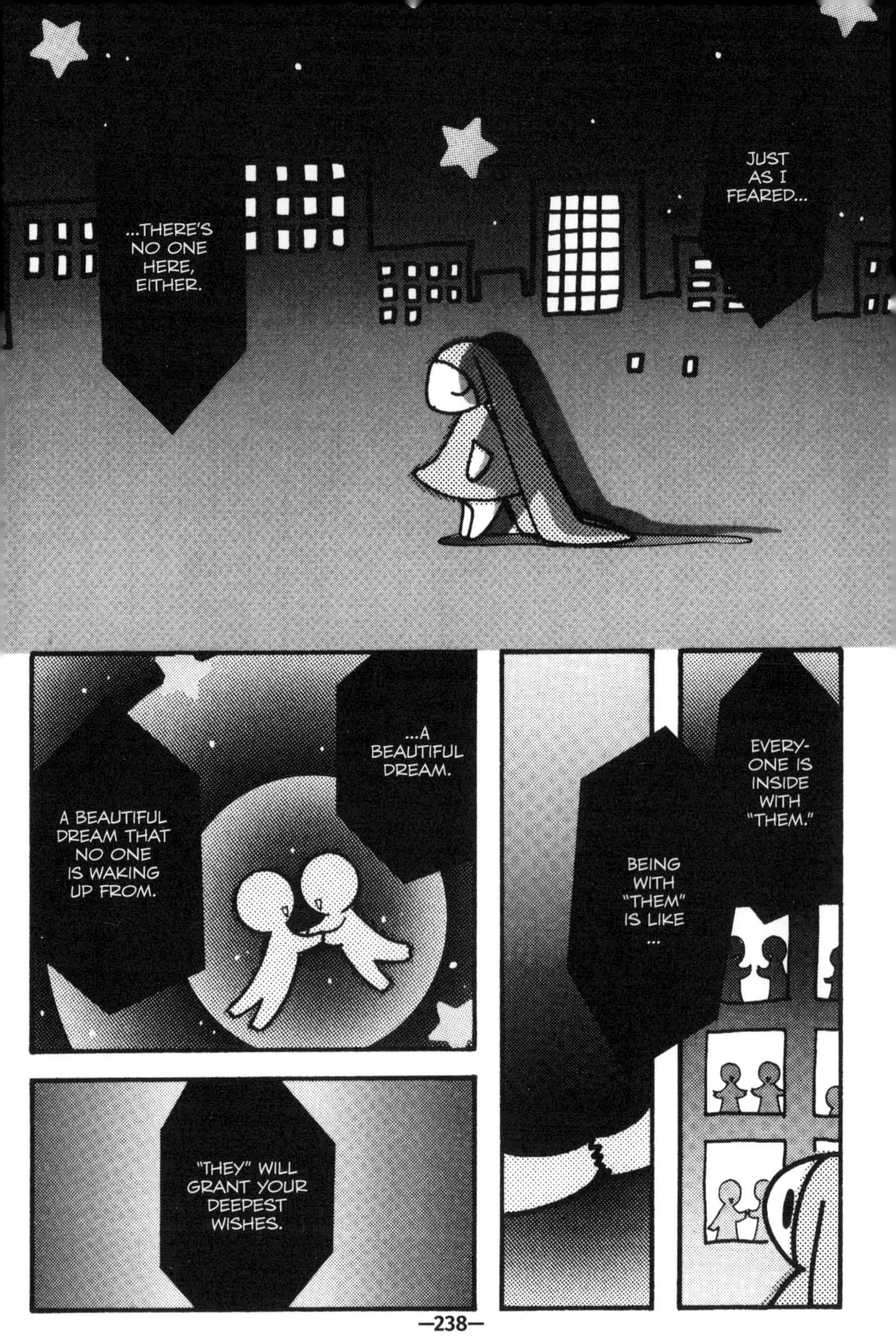
JUST AS I FEARED...
...THERE'S NO ONE HERE, EITHER.
EVERY-ONE IS INSIDE WITH "THEM."
BEING WITH "THEM" IS LIKE ...
...A BEAUTIFUL DREAM.
A BEAUTIFUL DREAM THAT NO ONE IS WAKING UP FROM.
"THEY" WILL GRANT YOUR DEEPEST WISHES.

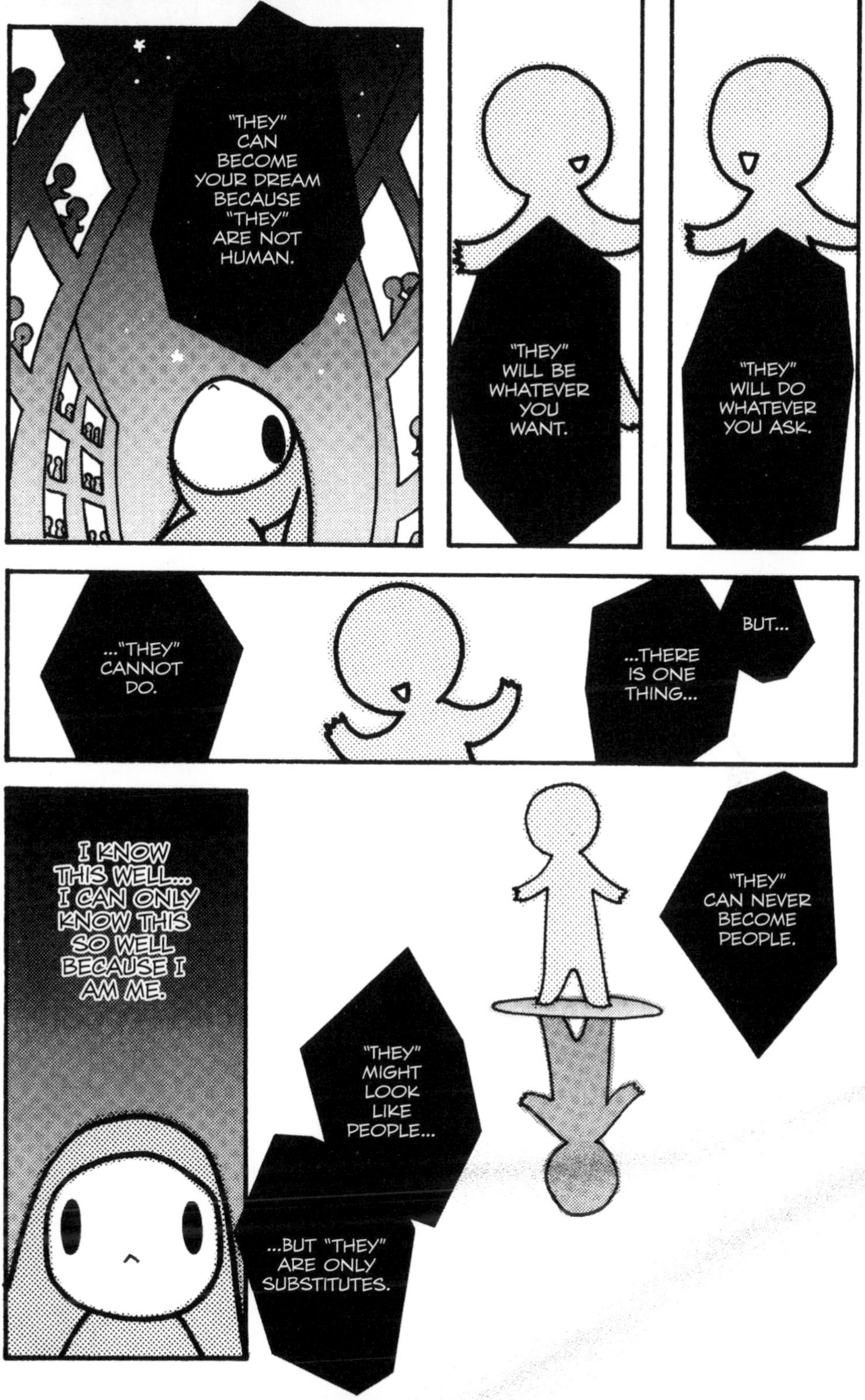
"THEY" WILL DO WHATEVER YOU ASK.
"THEY" WILL BE WHATEVER YOU WANT.
"THEY" CAN BECOME YOUR DREAM BECAUSE "THEY" ARE NOT HUMAN.
BUT...
...THERE IS ONE THING...
..."THEY" CANNOT DO.
"THEY" CAN NEVER BECOME PEOPLE.
"THEY" MIGHT LOOK LIKE PEOPLE...
...BUT "THEY" ARE ONLY SUBSTITUTES.
I KNOW THIS WELL... I CAN ONLY KNOW THIS SO WELL BECAUSE I AM ME.

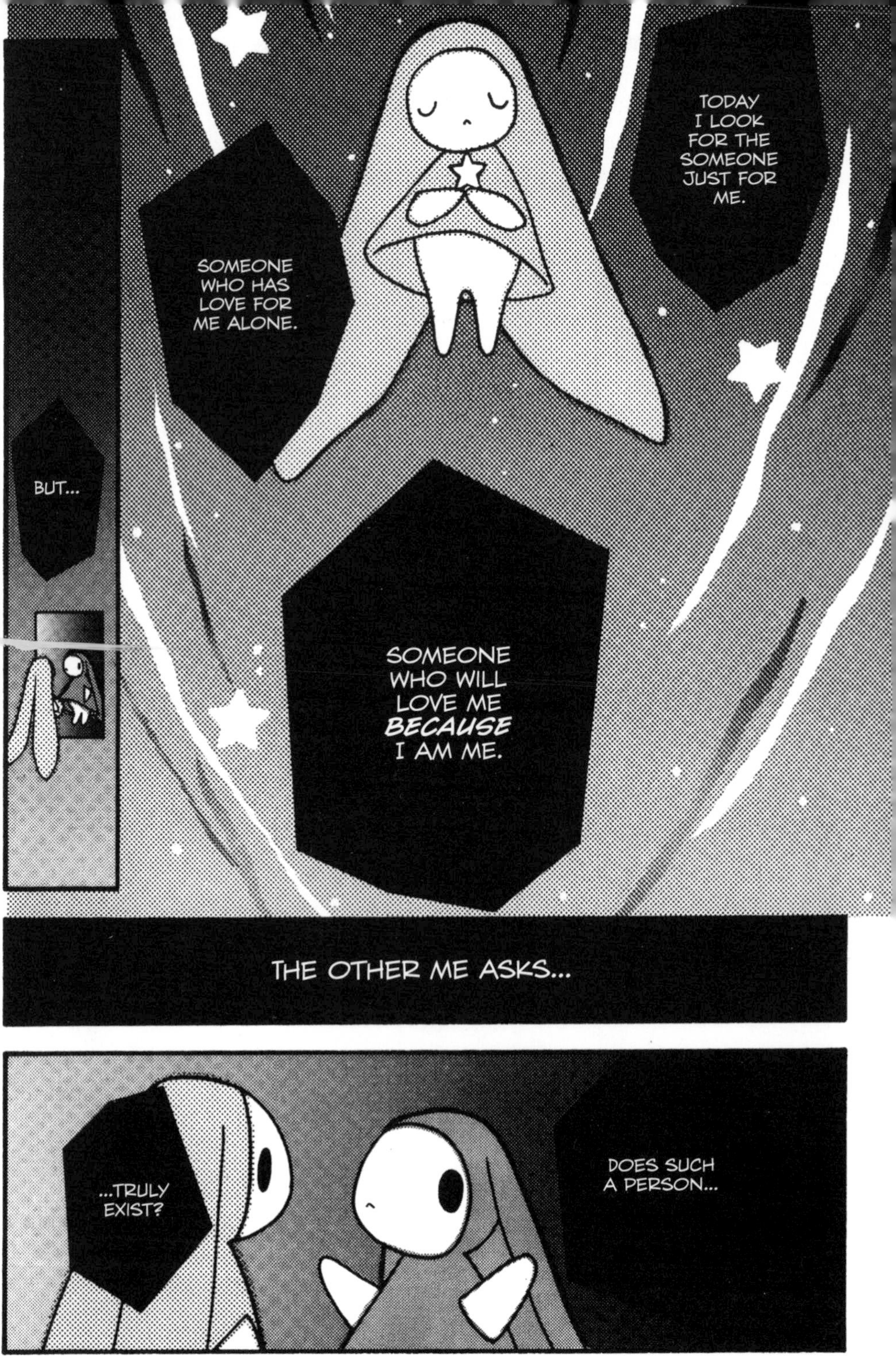
TODAY I LOOK FOR THE SOMEONE JUST FOR ME.
SOMEONE WHO HAS LOVE FOR ME ALONE.
SOMEONE WHO WILL LOVE ME *BECAUSE* I AM ME.
BUT...
THE OTHER ME ASKS...
DOES SUCH A PERSON...
...TRULY EXIST?

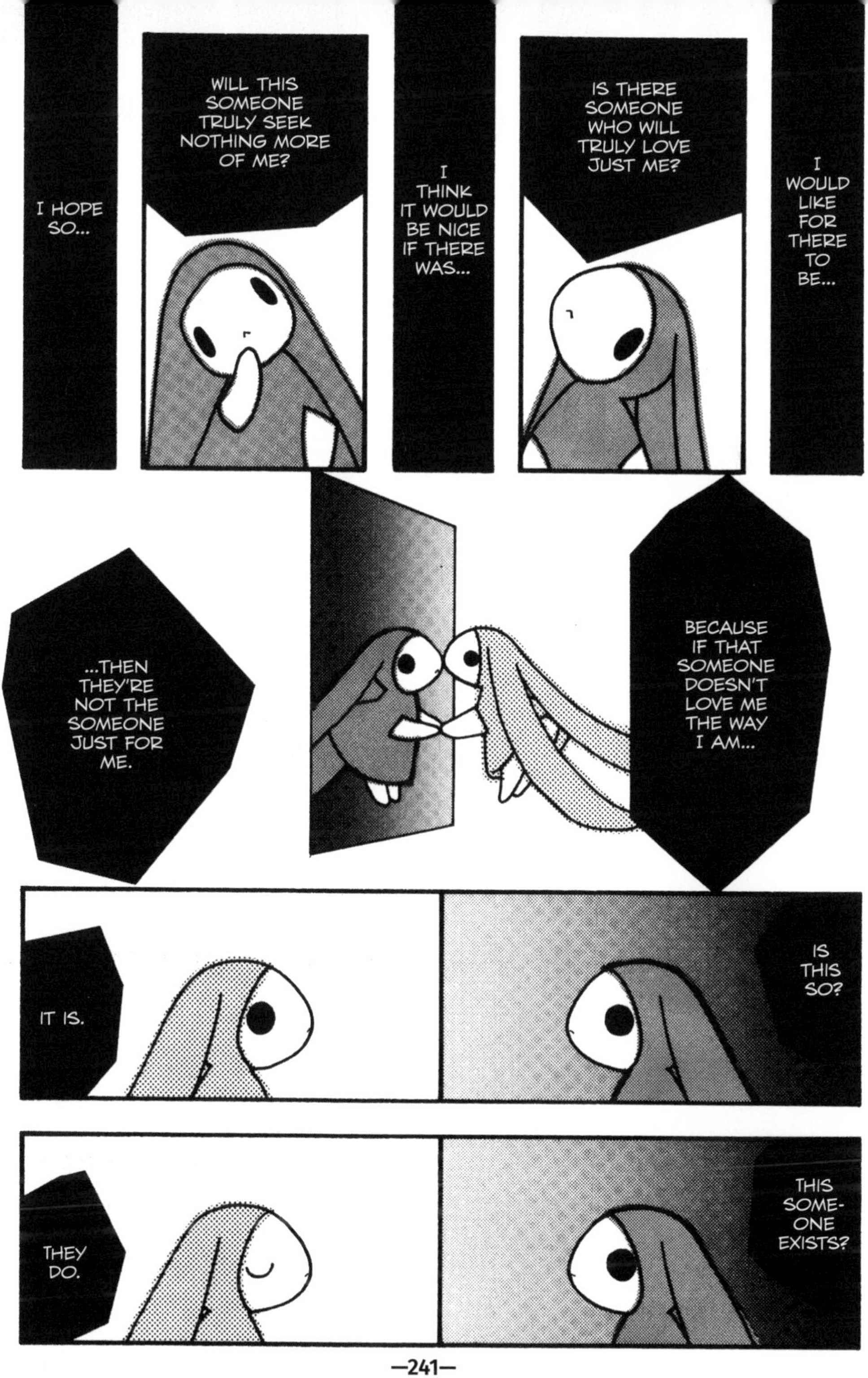
I WOULD LIKE FOR THERE TO BE...
IS THERE SOMEONE WHO WILL TRULY LOVE JUST ME?
I THINK IT WOULD BE NICE IF THERE WAS...
WILL THIS SOMEONE TRULY SEEK NOTHING MORE OF ME?
I HOPE SO...
BECAUSE IF THAT SOMEONE DOESN'T LOVE ME THE WAY I AM...
...THEN THEY'RE NOT THE SOMEONE JUST FOR ME.
IS THIS SO?
IT IS.
THIS SOME-ONE EXISTS?
THEY DO.

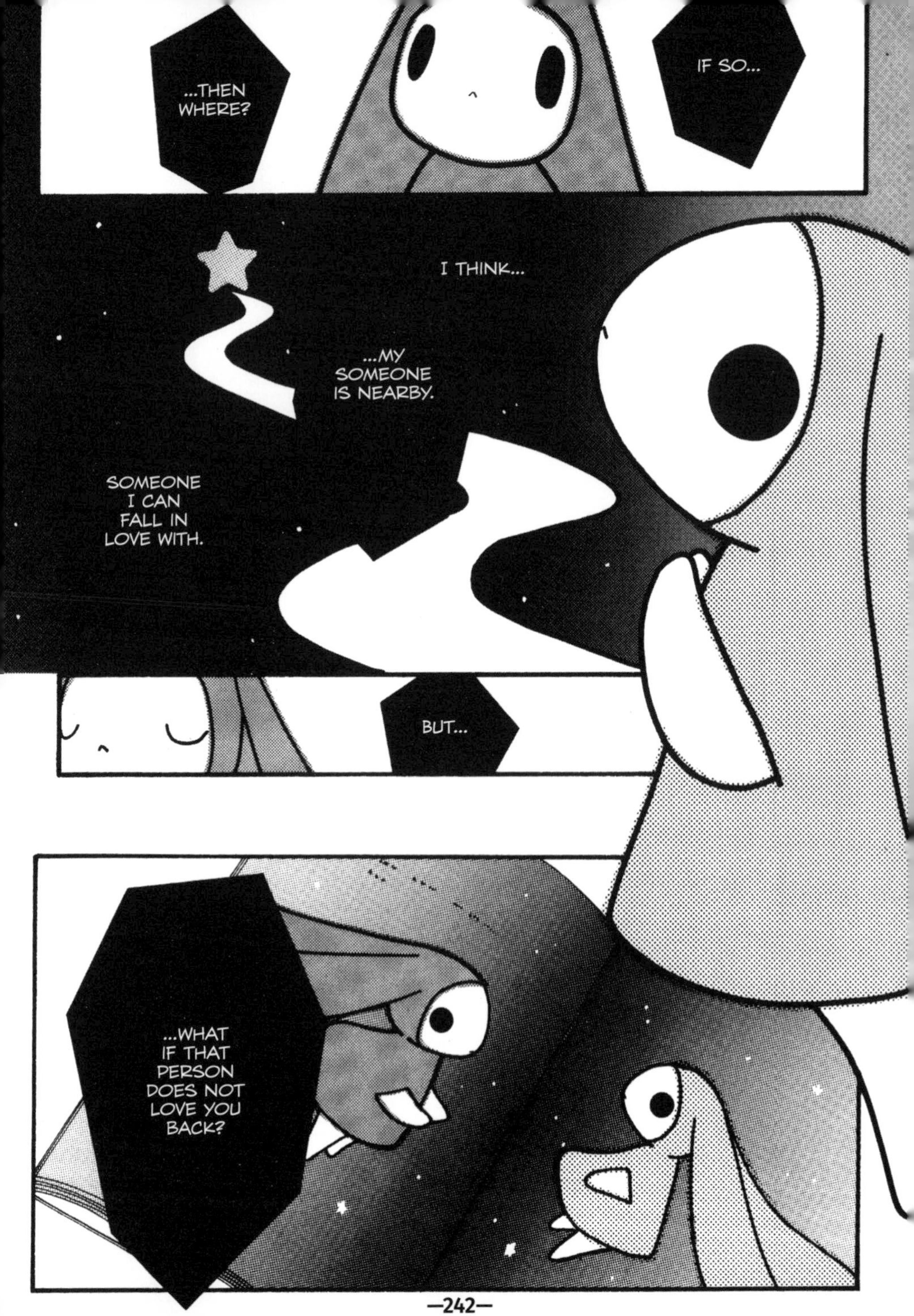
IF SO...
...THEN WHERE?
I THINK...
...MY SOMEONE IS NEARBY.
SOMEONE I CAN FALL IN LOVE WITH.
BUT...
...WHAT IF THAT PERSON DOES NOT LOVE YOU BACK?

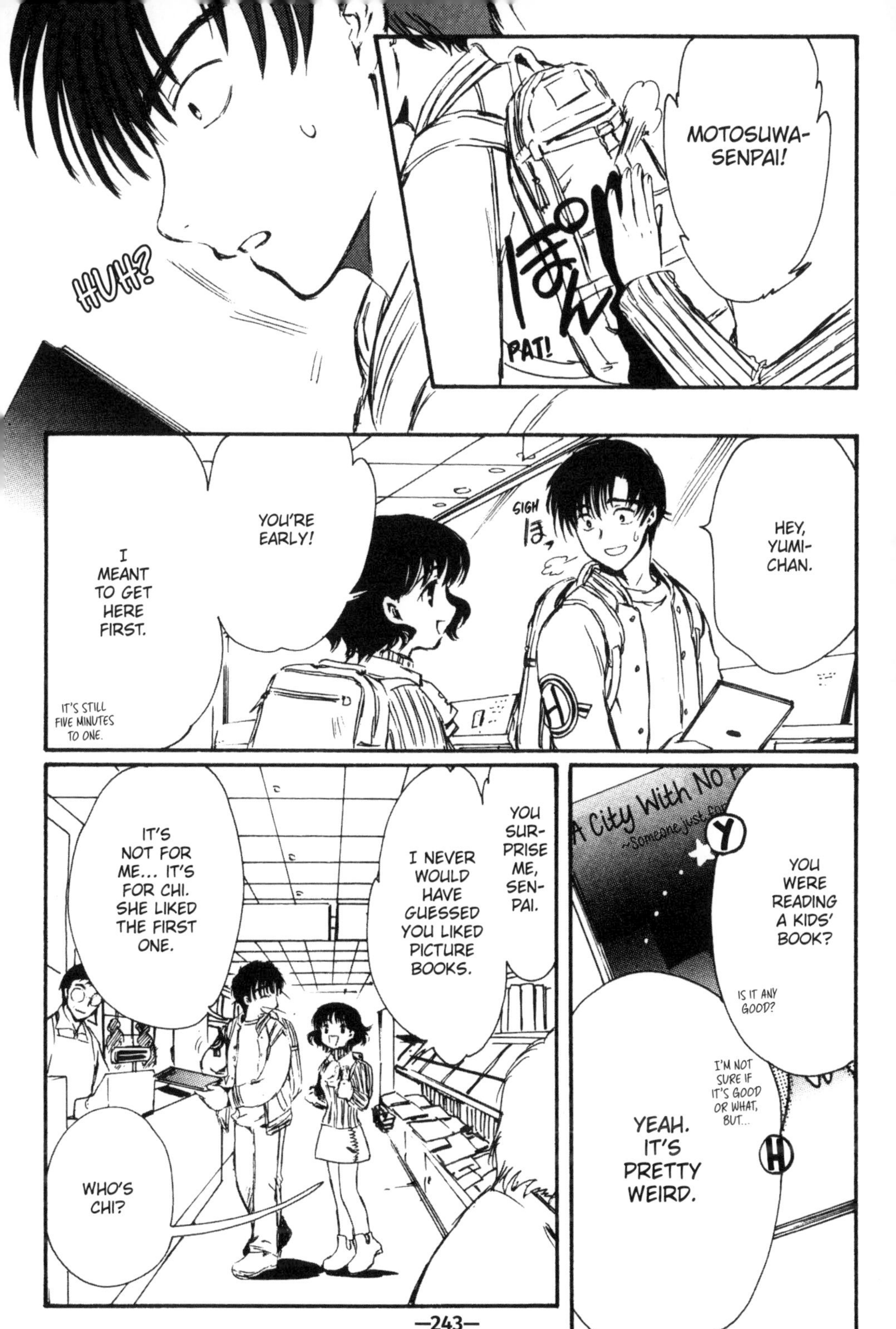

MOTOSUWA-SENPAI!
ぽん
PAT!
HUH?
HEY, YUMI-CHAN.
SIGH
ほっ
YOU'RE EARLY!
I MEANT TO GET HERE FIRST.
IT'S STILL FIVE MINUTES TO ONE.
YOU WERE READING A KIDS' BOOK?
IS IT ANY GOOD?
I'M NOT SURE IF IT'S GOOD OR WHAT, BUT...
YEAH. IT'S PRETTY WEIRD.
YOU SURPRISE ME, SEN-PAI.
I NEVER WOULD HAVE GUESSED YOU LIKED PICTURE BOOKS.
IT'S NOT FOR ME... IT'S FOR CHI. SHE LIKED THE FIRST ONE.
WHO'S CHI?

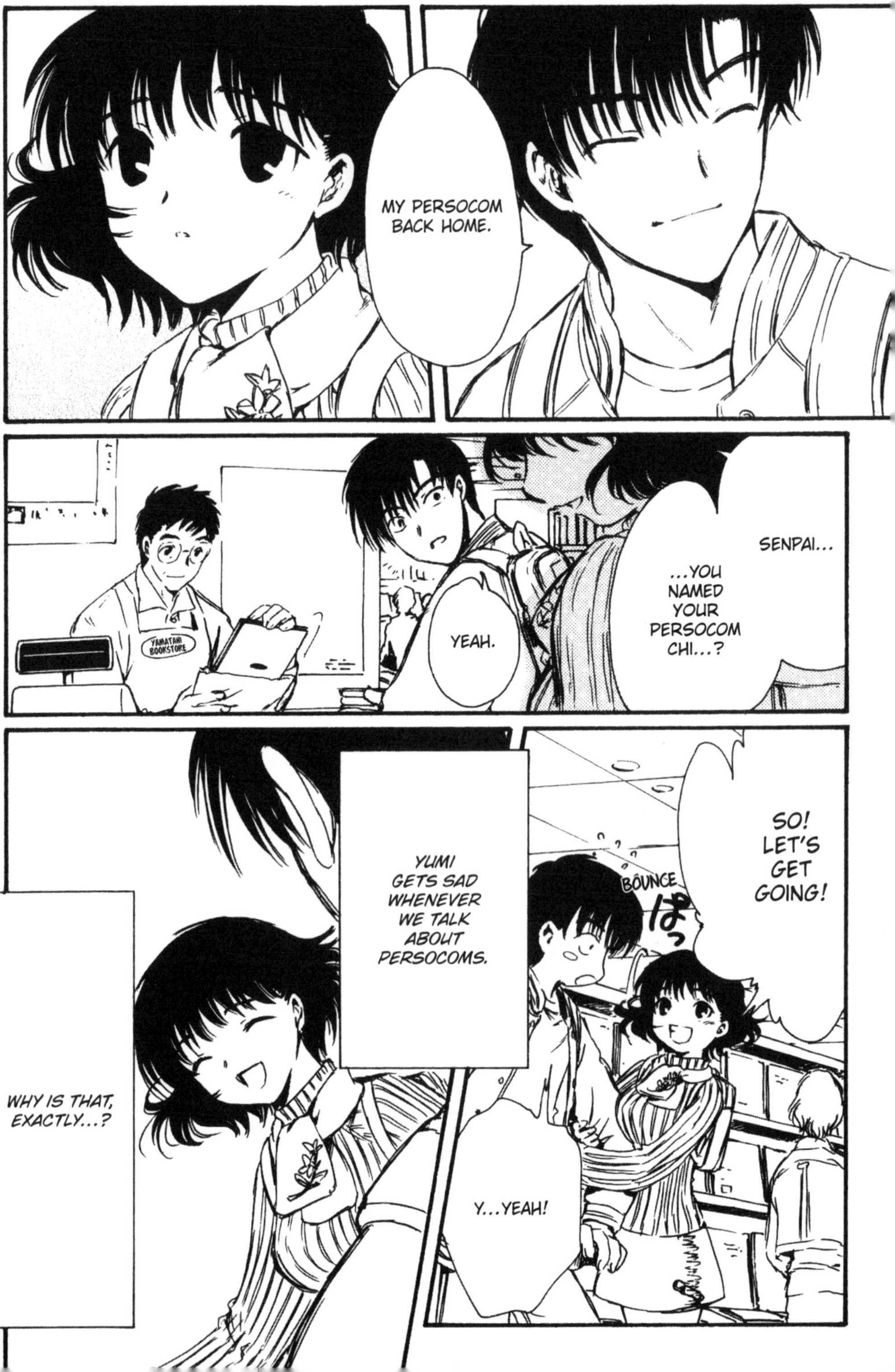
MY PERSOCOM BACK HOME.
SENPAI...
...YOU NAMED YOUR PERSOCOM CHI...?
YEAH.
YAMATANI BOOKSTORE
SO! LET'S GET GOING!
BOUNCE
ぱっ
Y...YEAH!
YUMI GETS SAD WHENEVER WE TALK ABOUT PERSOCOMS.
WHY IS THAT, EXACTLY...?

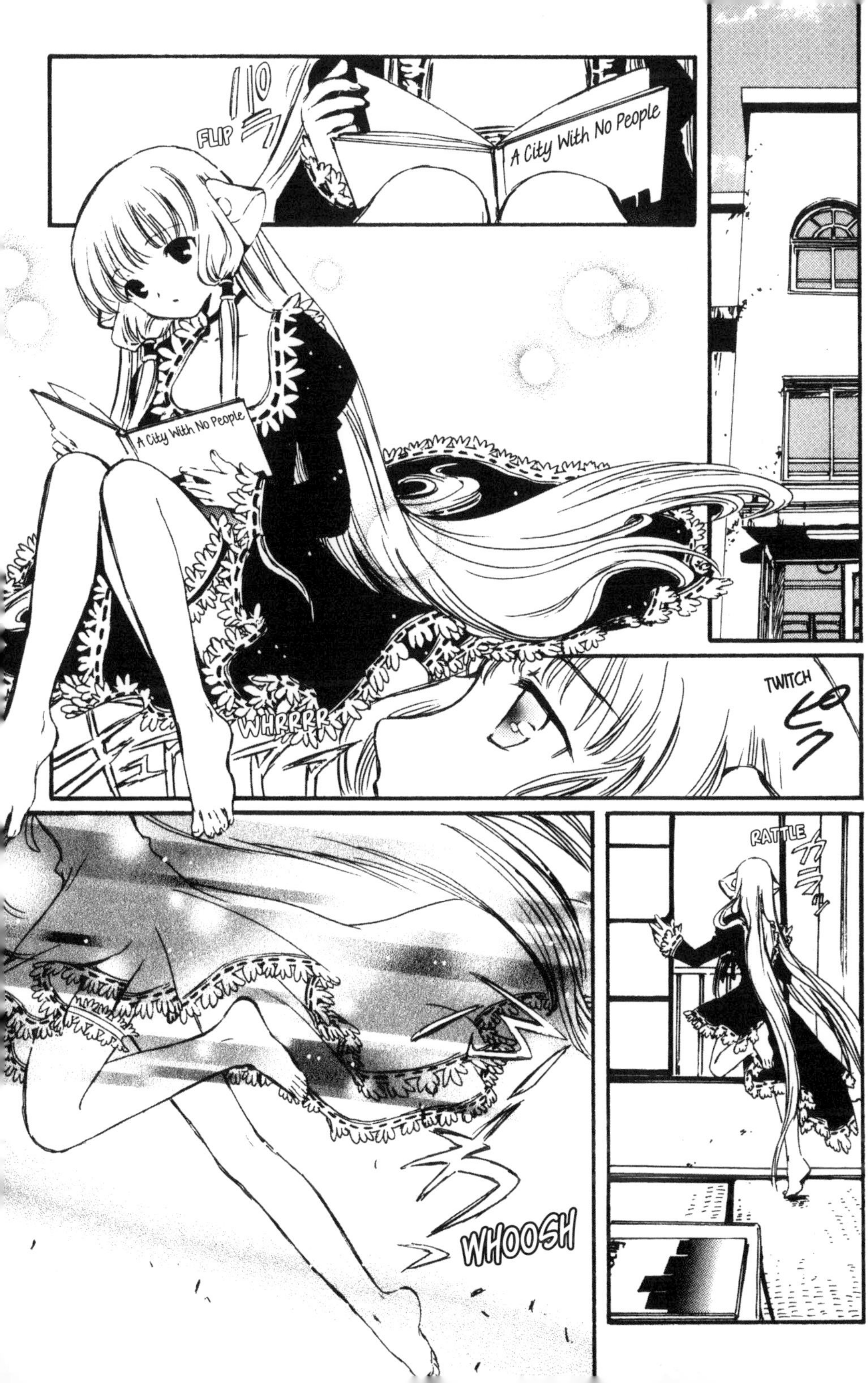
A City With No People
FLIP
A City With No People
WHRRRR
TWITCH
RATTLE
WHOOSH

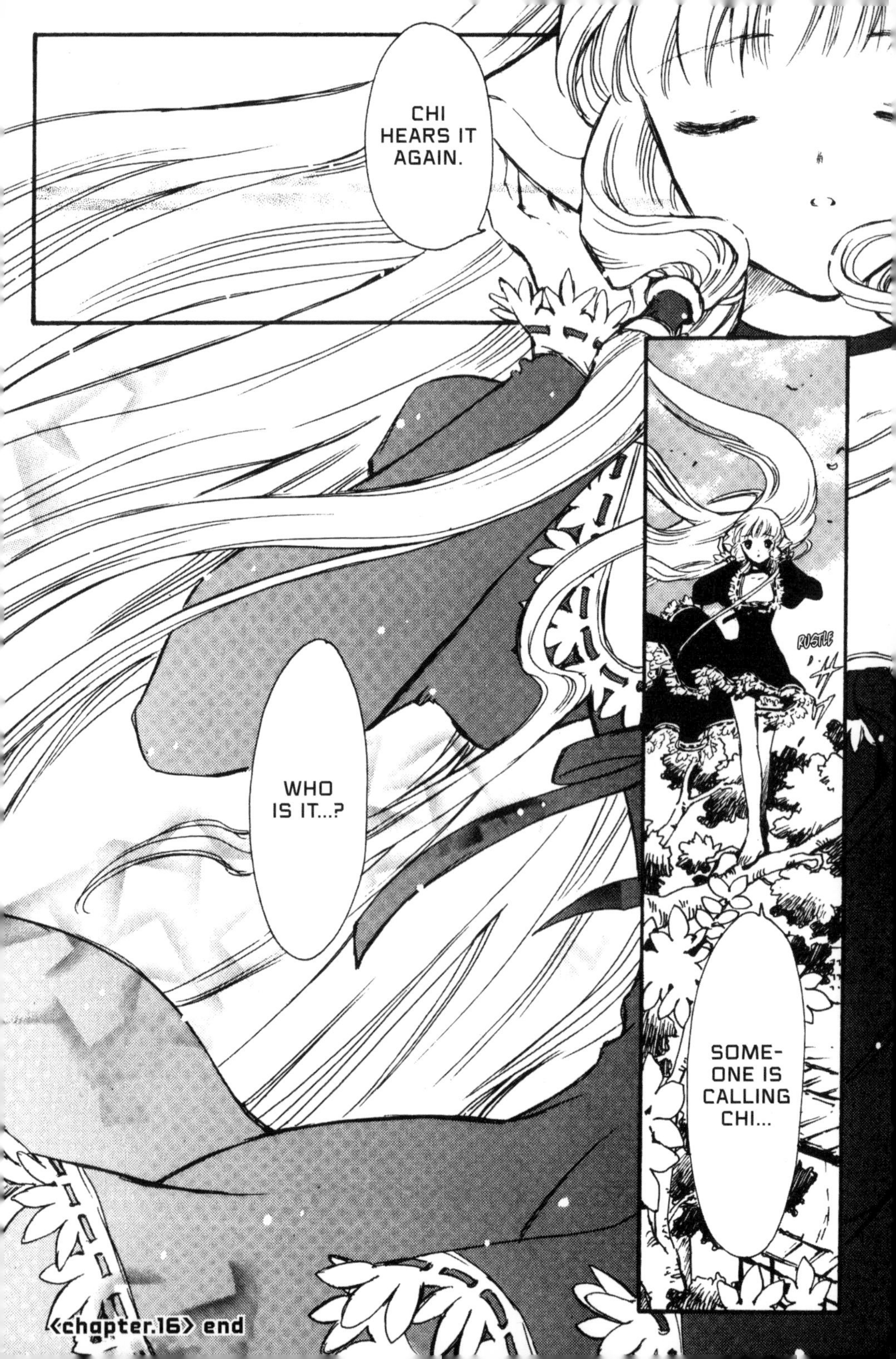
CHI HEARS IT AGAIN.
WHO IS IT...?
RUSTLE
SOME-ONE IS CALLING CHI...

«chapter.16» end

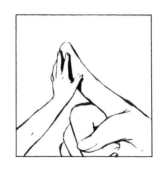

⟨chapter.17⟩

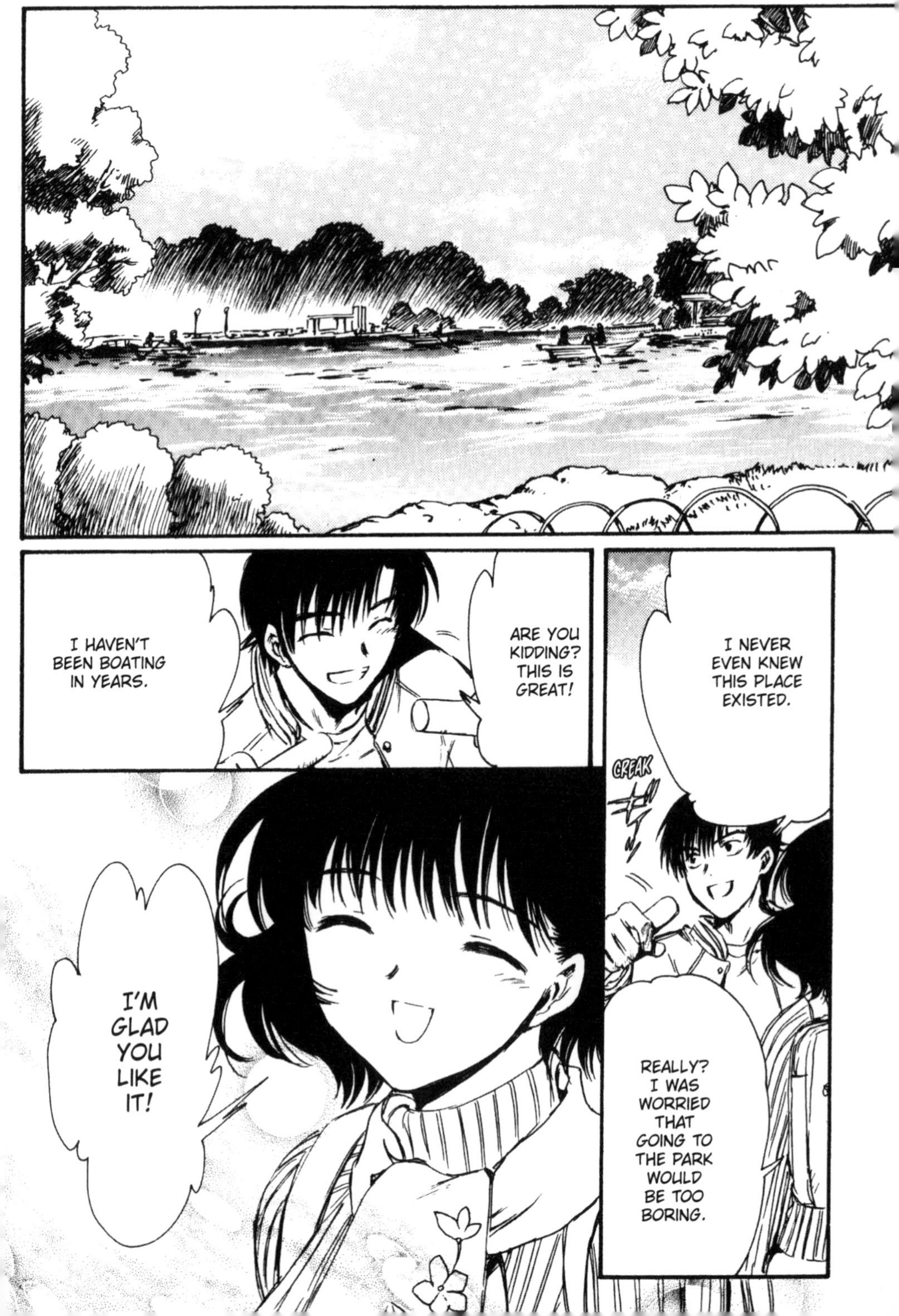
I NEVER EVEN KNEW THIS PLACE EXISTED.
CREAK
REALLY? I WAS WORRIED THAT GOING TO THE PARK WOULD BE TOO BORING.
ARE YOU KIDDING? THIS IS GREAT!
I HAVEN'T BEEN BOATING IN YEARS.
I'M GLAD YOU LIKE IT!

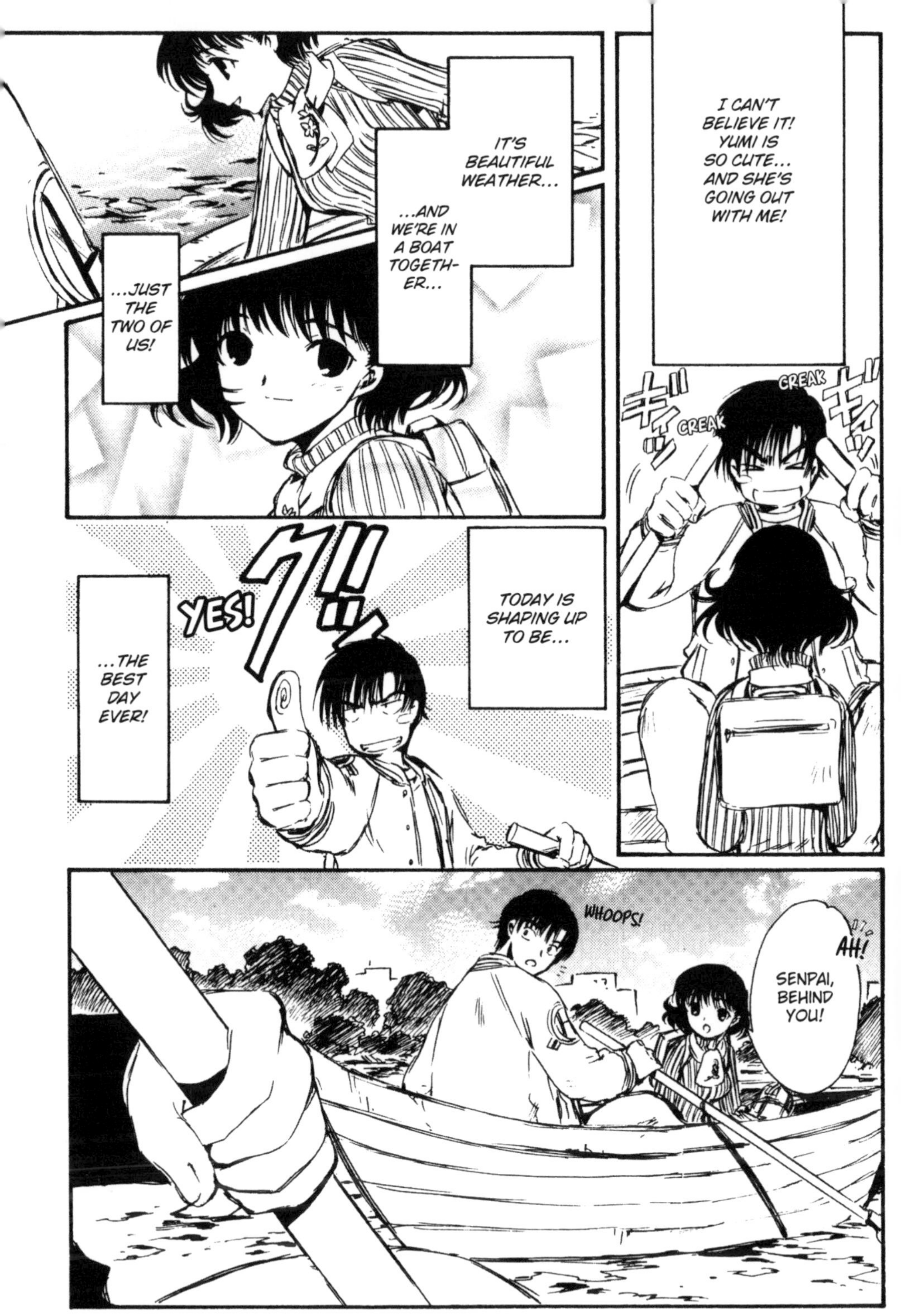
I CAN'T BELIEVE IT! YUMI IS SO CUTE... AND SHE'S GOING OUT WITH ME!
CREAK
CREAK
IT'S BEAUTIFUL WEATHER...
...AND WE'RE IN A BOAT TOGETH-ER...
...JUST THE TWO OF US!
TODAY IS SHAPING UP TO BE...
YES!
...THE BEST DAY EVER!
AH!
SENPAI, BEHIND YOU!
WHOOPS!

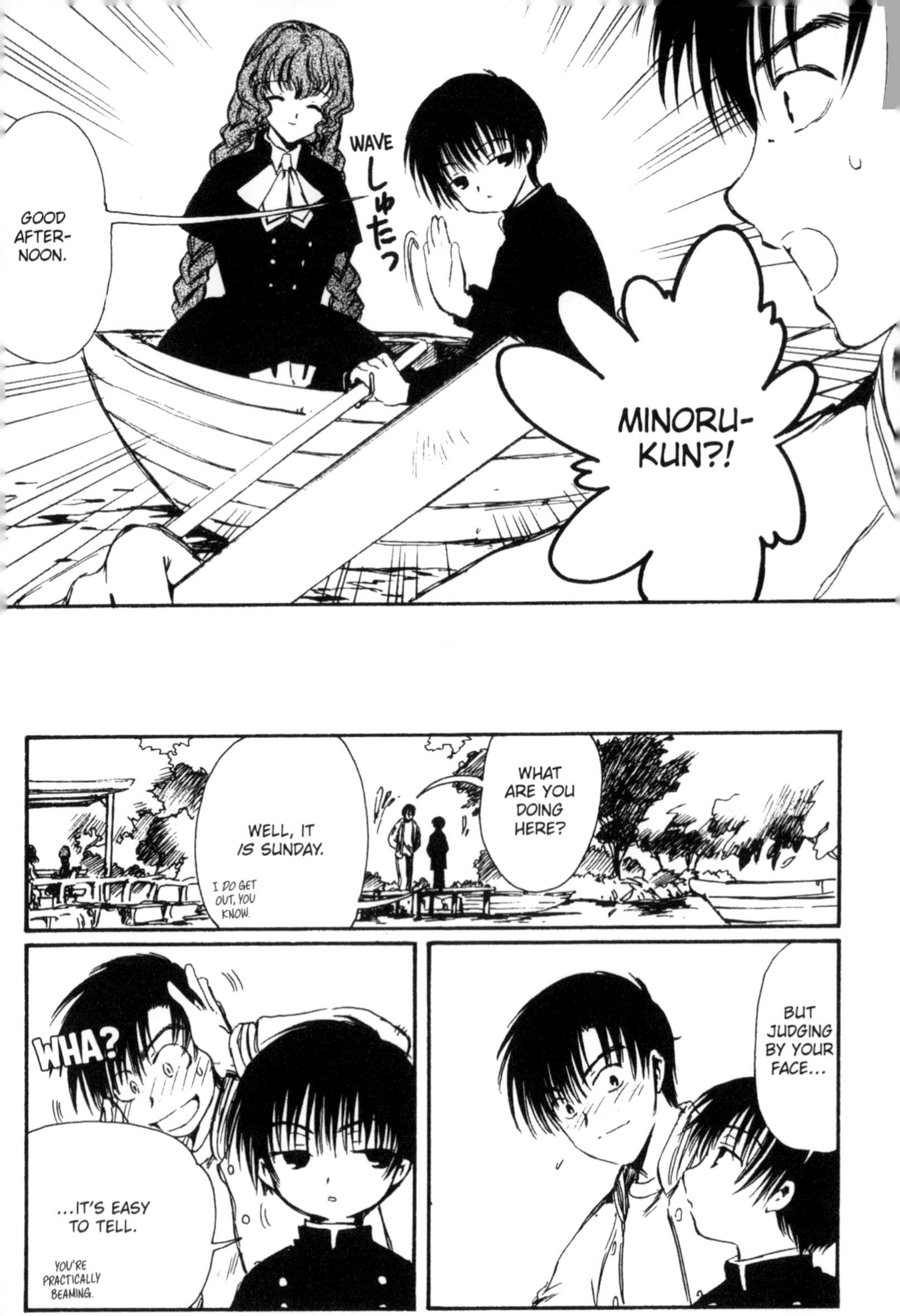
MINORU-KUN?!
WAVE しゅたっ
GOOD AFTERNOON.
WHAT ARE YOU DOING HERE?
WELL, IT IS SUNDAY.
I DO GET OUT, YOU KNOW.
BUT JUDGING BY YOUR FACE...
WHA?
...IT'S EASY TO TELL.
YOU'RE PRACTICALLY BEAMING.

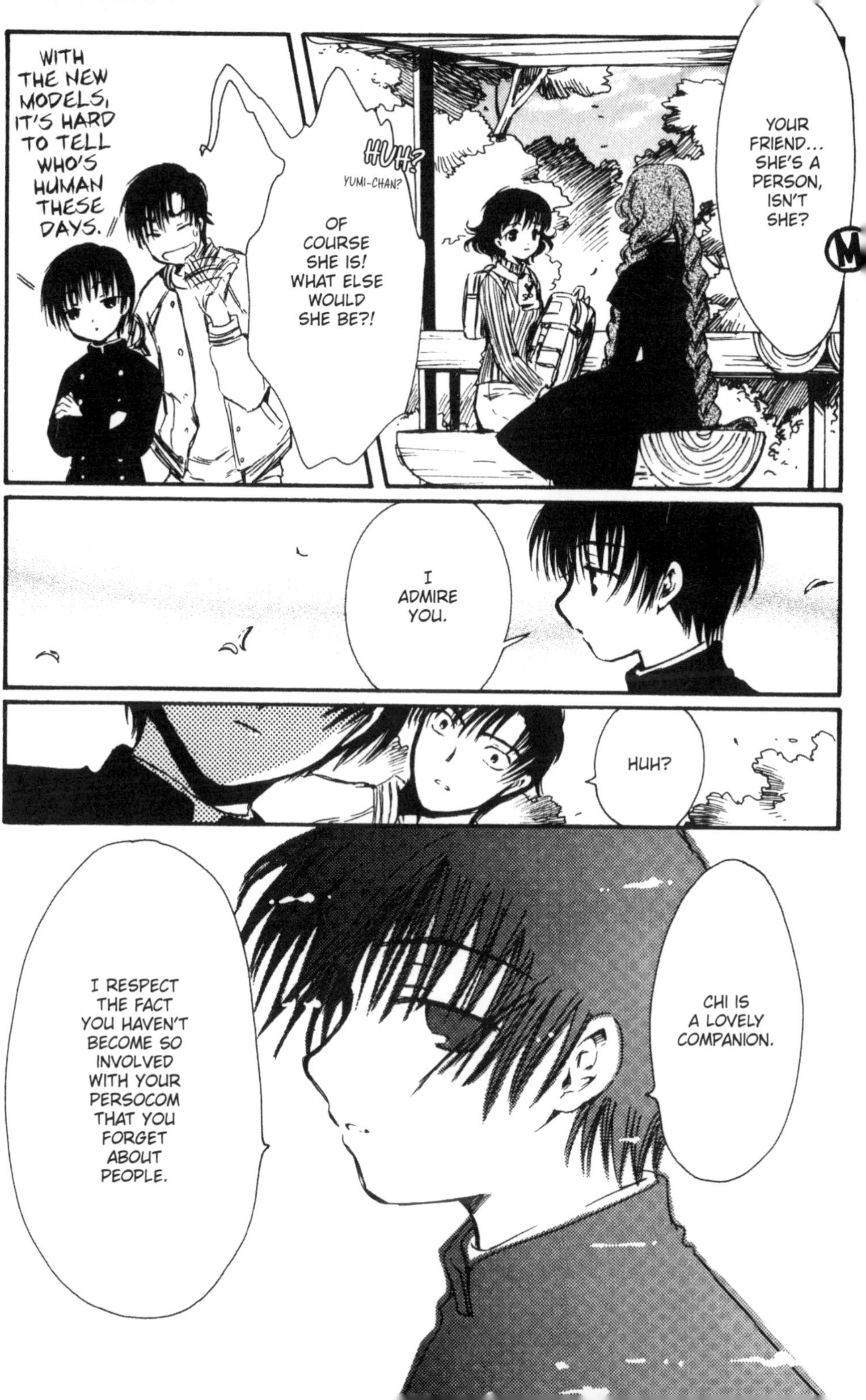

YOUR FRIEND... SHE'S A PERSON, ISN'T SHE?
HUH?
YUMI-CHAN?
OF COURSE SHE IS! WHAT ELSE WOULD SHE BE?!
WITH THE NEW MODELS, IT'S HARD TO TELL WHO'S HUMAN THESE DAYS.
I ADMIRE YOU.
HUH?
CHI IS A LOVELY COMPANION.
I RESPECT THE FACT YOU HAVEN'T BECOME SO INVOLVED WITH YOUR PERSOCOM THAT YOU FORGET ABOUT PEOPLE.

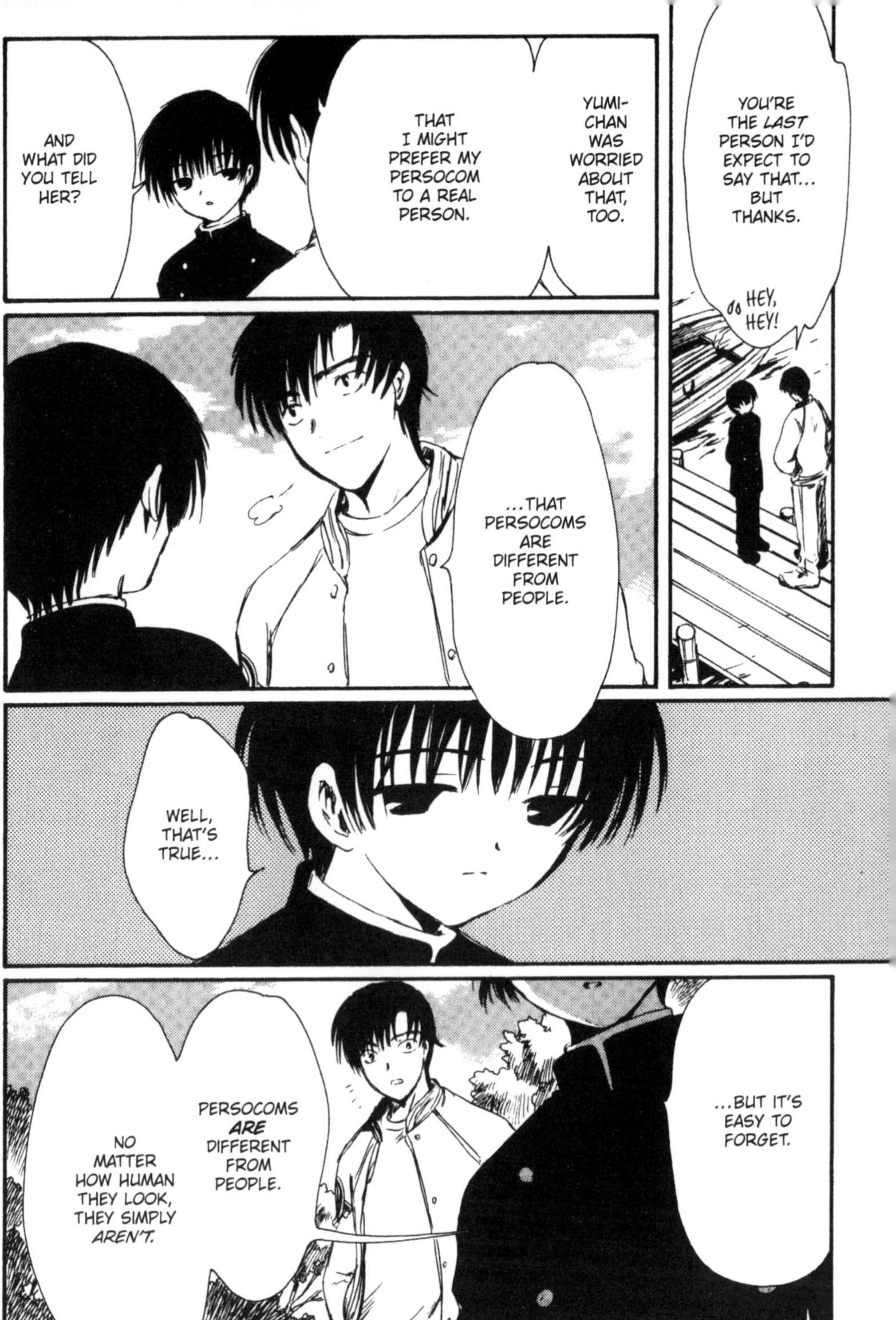
YOU'RE THE *LAST* PERSON I'D EXPECT TO SAY THAT... BUT THANKS.
HEY, HEY!
YUMI-CHAN WAS WORRIED ABOUT THAT, TOO.
THAT I MIGHT PREFER MY PERSOCOM TO A REAL PERSON.
AND WHAT DID YOU TELL HER?
...THAT PERSOCOMS ARE DIFFERENT FROM PEOPLE.
WELL, THAT'S TRUE...
...BUT IT'S EASY TO FORGET.
PERSOCOMS ***ARE*** DIFFERENT FROM PEOPLE.
NO MATTER HOW HUMAN THEY LOOK, THEY SIMPLY *AREN'T.*

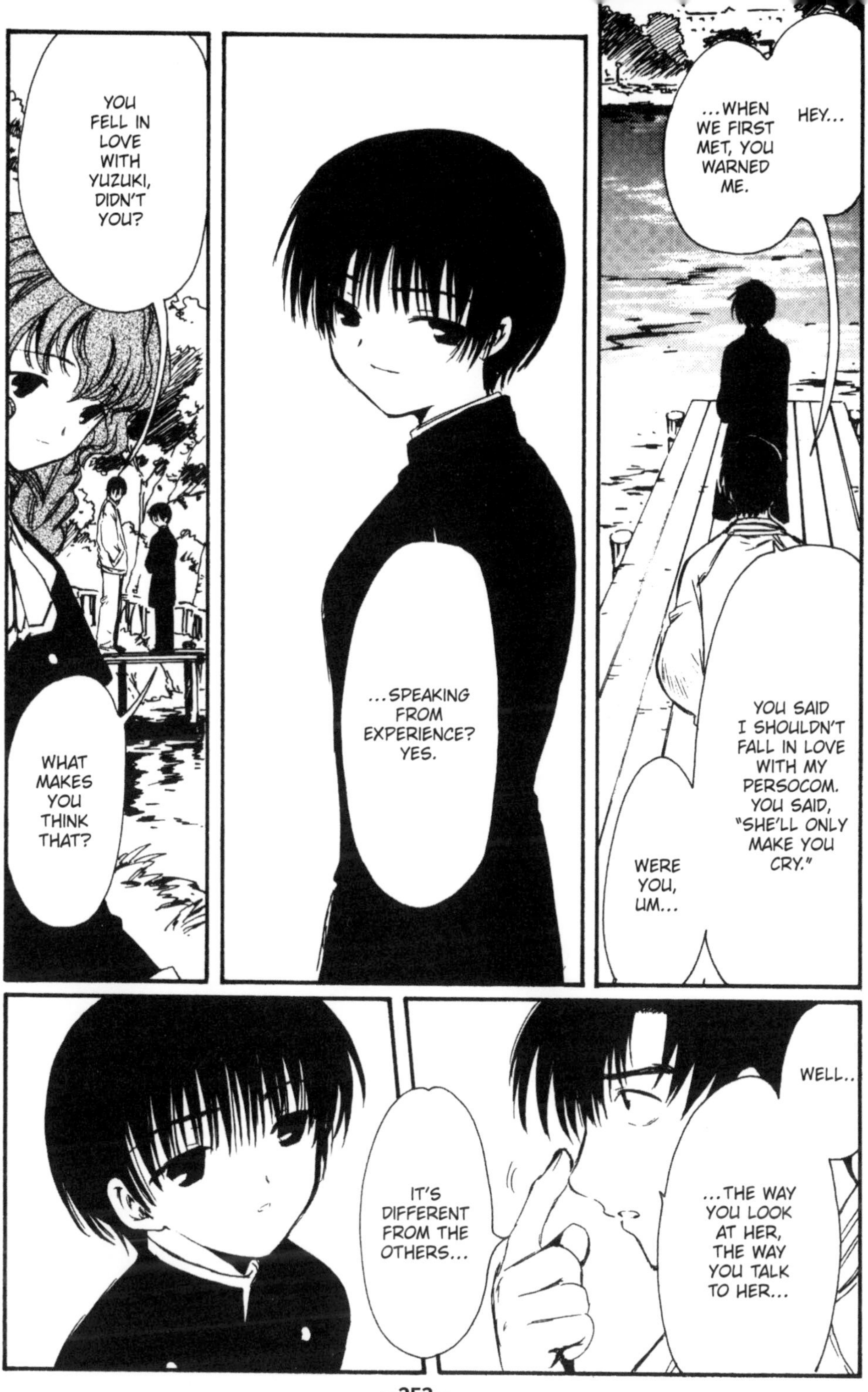
HEY...
...WHEN WE FIRST MET, YOU WARNED ME.
YOU SAID I SHOULDN'T FALL IN LOVE WITH MY PERSOCOM. YOU SAID, "SHE'LL ONLY MAKE YOU CRY."
WERE YOU, UM...
...SPEAKING FROM EXPERIENCE? YES.
YOU FELL IN LOVE WITH YUZUKI, DIDN'T YOU?
WHAT MAKES YOU THINK THAT?
WELL...
...THE WAY YOU LOOK AT HER, THE WAY YOU TALK TO HER...
IT'S DIFFERENT FROM THE OTHERS...

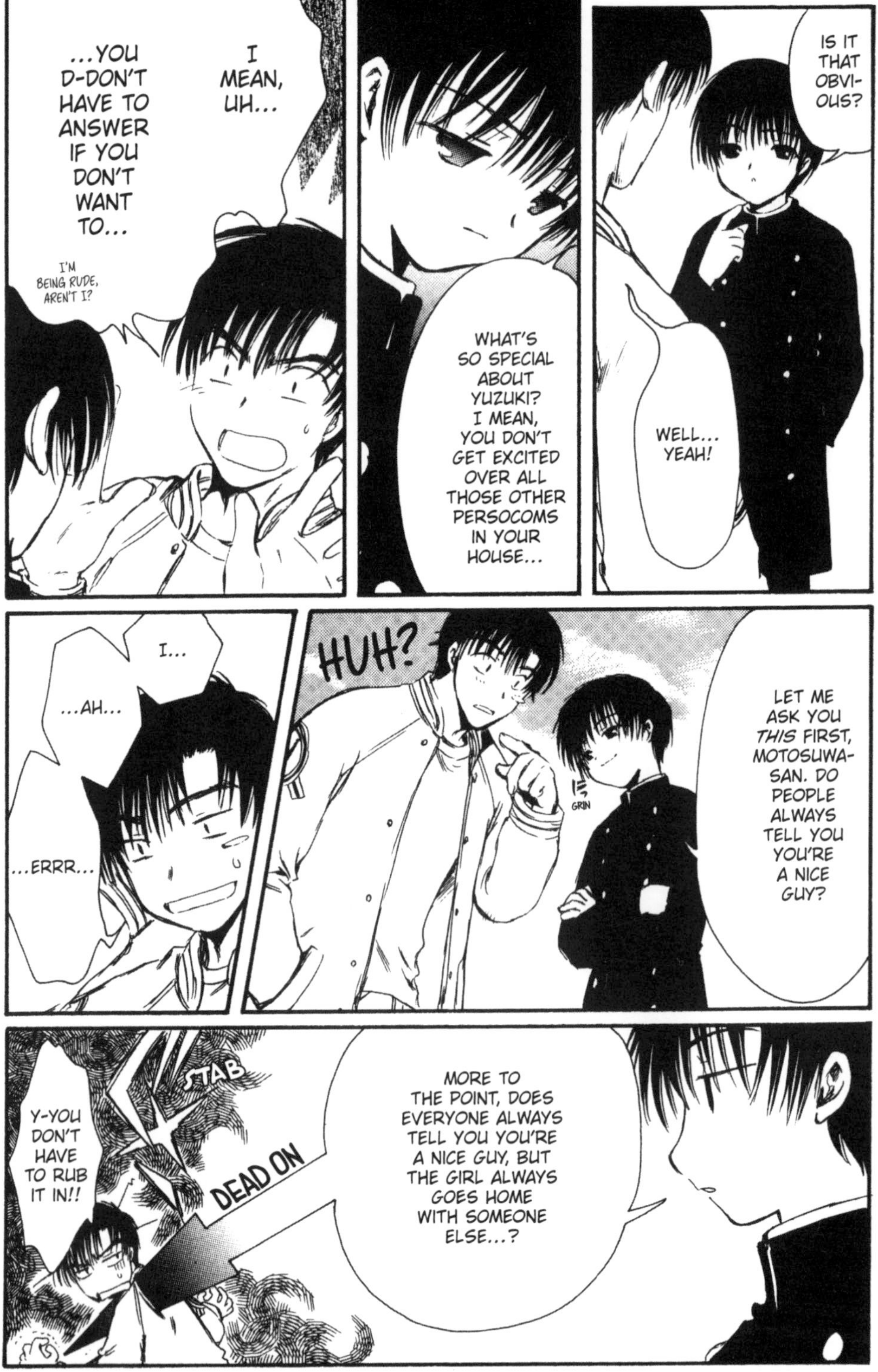
IS IT THAT OBVIOUS?
WELL... YEAH!
WHAT'S SO SPECIAL ABOUT YUZUKI? I MEAN, YOU DON'T GET EXCITED OVER ALL THOSE OTHER PERSOCOMS IN YOUR HOUSE...
I MEAN, UH...
...YOU D-DON'T HAVE TO ANSWER IF YOU DON'T WANT TO...
I'M BEING RUDE, AREN'T I?
LET ME ASK YOU THIS FIRST, MOTOSUWA-SAN. DO PEOPLE ALWAYS TELL YOU YOU'RE A NICE GUY?
HUH?
GRIN
I...
...AH...
...ERRR...
MORE TO THE POINT, DOES EVERYONE ALWAYS TELL YOU YOU'RE A NICE GUY, BUT THE GIRL ALWAYS GOES HOME WITH SOMEONE ELSE...?
STAB
DEAD ON
Y-YOU DON'T HAVE TO RUB IT IN!!

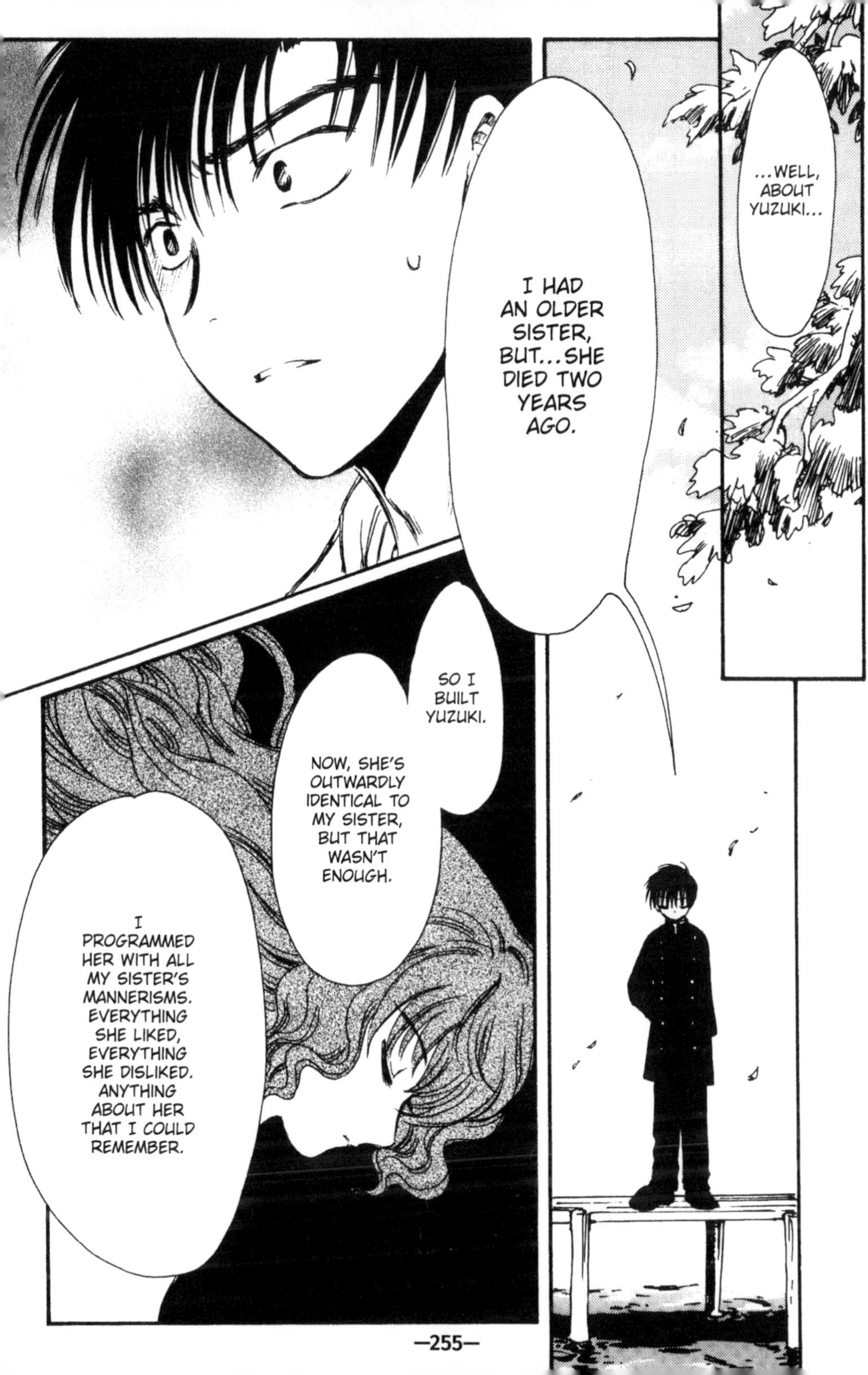
...WELL, ABOUT YUZUKI...
I HAD AN OLDER SISTER, BUT...SHE DIED TWO YEARS AGO.
SO I BUILT YUZUKI.
NOW, SHE'S OUTWARDLY IDENTICAL TO MY SISTER, BUT THAT WASN'T ENOUGH.
I PROGRAMMED HER WITH ALL MY SISTER'S MANNERISMS. EVERYTHING SHE LIKED, EVERYTHING SHE DISLIKED. ANYTHING ABOUT HER THAT I COULD REMEMBER.

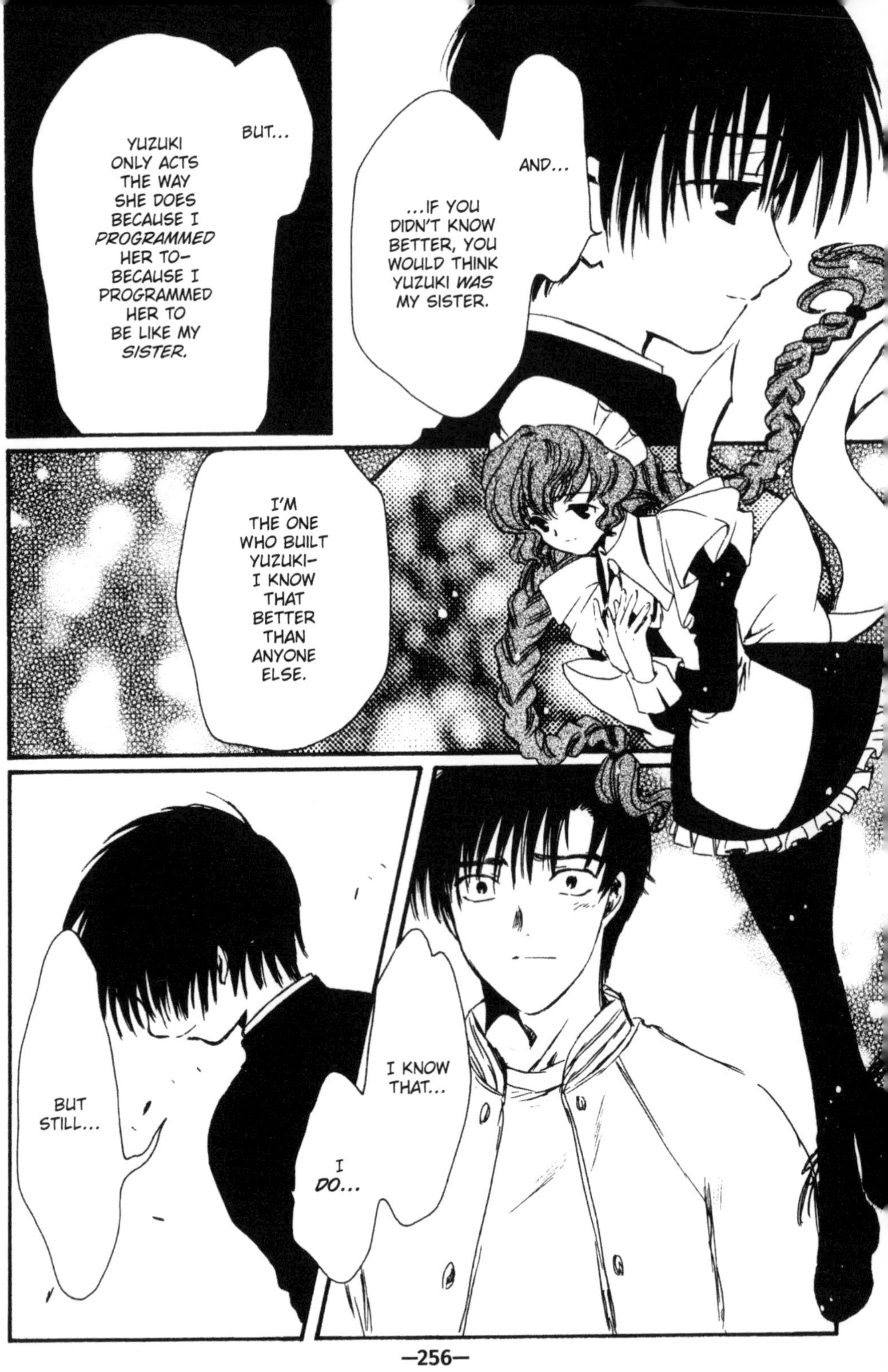
AND...
...IF YOU DIDN'T KNOW BETTER, YOU WOULD THINK YUZUKI *WAS* MY SISTER.
BUT...
YUZUKI ONLY ACTS THE WAY SHE DOES BECAUSE I *PROGRAMMED* HER TO– BECAUSE I PROGRAMMED HER TO BE LIKE MY *SISTER*.
I'M THE ONE WHO BUILT YUZUKI– I KNOW THAT BETTER THAN ANYONE ELSE.
I KNOW THAT...
I *DO*...
BUT STILL...

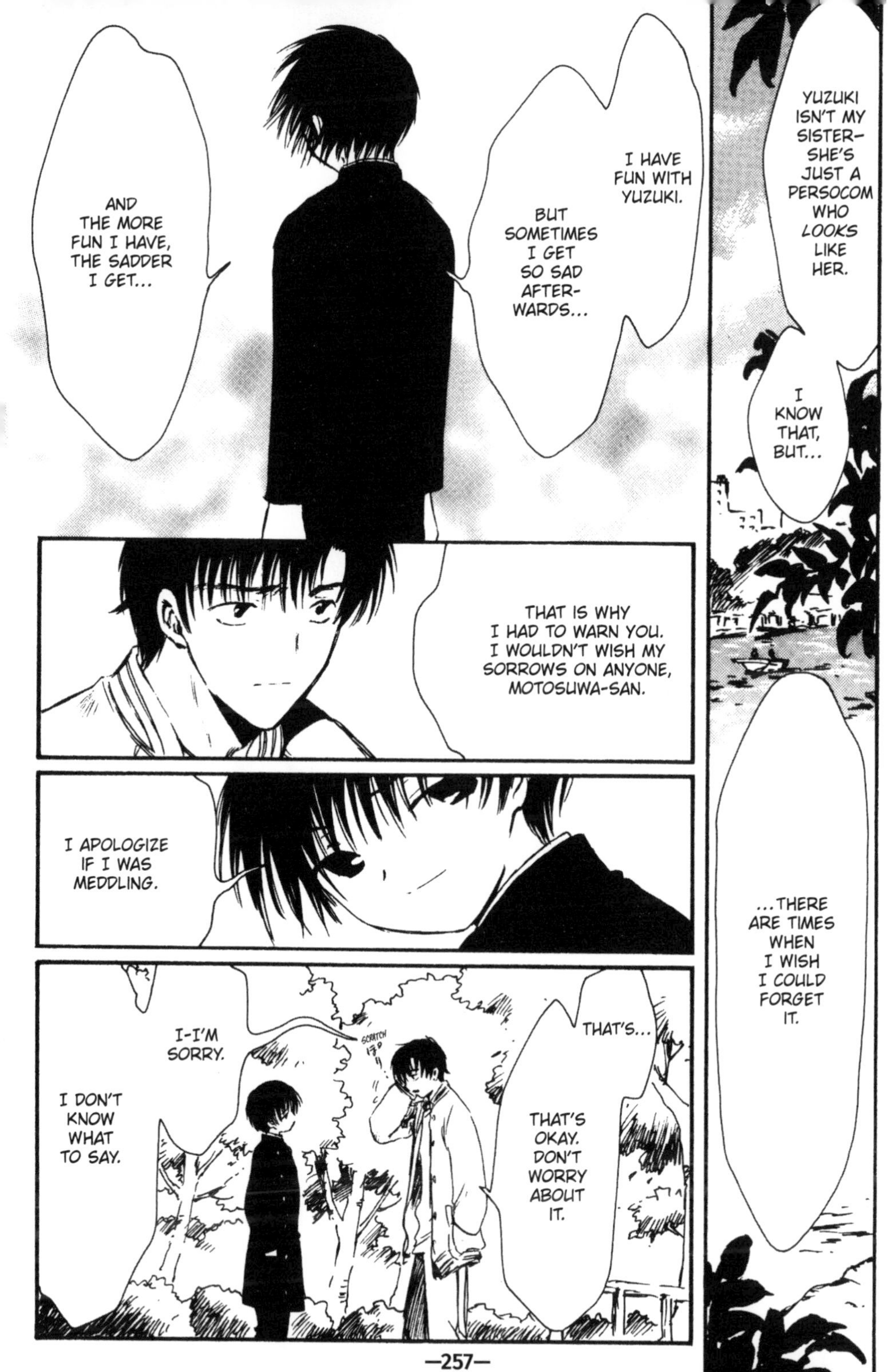
YUZUKI ISN'T MY SISTER–SHE'S JUST A PERSOCOM WHO LOOKS LIKE HER.
I KNOW THAT, BUT...
...THERE ARE TIMES WHEN I WISH I COULD FORGET IT.
I HAVE FUN WITH YUZUKI.
BUT SOMETIMES I GET SO SAD AFTER-WARDS...
AND THE MORE FUN I HAVE, THE SADDER I GET...
THAT IS WHY I HAD TO WARN YOU. I WOULDN'T WISH MY SORROWS ON ANYONE, MOTOSUWA-SAN.
I APOLOGIZE IF I WAS MEDDLING.
THAT'S...
THAT'S OKAY. DON'T WORRY ABOUT IT.
SCRATCH
I-I'M SORRY.
I DON'T KNOW WHAT TO SAY.

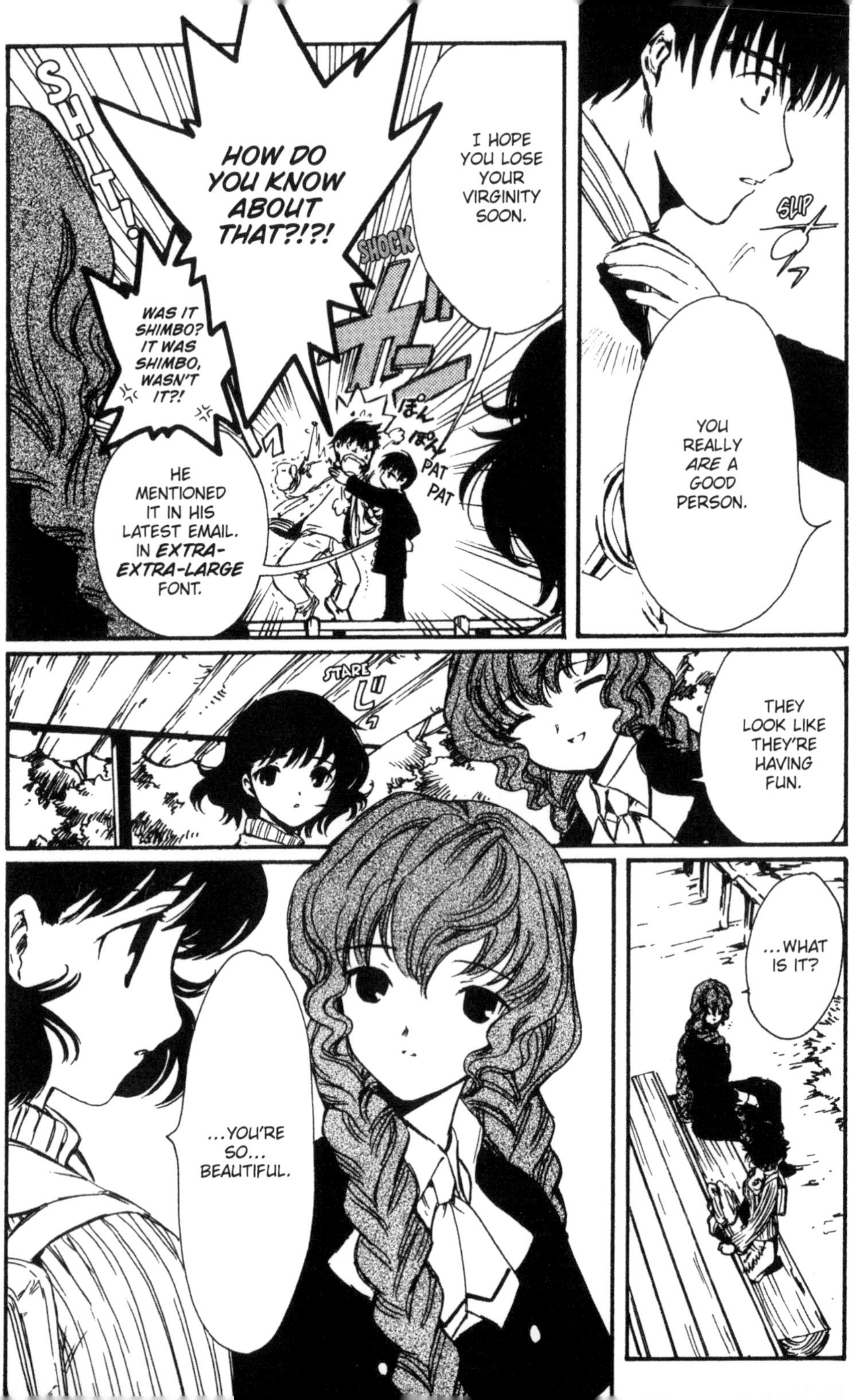
SLIP
YOU REALLY ARE A GOOD PERSON.
I HOPE YOU LOSE YOUR VIRGINITY SOON.
HOW DO YOU KNOW ABOUT THAT?!?!
SHIT!
SHOCK
WAS IT SHIMBO? IT WAS SHIMBO, WASN'T IT?!
HE MENTIONED IT IN HIS LATEST EMAIL. IN EXTRA-EXTRA-LARGE FONT.
PAT PAT
THEY LOOK LIKE THEY'RE HAVING FUN.
STARE
...WHAT IS IT?
...YOU'RE SO... BEAUTIFUL.

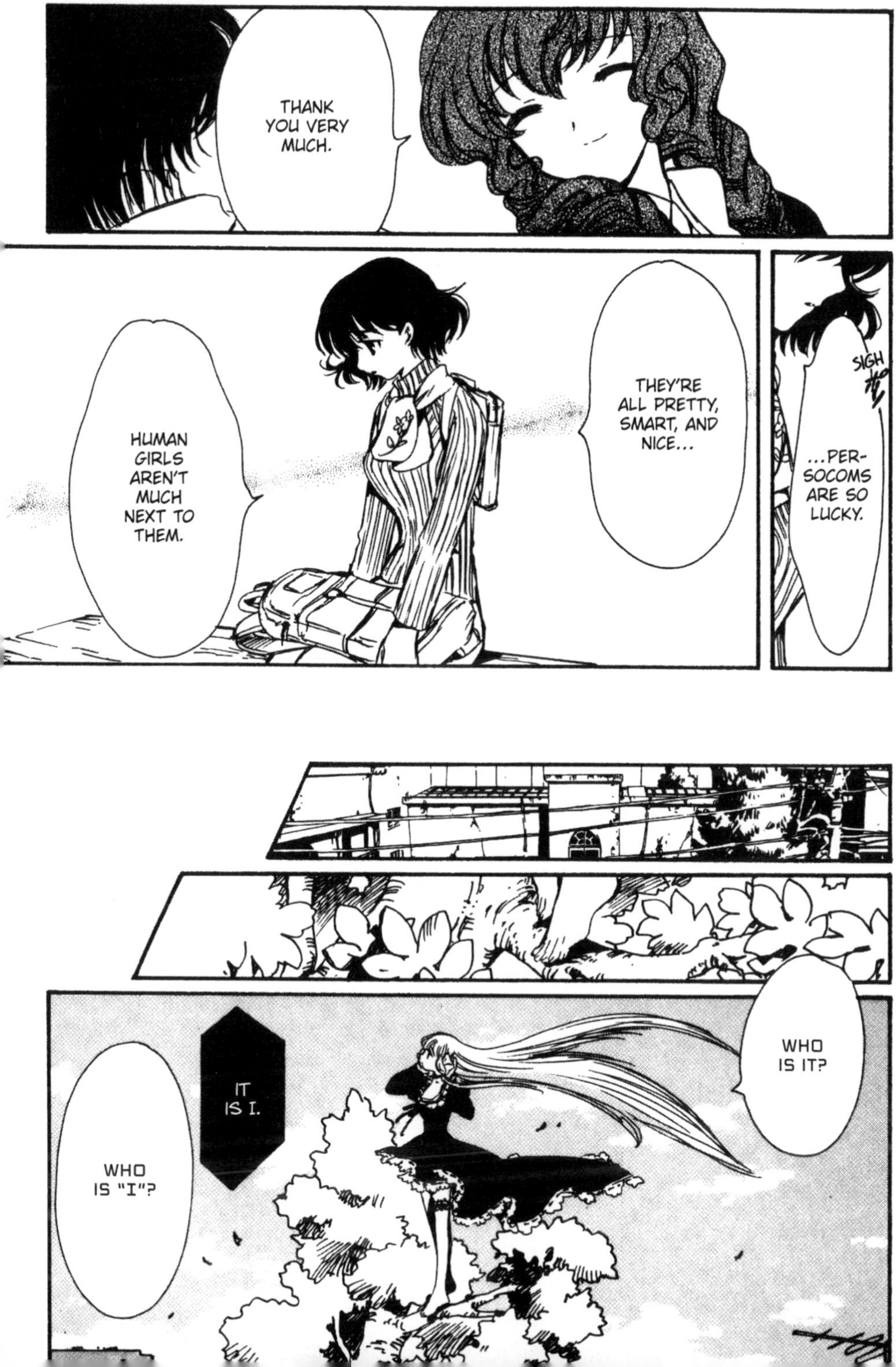
THANK YOU VERY MUCH.
SIGH
...PER-SOCOMS ARE SO LUCKY.
THEY'RE ALL PRETTY, SMART, AND NICE...
HUMAN GIRLS AREN'T MUCH NEXT TO THEM.
WHO IS IT?
IT IS I.
WHO IS "I"?

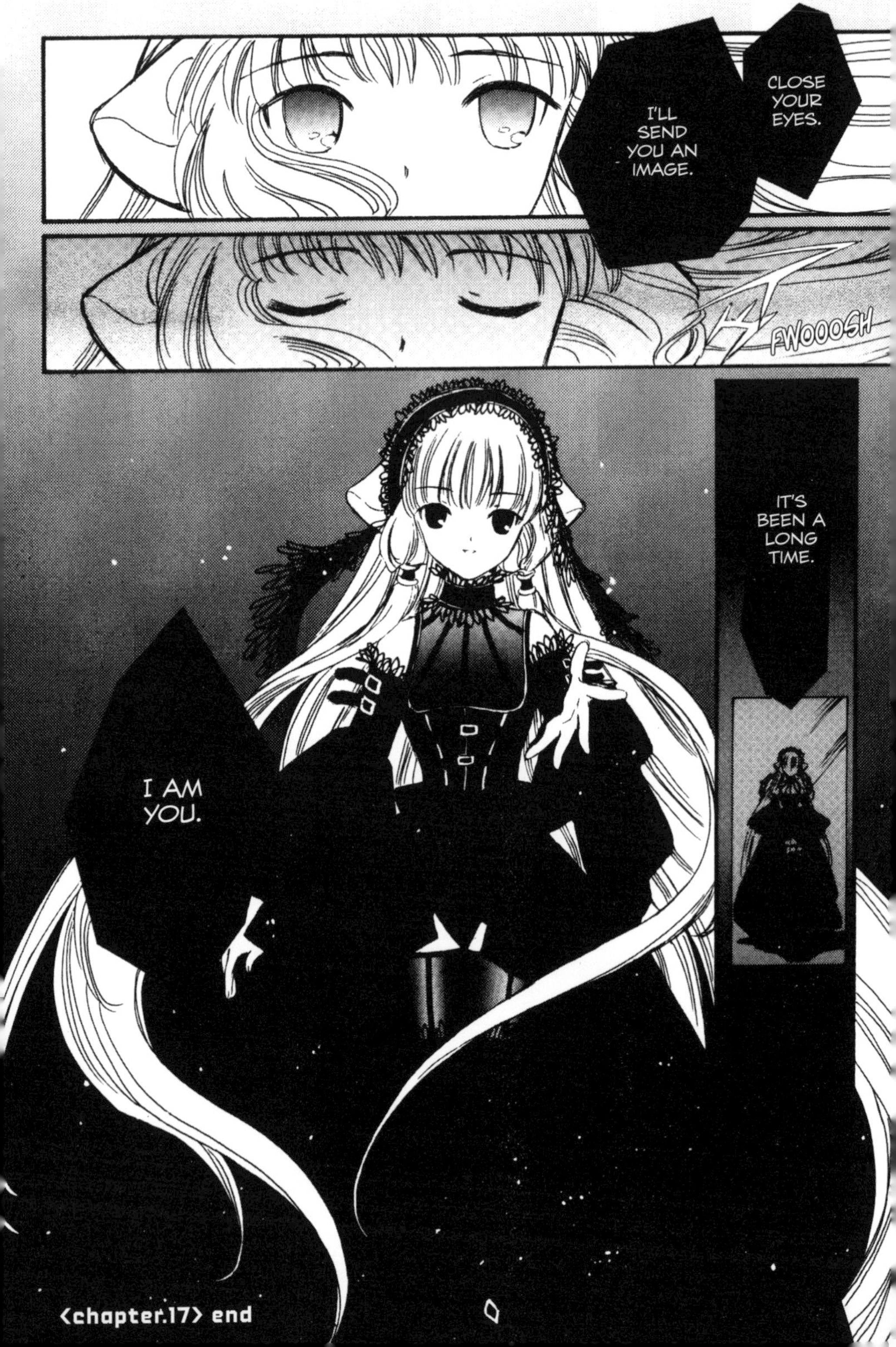
CLOSE YOUR EYES.
I'LL SEND YOU AN IMAGE.
FWOOOSH
IT'S BEEN A LONG TIME.
I AM YOU.
<chapter.17> end

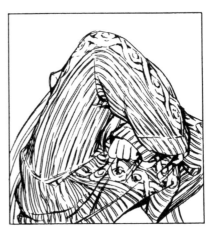

Chobits

〈chapter.18〉

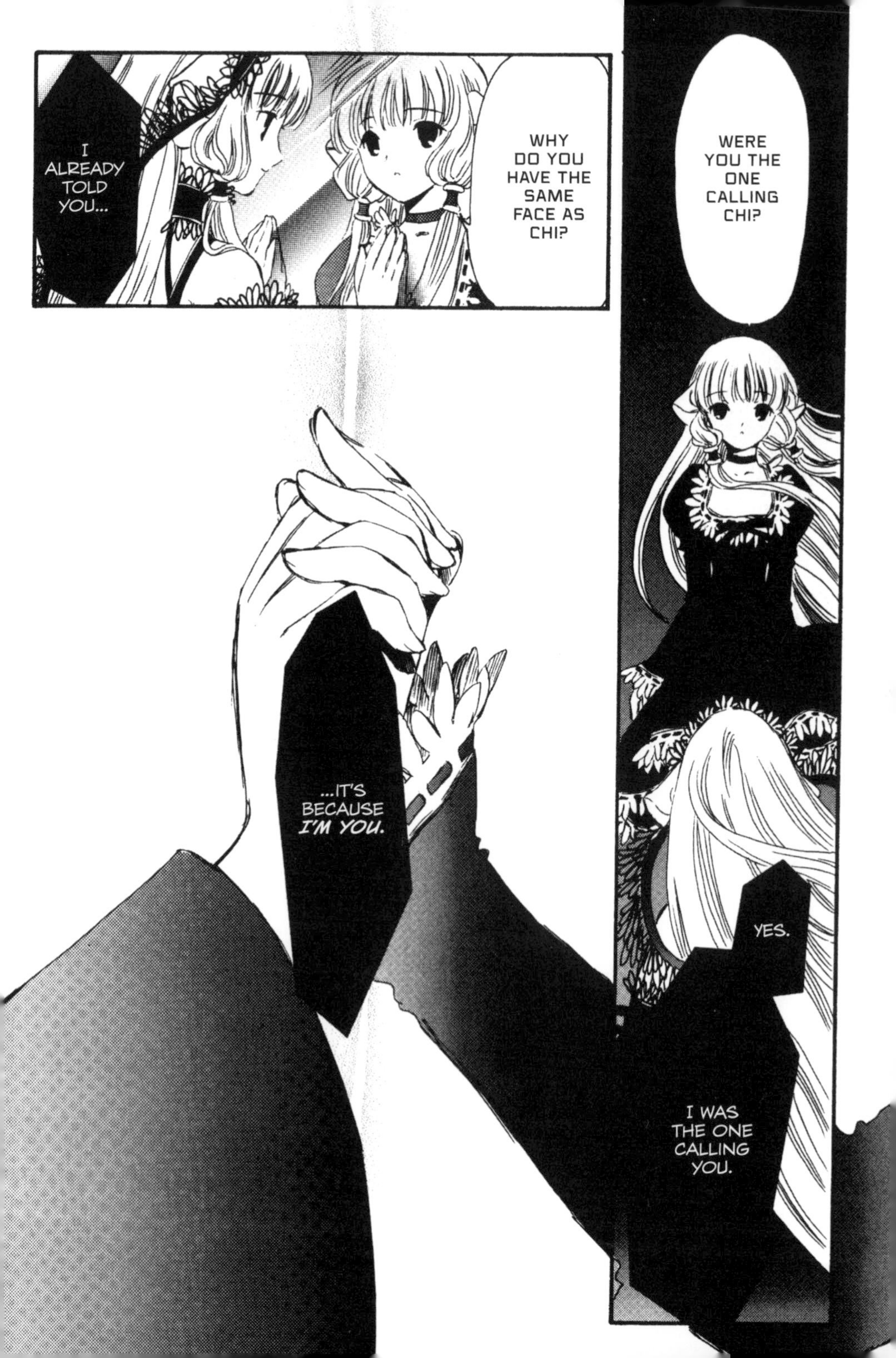
WERE YOU THE ONE CALLING CHI?
YES.
I WAS THE ONE CALLING YOU.
WHY DO YOU HAVE THE SAME FACE AS CHI?
I ALREADY TOLD YOU...
...IT'S BECAUSE *I'M YOU.*

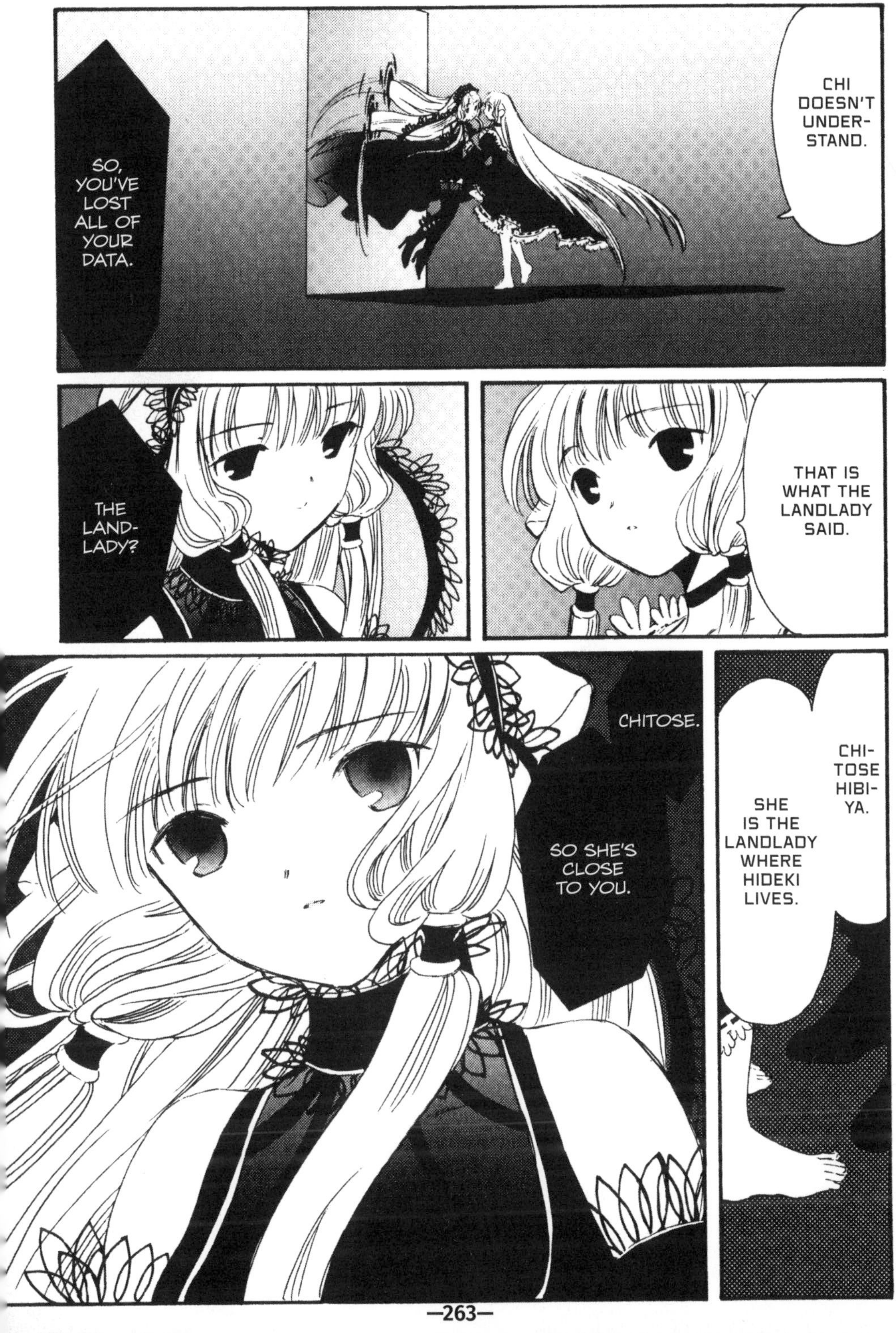
CHI DOESN'T UNDER-STAND.
SO, YOU'VE LOST ALL OF YOUR DATA.
THAT IS WHAT THE LANDLADY SAID.
THE LAND-LADY?
CHI-TOSE HIBI-YA.
SHE IS THE LANDLADY WHERE HIDEKI LIVES.
CHITOSE.
SO SHE'S CLOSE TO YOU.

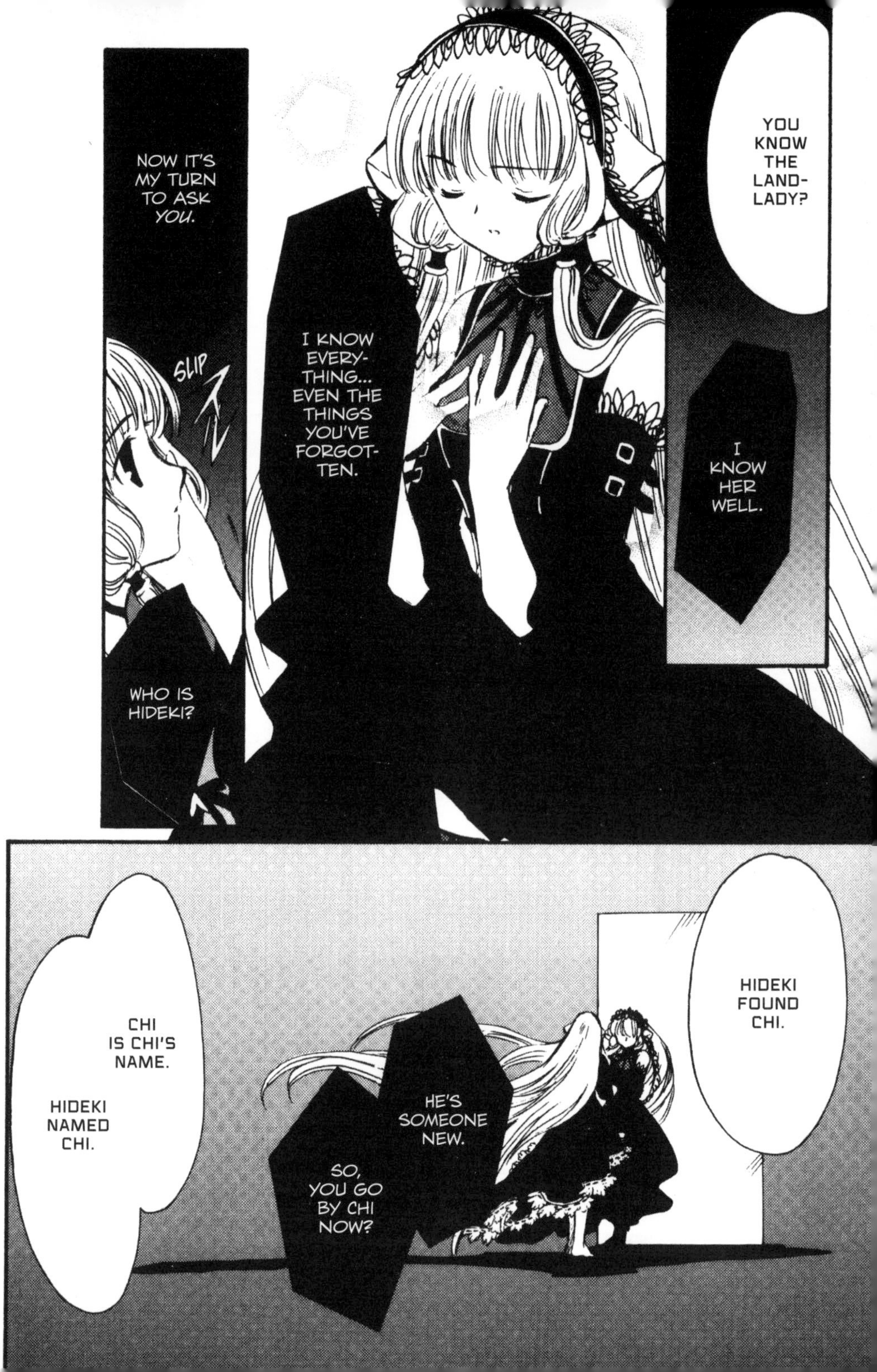
YOU KNOW THE LAND-LADY?
I KNOW HER WELL.
I KNOW EVERY-THING... EVEN THE THINGS YOU'VE FORGOT-TEN.
NOW IT'S MY TURN TO ASK *YOU*.
SLIP
WHO IS HIDEKI?
HIDEKI FOUND CHI.
HE'S SOMEONE NEW.
SO, YOU GO BY CHI NOW?
CHI IS CHI'S NAME.
HIDEKI NAMED CHI.

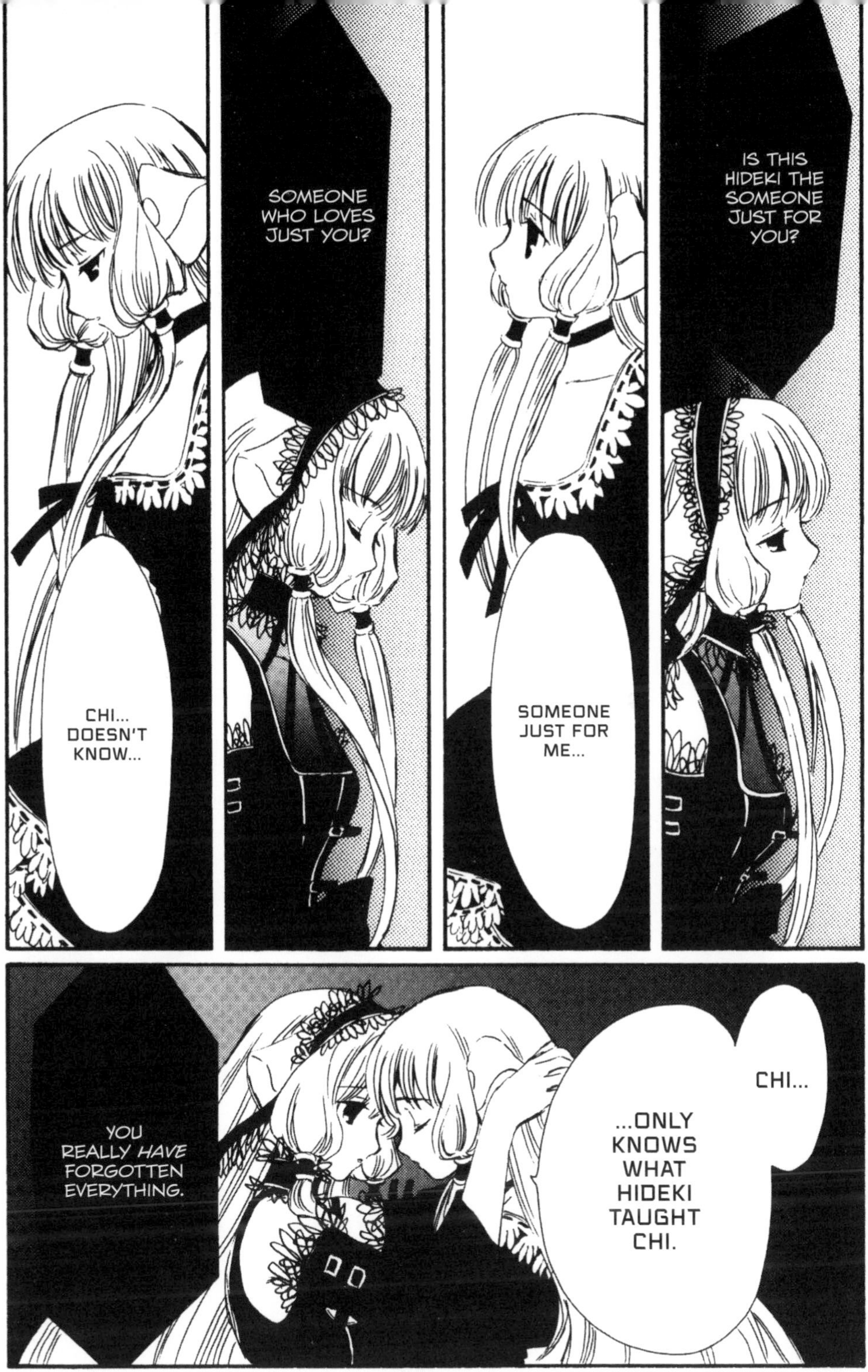
IS THIS HIDEKI THE SOMEONE JUST FOR YOU?
SOMEONE JUST FOR ME...
SOMEONE WHO LOVES JUST YOU?
CHI... DOESN'T KNOW...
CHI...
...ONLY KNOWS WHAT HIDEKI TAUGHT CHI.
YOU REALLY *HAVE* FORGOTTEN EVERYTHING.

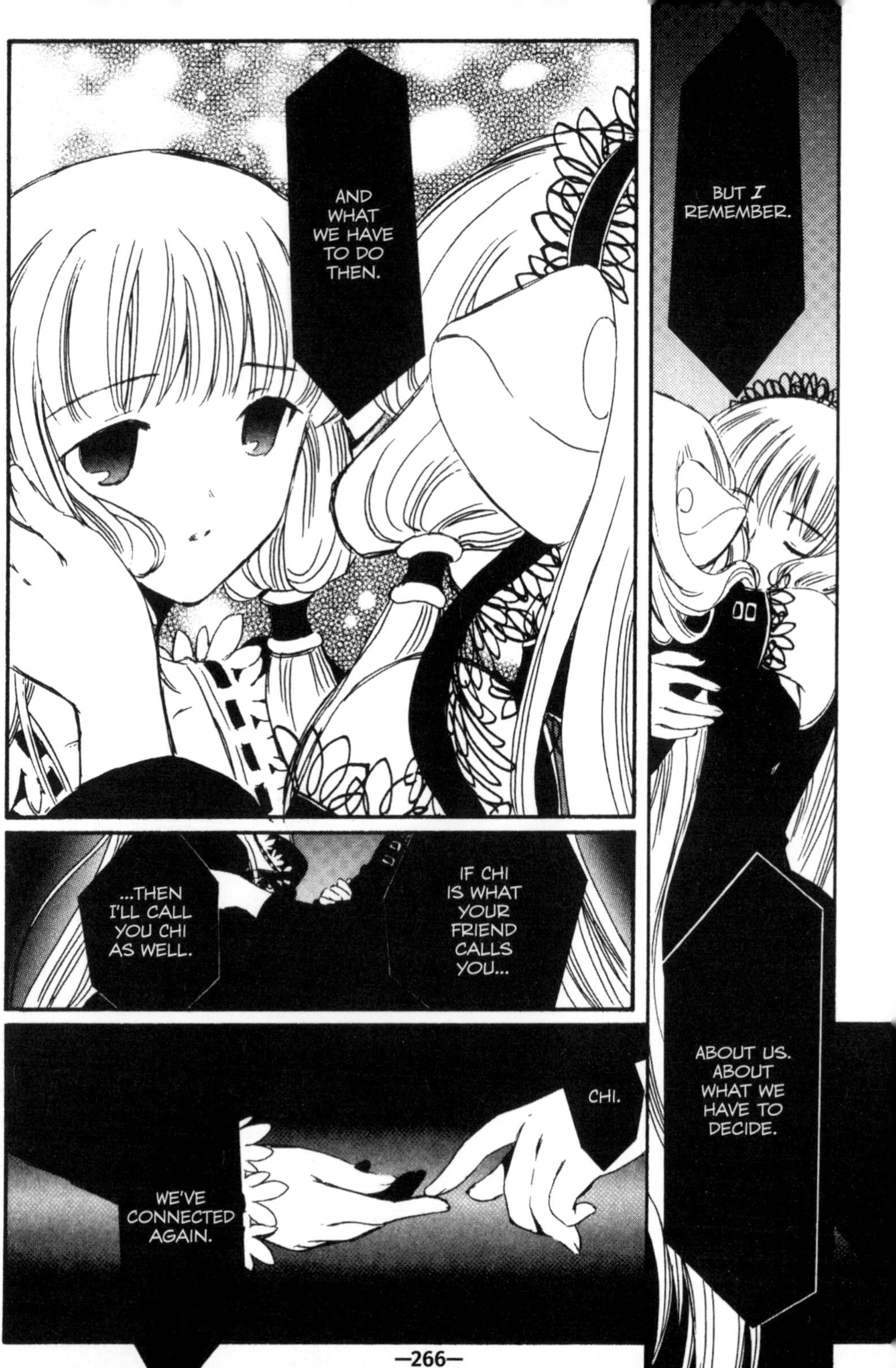
BUT I REMEMBER.
ABOUT US. ABOUT WHAT WE HAVE TO DECIDE.
AND WHAT WE HAVE TO DO THEN.
IF CHI IS WHAT YOUR FRIEND CALLS YOU...
...THEN I'LL CALL YOU CHI AS WELL.
CHI.
WE'VE CONNECTED AGAIN.

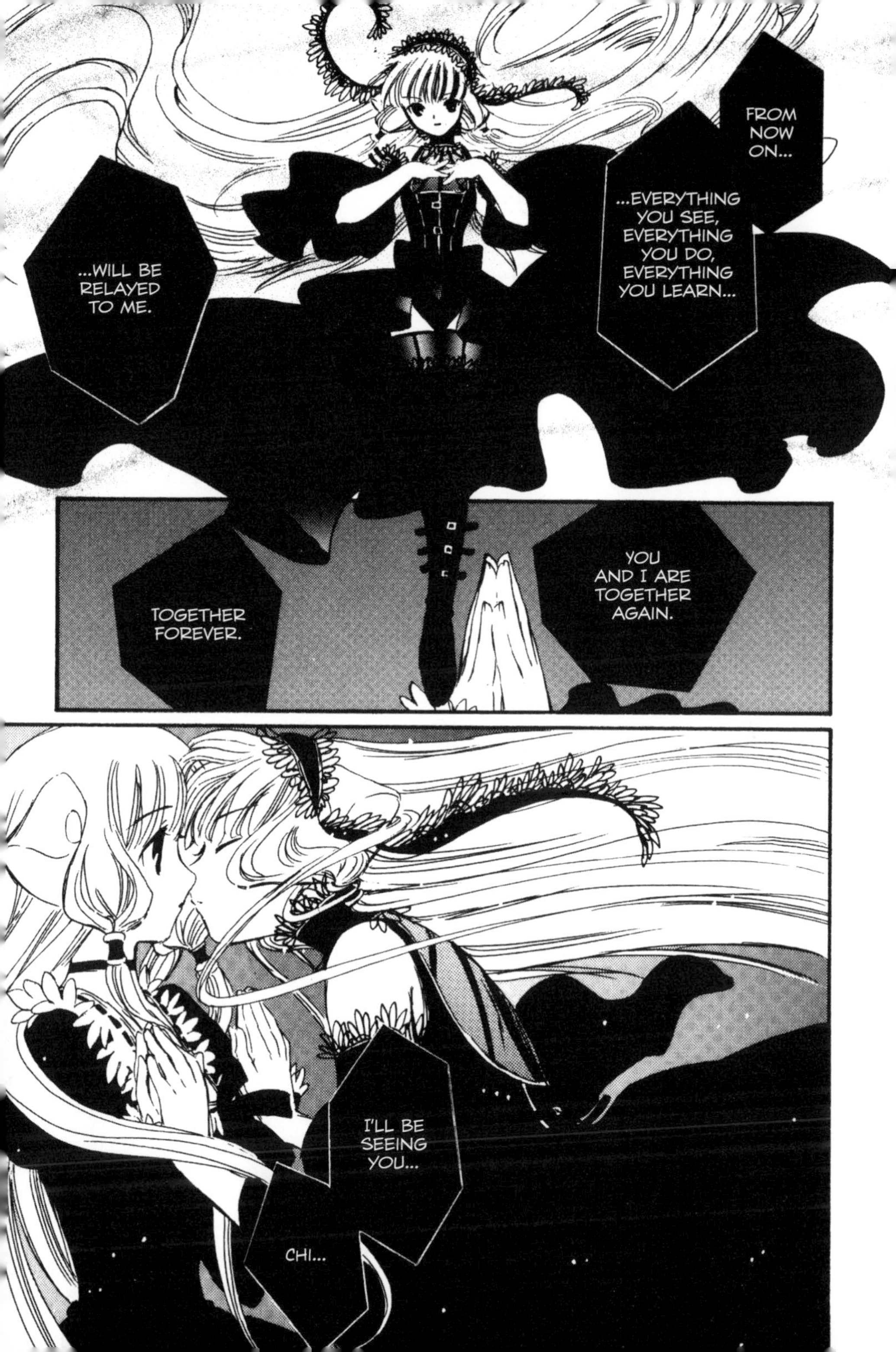
FROM NOW ON...
...EVERYTHING YOU SEE, EVERYTHING YOU DO, EVERYTHING YOU LEARN...
...WILL BE RELAYED TO ME.
YOU AND I ARE TOGETHER AGAIN.
TOGETHER FOREVER.
I'LL BE SEEING YOU...
CHI...

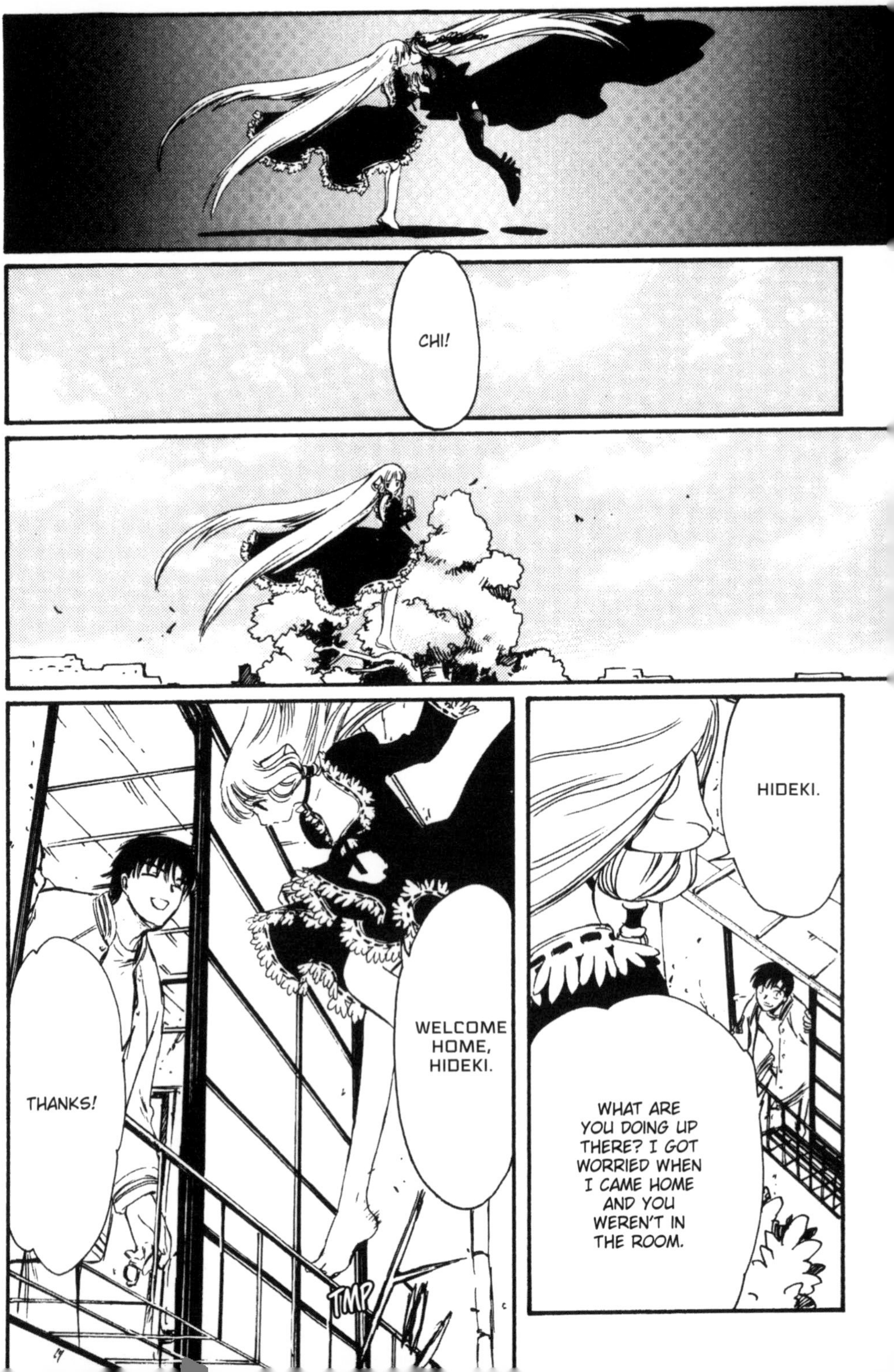
CHI!
HIDEKI.
WHAT ARE YOU DOING UP THERE? I GOT WORRIED WHEN I CAME HOME AND YOU WEREN'T IN THE ROOM.
WELCOME HOME, HIDEKI.
THANKS!
TMP

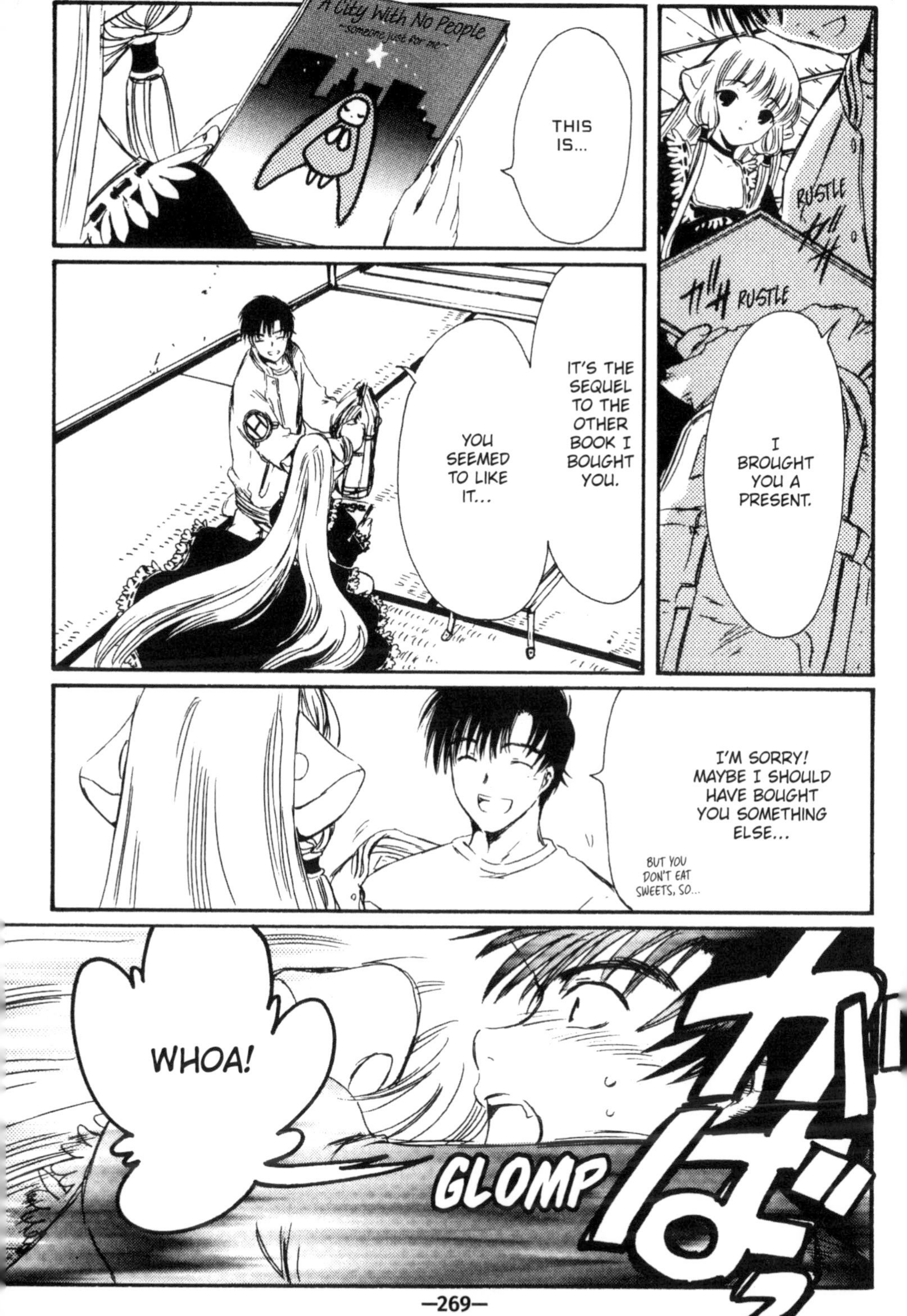
RUSTLE
RUSTLE
I BROUGHT YOU A PRESENT.
A City With No People
~someone just for me~
THIS IS...
IT'S THE SEQUEL TO THE OTHER BOOK I BOUGHT YOU.
YOU SEEMED TO LIKE IT...
I'M SORRY! MAYBE I SHOULD HAVE BOUGHT YOU SOMETHING ELSE...
BUT YOU DON'T EAT SWEETS, SO...
GLOMP
WHOA!

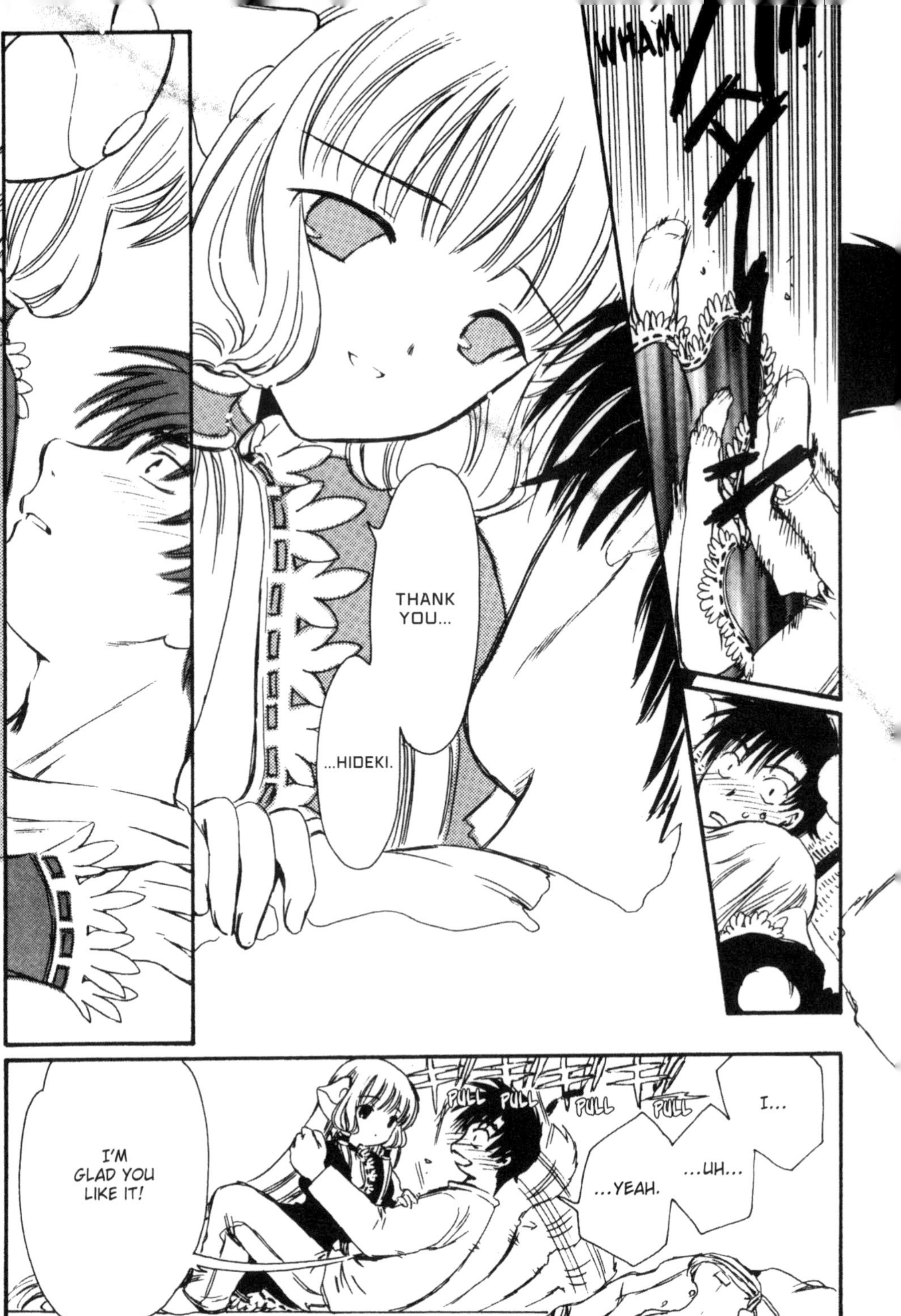
WHAM
THANK YOU...
...HIDEKI.
I...
PULL PULL PULL PULL
...UH...
...YEAH.
I'M GLAD YOU LIKE IT!

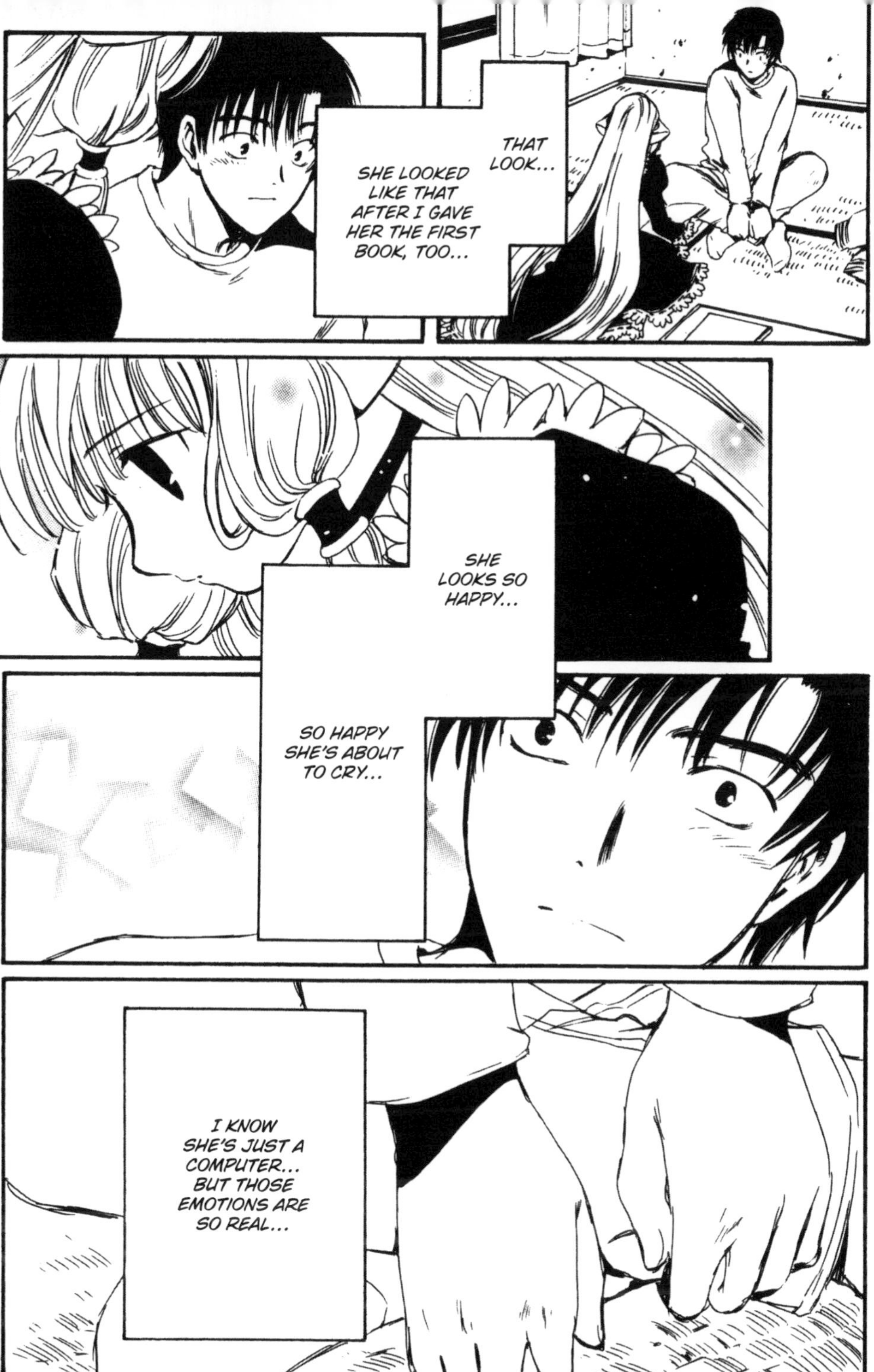
THAT LOOK...
SHE LOOKED LIKE THAT AFTER I GAVE HER THE FIRST BOOK, TOO...
SHE LOOKS SO HAPPY...
SO HAPPY SHE'S ABOUT TO CRY...
I KNOW SHE'S JUST A COMPUTER... BUT THOSE EMOTIONS ARE SO REAL...

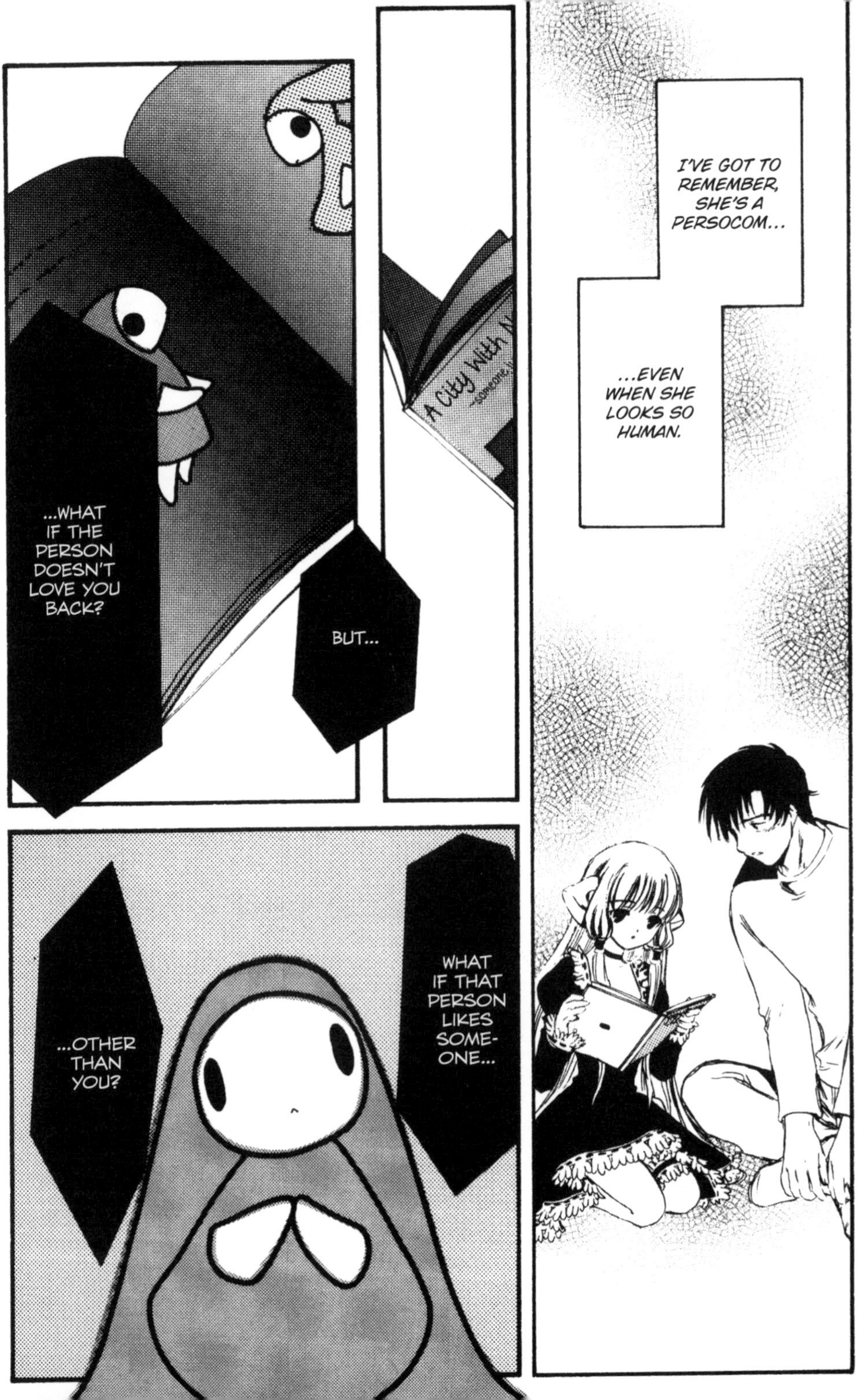
I'VE GOT TO REMEMBER, SHE'S A PERSOCOM...
...EVEN WHEN SHE LOOKS SO HUMAN.
A City With N
BUT...
...WHAT IF THE PERSON DOESN'T LOVE YOU BACK?
WHAT IF THAT PERSON LIKES SOME-ONE...
...OTHER THAN YOU?

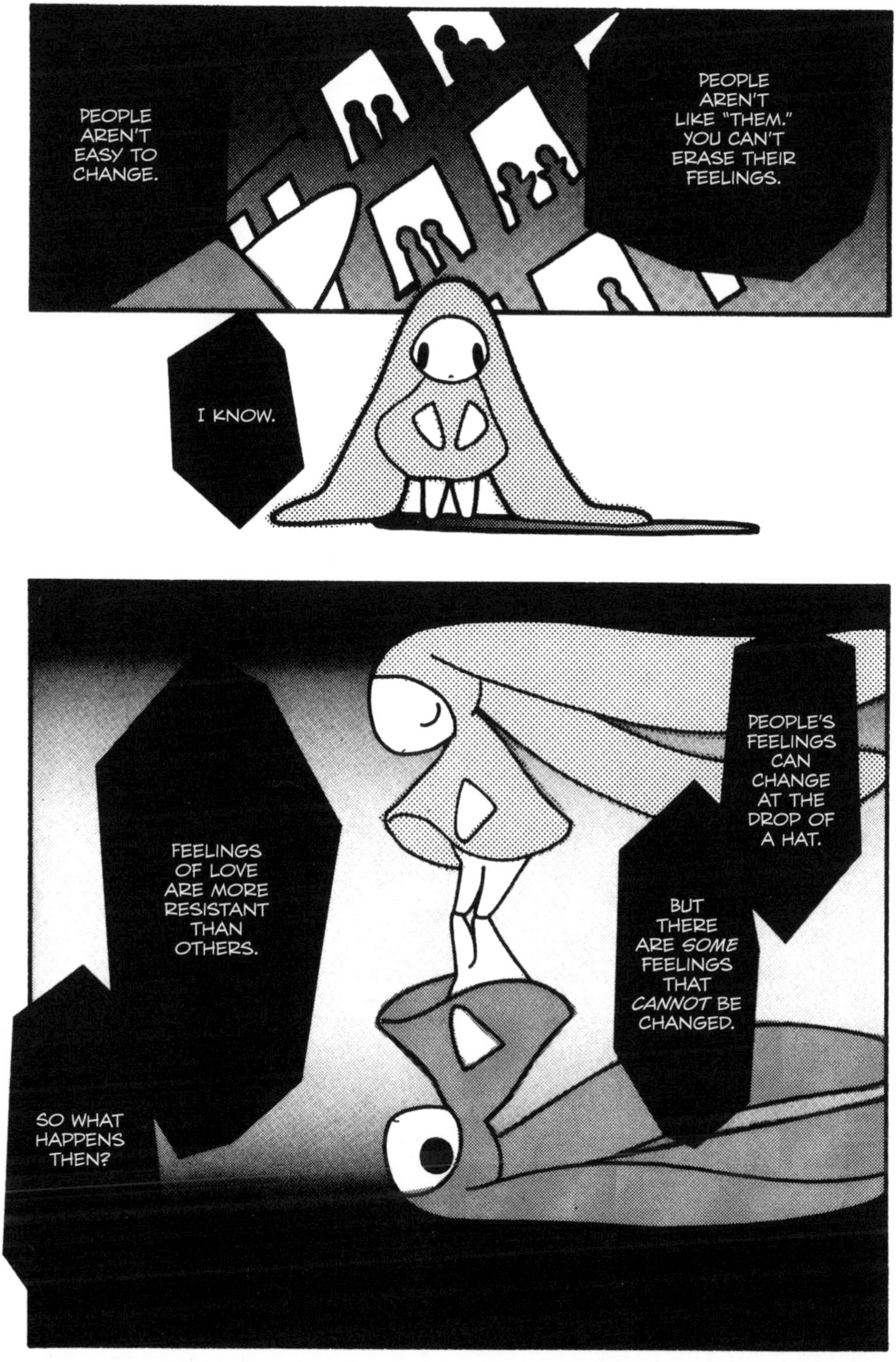
PEOPLE AREN'T LIKE "THEM." YOU CAN'T ERASE THEIR FEELINGS.
PEOPLE AREN'T EASY TO CHANGE.
I KNOW.
PEOPLE'S FEELINGS CAN CHANGE AT THE DROP OF A HAT.
BUT THERE ARE *SOME* FEELINGS THAT *CANNOT* BE CHANGED.
FEELINGS OF LOVE ARE MORE RESISTANT THAN OTHERS.
SO WHAT HAPPENS THEN?

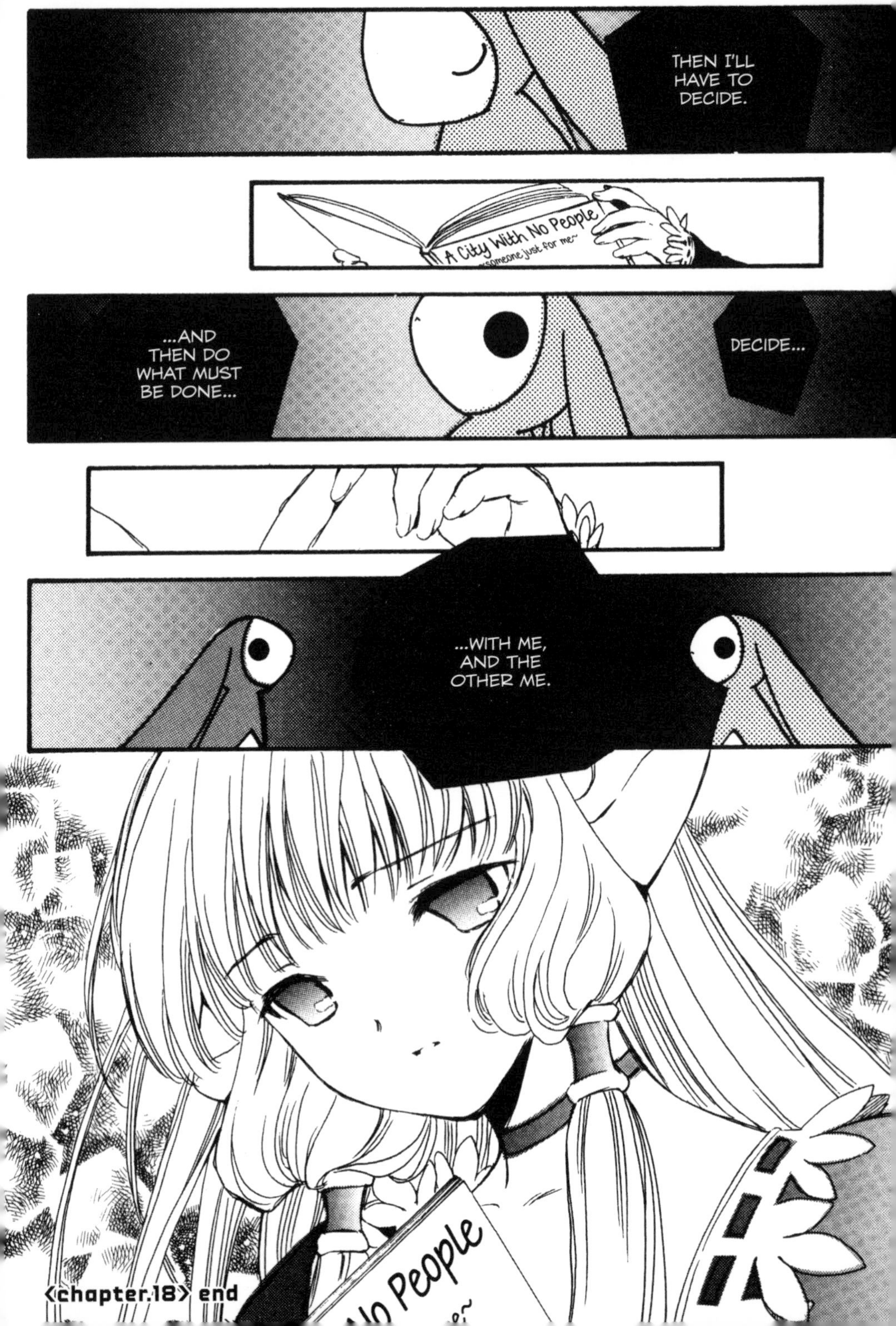
THEN I'LL HAVE TO DECIDE.
A City With No People
someone just for me~
DECIDE...
...AND THEN DO WHAT MUST BE DONE...
...WITH ME, AND THE OTHER ME.
No People
⟨chapter.18⟩ end

〈chapter.19〉

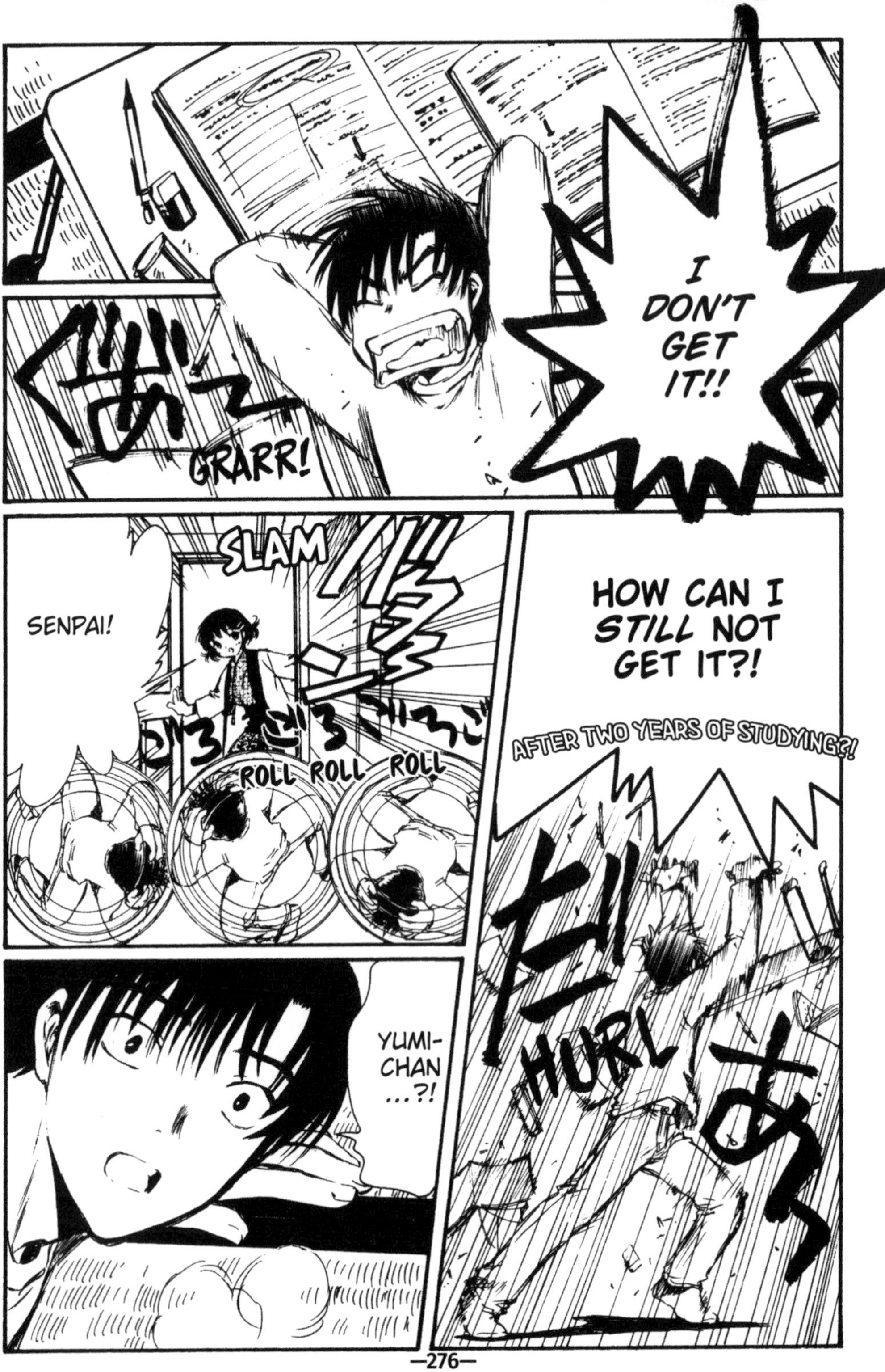
I DON'T GET IT!!
GRARR!
HOW CAN I STILL NOT GET IT?!
AFTER TWO YEARS OF STUDYING?!
HURL
SLAM
SENPAI!
ROLL ROLL ROLL
YUMI-CHAN ...?!

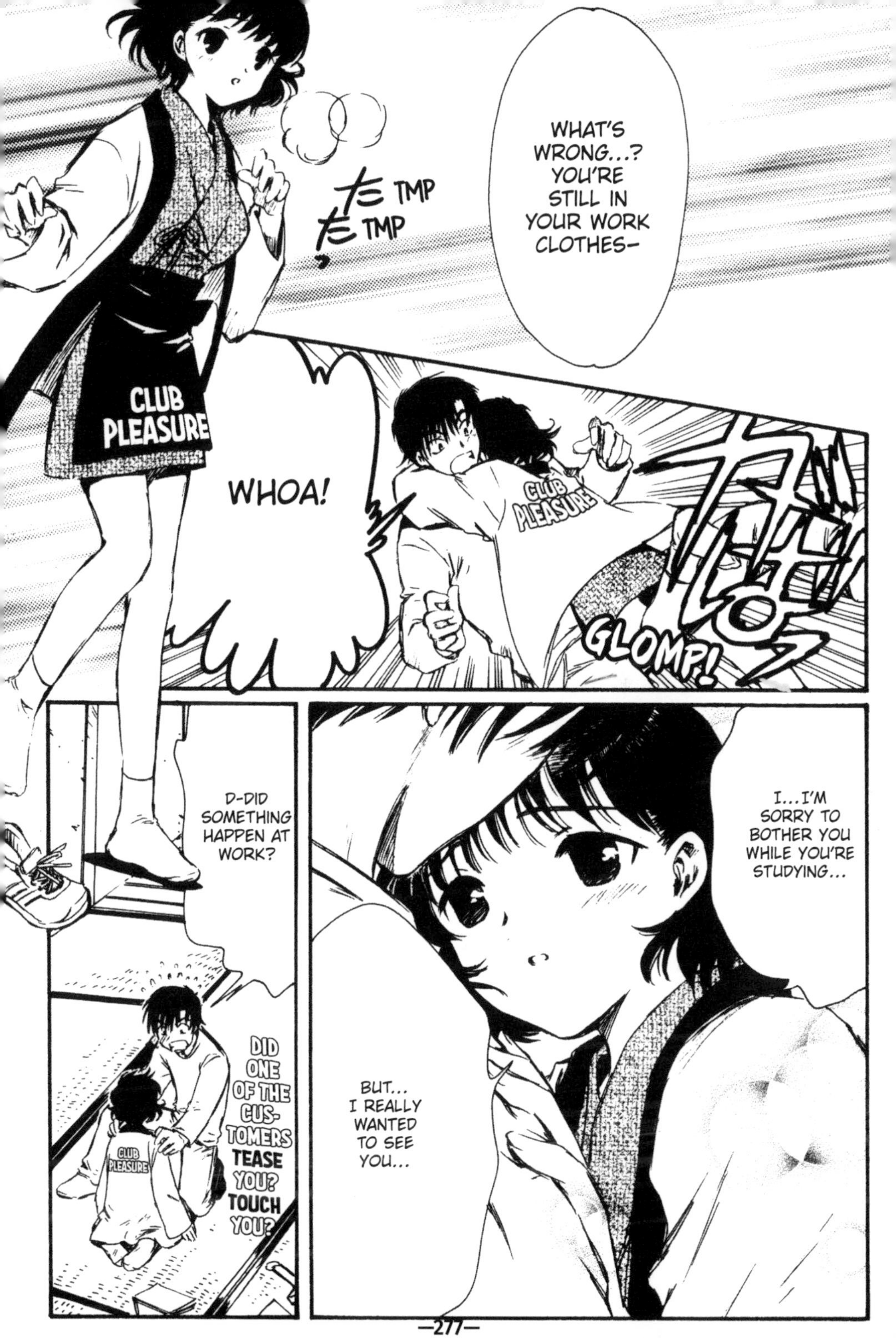
WHAT'S WRONG...? YOU'RE STILL IN YOUR WORK CLOTHES–
た TMP
た TMP
CLUB PLEASURE
WHOA!
CLUB PLEASURE
GLOMP!
I...I'M SORRY TO BOTHER YOU WHILE YOU'RE STUDYING...
BUT... I REALLY WANTED TO SEE YOU...
D-DID SOMETHING HAPPEN AT WORK?
DID ONE OF THE CUS-TOMERS TEASE YOU? TOUCH YOU?
CLUB PLEASURE

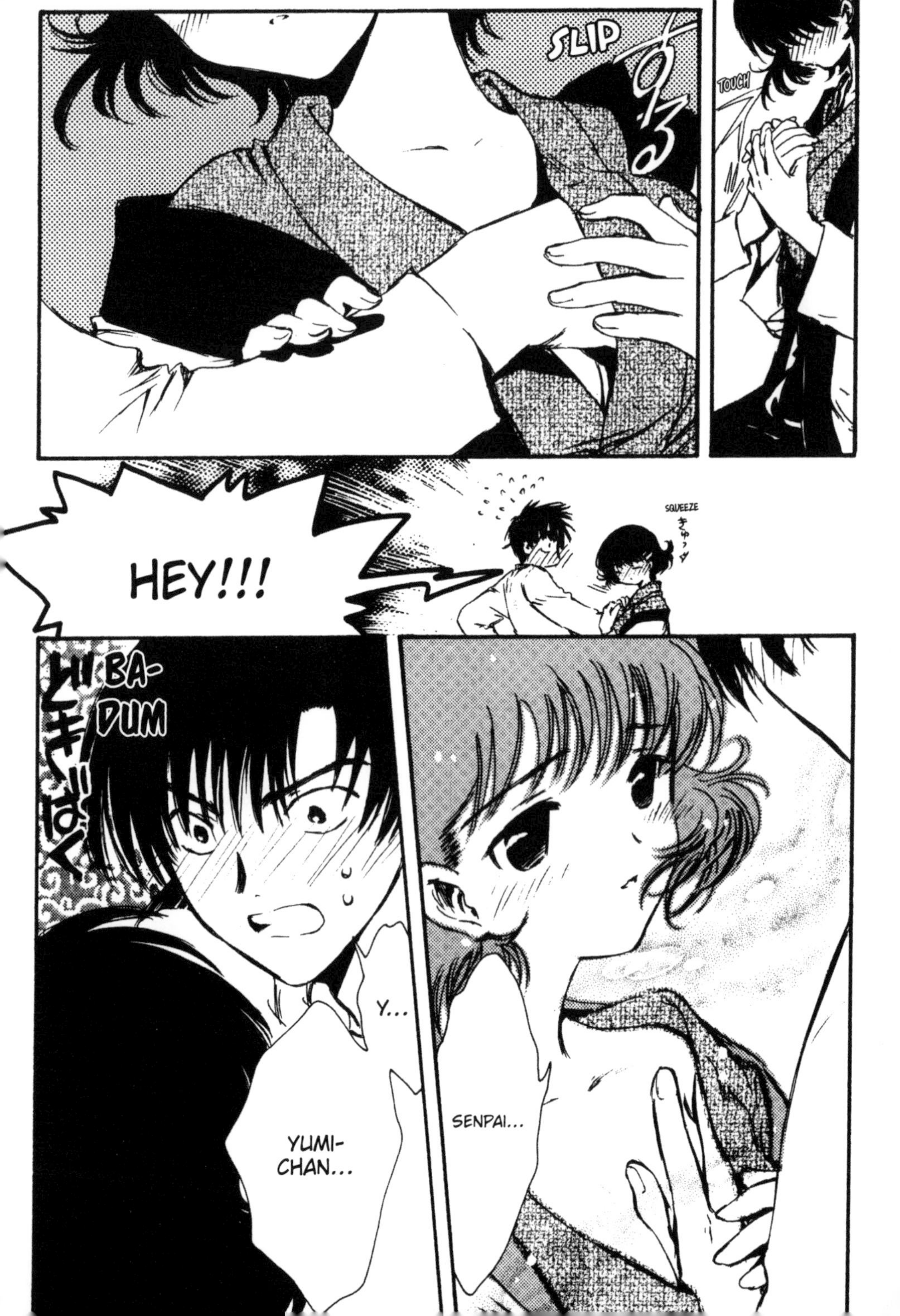
TOUCH
SLIP
SQUEEZE
HEY!!!
SENPAI...
BA-DUM
Y...
YUMI-CHAN...

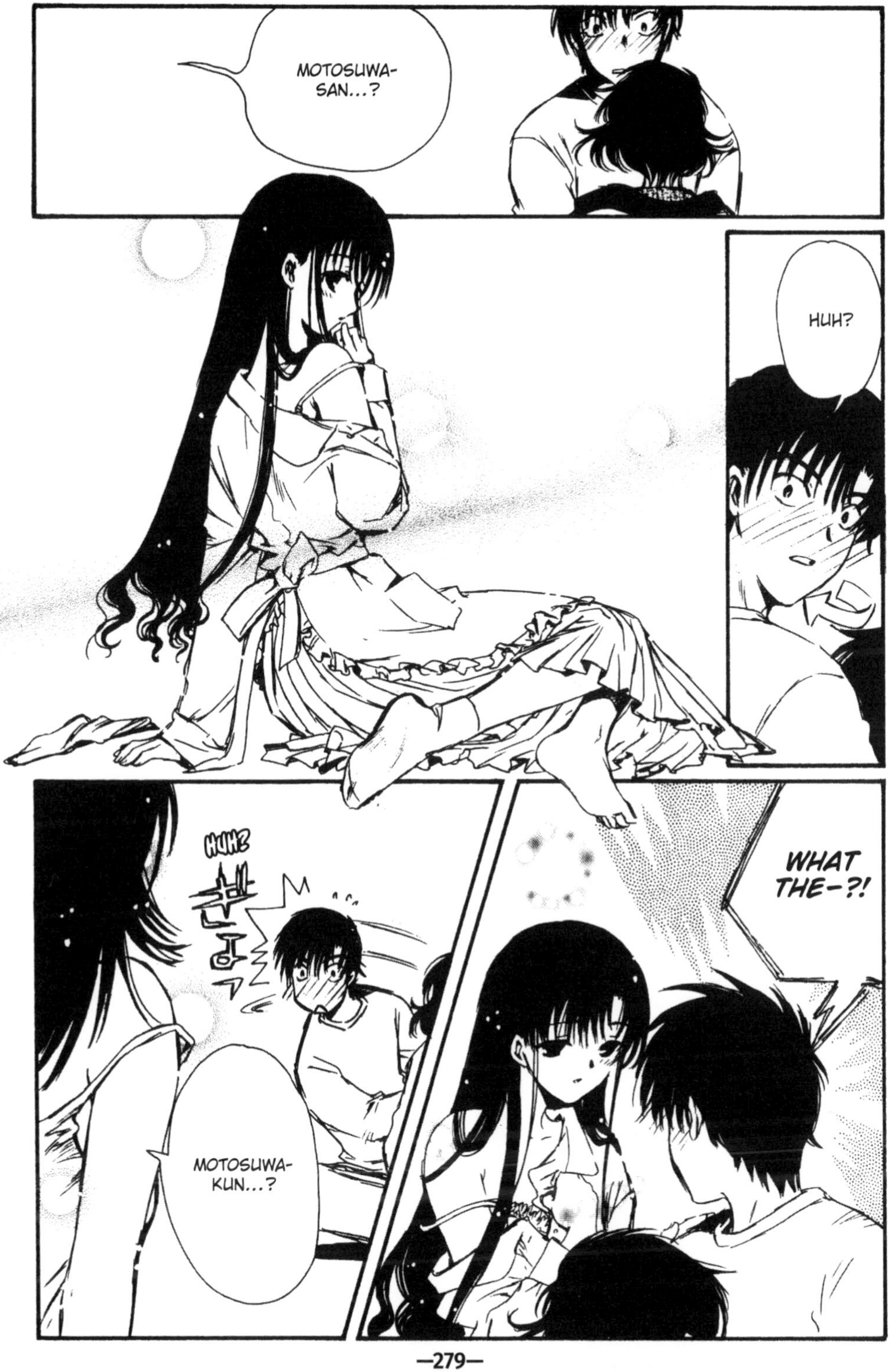
MOTOSUWA-SAN...?
HUH?
WHAT THE-?!
HUH?
MOTOSUWA-KUN...?

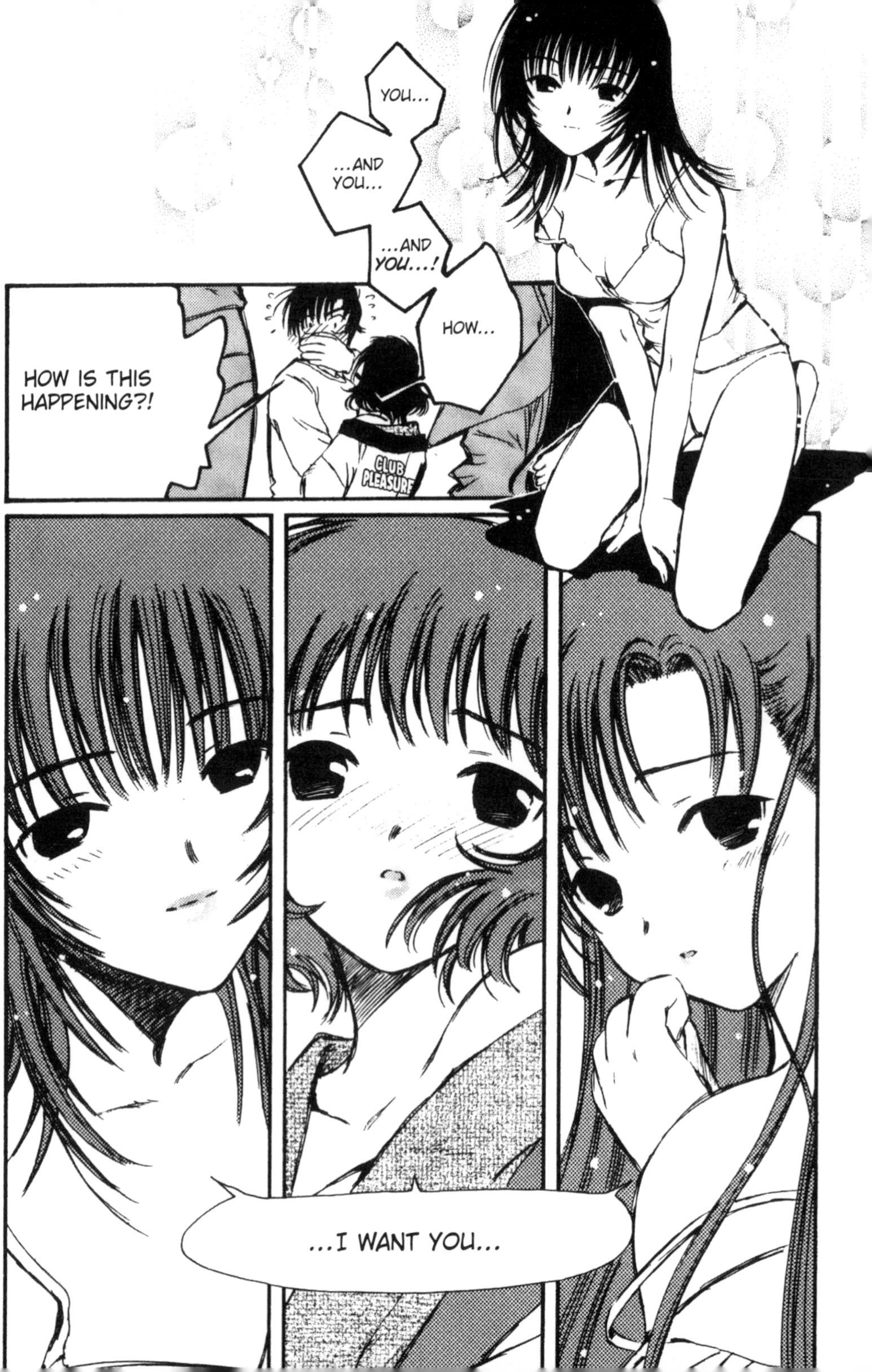
YOU...
...AND YOU...
...AND YOU...!
HOW...
HOW IS THIS HAPPENING?!
CLUB PLEASURE
...I WANT YOU...

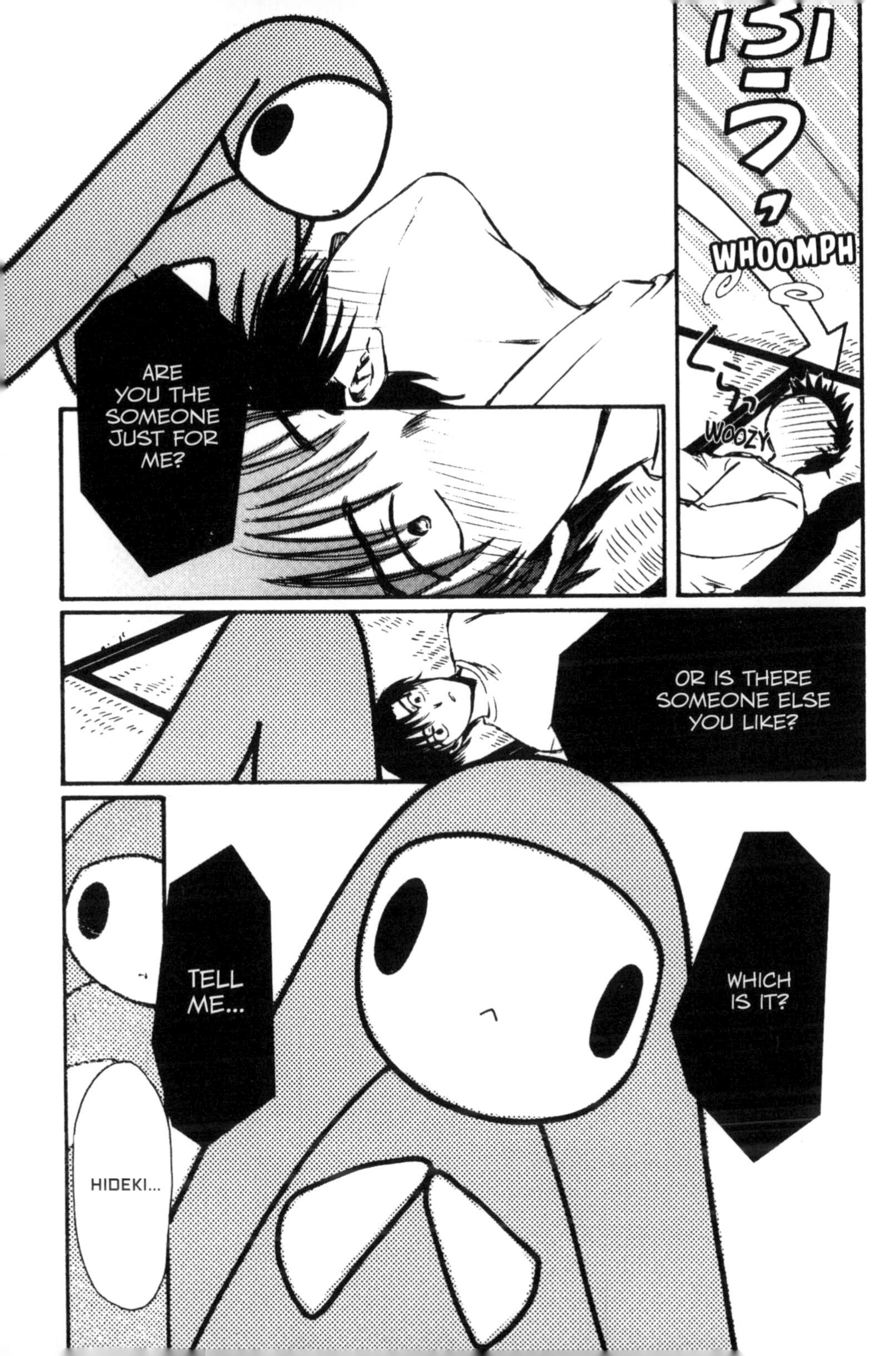
WHOOMPH
WOOZY
ARE YOU THE SOMEONE JUST FOR ME?
OR IS THERE SOMEONE ELSE YOU LIKE?
WHICH IS IT?
TELL ME...
HIDEKI...

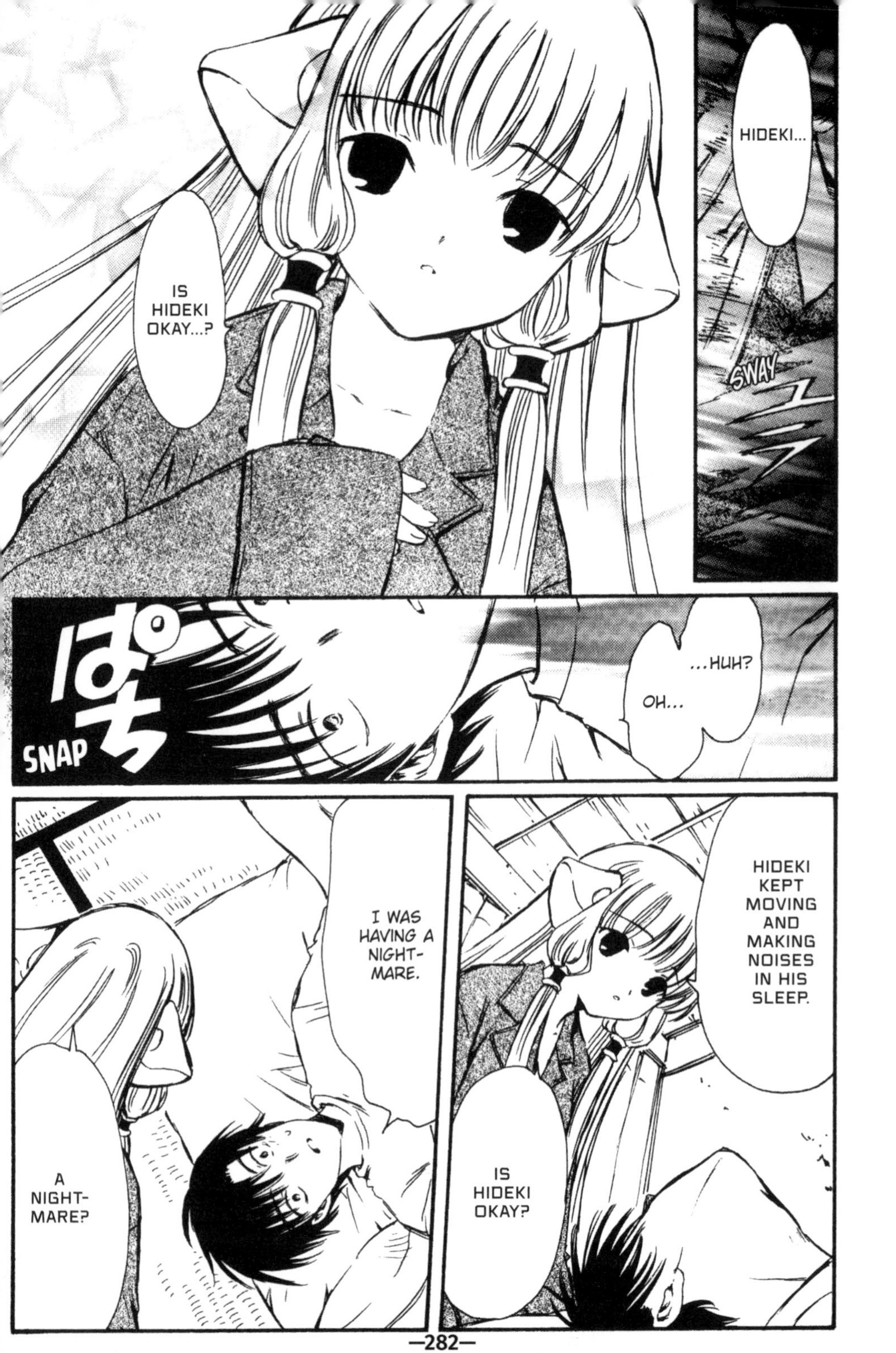
HIDEKI...
SWAY
IS HIDEKI OKAY...?
...HUH?
OH...
ぱち
SNAP
HIDEKI KEPT MOVING AND MAKING NOISES IN HIS SLEEP.
IS HIDEKI OKAY?
I WAS HAVING A NIGHT-MARE.
A NIGHT-MARE?

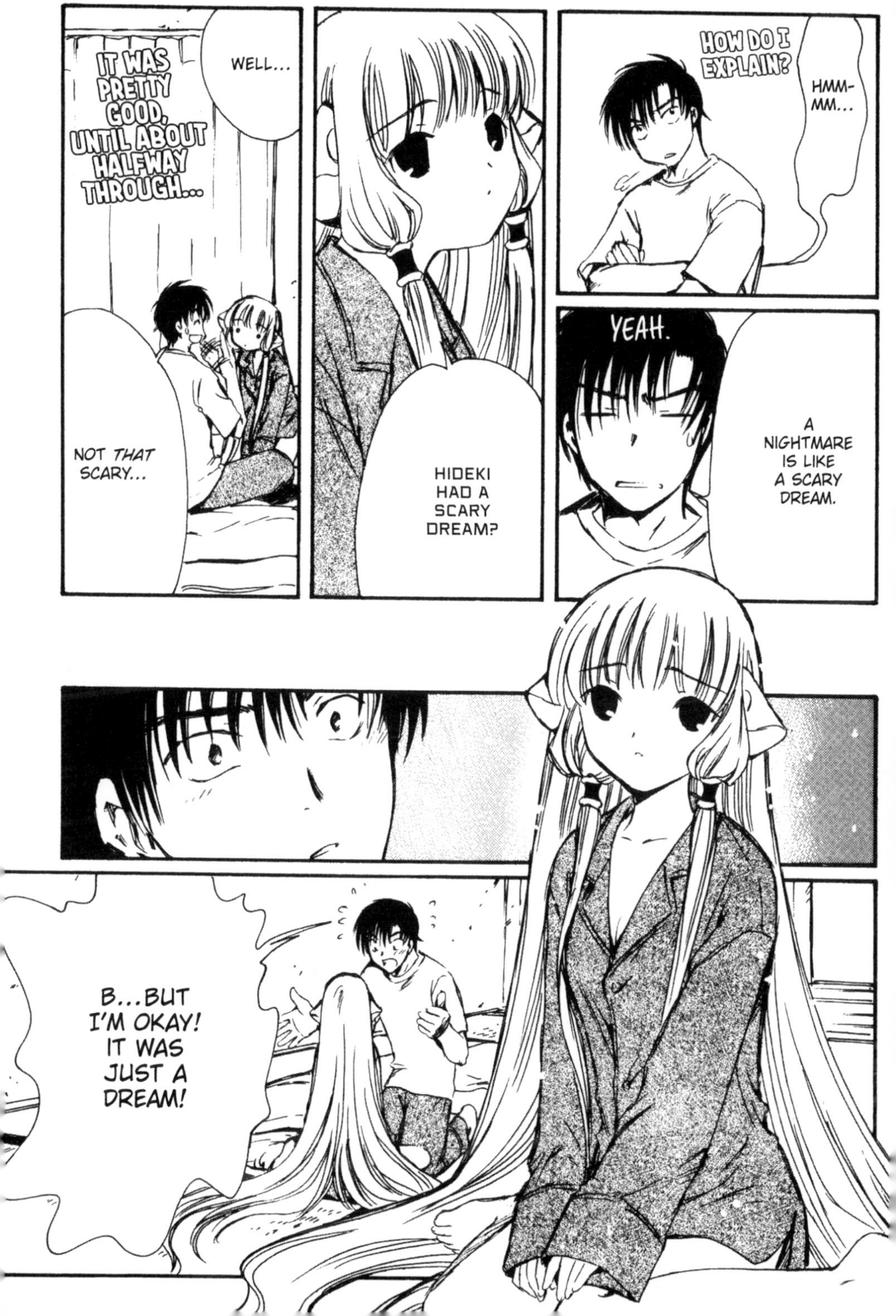
HMM-MM...
HOW DO I EXPLAIN?
YEAH.
A NIGHTMARE IS LIKE A SCARY DREAM.
HIDEKI HAD A SCARY DREAM?
WELL...
IT WAS PRETTY GOOD, UNTIL ABOUT HALFWAY THROUGH...
NOT *THAT* SCARY...
B...BUT I'M OKAY! IT WAS JUST A DREAM!

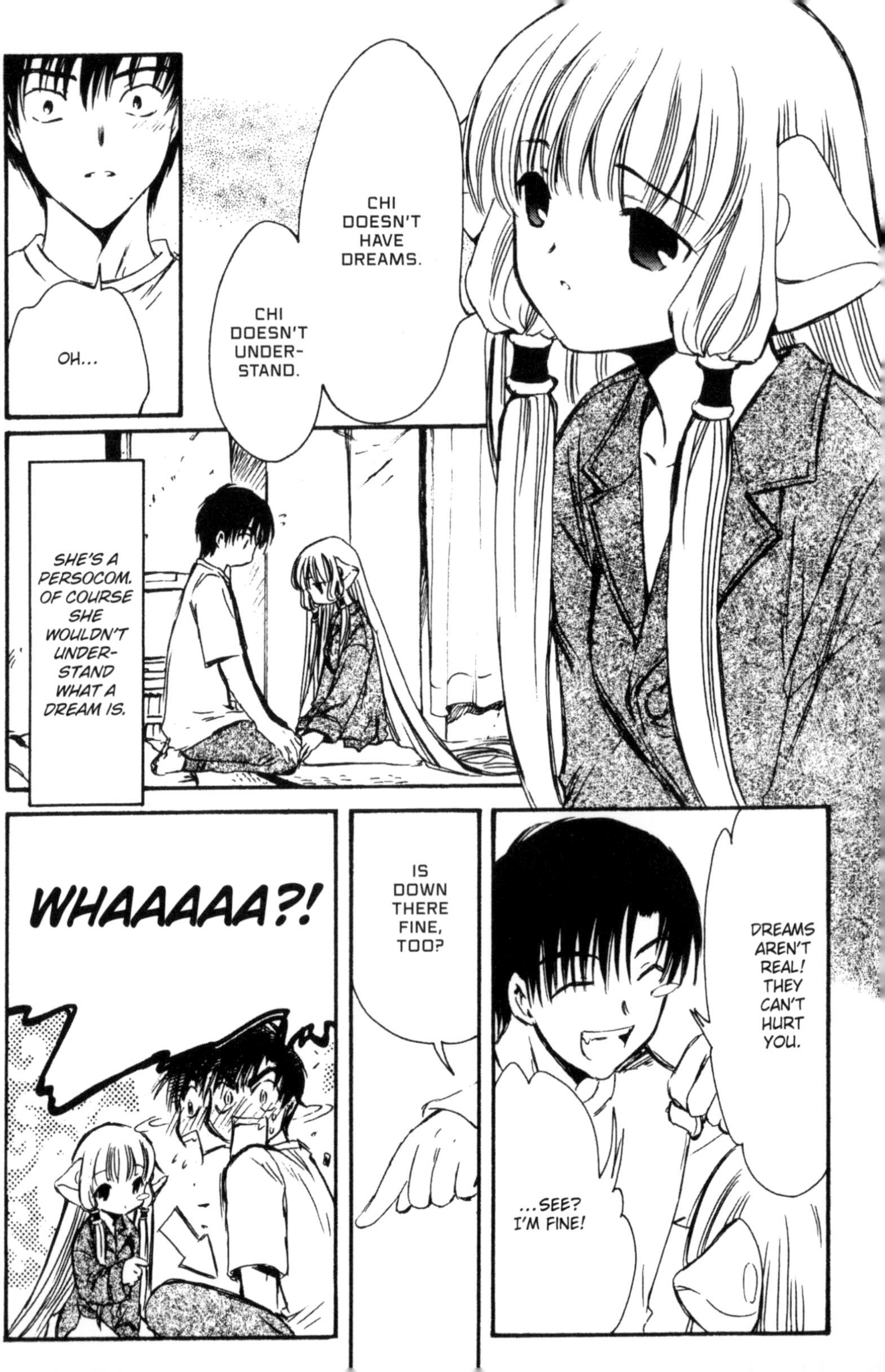
CHI DOESN'T HAVE DREAMS.
CHI DOESN'T UNDER-STAND.
OH...
SHE'S A PERSOCOM. OF COURSE SHE WOULDN'T UNDER-STAND WHAT A DREAM IS.
DREAMS AREN'T REAL! THEY CAN'T HURT YOU.
...SEE? I'M FINE!
IS DOWN THERE FINE, TOO?
WHAAAAAA?!

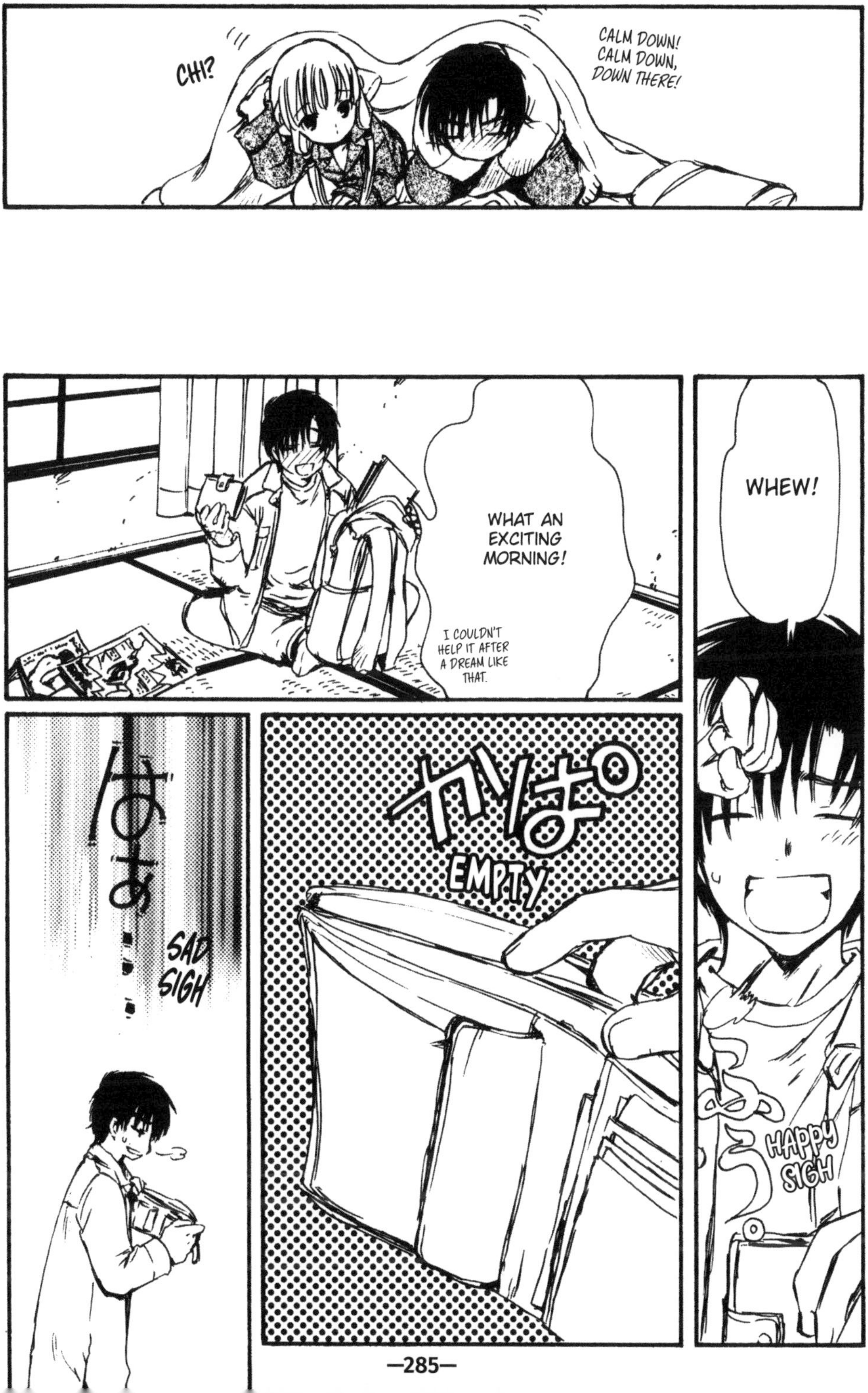
CALM DOWN! CALM DOWN, DOWN THERE!
CHI?
WHEW!
HAPPY SIGH
WHAT AN EXCITING MORNING!
I COULDN'T HELP IT AFTER A DREAM LIKE THAT.
EMPTY
SAD SIGH

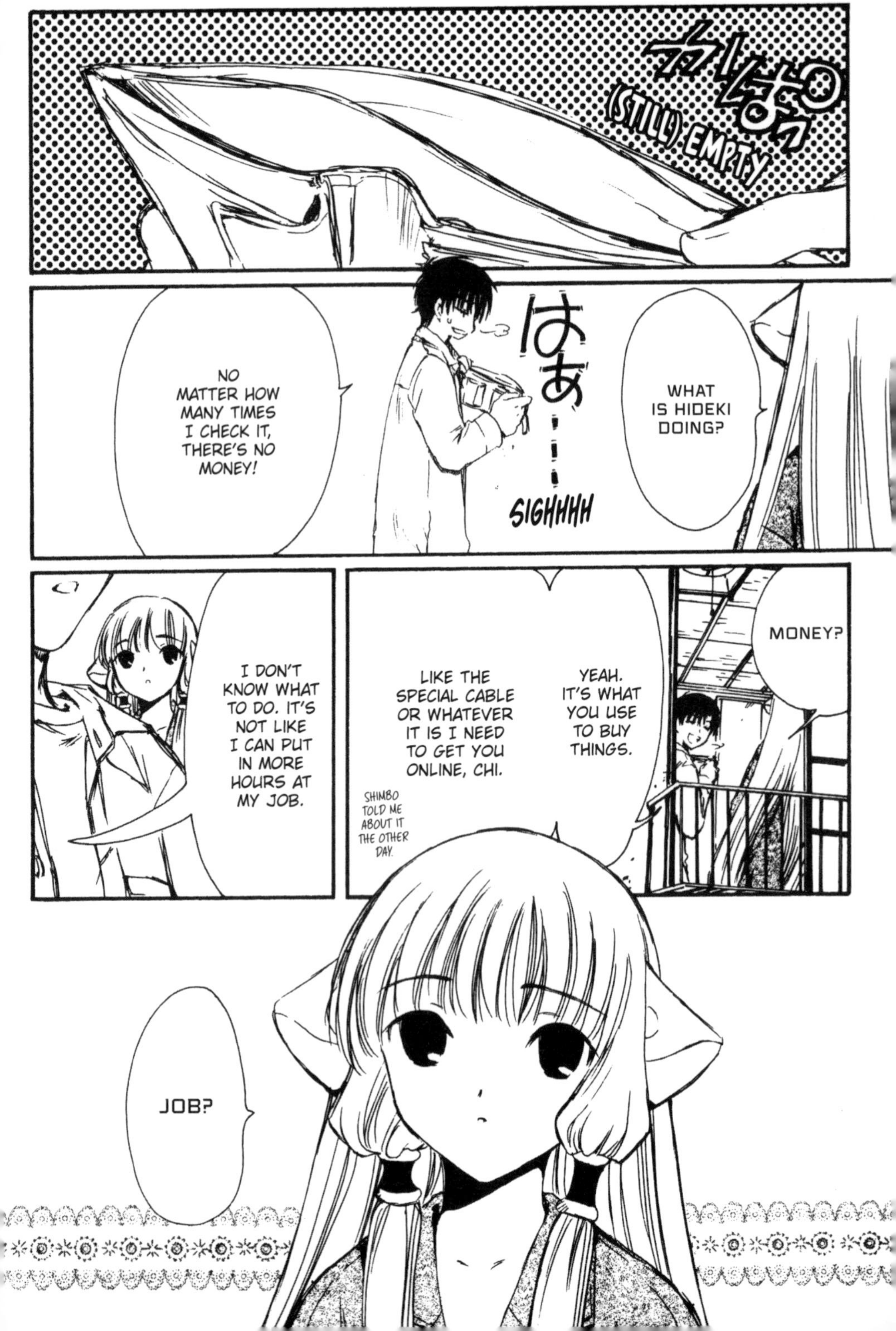
(STILL) EMPTY
WHAT IS HIDEKI DOING?
はぁ…
SIGHHHH
NO MATTER HOW MANY TIMES I CHECK IT, THERE'S NO MONEY!
MONEY?
YEAH. IT'S WHAT YOU USE TO BUY THINGS.
LIKE THE SPECIAL CABLE OR WHATEVER IT IS I NEED TO GET YOU ONLINE, CHI.
SHIMBO TOLD ME ABOUT IT THE OTHER DAY.
I DON'T KNOW WHAT TO DO. IT'S NOT LIKE I CAN PUT IN MORE HOURS AT MY JOB.
JOB?

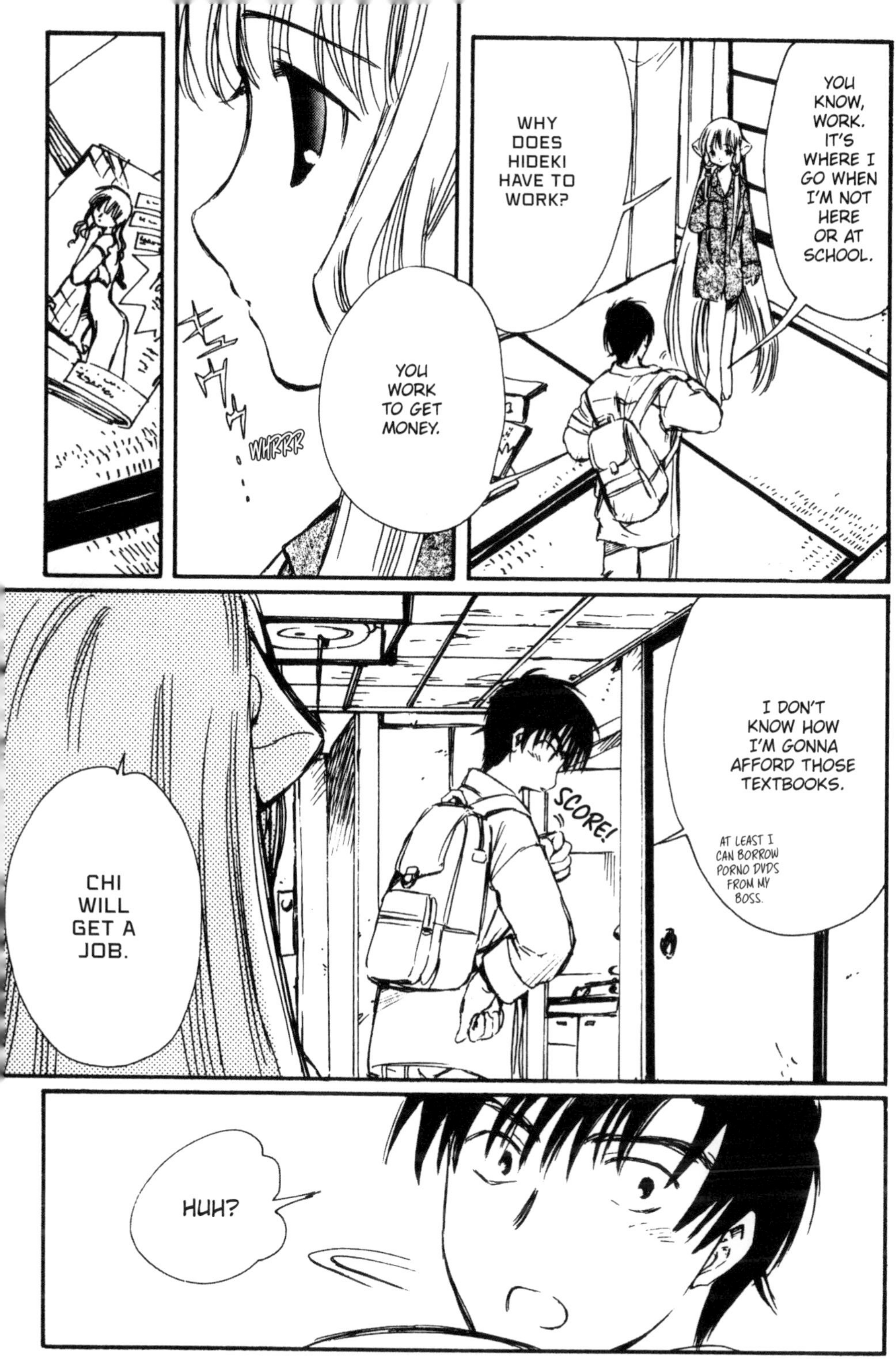
YOU KNOW, WORK. IT'S WHERE I GO WHEN I'M NOT HERE OR AT SCHOOL.
WHY DOES HIDEKI HAVE TO WORK?
YOU WORK TO GET MONEY.
WHRRR
I DON'T KNOW HOW I'M GONNA AFFORD THOSE TEXTBOOKS.
AT LEAST I CAN BORROW PORNO DVDS FROM MY BOSS.
SCORE!
CHI WILL GET A JOB.
HUH?

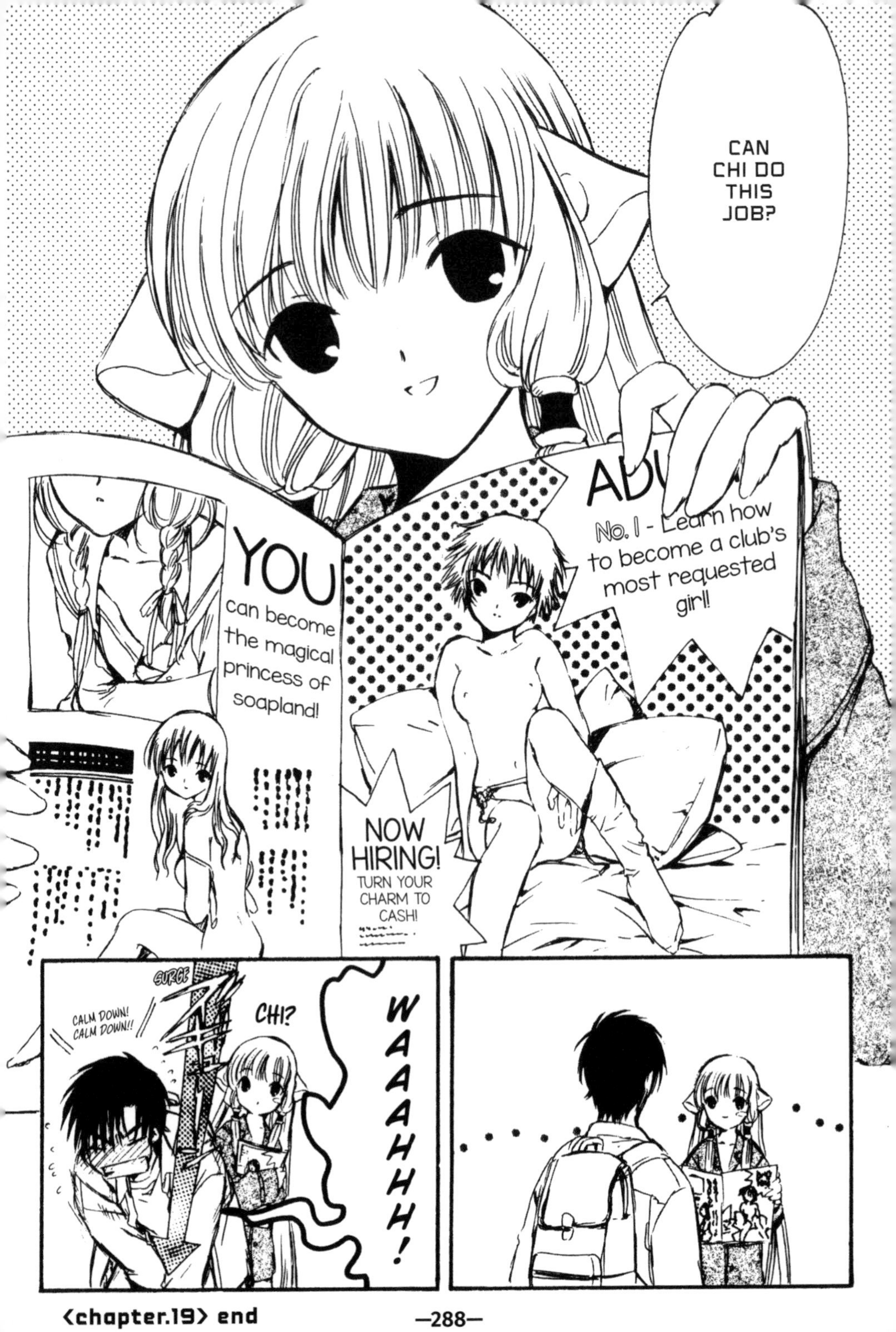
CAN CHI DO THIS JOB?
ADU
No. 1 - Learn how to become a club's most requested girl!
YOU can become the magical princess of soapland!
NOW HIRING!
TURN YOUR CHARM TO CASH!
WAAAAHHH!
CHI?
SURGE
CALM DOWN! CALM DOWN!!

<chapter.19> end

‹chapter.20›

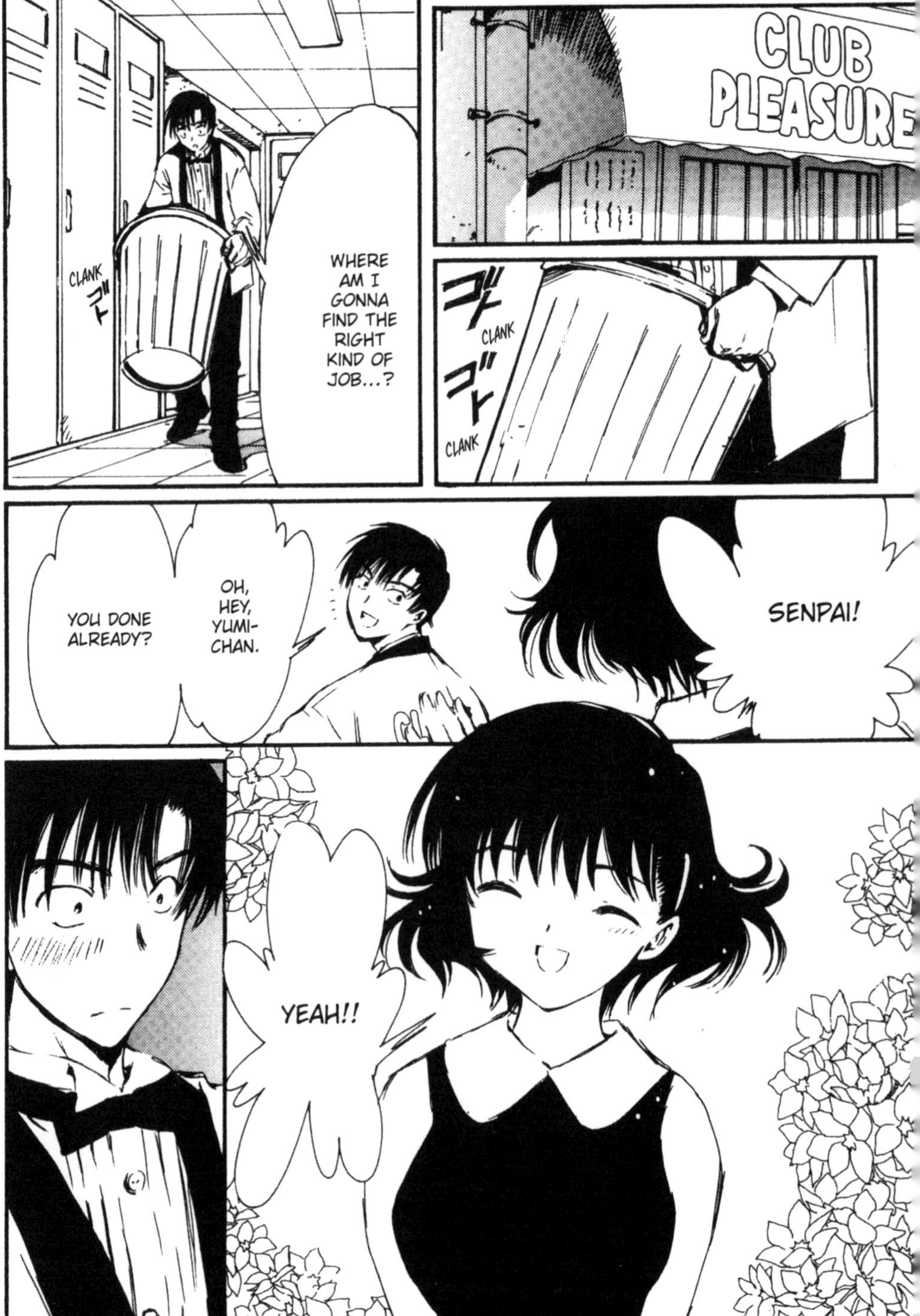
CLUB PLEASURE
ゴトッ
CLANK
ゴトッ
CLANK
WHERE AM I GONNA FIND THE RIGHT KIND OF JOB...?
CLANK
ゴトッ
SENPAI!
OH, HEY, YUMI-CHAN.
YOU DONE ALREADY?
YEAH!!

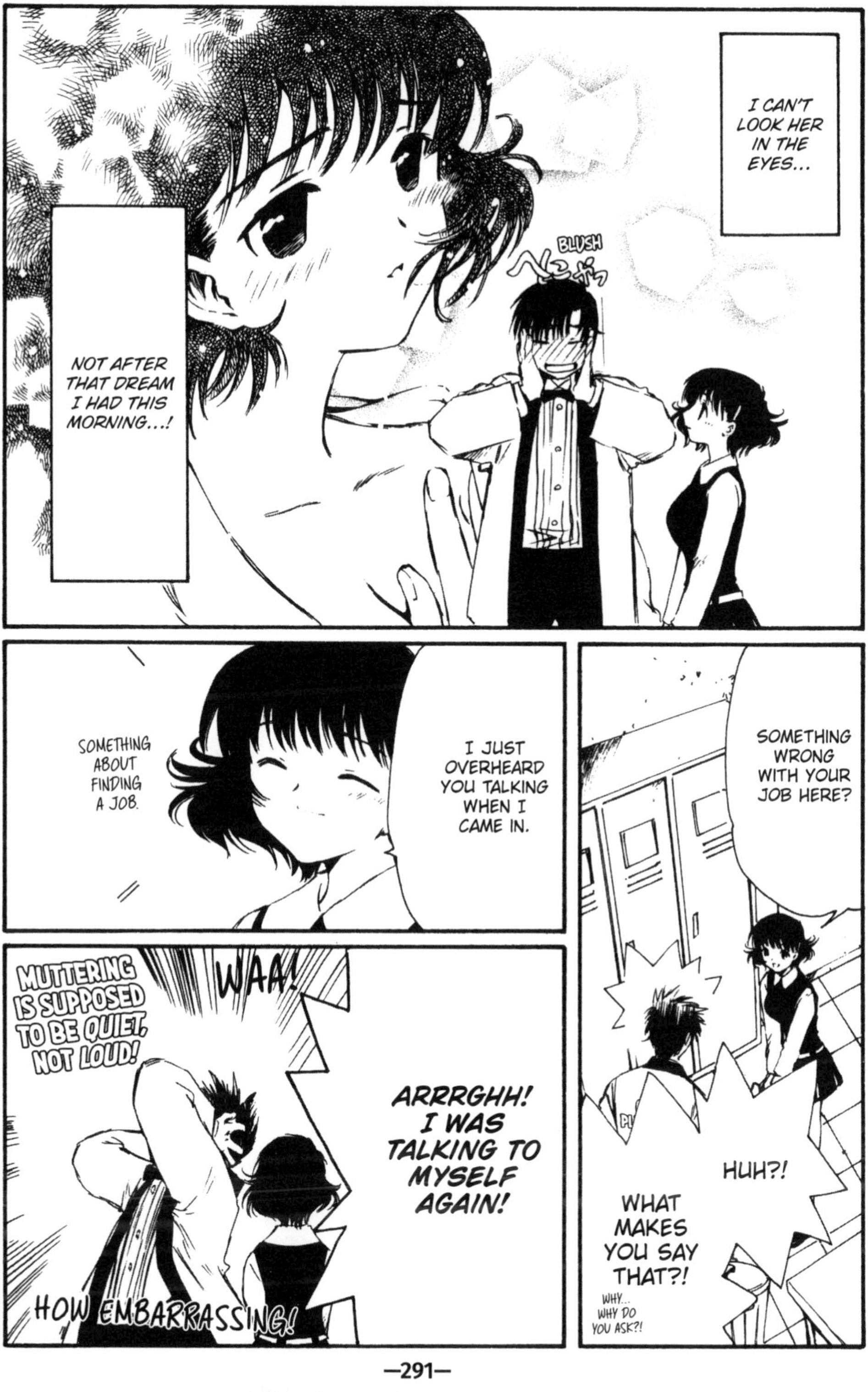

I CAN'T LOOK HER IN THE EYES...
BLUSH
NOT AFTER THAT DREAM I HAD THIS MORNING...!
SOMETHING WRONG WITH YOUR JOB HERE?
HUH?!
WHAT MAKES YOU SAY THAT?!
WHY... WHY DO YOU ASK?!
I JUST OVERHEARD YOU TALKING WHEN I CAME IN.
SOMETHING ABOUT FINDING A JOB.
ARRRGHH! I WAS TALKING TO MYSELF AGAIN!
WAA!
MUTTERING IS SUPPOSED TO BE QUIET, NOT LOUD!
HOW EMBARRASSING!

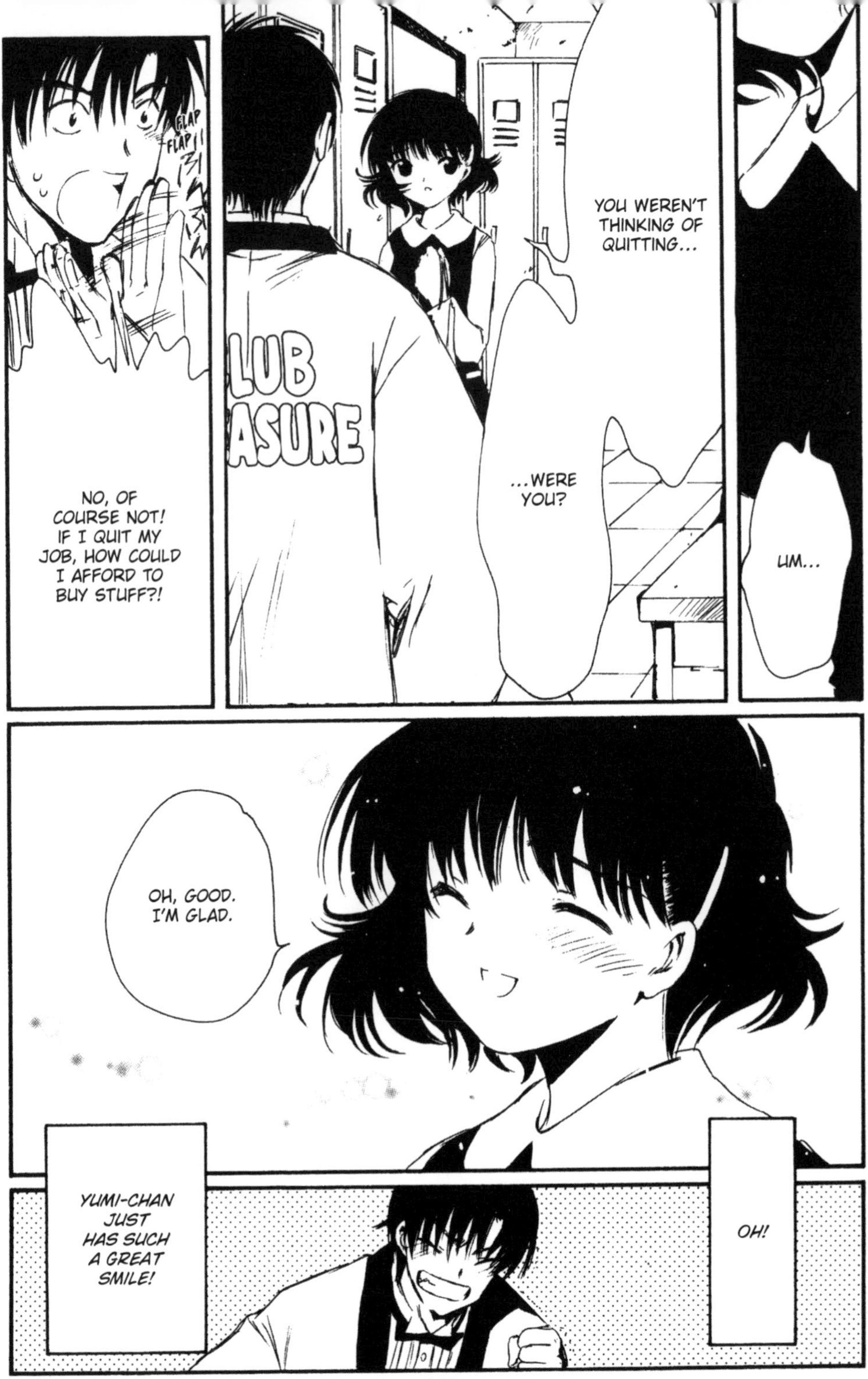
UM...
YOU WEREN'T THINKING OF QUITTING...
...WERE YOU?
FLAP FLAP
NO, OF COURSE NOT! IF I QUIT MY JOB, HOW COULD I AFFORD TO BUY STUFF?!
OH, GOOD. I'M GLAD.
OH!
YUMI-CHAN JUST HAS SUCH A GREAT SMILE!

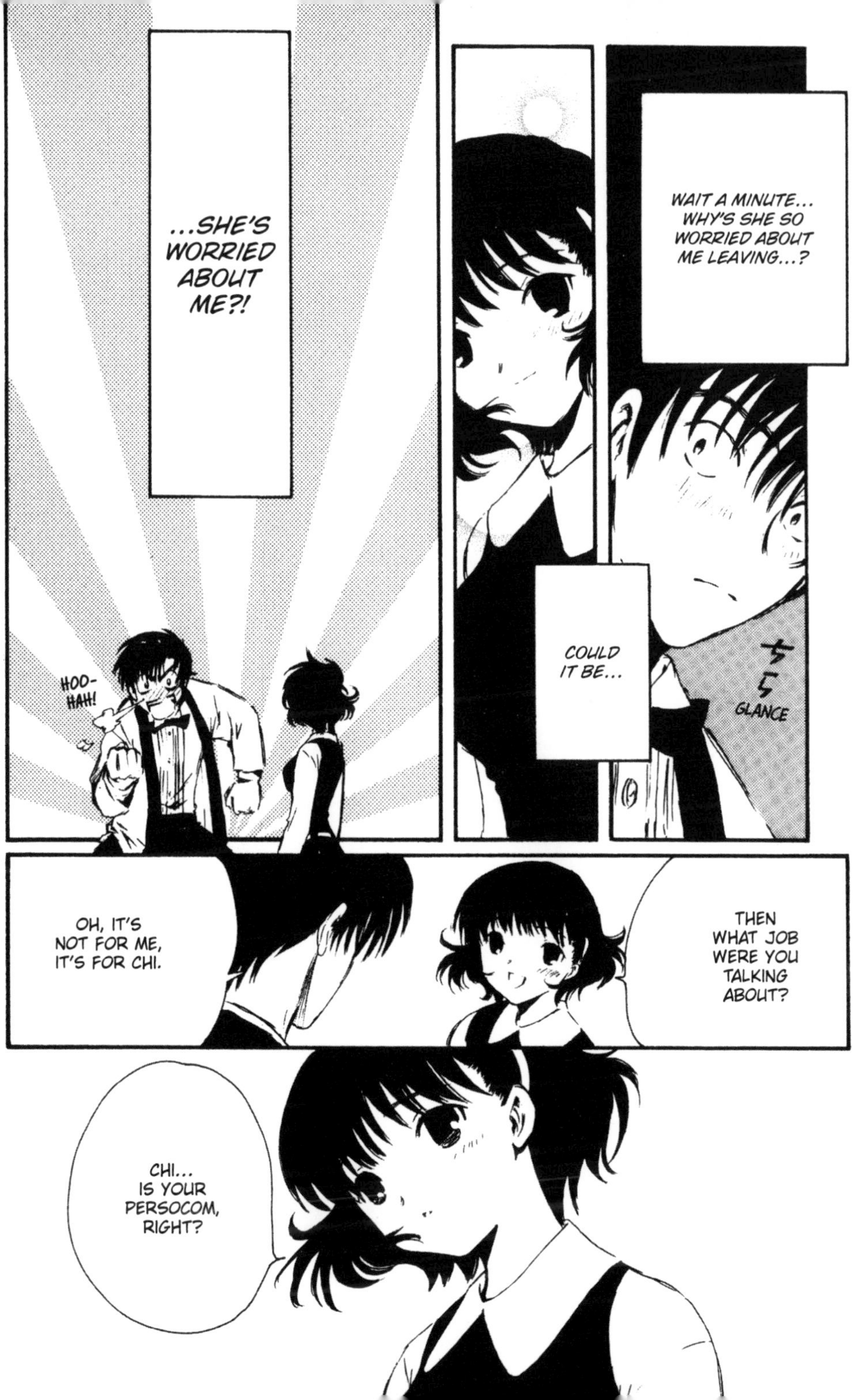

WAIT A MINUTE... WHY'S SHE SO WORRIED ABOUT ME LEAVING...?
COULD IT BE...
ちら
GLANCE
...SHE'S WORRIED ABOUT ME?!
HOO-HAH!
THEN WHAT JOB WERE YOU TALKING ABOUT?
OH, IT'S NOT FOR ME, IT'S FOR CHI.
CHI... IS YOUR PERSOCOM, RIGHT?

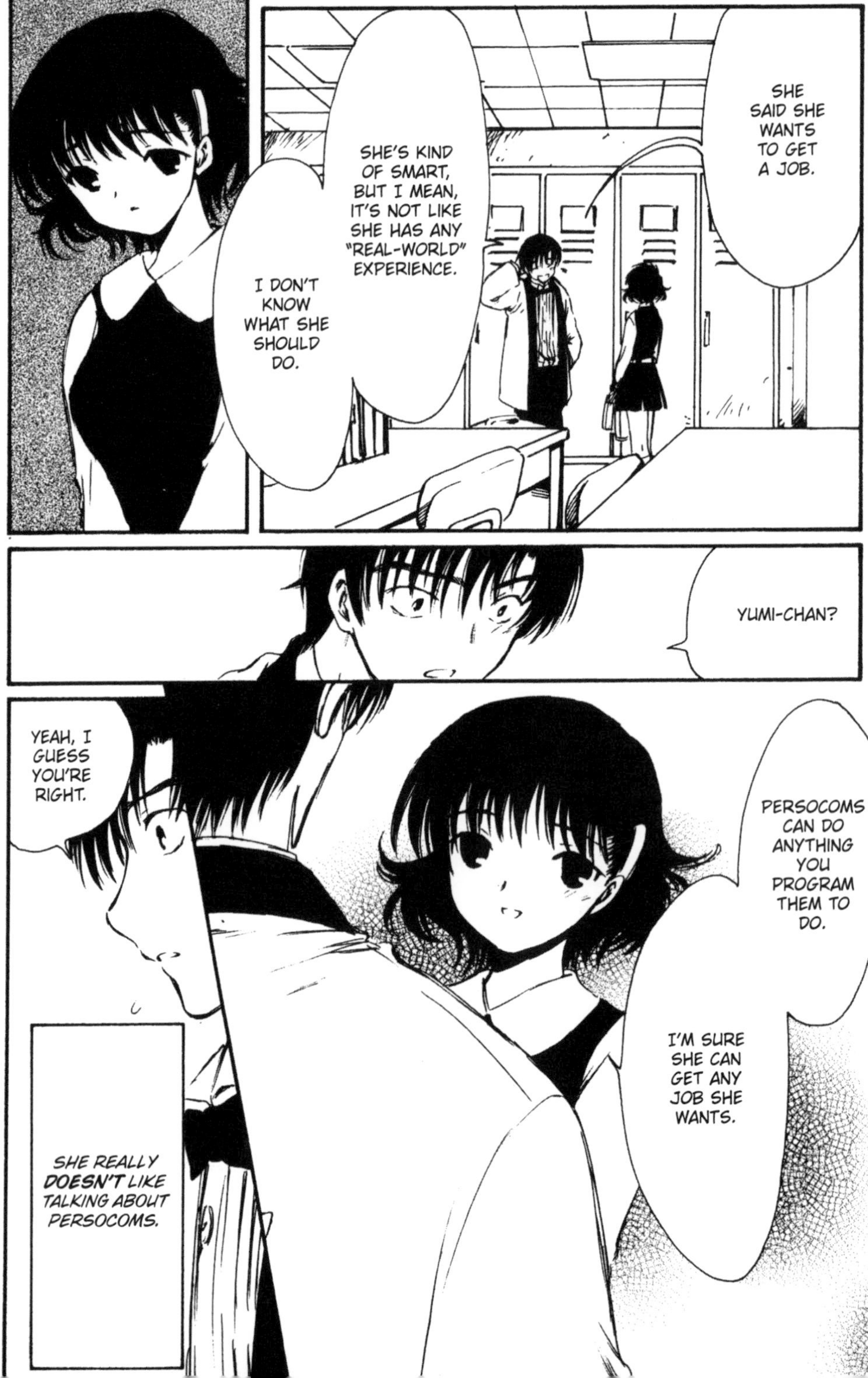
SHE SAID SHE WANTS TO GET A JOB.
SHE'S KIND OF SMART, BUT I MEAN, IT'S NOT LIKE SHE HAS ANY "REAL-WORLD" EXPERIENCE.
I DON'T KNOW WHAT SHE SHOULD DO.
YUMI-CHAN?
PERSOCOMS CAN DO ANYTHING YOU PROGRAM THEM TO DO.
I'M SURE SHE CAN GET ANY JOB SHE WANTS.
YEAH, I GUESS YOU'RE RIGHT.
SHE REALLY **DOESN'T** LIKE TALKING ABOUT PERSOCOMS.

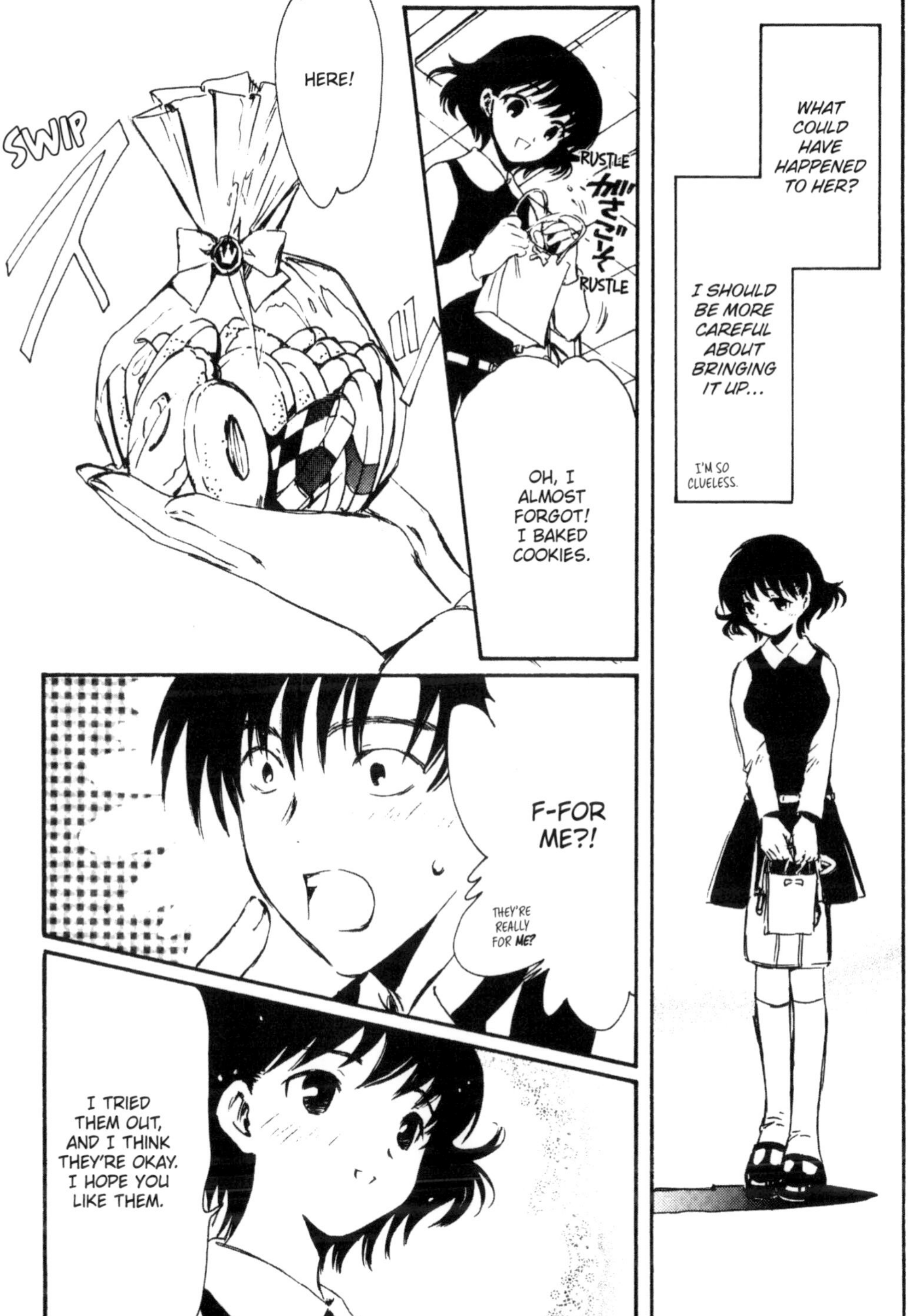
WHAT COULD HAVE HAPPENED TO HER?
I SHOULD BE MORE CAREFUL ABOUT BRINGING IT UP...
I'M SO CLUELESS.
RUSTLE
RUSTLE
OH, I ALMOST FORGOT! I BAKED COOKIES.
HERE!
SWIP
F-FOR ME?!
THEY'RE REALLY FOR ME?
I TRIED THEM OUT, AND I THINK THEY'RE OKAY. I HOPE YOU LIKE THEM.

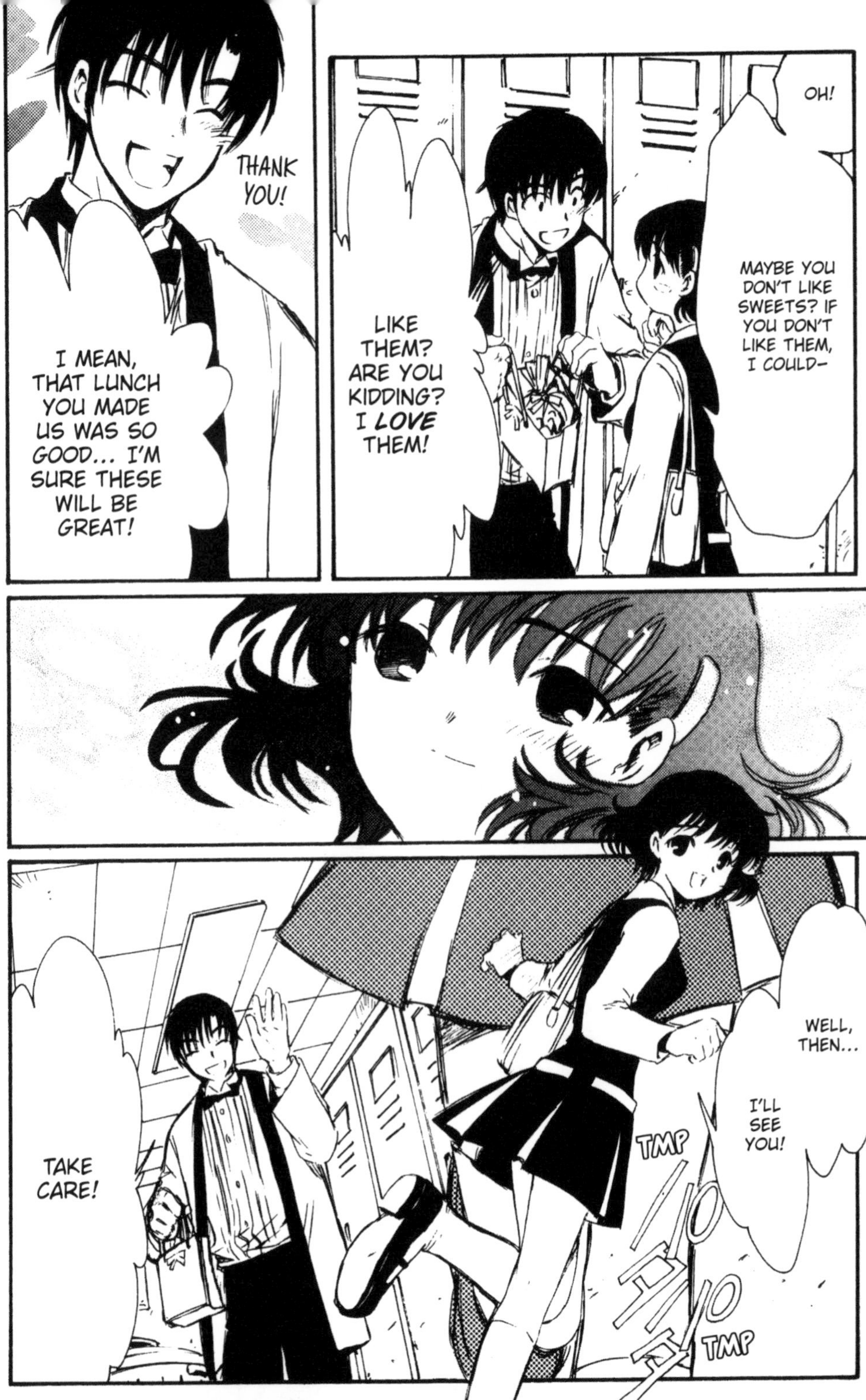
OH!
MAYBE YOU DON'T LIKE SWEETS? IF YOU DON'T LIKE THEM, I COULD–
LIKE THEM? ARE YOU KIDDING? I *LOVE* THEM!
THANK YOU!
I MEAN, THAT LUNCH YOU MADE US WAS SO GOOD... I'M SURE THESE WILL BE GREAT!
WELL, THEN...
I'LL SEE YOU!
TMP
TMP
TAKE CARE!

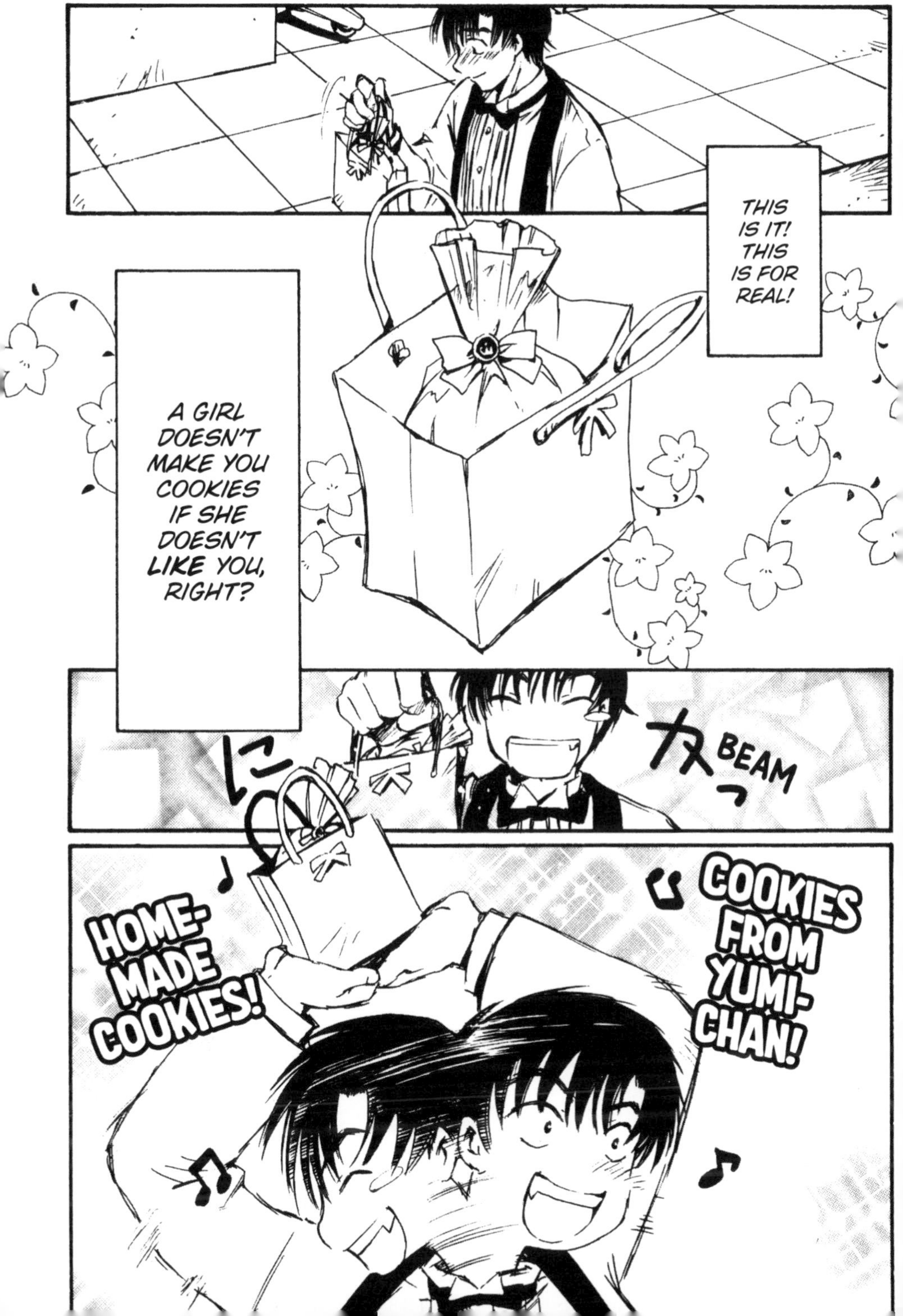
THIS IS IT! THIS IS FOR REAL!
A GIRL DOESN'T MAKE YOU COOKIES IF SHE DOESN'T LIKE YOU, RIGHT?
BEAM
COOKIES FROM YUMI-CHAN!
HOME-MADE COOKIES!

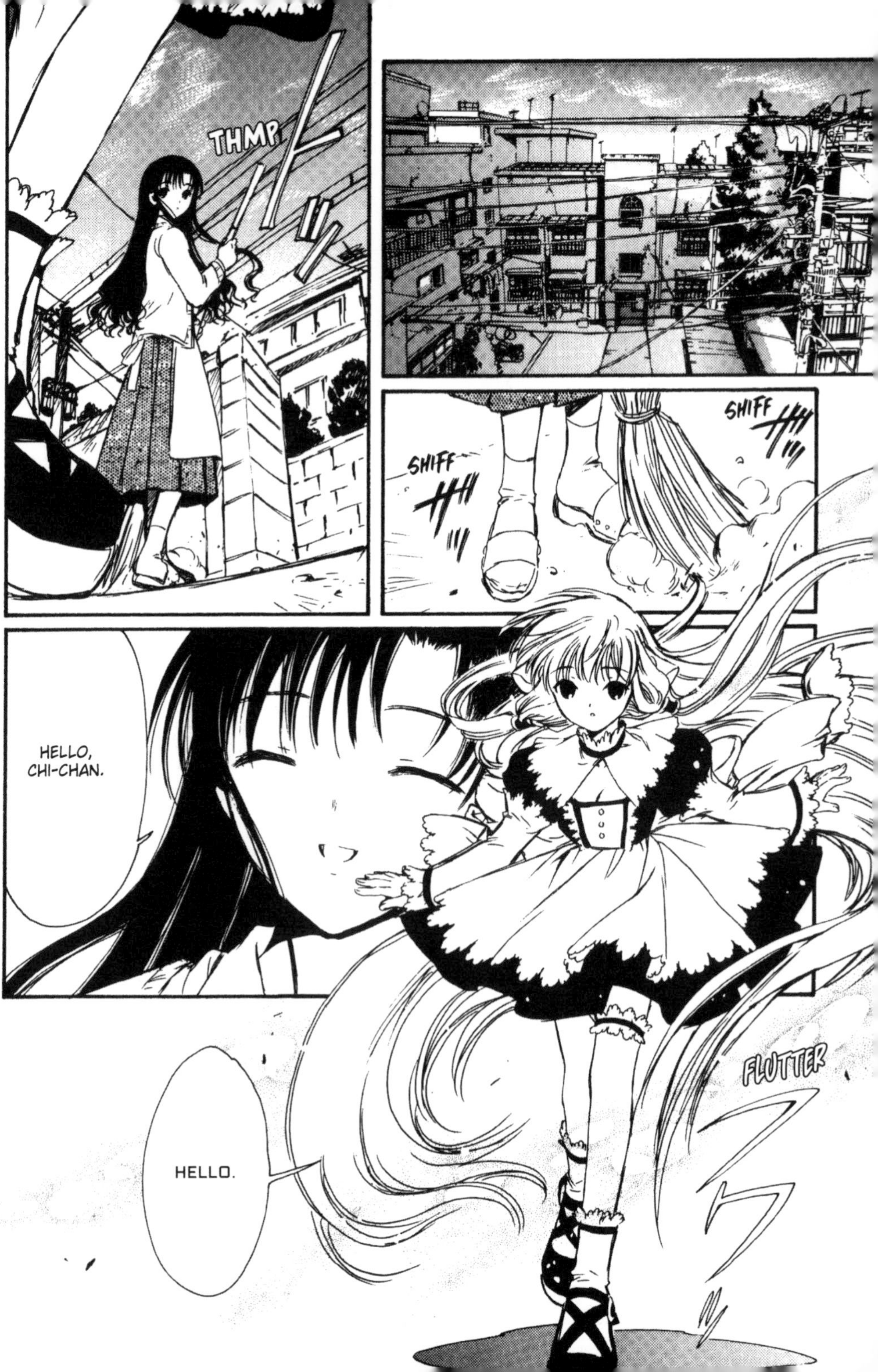
SHIFF
SHIFF
THMP
HELLO, CHI-CHAN.
FLUTTER
HELLO.

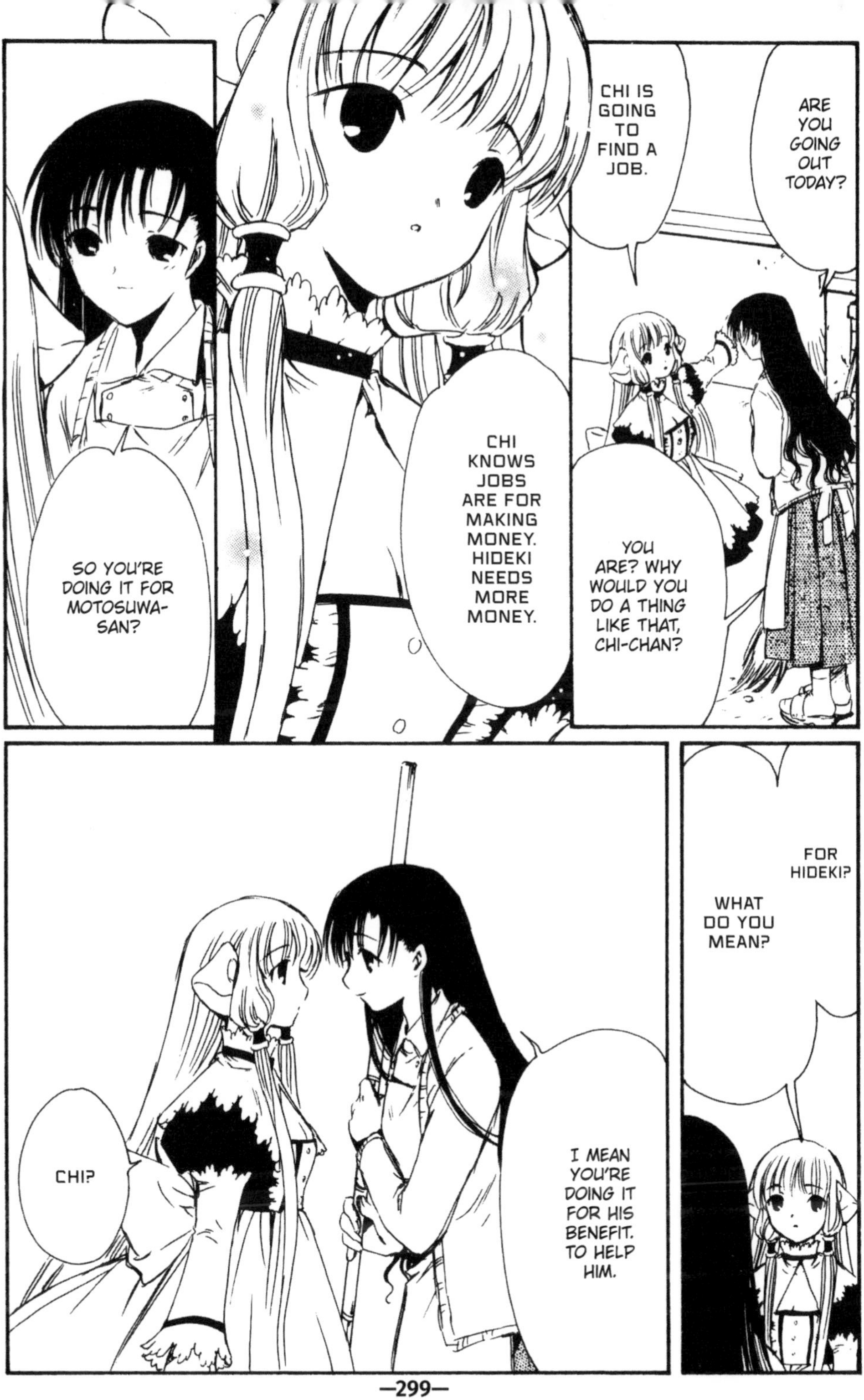
ARE YOU GOING OUT TODAY?
CHI IS GOING TO FIND A JOB.
YOU ARE? WHY WOULD YOU DO A THING LIKE THAT, CHI-CHAN?
CHI KNOWS JOBS ARE FOR MAKING MONEY. HIDEKI NEEDS MORE MONEY.
SO YOU'RE DOING IT FOR MOTOSUWA-SAN?
FOR HIDEKI?
WHAT DO YOU MEAN?
I MEAN YOU'RE DOING IT FOR HIS BENEFIT. TO HELP HIM.
CHI?

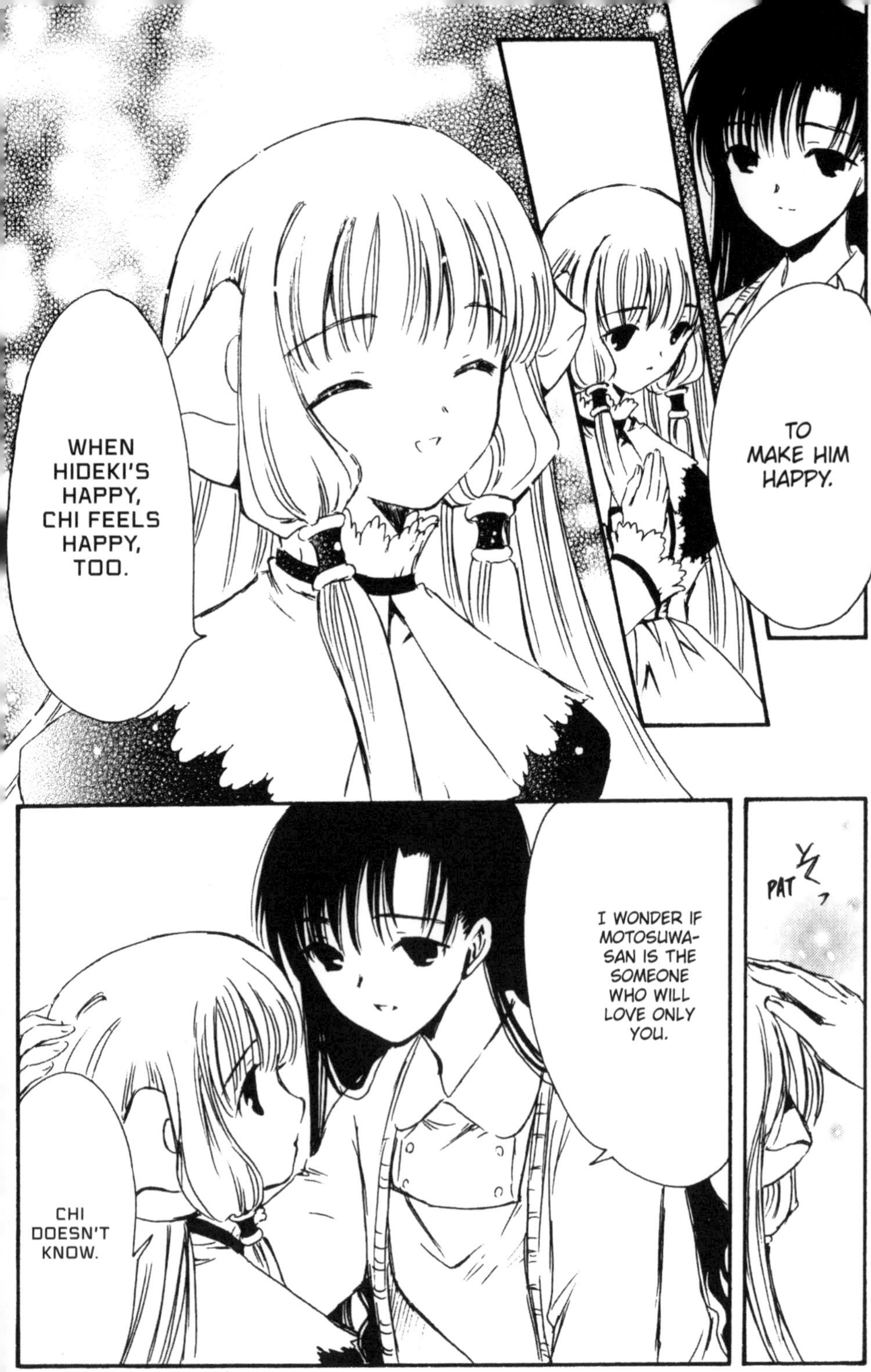
TO MAKE HIM HAPPY.
WHEN HIDEKI'S HAPPY, CHI FEELS HAPPY, TOO.
PAT
I WONDER IF MOTOSUWA-SAN IS THE SOMEONE WHO WILL LOVE ONLY YOU.
CHI DOESN'T KNOW.

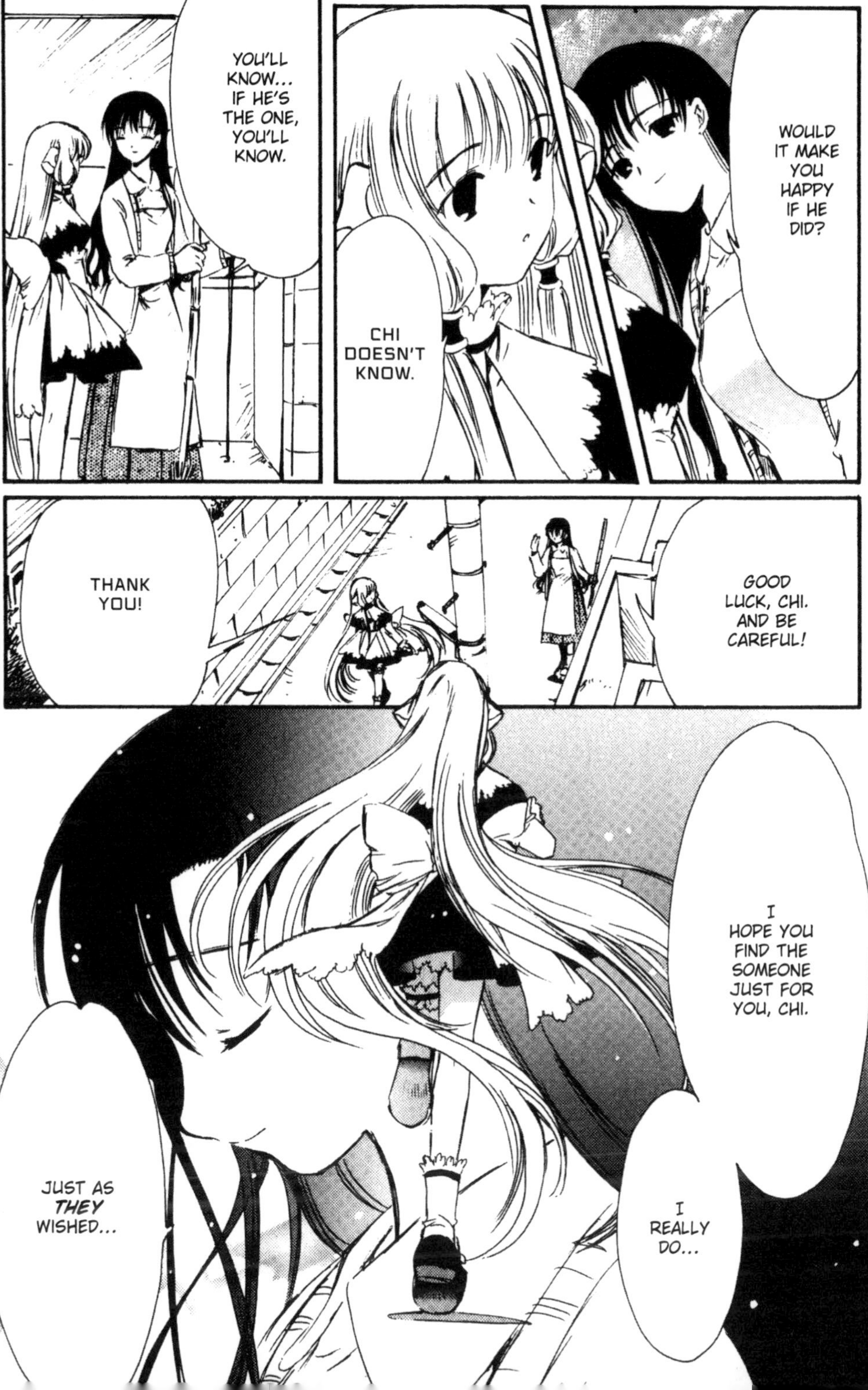
WOULD IT MAKE YOU HAPPY IF HE DID?
CHI DOESN'T KNOW.
YOU'LL KNOW... IF HE'S THE ONE, YOU'LL KNOW.
GOOD LUCK, CHI. AND BE CAREFUL!
THANK YOU!
I HOPE YOU FIND THE SOMEONE JUST FOR YOU, CHI.
I REALLY DO...
JUST AS THEY WISHED...

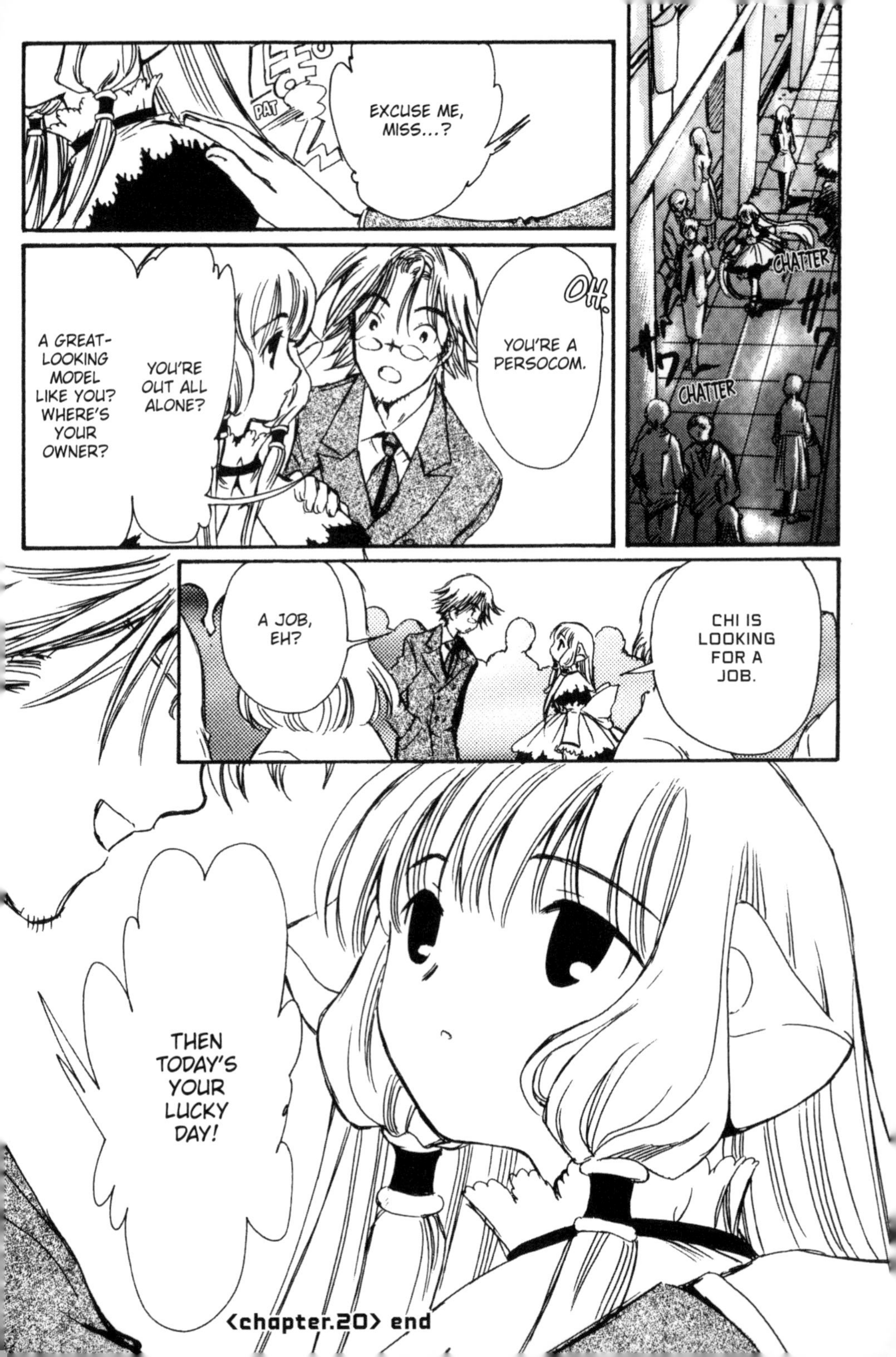
CHATTER
CHATTER
PAT
EXCUSE ME, MISS...?
OH.
YOU'RE A PERSOCOM.
YOU'RE OUT ALL ALONE?
A GREAT-LOOKING MODEL LIKE YOU? WHERE'S YOUR OWNER?
CHI IS LOOKING FOR A JOB.
A JOB, EH?
THEN TODAY'S YOUR LUCKY DAY!
‹chapter.20› end

<chapter.21>

Chobits

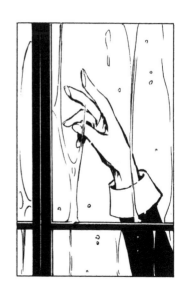

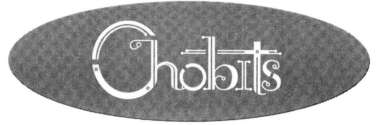

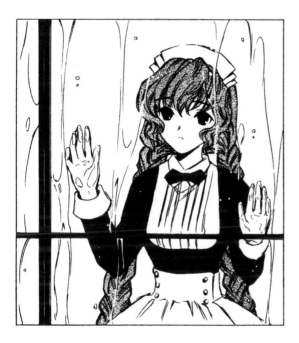

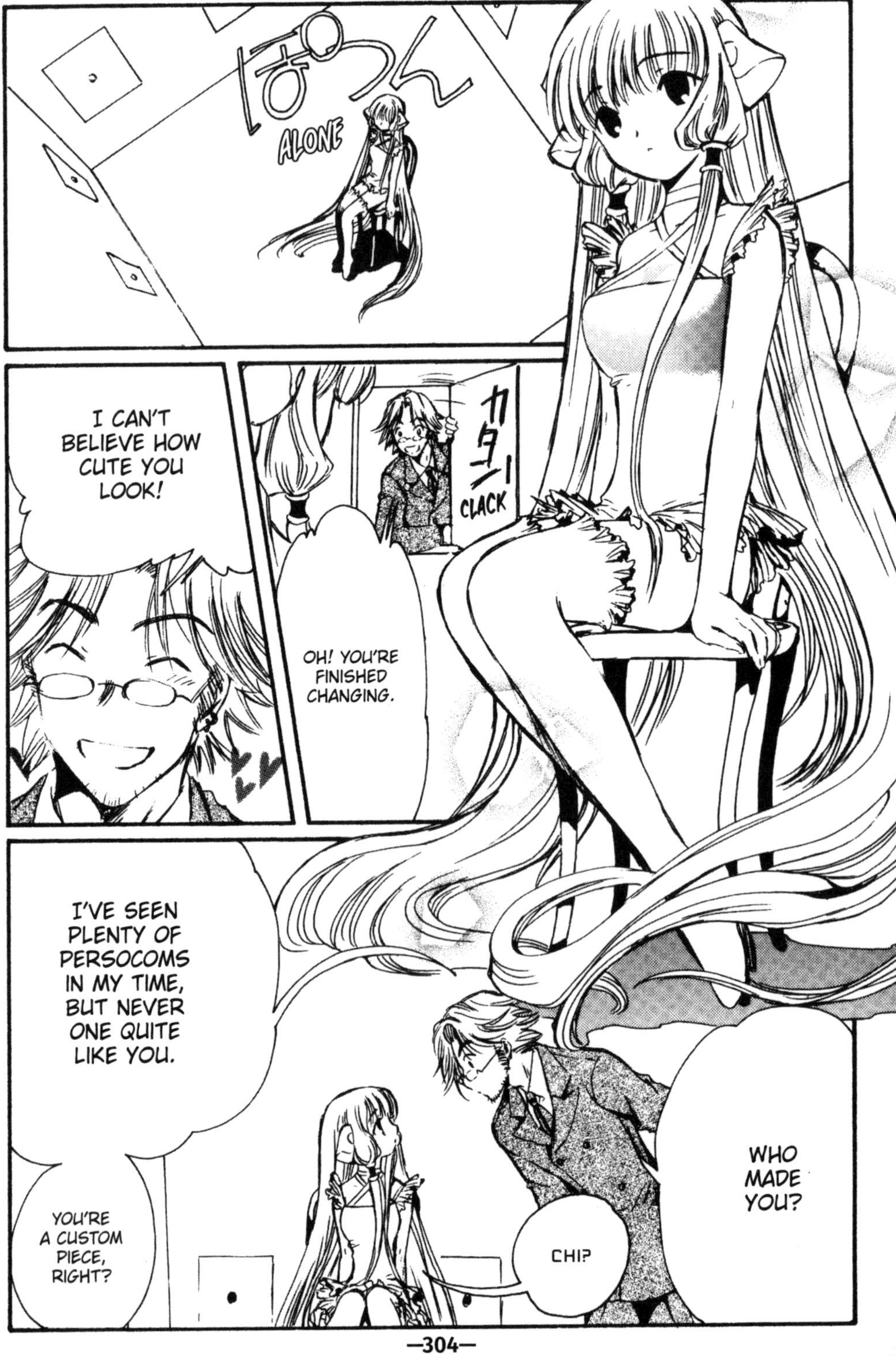
ぽつん
ALONE
カタン
CLACK
OH! YOU'RE FINISHED CHANGING.
I CAN'T BELIEVE HOW CUTE YOU LOOK!
I'VE SEEN PLENTY OF PERSOCOMS IN MY TIME, BUT NEVER ONE QUITE LIKE YOU.
YOU'RE A CUSTOM PIECE, RIGHT?
WHO MADE YOU?
CHI?

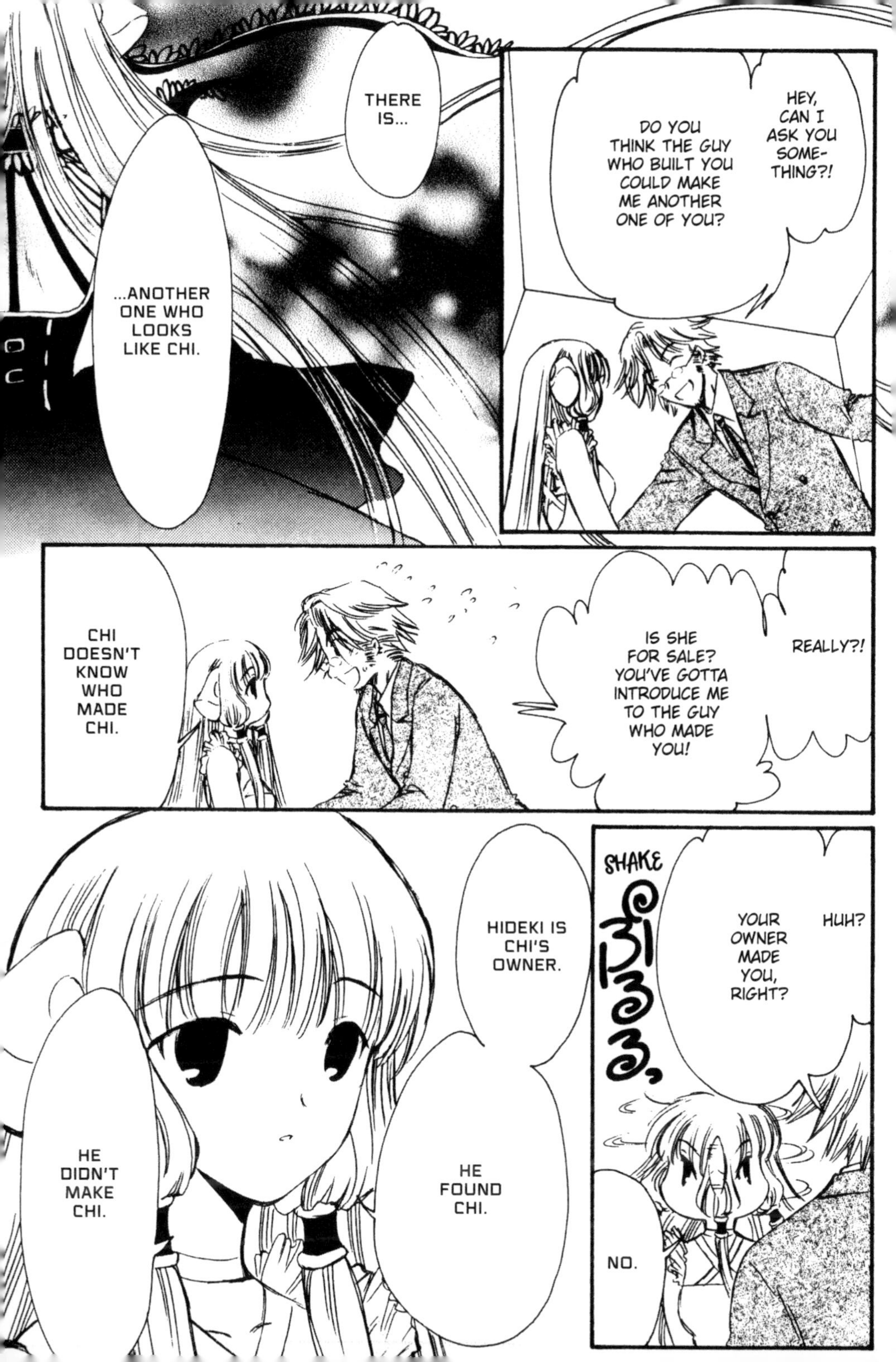
HEY, CAN I ASK YOU SOME-THING?!
DO YOU THINK THE GUY WHO BUILT YOU COULD MAKE ME ANOTHER ONE OF YOU?
THERE IS...
...ANOTHER ONE WHO LOOKS LIKE CHI.
REALLY?!
IS SHE FOR SALE? YOU'VE GOTTA INTRODUCE ME TO THE GUY WHO MADE YOU!
CHI DOESN'T KNOW WHO MADE CHI.
HUH?
YOUR OWNER MADE YOU, RIGHT?
SHAKE
NO.
HIDEKI IS CHI'S OWNER.
HE FOUND CHI.
HE DIDN'T MAKE CHI.

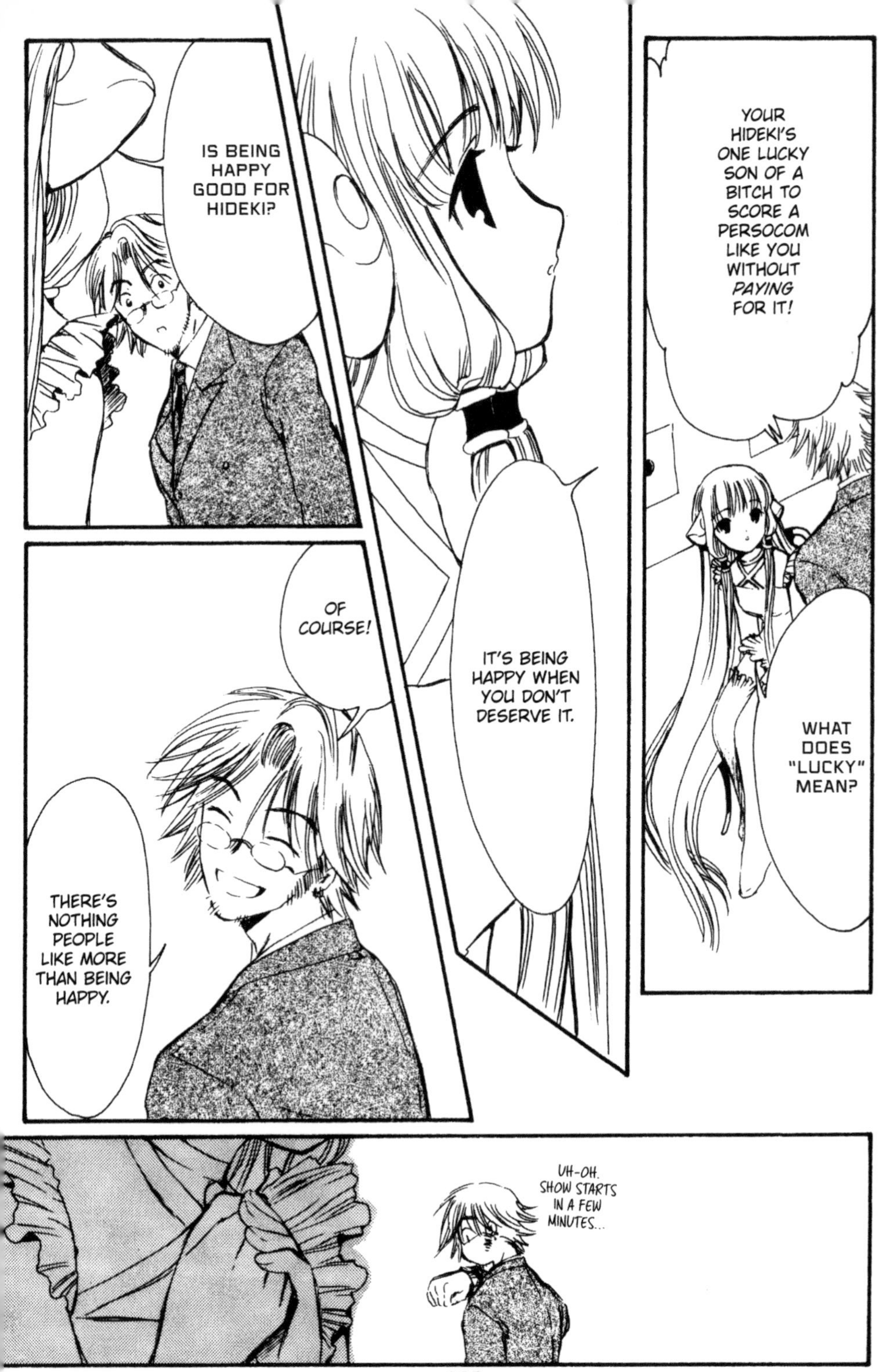
YOUR HIDEKI'S ONE LUCKY SON OF A BITCH TO SCORE A PERSOCOM LIKE YOU WITHOUT *PAYING* FOR IT!
WHAT DOES "LUCKY" MEAN?
IT'S BEING HAPPY WHEN YOU DON'T DESERVE IT.
IS BEING HAPPY GOOD FOR HIDEKI?
OF COURSE!
THERE'S NOTHING PEOPLE LIKE MORE THAN BEING HAPPY.
UH-OH. SHOW STARTS IN A FEW MINUTES...

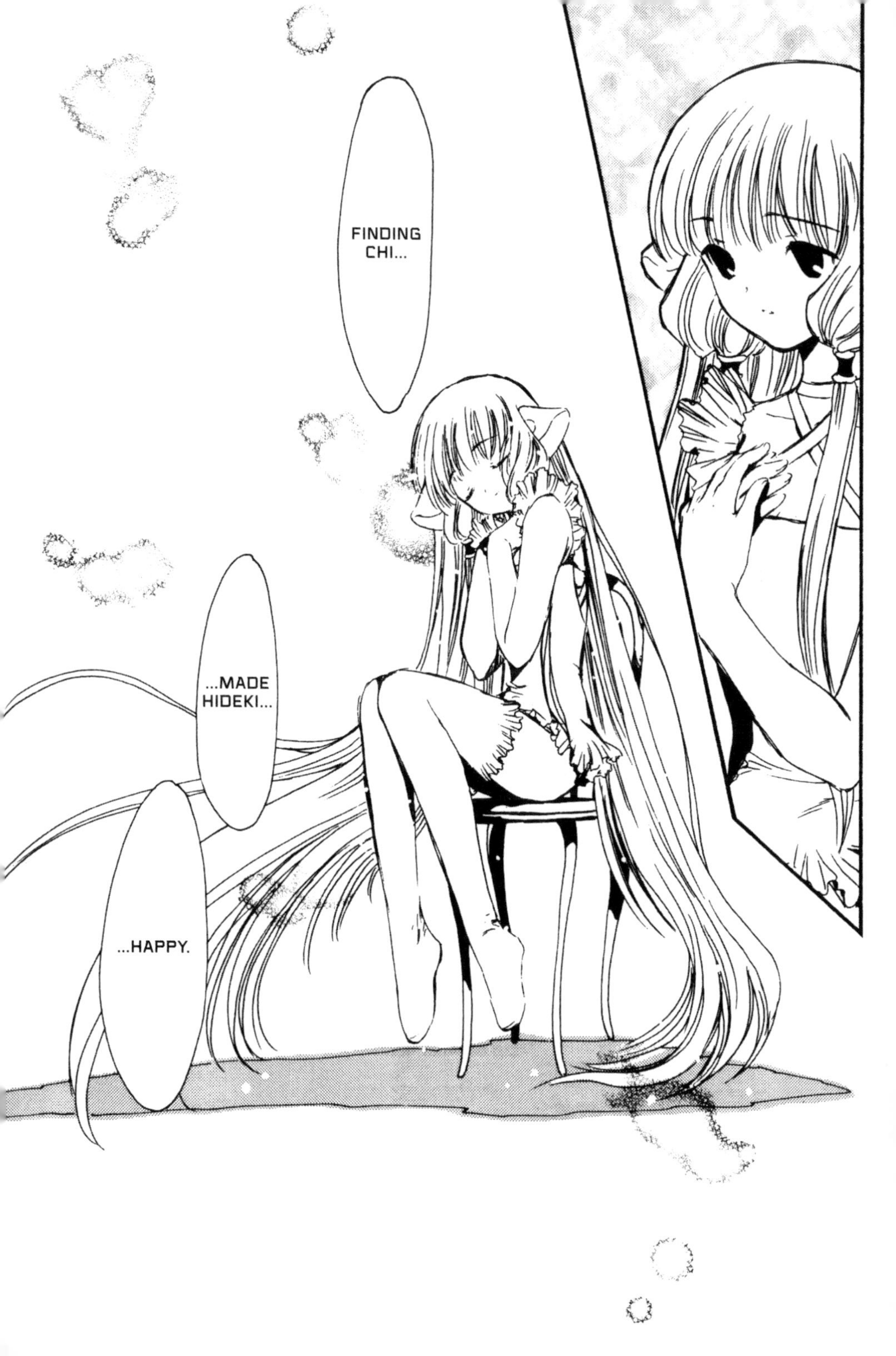
FINDING CHI...
...MADE HIDEKI...
...HAPPY.

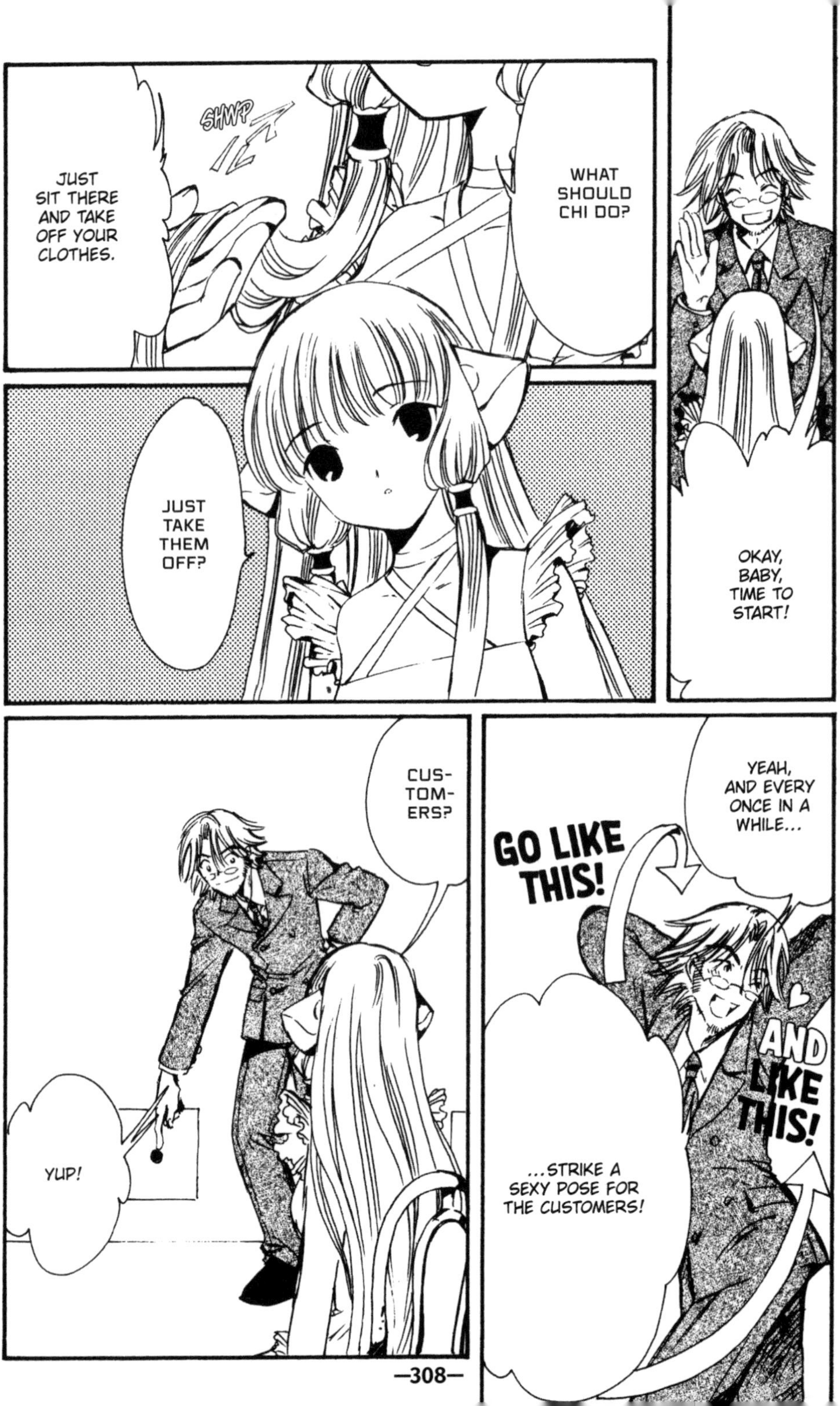
OKAY, BABY, TIME TO START!
WHAT SHOULD CHI DO?
SHWP
JUST SIT THERE AND TAKE OFF YOUR CLOTHES.
JUST TAKE THEM OFF?
YEAH, AND EVERY ONCE IN A WHILE...
GO LIKE THIS!
AND LIKE THIS!
...STRIKE A SEXY POSE FOR THE CUSTOMERS!
CUS-TOM-ERS?
YUP!

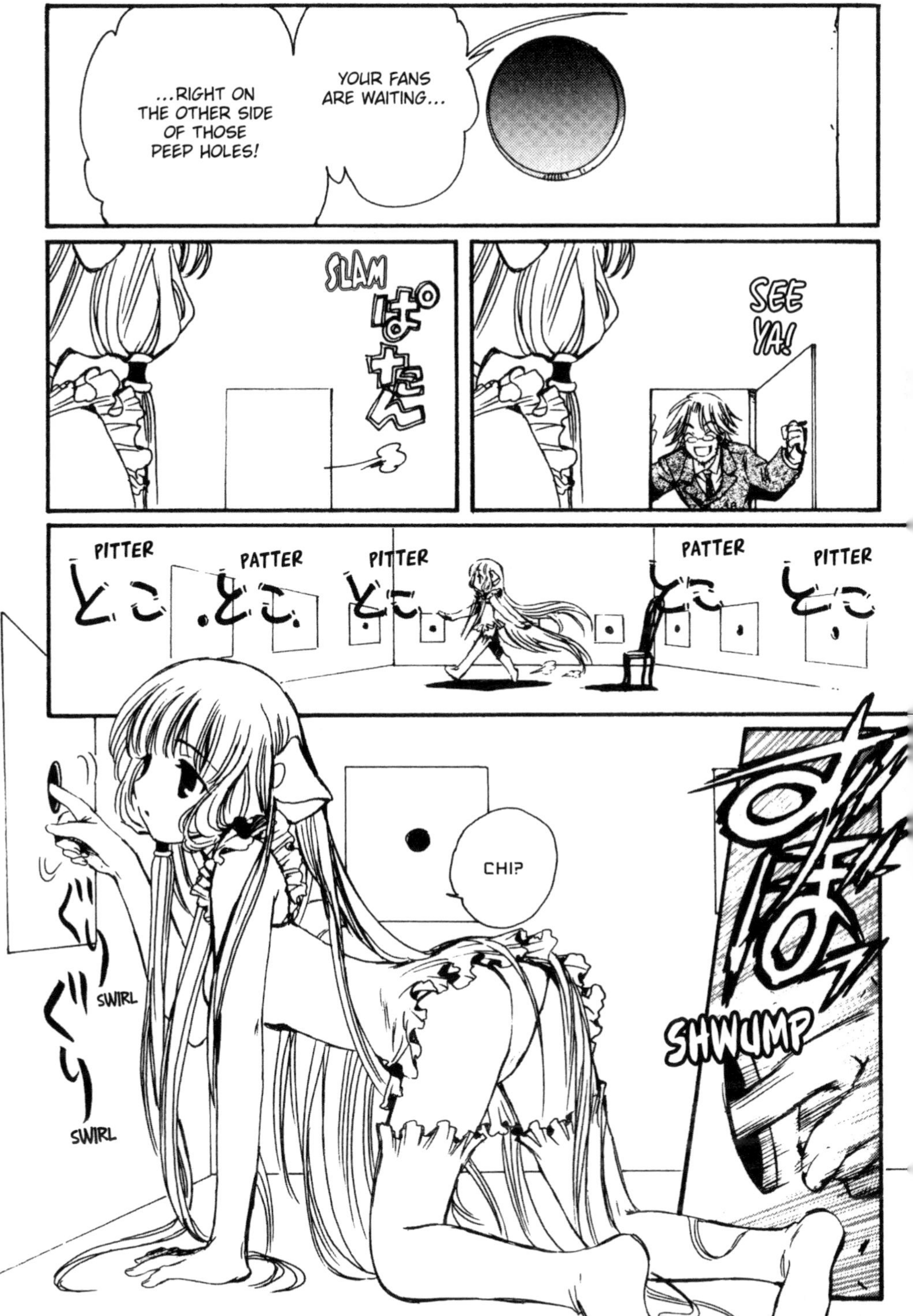
YOUR FANS ARE WAITING...
...RIGHT ON THE OTHER SIDE OF THOSE PEEP HOLES!
SEE YA!
ぱたん
SLAM
とこ
PITTER
とこ
PATTER
とこ
PITTER
とこ
PATTER
とこ
PITTER
SHWUMP
CHI?
ぐりぐり
SWIRL
SWIRL

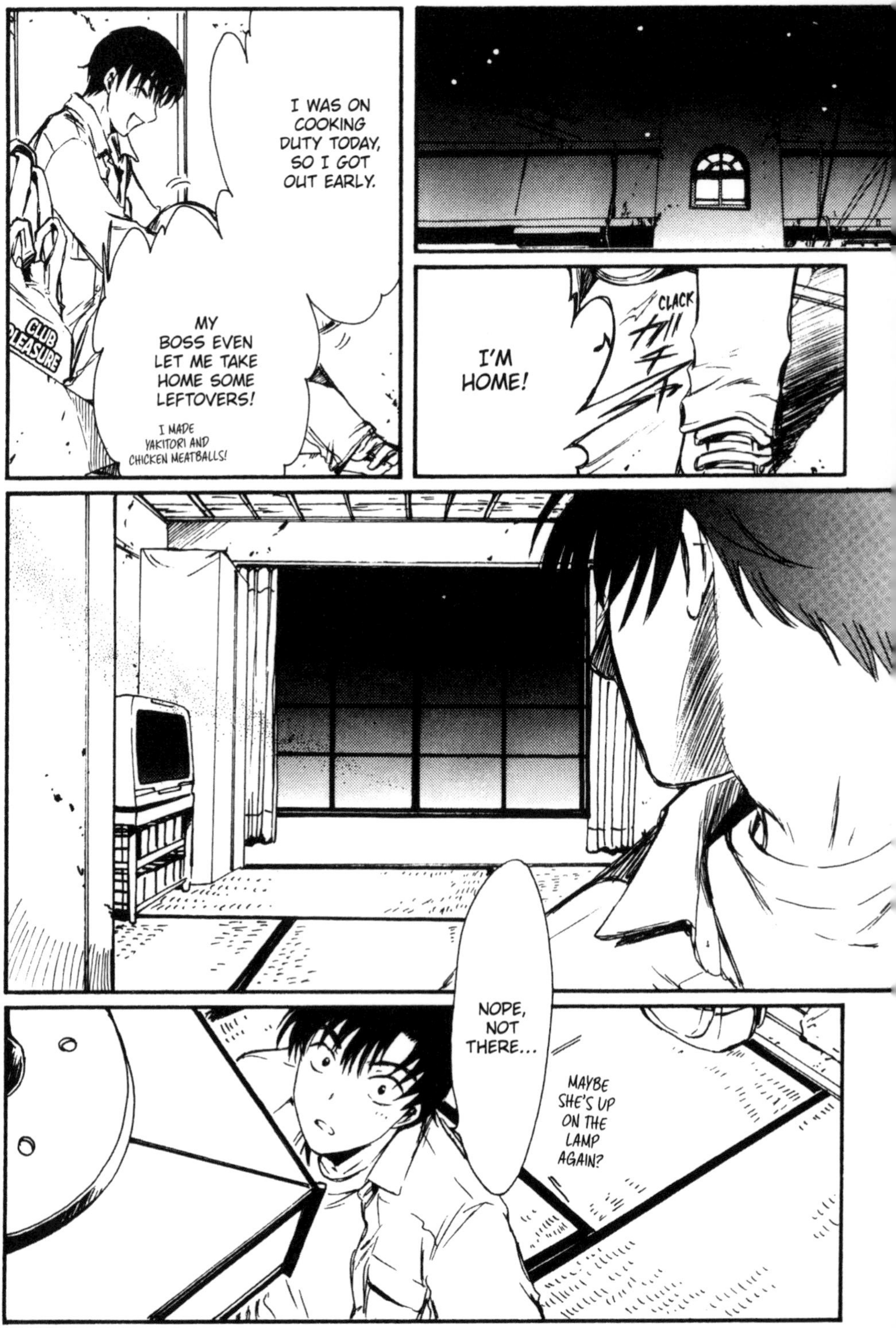
CLACK
I'M HOME!
I WAS ON COOKING DUTY TODAY, SO I GOT OUT EARLY.
MY BOSS EVEN LET ME TAKE HOME SOME LEFTOVERS!
I MADE YAKITORI AND CHICKEN MEATBALLS!
CLUB PLEASURE
NOPE, NOT THERE...
MAYBE SHE'S UP ON THE LAMP AGAIN?

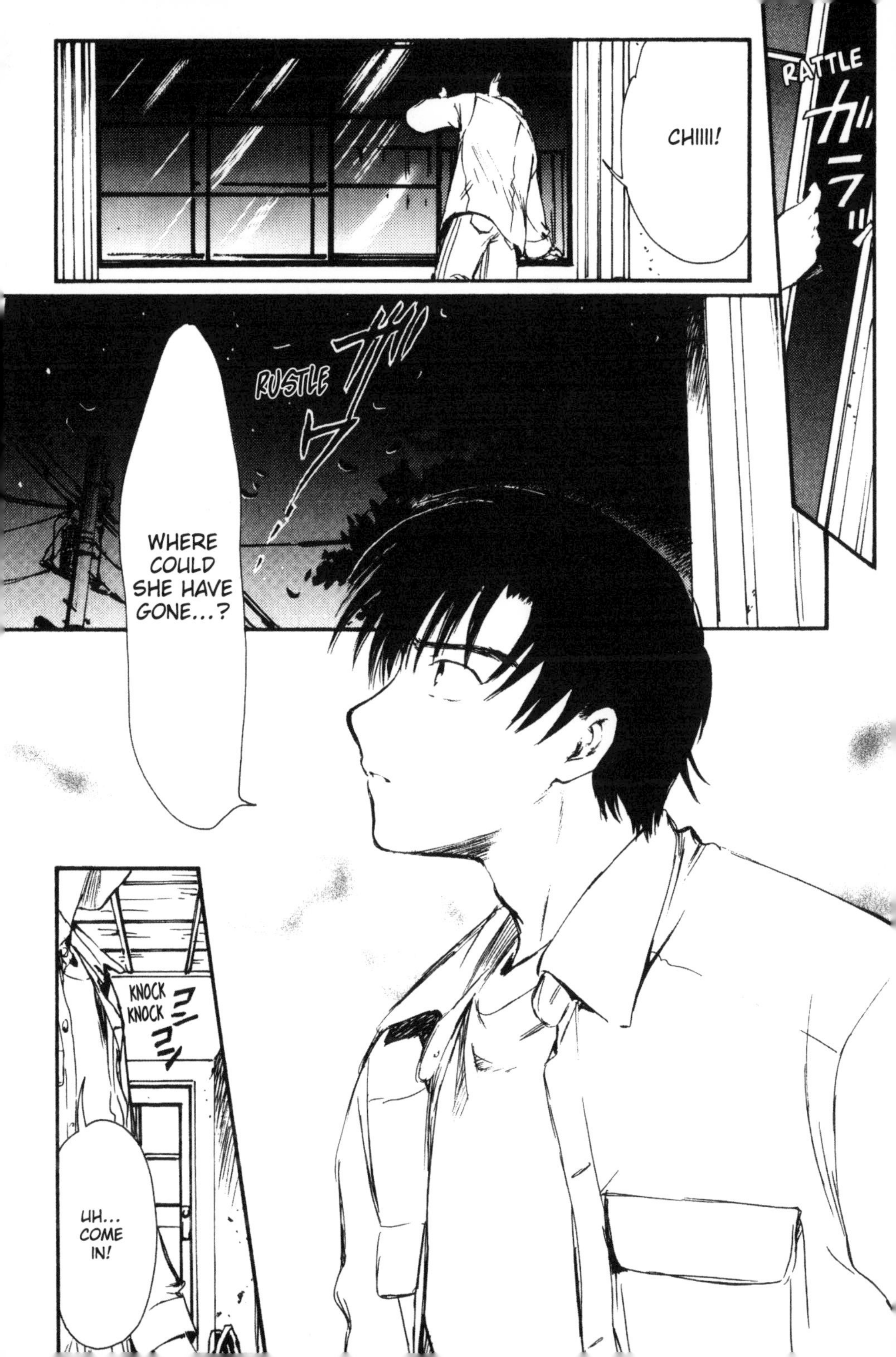
RATTLE
ガラッ
CHIIII!
RUSTLE
ブワッ
WHERE COULD SHE HAVE GONE...?
KNOCK KNOCK
コンコン
UH... COME IN!

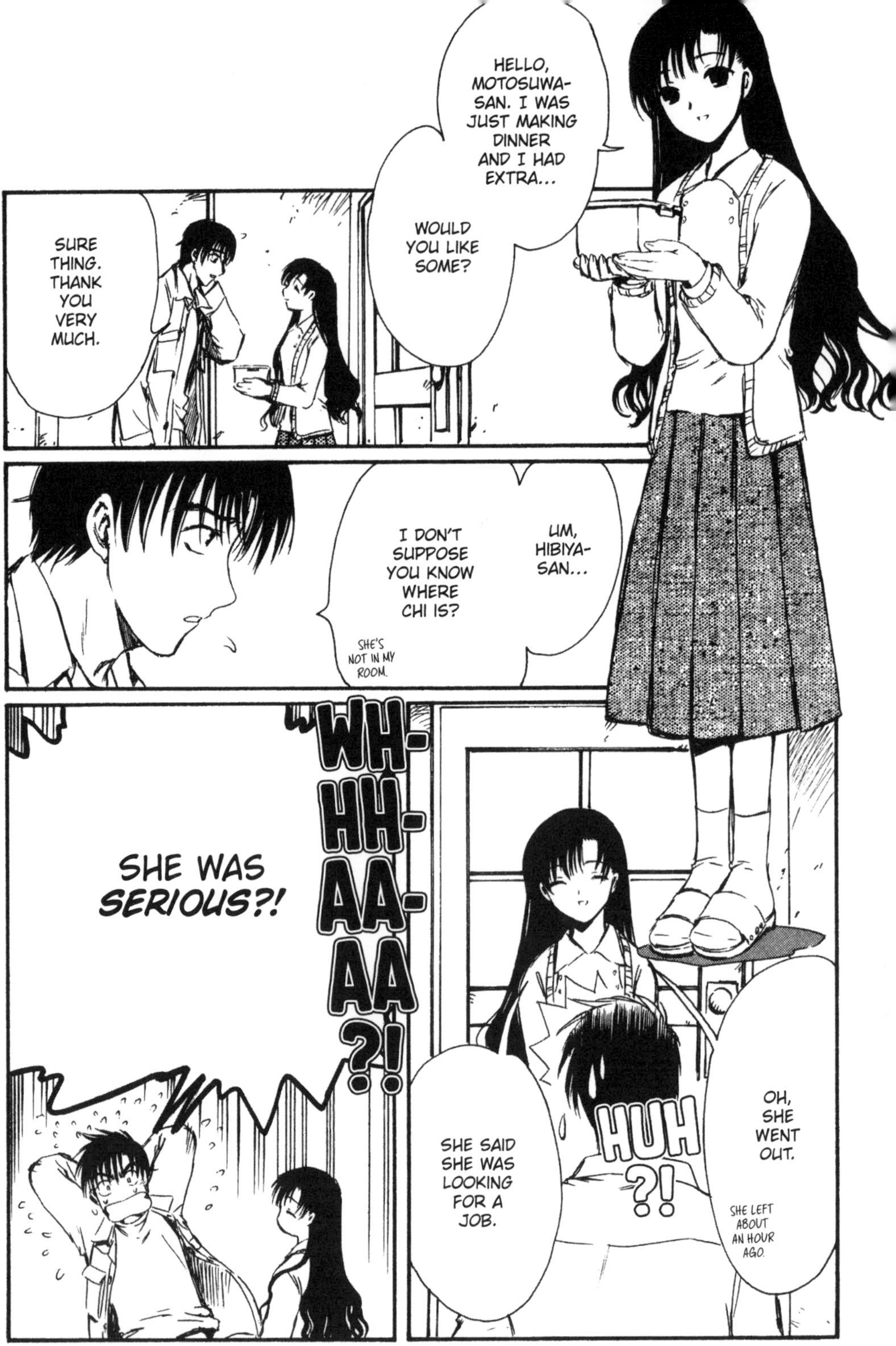
HELLO, MOTOSUWA-SAN. I WAS JUST MAKING DINNER AND I HAD EXTRA...
WOULD YOU LIKE SOME?
SURE THING. THANK YOU VERY MUCH.
UM, HIBIYA-SAN...
I DON'T SUPPOSE YOU KNOW WHERE CHI IS?
SHE'S NOT IN MY ROOM.
OH, SHE WENT OUT.
SHE LEFT ABOUT AN HOUR AGO.
HUH?!
SHE SAID SHE WAS LOOKING FOR A JOB.
WH-HH-AA-AA?!
SHE WAS SERIOUS?!

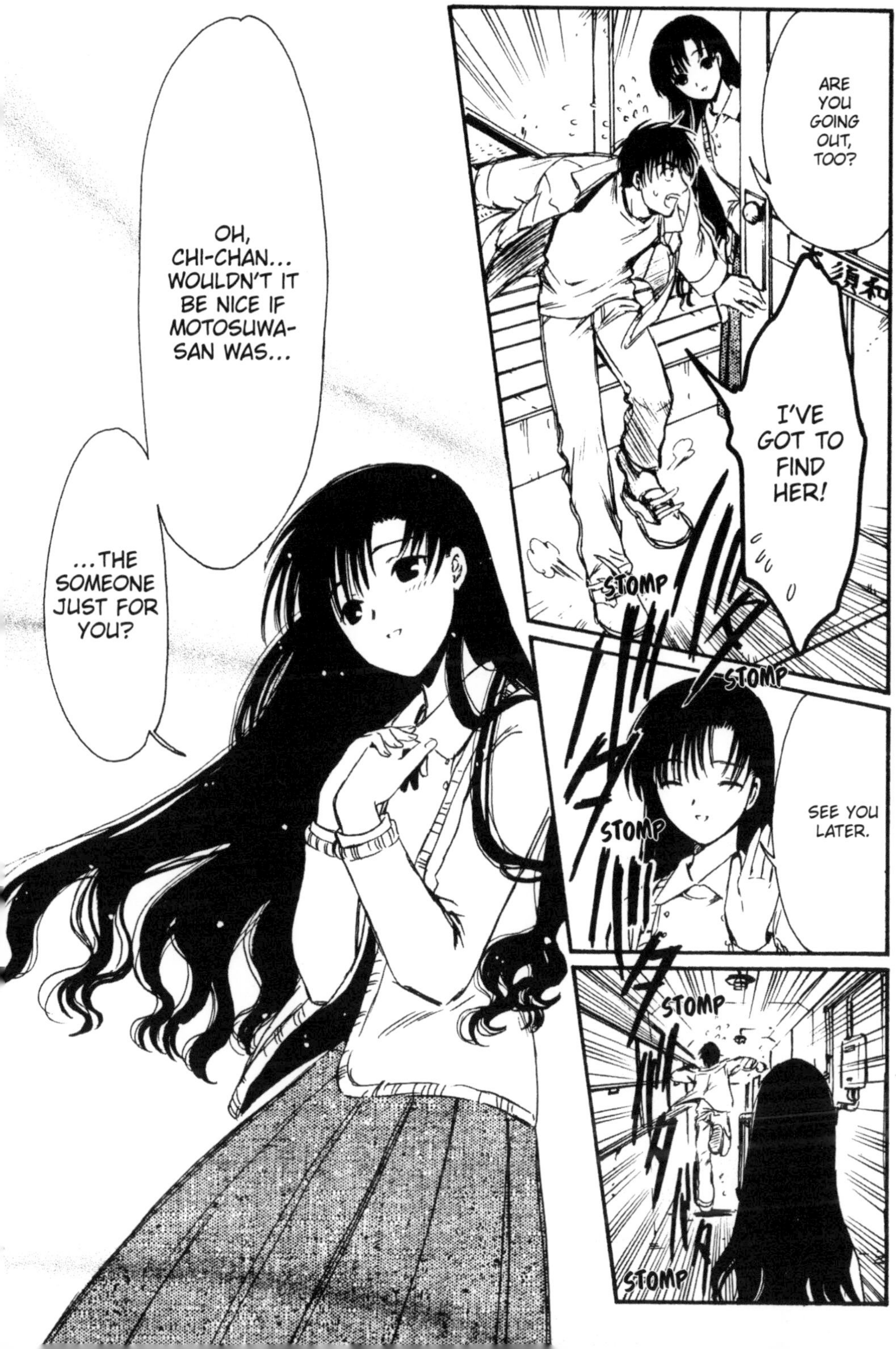
ARE YOU GOING OUT, TOO?
I'VE GOT TO FIND HER!
STOMP
STOMP
STOMP
SEE YOU LATER.
STOMP
STOMP
OH, CHI-CHAN... WOULDN'T IT BE NICE IF MOTOSUWA-SAN WAS...
...THE SOMEONE JUST FOR YOU?

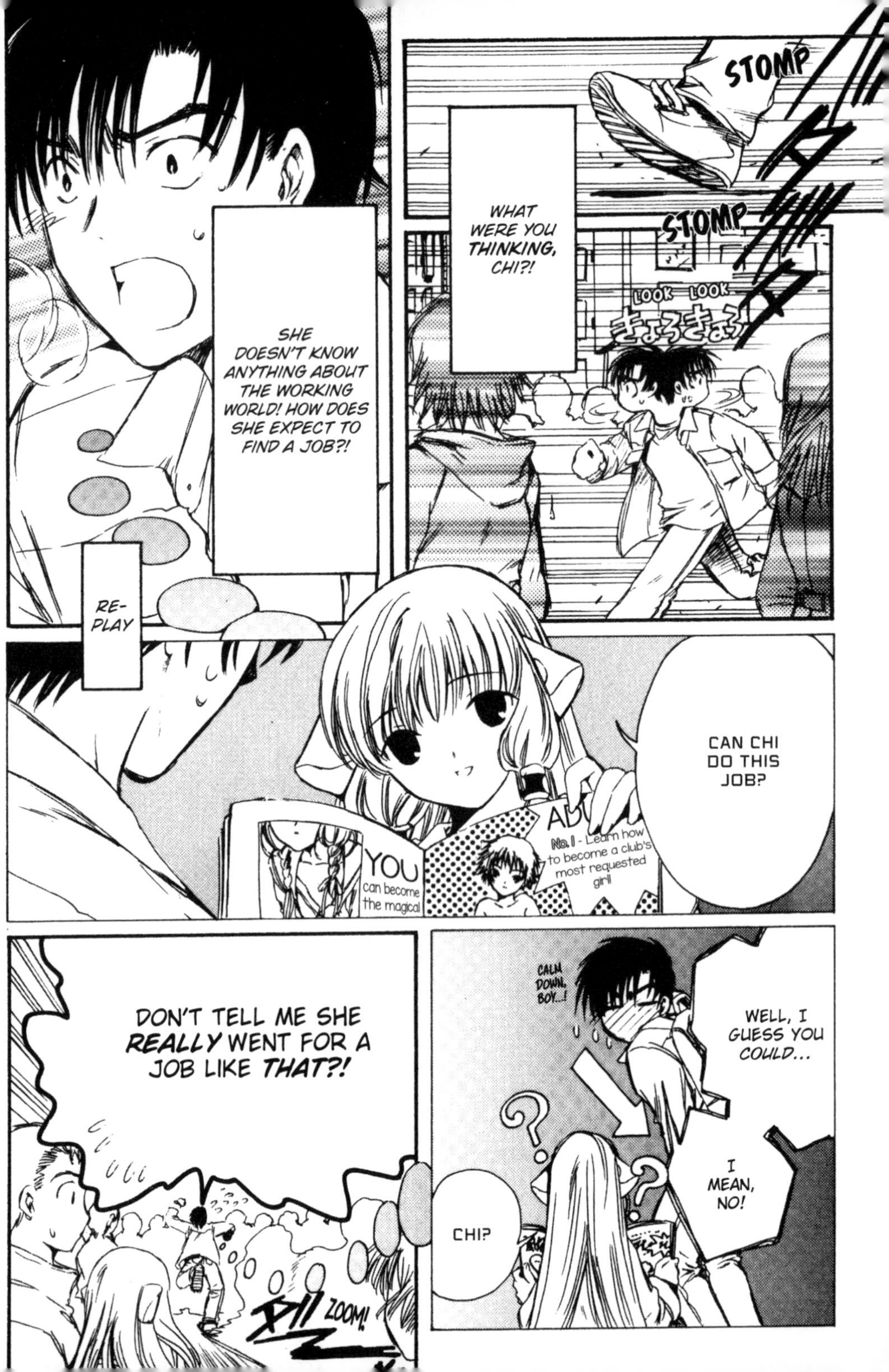
STOMP
STOMP
WHAT WERE YOU THINKING, CHI?!
LOOK LOOK
きょろきょろ
SHE DOESN'T KNOW ANYTHING ABOUT THE WORKING WORLD! HOW DOES SHE EXPECT TO FIND A JOB?!
RE-PLAY
CAN CHI DO THIS JOB?
No.1 - Learn how to become a club's most requested girl
YOU can become the magical
WELL, I GUESS YOU COULD...
CALM DOWN, BOY...!
I MEAN, NO!
CHI?
DON'T TELL ME SHE ***REALLY*** WENT FOR A JOB LIKE ***THAT?!***
ZOOM!

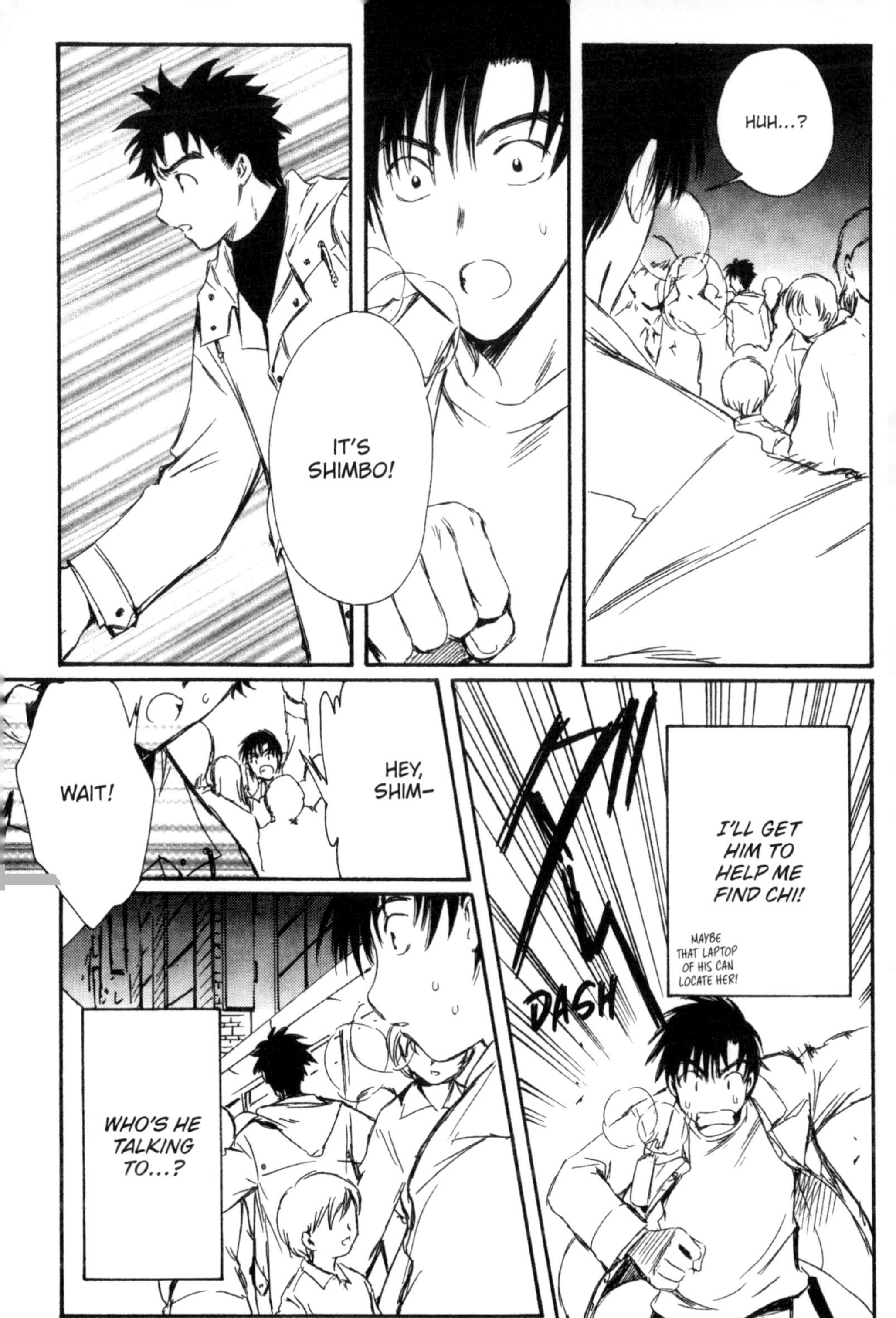
HUH...?
IT'S SHIMBO!
I'LL GET HIM TO HELP ME FIND CHI!
MAYBE THAT LAPTOP OF HIS CAN LOCATE HER!
DASH
HEY, SHIM-
WAIT!
WHO'S HE TALKING TO...?

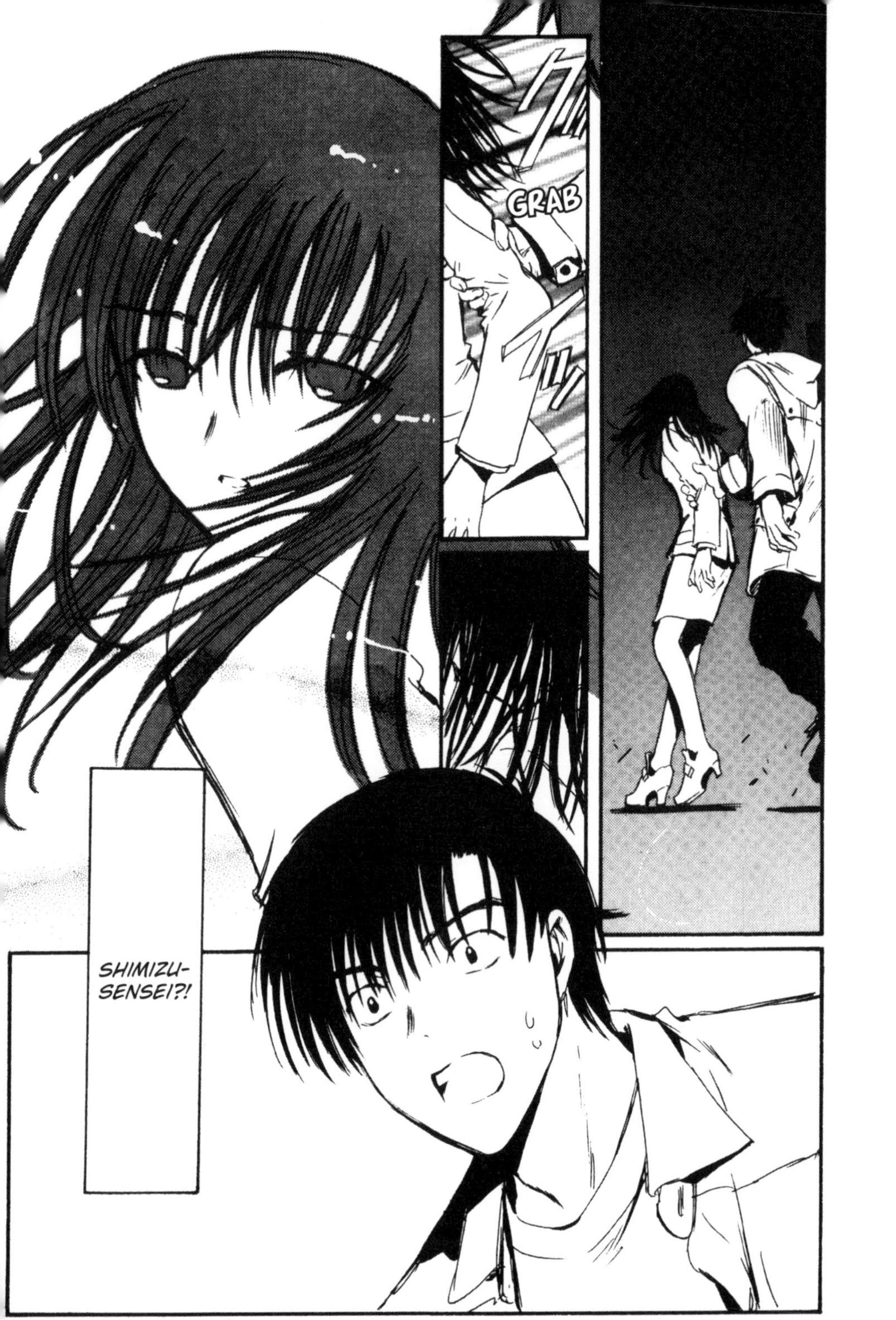
GRAB
SHIMIZU-SENSEI?!

Chobits

〈chapter.22〉

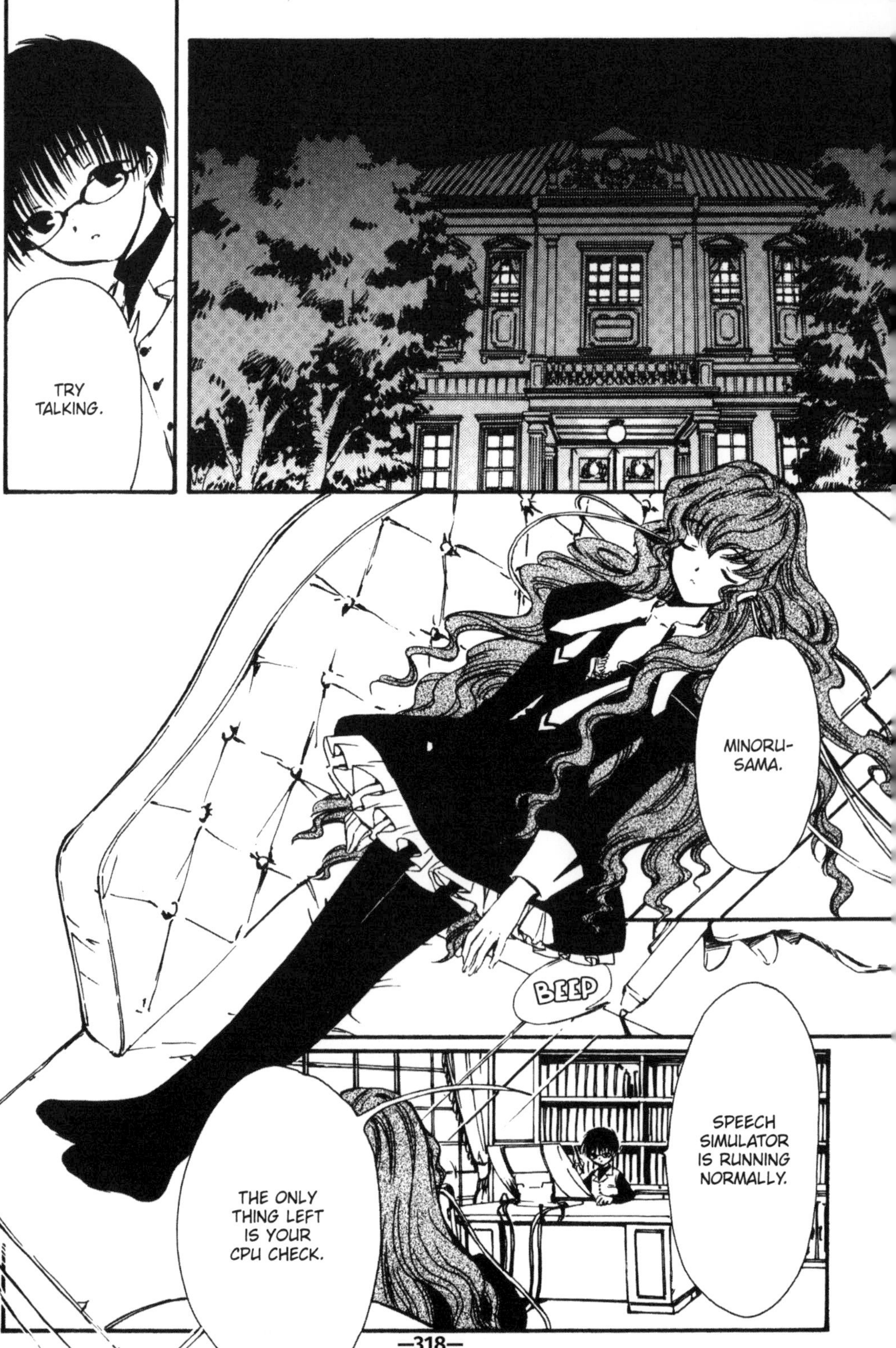
TRY TALKING.
MINORU-SAMA.
BEEP
SPEECH SIMULATOR IS RUNNING NORMALLY.
THE ONLY THING LEFT IS YOUR CPU CHECK.

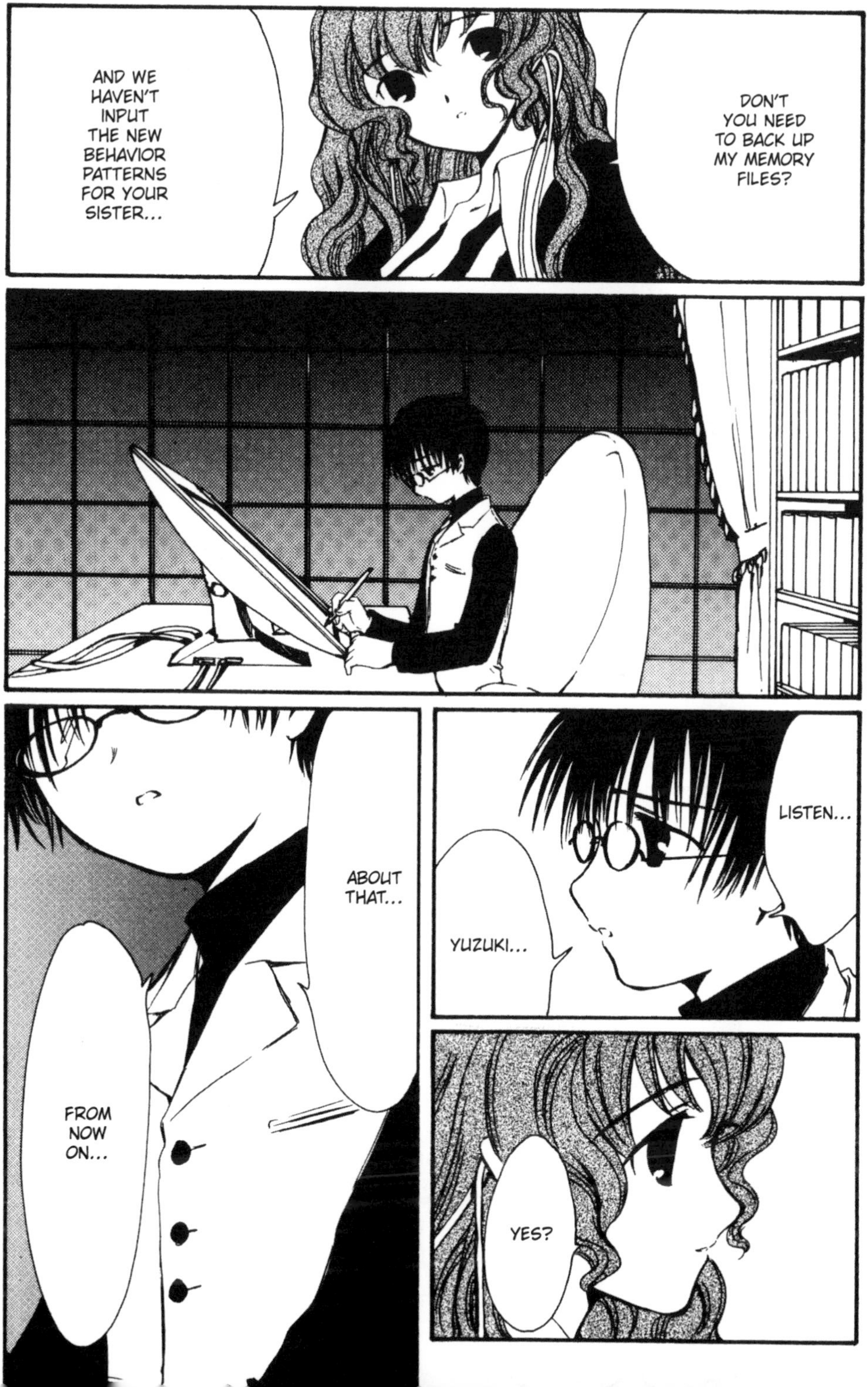
DON'T YOU NEED TO BACK UP MY MEMORY FILES?
AND WE HAVEN'T INPUT THE NEW BEHAVIOR PATTERNS FOR YOUR SISTER...
LISTEN...
YUZUKI...
YES?
ABOUT THAT...
FROM NOW ON...

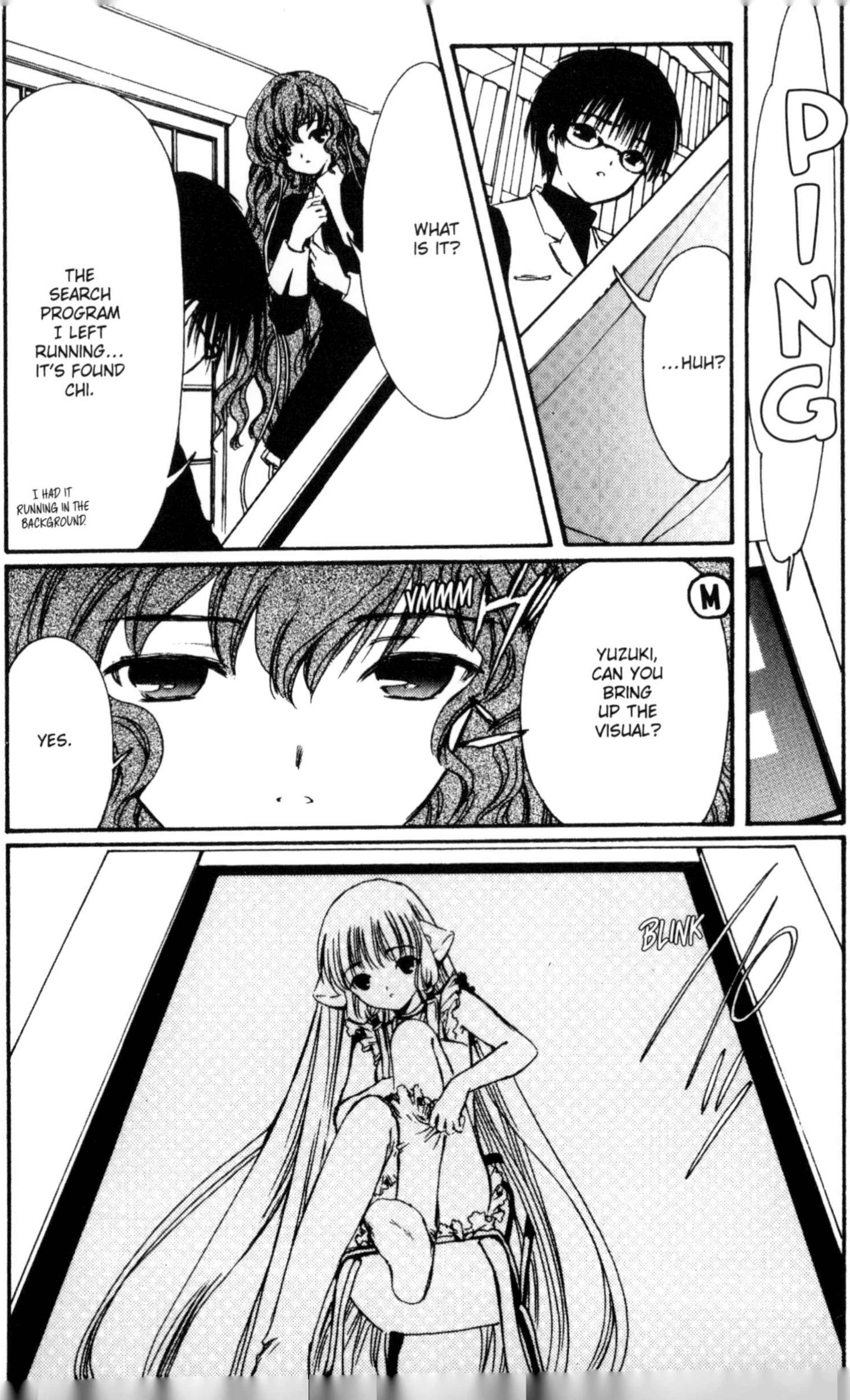
PING
...HUH?
WHAT IS IT?
THE SEARCH PROGRAM I LEFT RUNNING... IT'S FOUND CHI.
I HAD IT RUNNING IN THE BACKGROUND.
M
YUZUKI, CAN YOU BRING UP THE VISUAL?
VMMM
YES.
BLINK

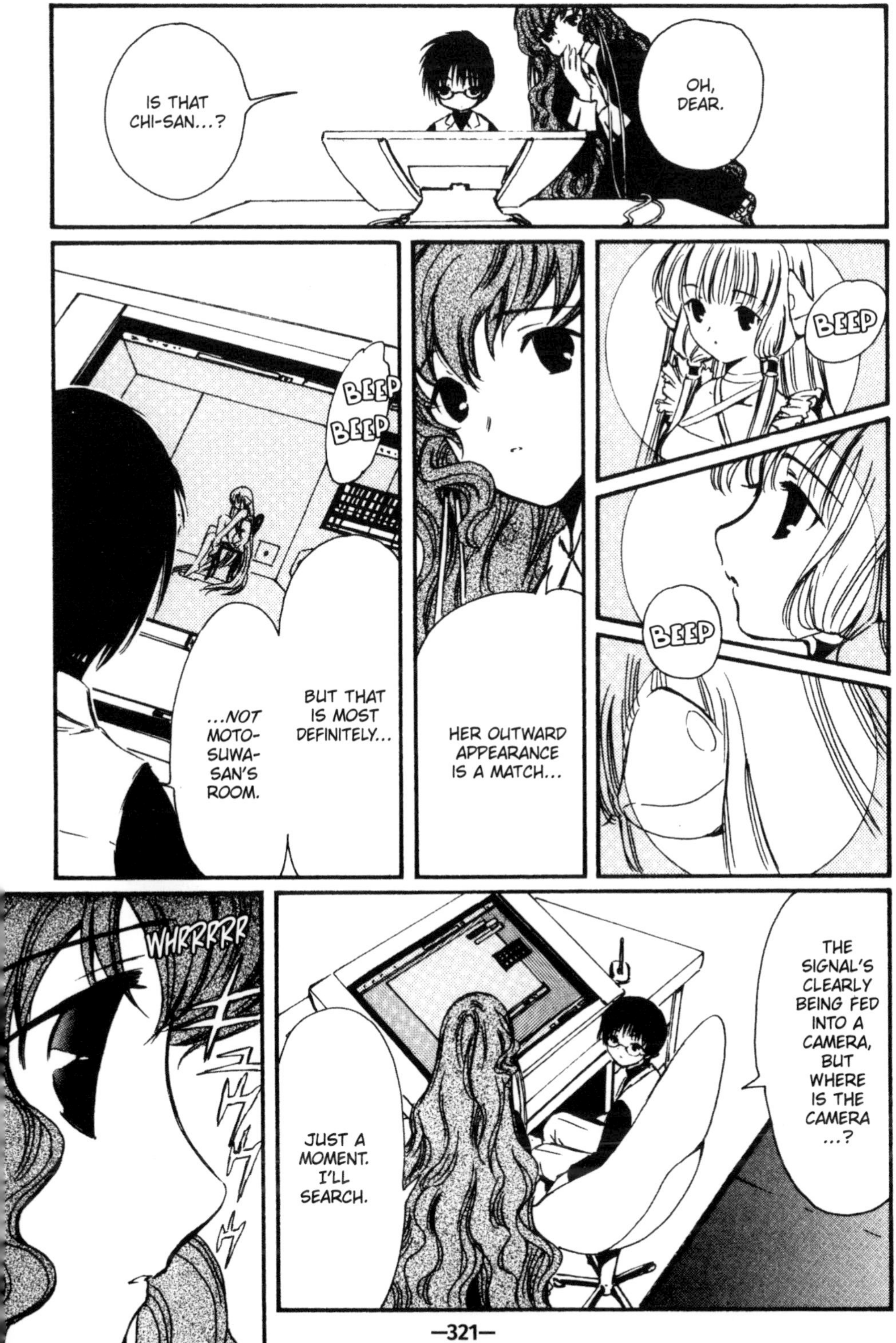
OH, DEAR.
IS THAT CHI-SAN...?
BEEP
BEEP
HER OUTWARD APPEARANCE IS A MATCH...
BEEP
BEEP
BUT THAT IS MOST DEFINITELY...
...NOT MOTO-SUWA-SAN'S ROOM.
THE SIGNAL'S CLEARLY BEING FED INTO A CAMERA, BUT WHERE IS THE CAMERA ...?
JUST A MOMENT. I'LL SEARCH.
WHRRRRR

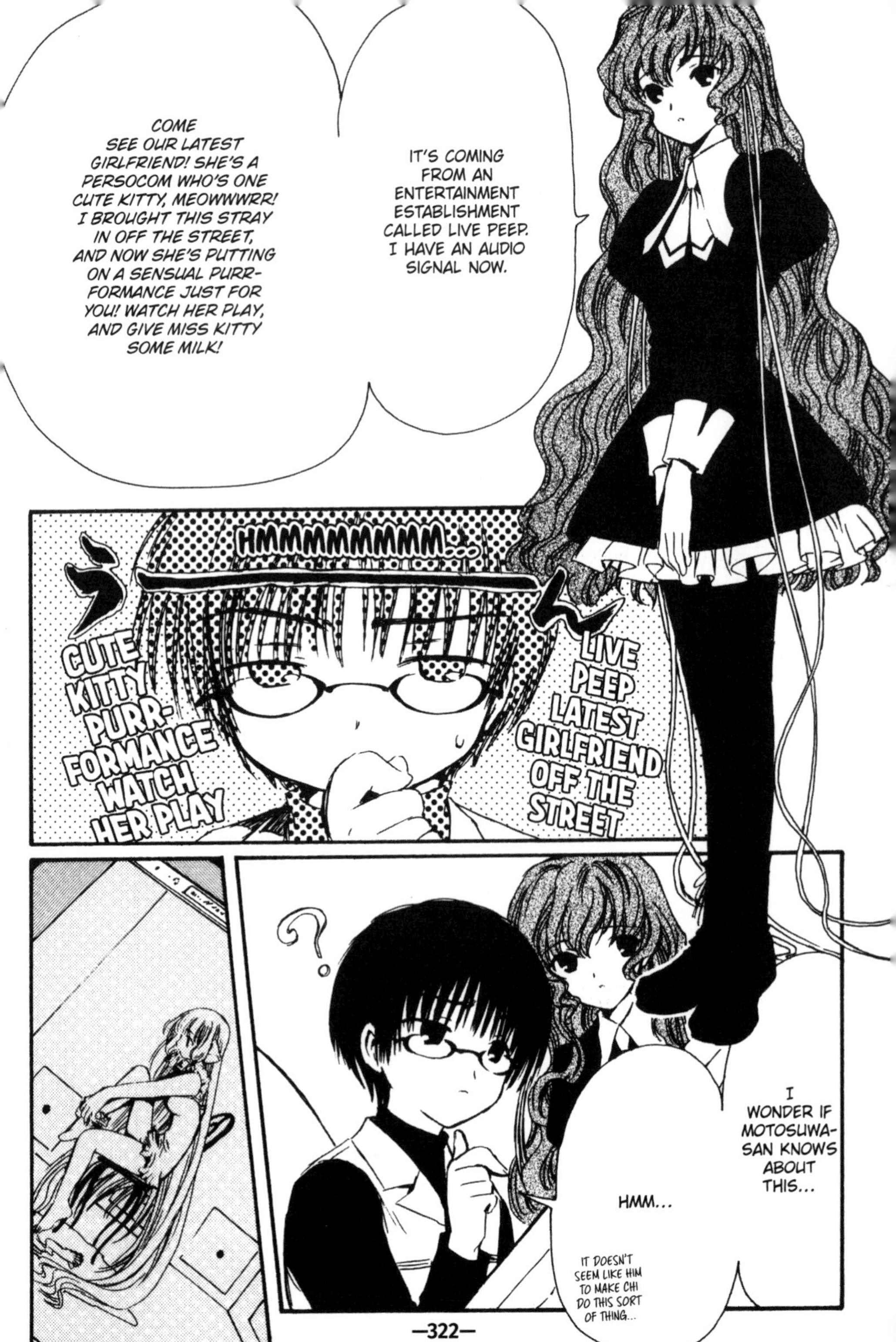
IT'S COMING FROM AN ENTERTAINMENT ESTABLISHMENT CALLED LIVE PEEP. I HAVE AN AUDIO SIGNAL NOW.
COME SEE OUR LATEST GIRLFRIEND! SHE'S A PERSOCOM WHO'S ONE CUTE KITTY, MEOWWWRR! I BROUGHT THIS STRAY IN OFF THE STREET, AND NOW SHE'S PUTTING ON A SENSUAL PURR-FORMANCE JUST FOR YOU! WATCH HER PLAY, AND GIVE MISS KITTY SOME MILK!
HMMMMMMMM...
LIVE PEEP LATEST GIRLFRIEND OFF THE STREET
CUTE KITTY PURR-FORMANCE WATCH HER PLAY
I WONDER IF MOTOSUWA-SAN KNOWS ABOUT THIS...
HMM...
IT DOESN'T SEEM LIKE HIM TO MAKE CHI DO THIS SORT OF THING...

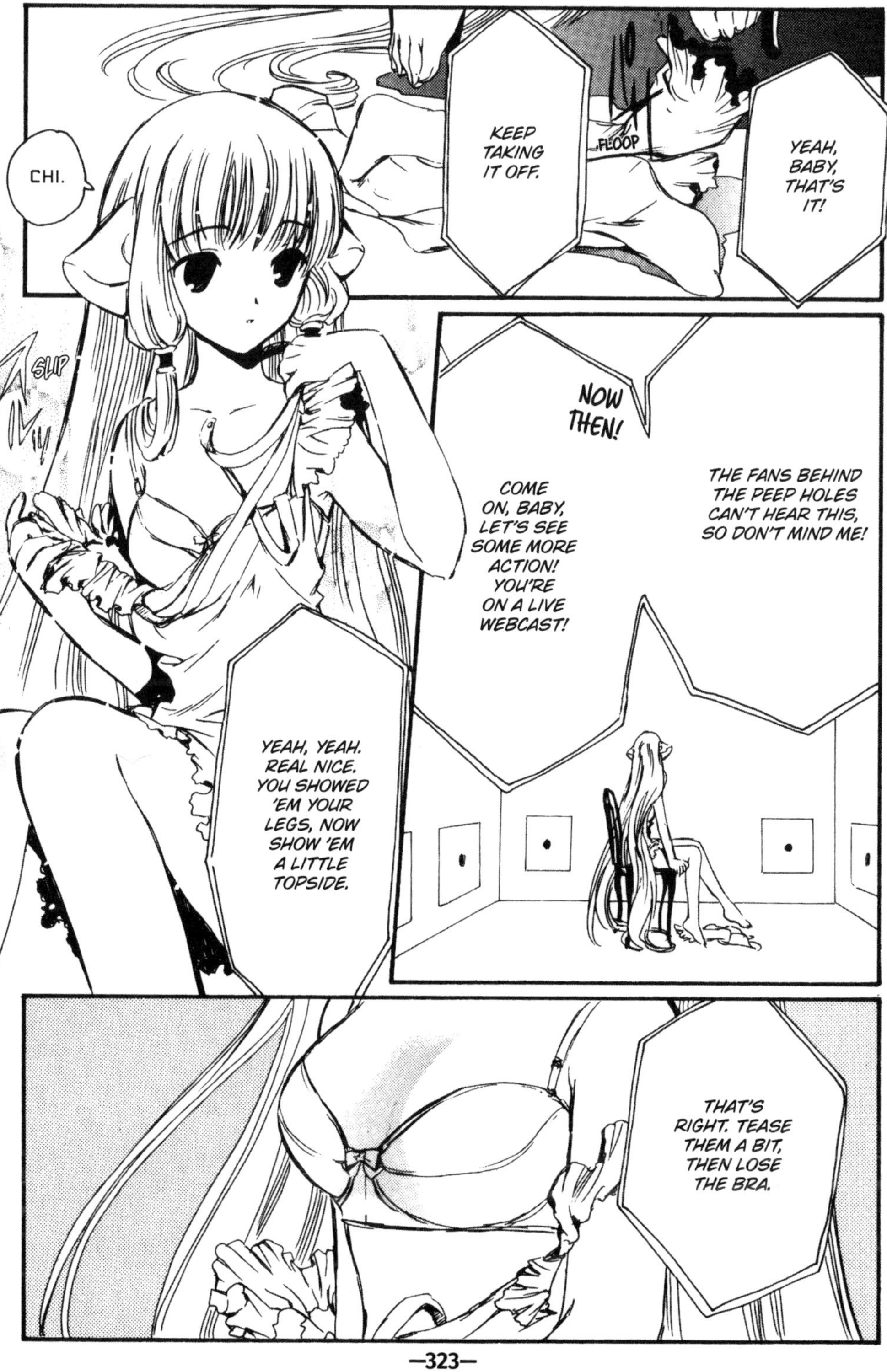
YEAH, BABY, THAT'S IT!
FLOOP
KEEP TAKING IT OFF.
CHI.
NOW THEN!
THE FANS BEHIND THE PEEP HOLES CAN'T HEAR THIS, SO DON'T MIND ME!
COME ON, BABY, LET'S SEE SOME MORE ACTION! YOU'RE ON A LIVE WEBCAST!
SLIP
YEAH, YEAH. REAL NICE. YOU SHOWED 'EM YOUR LEGS, NOW SHOW 'EM A LITTLE TOPSIDE.
THAT'S RIGHT. TEASE THEM A BIT, THEN LOSE THE BRA.

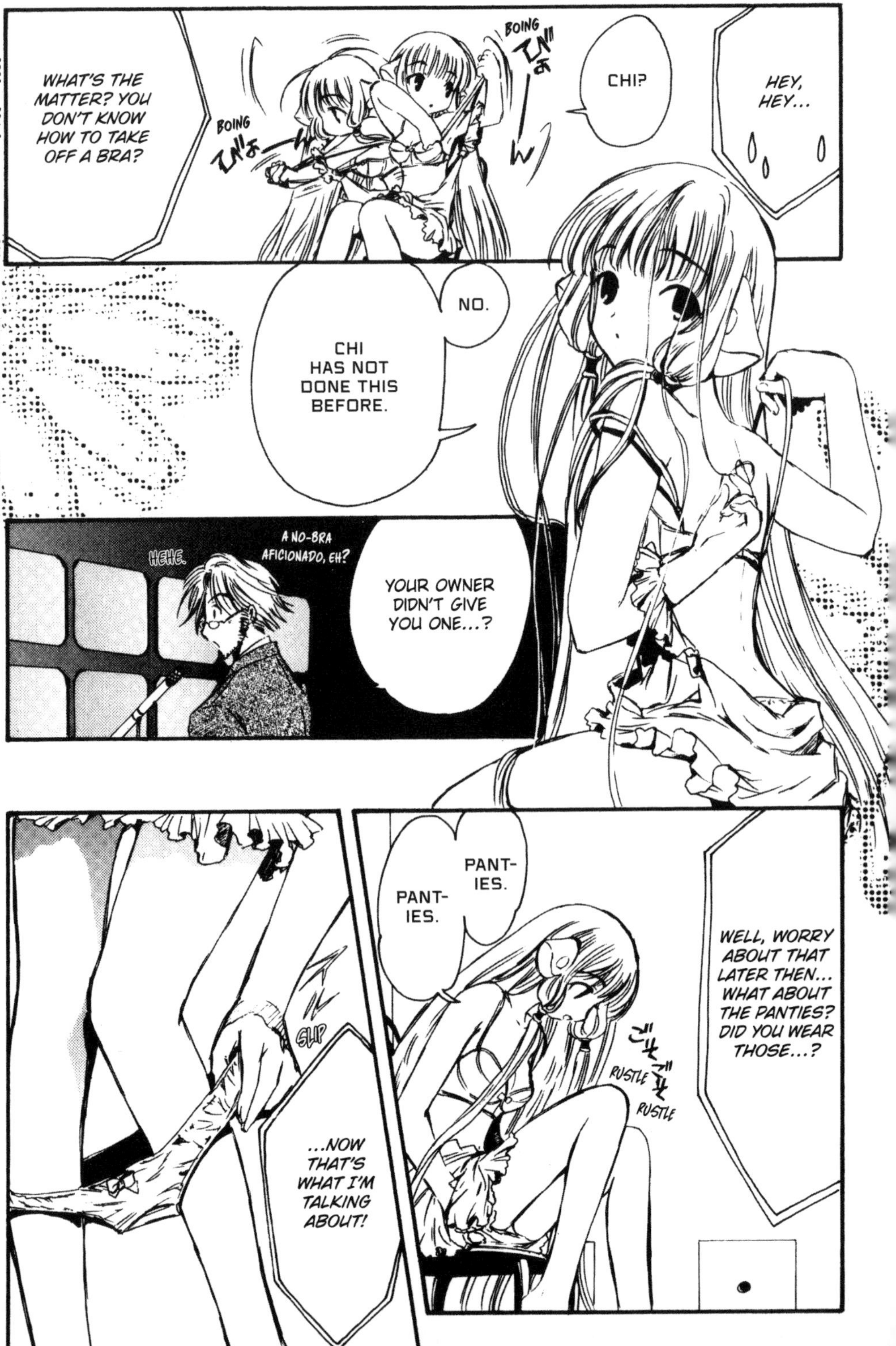
HEY, HEY...
CHI?
BOING
BOING
WHAT'S THE MATTER? YOU DON'T KNOW HOW TO TAKE OFF A BRA?
NO.
CHI HAS NOT DONE THIS BEFORE.
YOUR OWNER DIDN'T GIVE YOU ONE...?
A NO-BRA AFICIONADO, EH?
HEHE.
WELL, WORRY ABOUT THAT LATER THEN... WHAT ABOUT THE PANTIES? DID YOU WEAR THOSE...?
RUSTLE
RUSTLE
PANT-IES.
PANT-IES.
SLIP
...NOW THAT'S WHAT I'M TALKING ABOUT!

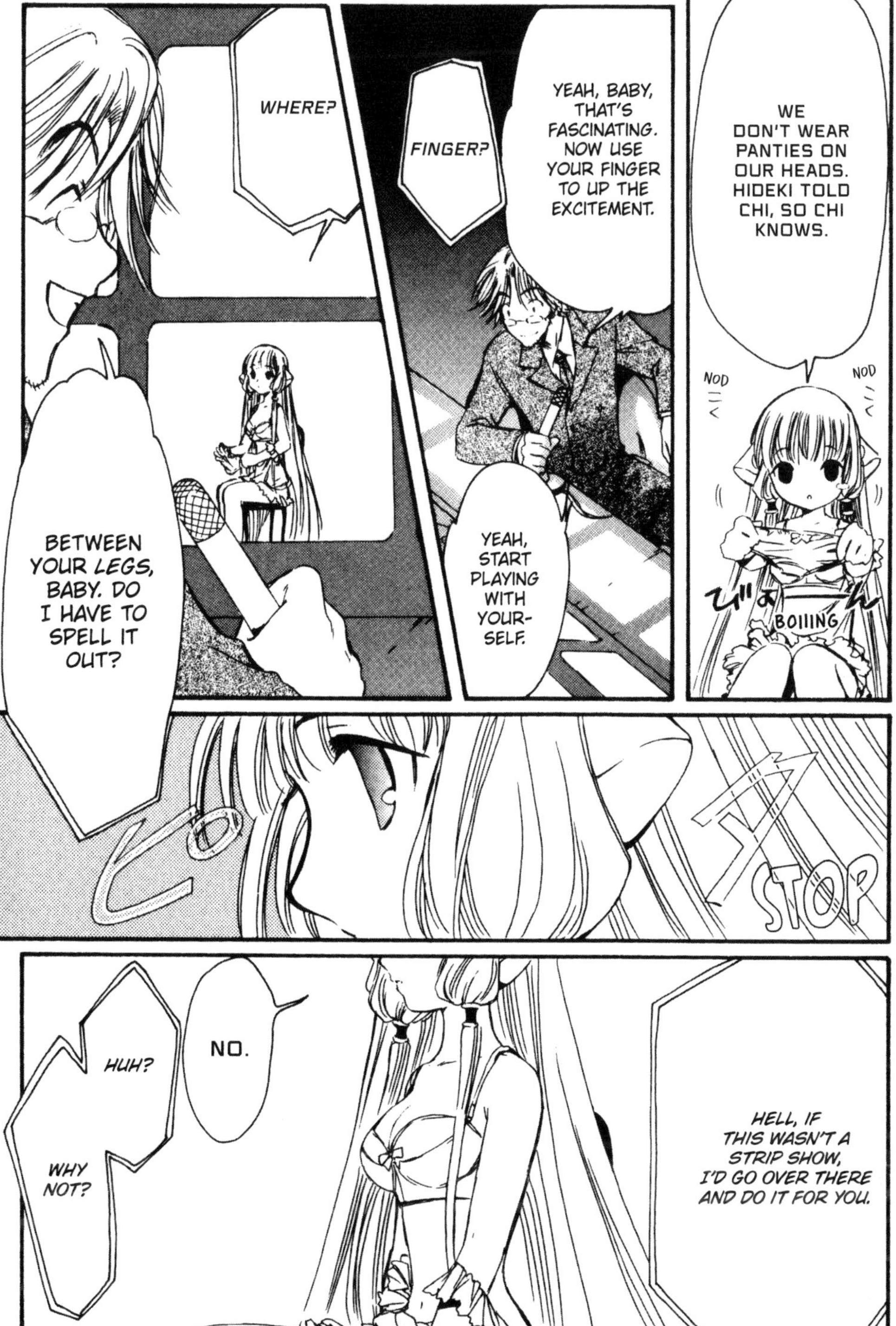
WE DON'T WEAR PANTIES ON OUR HEADS. HIDEKI TOLD CHI, SO CHI KNOWS.
NOD
NOD
BOIIING
YEAH, BABY, THAT'S FASCINATING. NOW USE YOUR FINGER TO UP THE EXCITEMENT.
FINGER?
YEAH, START PLAYING WITH YOUR-SELF.
WHERE?
BETWEEN YOUR LEGS, BABY. DO I HAVE TO SPELL IT OUT?
STOP
HELL, IF THIS WASN'T A STRIP SHOW, I'D GO OVER THERE AND DO IT FOR YOU.
NO.
HUH?
WHY NOT?

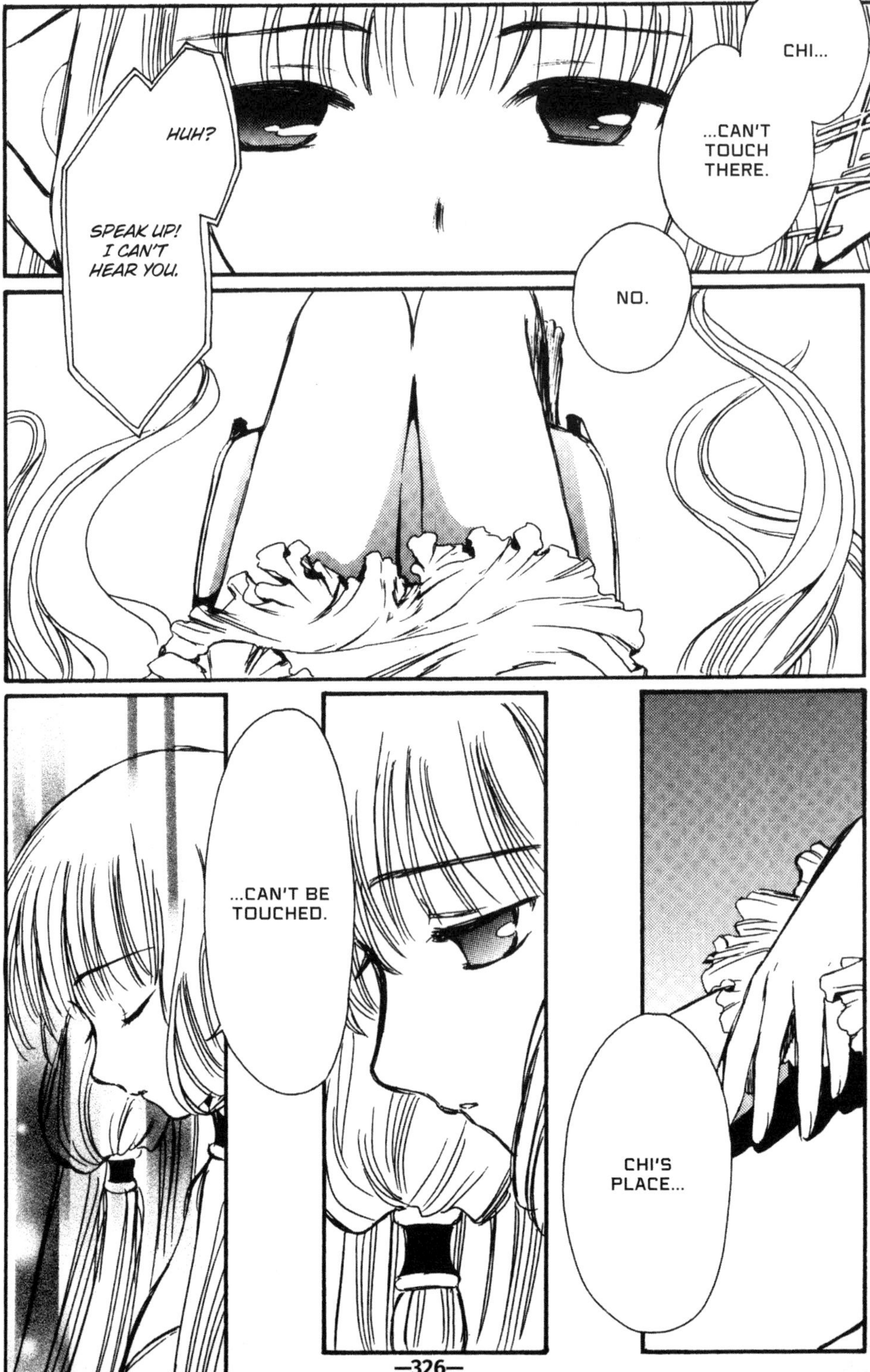
CHI...
...CAN'T TOUCH THERE.
HUH?
SPEAK UP! I CAN'T HEAR YOU.
NO.
CHI'S PLACE...
...CAN'T BE TOUCHED.

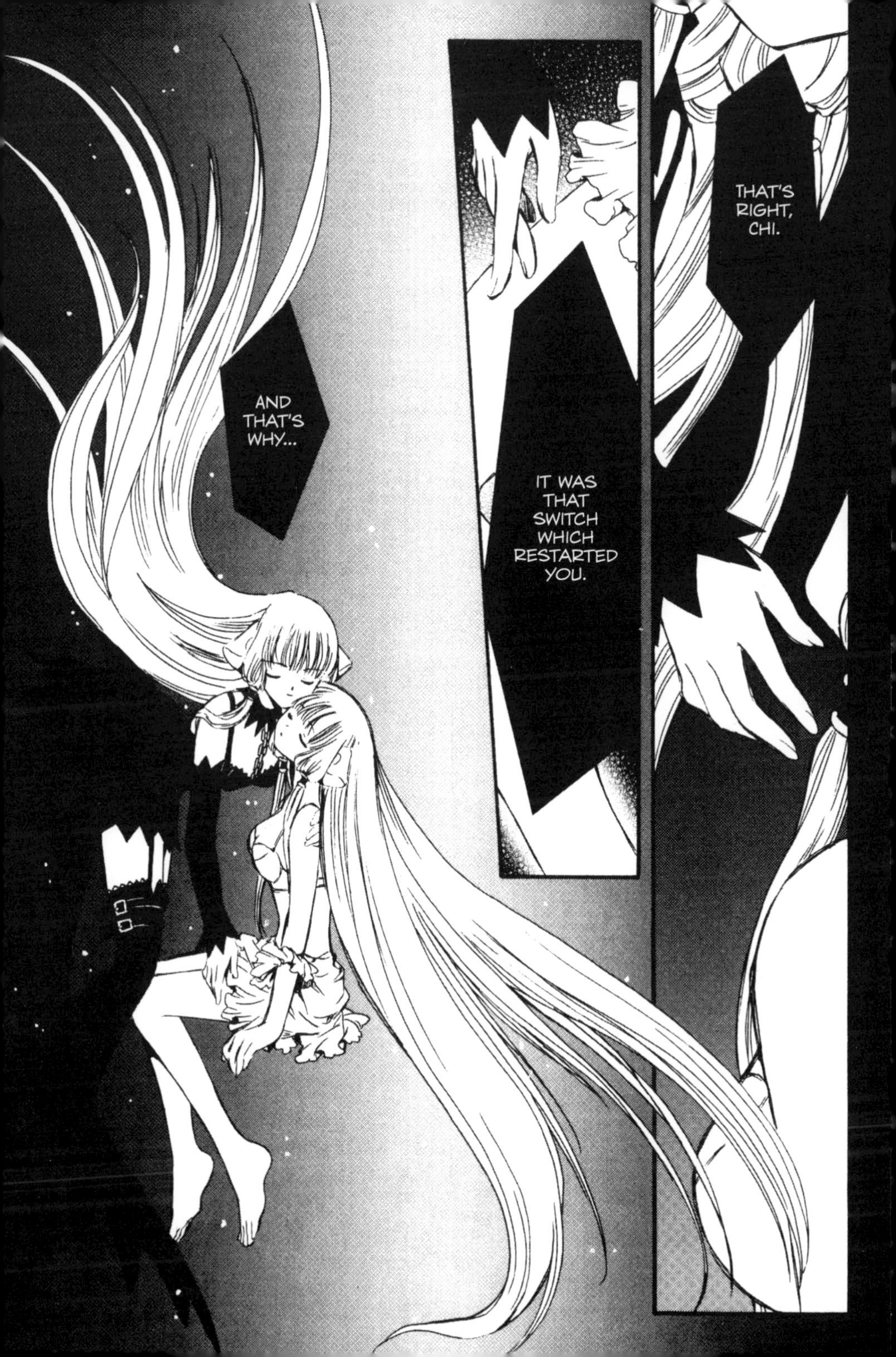
THAT'S RIGHT, CHI.
IT WAS THAT SWITCH WHICH RESTARTED YOU.
AND THAT'S WHY...

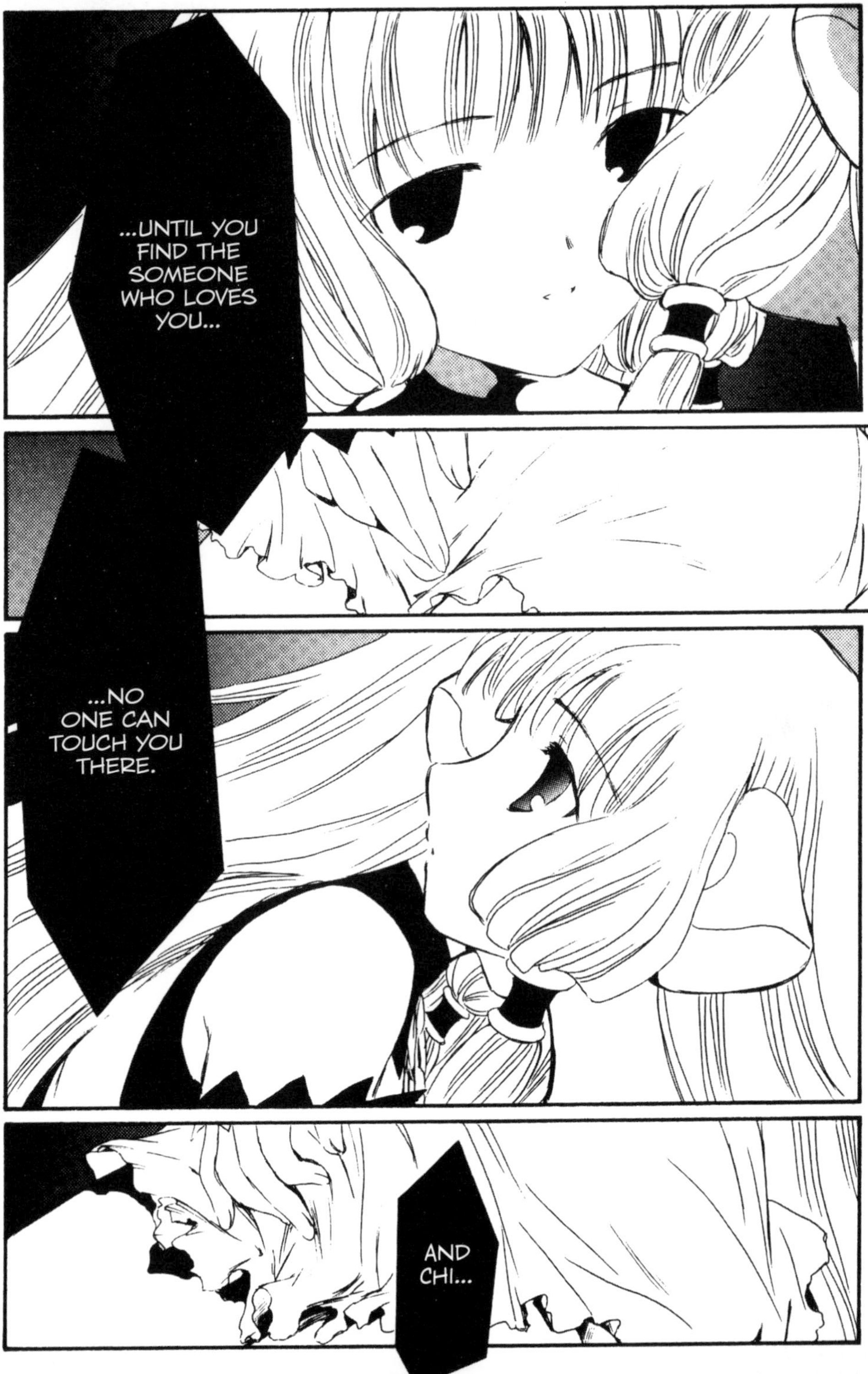
...UNTIL YOU FIND THE SOMEONE WHO LOVES YOU...
...NO ONE CAN TOUCH YOU THERE.
AND CHI...

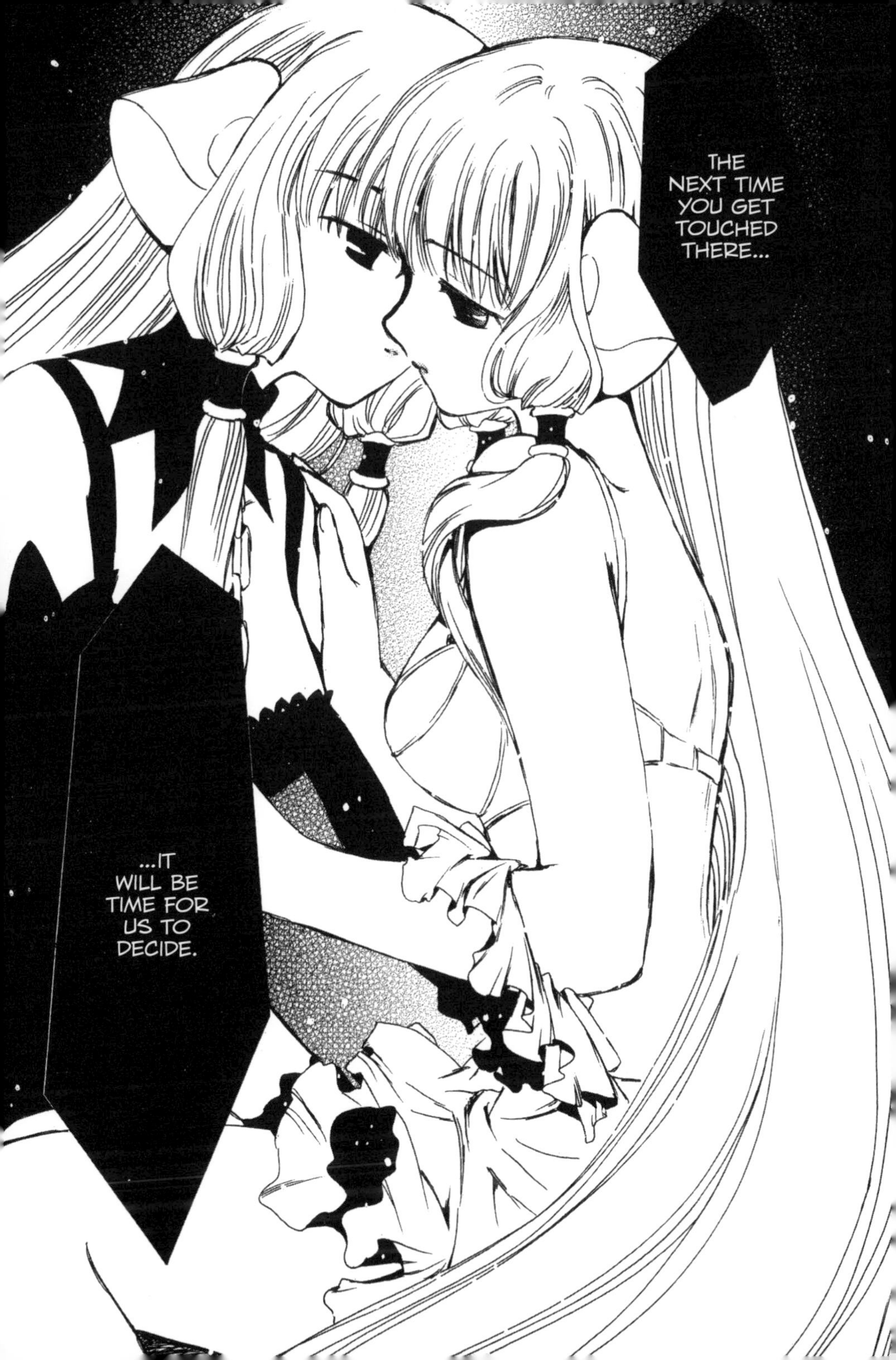
THE NEXT TIME YOU GET TOUCHED THERE...
...IT WILL BE TIME FOR US TO DECIDE.

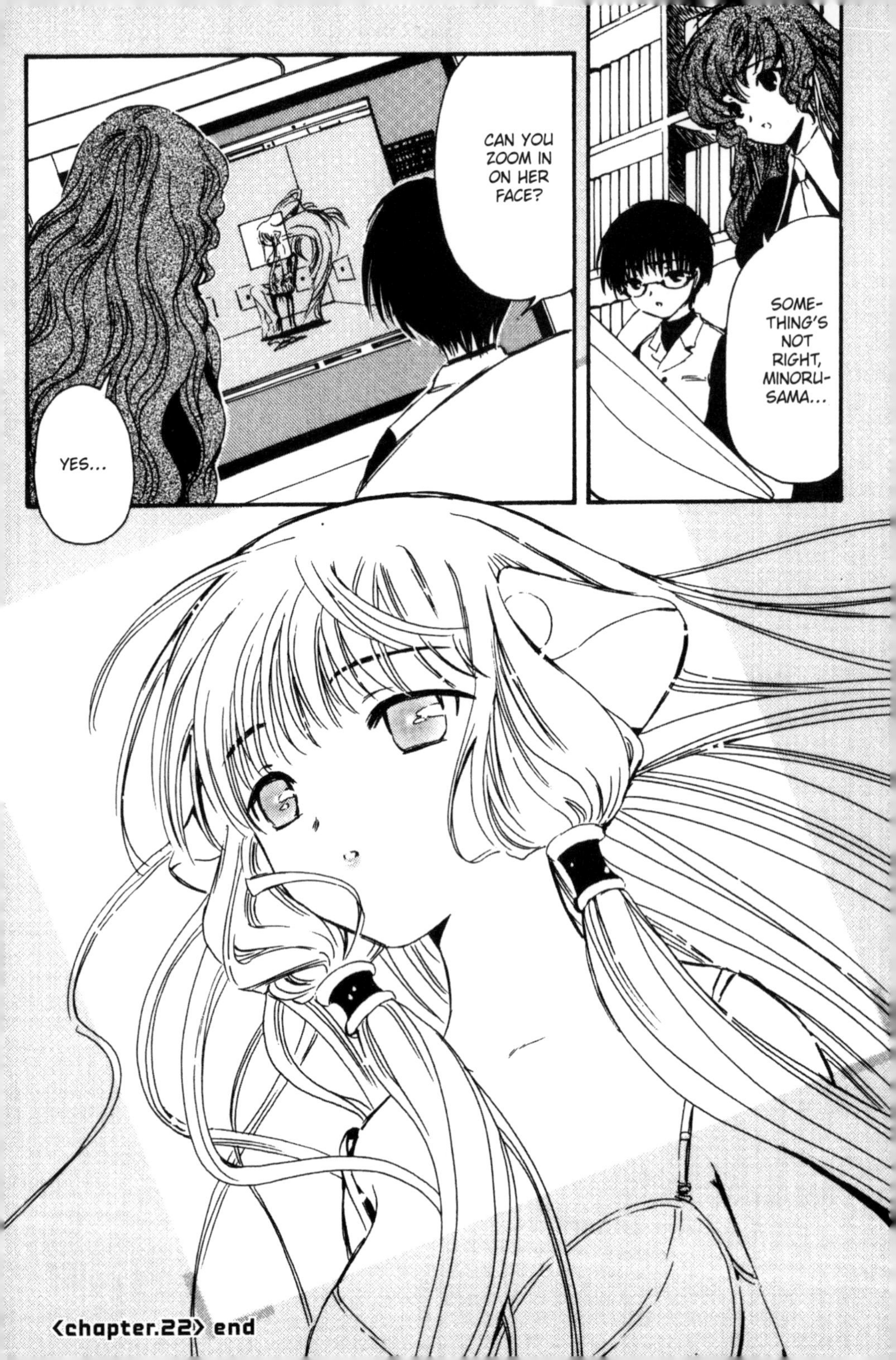
SOME-THING'S NOT RIGHT, MINORU-SAMA...
CAN YOU ZOOM IN ON HER FACE?
YES...
<chapter.22> end

Chobits

⟨chapter.23⟩

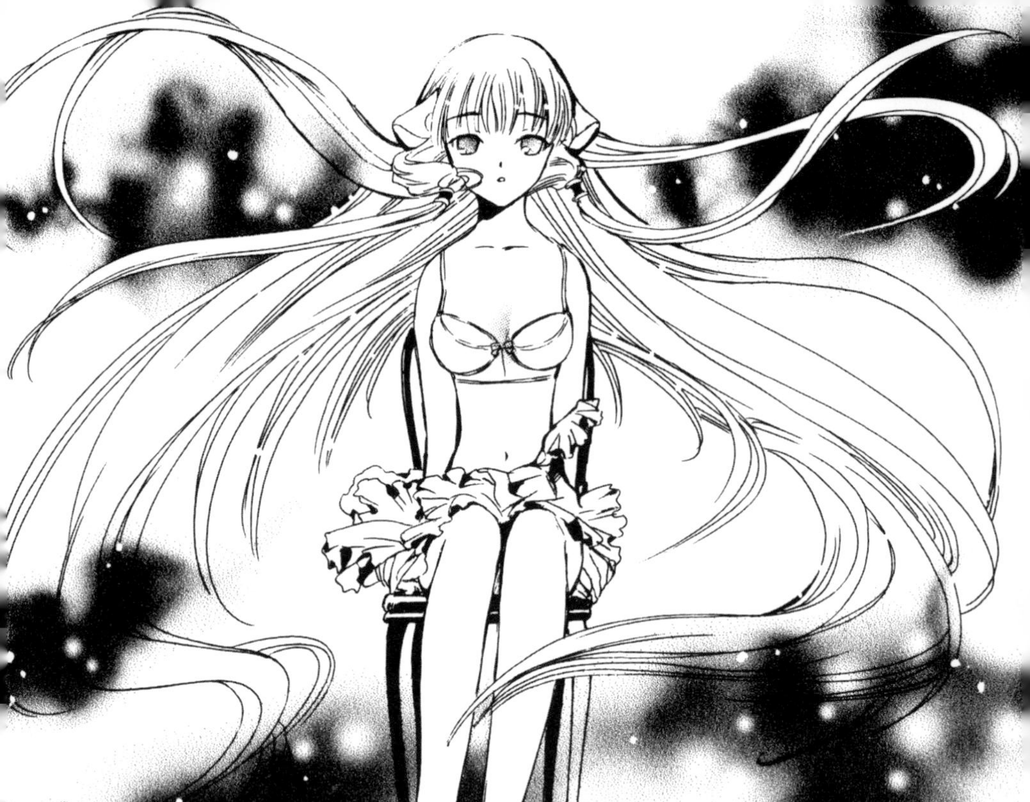

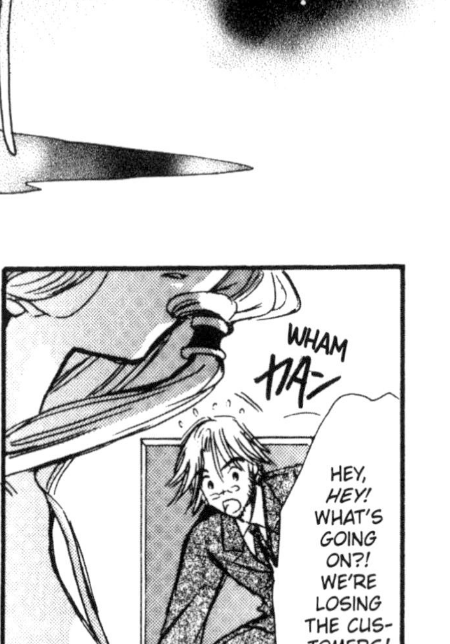
WHAM
HEY, HEY! WHAT'S GOING ON?! WE'RE LOSING THE CUS-TOMERS!

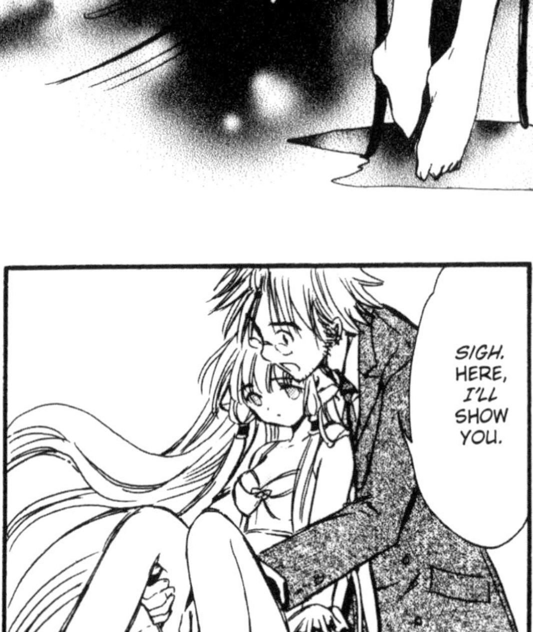
SIGH. HERE, I'LL SHOW YOU.

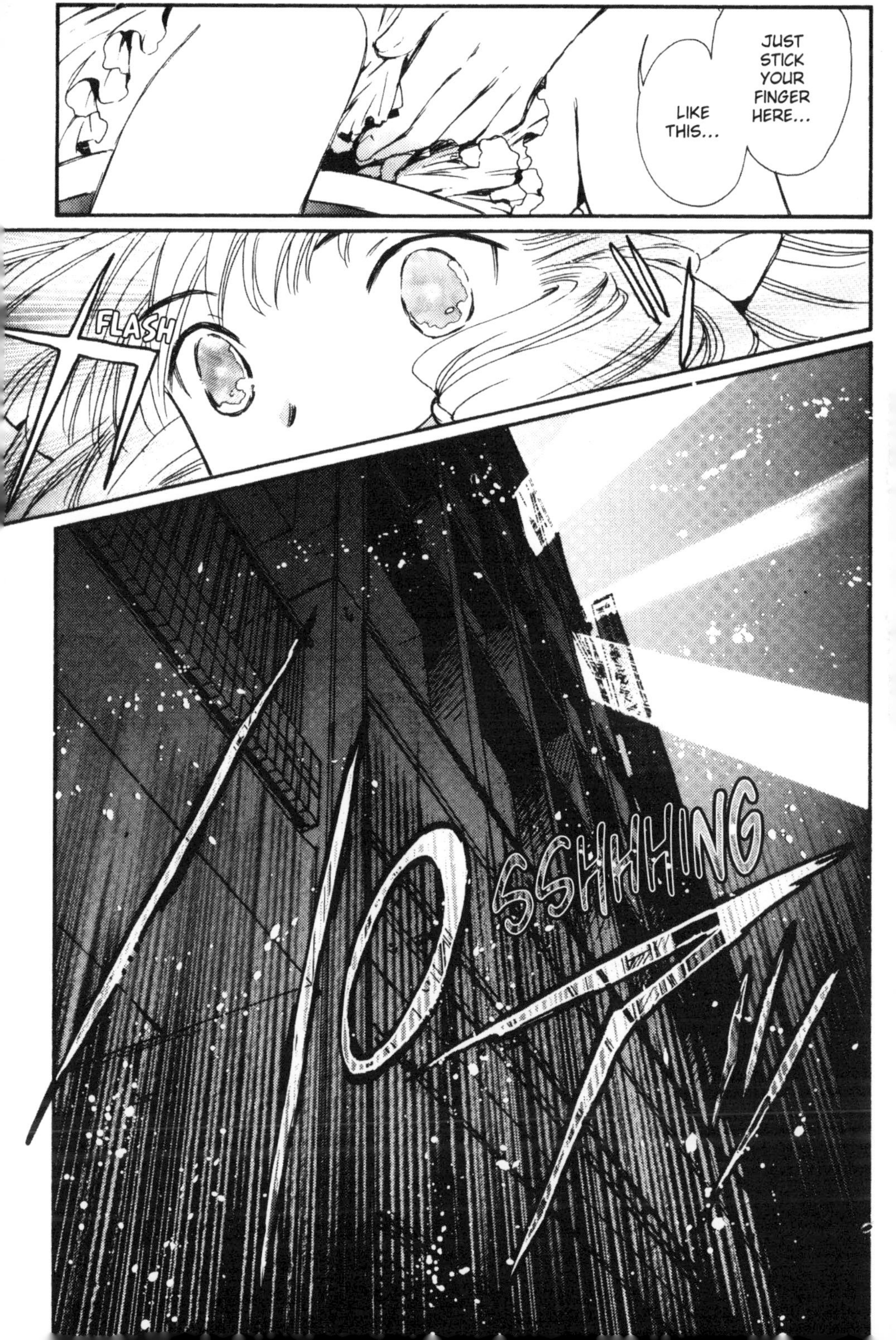
JUST STICK YOUR FINGER HERE...
LIKE THIS...
FLASH
SSHHHING

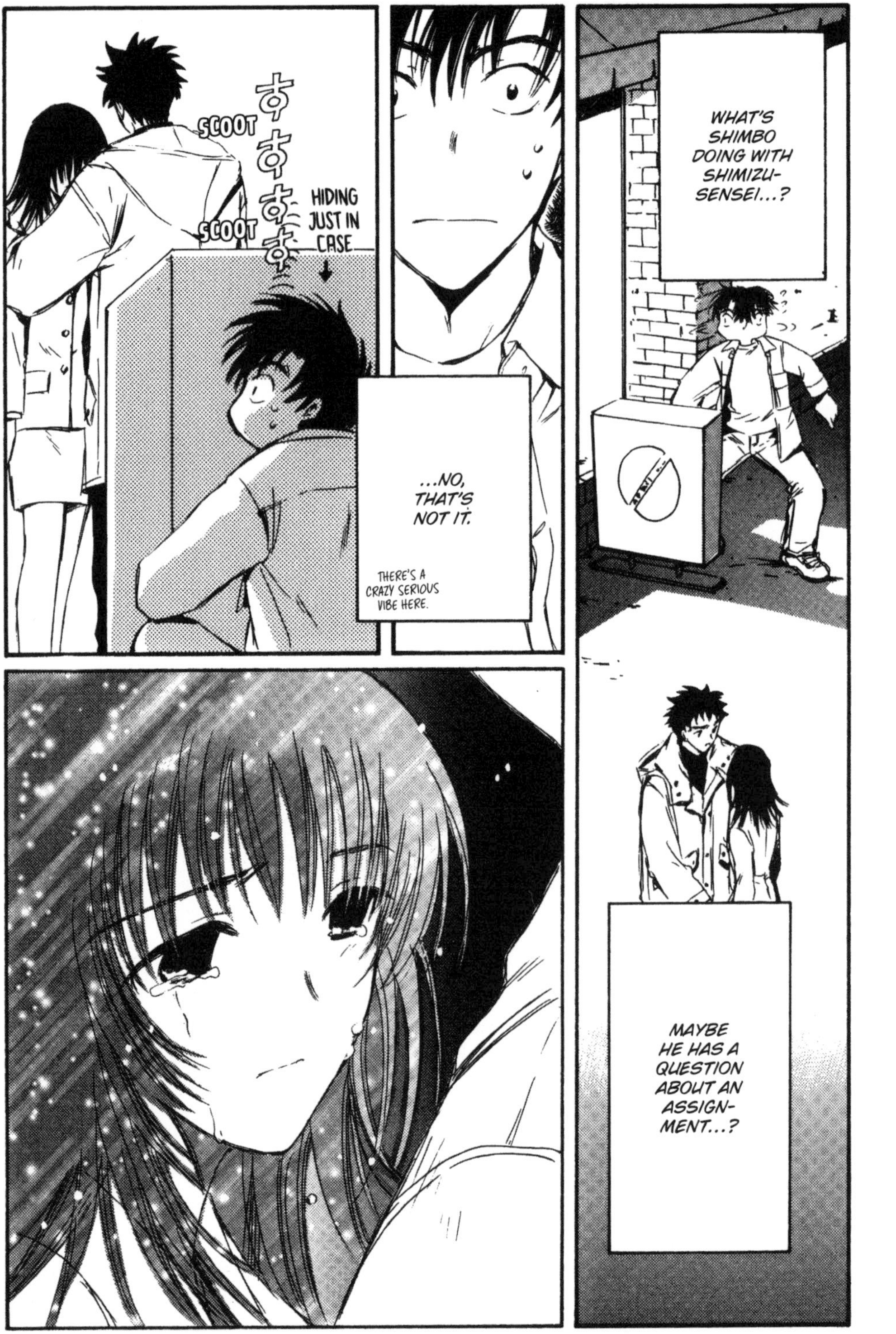
WHAT'S SHIMBO DOING WITH SHIMIZU-SENSEI...?
MAYBE HE HAS A QUESTION ABOUT AN ASSIGNMENT...?
...NO, THAT'S NOT IT.
THERE'S A CRAZY SERIOUS VIBE HERE.
すすすす
SCOOT
SCOOT
HIDING JUST IN CASE

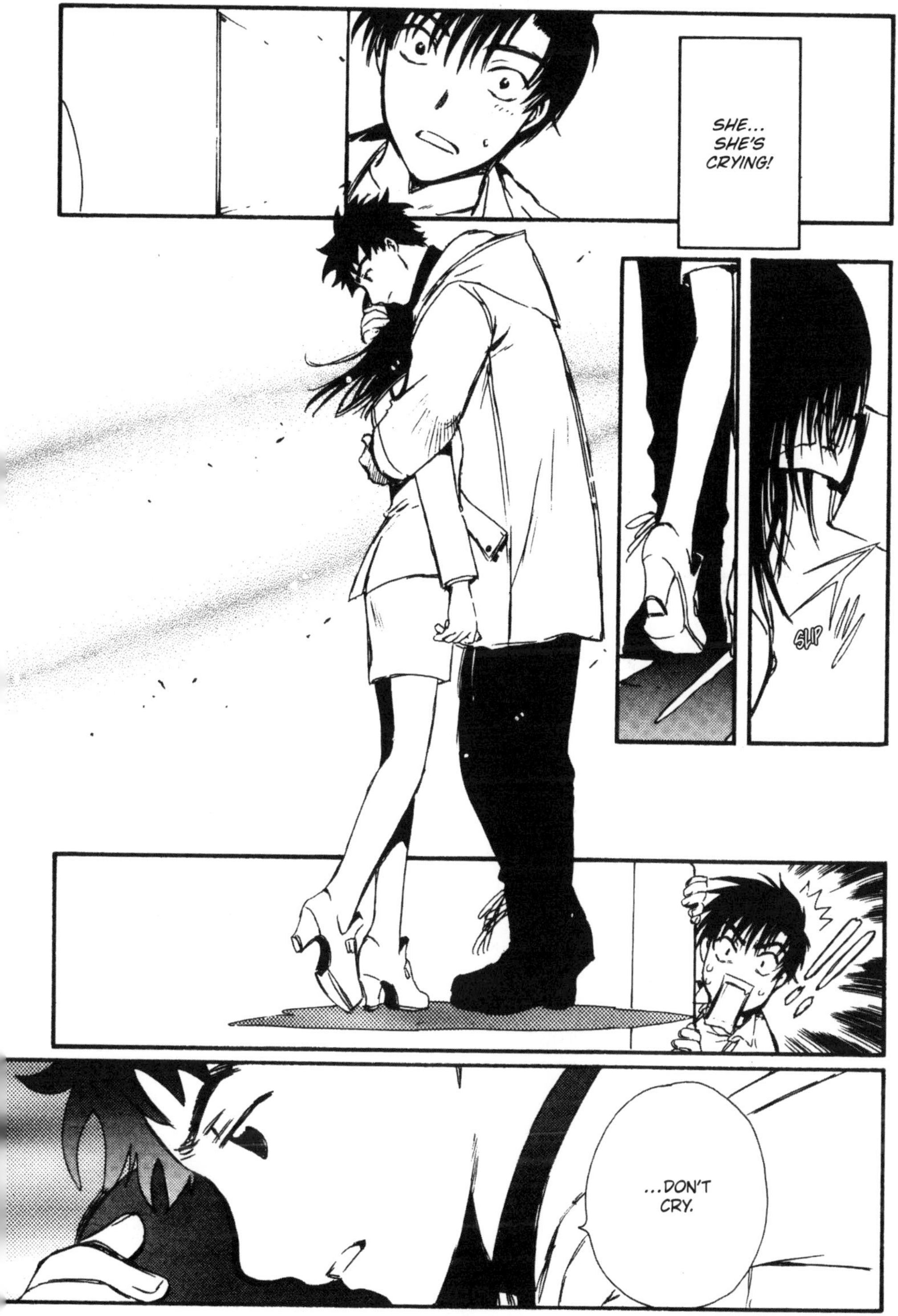
SHE... SHE'S CRYING!
SLIP
...DON'T CRY.

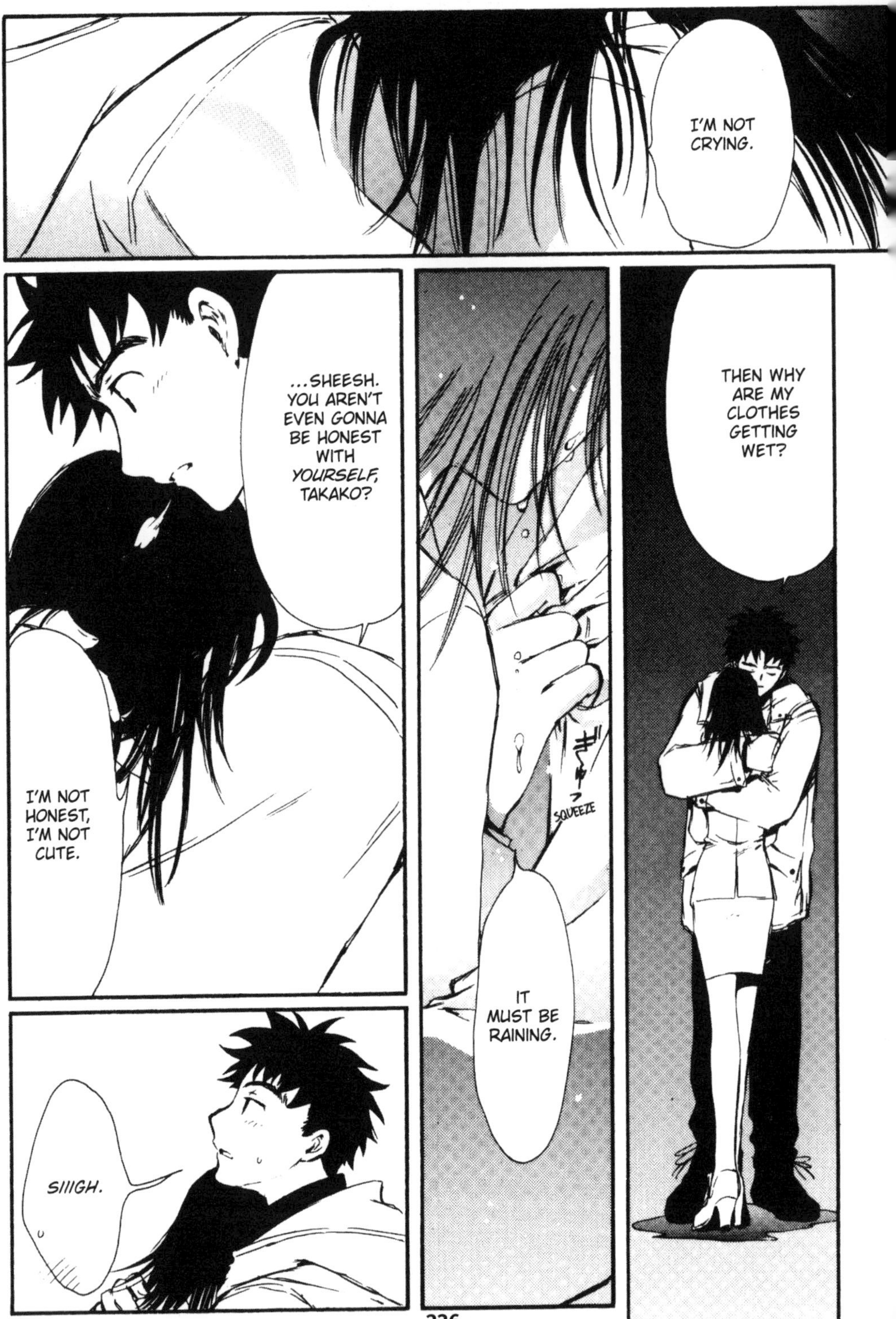
I'M NOT CRYING.
THEN WHY ARE MY CLOTHES GETTING WET?
SQUEEZE
IT MUST BE RAINING.
...SHEESH. YOU AREN'T EVEN GONNA BE HONEST WITH *YOURSELF,* TAKAKO?
I'M NOT HONEST, I'M NOT CUTE.
SIIIGH.

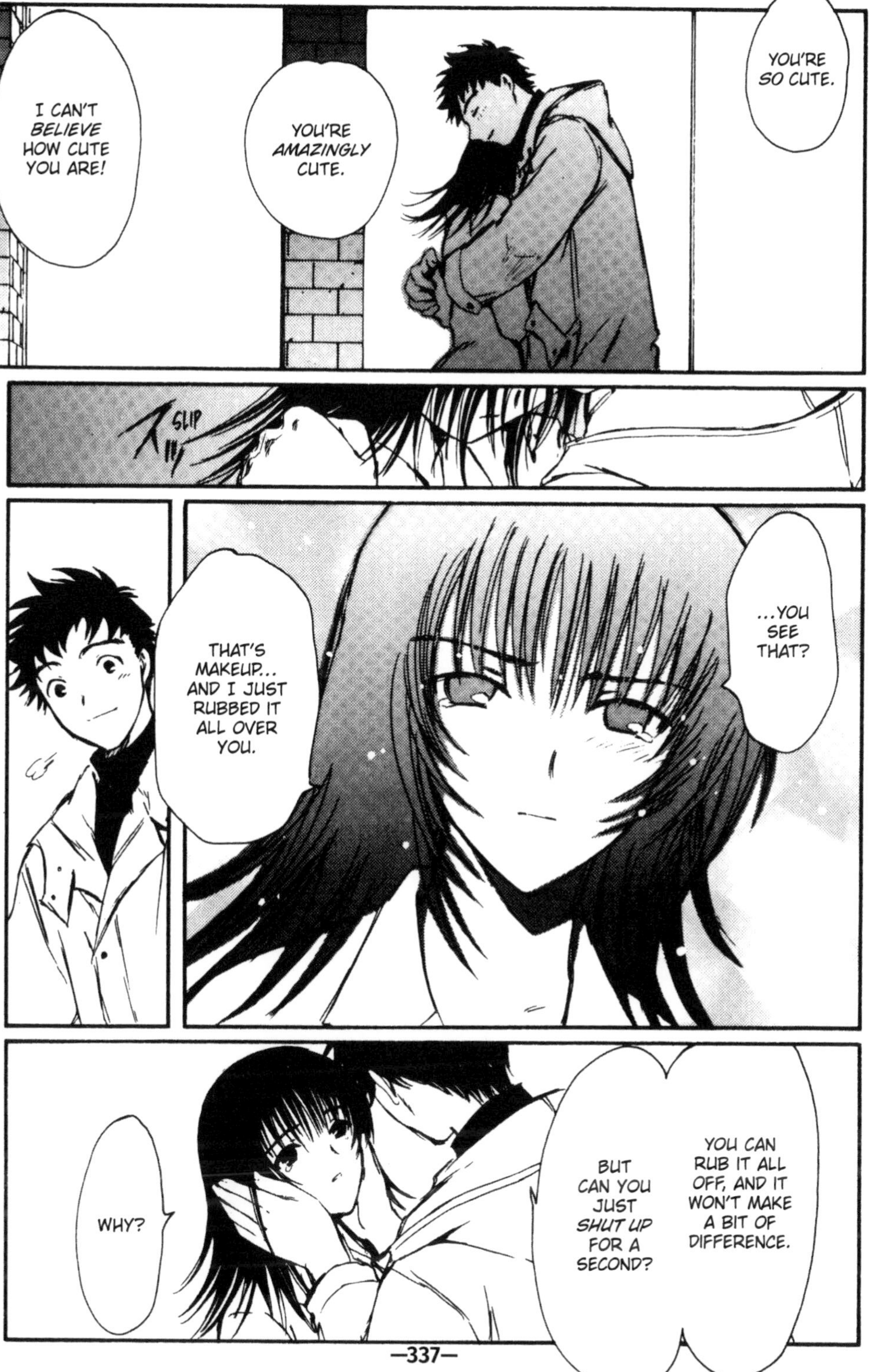
YOU'RE SO CUTE.
YOU'RE AMAZINGLY CUTE.
I CAN'T BELIEVE HOW CUTE YOU ARE!
SLIP
...YOU SEE THAT?
THAT'S MAKEUP... AND I JUST RUBBED IT ALL OVER YOU.
YOU CAN RUB IT ALL OFF, AND IT WON'T MAKE A BIT OF DIFFERENCE.
BUT CAN YOU JUST SHUT UP FOR A SECOND?
WHY?

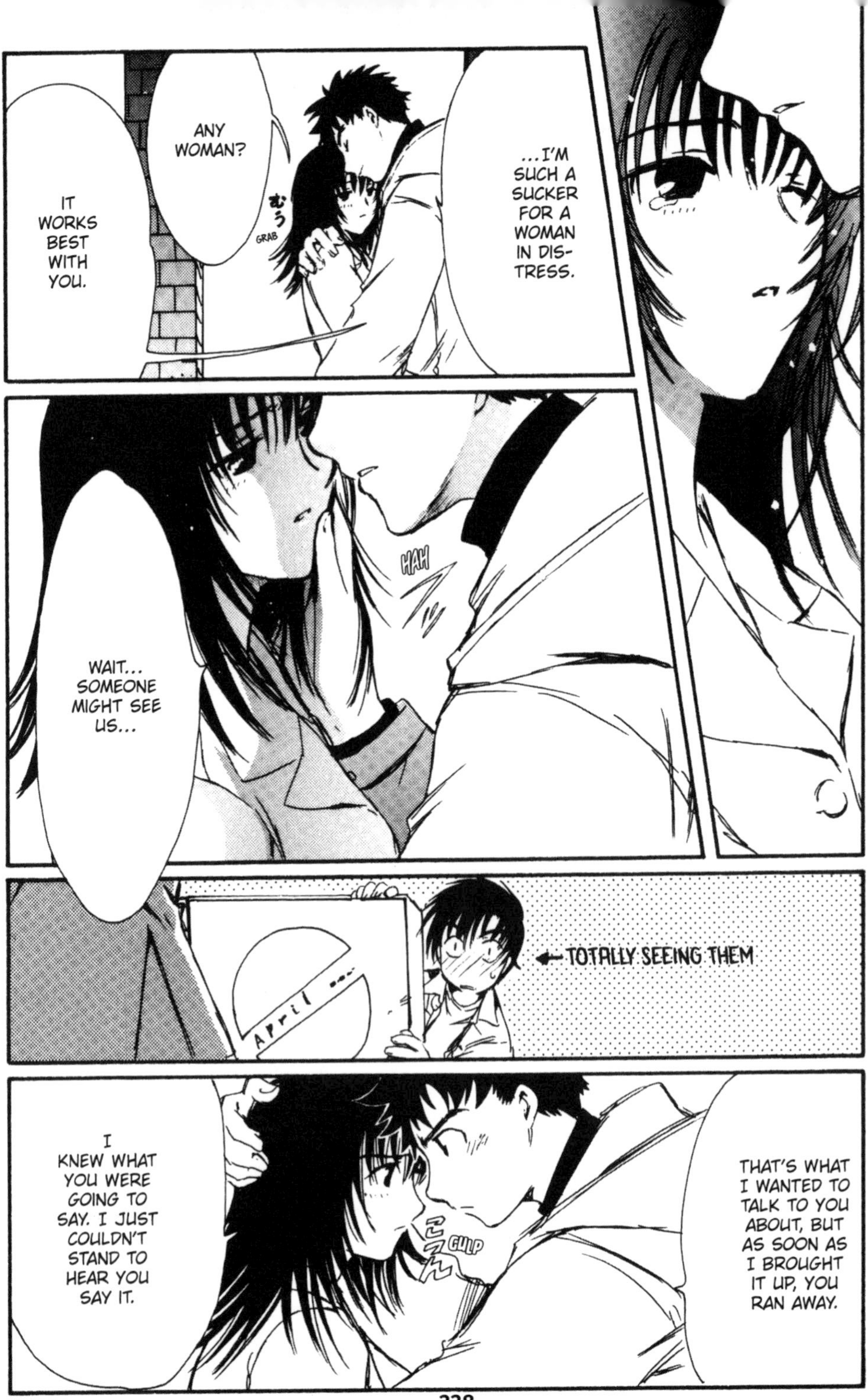
...I'M SUCH A SUCKER FOR A WOMAN IN DIS-TRESS.
ANY WOMAN?
GRAB
IT WORKS BEST WITH YOU.
HAH
WAIT... SOMEONE MIGHT SEE US...
TOTALLY SEEING THEM
April
THAT'S WHAT I WANTED TO TALK TO YOU ABOUT, BUT AS SOON AS I BROUGHT IT UP, YOU RAN AWAY.
GULP
I KNEW WHAT YOU WERE GOING TO SAY. I JUST COULDN'T STAND TO HEAR YOU SAY IT.

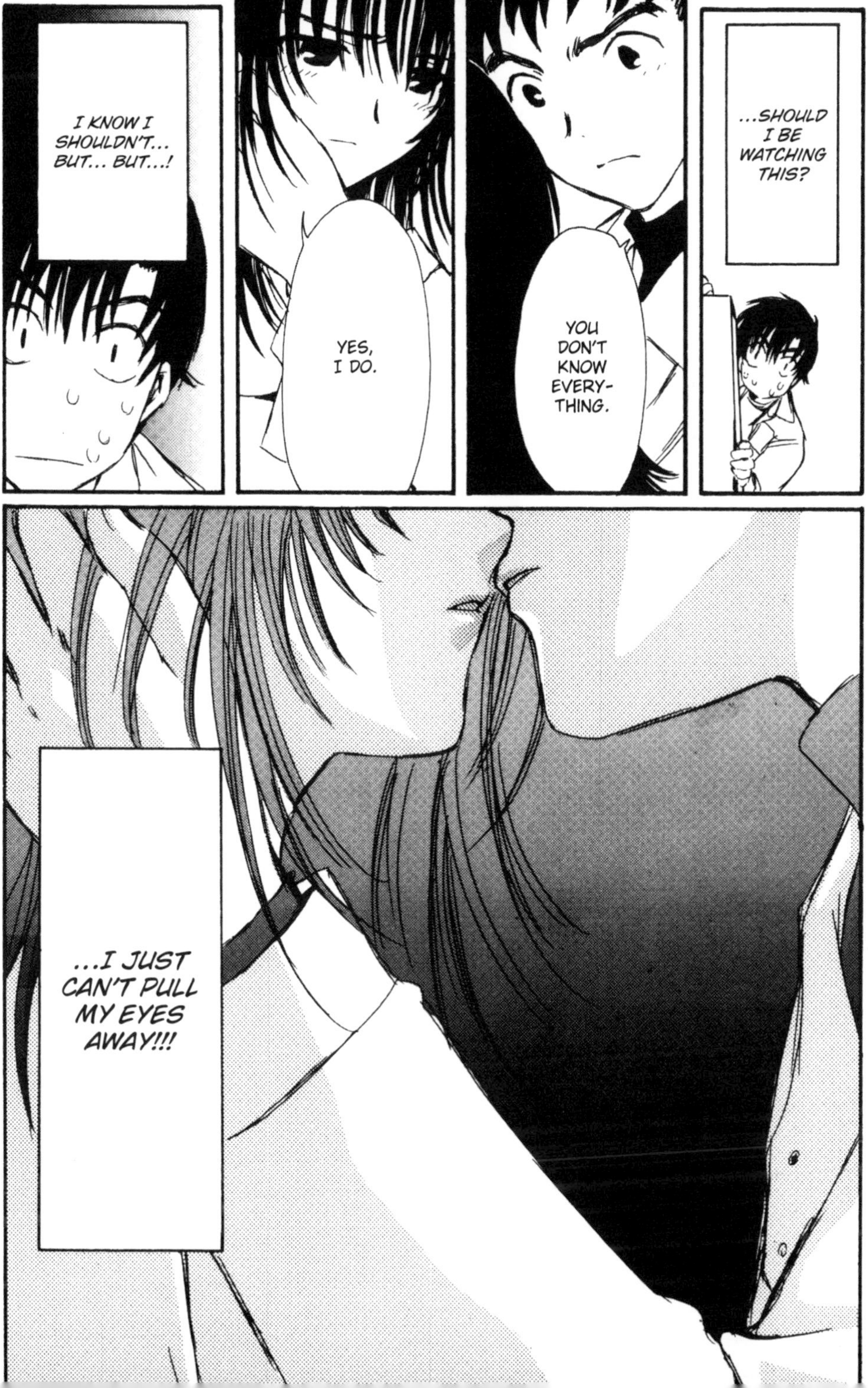
...SHOULD I BE WATCHING THIS?
YOU DON'T KNOW EVERY-THING.
YES, I DO.
I KNOW I SHOULDN'T... BUT... BUT...!
...I JUST CAN'T PULL MY EYES AWAY!!!

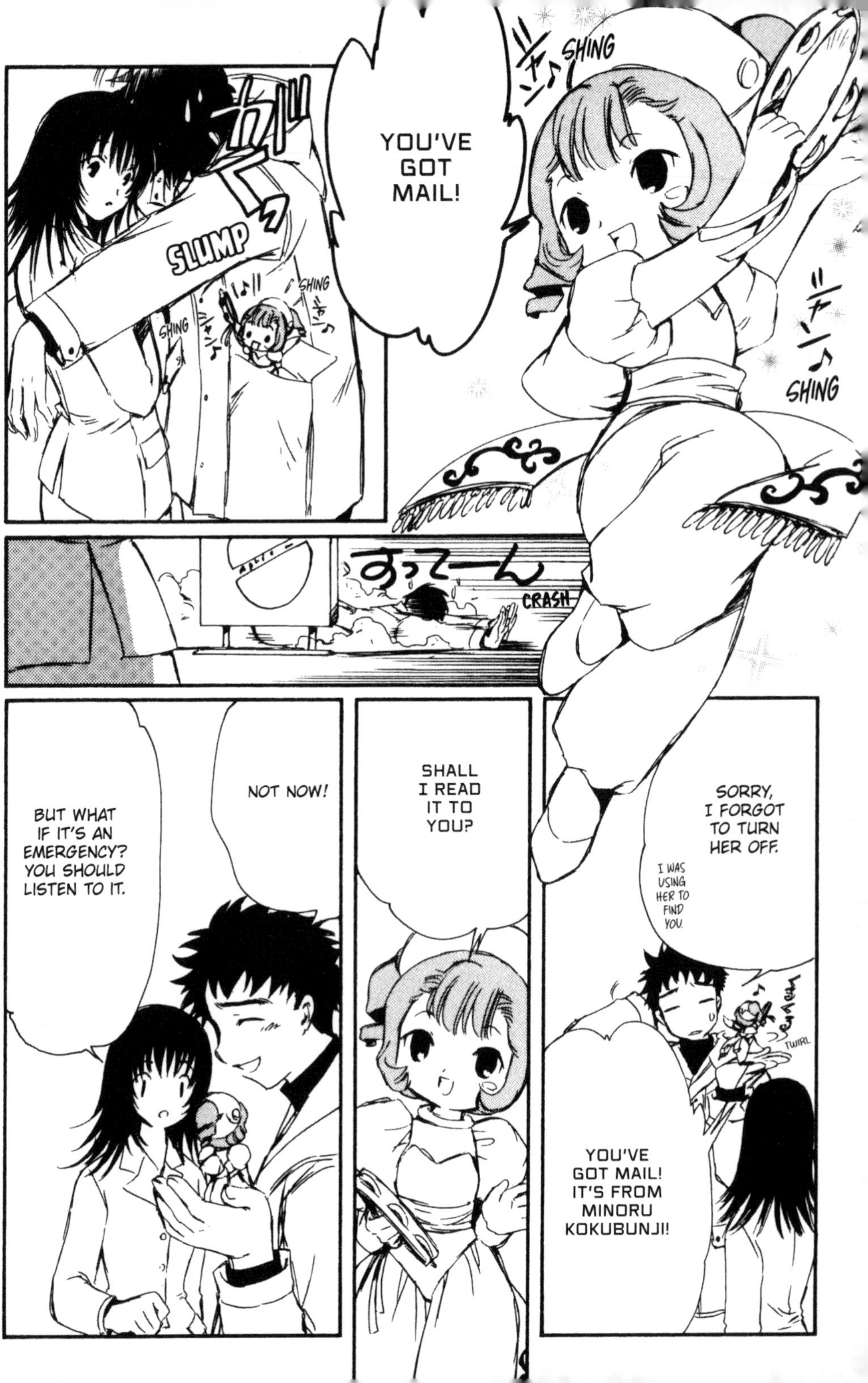
SHING
YOU'VE GOT MAIL!
SHING
SLUMP
SHING
SHING
すってーん
CRASH
SORRY, I FORGOT TO TURN HER OFF.
I WAS USING HER TO FIND YOU.
TWIRL
YOU'VE GOT MAIL! IT'S FROM MINORU KOKUBUNJI!
SHALL I READ IT TO YOU?
NOT NOW!
BUT WHAT IF IT'S AN EMERGENCY? YOU SHOULD LISTEN TO IT.

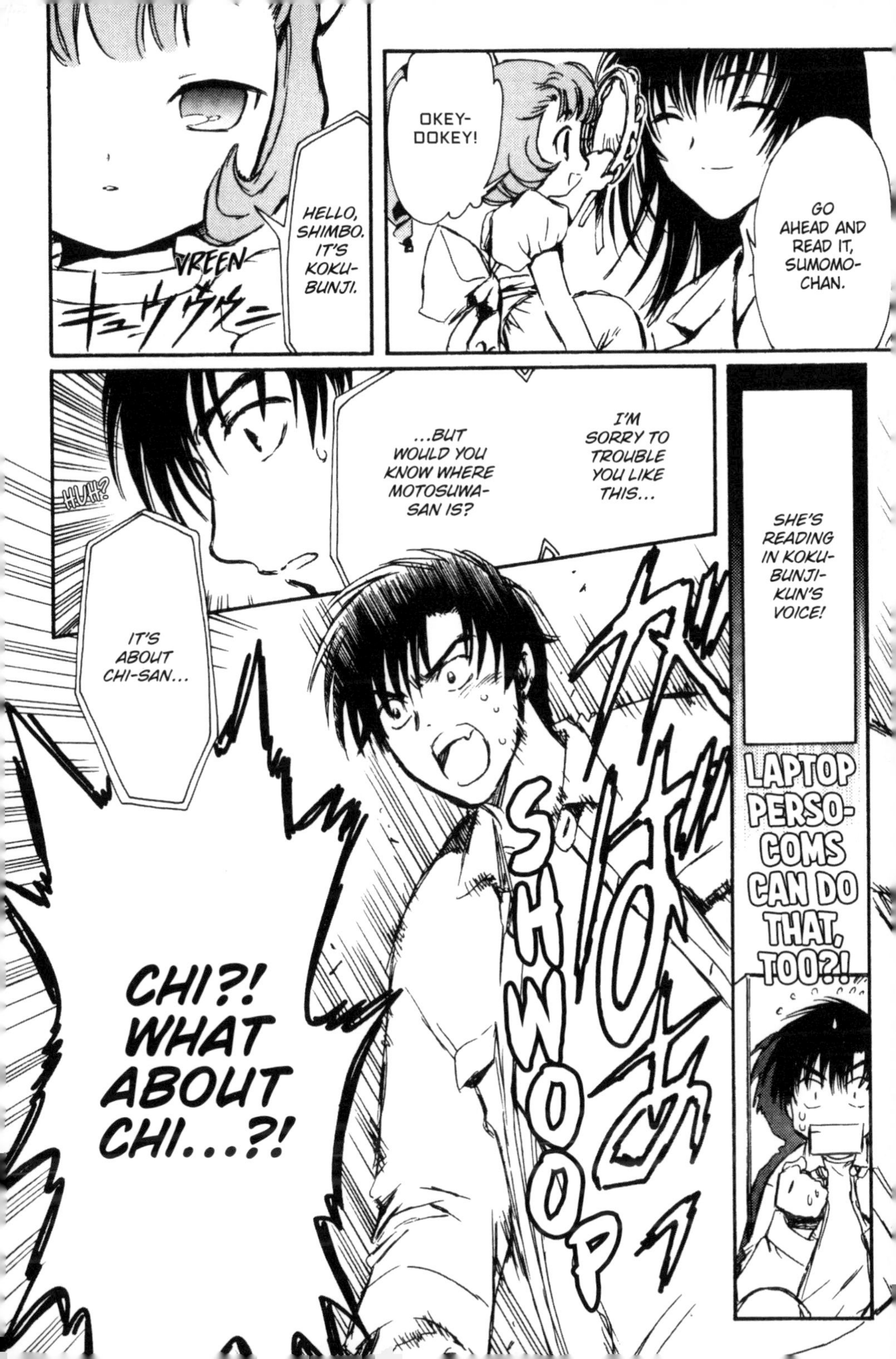
GO AHEAD AND READ IT, SUMOMO-CHAN.
OKEY-DOKEY!
HELLO, SHIMBO. IT'S KOKU-BUNJI.
VREEN
SHE'S READING IN KOKU-BUNJI-KUN'S VOICE!
LAPTOP PERSO-COMS CAN DO THAT, TOO?!
I'M SORRY TO TROUBLE YOU LIKE THIS...
...BUT WOULD YOU KNOW WHERE MOTOSUWA-SAN IS?
HUH?
IT'S ABOUT CHI-SAN...
SHWOOOP
CHI?! WHAT ABOUT CHI...?!

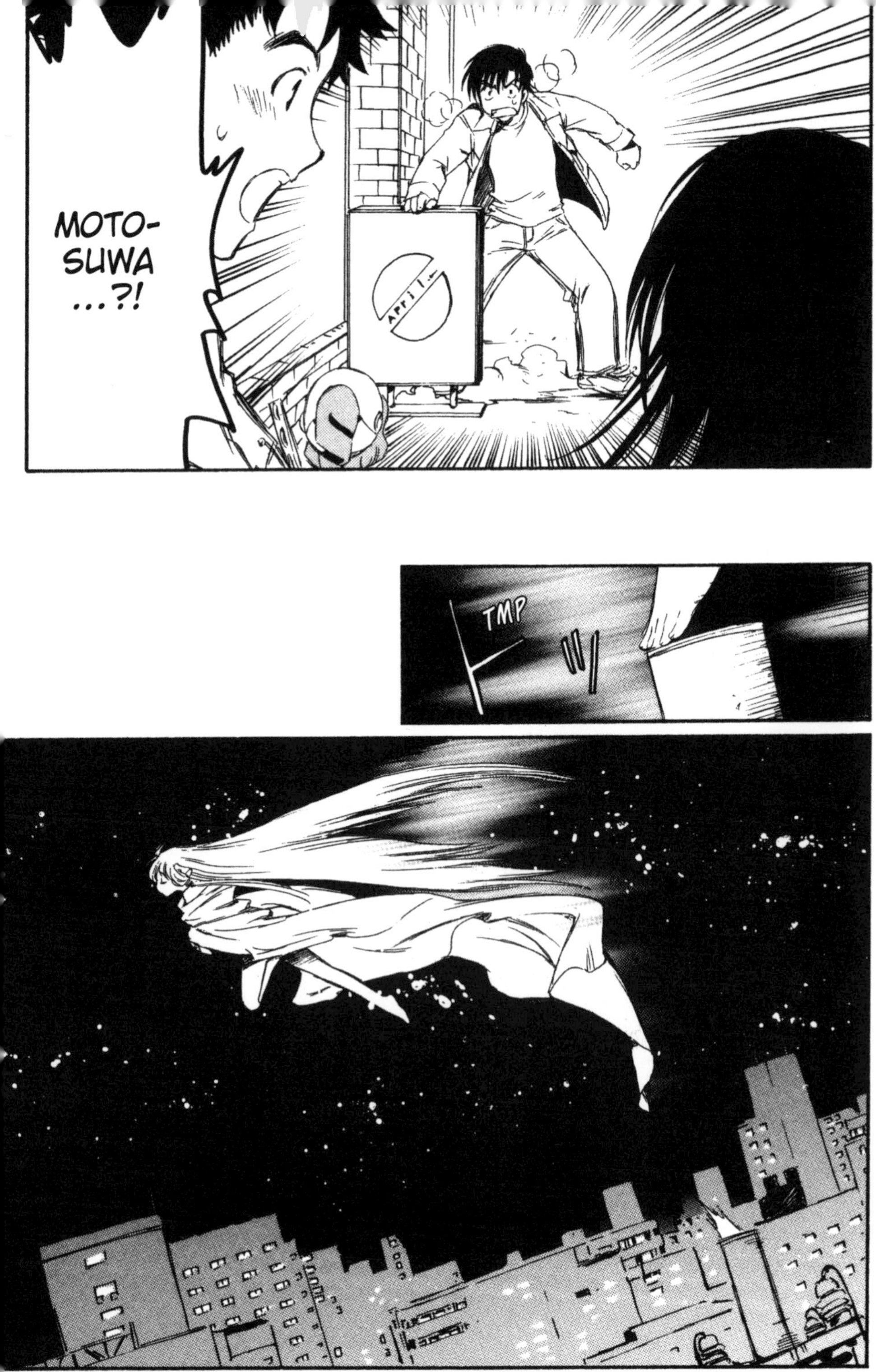
MOTO-
SUWA
...?!
April 1
TMP

<chapter.23> end

⟨chapter.24⟩

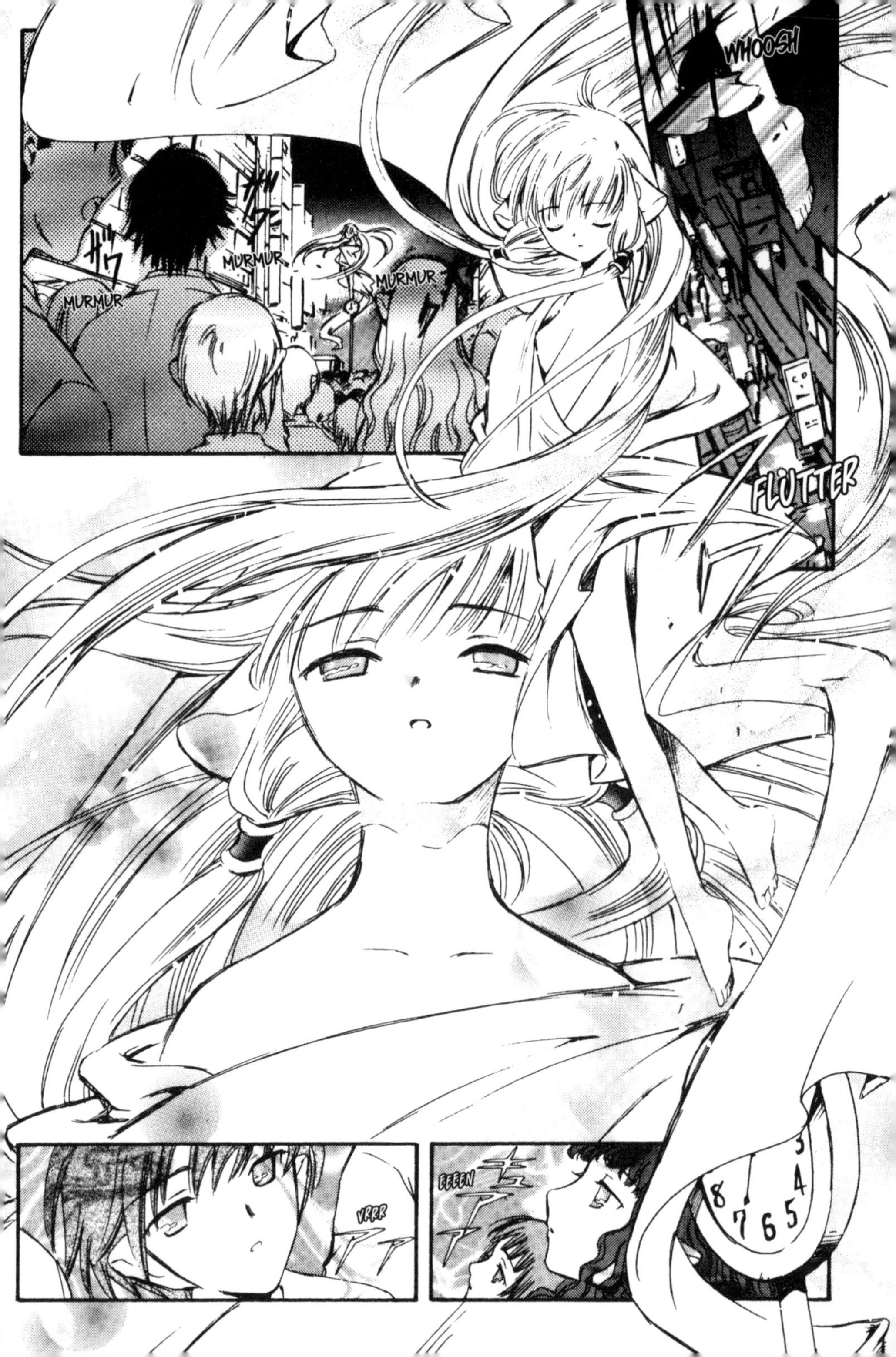
WHOOSH
FLUTTER
MURMUR
MURMUR
MURMUR
EEEEN
VRRR

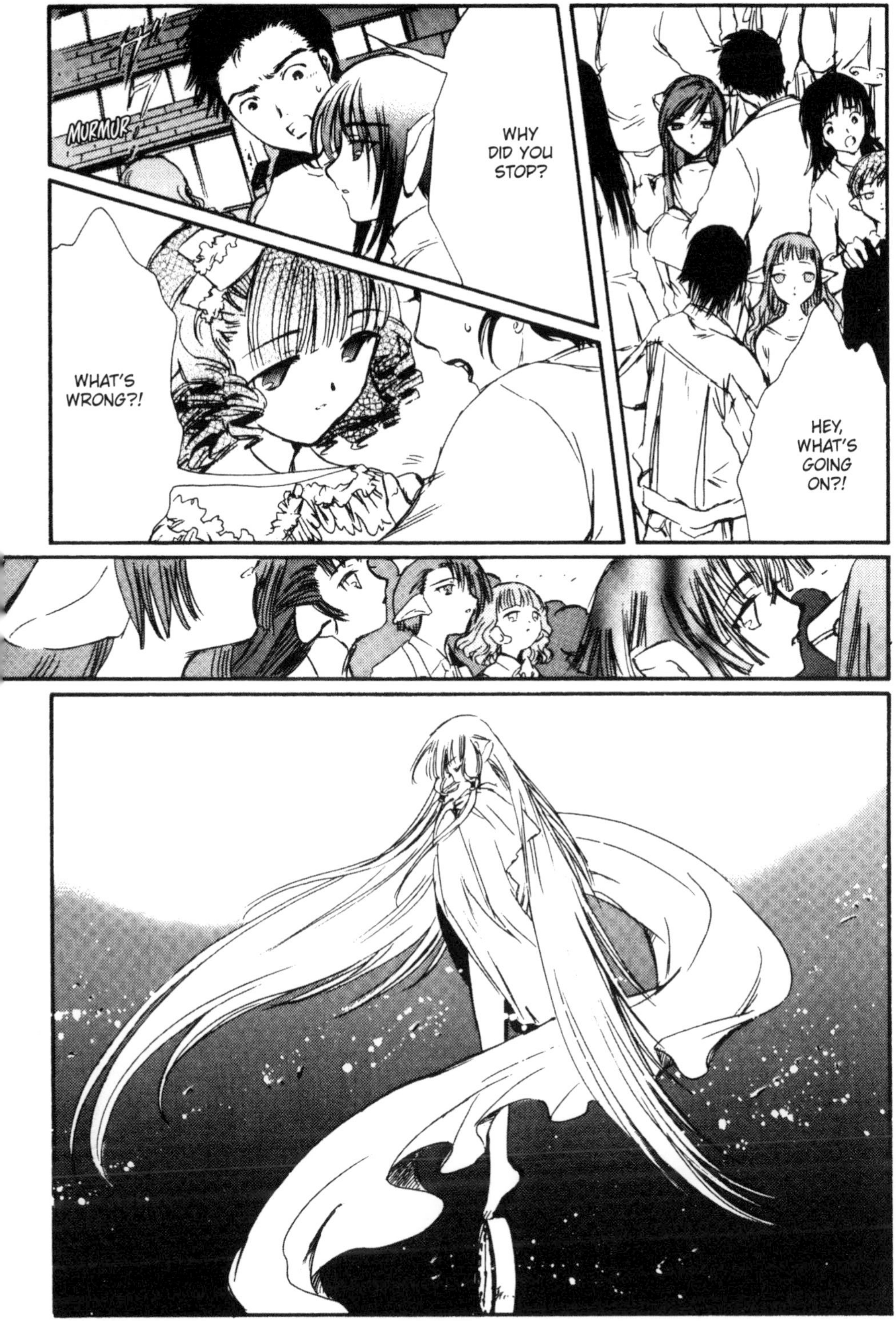
HEY, WHAT'S GOING ON?!
WHY DID YOU STOP?
MURMUR
WHAT'S WRONG?!

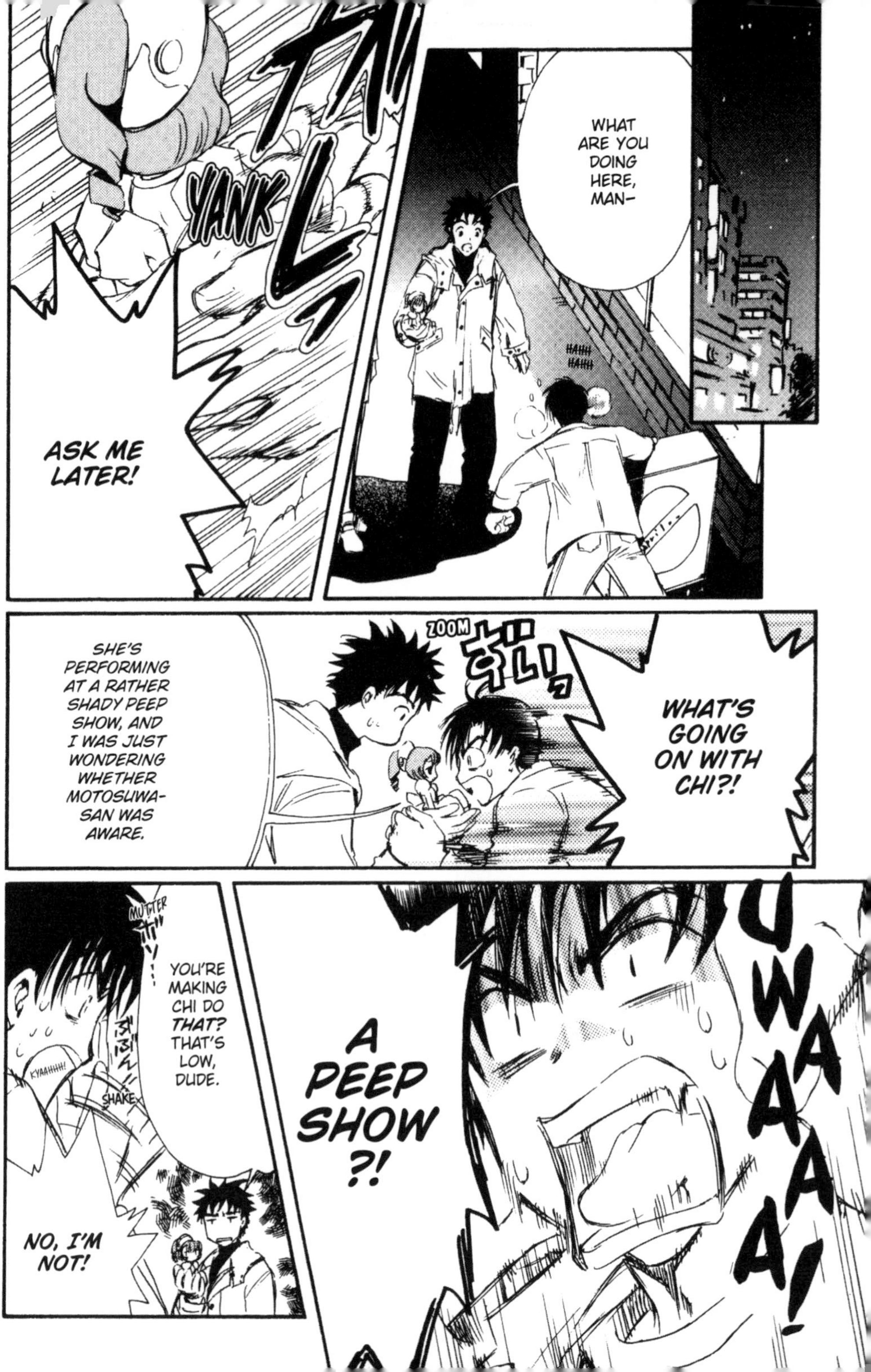
WHAT ARE YOU DOING HERE, MAN–
HAHH HAHH
YANK
ASK ME LATER!
ZOOM
WHAT'S GOING ON WITH CHI?!
SHE'S PERFORMING AT A RATHER SHADY PEEP SHOW, AND I WAS JUST WONDERING WHETHER MOTOSUWA-SAN WAS AWARE.
UWAAAAAA!
A PEEP SHOW?!
MUTTER
YOU'RE MAKING CHI DO *THAT*? THAT'S LOW, DUDE.
KYAAHHH!
SHAKE
NO, I'M NOT!

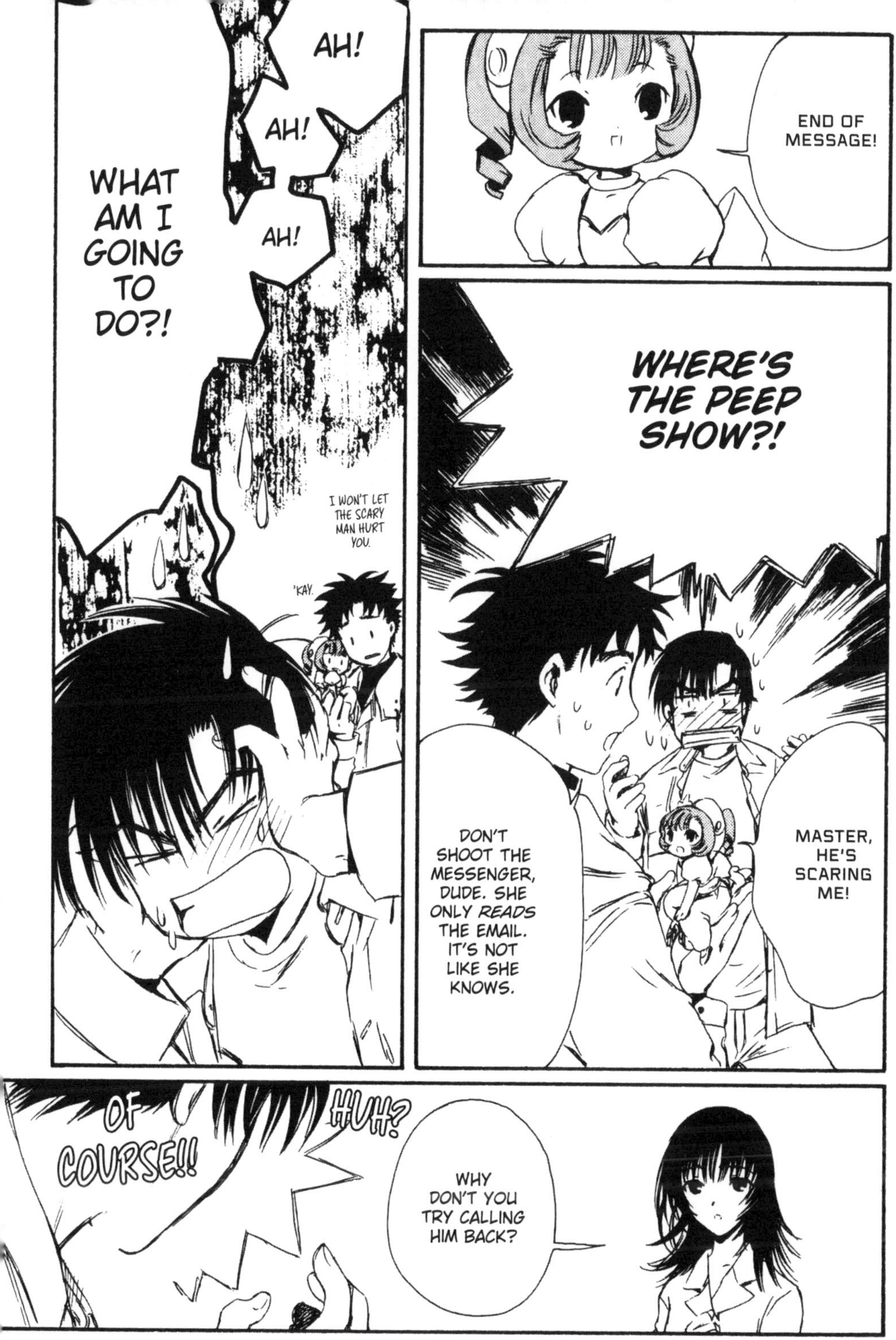
END OF MESSAGE!
WHERE'S THE PEEP SHOW?!
MASTER, HE'S SCARING ME!
DON'T SHOOT THE MESSENGER, DUDE. SHE ONLY *READS* THE EMAIL. IT'S NOT LIKE SHE KNOWS.
AH!
AH!
AH!
WHAT AM I GOING TO DO?!
I WON'T LET THE SCARY MAN HURT YOU.
'KAY.
WHY DON'T YOU TRY CALLING HIM BACK?
HUH?
OF COURSE!!

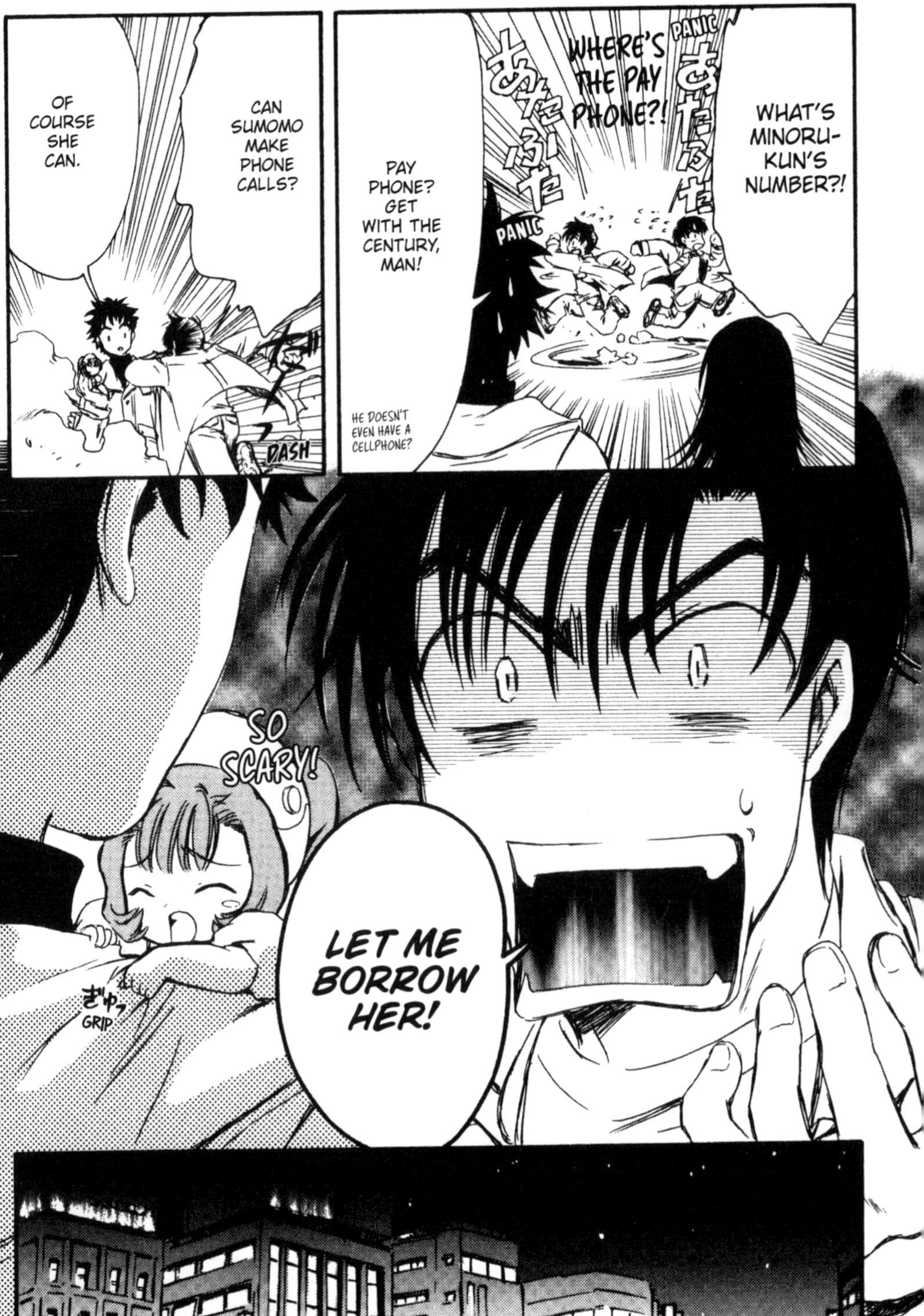
WHAT'S MINORU-KUN'S NUMBER?!
PANIC
あたふた
WHERE'S THE PAY PHONE?!
あたふた
PANIC
PAY PHONE? GET WITH THE CENTURY, MAN!
HE DOESN'T EVEN HAVE A CELLPHONE?
CAN SUMOMO MAKE PHONE CALLS?
OF COURSE SHE CAN.
DASH
LET ME BORROW HER!
SO SCARY!
ぎゅっ
GRIP

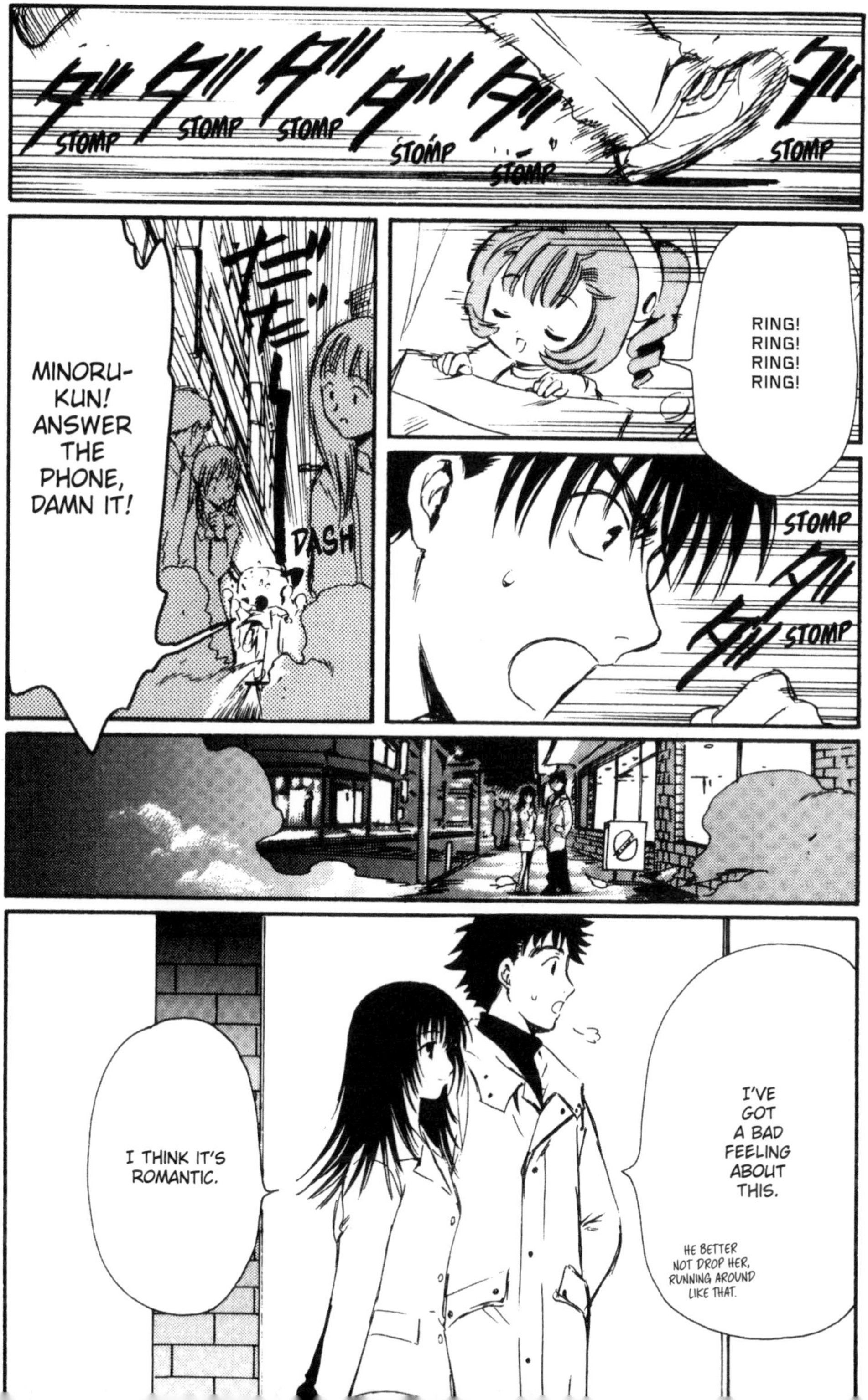
STOMP
STOMP
STOMP
STOMP
STOMP
STOMP
RING! RING! RING! RING!
STOMP
STOMP
MINORU-KUN! ANSWER THE PHONE, DAMN IT!
DASH
I'VE GOT A BAD FEELING ABOUT THIS.
HE BETTER NOT DROP HER, RUNNING AROUND LIKE THAT.
I THINK IT'S ROMANTIC.

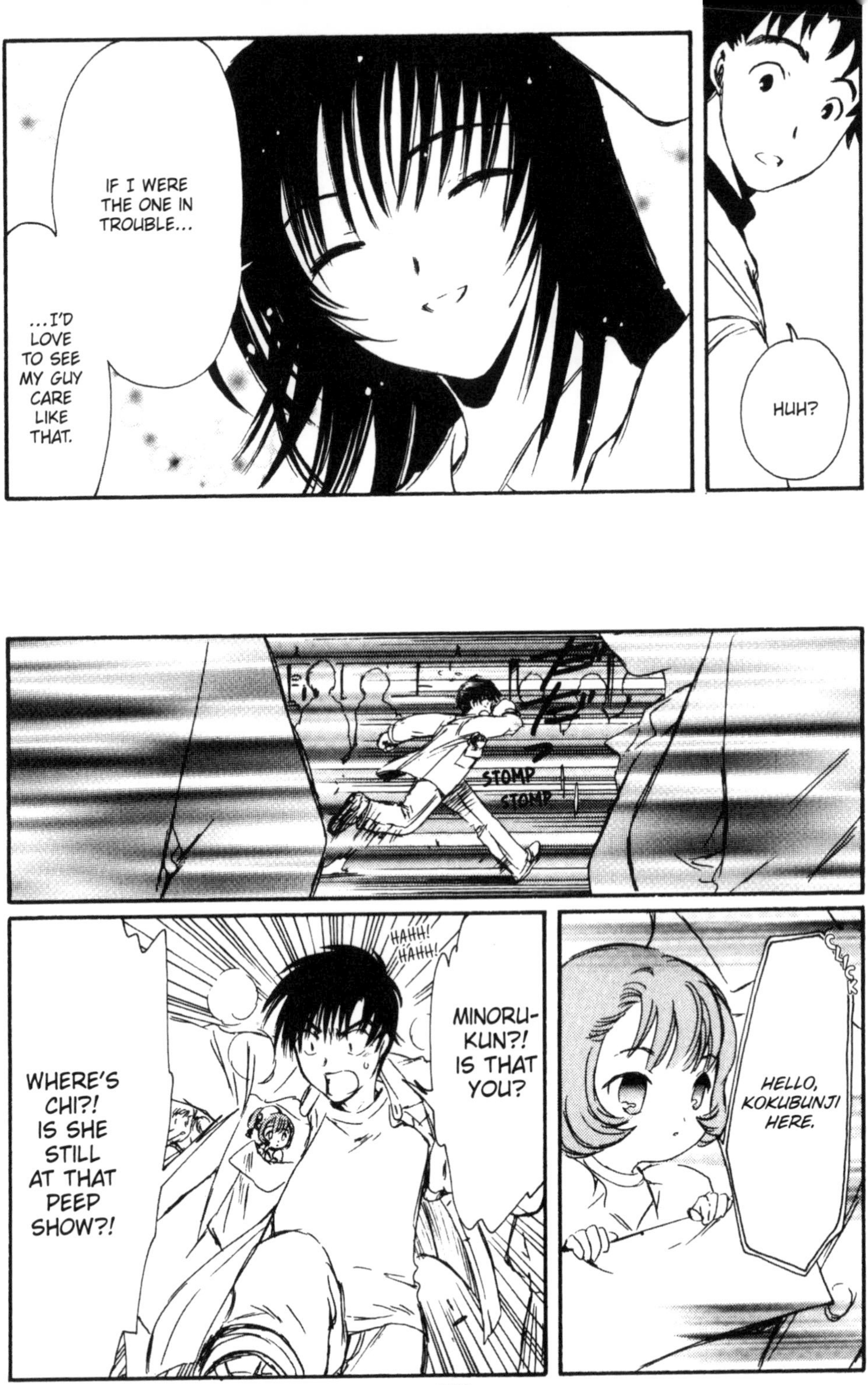
HUH?
IF I WERE THE ONE IN TROUBLE...
...I'D LOVE TO SEE MY GUY CARE LIKE THAT.
STOMP
STOMP
CLICK
HELLO, KOKUBUNJI HERE.
HAHH! HAHH!
MINORU-KUN?! IS THAT YOU?
WHERE'S CHI?! IS SHE STILL AT THAT PEEP SHOW?!

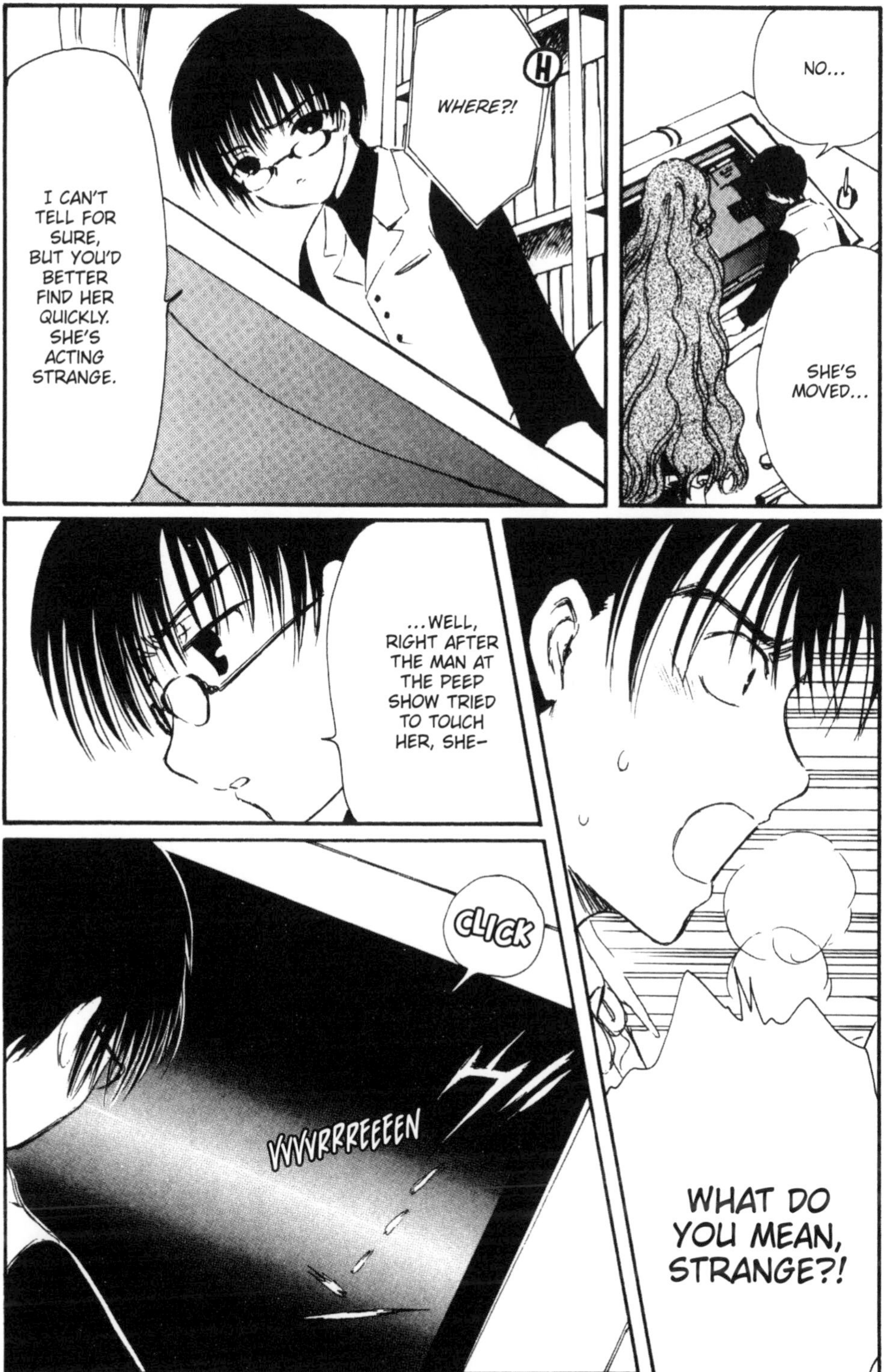
NO...
SHE'S MOVED...
H
WHERE?!
I CAN'T TELL FOR SURE, BUT YOU'D BETTER FIND HER QUICKLY. SHE'S ACTING STRANGE.
WHAT DO YOU MEAN, STRANGE?!
...WELL, RIGHT AFTER THE MAN AT THE PEEP SHOW TRIED TO TOUCH HER, SHE-
CLICK
VVVVRRREEEEN

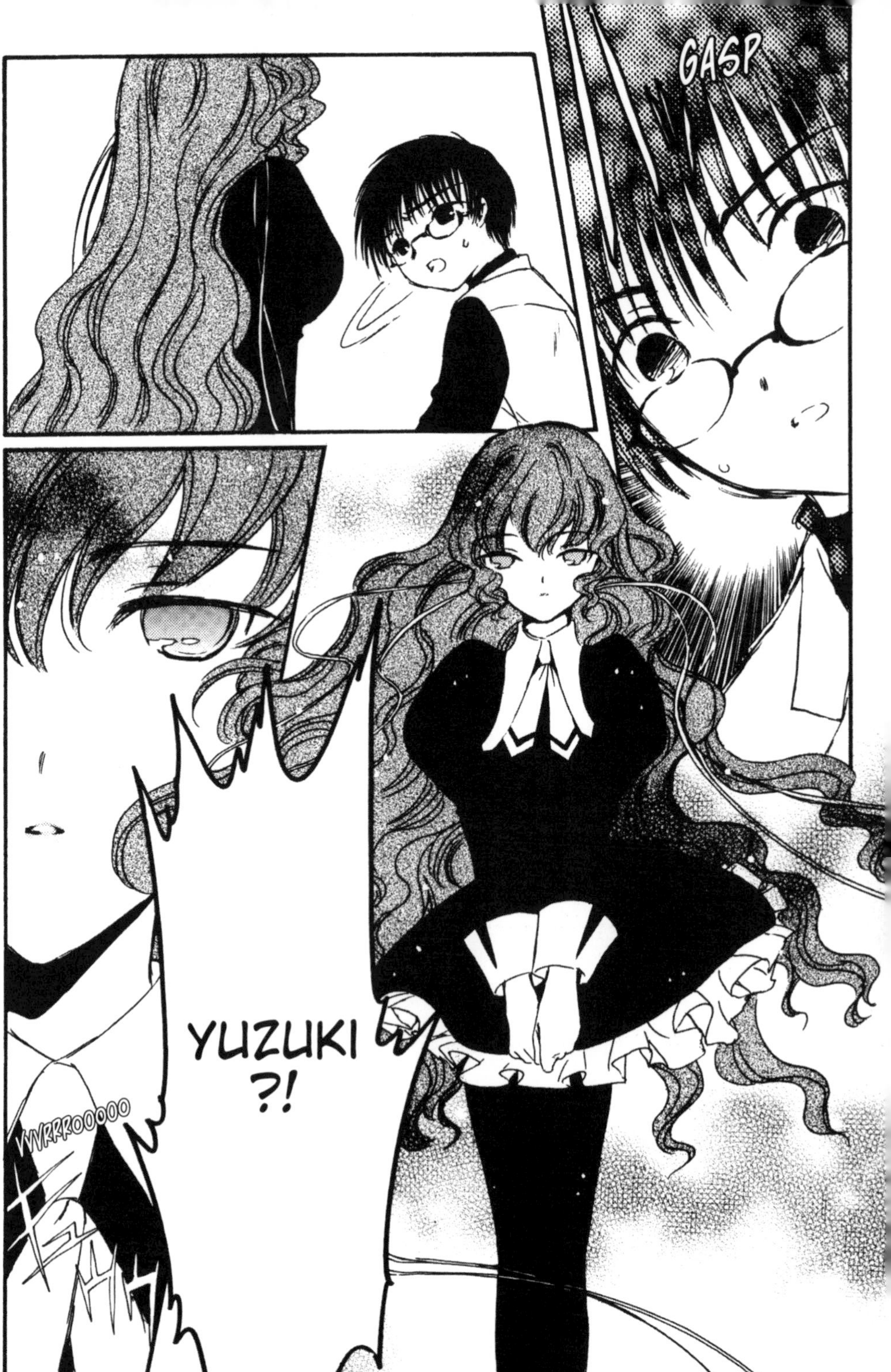
GASP
YUZUKI ?!
VVVRRROOOOO

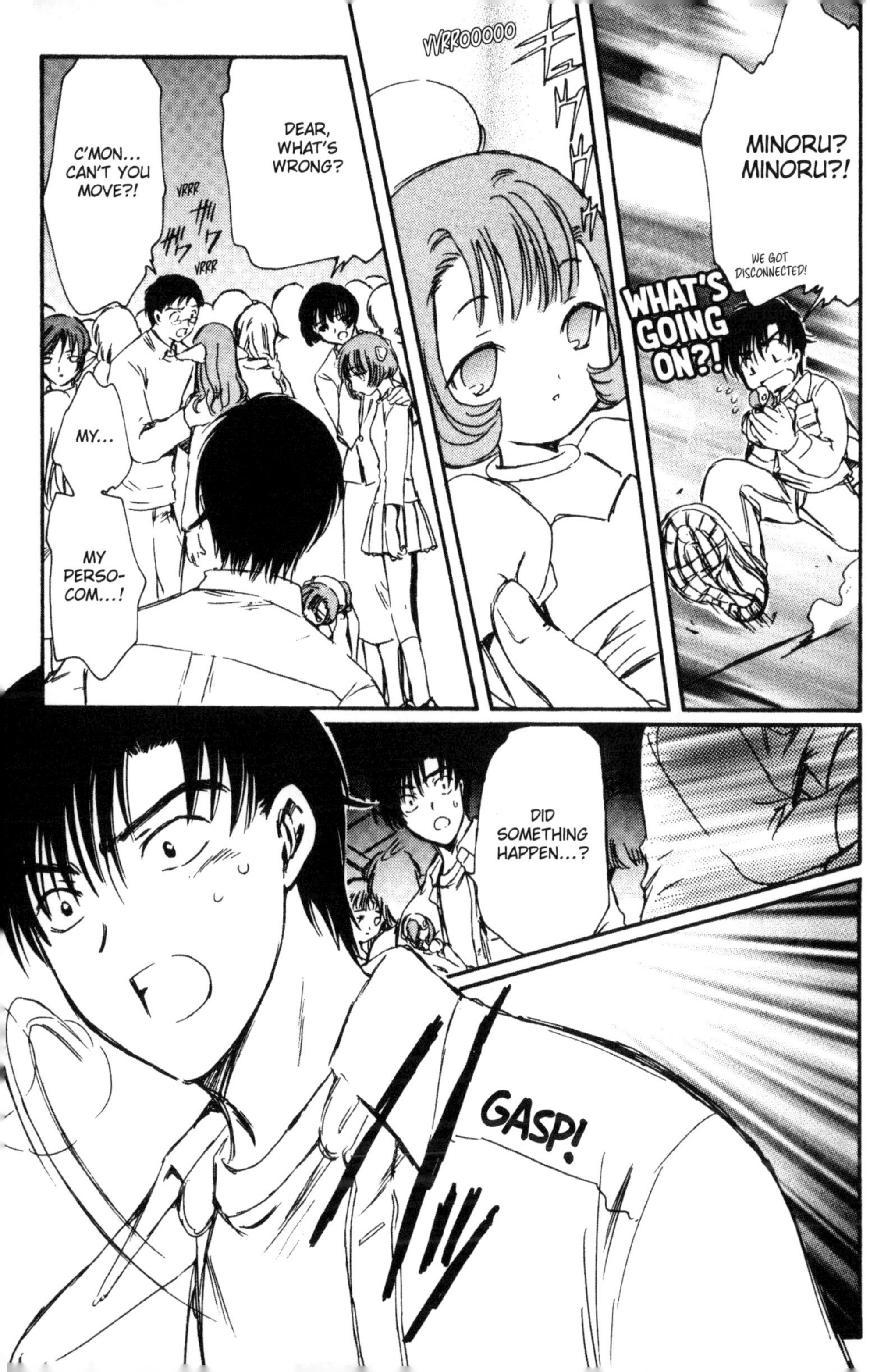
MINORU? MINORU?!
WHAT'S GOING ON?!
WE GOT DISCONNECTED!
VVRROOOOO
DEAR, WHAT'S WRONG?
C'MON... CAN'T YOU MOVE?!
VRRR
VRRR
MY...
MY PERSO-COM...!
DID SOMETHING HAPPEN...?
GASP!

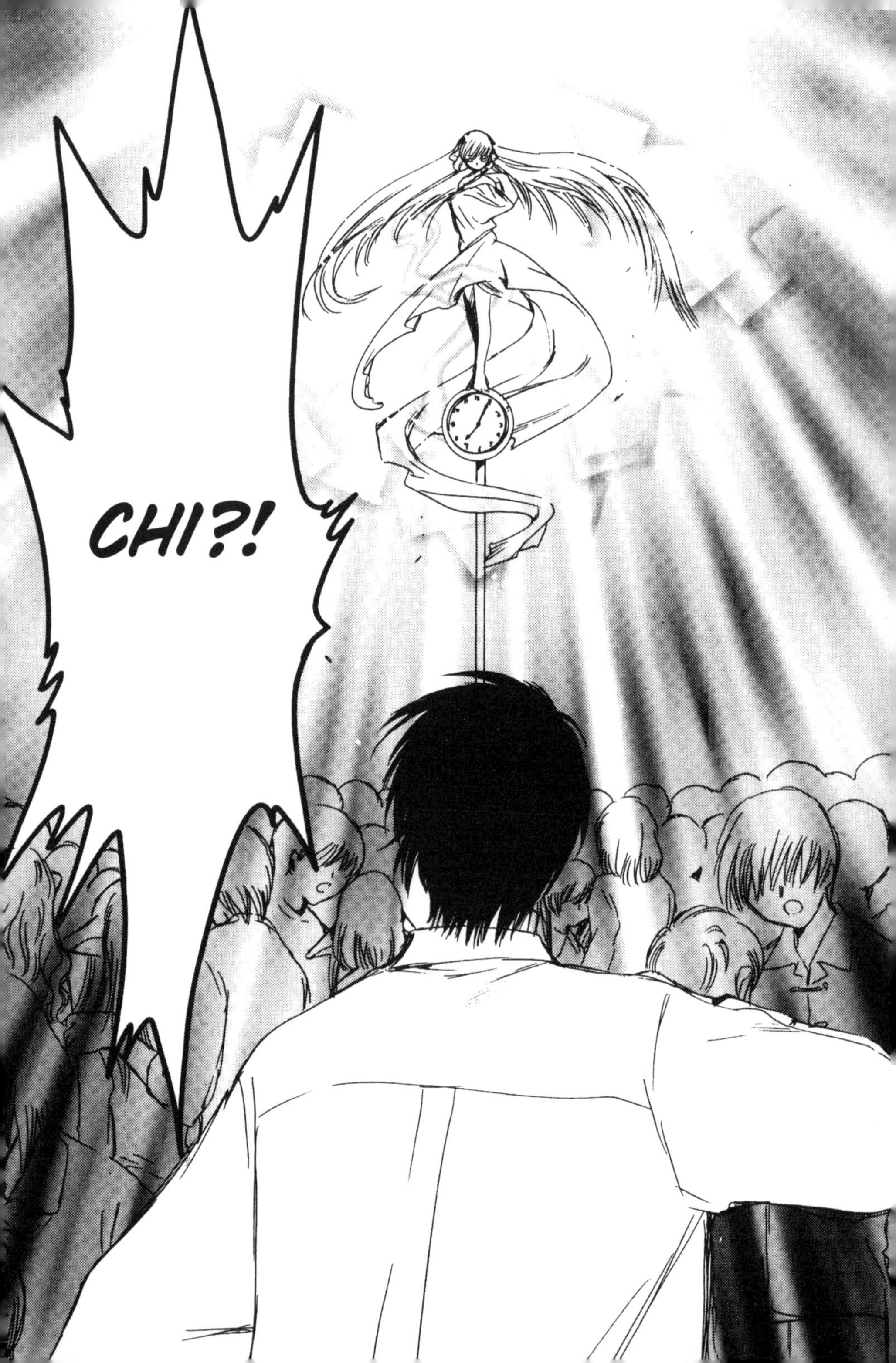
CHI?!

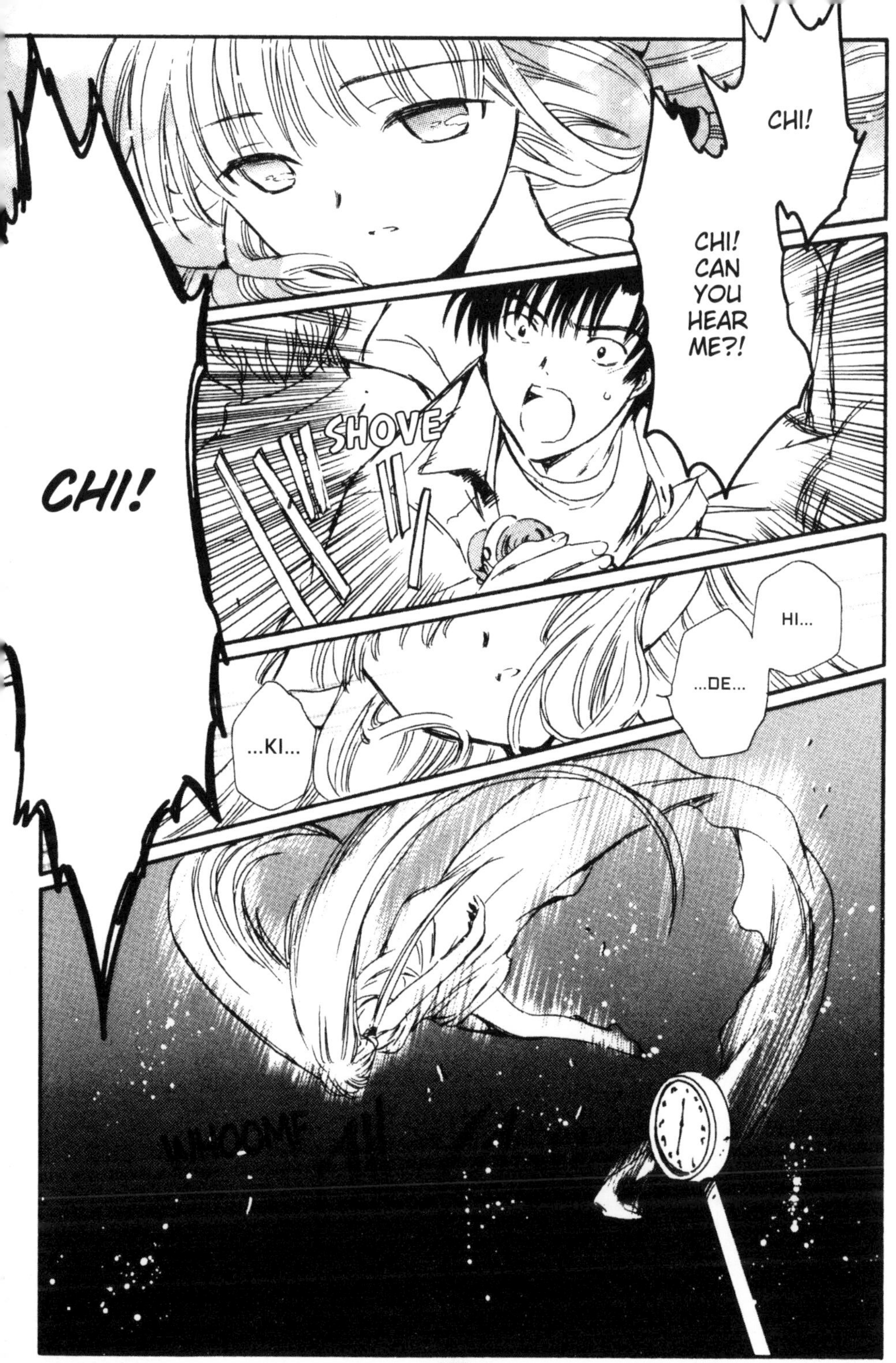
CHI!
CHI! CAN YOU HEAR ME?!
SHOVE
CHI!
HI...
...DE...
...KI...
WHOOMF

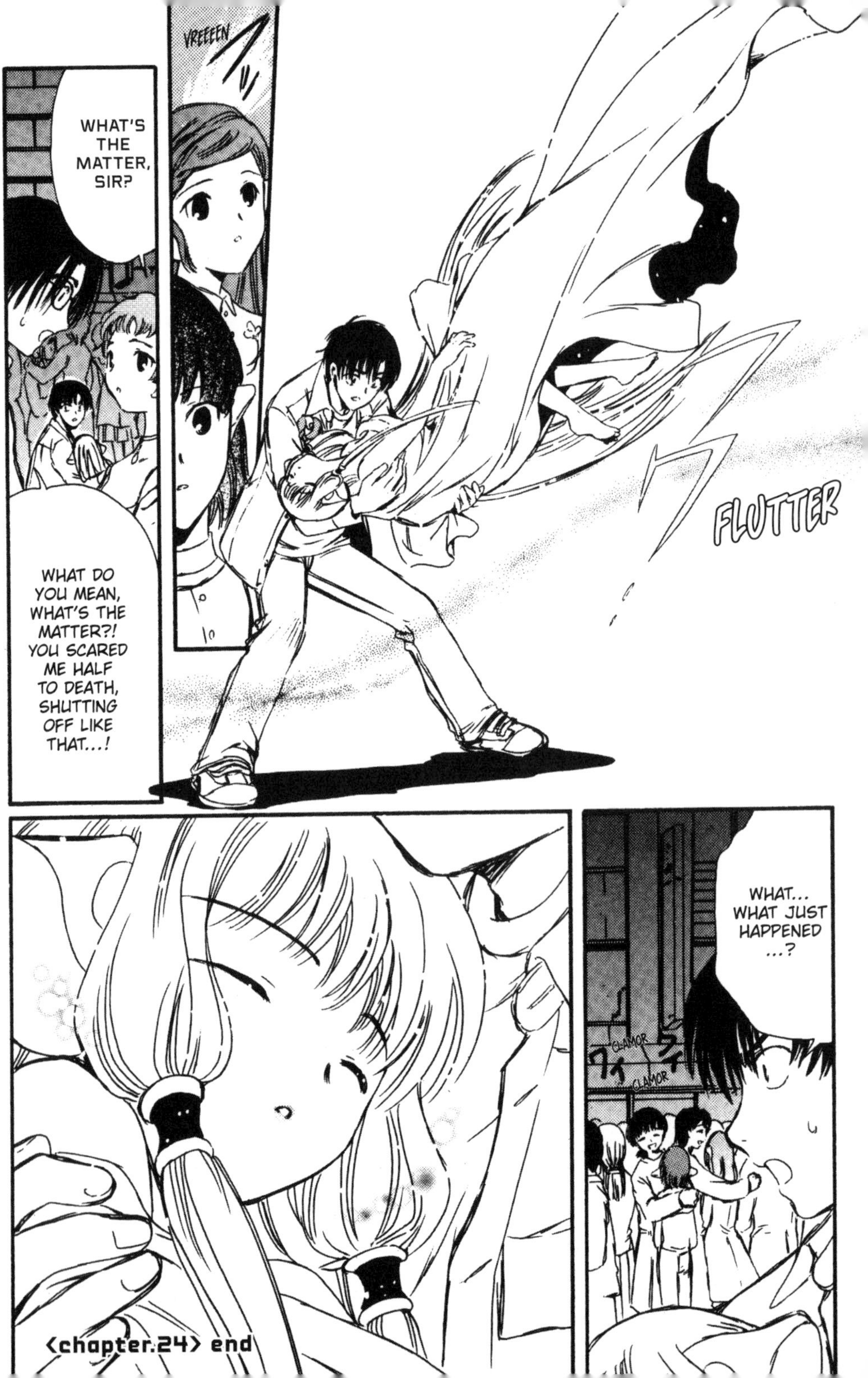
FLUTTER
VREEEEN
WHAT'S THE MATTER, SIR?
WHAT DO YOU MEAN, WHAT'S THE MATTER?! YOU SCARED ME HALF TO DEATH, SHUTTING OFF LIKE THAT...!
WHAT... WHAT JUST HAPPENED ...?
CLAMOR
CLAMOR
<chapter.24> end

Chobits

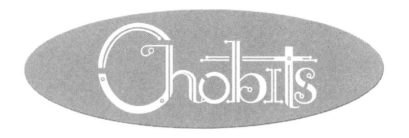

Translation Notes

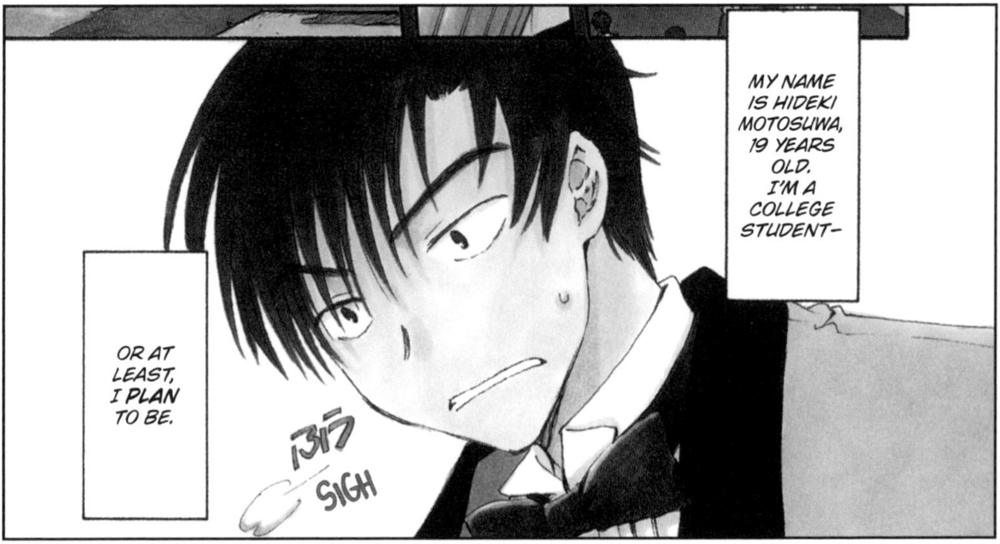
MY NAME IS HIDEKI MOTOSUWA, 19 YEARS OLD. I'M A COLLEGE STUDENT–
SIGH
OR AT LEAST, I PLAN TO BE.

"I'm a college student—or at least, I plan to be.", page 6
In Japanese, Hideki describes himself as a *ronin*, or someone who has taken a year (or multiple years) off after high school to cram for college entrance exams after failing to enter their school of choice, rather than settling for a backup choice.

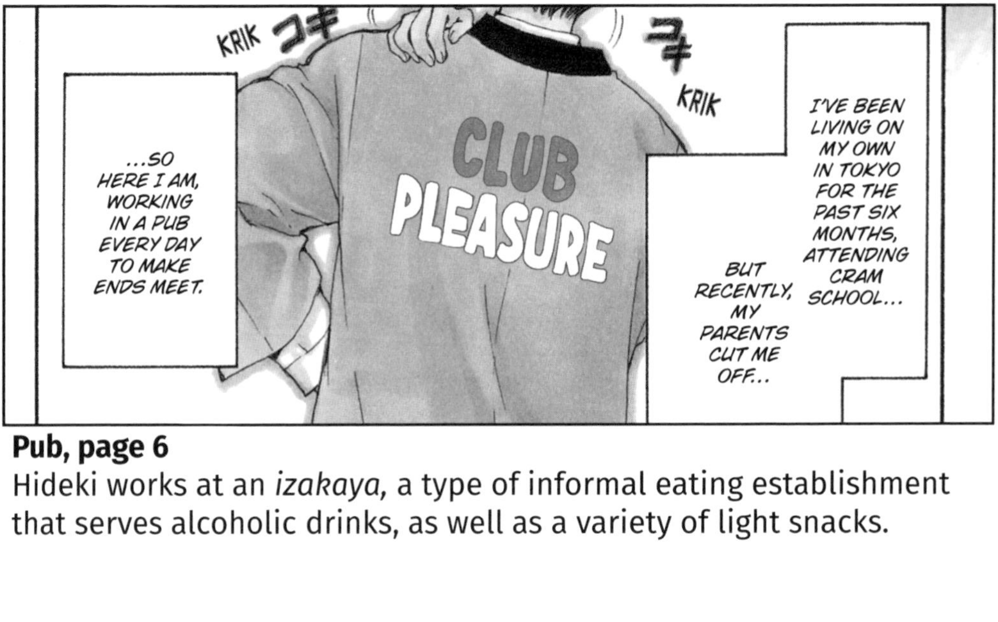
コキ
KRIK
I'VE BEEN LIVING ON MY OWN IN TOKYO FOR THE PAST SIX MONTHS, ATTENDING CRAM SCHOOL...
BUT RECENTLY, MY PARENTS CUT ME OFF...
KRIK コキ
CLUB PLEASURE
...SO HERE I AM, WORKING IN A PUB EVERY DAY TO MAKE ENDS MEET.

Pub, page 6
Hideki works at an *izakaya*, a type of informal eating establishment that serves alcoholic drinks, as well as a variety of light snacks.

Signs, page 11
All the signs in the first panel on this page seem to be advertising, promoting, or otherwise related to persocoms and technology.

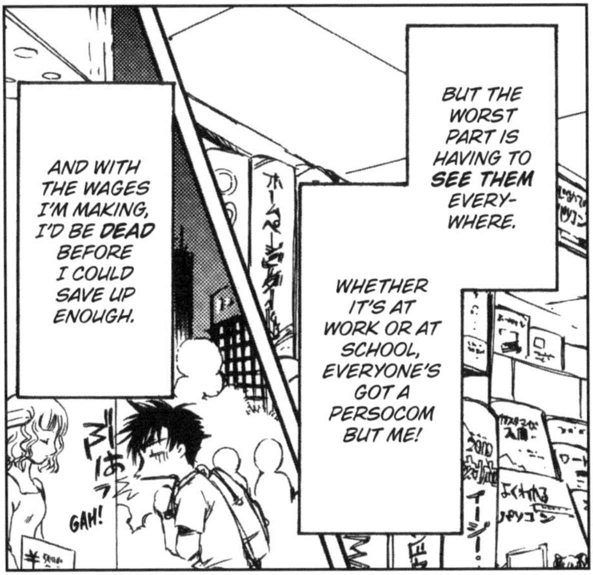
BUT THE WORST PART IS HAVING TO SEE THEM EVERY-WHERE.
WHETHER IT'S AT WORK OR AT SCHOOL, EVERYONE'S GOT A PERSOCOM BUT ME!
AND WITH THE WAGES I'M MAKING, I'D BE DEAD BEFORE I COULD SAVE UP ENOUGH.
GAH!

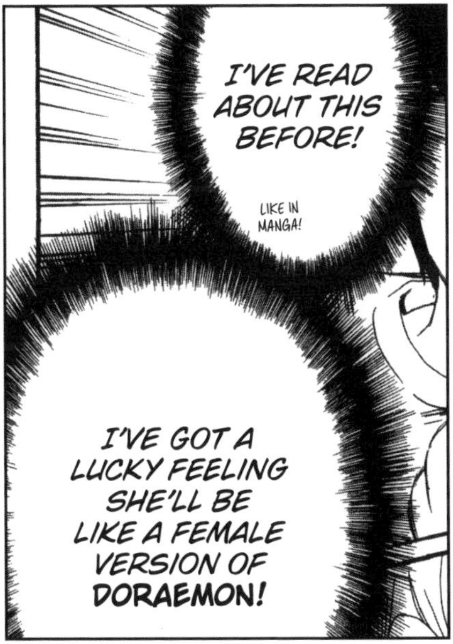
I'VE READ ABOUT THIS BEFORE!
LIKE IN MANGA!
I'VE GOT A LUCKY FEELING SHE'LL BE LIKE A FEMALE VERSION OF DORAEMON!

***Doraemon*, page 38**
Doraemon is a famous and very long-running Japanese children's show. The title character, Doraemon, is a robot cat from the future who produces an endless array of gadgets from a pouch on his belly to cater to the interests of his human friends.

Boobs, page 62
There's arguably a naughty little pun in Hideki's aside here: he worries Hibiya-san thinks he is trying to get a peek at Chi's *chichi*, or boobs. (To be fair, though, the name Chi has a long vowel in Japanese: *Chii*.)

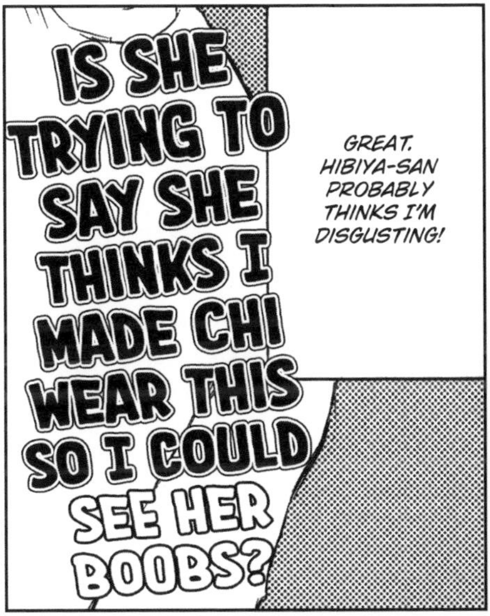
GREAT. HIBIYA-SAN PROBABLY THINKS I'M DISGUSTING!
IS SHE TRYING TO SAY SHE THINKS I MADE CHI WEAR THIS SO I COULD SEE HER BOOBS?

C'mere, page 91
Minoru beckons Hideki over with his palm down and using his whole hand. To beckon with the palm up, or worse, with just one finger, is considered rude in Japan—which is why you so often see characters in manga starting fights that way!

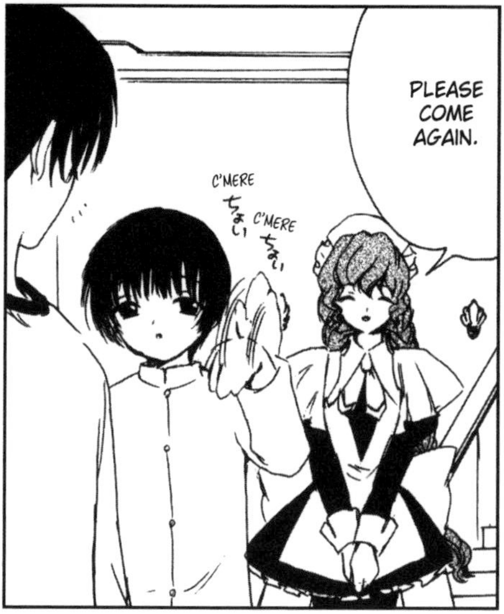
PLEASE COME AGAIN.
C'MERE
C'MERE

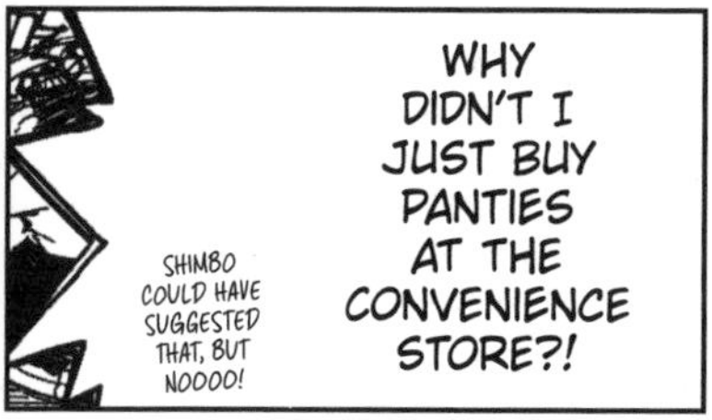
WHY DIDN'T I JUST BUY PANTIES AT THE CONVENIENCE STORE?!
SHIMBO COULD HAVE SUGGESTED THAT, BUT NOOOO!

Convenience store, page 109
Convenience stores in Japan have a considerably wider inventory than many similar places in the US. They stock not just sandwiches and candy, but kitchen supplies, personal grooming products, and even sometimes, as Hideki suddenly remembers here, clothing items like socks and underwear.

Gym uniform, page 162
Most Japanese schools require students to wear uniforms, including a separate outfit for gym class. Hibiya-san's old uniform still indicates her class (presumably second-year, group 3) and name. On the next page, you can see it comes complete with the very short "bloomer" pants that used to be characteristic of girls' gym uniforms. In the face of mounting discontent from the women who had to wear them, bloomers were phased out in favor of longer shorts by about the early 2000s, but between this series' publication date (the very beginning of the 21st century) and manga's continuing penchant for bloomers regardless of real-world fashion, it's not surprising to see Chi wearing them.

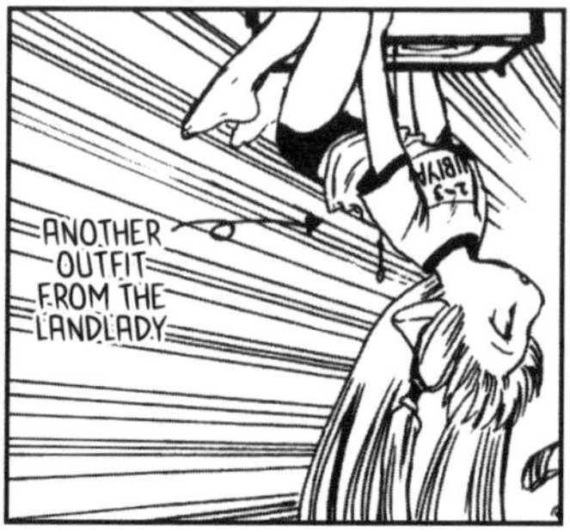
ANOTHER OUTFIT FROM THE LANDLADY

Drinks and snacks, page 173
Shimizu-sensei presents Hideki with a can of Kirin, a prominent brand of beer in Japan, and a package of *onigiri,* or rice balls. Kirin Lager Special Light was a variety of beer Kirin produced for just a couple of years starting in 1999, right around the time *Chobits* was debuting. Special Light had 50% less sugar than usual, and fewer calories.

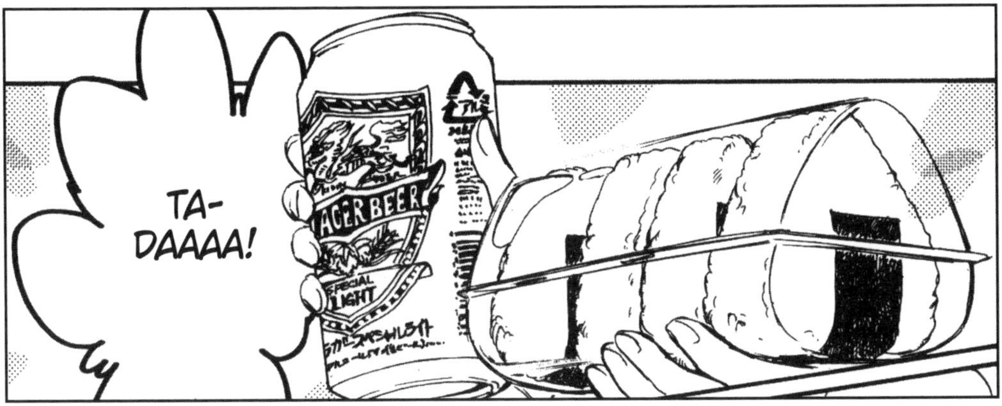
TA-
DAAAA!
LAGER BEER
SPECIAL
LIGHT

Soapland, page 288
Soaplands are businesses where clients pay to have a woman wash their body. The specifics of this business model have to do with exploiting the language of Japan's anti-prostitution laws, and the women at soaplands sometimes offer services beyond simple hygiene.

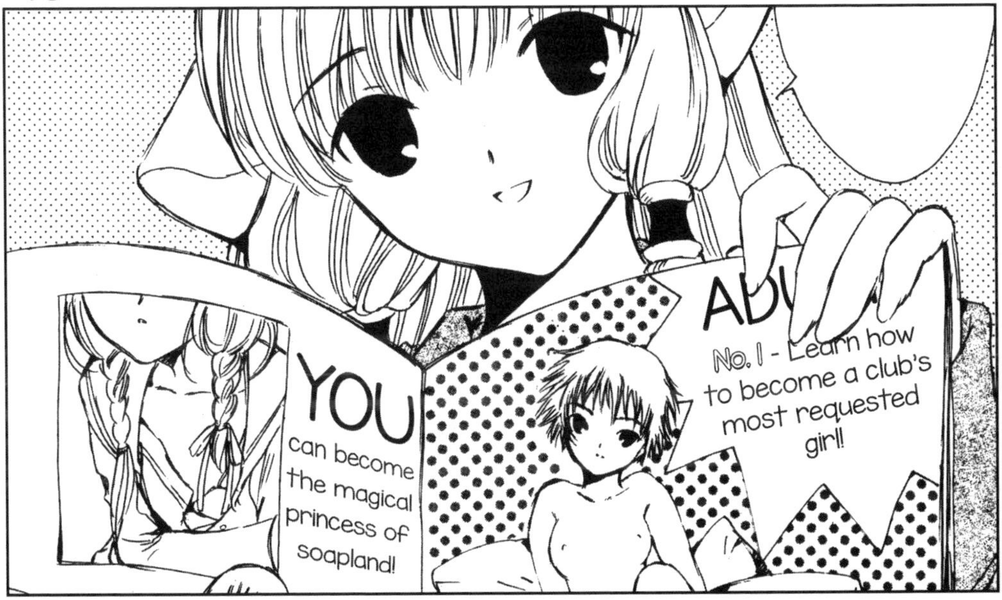
ADV
No. 1 - Learn how to become a club's most requested girl!
YOU
can become the magical princess of soapland!

A Kodansha Comics Hardcover Original
Chobits 20th Anniversary Edition volume 1 copyright © 2001
CLAMP · Shigatsu Tsuitachi Co., Ltd. / Kodansha Ltd.
English translation copyright © 2020
CLAMP · Shigatsu Tsuitachi Co., Ltd. / Kodansha Ltd.

Published in the United States by Kodansha Comics, an imprint of Kodansha USA Publishing, LLC, New York.

Publication rights for this English edition arranged through Kodansha Ltd., Tokyo.

First published in Japan in 2001 by Kodansha Ltd., Tokyo as *Chobittsu*, volumes 1 and 2.

ISBN 978-1-63236-816-4

Printed in China.

www.kodanshacomics.com

9 8 7 6 5 4 3 2 1
Translation: Shirley Kubo
Additional Translation: Kevin Steinbach, Tiff Ferentini, Haruko Hashimoto
Lettering: Michael Martin
Editing: Tiff Ferentini
Kodansha Comics edition cover design: Phil Balsman

Publisher: Kiichiro Sugawara
Managing editor: Maya Rosewood
Vice president of marketing & publicity: Naho Yamada

Director of publishing services: Ben Applegate
Associate director of operations: Stephen Pakula
Publishing services managing editor: Noelle Webster
Assistant production manager: Emi Lotto, Angela Zurlo

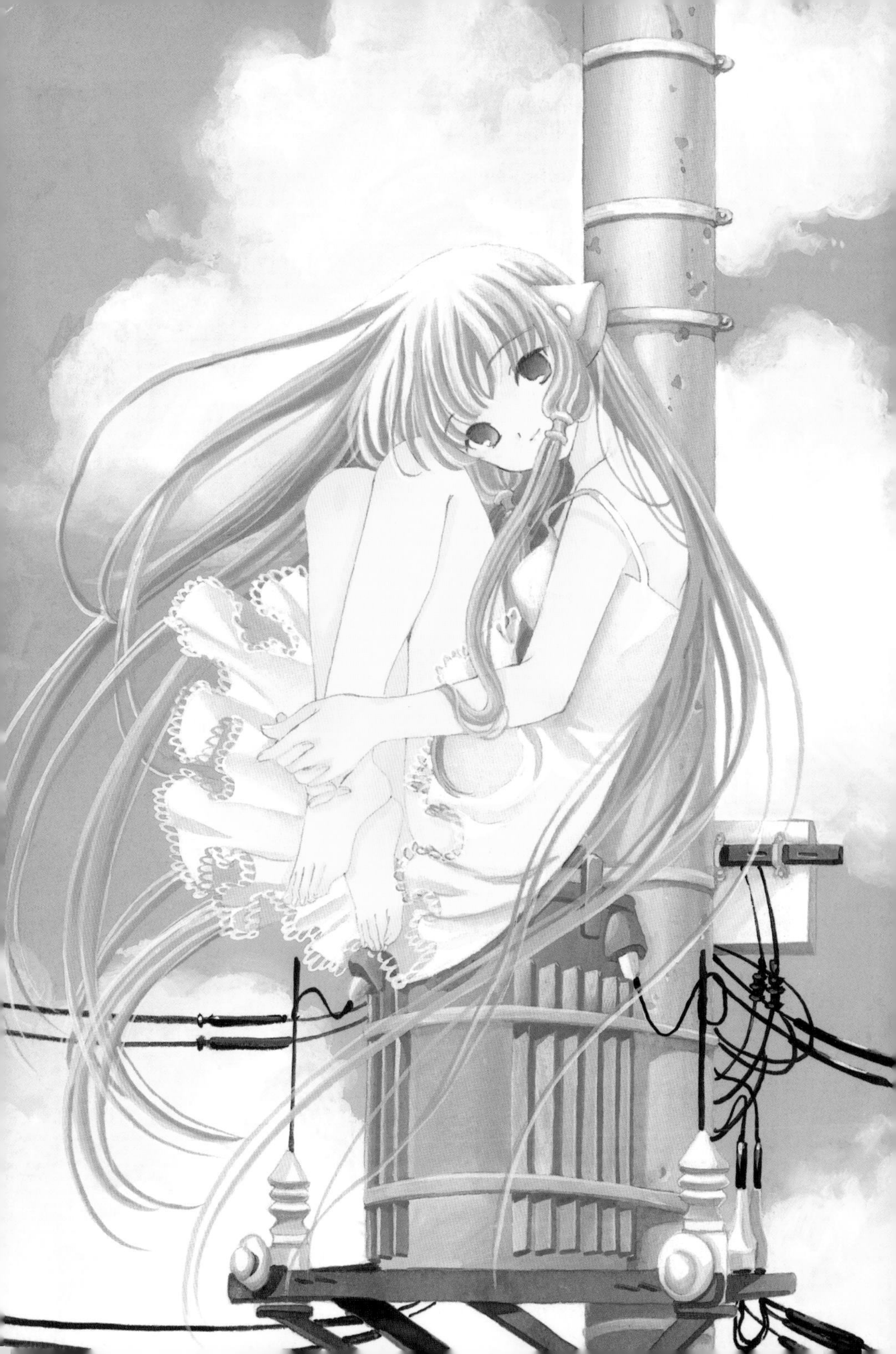

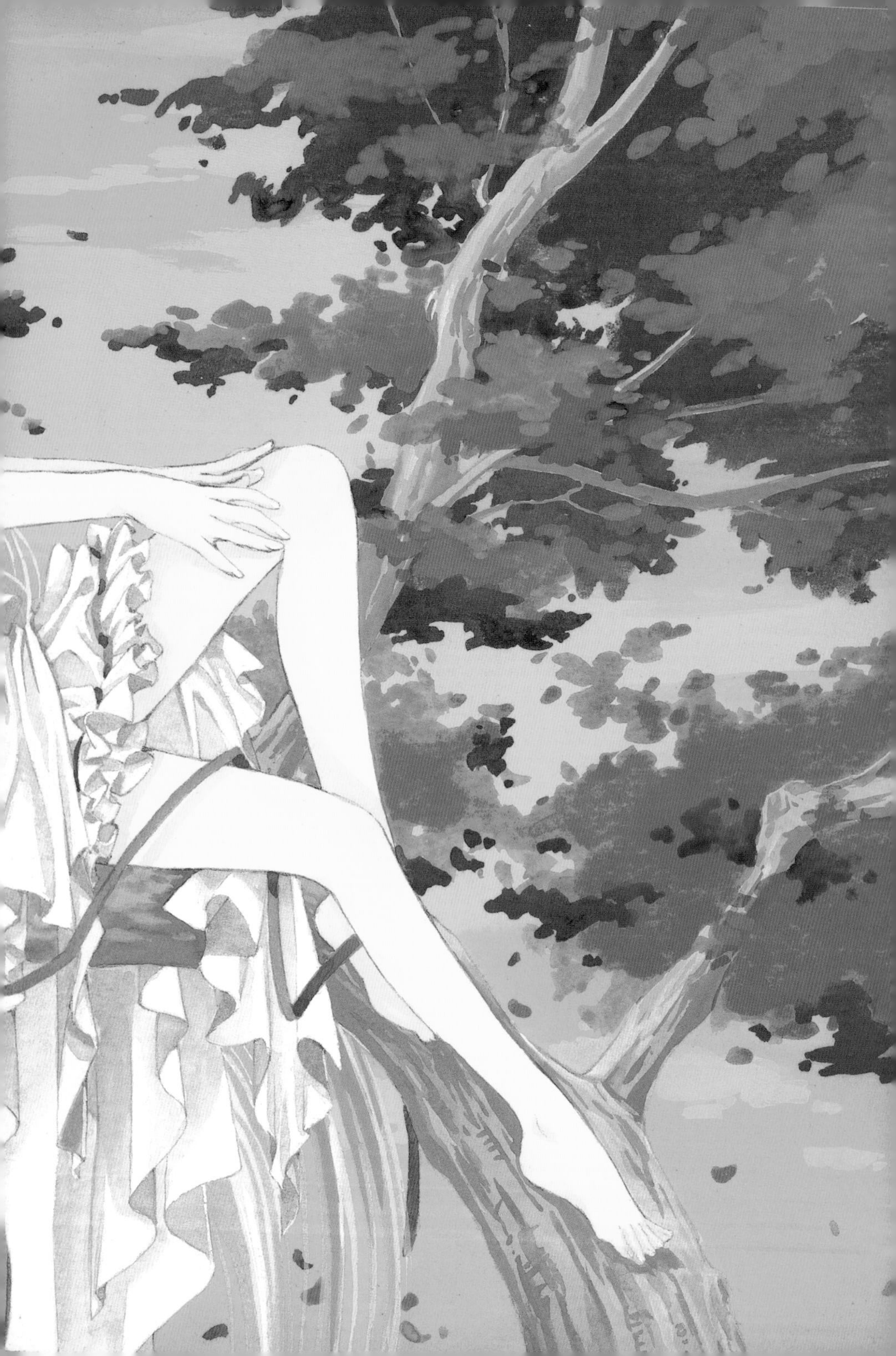

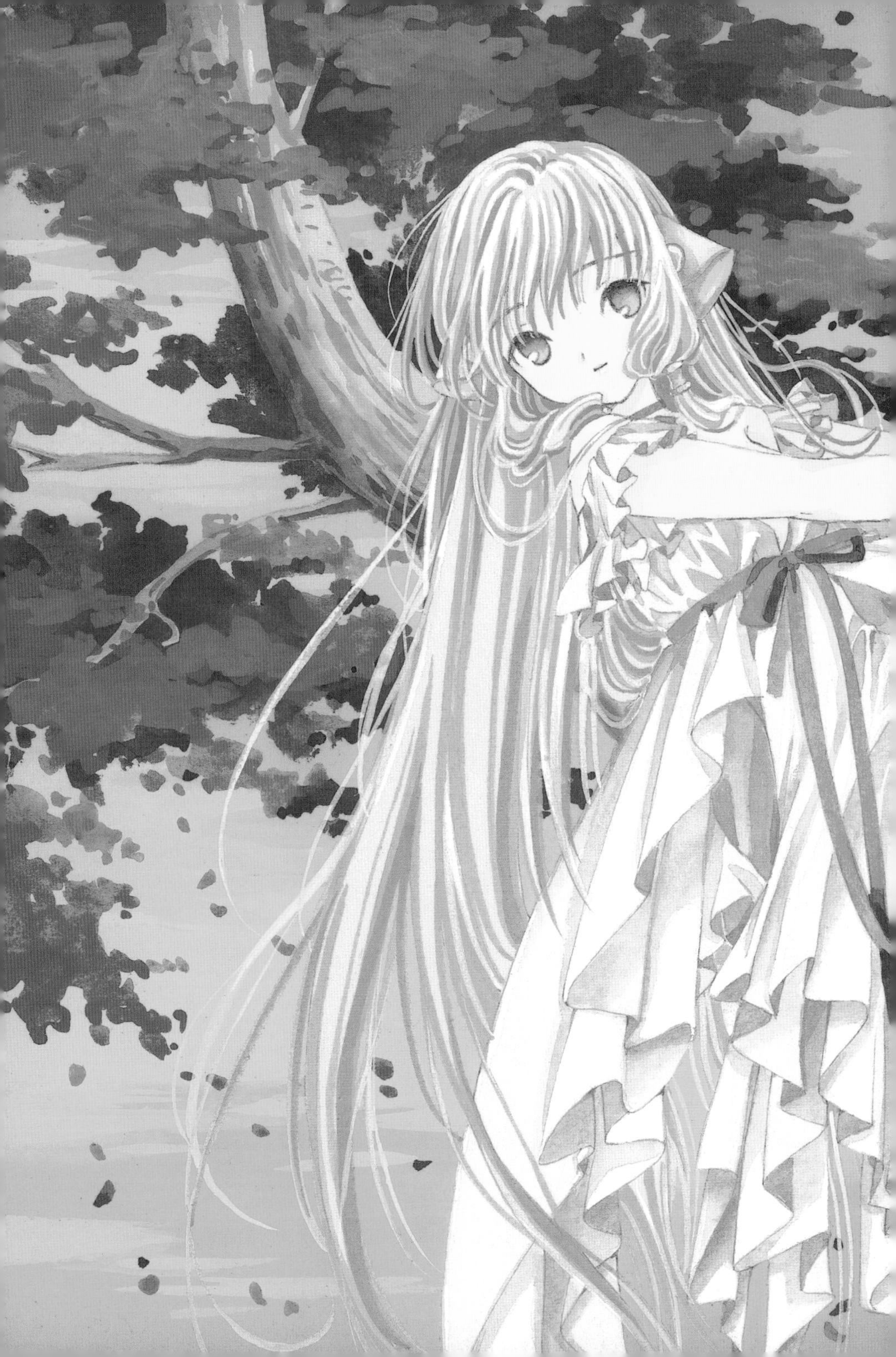

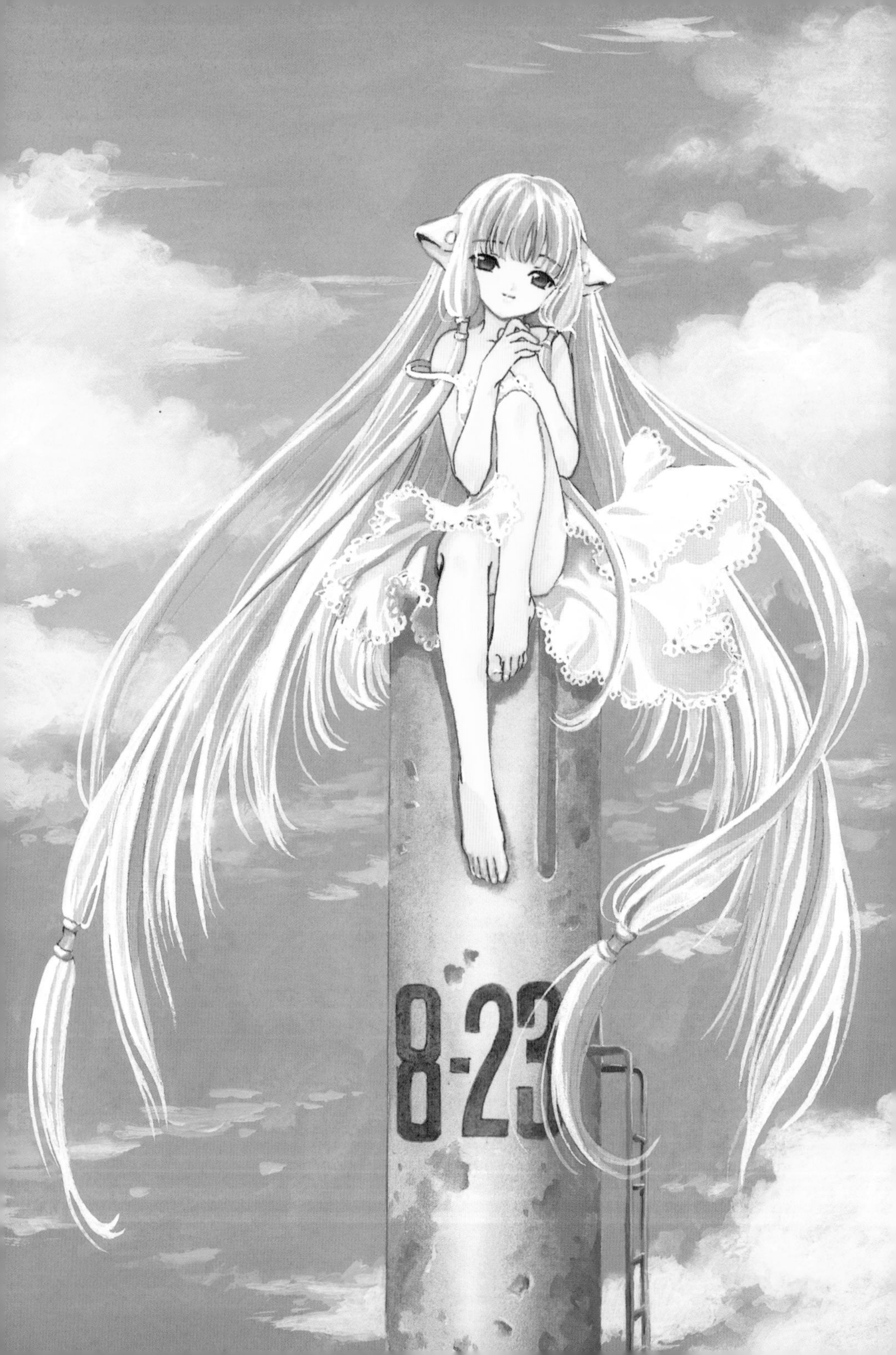
8-23

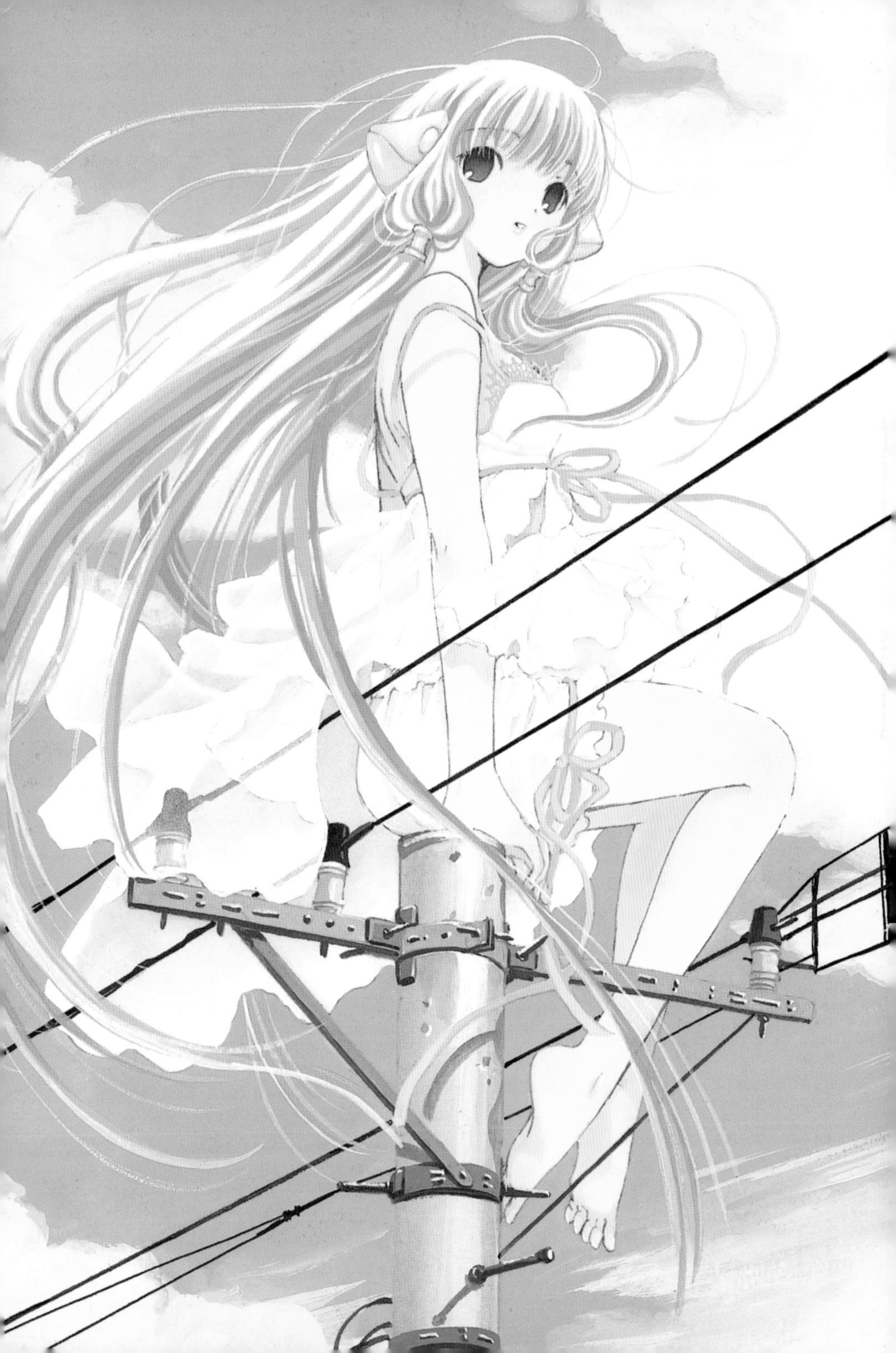

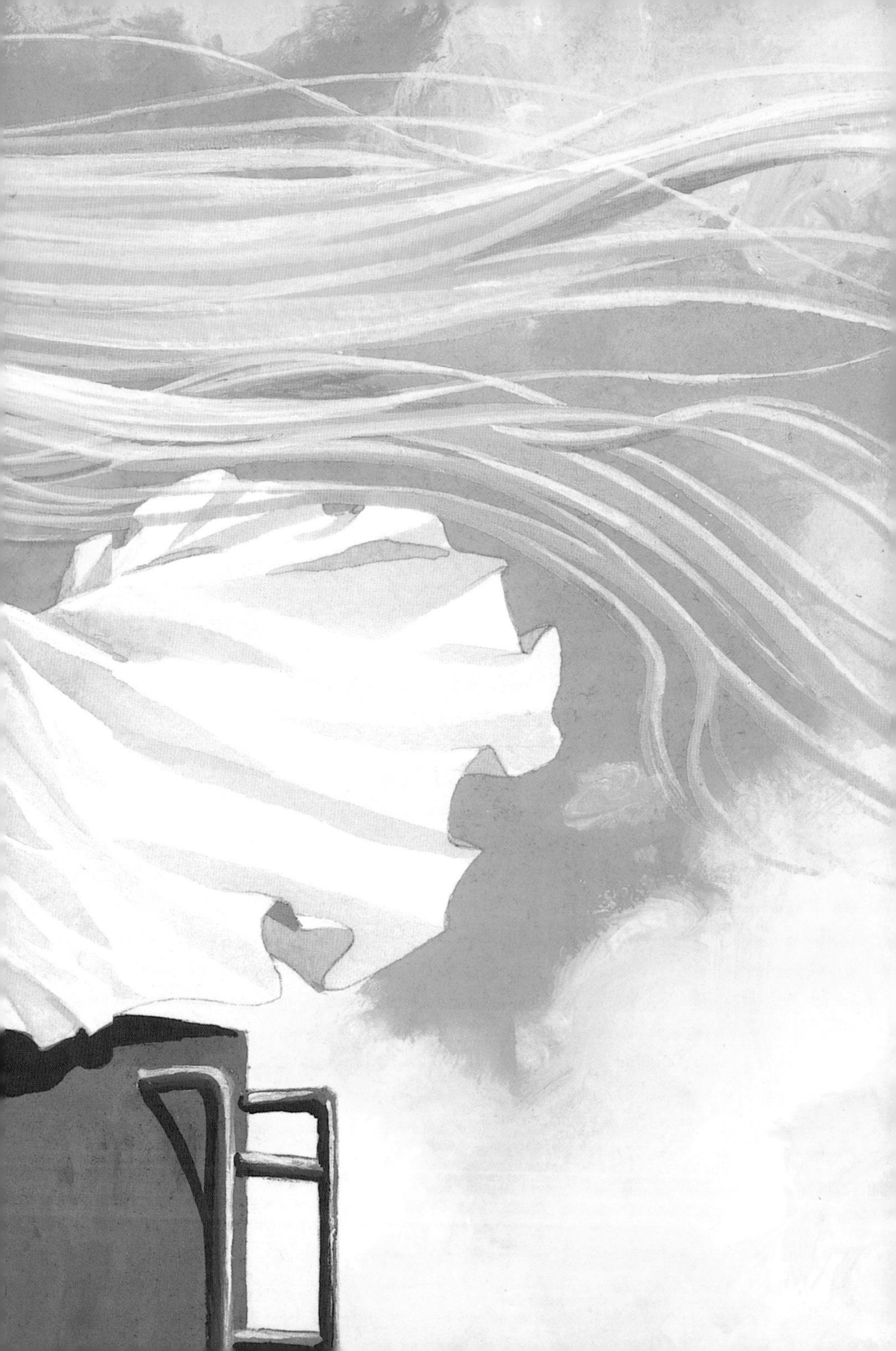

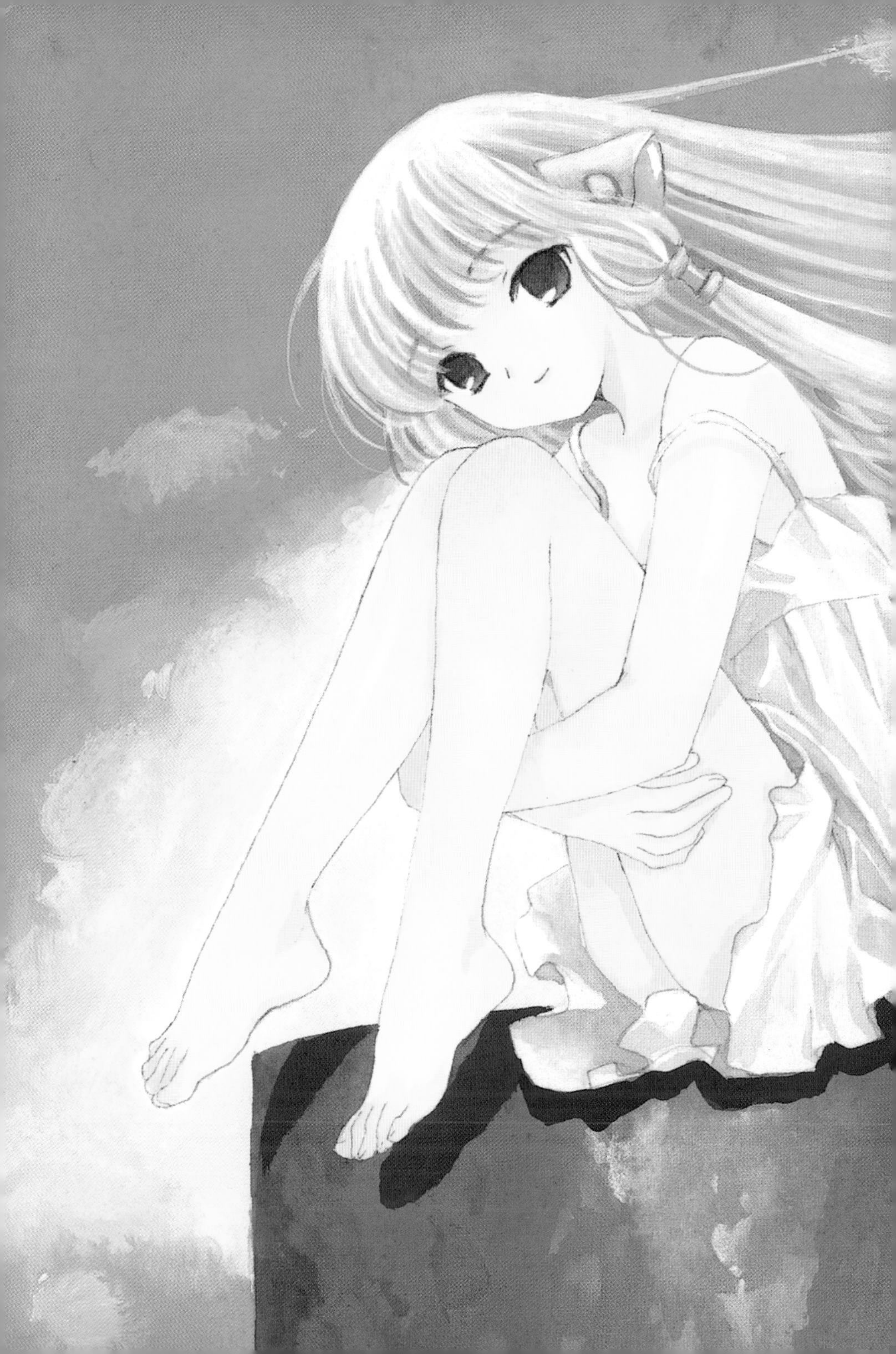

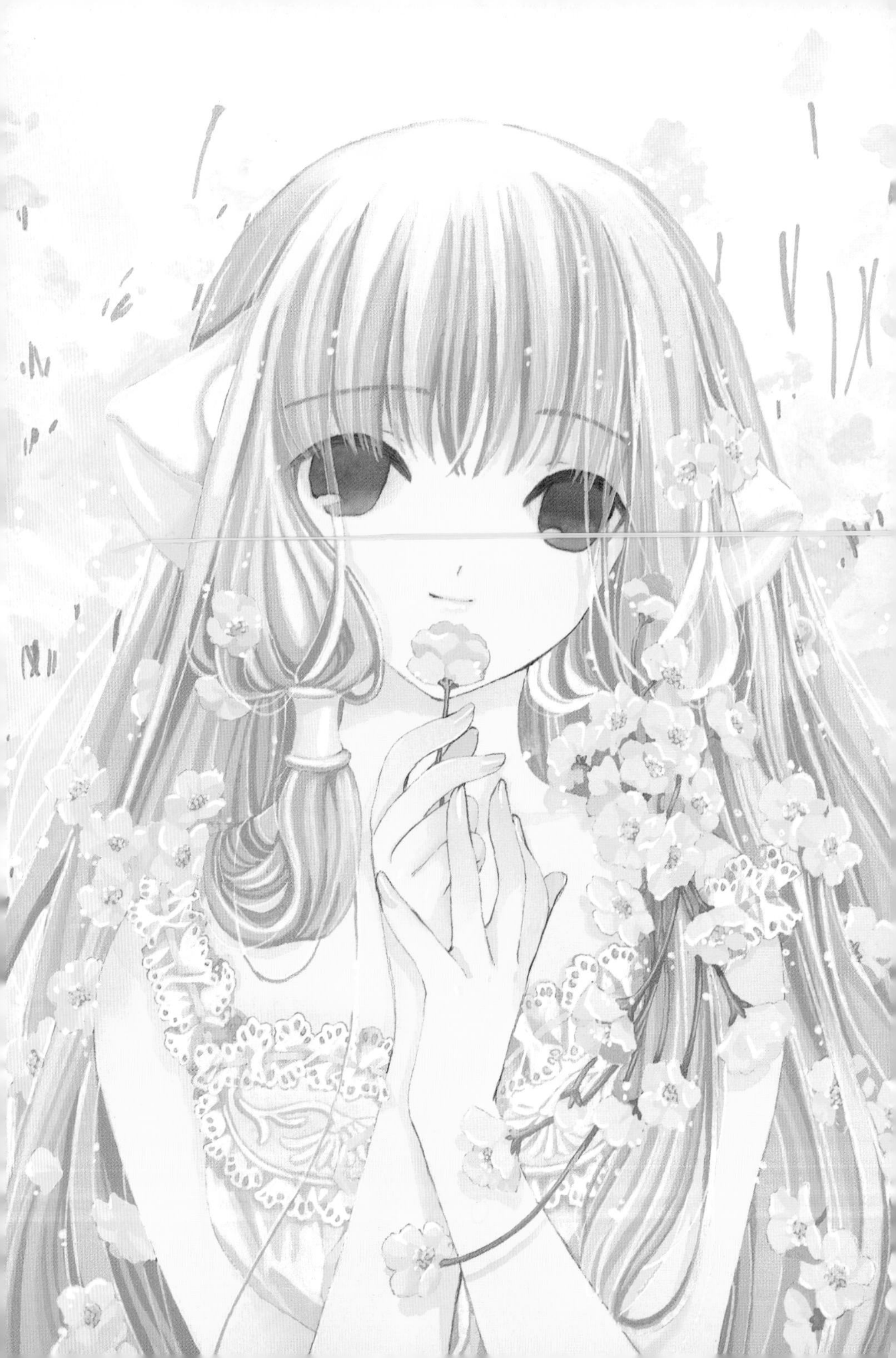

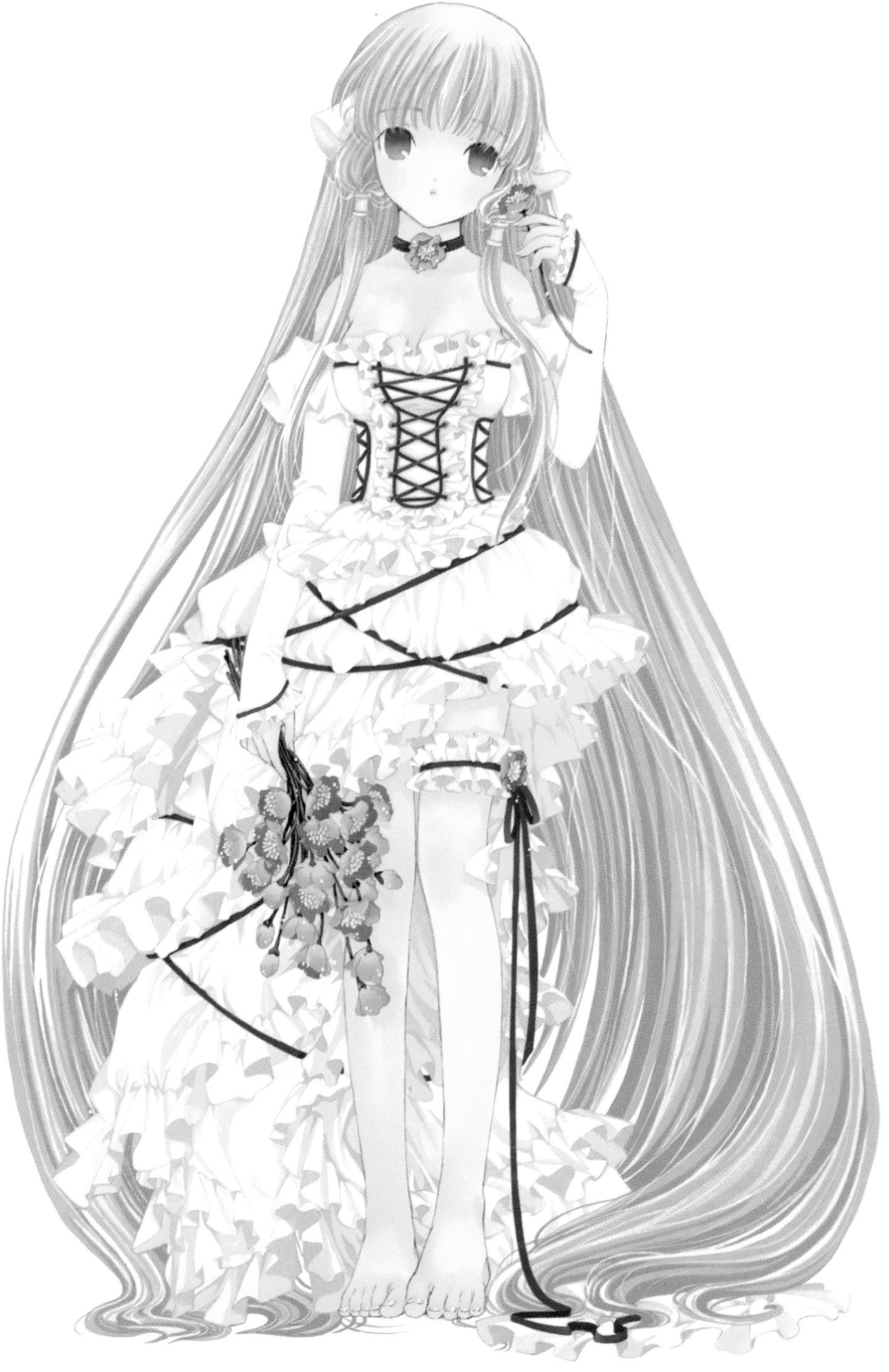

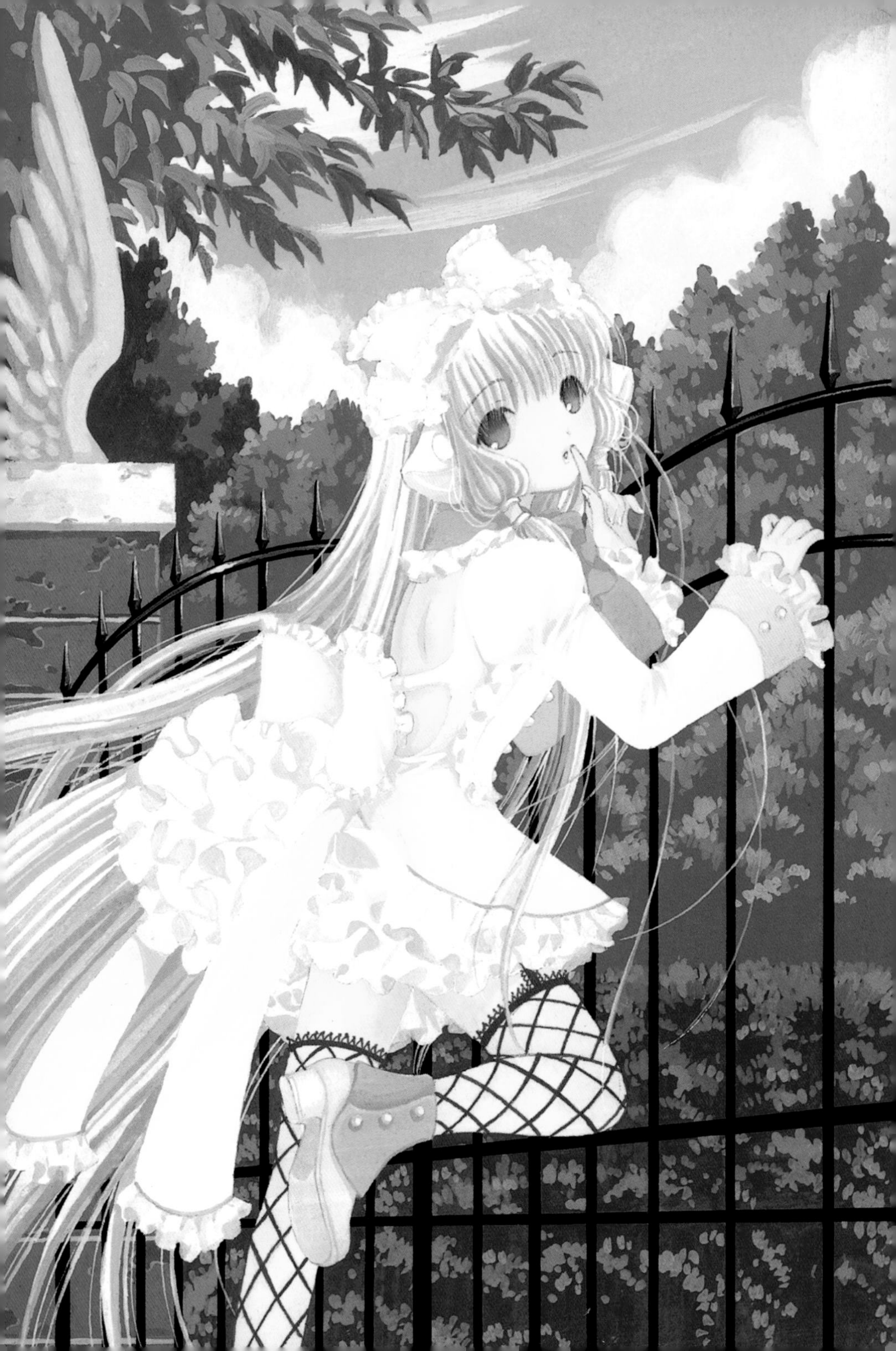

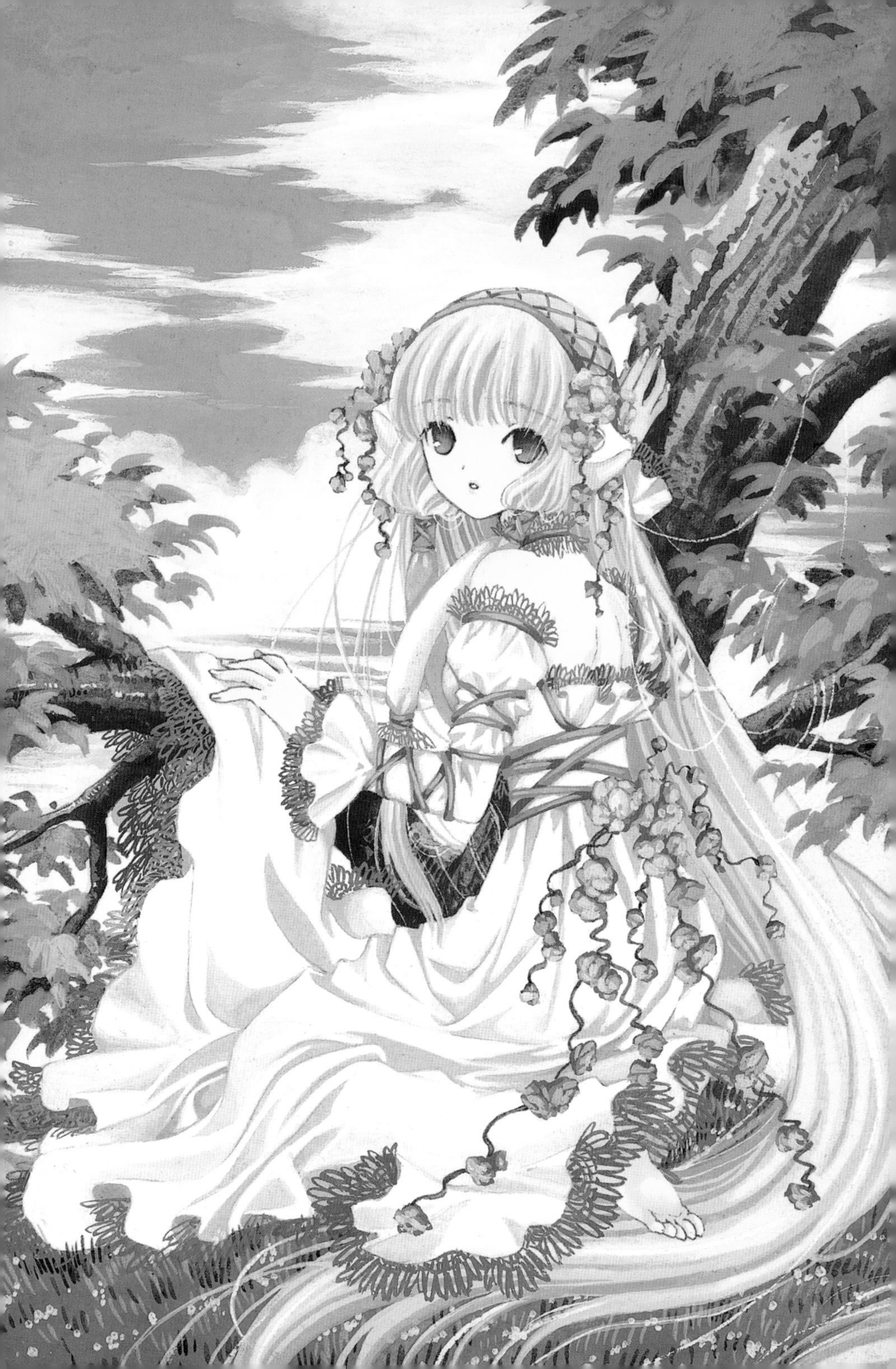

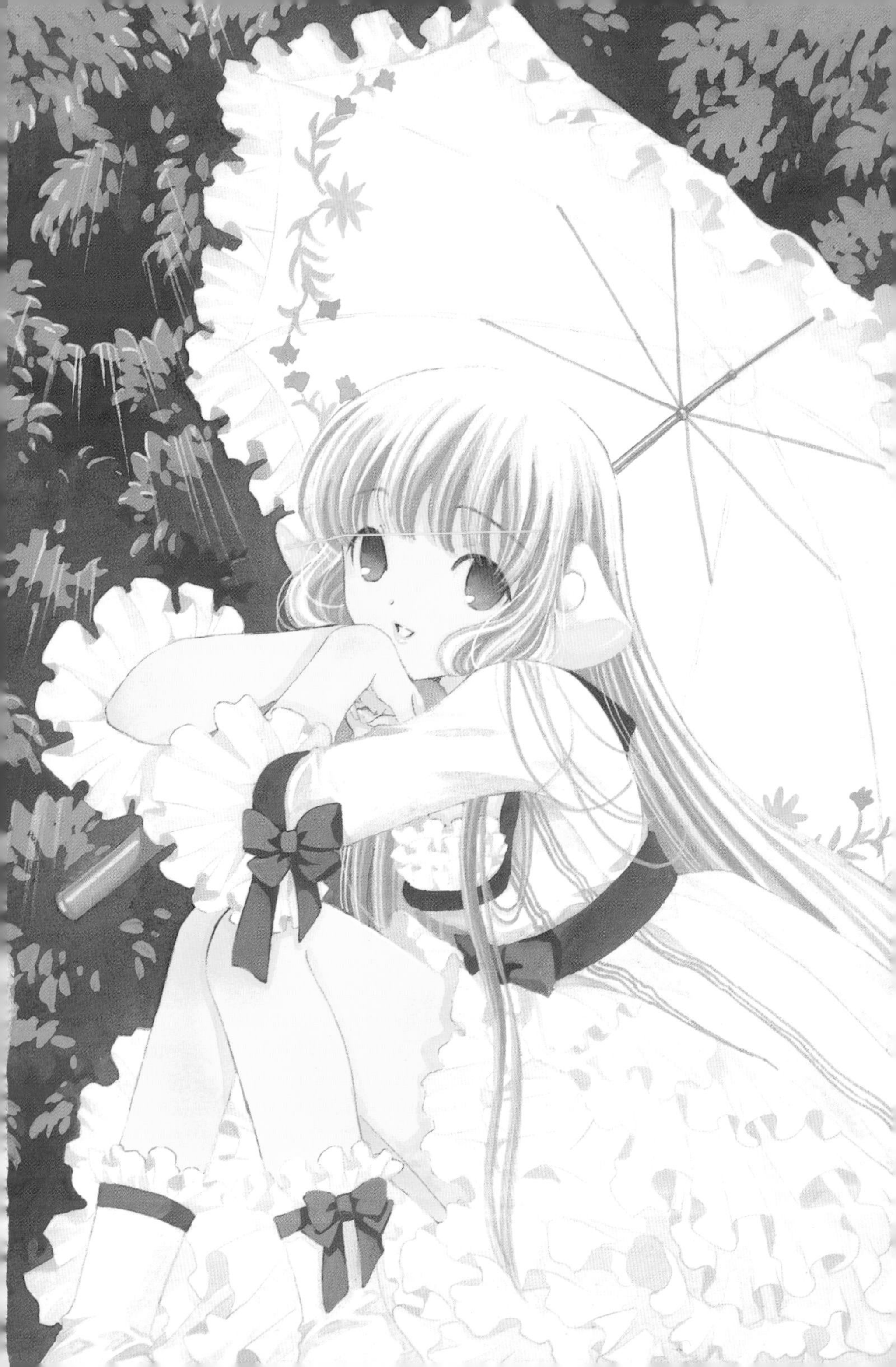

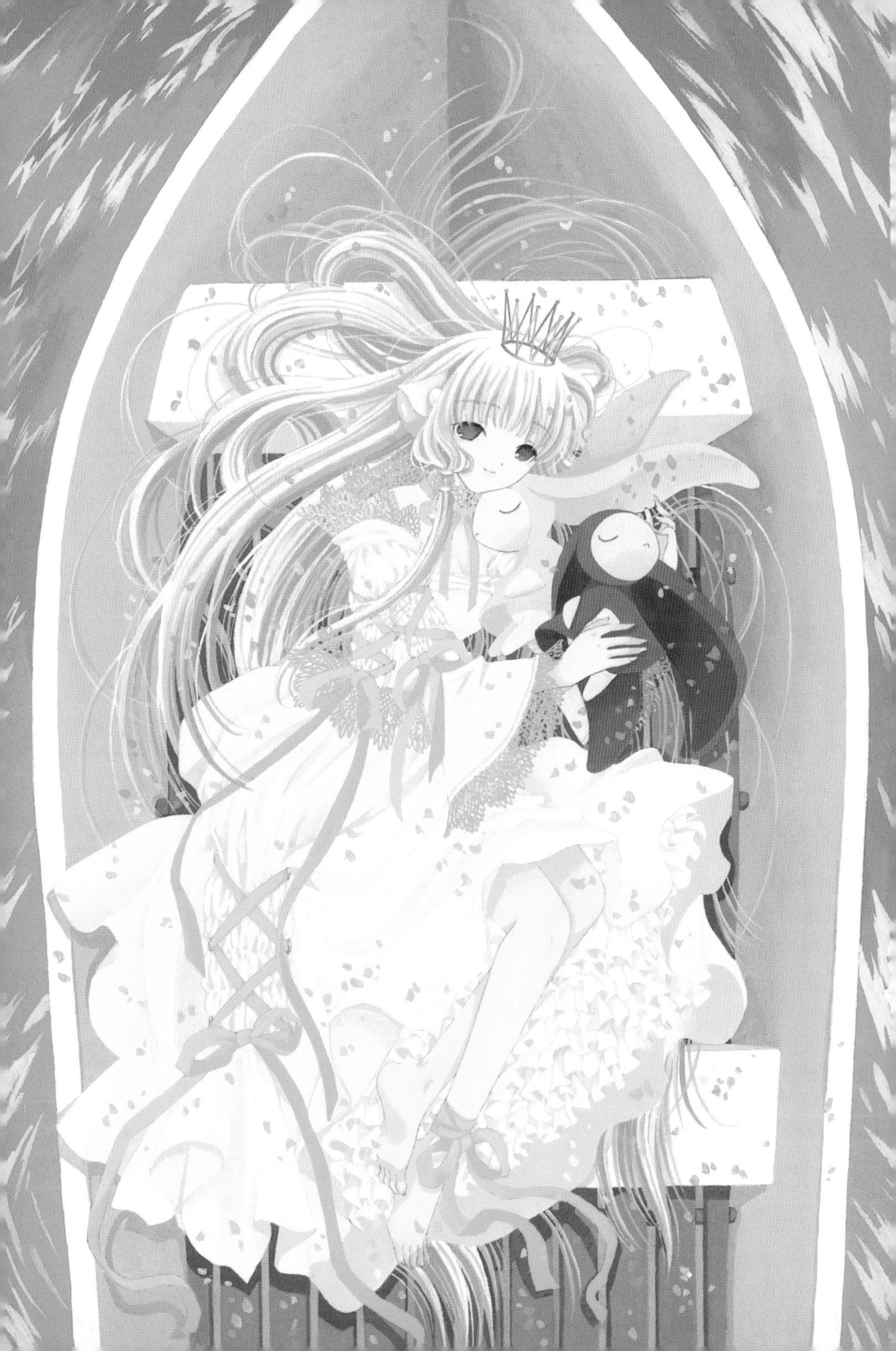

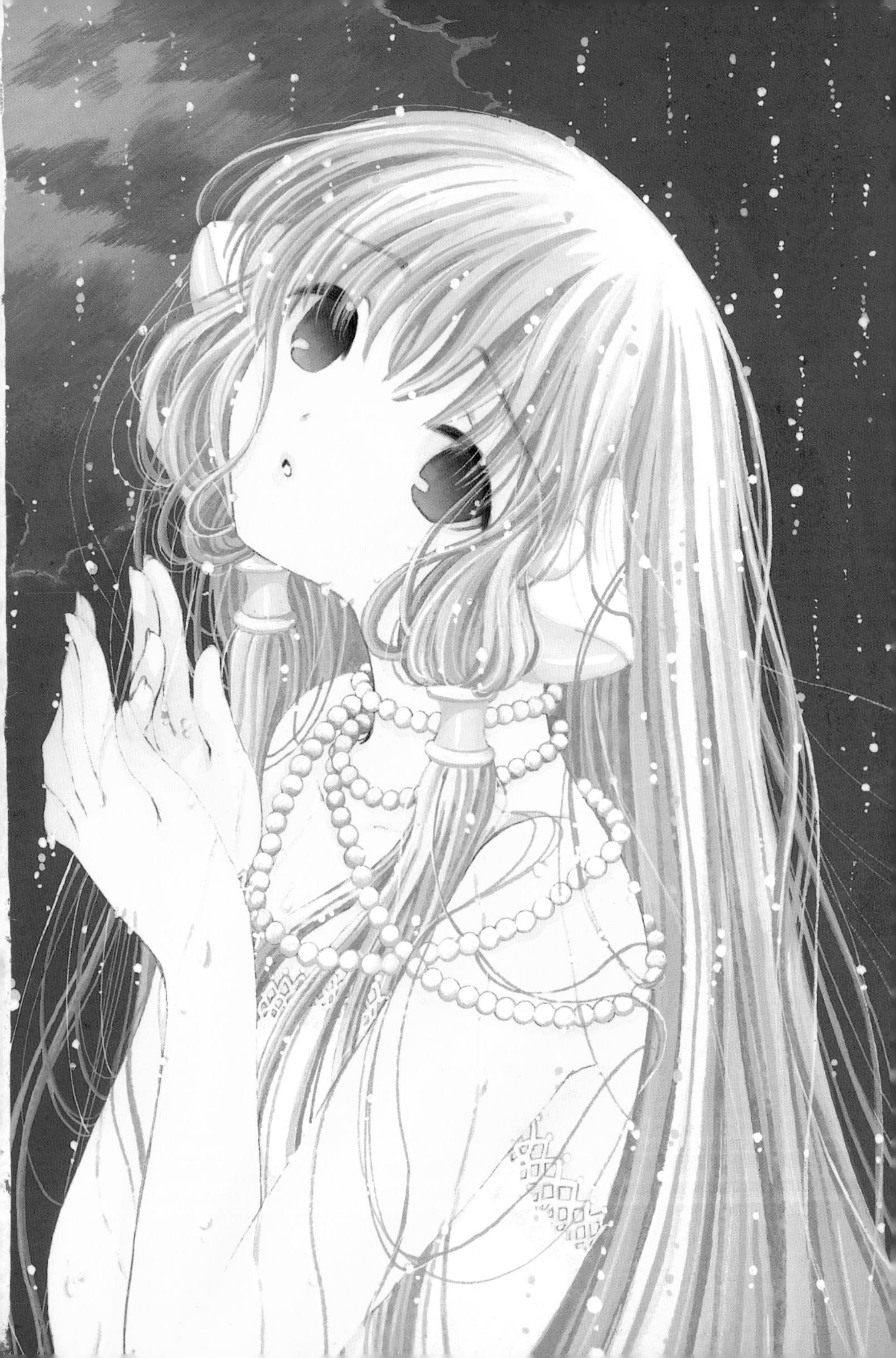